D1451375

FLORIDA Treasures

A Reading/Language Arts Program

Macmillan/McGraw-Hill

Acknowledgments

The publisher gratefully acknowledges permission to reprint the following copyrighted material:

"Adelina's Whales" text and photographs by Richard Sobol. Text and photographs copyright © 2003 by Richard Sobol. Reprinted by permission of Dutton Children's Books, a division of Penguin Books USA Inc.

"The Ant and the Grasshopper" retold and illustrated by Amy Lowry Poole. Copyright © 2000 by Amy Lowry Poole. Reprinted by permission of Holiday House.

"The Astronaut and the Onion" by Ann Cameron from GLORIA RISING. Text copyright © 2002 by Ann Cameron. Reprinted by permission of Frances Foster Books, an imprint of Farrar, Straus and Giroux.

"At Home in the Coral Reef" by Katy Muzik, illustrated by Katherine Brown-Wing. Text and illustrations copyright © 1992 by Charlesbridge Publishing. Reprinted by permission.

"Because of Winn-Dixie" by Kate DiCamillo from BECAUSE OF WINN-DIXIE. Copyright © 2000 by Kate DiCamillo. Reprinted by permission of Candlewick Press.

"The Blind Hunter" written and illustrated by Kristina Rodanas. Text and illustrations copyright © 2003 by Kristina Rodanas. Reprinted by permission of Marshall Cavendish.

"Brave New Heights" by Monica Kulling from MORE SPICE THAN SUGAR: POEMS ABOUT FEISTY FEMALES compiled by Lillian Morrison. Compilation copyright © 2001 by Lillian Morrison. Used by permission of Marian Reiner from the author.

"The Cricket in Times Square" by George Selden, illustrated by Garth Williams from THE CRICKET IN TIMES SQUARE. Copyright © 1960 by George Selden Thompson and Garth Williams. Reprinted by permission of Farrar, Straus and Giroux.

"Dear Mr. Winston" by Ken Roberts from WHEN I WENT TO THE LIBRARY edited by Debora Pearson. Copyright © 2001 by Ken Roberts. Reprinted by permission of Groundwood Books/Douglas & McIntyre.

"Dear Mrs. LaRue" written and illustrated by Mark Teague. Copyright © 2002 by Mark Teague. Reprinted by permission of Scholastic Press, a division of Scholastic, Inc.

"Dear Mrs. Parks" by Rosa Parks with Gregory J. Reed from DEAR MRS. PARKS: A DIALOGUE WITH TODAY'S YOUTH. Text copyright © 1996 by Rosa L. Parks, jacket photo copyright © 1996 by Mark. T. Kerrin. Reprinted by permission of Lee & Low Books, Inc.

"How Ben Franklin Stole the Lightning" by Rosalyn Schanzer. Copyright © 2003 by Rosalyn Schanzer. Reprinted by permission of HarperCollins Publishers.

(Acknowledgments continued on page 815.)

Contributors

Time Magazine, Accelerated Reader

Students with print disabilities may be eligible to obtain an accessible, audio version of the pupil edition of this textbook. Please call Recording for the Blind & Dyslexic at 1-800-221-4792 for complete information.

B

The McGraw·Hill Companies

Macmillan McGraw-Hill

Published by Macmillan/McGraw-Hill, of McGraw-Hill Education, a division of The McGraw-Hill Companies, Inc., Two Penn Plaza, New York, New York 10121.

Copyright © 2009 by Macmillan/McGraw-Hill. All rights reserved. No part of this publication may be reproduced or distributed in any form or by any means, or stored in a database or retrieval system, without the prior written consent of The McGraw-Hill Companies, Inc., including, but not limited to, network storage or transmission, or broadcast for distance learning.

Printed in the United States of America

ISBN-13: 978-0-02-198766-5/4

ISBN-10: 0-02-198766-1/4

2 3 4 5 6 7 8 9 (027/043) 11 10 09 08

FLORIDA Treasures

A Reading/Language Arts Program

Program Authors

Dr. Donald R. Bear
University of Nevada, Reno
Reno, Nevada

Dr. Janice A. Dole
University of Utah
Salt Lake City, Utah

Dr. Douglas Fisher
San Diego State University
San Diego, California

Dr. Vicki Gibson
Longmire Learning Center, Inc.
College Station, Texas

Dr. Jana Echevarria
California State University, Long Beach
Long Beach, California

Dr. Jan E. Hasbrouck
Educational Consultant - J.H. Consulting
Seattle, Washington

Dr. Scott G. Paris
University of Michigan
Ann Arbor, Michigan

Dr. Timothy Shanahan
University of Illinois at Chicago
Chicago, Illinois

Dr. Josefina V. Tinajero
University of Texas at El Paso
El Paso, Texas

Macmillan/McGraw-Hill

Unit 1 Let's Explore

THEME: Mysteries

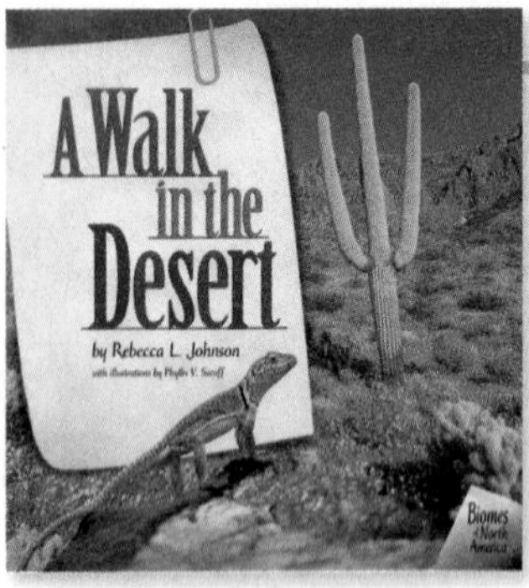

THEME: Adapting to Survive

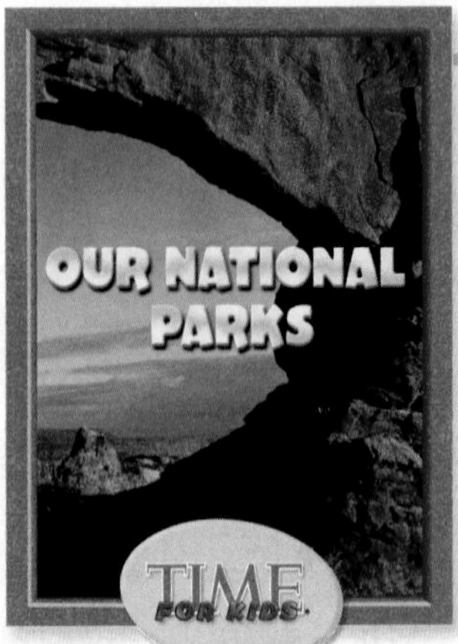

THEME: Our National Parks

The Astronaut and the Onion
by Ann Cameron
illustrated by
Anna Rich
Award Winning Author

THE RAFT
Award Winning Author and Illustrator

Unit 2 Take a Stand

THEME: Baseball

THEME: New Places, New Faces

THEME: Focus on China

THEME: Bright Ideas

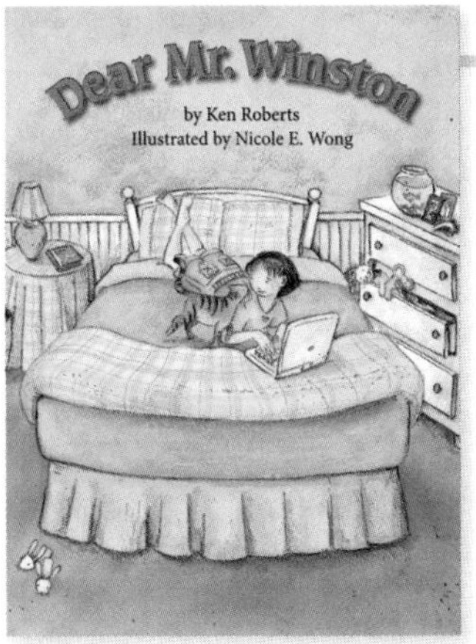

THEME: Snakes

FCAT

Show What You Know

Unit 3 Making a Difference

THEME: Friend or Foe?

THEME: People Who Made a Difference

THEME: Kids Get It Done

THEME: Great Plains Indians

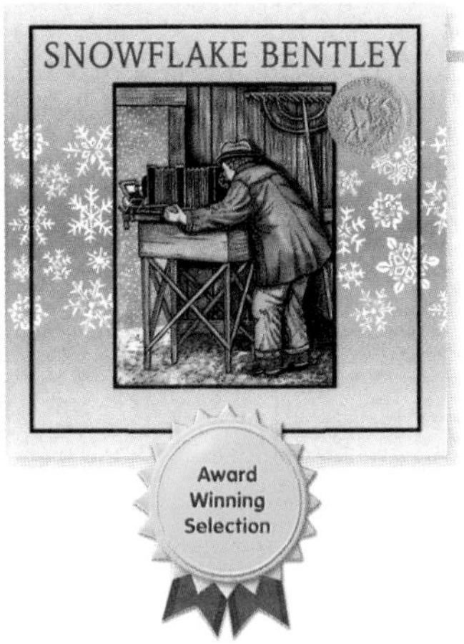

THEME: Precipitation

FCAT

Show What You Know

Unit 4 Viewpoints

THEME: Man's Best Friend

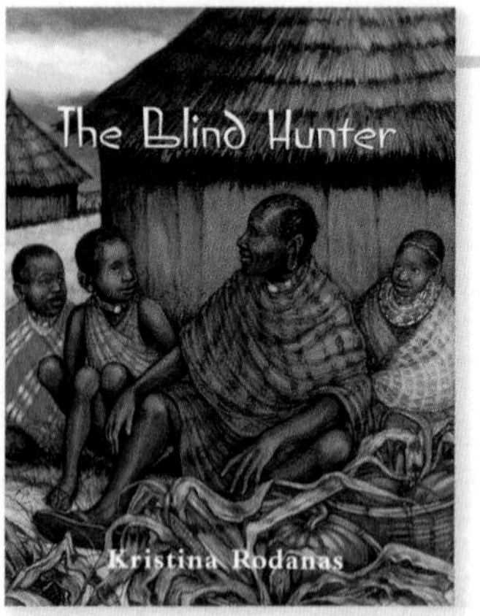

THEME: Creative Solutions

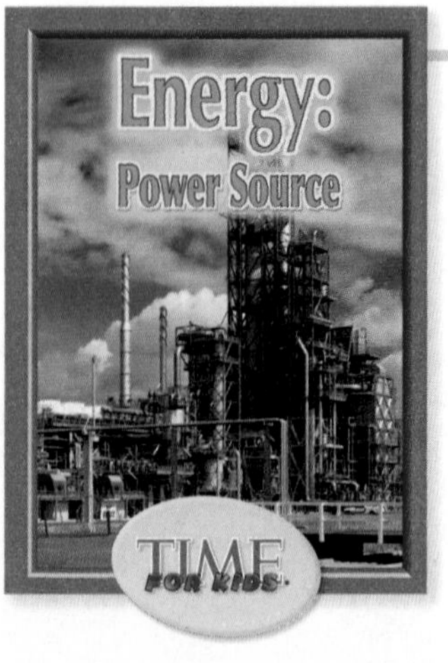

THEME: Energy: Power Source

THEME: Whales

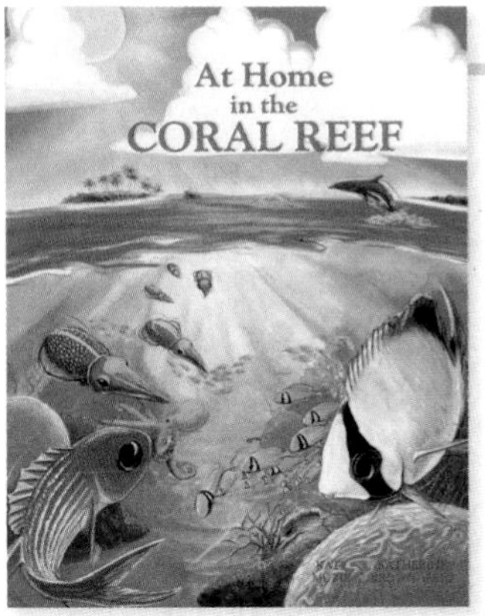

THEME: The Sea

FCAT

Show What You Know

Unit 5 Relationships

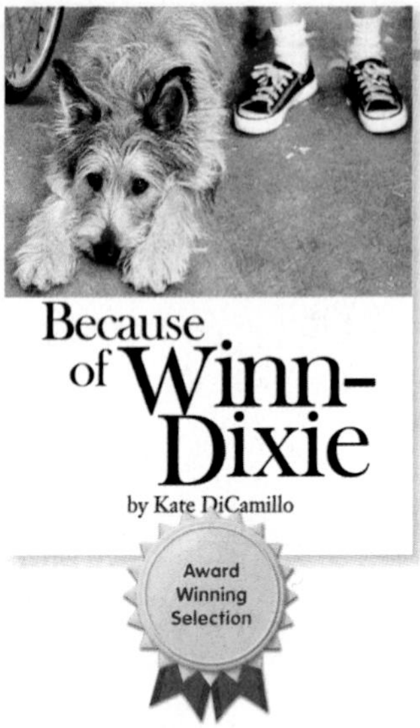

THEME: Going to the Library

THEME: Putting on a Play

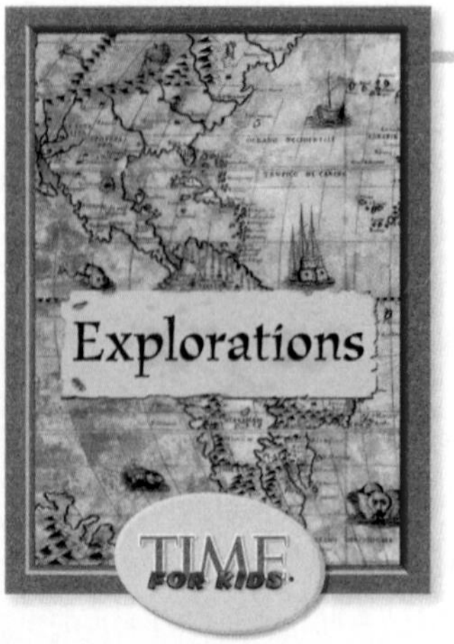

THEME: Explorations

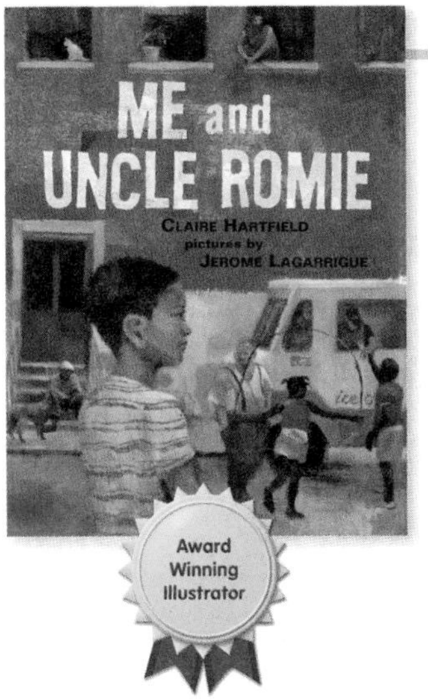
ME and
UNCLE ROMIE
CLAIRE HARTFIELD
pictures by
JEROME LAGARRIGUE
Award Winning Illustrator

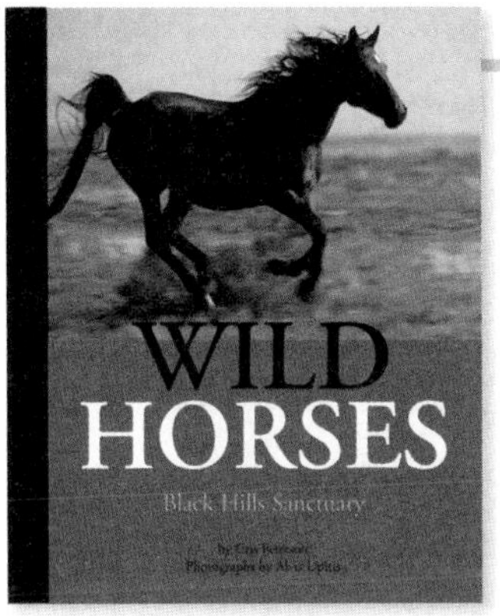
WILD
HORSES
Black Hills Sanctuary

Unit 6

Discovery

THEME: The Gold Rush

THEME: Wild Visitors

THEME: Discovering Nature's Secrets

THEME: Airplanes

THEME: Ants

FCAT

Show What You Know

Talk About It

What mysteries do you think surround these stones?

LOG ON Find out more about mysteries at **www.macmillanmh.com**

MYSTERIES

Vocabulary

assignments
consideration
allergies
accuse
suspicious
evidence
consume

FCAT Dictionary

Unfamiliar Words are words you do not know. You can find the meanings of unfamiliar words in a dictionary. Use a dictionary to figure out the meaning of the word *assignment*.

The Case of the Blurry Board

by Jaime Beaurline

Blurry Vision

After collecting homework **assignments**, Mrs. Morris said, "Jason, would you please read the first problem on the board?"

Jason put on his glasses. "That's weird," he said.

"What's the matter?" Mrs. Morris asked.

"I can't see the board. Everything is blurry," explained Jason.

Mrs. Morris thought a moment. After some **consideration**, she suggested, "Why don't you go see the school nurse? Maybe you have **allergies** to something that's blooming now."

Colliding Classmates

Jason walked down the hall. He turned the corner and BAM! He and Susie Hu bumped into each other. Their glasses went flying.

Susie was about to **accuse** Jason of not looking where he was going, but she had been on her way to clean her own glasses.

"That's weird," said Jason, as soon as they had put on their glasses. "Now I can see just fine."

"Me too!" Susie exclaimed.

"Something **suspicious** is going on," said Jason.

Mystery Solved

"Our glasses must have gotten switched when we bumped into each other earlier today," Jason said.

"Hmmm..." said Susie. "What's your proof? I need **evidence**!"

"Look, our glasses are exactly the same," noted Jason.

"You're right!" said Susie. "I'm very glad you solved the mystery. Lunch period is next and I would have hated to **consume** a pencil instead of a pretzel rod!"

Reread for **Comprehension**

FCAT

Make Inferences and Analyze

Problem and Solution The plot is what happens in a story. The plot often includes a **problem** and a **solution** to the problem. Reread the story to find the problem and what the character does to solve it. Fill in your Problem and Solution Chart.

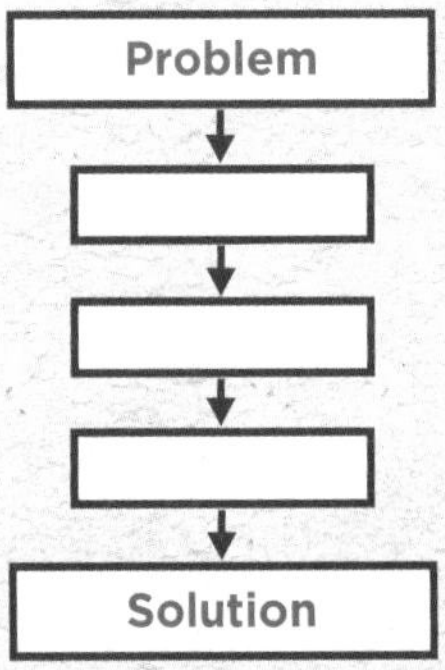

Comprehension

Genre

A **Mystery** is a story in which the characters and the reader must use clues to find the explanation for a troubling event.

Make Inferences and Analyze

FCAT **Problem and Solution**

As you read, fill in your Problem and Solution Chart.

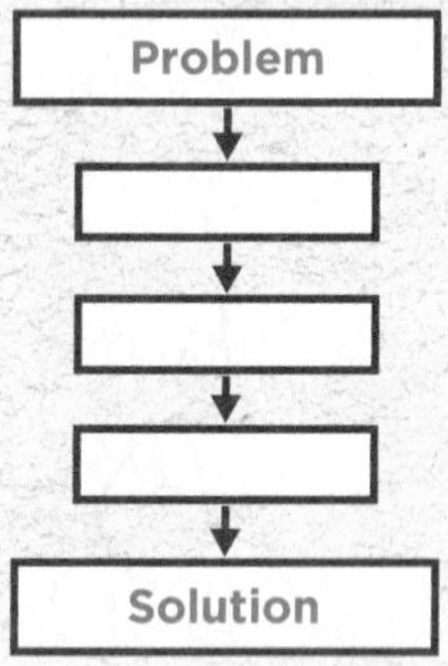

Read to Find Out

Can you solve the mystery before Ramón does?

The Mystery of the Missing Lunch

by Johanna Hurwitz

illustrated by Joe Cepeda

Award Winning Author

At noon, on the first day of school, a very hungry Ramón García looked for his lunch bag in the coat closet. He searched the shelf above the coat hooks but couldn't find his lunch. "My bag isn't here," he complained.

"Are you sure you brought it?" asked his friend Emily Wilson. "Maybe you left it at home."

Ramón was sure. His mom had made him his favorite sandwich—salami—and he knew he hadn't forgotten it.

"Here's my lunch box," reported Ted Collins between sneezes. Ted had been sneezing all morning. "**Allergies**," he explained, apologetically.

Ramón didn't hear him. He was too angry. "Someone took my salami sandwich!" he said to Emily. "And I'm going to find out who!"

FCAT Problem and Solution
Ramón has a big problem. What is it?

“Maybe it was Jack Crawford,” Emily whispered. “He’s always hungry.”

Ramón took out the little notebook he had bought to write down homework **assignments**. It would be good for keeping track of any clues. Then he went over to Jack. He noticed at once that there was no lunch bag or box on Jack’s desk.

“Where’s your lunch?” he asked.

“I don’t have one,” answered Jack.

“Why not?” asked Ramón.

Jack pulled a couple of dollars out of his pocket. “I’m buying today,” he said.

Ramón leaned closer to Jack and sniffed deeply. He couldn’t smell any salami on his classmate’s breath.

“What’s that?” asked Emily. She pointed to a brown smudge on Jack’s shirt. “It looks like mustard.”

“It’s just an old paint stain,” claimed Jack. “I got it when I helped my dad during the summer. It may look like mustard, but it’s called ‘golden oak’ on the paint can.”

“A likely alibi,” Ramón muttered to himself. He made a note of the stain on Jack’s shirt.

"All right, what's going on here?" asked Mrs. Richmond, their fourth-grade teacher.

"Someone took my lunch," said Ramón.

"Don't look at me," said Jack. "I'm innocent."

Mrs. Richmond clapped her hands. "Everyone in your seats," she shouted. "A lunch is missing. We can't leave for the cafeteria until we find it."

"Awww," grumbled all the students together. By now, everyone was hungry. Ted sneezed three times in succession.

No one knew anything about Ramón's lunch bag. The whole class waited while Mrs. Richmond checked the coat closet, but she didn't find Ramón's lunch.

By this time Ramón was so hungry, his stomach was growling. Mrs. Richmond must have been hungry herself, because she solved the problem by handing Ramón a five dollar bill. "Buy something with this," she told him. "You can pay me back tomorrow. I have a feeling that you left your lunch on the bus. I can't imagine any of your classmates taking it."

Of course, it was a relief that Ramón could buy some food. However, he was 100% certain that he had put the bag in the closet. He was determined to discover who had taken it.

In the cafeteria, while he was eating the soggy tuna fish sandwich he had bought, Ramón wrote again in his notebook. He made a list of all his classmates. Any one of them could be the culprit.

Emily leaned forward to see. "Just because you like salami doesn't mean that everyone else does," she pointed out. "Josh, Tina, and Margaret are vegetarians. They wouldn't eat a salami sandwich."

"You're right," agreed Ramón, crossing out their names. "Sarah thinks salami is smelly. She holds her nose whenever she's around it. And all Max ever eats is peanut butter and jelly," he added. He crossed out their names too. After a minute's **consideration**, he crossed Jack's name off his list.

Ted had been too busy sneezing all morning to secretly **consume** a salami sandwich, Ramón decided. Off went his name too.

"Cross me off the list of suspects, too," said Emily. "I don't even like salami."

So far, out of a class of eighteen, eight were definitely innocent. Then there were Beverly and Grace. Neither of them was tall enough to reach the shelf where Ramón put his lunch. He crossed off their names too. The list of potential suspects kept getting shorter. It got even shorter when Ramón realized that he was one of the eighteen students in the class. And he knew for certain that he had not eaten the salami sandwich.

Ramón sighed deeply. His chances of solving this case were getting slimmer and slimmer.

Then, after lunch, when the students were given quiet time for reading, Ramón went back to the closet to see if he could find any clues that he hadn't noticed earlier. He looked under the book bags but found nothing **suspicious** there.

On his way back to his desk, Ramón passed the library corner. He stopped. What was that scratching sound? Could there be a mouse in the classroom? Mice eat anything.

Looking around, he saw poor Ted was still blowing his nose. Then he spotted something! Pieces of torn brown paper lay on the floor near Ted's desk. Ramón picked them up. Immediately, he noticed that there were ink markings on the papers. He placed them together, like puzzle pieces, to form the picture of a smiley face. Ramón recognized it at once. It was the same smiley face his mom had drawn on his lunch bag that morning!

This was a very important clue. Whoever had taken his lunch had torn up the **evidence**!

Just then, Mr. Gordon, the Assistant Principal, knocked and came into the classroom. "Here's the new computer we ordered for you, Mrs. Richmond." He placed it on the counter.

As he started to leave, Mr. Gordon said, "By the way, has anyone seen a stray cat? She sneaked into the school building a few weeks ago when we were painting, and I think she's still hiding somewhere." The kids looked at each other and shook their heads.

"Please let me know if you do. I want to find her a home," Mr. Gordon added.

Mrs. Richmond looked around with a little chuckle. "I don't see any cat in this room," she said.

At that moment, Ted gave three more loud sneezes.

"Wait a minute," Ramón called out. The biggest clue had been right there under his nose all this time. "Ted, what kind of allergy do you have?" he asked. "Could you be allergic to cats?"

"How did you know?" Ted asked when he stopped blowing his nose.

"Your nose gave it away," said Ramón.

Ted grinned. "I'm very allergic to any animal with fur," he admitted.

Mrs. Richmond turned to Mr. Gordon, "And I was worried that he was allergic to fourth grade!"

Ramón started pulling all the books out of the shelves in the library corner. The other students and Mr. Gordon helped. Sure enough, there behind the mystery books was the solution to the mystery of the missing lunch. Three little kittens were hiding amid the remains of Ramón's salami sandwich.

"But where's the mother cat?" asked Mrs. Richmond.

"She won't be far away from her kittens," Mr. Gordon said.

A loud hiss confirmed his words. On top of the closet stood the anxious mother cat.

"You stole my lunch!" Ramón scolded the cat, but he was smiling. He was pleased that he did not have to **accuse** one of his classmates.

The mother cat jumped off the closet and slipped out the door.

"There she goes!" said Mr. Gordon. "Well, I'll take these kittens to my office until we find good homes for them. Their mama will find them. Cats have a good sense of smell."

"*And* they like salami!" said Ramón.

FCAT **Problem and Solution**

Ramón solved the problem. What was the solution?

Clues About the Author and Illustrator

Johanna Hurwitz likes to write about everyday boys and girls, like the ones in this story, and their funny adventures. Johanna gets her story ideas from many places. She thinks about children she knew as a librarian and about people and places she's seen on her trips. She also gets ideas from her family, and, as proven in this story, her cats.

Other books by Johanna Hurwitz and Joe Cepeda

Joe Cepeda did not plan on becoming a children's book illustrator. He planned to be an engineer, but then he went back to school to study illustration. Joe thinks that children who want to be artists should spend a lot of time reading and studying math.

LOG ON Find out more about Johanna Hurwitz and Joe Cepeda at **www.macmillanmh.com**

FCAT Author's Purpose

What clues can you use to figure out Johanna Hurwitz's purpose for writing *The Mystery of the Missing Lunch*? Did she want to inform or entertain? How do you know?

FCAT Comprehension Check

Summarize

Use your Problem and Solution Chart to help you summarize *The Mystery of the Missing Lunch.* Describe Ramón's problem and the steps he took to solve it.

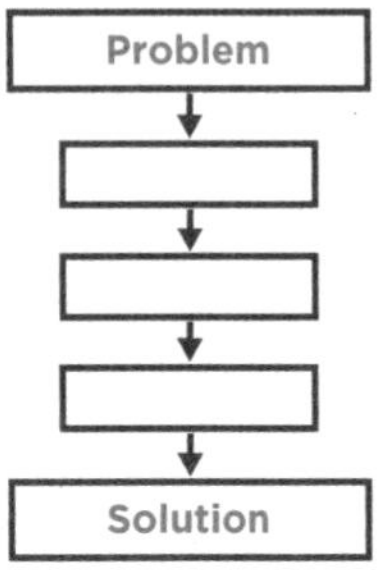

Think and Compare

1. Describe one piece of **evidence** Ramón gathered to solve the mystery. How did that piece of evidence help him? Use details from the story to explain. **Make Inferences and Analyze: Problem and Solution**

2. Why does Ramón eventually cross Jack off the suspect list? Describe the events that led him to make that decision. Provide details from the story. **Analyze**

3. How would you have tried to solve this mystery? Explain. **Apply**

4. Think about Ramón's problem-solving methods. Were they effective? Why or why not? **Evaluate**

5. Read "The Case of the Blurry Board" on pages 18–19. How is Jason's method of solving a problem similar to Ramón's? Explain using details from both stories. **Reading/Writing Across Texts**

Putting Together the Pieces of the Puzzle

by Timothy Grey

Science

Genre

Magazine Articles present facts and photographs of the people and places that are being discussed.

FCAT Text Feature

Charts give the reader information in easy-to-read columns and rows.

Content Vocabulary

investigation **analysis** **forensic**

Police secure a crime scene using official police tape.

A computer is stolen from a woman's house in the middle of the day. No one saw it happen. It is the job of the police to figure out who committed this crime. Without a witness, where will they start? Where would *you* start? With science, of course! Mysteries like these are solved every day with the help of scientists who, like the police, want to catch criminals.

When a crime is committed, the first person called in is a crime scene investigator. Investigators often work in teams made up of scientists and police detectives. Together they try to solve mysteries. Each **investigation** is different. The team of investigators must use different groups of people and create new ways to solve each case.

What is a Crime Scene?

A crime scene is the place where the crime was committed. Each crime scene is handled differently, but there are steps that investigators should follow. First the team of investigators look at the scene to gather information. They have to decide how much of the area can be considered the crime scene. If something was stolen, can investigators see a path that the thief used? If so, the whole path is part of the crime scene. Next they will block off an area larger than the crime scene to protect the scene. Investigators need to make sure that no one touches or moves anything that could have been part of the crime.

Searching for and Collecting Evidence

Investigators search every inch of a crime scene for evidence. To search thoroughly, they follow a pattern. Sometimes, they search an area in a circle. Other times, investigators search in a back and forth pattern. The first evidence they collect is a description of the scene. What do investigators see, smell, or hear? They take pictures and write down anything important. Detectives also collect other evidence from witnesses. Investigators then use the evidence from the crime scene to decide what kinds of scientists and tools will be needed to complete their investigation.

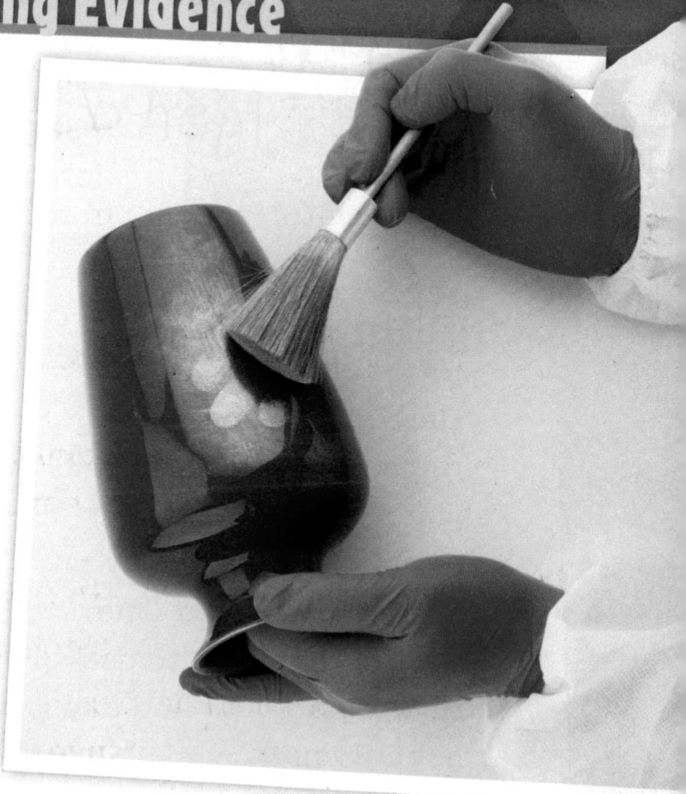

Any bit of evidence, such as a fingerprint, can lead the police to the person who committed the crime.

Types of Physical Evidence

Investigators collect physical evidence. They look for small pieces of evidence like paint chips, grass pieces, and broken glass. They also look for footprints, fingerprints, and marks from any tools that may have been used. Fibers and hairs are also collected. This evidence is brought to scientists in a lab for **analysis**.

This scientist is testing evidence collected at a crime scene.

The Scientist's Job

The scientists who study evidence are called **forensic** scientists. They test all the evidence to get exact measurements to make comparisons. Once they have their test results, the scientists often give opinions about the evidence. Their opinions and the test results are put together and given to the detectives on the case.

Solving the Case

Detectives use the evidence they gathered and the information from the scientists to figure out what happened in a crime. The police are then able to use all that information to find and arrest criminals.

In court the evidence and scientists' findings are presented to a judge and jury.

Reading a Chart

This chart shows the steps for solving a crime.
The steps are presented in columns and rows.

Steps for Solving a Crime	
Step 1	Investigators look at the scene and gather information.
Step 2	Investigators decide how large the crime scene area is.
Step 3	The team of investigators protect the crime scene.
Step 4	Investigators search for and collect evidence.
Step 5	Detectives interview witnesses.
Step 6	Investigators give evidence to scientists for analysis.
Step 7	Scientists perform tests on all the evidence.
Step 8	Scientists give test results and opinions to the detectives.
Step 9	Police use the evidence to find and arrest criminals.

FCAT Connect and Compare

1. At what step in the process do detectives interview the witnesses? **Reading a Chart**
2. Why does the investigation team collect things like fibers and hairs? How does this evidence help scientists? **Evaluate**
3. Think about this article and *The Mystery of the Missing Lunch*. How is Ramón like a crime scene investigator? **Reading/ Writing Across Texts**

Research Inquiry — Science Activity

Research the types of tools used to solve crimes. Make a chart showing the information you gathered about the different tools, what they are used for, and who uses them.

LOG ON Find out more about investigators at **www.macmillanmh.com**

Write About a Problem

Writer's Craft

FCAT A Good Paragraph

A good paragraph has a topic sentence that tells what the paragraph will be about. The other sentences provide details about the topic sentence.

I wrote about a problem and how I solved it. Here's my topic sentence.

The other sentences give details about what happened.

What's That Noise?

by Indira S.

Last weekend, all of a sudden, a loud banging woke me up. Thump, thump! I was at Grandma's house in Pennsylvania. I was scared – I thought a bear was trying to get into the house! I thought a light might scare the bear. I put on the lamp, but the thumping got louder.

Then I heard a small woof. I looked over the side of the bed and saw Grandma's dog, Rusty, lying on the floor. The thumping was her tail wagging!

Writing Prompt

Most people have faced a problem they needed to solve.

Think about a time you had a problem you needed to solve.

Now write a story about a time you had a problem and how you solved it.

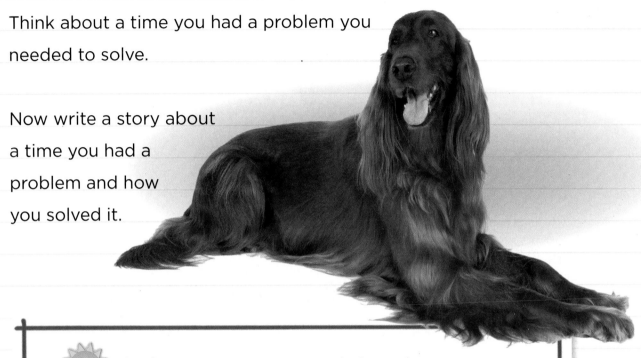

FCAT Writer's Checklist

- ☑ **Focus:** My topic sentence clearly presents the main idea.
- ☐ **Organization:** My good paragraph begins with a topic sentence and provides supporting details.
- ☑ **Support:** I include details that support my topic sentence and clearly show the reader what happened.
- ☑ **Conventions:** My sentences are complete. My spelling is correct and I use proper punctuation.

Adapting to Survive

Talk About It

How is the insect in the photograph adapting to survive? How do you adapt to your surroundings?

LOG ON Find out more about adaptation at **www.macmillanmh.com**

Vocabulary

shimmer **climate**
eerie **silken**
lurk **lumbering**
swallows

FCAT Context Clues

Surrounding Words can often help you figure out the meaning of unfamiliar words. Read through the story and find the sentence where the word *shimmer* appears. Read the sentence slowly. Use the surrounding words to help you figure out the meaning of *shimmer*.

Living in Alaska

by Marsha Adams

Another World

In some ways, living in Alaska is like living in another world. Winter lasts for about nine months. For more than two months each year, the northern lights that **shimmer** in the sky are the only source of light.

For the people there, it can be **eerie** to go so long without seeing the sun. For the animals, it can be dangerous. Such dim light makes it difficult to see whether predators **lurk** in the shadows, waiting for their next meal. It may be a snowy owl that swoops down on silent wings and **swallows** its prey whole!

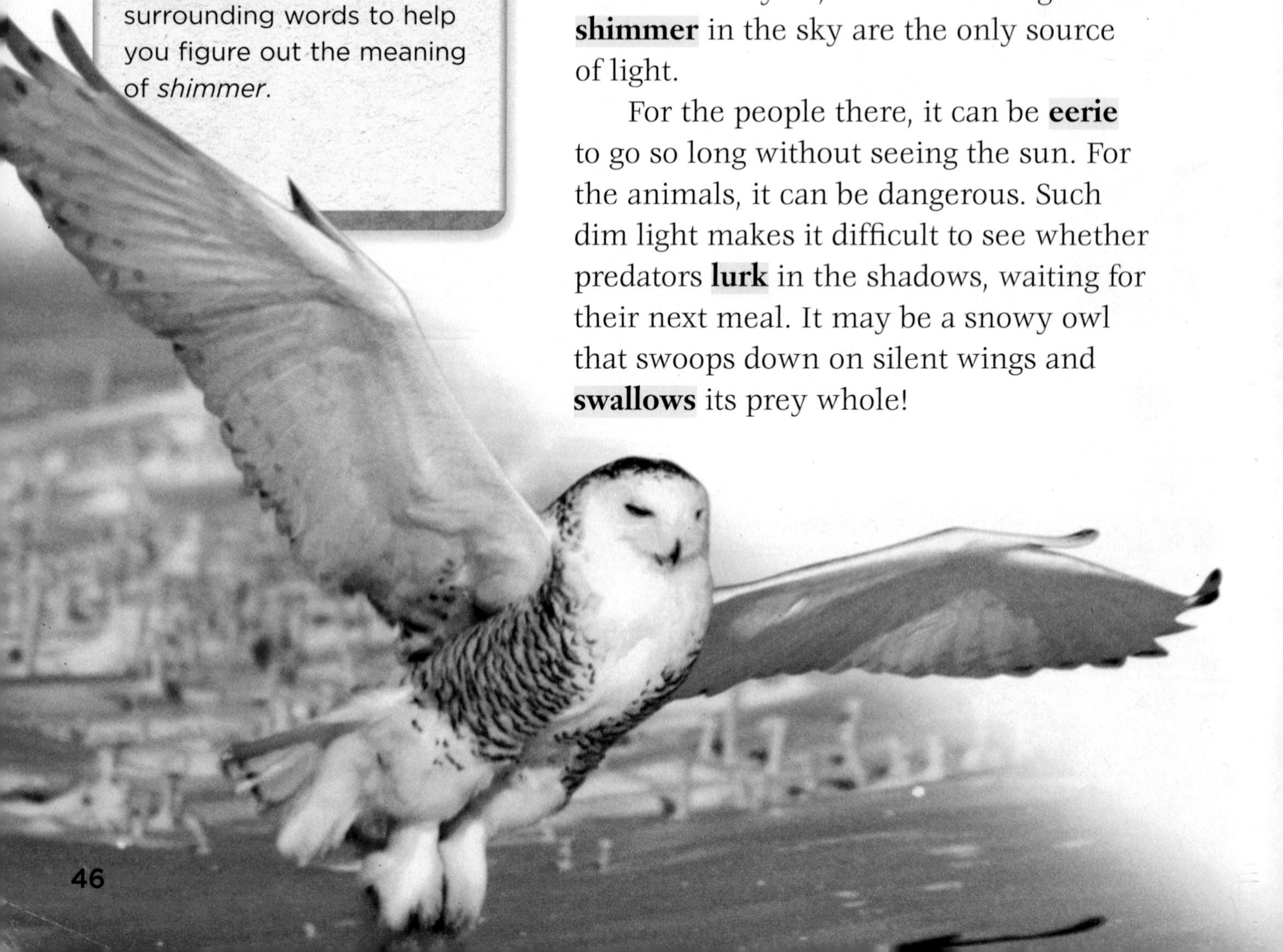

Winter Coats

Beavers, sea otters, and other mammals are adapted to survive in the cold Alaskan **climate**. They grow two layers of fur. The thick bottom layer is soft, **silken** fur that helps trap body heat. Longer, coarse hairs that form the outer layer act as a barrier against water, snow, and wind.

The ptarmigan, Alaska's state bird, has a special way to keep warm. It grows feathers down its legs, over its toes, and on the soles of its feet!

A Winter Nap

You won't find **lumbering** black or brown bears when the frigid weather arrives. Bears, mice, and other animals hibernate, or go into a deep sleep, during the winter. When they hibernate, their bodies don't need food or water. Other animals, such as some caterpillars, fish, and houseflies, actually freeze during the winter. Then they thaw out in the spring!

A Low Profile

Arctic plants have their own special traits that help them survive. During the summer months, the dark soil absorbs the sun's heat. So plants grow close to the ground, where it's warmer. When snow falls, it protects the plants from the cold winds above.

Reread for Comprehension

Summarize

FCAT **Main Idea and Details** The **main idea** is the most important point in a paragraph or section. **Details** give information that support the main idea. To summarize a passage, use your own words to describe the main idea and important details. Reread the selection to find the main idea and supporting details.

Main Ideas	Details

Comprehension

Genre

Informational Nonfiction is a detailed composition that sets out to explain something by presenting facts about it.

Summarize

FCAT

Main Idea and Details
As you read, fill in your Main Idea Chart.

Main Ideas	Details

Read to Find Out

What characteristics allow desert animals to live in such a hot, dry place?

A Walk in the Desert

by Rebecca L. Johnson

with illustrations by Phyllis V. Saroff

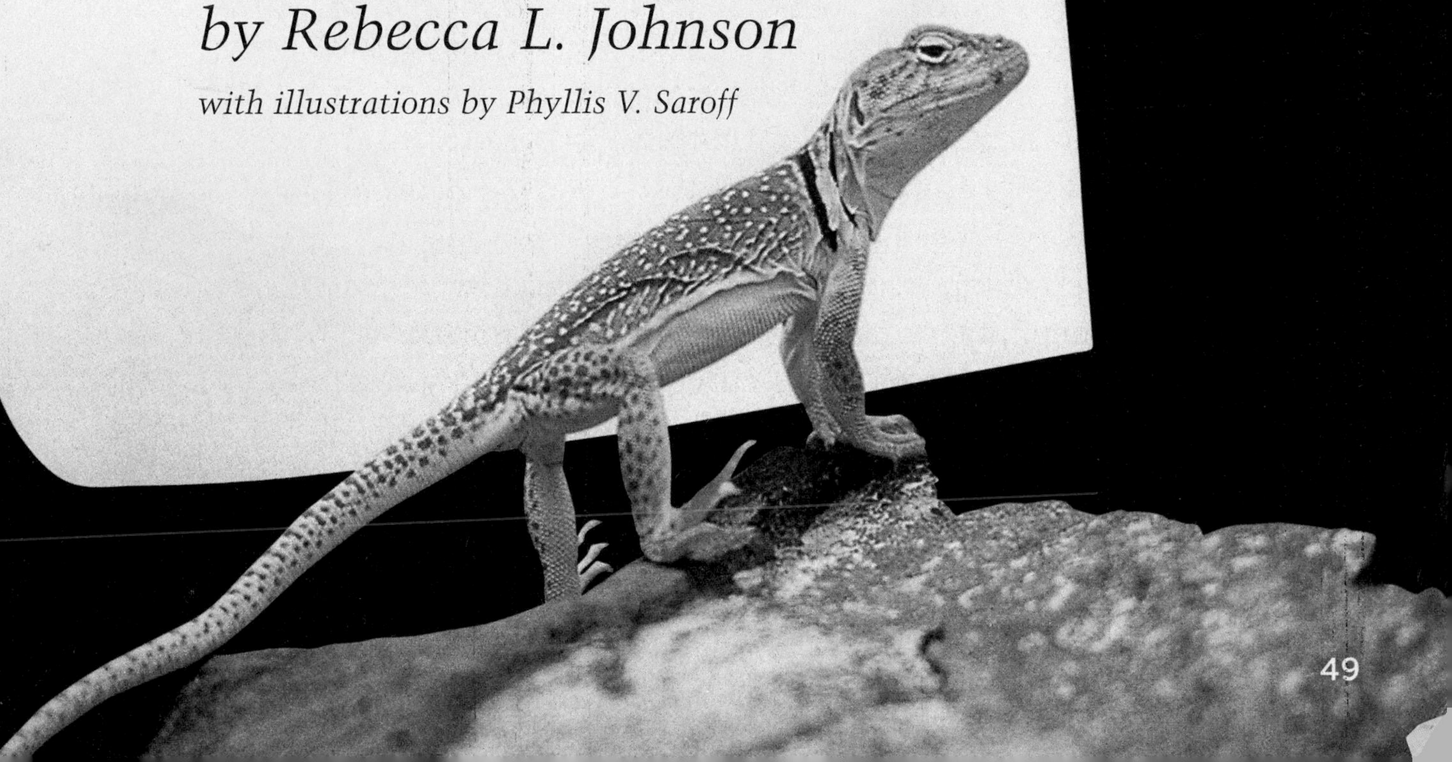

Biomes of North America

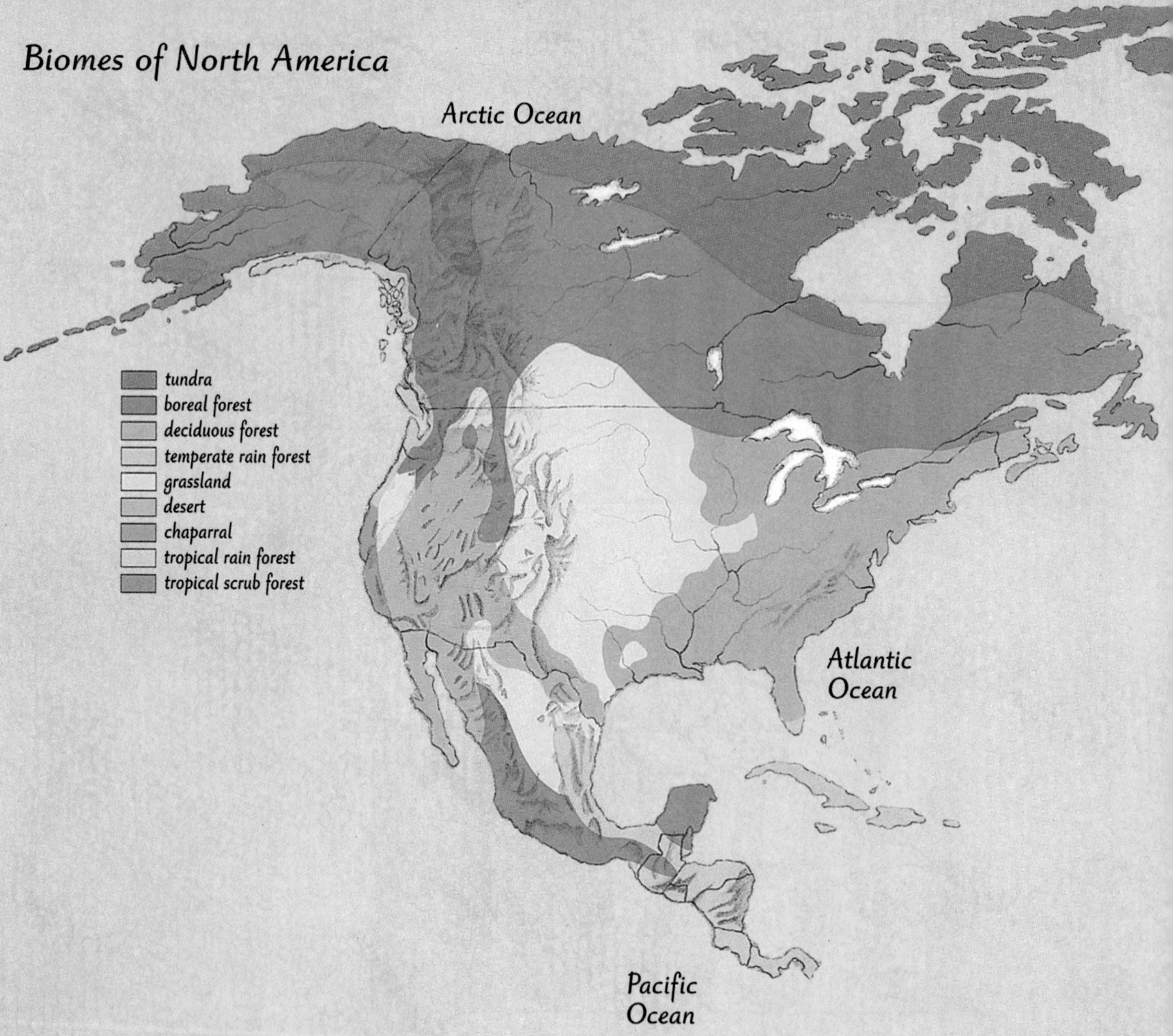

*S*unbeams are flickering over the landscape as the sun rises. A kit fox heads for her den as another day in the desert begins.

Deserts are surrounded by other kinds of landscapes. Scientists call these different land zones biomes. All the plants and animals in a biome form a community. In that community, every living thing depends on other community members for its survival. A biome's **climate**, soil, plants, and animals are all connected this way.

Deserts have a very dry climate. They do get a little rain, but it doesn't come regularly. One storm might drench a desert with several inches of rain in just a few hours. It might not rain again for months—even years.

A mother desert tortoise lays her eggs in sandy soil. The sun warms the eggs until they hatch.

Desert plants provide many animals with food and water. Here comes a desert tortoise. It shuffles slowly along and stops often to rest. The tortoise stretches its long neck to nibble a wildflower. Tortoises rarely drink. They get nearly all the water they need from the plants they eat.

Cacti also provide homes for desert animals. Halfway down a nearby saguaro's thick stem, a Gila woodpecker pecks a hole in the juicy flesh. It is making a nest for its eggs. Woodpeckers have nested in this cactus for many years, so they've made many holes in it.

Other creatures have moved into some of the old woodpecker holes. A pair of flycatchers lives in one. Another is home to a hive of honeybees. And peeking out of still another hole is an elf owl. It has white eyebrows and fierce yellow eyes.

Saguaro cacti grow very slowly. But they may live for 200 years.

A wood rat nibbles on the sweet fruit of a prickly pear cactus.

Not far from the saguaro, you see a very different kind of desert home. Jammed between a dead cactus and a fallen tree is a huge mound of tangled twigs. It's the nest of a wood rat.

Wood rats are also called pack rats. They use anything they can find to build enormous nests. A wood rat's nest might be made of sticks, rocks, leaves, cactus spines, or even bones. It may be as tall as a person and just as wide. The nest protects the wood rat from foxes, hawks, and other predators. It is also a cool place to hide from the hot sun.

FCAT Main Idea and Details
What is the main idea in the second paragraph?

Many desert animals are nocturnal. They are active only at night, when it is cooler. Nocturnal desert-dwellers spend their days in burrows, dens, and other sheltered places. The kangaroo rat and the kit fox are nocturnal. They stay underground until the sun goes down.

Elf owls are the smallest owls in the world. They are about the size of sparrows.

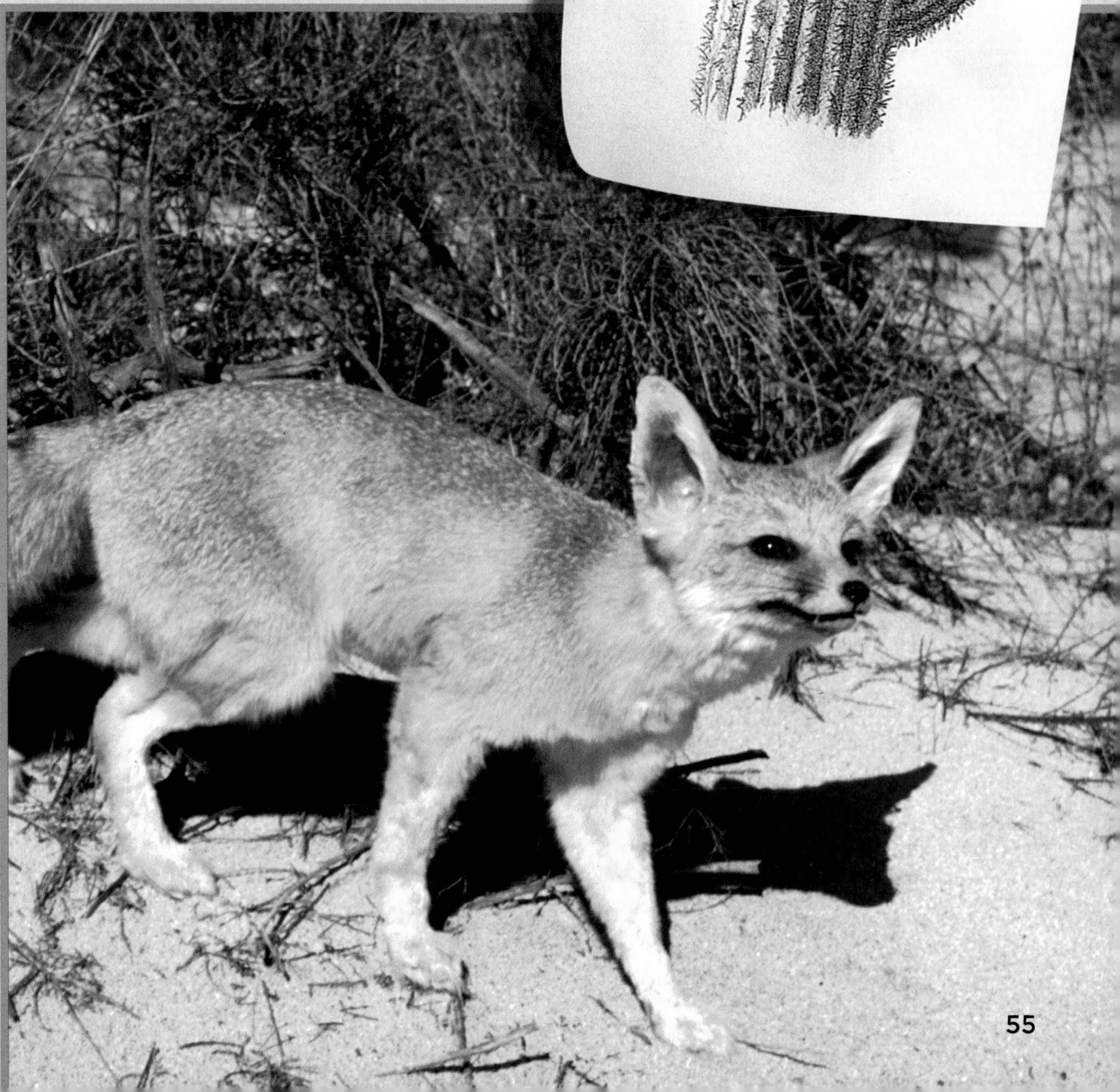

A painted grasshopper uses its long legs to hop from plant to plant—and to escape being eaten.

But some desert animals are active during the day. Insects are on the move everywhere. Columns of ants march across the ground. Colorful beetles crawl up and down stems. Grasshoppers spring from leaf to leaf. Insect-eating spiders are busy, too. They spin **silken** webs among cactus spines.

The sun has climbed higher in the clear blue sky. Can you feel the heat? Desert lizards don't seem to mind. Their tough, scaly skin seals water inside their bodies and keeps them from drying out. Lizards rest on rocks, hunt insects, and cling to cactus stems. In one small patch of desert, you could see tiny skinks, chunky chuckwallas, spiny horned lizards, and **lumbering** Gila monsters.

A horned lizard's spiny scales are a good defense against desert predators.

Suddenly, something streaks across your path. It's a speedy lizard, and right on its heels is a roadrunner. Roadrunners can fly. But these desert birds prefer to run after lizards and the other small animals they hunt.

Roadrunners have long, strong legs. They can run as fast as many lizards can. In fact, this time the bird is faster. The roadrunner catches the lizard by its tail and **swallows** it in one gulp.

A roadrunner's feet have two toes that point forward and two that point backward. This shape helps the bird grip the ground when it runs.

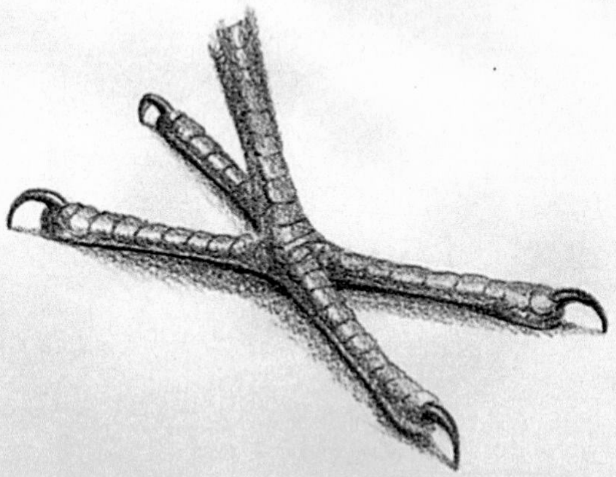

Desert jackrabbits have longer ears than rabbits from other biomes. Long ears release heat and help jackrabbits stay cool.
cottontail rabbit
jackrabbit

Nearby, a jackrabbit looks for plants to nibble. Jackrabbits are even faster than roadrunners. They can outrun almost everything in the desert. They can even outrun coyotes—most of the time!

Coyotes eat rabbits when they can catch them. But they will eat just about anything, from birds and lizards to berries. To find underground water, they dig holes in dry streambeds. Coyotes can survive almost anywhere.

A mother scorpion carries her babies around on her back until they can survive on their own.

By noon, even the coyotes are panting. It's well over 100 degrees. The sun is a fireball overhead. Nearly all the daytime animals move into the shade of rocks and cacti during the hottest part of the day.

A rattlesnake's rattle is made up of a row of large, dry scales.

Take a tip from the animals. Find a place out of the sun to rest. Just be careful where you sit. Scorpions often **lurk** in crevices or under rocks during the day. A scorpion's tail has a stinger filled with poison. Few kinds of scorpions can kill a person. But the sting of any scorpion is very painful.

Watch out for hiding rattlesnakes and coral snakes, too. Their poison is deadly. You don't want to get within striking distance of either one.

Heat waves **shimmer** above the landscape. The leaves of the mesquite trees curl up. Curled leaves lose less water to the hot, dry air. The desert is very quiet. Most of the birds are silent. They seem to be waiting for the sun's fierce heat to fade.

Gradually, the sun moves lower in the sky. As shadows grow longer, the temperature starts to drop. Desert birds begin to sing again. At sunset, coyotes call to each other, barking and yelping. They join voices in an **eerie**, wailing song.

FCAT **Main Idea and Details**

Name the main idea on these two pages. Which details support the main idea?

The hot desert day is over. The cool night is about to begin. Birds, lizards, and other daytime animals retreat to snug nests and safe hiding places. There they will sleep the night away.

Take a Walk with Rebecca

Rebecca L. Johnson grew up in South Dakota. Harsh prairie winters helped her prepare for working with scientists in Antarctica. Ms. Johnson has traveled to Antarctica twice and has written three books on the experience: *Braving the Frozen Frontier*, *Investigating the Ozone Hole*, and *Science on the Ice* (winner of the *Scientific American* Young Readers Award). She has also "walked" in several other biomes—the tundra, the rain forest, the prairie, and others—for the "Biomes of North America" series.

Rebecca studied Biology at Augustana College and has worked as a teacher and a museum curator. She enjoys scuba diving, water color painting, and cross country skiing, and lives in South Dakota with her husband.

LOG ON Find out more about Rebecca L. Johnson at **www.macmillanmh.com**

FCAT Author's Purpose

How do you think the author's own experiences influenced her purpose for writing *A Walk in the Desert*? Did she want to entertain or to inform the reader?

FCAT Comprehension Check

Summarize

Use your Main Idea Chart to summarize *A Walk in the Desert.* State the main ideas and the details that support those main ideas.

Main Ideas	Details

Think and Compare

1. What is the main idea of the story? Include details from the story that support the main idea. **Summarize: Main Idea and Details**

2. Describe the different physical features of some of the animals in this selection. How do these features help them survive in the desert climate? Explain using story details. **Analyze**

3. If you were taking a walk in the desert, which of the plants and animals described in this selection would you most want to see? Why? **Apply**

4. How could people living in the desert adapt to the **climate**? Explain using story details. **Apply**

5. Read "Living in Alaska" on pages 46-47. Compare the plants and animals in Alaska's environment with those in the desert. How are they similar? Use details from both selections to explain. **Reading/Writing Across Texts**

Cinquains

by Polly Peterson

FCAT

Poetry

A **Cinquain** has five lines of two, four, six, eight, and two syllables. The first line may also be the title.

Literary Elements

Assonance is created by repeating similar vowel sounds in two or more words. An example is ***green cream***. These words share the vowel sound ***e***.

A **Metaphor** is a figure of speech in which two very different objects or ideas are said to be alike. An example of a metaphor is ***Life is a beach***.

FAT FROG

Fat frog
Murky as mud
Hides all but his high eyes.
Flash! Flick! Flies cannot flee from that
Fast tongue.

You can hear assonance in the words "high eyes," which both have the long *i* sound.

White Swans

White swans,
Awkward on land,
Glide through water with ease.
Wide webbed feet grant them the grace of
Dancers.

The poet creates a metaphor by comparing swans to dancers.

GRASS SNAKE

Grass snake
Graceful and quick
Slithers, slips, slides away —
Disappears quietly as a
Daydream.

FCAT Connect and Compare

1. Besides "high eyes," find an example of assonance in one of these cinquains. What vowel sound do the words share? **Assonance**

2. Which cinquain best captures the animal it describes? Explain. **Analyze**

3. How are the animals in these poems well adapted to their environments? Compare them with animals from *A Walk in the Desert*. **Reading/Writing Across Texts**

LOG ON Find out more about cinquains at **www.macmillanmh.com**

Write About an Animal

Writer's Craft

FCAT **Topic Sentence**

A **topic sentence** is the first sentence of a paragraph. It lets readers know what the rest of the paragraph is going to be about.

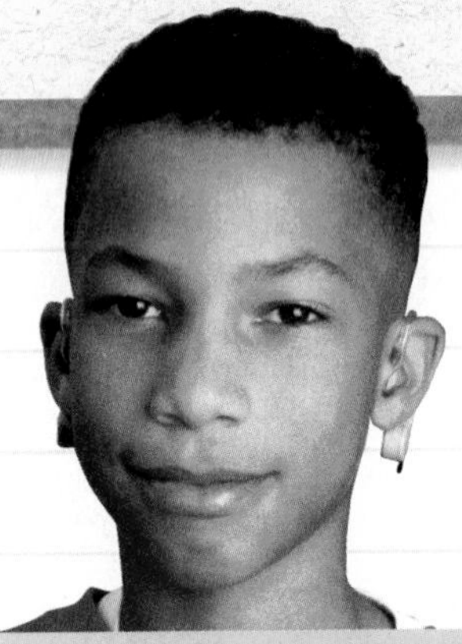

My topic sentence tells what I am writing about.

In the other sentences, I explain why I would like to be a pelican.

Why I'd be a Pelican

by Joshua M.

If I could be any animal, I'd be a pelican. Pelicans live by the ocean, which is my favorite place to be. They fly in the air and dive into the water to catch fish. I've always wanted to fly and I love eating fish.

Pelicans like to be in a group. Most pelicans live with their family and friends. I like to be with my family and friends. If I were a pelican I could be with them all of the time! I think I would enjoy being a pelican.

Writing Prompt

Imagine you could be any kind of animal in the world.

Think about what animal you would want to be.

Now write to explain why you would want to be this animal.

FCAT Writer's Checklist

- [ ] **Focus:** My topic sentence is the first sentence. It clearly tells readers what my main idea is.
- [x] **Organization:** I present my reasons in order, saving my strongest reason for last.
- [x] **Support:** In my detail sentences, I use facts to support my reasons.
- [x] **Conventions:** I use complete sentences and proper punctuation. My grammar and spelling is correct.

Talk About It

National parks are full of history and life. What things can you learn about at a national park?

LOG ON Find out more about our national parks at **www.macmillanmh.com**

OUR NATIONAL PARKS

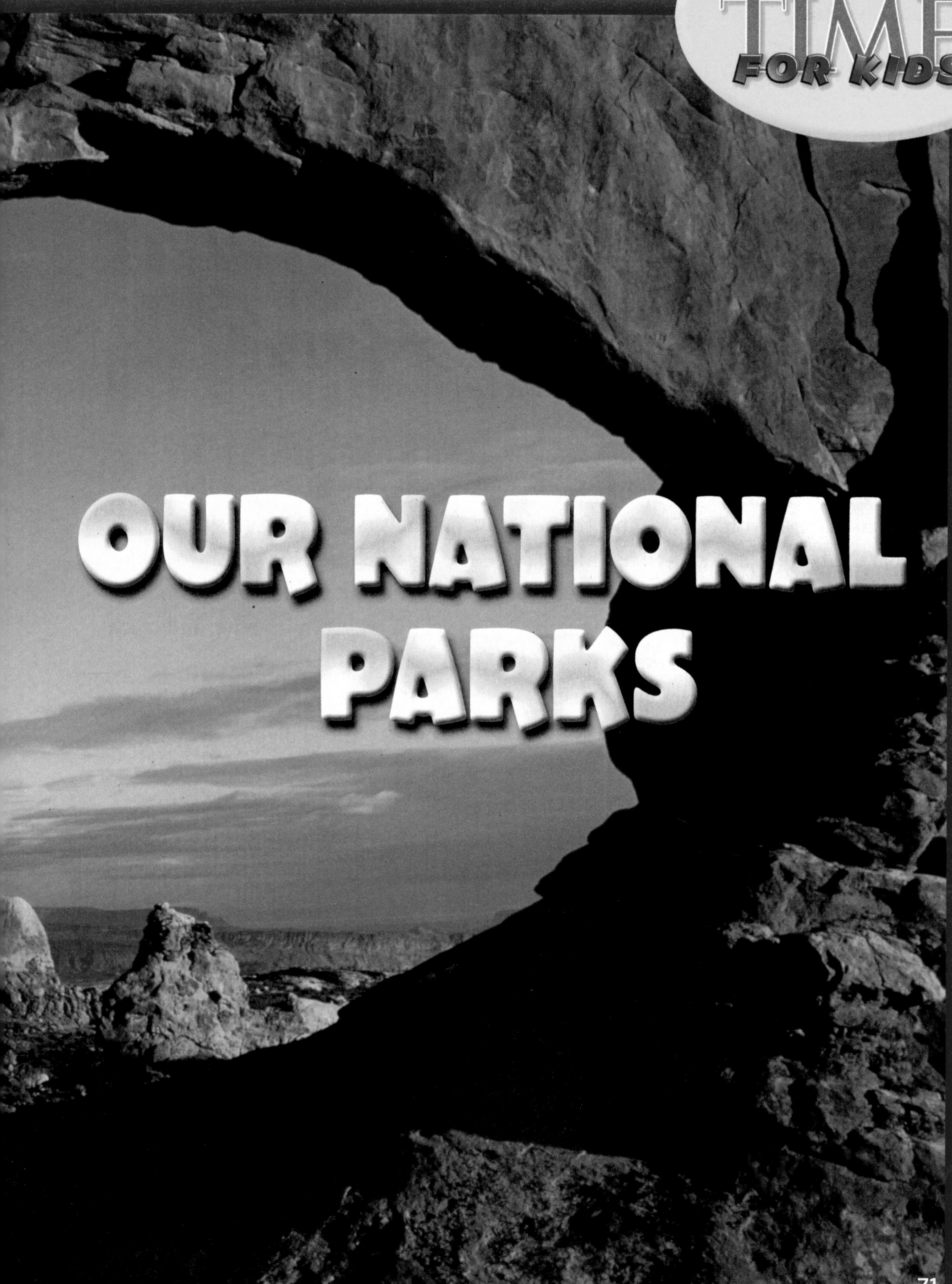

Vocabulary

roamed
completed
journey
natural
wildlife

A Prehistoric Park

More than 200 million years ago, dinosaurs **roamed** freely over the earth. Have you ever wondered what the land was like or what kind of trees there were then? You can see some of these trees today in Arizona! Throughout 28 miles of desert in Petrified Forest National Park, you can see 225-million-year-old fossil trees. Visitors are amazed to see these trees that have turned to stone.

How did it happen? Millions of years ago, water filled with minerals flowed into the area. Over time the minerals seeped into fallen trees and turned them into rock-hard logs. Some of these logs are 100 feet long! Today they create a colorful and amazing sight in Arizona's desert. The petrified logs look like wooden rainbows. The colors range from red, to yellow, to green, to blue, and black and white.

Petrified Forest National Park is one of the world's biggest displays of petrified wood. Nearly one million people visit the park every year to get an up-close look at these fossils of prehistoric trees.

These logs were trees 225 million years ago. Now they are stone in the Petrified Forest National Park in Arizona.

King of the Mountain

By the time Scott Cory was 13 years old, he had already scaled two major peaks in California's Yosemite National Park. One was the 2,900-foot "Nose" of El Capitan. The other was the 2,000-foot face of Half Dome. The first time Scott climbed the Nose, it took him three days and two nights. One month later he **completed** that climb in one day! Scott later became the youngest person to climb Half Dome in only one day. The **journey** to the top usually takes three days!

Scott started climbing when he was seven years old. When he's not on the peaks, he hits the gym for push-ups and pull-ups. What's next for this peak pro? Scott wants to climb to the top of the Nose and Half Dome together in just 24 hours. You could say this kid really sets a goal and then climbs for it!

LOG ON Find out more about Yosemite National Park at **www.macmillanmh.com**

The Top 5 Most Visited National Parks

In 1872 Yellowstone National Park became the first national park in the United States. Since then more than 383 parks have been added to the list. More than three million people visit these natural, unspoiled places every year. They take thousands of photos of the wildlife. Which parks recently brought in the most visitors in a year? Here's how they ranked.

1. **Great Smoky Mountains National Park, North Carolina and Tennessee**
2. **Grand Canyon National Park, Arizona**
3. **Yosemite National Park, California**
4. **Olympic National Park, Washington**
5. **Rocky Mountain National Park, Colorado**

Comprehension

Genre

A **Nonfiction Article** tells facts about a person, place, or event.

Summarize

FCAT **Main Idea and Details**

The main idea of an article is what it is mostly about. Details support and give information about the main idea.

A male and female elk graze in the Great Smoky Mountains National Park. Female elk are called cows.

Animals Come Home to Our National Parks

How did the return of elk to one national park and gray wolves to another affect the ecosystems of those parks?

National parks protect **wildlife**, history, and culture. Still, hundreds of plants and animals have disappeared from our national parks. That's because their environment has changed, mostly because of human activities.

Today park rangers work to restore the balance of each park ecosystem. They are bringing plants and animals back into their **natural** environments. So far the programs are working—especially for elk and wolves.

Long Journey Home

It was a cold morning in January when 28 elk had finally **completed** a long **journey**. They had traveled 2,500 miles by truck from Elk Island National Park in Canada to the Great Smoky Mountains National Park in North Carolina. They were the first of 52 elk to be reintroduced into the park.

Ten million elk once **roamed** all over North America. Now there are only about one million. Elk disappeared from North Carolina more than 150 years ago. Many were killed by hunters. Others died as people built farms, towns, and roads where elk once grazed.

Elk munch on trees and bushes, allowing more sunlight into the park so ground-level plants can grow. Smaller animals, like chipmunks, can then flourish. Chipmunks are food for larger animals, like wolves. Without the elk, the park's ecosystem didn't function as well. "We are trying to restore the ecosystem to what it was 200 years ago," said Lawrence Hartman of the National Park Service.

Park workers watch as relocated elk dash for freedom.

Have they achieved their goal? So far, so good. Researchers have been studying the elks' progress. Jennifer Murrow is leading the research. She tracks the elk using special radio collars that are placed around the elks' necks. The collars send signals that show researchers where the elk are and how they are doing.

Researchers also keep track of the number of elk calves that are born each year. In the first year, 11 calves were born in the park. Eight survived, but some were preyed upon by bears. It's all part of the natural balance—and that's exactly what wildlife researchers like to see.

Yellowstone Food Chain

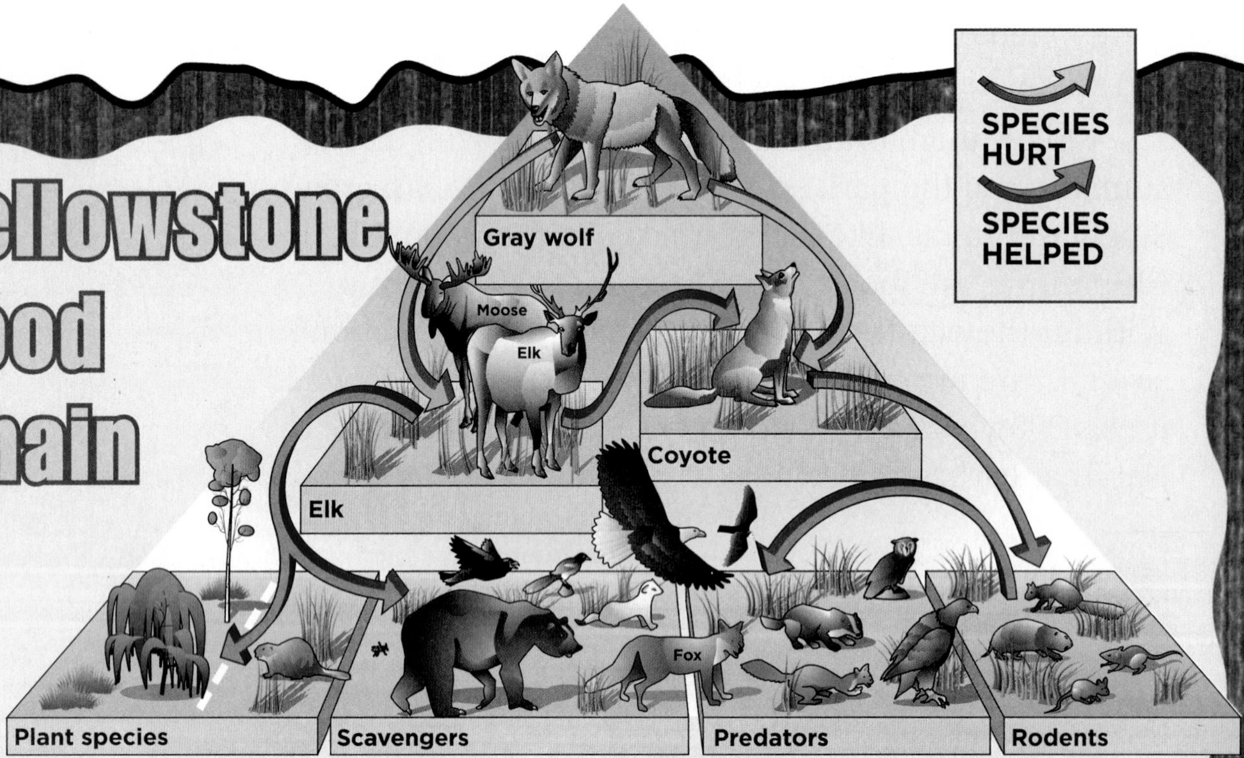

The disappearance of wolves left a big hole in Yellowstone's ecosystem. Coyotes and elk, which are hunted by wolves, became too numerous. Plants began to disappear because the elk population had grown so large. Foxes, which eat the same rodents as coyotes, were starving because the coyotes were catching most of the prey. The ecosystem of the park was badly out of balance.

The government wanted to fix the park's ecosystem. They decided to bring back the wolves. The goal was to put nature back into balance. Now Yellowstone is howling with life once again, and nature is taking its course.

Gray wolves live in packs that can have as few as 8 members or as many as 35.

Howling Back to Life

For centuries, packs of wolves lived in the West. When settlers came in the 1800s, they hunted these wild animals. By the 1970s, the wolves had completely disappeared from Yellowstone National Park. They had also become endangered in much of the United States.

In 1995, 31 gray wolves were released into the park. Now, more than a decade later, there are more than five times as many wolves roaming through Yellowstone.

FCAT

Think and Compare

1. What animal was returned to Great Smoky Mountains National Park? What animal was brought back into Yellowstone National Park? Why was this done?
2. How does the disappearance of one animal affect the other animals and plants in an ecosystem? Explain.
3. If you could visit any national park in the United States, which one would you choose, and why?
4. Compare the problems a park ranger at Yellowstone might face with those of a ranger in Yosemite or Petrified Forest National Park.

Saving a National Park

FCAT Test Strategy

Right There

You can put your finger on the answer. Look for key words in the question. Then find those key words in the selection.

The Florida Panther is on the endangered species list. Human development in Florida destroyed much of its habitat.

The early settlers of Florida's Everglades declared the area a worthless swamp. In fact the Everglades is a unique paradise that is home to thousands of species of plants and animals. The plants and animals living in the Everglades form a delicate food chain where they rely on each other—and a steady supply of precious water—for survival. However, human development in the Everglades has threatened to disrupt the water supply and the ecosystem.

In order to develop within the Everglades, people needed dry land to build homes and plant farms. A small portion of the Everglades was dedicated as a National Park in 1947, which meant people could not develop on this land. The rest of the Everglades was not protected from human development, so people began draining water from many different areas. This began a chain reaction that upset the delicate ecosystem of the Everglades.

The Everglades wetlands are now only half their original size. From 1900 to 2000, the number of wading birds decreased by 90 percent. Human development had a major effect on the National Park. It is now considered one of the ten most endangered parks in the United States.

Now there is a plan to save the Everglades. Engineers have designed wells and pumps to capture water before it flows out of the Everglades. Many canals built to support human development are being removed. The removal of the canals allows water to follow its natural course. The plan may take as many as 50 years to complete. However, saving this unique ecosystem is an important goal, no matter how long it takes.

Go on

FCAT **Now answer Numbers 1 through 5. Base your answers on the article "Saving a National Park."**

1 What do plants and animals rely on for survival?

(A) dry land to build homes
(B) canals that let water flow naturally
(C) wells and pumps that capture water
(D) one another and a steady supply of water

2 The Everglades ecosystem was upset by human development because people

(F) made it into a national park.
(G) drained water from many different areas.
(H) hunted many of the animals that live there.
(I) removed the canals that had been placed there.

Tip
Look for key words.

3 The new plan for the Everglades shows that

(A) people value new homes over national parks.
(B) people want to save it, no matter how long it takes.
(C) engineers will replace the park with wells and pumps.
(D) people keep wasting natural resources, such as water.

4 READ THINK EXPLAIN Describe the plan that was developed to save the Everglades. How long will it take to complete? Use details from the article to explain.

5 READ THINK EXPLAIN What is the main idea of this article? Explain using the most important details from the article.

STOP

Write to a Prompt

FCAT

Most people do several things to get ready to go on a trip.

Think about what you would do to get ready for a trip.

Now write to tell how you get ready for a trip.

Expository writing explains, defines, or tells how to do something.

To figure out if a writing prompt asks for expository writing, look for clue words, such as explain, tell how, or define.

Below see how one student begins a response to the prompt above.

In response to the prompt, the writer included specific details.

On Saturdays my family goes to our city park. We always have a lot of things to do before we are ready to go.

First I help my sister make sandwiches. We always make two different sandwiches for each person. That is a total of twelve sandwiches for the whole family.

Then I pack my backpack. I always put in binoculars so I can watch the birds. I put in an extra sweater so I won't be cold and if it's warm, I pack my softball and mitt. This way I can play catch with my sister.

The last thing I do before we leave is put the leash on my dog, Chief.

Writing Prompt

Respond in writing to the prompt below. Before you write, read the Writing Hints below. Review the hints after you finish writing.

FCAT

There are things people do after returning from a trip.
Think about what you would do after returning from a trip.
Write to tell what you would do after returning from a trip.

Writing Hints for Prompts

- ☑ Read the prompt carefully.
- ☑ Plan your writing by organizing your ideas.
- ☑ Support your ideas by telling more about each event or reason.
- ☑ Use compound sentences to add variety.
- ☑ Choose words that help others understand what you mean.
- ☑ Review and edit your writing.

Astronauts

Talk About It

What do you think is happening in this photograph?

LOG ON Find out more about astronauts at **www.macmillanmh.com**

Vocabulary

endless **sensible**
realistic **protested**
universe **paralyzed**
astronaut

FCAT Dictionary

Using a Dictionary will help you to learn the pronunciation and meaning of a word you may not know.

Look up the meaning and pronunciation of *sensible.*

Astronauts in Training

by Benjamin Telicki

Ana Gomez spotted Larry Waters looking for a table in the cafeteria. "Hi, Larry!" she called out.

Larry smiled and brought his tray over. "Hi, Ana. You're looking especially cheerful this morning," he remarked as he sat.

Ana smiled broadly.

"You got your launch date, didn't you?" Larry exclaimed.

"Yes, I did," Ana replied. "Finally! The wait seemed **endless**. I have been curious about that planet since I was ten and now I'll be on our first mission to Venus. We're leaving ten months from now on April 17, 2016."

"That's **realistic**. You'll have plenty of time to train your crew, and they'll have time to review the virtual trip before the actual flight. Congratulations, Ana. It sounds like you would have picked this mission if you had your choice of any planet in the whole **universe**."

"Well," replied Ana, "if I could go anywhere in the solar system, I'd pick Neptune. But that wouldn't be a wise choice for a middle-aged **astronaut**. By the time we're able to go there, I'll be out of the space program! I'll be **sensible** and stick to Venus. What about you, Larry? You applied for the next trip to Mars. It's time you went as the commander."

Larry **protested.** "I wish I could but sometimes I feel **paralyzed** during training. It's like I can't move or breathe! I doubt I'll be commander anytime soon. I'm going to keep working at it though and maybe I'll be able to go to Mars in April."

"Wouldn't it be great if we were headed for Earth's nearest neighbors at the same time?"

Reread for Comprehension

Make Inferences and Analyze

FCAT **Plot Development** The plot tells what happens to a **character** in a story. To learn more about a character, pay attention to traits and actions throughout the story. Use a Character Web to help you better understand a character. Reread the selection and fill in your web to find the character's traits.

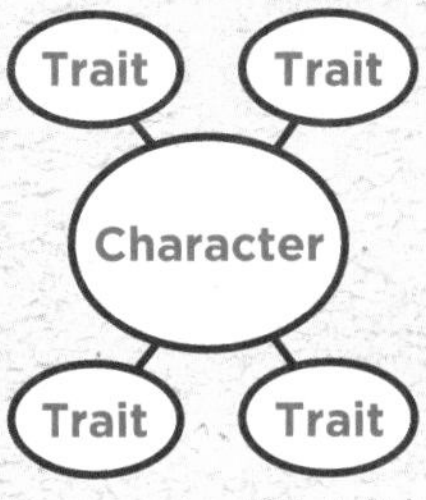

Comprehension

Genre

Realistic Fiction is a made-up story that could have happened in real life.

Make Inferences and Analyze

FCAT **Plot Development**

As you read, fill in your Character Web.

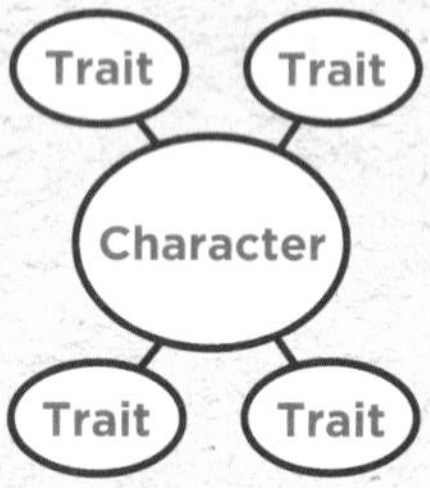

Read to Find Out

How does a trip to the supermarket change Gloria?

The Astronaut and the Onion

BY Ann Cameron

ILLUSTRATED BY Anna Rich

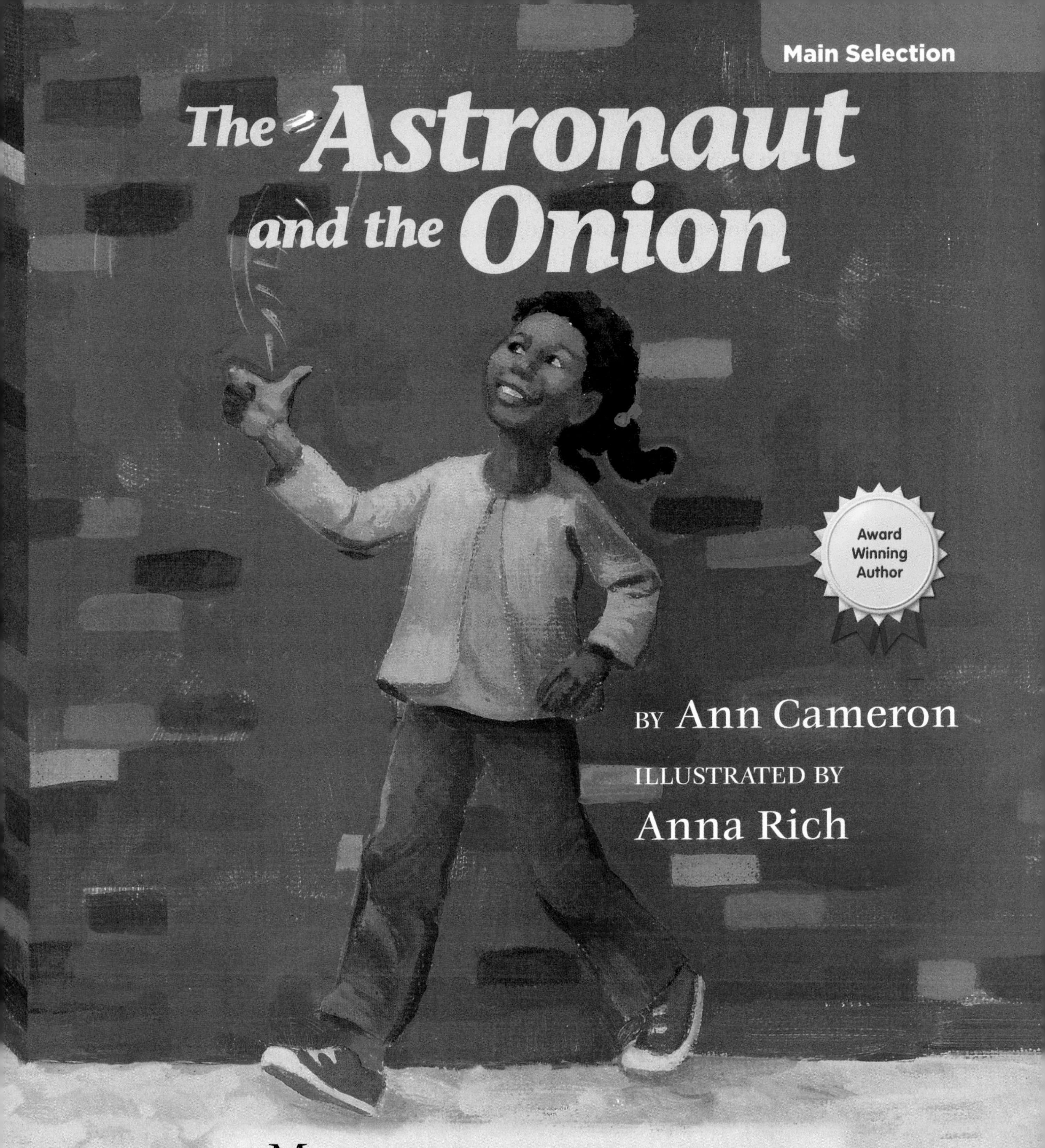

MY MOTHER was making spaghetti sauce. She said, "Gloria, honey, would you go buy me an onion?"

"Sure," I said. She gave me some money, and I went.

The store was crowded with old people holding tightly to their shopping carts, little kids hollering to their parents for candy, and lots of people staring at shopping lists and blocking the aisles.

I ducked around all the carts and went to the back where the vegetables are. From all the onions in the bin, I took the prettiest—a big round one, light tan and shiny, with a silvery glow to its skin.

I carried it to the express checkout and stood at the end of a very long line.

Next to me there was a giant Berkbee's Baby Food display. It was like a wall of glass, and taller than I am. All the little jars were stacked up to look like a castle, with pennants that said "Baby Power" sticking out above the castle doorways and windows. At the top there was a high tower with a red-and-white flag that said "Berkbee's Builds Better Babies!" I started counting the jars, but when I got to 346, I gave up. There must have been at least a thousand.

The checkout line didn't move. To pass the time, I started tossing my onion from hand to hand. I tried to improve and make my throws harder to catch.

A woman wearing a sky-blue jogging suit got in line behind me. She was holding a cereal box. She smiled at me, and I smiled back.

I decided to show her what a really good catcher I am. I made a wild and daring onion throw.

FCAT Plot Development
What was wild and daring about Gloria's actions?

I missed the catch. The onion kept going, straight for the middle of the baby food castle. The castle was going to fall!

My folks would have to pay for every broken jar! The store manager would kill me. After that, my folks would bring me back to life to tell me things that would be much worse than death.

I was **paralyzed**. I shut my eyes.

I didn't hear a crash. Maybe I had gone deaf from fright. Or maybe I was in a time warp because of my fear. In fifty years the onion would land, and that would be the end of me.

I felt a tap on my shoulder. If I opened my eyes, I would see the store manager and all the broken jars.

I didn't want to see him. I didn't want to know how bad it was.

There came a tap again, right on the top of my head.

I heard a woman's voice. "I have your onion."

I opened my eyes. The woman in the jogging suit handed the onion to me.

"Lucky I used to play baseball," she said.

"O-o-o-h," I said. I clutched the onion.

"O-o-o-h," I moaned again.

"You're welcome," was all she said.

She had brown eyes with a sparkle in them, and her hair was in shiny black ringlets. She wore blue-green earrings that hung on tiny gold chains. When she tilted her head, her earrings spun around, and I saw they were the Earth—I mean, made to look like the Earth, jeweled with green continents and blue oceans.

"Your earrings are beautiful," I said.

She smiled. "Some friends got them for me," she said, "to remind me of a trip we made."

When she said "trip," her face started to look familiar, but I didn't know why. Then I remembered.

"I've seen you!" I said. "I saw you on TV!"

She smiled. "Could be."

"And you come from right here in town, but you don't live here anymore," I said.

"That's right," she said.

"And you are—aren't you?—Dr. Grace Street, the **astronaut**!"

She tilted her head, and the little Earths on both her ears spun round. "That's me," she said.

I was amazed, because I never thought I would meet a famous person in my life, and yet one was right beside me in the supermarket, and I myself, Gloria Jones, was talking to her, all because of my onion throw.

"We learned about the space station in school last year," I said. "You were up there, orbiting the Earth."

"My team and I were there," Dr. Street said.

"What is space like?"

"You know," she said.

"How could I know?" I said.

"We're always in space," Dr. Street said. "We're in space right now."

"Yes," I said, "but what was it like out there, where you went? Out there it must seem different."

"Do you really want to know?" she asked, and I said yes.

Q's!

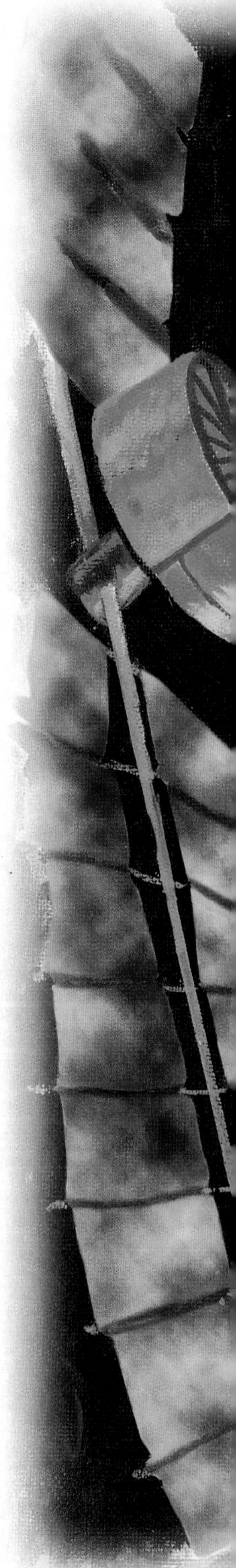

"The most awesome part was when we had to fix things on the outside of the station. We got our jobs done and floated in our space suits, staring out into the **universe**. There were zillions of stars—and space, deep and black, but it didn't seem exactly empty. It seemed to be calling to us, calling us to go on an **endless** journey. And that was very scary.

"So we turned and looked at Earth. We were two hundred miles above it. We saw enormous swirls of clouds and the glow of snowfields at the poles. We saw water like a giant blue cradle for the land. One big ocean, not 'oceans.' The Earth isn't really chopped up into countries, either. Up there you see it is one great big powerful living being that knows a lot, lot more than we do."

"What does it know?" I said.

"It knows how to be Earth," Dr. Street said. "And that's a lot."

I tried to imagine everything she had seen. It gave me a shiver.

"I wish I could see what you saw," I said. "I'd like to be an astronaut. Of course, probably I couldn't."

Dr. Street frowned. "Why do you say 'Probably I couldn't?' "

"Practically nobody gets to do that," I said.

"You might be one of the people who do," she said. "But you'll never do anything you want to do if you keep saying 'Probably I couldn't.'"

"But maybe I can't!" I **protested**. I looked down at my onion. I didn't think a very poor onion thrower had a chance to be an astronaut.

5555

Dr. Street looked at my onion, too. "It was a good throw—just a bad catch," she said. "Anyhow—saying 'Maybe I can't' is different. It's okay. It's **realistic**.

"Even 'I can't' can be a good, **sensible** thing to say. It makes life simpler. When you really know you can't do one thing, that leaves you time to try some of the rest. But when you don't even know what you can do, telling yourself 'Probably I couldn't' will stop you before you even start. It's paralyzing. You don't want to be paralyzed, do you?"

"I just was paralyzed," I said. "A minute ago, when I threw my onion. I didn't enjoy it one bit."

"If you don't want to be paralyzed," Dr. Street said, "be careful what you tell yourself—because whatever you tell yourself you're very likely to believe."

I thought about what she said. "If maybe I could be an astronaut," I asked, "how would I get to be one?"

"You need to do well in school," she said. "And you need to tame your fears. Not get rid of them—just tame them."

The line moved forward suddenly, and we moved up. Maybe the people in line behind us thought Dr. Street and I were mother and daughter having a serious conversation, because they left some space around us.

"So how does a person tame fears?"

"By doing things that are difficult, and succeeding," Dr. Street said. "That's how you learn you can count on yourself. That's how you get confidence. But even then, you keep a little bit of fear inside—a fear that keeps you careful."

FCAT Plot Development
How did Dr. Street's experience in outer space help influence the plot?

The checkout line moved again, and we moved with it.

"Big things are really little," Dr. Street said. "That's a great secret of life."

"How—" I began. But I never got to ask how big things are really little, because I was the first person in line.

The checkout man looked at my onion.

"Young lady, didn't you weigh that?" he asked.

"No, sir," I said.

"Go back to Produce and have it weighed."

So I had to go.

"Goodbye," Dr. Street said.

"Goodbye," I said. On the way to Produce, I looked back at her. She was walking toward the exit with her cereal box. I waved, but she didn't notice.

And I could see how little things are really big. Just on account of an onion, I had met an astronaut, and on account of that same onion, I had to stop talking to her.

But how big things are really little I couldn't understand at all.

Blast Off with Ann and Anna

Ann Cameron is a well-known writer. When she was a young girl, like Gloria, she was always outside exploring and wondering about the world around her. Ann did not have a TV until she was nine years old. She spent time listening to stories on the radio and reading books. Today Ann still loves nature and books. She lives in Guatemala, near a waterfall and volcanoes.

Other books by Ann Cameron

Anna Rich has always loved to draw. From an early age, her mother saw her talent and encouraged Anna to follow her dream. Her passion for illustration eventually became a full-time job. Good thing, too, because Anna has never considered doing anything else as a career. Anna, a native New Yorker, still lives there with her family.

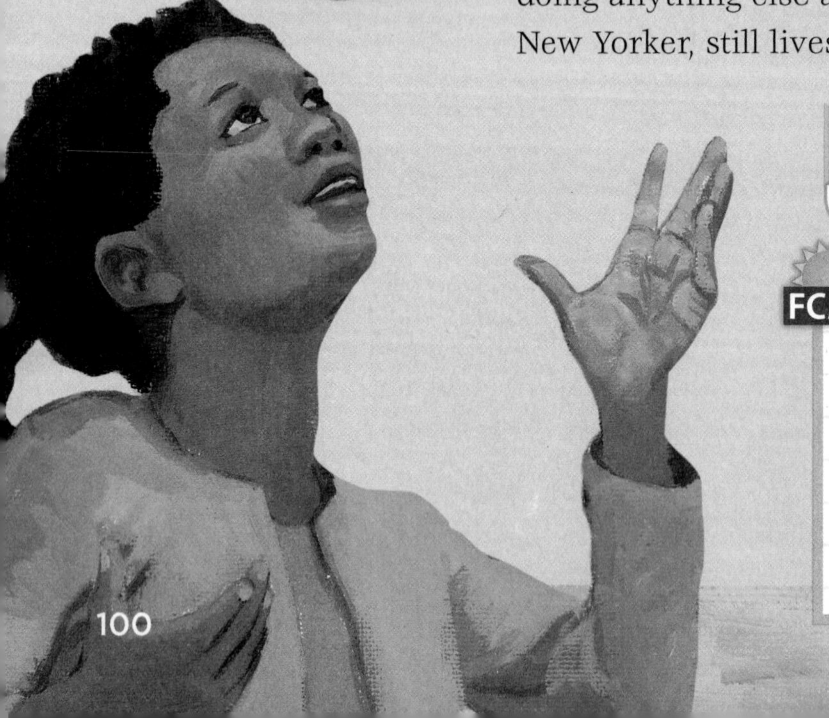

LOG ON Find out more about Ann Cameron and Anna Rich at **www.macmillanmh.com**

FCAT **Author's Purpose**

Think about Ann Cameron's purpose for writing *The Astronaut and the Onion*. Did she mainly write the story to entertain the reader or to inform the reader? How do you know?

FCAT Comprehension Check

Summarize

Summarize the plot of *The Astronaut and the Onion*. Use your Character Web to include information about Gloria's character traits in your summary.

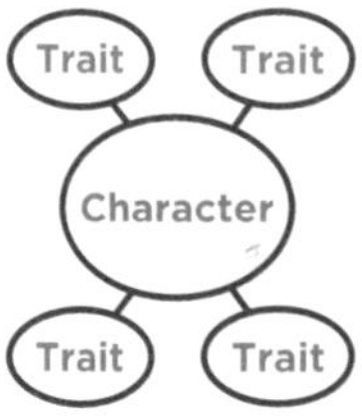

Think and Compare

READ THINK EXPLAIN

1. How was Gloria's onion important to the development of this story's plot? Explain using details from the story. **Make Inferences and Analyze: Plot Development**

READ THINK EXPLAIN

2. Reread page 94. What did the astronauts see in space? Why did Dr. Street say Earth knows more than people? Use story details about her character traits to explain. **Analyze**

3. Suppose you meet someone who has a career that interests you. What kind of questions would you ask that person? **Apply**

4. Why does Dr. Street tell Gloria not to be **paralyzed** by her fears? Use details from the story to explain. **Evaluate**

5. Read "Astronauts in Training" on pages 84–85. Compare Ana's character to Dr. Street's character. In what ways are they alike? How are they different? **Reading/Writing Across Texts**

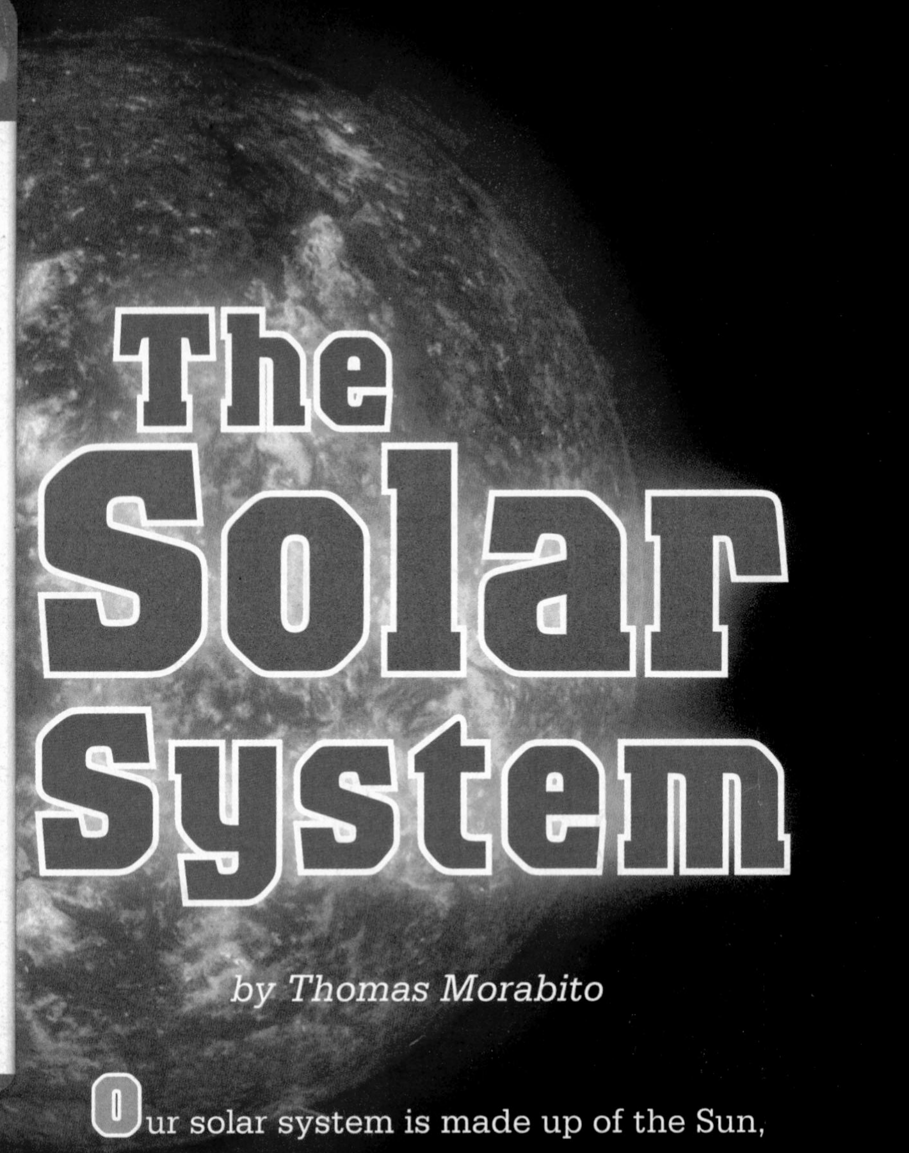

Science

Genre

Nonfiction Articles explain a topic by presenting facts about it in the text. They also provide informative photos and graphic aids.

FCAT Text Feature

Diagrams are graphic aids that show how things relate to each other.

Content Vocabulary

orbits
craters
rotate
exploration

The Solar System

by Thomas Morabito

Our solar system is made up of the Sun, Earth, our moon, seven other planets and their moons, meteors, asteroids, and all the space around them. All eight planets move in **orbits** around the Sun, which is the center of our solar system.

The Sun

The Sun is a medium-size star made up of very hot gases. The temperature of the Sun is almost 10,000°F! The closer a planet is to the Sun, the higher the temperatures are on its surface. The farther away a planet is from the Sun, the lower the temperatures are on its surface.

The Inner Planets

The inner planets are those closest to the Sun. They are made of solid rock.

Mercury

Mercury is the planet closest to the Sun. It is about one-third the size of Earth. Covered with **craters**, it looks a lot like the Moon. Mercury has no water and very little air.

Venus

Venus, the second planet from the Sun, is veiled in thick, swirling clouds. About the same size as Earth, Venus is sometimes called a sister planet.

Venus, though, is very different from Earth. It has no oceans and no life. The air is made up of carbon dioxide. This layer traps heat. That makes Venus the hottest planet in the solar system. With temperatures of 900°F, Venus is even hotter than Mercury!

Earth

Earth is the third planet from the Sun. In addition to having the most comfortable temperatures, Earth has water and oxygen. As far as we know, Earth is the only planet able to sustain life.

Besides heat, we also get light from the Sun. It takes about 24 hours for Earth to spin, or **rotate**, all the way around. For half of that time, a side of Earth faces the Sun and it is day. At the same time, the other side faces away from the Sun and it is night.

It takes Earth about 365 days to move around the Sun. We call this time period a year.

Distance from the Sun

Reading a Diagram

This diagram shows the distance from the Sun to each of the eight planets in miles and kilometers.

Mars

Mars, the planet next farthest from the Sun, is often called the Red Planet. The rocks, soil, and sky are red in color. Before space exploration, people thought there might be life on Mars. They thought the lines on Mars's surface were canals made by intelligent life-forms. Traces of shorelines, riverbeds, and islands may suggest that there was water on Mars at one time and perhaps life. Craters and inactive volcanoes cover most of its surface today.

The Outer Planets

In addition to being farther away from the Sun, these planets are not made of rock. Although they may have solid centers, these planets are made up of gases. They are dark and cold.

Jupiter

Jupiter is the largest planet. If Jupiter were hollow, more than one thousand Earths could fit inside. It is the fifth planet from the Sun and is famous for its great red spot. Scientists believe this spot to be a storm.

Saturn

Saturn, the sixth planet from the Sun, is the second-largest planet. It has thousands of beautiful shiny rings. These rings are made up of chunks of ice, rock, and dust. Saturn is also very windy. Near the equator the wind blows at speeds of up to 1,100 miles an hour!

Saturn

Uranus

Uranus, the third-largest planet, has at least 22 moons. Like Saturn, Uranus has faint gray rings that might be made of graphite, the black material inside a pencil.

Neptune

Neptune has a great dark spot, about the size of Earth. Neptune's spot, like the one on Jupiter, is thought to be a storm. The winds there are the strongest on any planet. They have been found to reach speeds of 1,200 miles per hour. Neptune has faint rings and eight moons.

Pluto

Discovered in 1930, Pluto was called the ninth planet. In 2006 the International Astronomical Union said planets must orbit the Sun, have a nearly round shape, and clear other objects in their orbital neighborhood. Because Pluto's orbit intersects Neptune's, it was renamed a dwarf planet.

Pluto

FCAT Connect and Compare

1. Look at the diagram. Which planet is farther away from the Sun: Mars or Neptune? How do you know? **Reading a Diagram**

2. Using information from the article and the latest findings about the solar system, make three observations about the planets. **Synthesize**

3. Think about Gloria from *The Astronaut and the Onion*. What do you know about her that tells you Gloria would probably like to visit the solar system? **Reading/Writing Across Texts**

Science Activity

Research any U.S. mission to space. Find out all the details of the mission especially any special preparations that were made. Write a brief summary and draw a diagram of the trip's route.

LOG ON Find more about space travel at **www.macmillanmh.com**

Write an E-Mail

Writer's Craft

FCAT Important Details

Important details support your main idea and are important, or relevant, to the topic.

I wanted to tell a friend about my trip to Space Camp. This is the e-mail I wrote.

I chose the most important details about what I did.

e-mail

Write | Send | Reply | Print | Delete | Address

TO: Chanell97@example.com

FROM: Taqoya123@example.com

SUBJECT: Space Camp

Dear Chanell,

While I was at Space Camp, I felt what it's like to be an astronaut on the moon. At first, I just hopped a bit. Then I bounced high in the air! It was awesome. I hope you and I can leap across the moon together someday for real. Write soon!

Your friend,

Taqoya

Writing Prompt

Most people have something they enjoy doing.

Think about something you enjoy doing.

Now write about something you enjoy doing.

FCAT Writer's Checklist

- ☑ **Focus:** My writing clearly describes my experience.
- ☑ **Organization:** I use words like *first* and *then* to describe my experience in the order that it happened.
- ☐ **Support:** I use important details to support my main idea.
- ☑ **Conventions:** My punctuation, grammar, and spelling is correct. I use the proper greeting and closing for a letter.

Talk About It

What do you think the girl is thinking? What could the frog be thinking about?

LOG ON Find out more about **wildlife** at **www.macmillanmh.com**

WILDLIFE WATCHERS

Vocabulary

disguested **cluttered**

raft **downstream**

scattered **nuzzle**

FCAT **Context Clues**

Paragraph Clues are words or phrases within the same paragraph that help readers figure out the meaning of an unfamiliar word. Figure out what *cluttered* means by using paragraph clues.

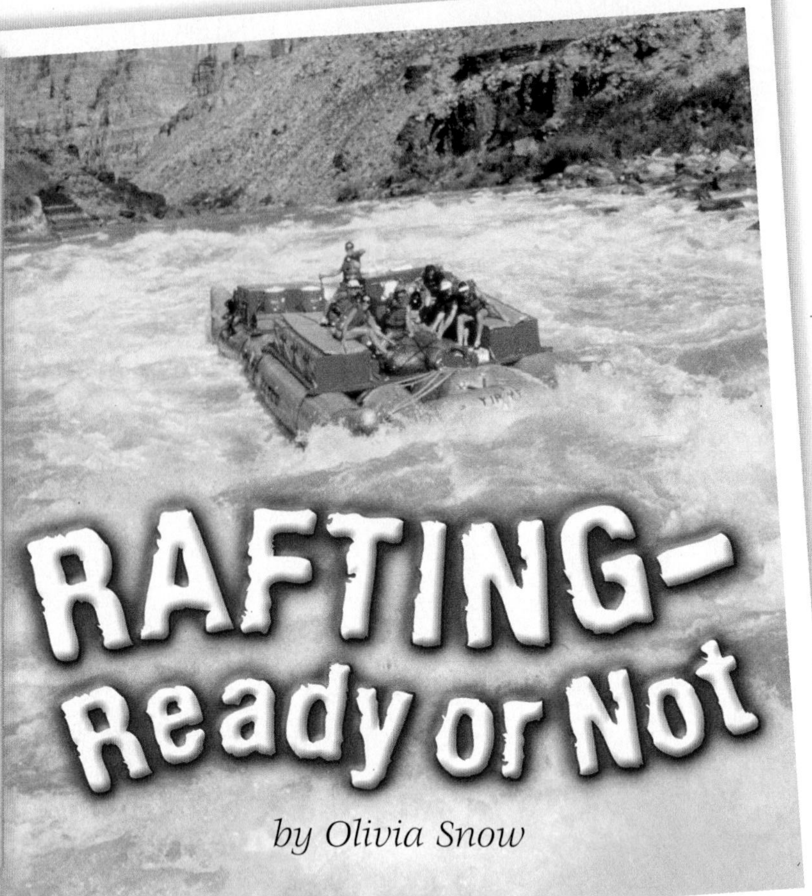

RAFTING–Ready or Not

by Olivia Snow

Dear Diary,

What an amazing day! I never thought rafting could be so much fun. Wait... I should probably back up and explain what I was doing on a raft in the first place.

Today my family and I started our vacation. We're taking a rafting trip down the Colorado River. I have to admit, it didn't sound like my idea of fun. The thought of getting drenched by the river and sleeping in tents with creepy bugs and spiders kind of **disgusted** me. But, unless I wanted to be left behind, I had to put on my life jacket and join in.

Lisa, our guide, helped us get our big, rubber **raft** into the river. We joined the others, **scattered** here and there along the river. There were so many, it felt like we were playing bumper boats! Lisa had told us that the river would narrow and we would be a bit **cluttered**. Then the river widened, and the rafts spread out as we were carried in the water's flow **downstream**. At first I just sat in the raft and listened to my music. But when we picked up speed, I realized my help was needed.

Before long I was paddling away and enjoying the amazing wildlife overhead and along the shore. We spotted a great blue heron and a coyote. Then we watched a mother beaver **nuzzle** her young gently with her snout. Lisa said that if we looked carefully, we might even see a mountain lion!

I have to admit that when it was time to get off the river and set up camp, I actually felt disappointed. But it gave us a chance to appreciate the beauty of the Grand Canyon. The sunset was amazing. It made the red and gold colors of the canyon walls positively glow.

We'll be back on the river early tomorrow, so I'd better zip up my sleeping bag and get to sleep.

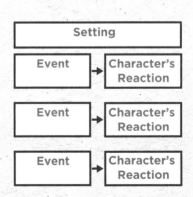

Reread for **Comprehension**

Make Inferences and Analyze

FCAT **Plot Development**

A plot is a series of **events** in a story that give it a beginning, middle, and end. A story has **characters** and a **setting** where the story takes place. Reread the selection and fill in your Setting Chart to help you learn how a story's characters and setting affect the plot.

Setting		
Event	→	Character's Reaction
Event	→	Character's Reaction
Event	→	Character's Reaction

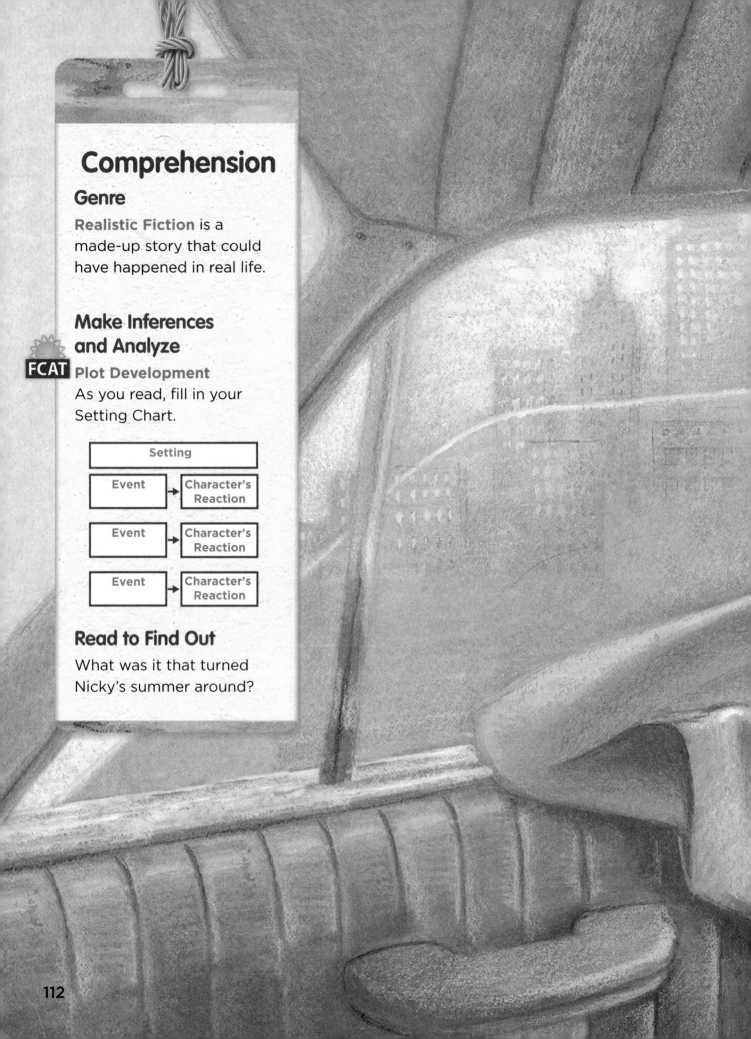

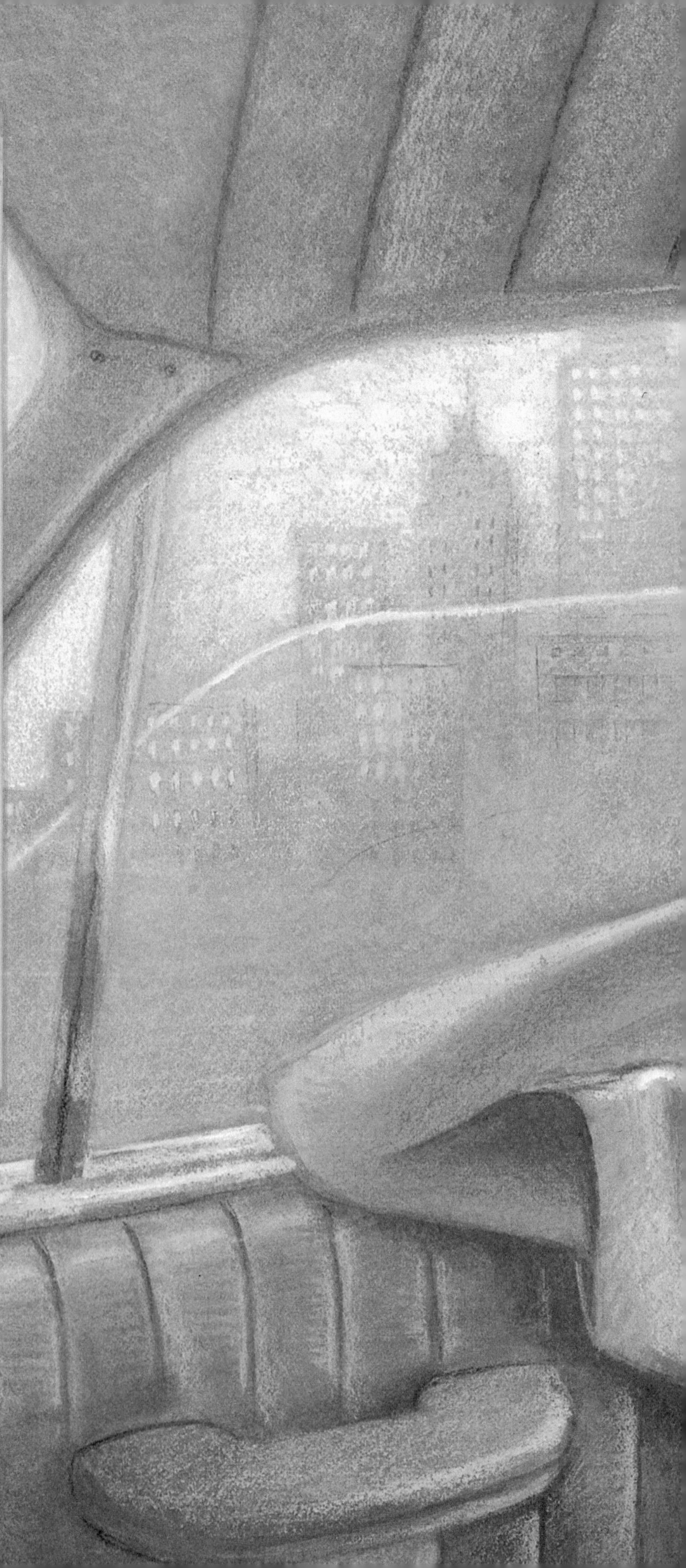

Comprehension

Genre

Realistic Fiction is a made-up story that could have happened in real life.

Make Inferences and Analyze

FCAT

Plot Development

As you read, fill in your Setting Chart.

Setting	
Event	→ Character's Reaction
Event	→ Character's Reaction
Event	→ Character's Reaction

Read to Find Out

What was it that turned Nicky's summer around?

THE RAFT

Award Winning Author and Illustrator

BY JIM LAMARCHE

"There's nobody to play with," I complained. "She doesn't even have a T.V."

Dad grinned. "Well, she's not your normal kind of grandma, I guess," he said. "Calls herself a river rat." He chuckled. "But I promise, she'll find plenty for you to do. And you know I can't take you with me this summer, Nicky. There'll be no kids there, and I'll be spending all my time at the plant."

I felt tears starting again, but I blinked hard and looked out the window.

That afternoon, I stood in Grandma's yard and watched my dad drive away. Dust rose up behind our car as it disappeared into the pines.

"Well, we can't stand here all summer," said Grandma. "C'mon, Nicky, it's time for supper."

"Honey or maple syrup on your cornbread?" Grandma asked.

"I don't like cornbread," I mumbled, poking my finger into the syrup pitcher when she wasn't looking.

"If you're going to do that, you'd better wash up first," she said. She had eyes in the back of her head. "Bathroom's through there."

FCAT Plot Development
How does Nicky feel about spending the summer with his grandmother in her cottage?

I pushed the doorway curtain aside and walked into what would have been a living room in anyone else's house. Books were **scattered** everywhere—on the tables, on the chairs, even on the floor. Three of the walls were **cluttered** with sketches and stuffed fish and charts of the river. Several fishing poles hung from the fourth with a tackle box, a snorkel, and a mask on the floor beneath them. It looked like a river rat's workroom, all right, except that in the middle of everything was a half-finished carving of a bear.

"Been carving that old fellow for years," Grandma called from the kitchen. "The real one hangs out at the dump. Now come get your supper, before I feed it to him."

B

Dad was right—Grandma found plenty for me to do. In the morning, I stacked firewood, then helped her clean out the rain gutters and change the spark plugs on her truck. The afternoon was almost over when she handed me a cane pole, a bobber, and some red worms.

"Fish fry tonight!" she said, showing me how to bait the hook. "That river's full of fat bluegills. Drop your line near the lily pads and you'll find 'em."

Down at the dock, I looked things over. The lily pads were too close to shore. There couldn't be fish there. I walked to the end of the dock and threw my line out as far as I could. Then I sat down to wait. And wait. And wait. My bobber never moved.

"There's no fish in this stupid river," I said out loud, **disgusted**.

We had hamburgers for supper.

"Give it another try," said Grandma the next evening. "I'll bet you catch something."

Don't count on it, I thought, as I headed back to the dock. I threw my line in the water. Then I stretched out on the dock to wait. I must have fallen asleep, because I was awakened by loud chirping and chattering. I sat up and looked around. A flock of birds was moving toward me along the river, hovering over something floating on the water. It drifted **downstream**, closer and closer, until finally it bumped up against the dock.

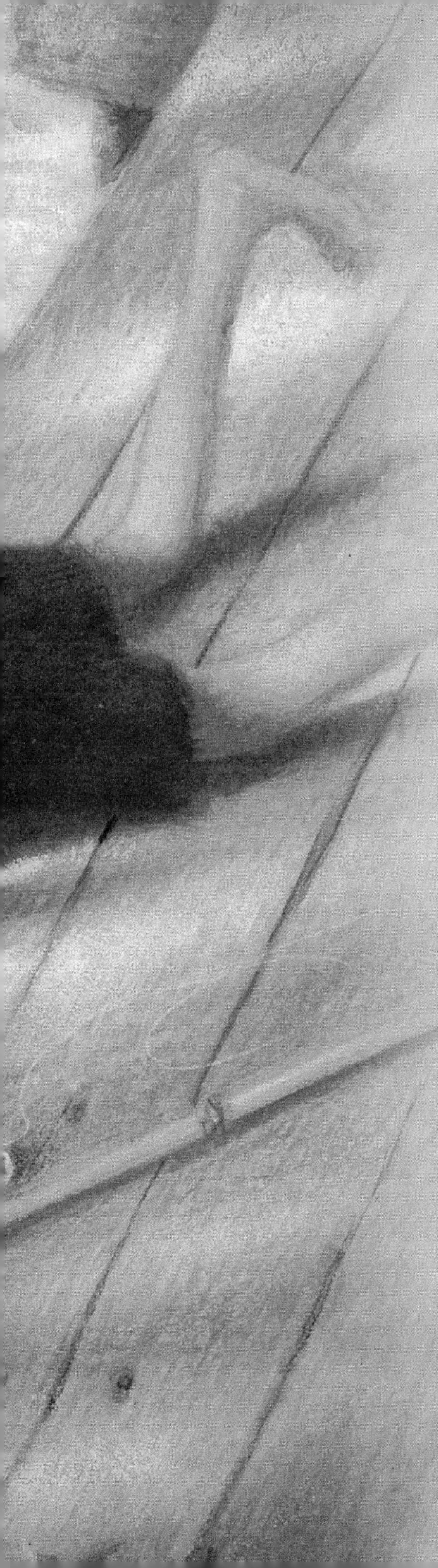

Though it was covered with leaves and branches, now I could tell that it was a **raft**. What was it doing floating down the river all by itself, I wondered. I reached down and pushed some of the leaves aside. Beneath them was a drawing of a rabbit. It looked like those ancient cave paintings I'd seen in books—just outlines, but wild and fast and free.

I cleaned away more leaves and it was like finding presents under the Christmas tree. A bear, a fox, a raccoon—all with the wild look of the rabbit. Who had drawn them, I wondered. Where had the raft come from?

I ran up to the cottage. Grandma was on the porch, reading.

"Do you have some rope I can use?" I asked.

"In the shed, hon," she said. "Help yourself." She didn't ask me what I needed it for, and I decided not to tell her yet.

I pushed the raft into the reeds along the river's edge, then tied it to the dock so it wouldn't drift away. All the while, birds flew over my head, every now and then swooping down to the raft as if it were a friend. A crane waded through the reeds to it. A turtle swam up from the bottom of the river.

The moon had risen yellow over the river by the time I went up to the cottage to go to bed.

I was already down at the dock the next morning when Grandma appeared with a life jacket and a long pole. She didn't seem surprised by the raft at all, or by the animal pictures all over it.

"How did you know . . . ?" I started.

"Let's go," Grandma interrupted, tossing me the life jacket and stepping onto the raft. She pushed the pole hard into the river bottom and we moved smoothly into the current.

"Your turn," she said after a few minutes. She showed me how to hold the pole and push, and I poled us to the middle of the river. Even there, the water wasn't over my head.

We poled the raft up the river, then let it slowly drift back down. The birds kept us company the whole time, soaring, swooping, singing. Some even landed on the raft and rode with us for a while. Hitchhikers, Grandma called them.

After that, I had little time for anything but the raft. I raced through whatever chores there were, then ran down to the dock, wondering what animals I'd see that day.

It wasn't just birds that the raft attracted. One morning three raccoons followed me along the shore. Another time a turtle climbed on board and spent the morning sunning itself. And one afternoon I saw a family of foxes slip through the trees along the river.

When the weather turned too hot and sticky to sleep indoors, Grandma helped me put up a small tent on the raft. I lay on top of the cool sheets and read comic books by flashlight until I fell asleep. One night, a noise woke me up. There in the moonlight stood a huge buck. He looked right at me, then lowered his head to drink, as if I wasn't there at all.

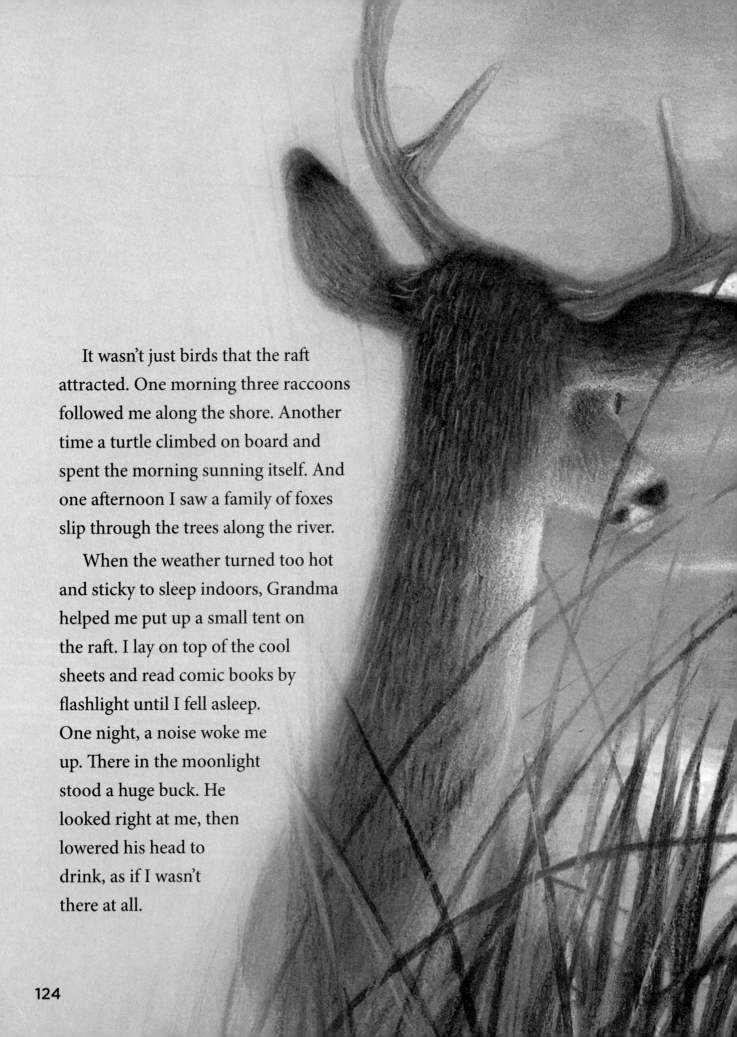

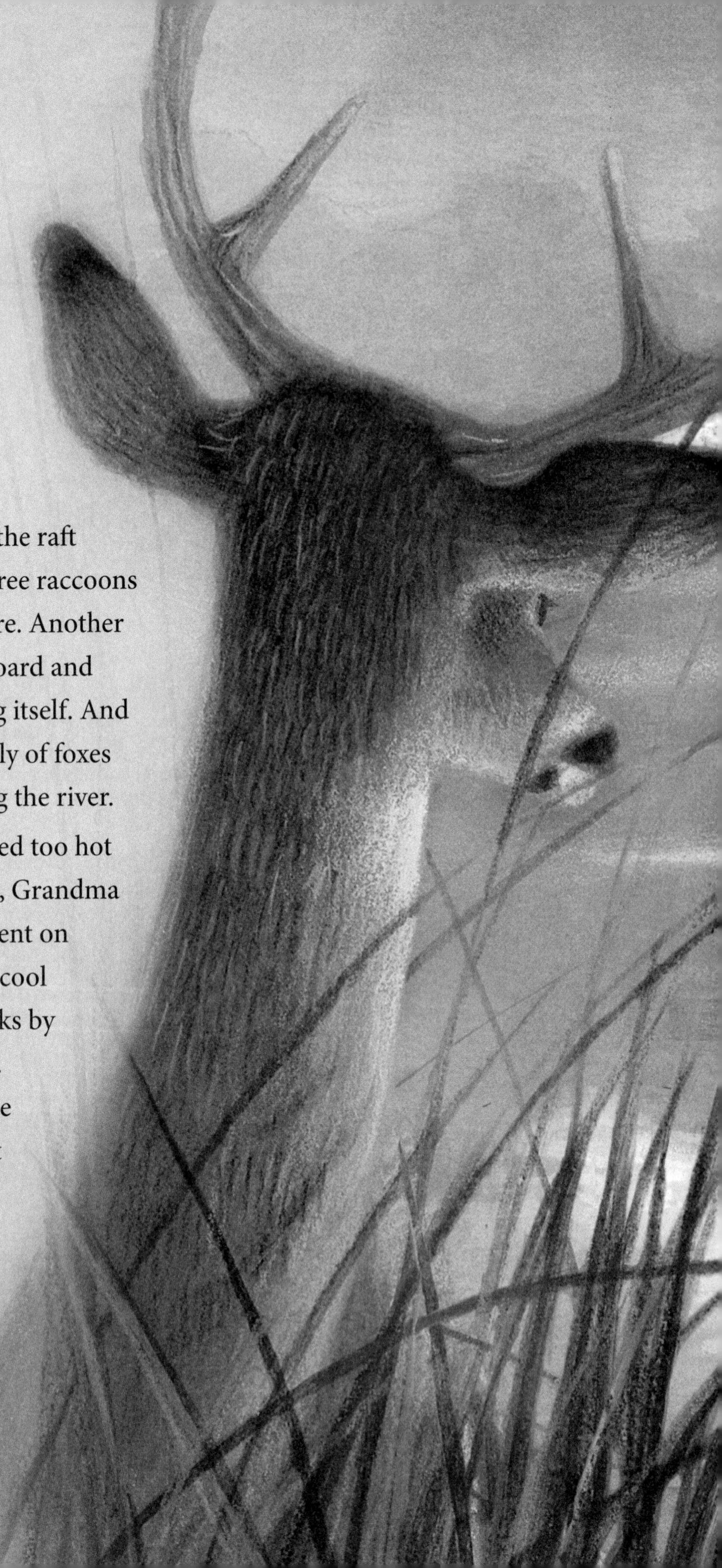

I found Grandma the next morning working on her bear carving.

"Do you have some extra paper I could draw on?" I asked her.

She brought out a big sketchpad and a pouch filled with thick pencils and crayons. "I've been saving these just for you," she said. "Better take these, too." She held out the snorkel and mask. "Never know when they might come in handy on a raft."

The sun was hot that afternoon, so I poled into the shade of a willow, then waited to see what animals the raft would bring. It wasn't long before a great blue heron whooshed down with a crayfish in its bill.

I grabbed a pencil and began to sketch. I felt invisible as the bird calmly ate its lunch right in front of me. Then it preened its feathers, looked back up the river, and flew off.

That night I showed my drawing to Grandma.

"Not bad," she said. "Not bad at all!" And she tacked it on the wall on top of one of her own sketches.

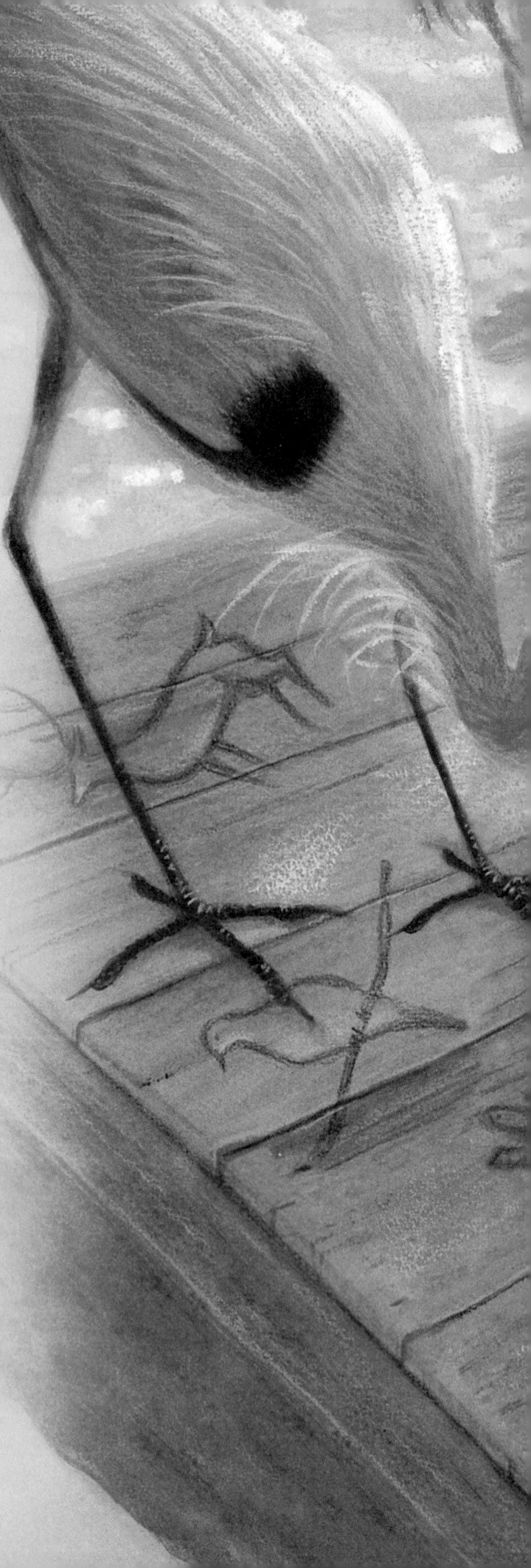

FCAT Plot Development
How do the setting and Nicky's character traits affect the plot of the story?

One day I poled upriver farther than I'd ever been. Near a clump of tall cattails, I startled an otter family. They dove underwater, but, as with the other animals, the raft seemed to calm them down. Soon they were playing all around me.

Grandma had been right about the mask and snorkel coming in handy. I slipped them on, then hung my head over the raft and watched the otters play—chasing fish, chasing each other, sometimes just chasing their own tails. I kept very still, but they didn't seem to mind me watching. They played keep away with a small stone, then tug-of-war with a piece of rope. It was like they were showing off for me. They even let me feed them right out of my hand.

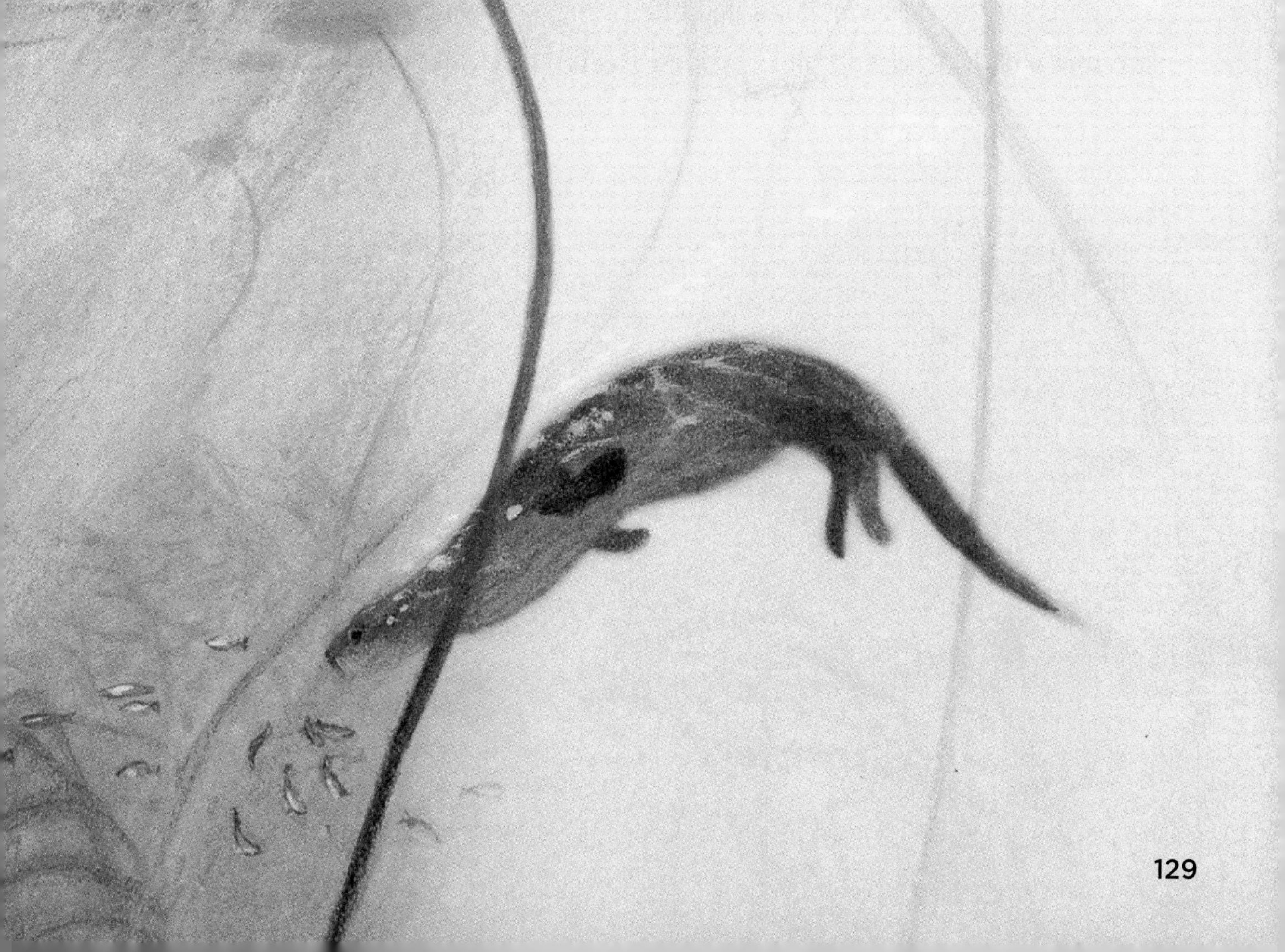

Some mornings, Grandma would make a bagful of sandwiches and a thermos of icy lemonade. Then we'd put on our bathing suits, grab some towels, a lawn chair, and an inner tube, and pole upriver to her favorite swimming spot. "I've come swimming here since I was a girl," she told me as we tied the raft to an old dock. "The Marshalls used to live here—all ten of them. What a herd of wild animals we were!"

While Grandma watched from the inner tube, I practiced my flying cannonballs. Then we'd eat our lunch, and she'd tell me stories about growing up on the river. My favorite was of the time she'd found a small black pearl inside a river clam. "I still have it," she said.

Somehow, on the river, it seemed like summer would never end. But of course it did.

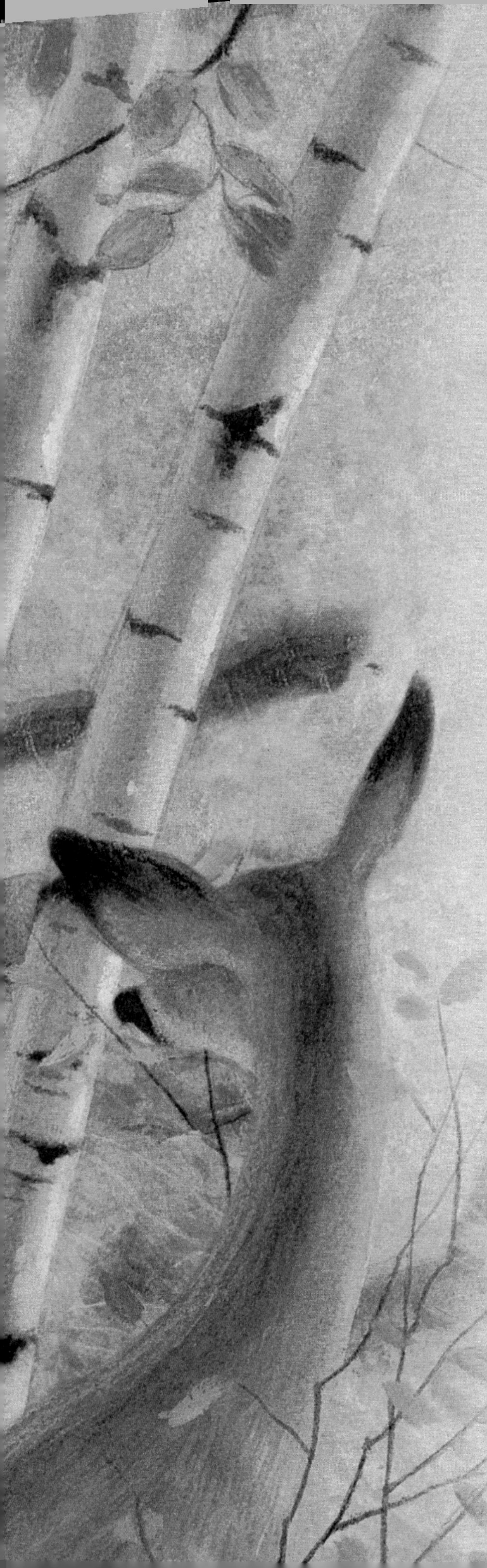

On my last day, I got up extra early and crept down to the dock. The air was cool and a low pearly fog hung over the river. I untied the raft and quietly drifted downstream.

Ahead of me, through the fog, I saw two deer moving across the river, a doe and her fawn. When they reached the shore, the doe leaped easily up the steep bank, then turned to wait for her baby. But the fawn was in trouble. It kept slipping down the muddy bank. The doe returned to the water to help, but the more the fawn struggled, the deeper it got stuck in the mud.

I pushed off the river bottom and drove the raft hard onto the muddy bank, startling the doe. Then I dropped into the water. I was ankle-deep in mud.

"You're okay," I whispered to the fawn, praying that the raft would calm it. "I won't hurt you."

Gradually the fawn stopped struggling, as if it understood that I was there to help. I put my arms around it and pulled. It barely moved. I pulled again, then again. Slowly the fawn eased out of the mud, and finally it was free. Carefully I carried the fawn up the bank to its mother.

Then, quietly, I returned to the raft. From there, I watched the doe **nuzzle** and clean her baby, and I knew what I had to do. I pulled the stub of a crayon from my pocket, and drew the fawn, in all its wildness, onto the old gray boards of the raft. When I had finished, I knew it was just right.

After supper, I showed Grandma my drawing of the fawn and told her my story.

"It's perfect," she said, "but we need to do one more thing." She hurried up to the cottage. When she came back, she had tubes of oil paint and two brushes.

Grandma helped me trace my drawing with the oil paint, which soaked deep into the wood. "That'll keep it," she said. "Now you'll always be part of the river."

"Just like you, Grandma," I told her. "A river rat."

Grandma laughed. "Just like me," she agreed.

A SKETCH OF JIM LAMARCHE

JIM LAMARCHE is a lot like the boy in this story. Jim spent his summers rafting on a river when he was a child. He grew up near the Milwaukee River in Wisconsin. All year round, the river was a special place to play. Jim also liked drawing and crafting things. Once he made a whole zoo out of clay that he dug up from a field. Even though Jim liked art, he didn't think about becoming an artist when he grew up. Back then, he really wanted to be a magician. Today Jim thinks that creating a book from just a blank piece of paper is not so different from being a magician.

Other books illustrated by Jim LaMarche

LOG ON Find out more about Jim LaMarche at **www.macmillanmh.com**

FCAT Author's Purpose

How might Jim LaMarche's own childhood experiences have influenced his purpose for writing *The Raft*? What story clues tell you if he was trying to explain, inform, or entertain?

FCAT Comprehension Check

Summarize

Use your Setting Chart to summarize *The Raft.* Describe the setting of the story and how it affects the plot and characters.

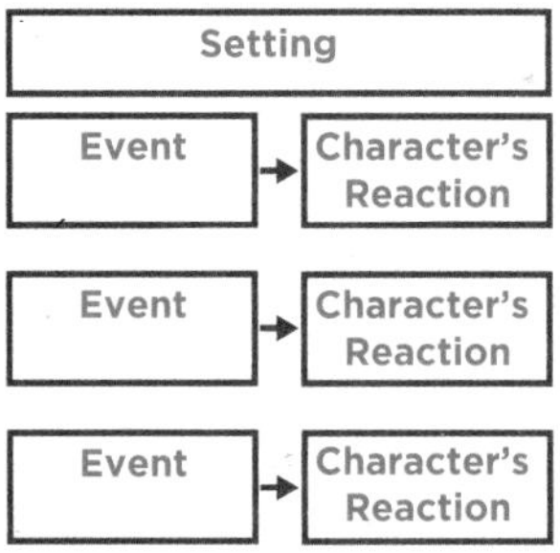

Think and Compare

1. How does the story's setting change Nicky? How does this change affect the plot? Explain using details from the story. **Make Inferences and Analyze: Plot Development**

2. Reread page 113 of *The Raft.* What does Nicky expect his vacation with his grandmother to be like? How is the actual vacation different from what he expected? Use story details to explain. **Analyze**

3. What would it be like if you were able to make use of a **raft** for the summer? Explain. **Apply**

4. What information from the story could be used to support the view that the raft was a gift from Nicky's grandmother? **Evaluate**

5. Read "Rafting—Ready or Not" on pages 110–111. How is the narrator's experience on a raft similar to Nicky's? What do the characters discover? Use details from both stories to explain. **Reading/Writing Across Texts**

THE EVERGLADES

A NATIONAL TREASURE

by Sunil Patel

Science

Genre

Magazine Articles give facts and information about interesting topics.

FCAT **Text Feature**

Maps are drawings of all or part of an area.

Content Vocabulary

environments
organisms
adapted
migrate

Ecosystems are **environments** formed by living and nonliving things working together. The parts of an ecosystem include soil, water, air, heat and light from the sun, and living **organisms**. All these parts work together to keep the ecosystem healthy. Water and soil work together to give plants and animals life. Heat and light from the sun allow algae to grow in water. The algae then give fish the oxygen they need to live. Fish absorb the oxygen and push out carbon dioxide through their gills. Plants then use the carbon dioxide and the sun's heat to grow. The sun's heat evaporates water or changes it to vapor. The vapor then joins the air so that the ecoystem's natural balance can continue.

Everglades National Park is the third-largest park in the United States.

Wet and Dry Seasons

The Everglades in Florida is an ecosystem that covers thousands of acres. It has more than 100 kinds of plants, more than 350 kinds of birds, and more than 40 kinds of animals. The plants and animals that live in the Everglades have **adapted** to the wet and dry seasons of the area. The dry season begins in December and ends in April. During this season water levels drop. Fish **migrate** to deeper water to find food. Animals and birds then gather near the pools of water to feed on the fish, amphibians, and reptiles that have moved into them.

The red-cockaded woodpecker is one of the many animals that live in the Everglades.

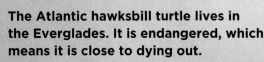

The wet season in the Everglades starts in May and ends in December. During this time the entire area is almost completely covered with water. Wildlife moves to outer areas that are drier. Fish, insects, and reptiles produce their young, and the food chain continues.

The Atlantic hawksbill turtle lives in the Everglades. It is endangered, which means it is close to dying out.

Protecting the Ecosystem

People have put the natural balance of the Everglades in danger by tearing parts of it down to make room for businesses and homes. Many animals started dying out, upsetting the ecosystem's natural balance. For these reasons, a part of the Everglades became a National Park in 1947. This means that the Everglades is protected by law and no one is allowed to tear down any part of it. The Everglades was saved because people finally recognized the beauty and importance of this ecosystem.

Reading a Map

This map shows the location of major cities, the Everglades, and other National Parks in Florida. In what part of the United States is Florida located?

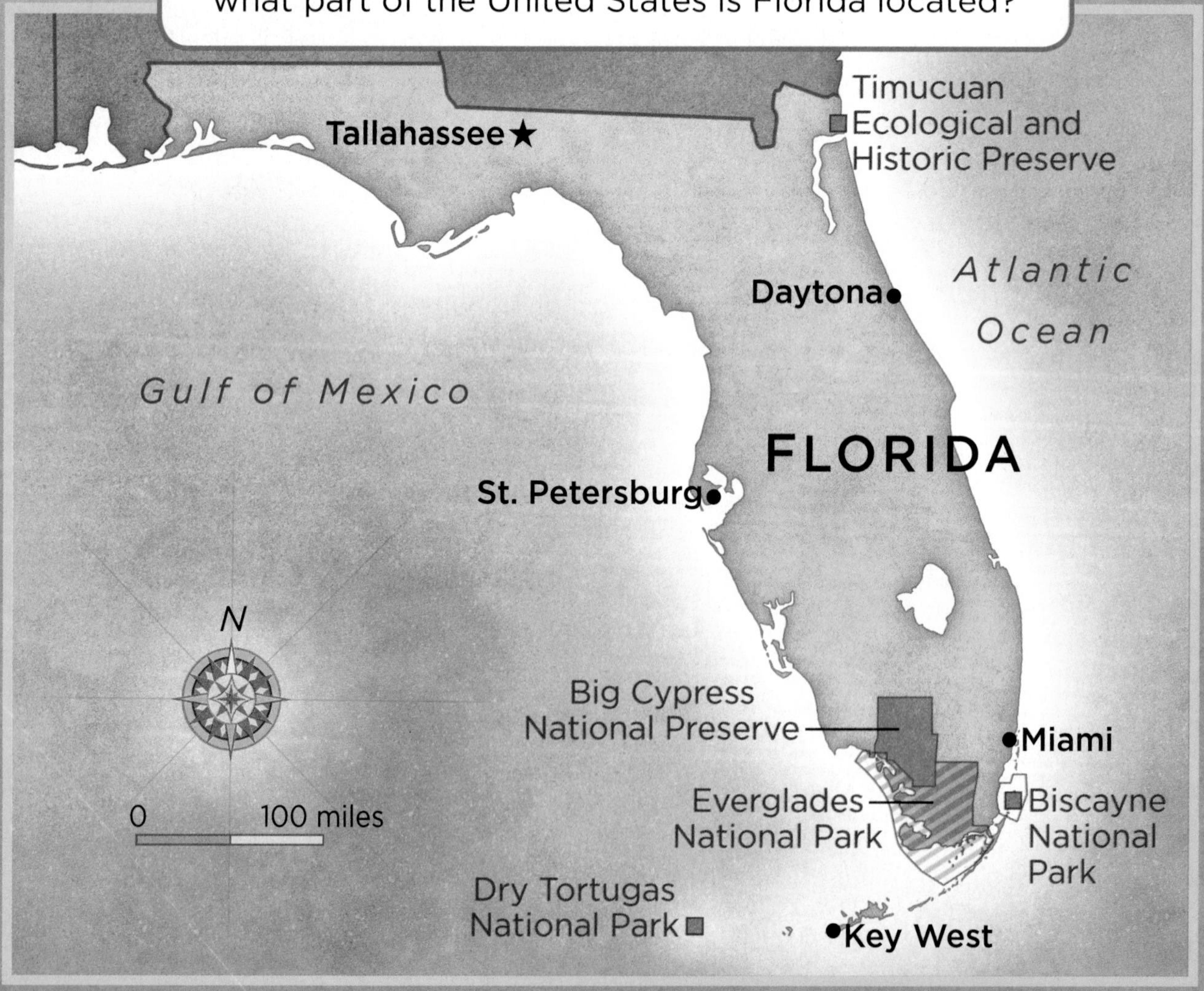

Everglades National Park offers tours both during the day and at night.

FCAT Connect and Compare

1. What National Parks are on the southernmost tip of Florida? In the northern part? **Reading a Map**
2. Why was making the Everglades a National Park in 1947 important? Use details from the article to explain. **Evaluate**
3. What similarities do the river from *The Raft* and the Everglades ecosystem have? **Reading/Writing Across Texts**

Science Activity

Research another national park in Florida. Draw a map of it and include its different sections.

LOG ON Find out more about the Everglades at **www.macmillanmh.com**

Write About an Interesting Walk

Writer's Craft

FCAT **Unimportant Details**

Unimportant details are statements and facts that do not support the main idea. Good writers make sure details in their writing support the main idea.

I made sure that the details support my main idea.

I wanted to tell the most important details.

Friday, October 25

Today Dad and I went on a fantastic hike in the foothills. After about ten minutes I saw some hoof prints in the soft dirt of the trail. Then I looked up, and I saw a doe and her tiny spotted fawn. Dad and I stood there quietly so we wouldn't disturb them. Then they turned and walked into some thick brush.

Wow! I had never been so close to a wild animal. Dad patted me on the shoulder and told me there's a first time for everything.

Writing Prompt

There are many interesting places to take a walk.

Think about an interesting place where you have taken a walk.

Now write a story about an interesting place where you have taken a walk.

FCAT Writer's Checklist

- ☑ **Focus:** My writing clearly shows the main idea and my feelings about the interesting walk.
- ☑ **Organization:** I use details that describe my experience in the order that it happened.
- ☑ **Support:** I make sure that I leave out **unimportant details** that don't support my main idea.
- ☑ **Conventions:** My sentences are complete and there are no run-ons. My spelling is correct.

Show What You Know

FCAT Review

- Problem and Solution
- Main Idea and Details
- Character
- Setting and Plot
- Context Clues
- Chart

A Walk on the Beach

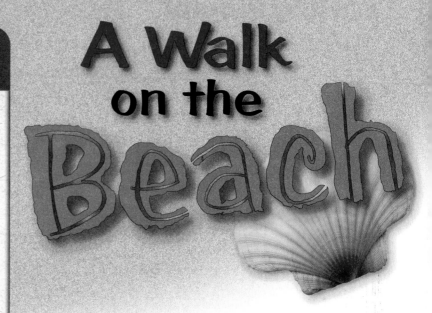

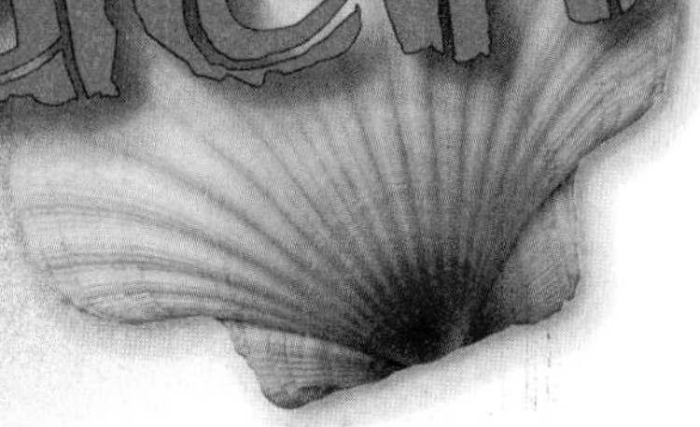

Jenny stared at her cousin disapprovingly. "Tony, is it true you've really never seen the ocean?"

Tony felt exhausted. Why had he told his parents he would come on this trip? It had seemed like a great idea last month. Now that he was actually here, he wasn't so sure. Jenny sounded mean. Tony felt like she wasn't happy to see him.

"No, I've never seen it," he answered quietly.

"Tony lives in New Mexico, Jen. Look it up on the map. It's nowhere near the ocean. That's one of the reasons your cousin came to visit us. Right, Tony?" asked Jen's dad.

"Right," said Tony. Then he thought of something. "Jenny, when was the last time you saw a desert?"

"I've never seen a desert but that doesn't matter. I mean, who would want to go to a desert anyway?" she said coldly.

"You've never seen a desert? Are you kidding?" said Tony, sounding as surprised as Jenny.

Jenny's dad smiled at them. "Okay, you two. Put your sneakers on. Mom's taking you to the beach."

Twenty minutes later, Tony stood on the beach staring at the Atlantic Ocean. He'd had no idea that it was so big.

"Beautiful, isn't it?" asked his aunt as she stood next to him. Tony nodded and watched in amazement as a line of pelicans swooped low over the waves.

"Check out the dunes, Tony. They're beautiful, too," said Jenny. She waved her hand at the huge hills of sand.

Tony turned to look behind him. "How can all those plants grow in the sand?" he asked.

"Some have leaves with a waxy coating or little hairs to keep the water inside," his aunt explained.

"Hey, desert plants do that too!" Tony exclaimed. He turned and looked at the ocean again. All of a sudden he saw three black fins in a row, swimming in a line.

"Sharks!" he yelled, pointing at the fins.

Jenny looked at where Tony was pointing. She laughed.

"Those aren't sharks, Tony. Those are dolphins. I don't see how you could mistake them."

Tony turned and started walking down the beach. *Jenny doesn't seem thrilled about my visit*, he thought. Maybe coming to visit his aunt and uncle was not such a great idea after all, but he had really wanted to see the ocean.

Jenny watched Tony walk away. "Tony, wait up." Jenny called. "I'm sorry. A lot of people think of sharks when they see dolphin fins. I bet if I went to New Mexico, I'd think everything in the desert was poisonous. I'd probably be too scared to get out of the car."

Tony laughed. "You probably would. One time this guy started yelling because he thought some tiny harmless spider was really a tarantula."

"Are you two ready for a swim?" Jenny's mother yelled from down the beach.

"Race you back," Tony grinned, and took off running down the beach.

"No fair, you got a head start!" shouted Jenny as she ran after him laughing.

CAVES

MYSTERIOUS UNDERGROUND WORLDS

ARE YOU LOOKING for something new to explore? Check out a cave! Caves are natural spaces, like rooms, that have openings you can reach from the inside. They are often so deep under the ground that natural light does not reach inside. There are about 40,000 caves in the United States. This means there is a very good chance you can find one somewhere near you. There are caves in every state except Louisiana and Rhode Island.

There are four basic types of caves: **solution caves, sea caves, lava caves,** and **glacier caves.** Solution and sea caves are both formed by water. The constant flow of water dissolves and wears away the rock. Over time, the path deepens and creates a cave. Lava caves are formed from volcanic eruptions. The outer layer of lava cools and hardens while the center stays hot and keeps flowing. When the lava in the center drains, it creates a cave. Glacier caves form when melting water runs through a glacier.

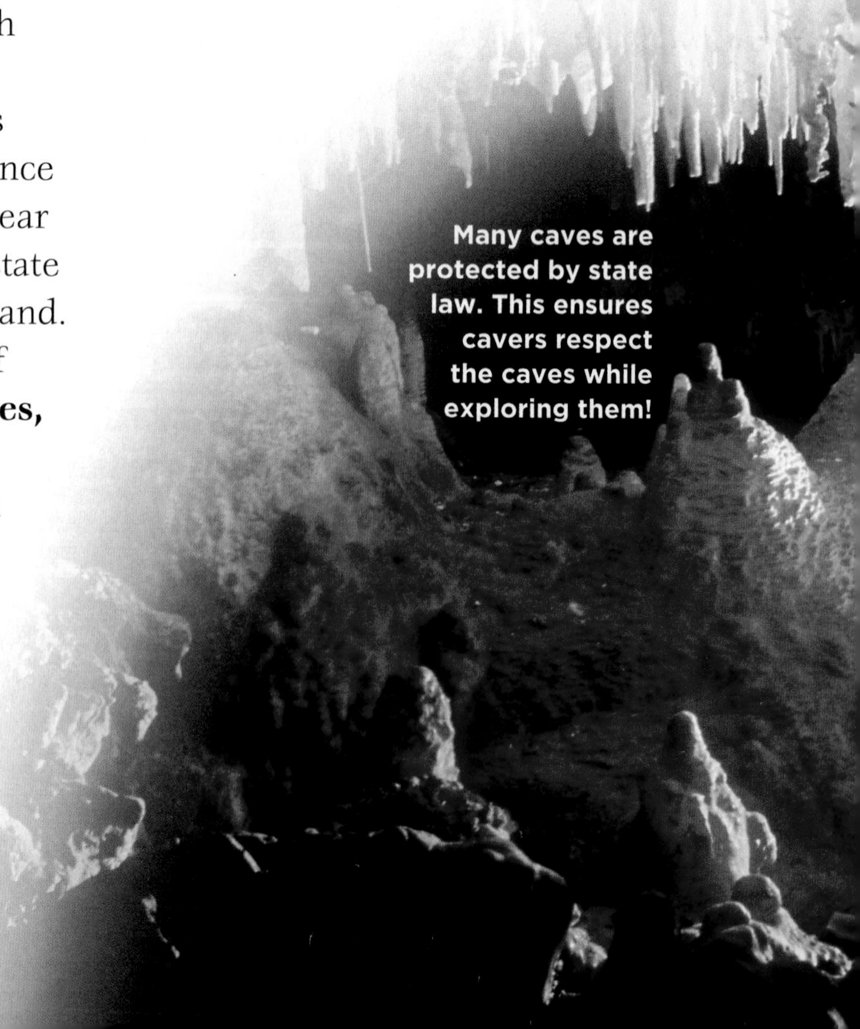

Many caves are protected by state law. This ensures cavers respect the caves while exploring them!

Caves can be exciting places to explore, but they can also be dangerous. The number one rule to remember is never to go in a cave alone. It is best to go with an expert who knows the cave well. You also need to be prepared. Remember, there is no natural light in a cave, so you need to bring your own light with you. Most cave explorers wear a helmet that has a light on the front. The light allows you to see and explore the wonders of the cave. It also helps you in tricky areas that might need more of your attention because you will not have to hold a light in your hands. This is important because then your hands are free to help you keep your balance.

Choose your clothing carefully before you go caving. Wear comfortable shoes that help you keep your balance on steep or slippery paths. Temperatures are often colder in caves, so wear layers of clothing that you can add or remove as necessary. Wearing cotton as the inside layer and wool as the outside layer will help you keep dry and trap in heat.

Finally, you also need to be sure not to cause any damage. Do not go off alone or remove any objects. Be sure to leave the cave exactly the way you found it. That way, other people can enjoy the same mysterious underground world!

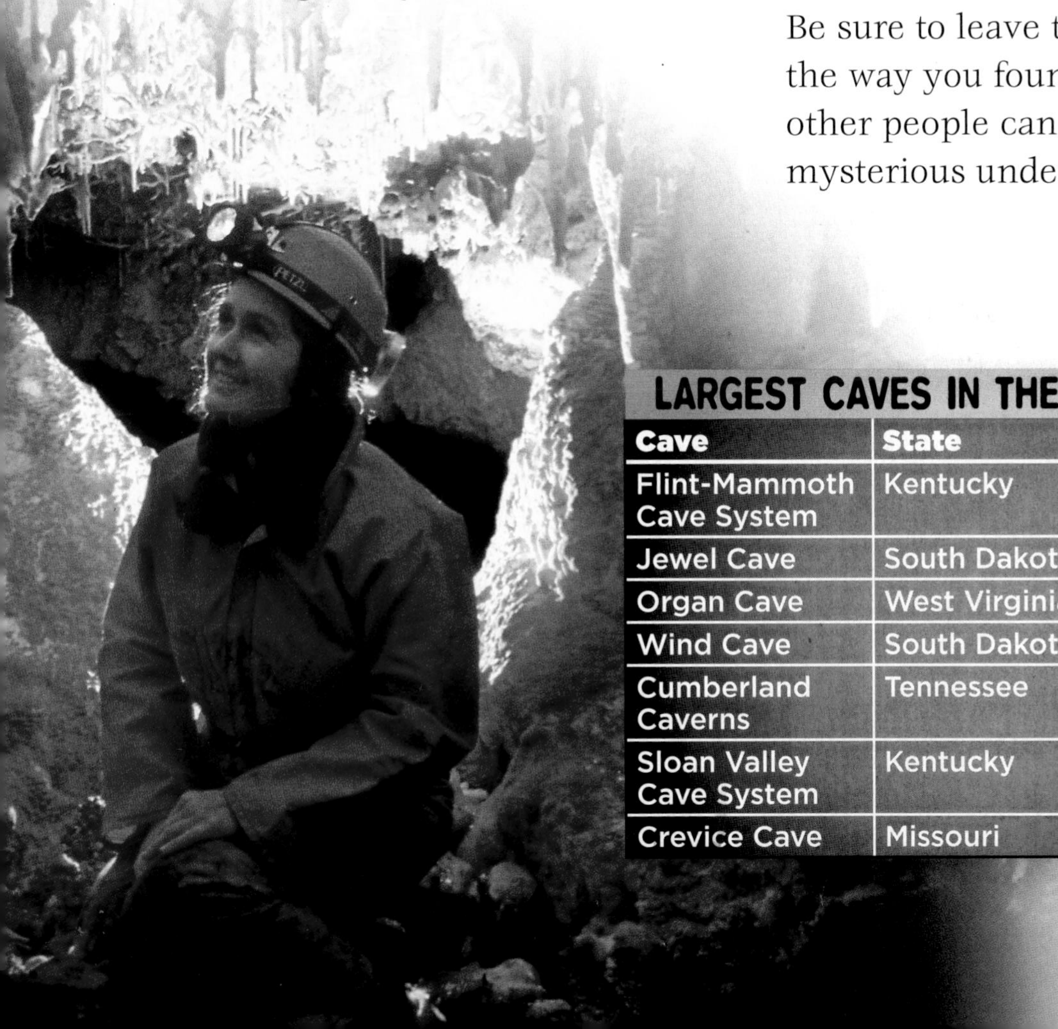

LARGEST CAVES IN THE UNITED STATES

Cave	State	Length
Flint-Mammoth Cave System	Kentucky	169 miles
Jewel Cave	South Dakota	54.4 miles
Organ Cave	West Virginia	32 miles
Wind Cave	South Dakota	28.7 miles
Cumberland Caverns	Tennessee	23.2 miles
Sloan Valley Cave System	Kentucky	22.4 miles
Crevice Cave	Missouri	20.8 miles

BASEBALL

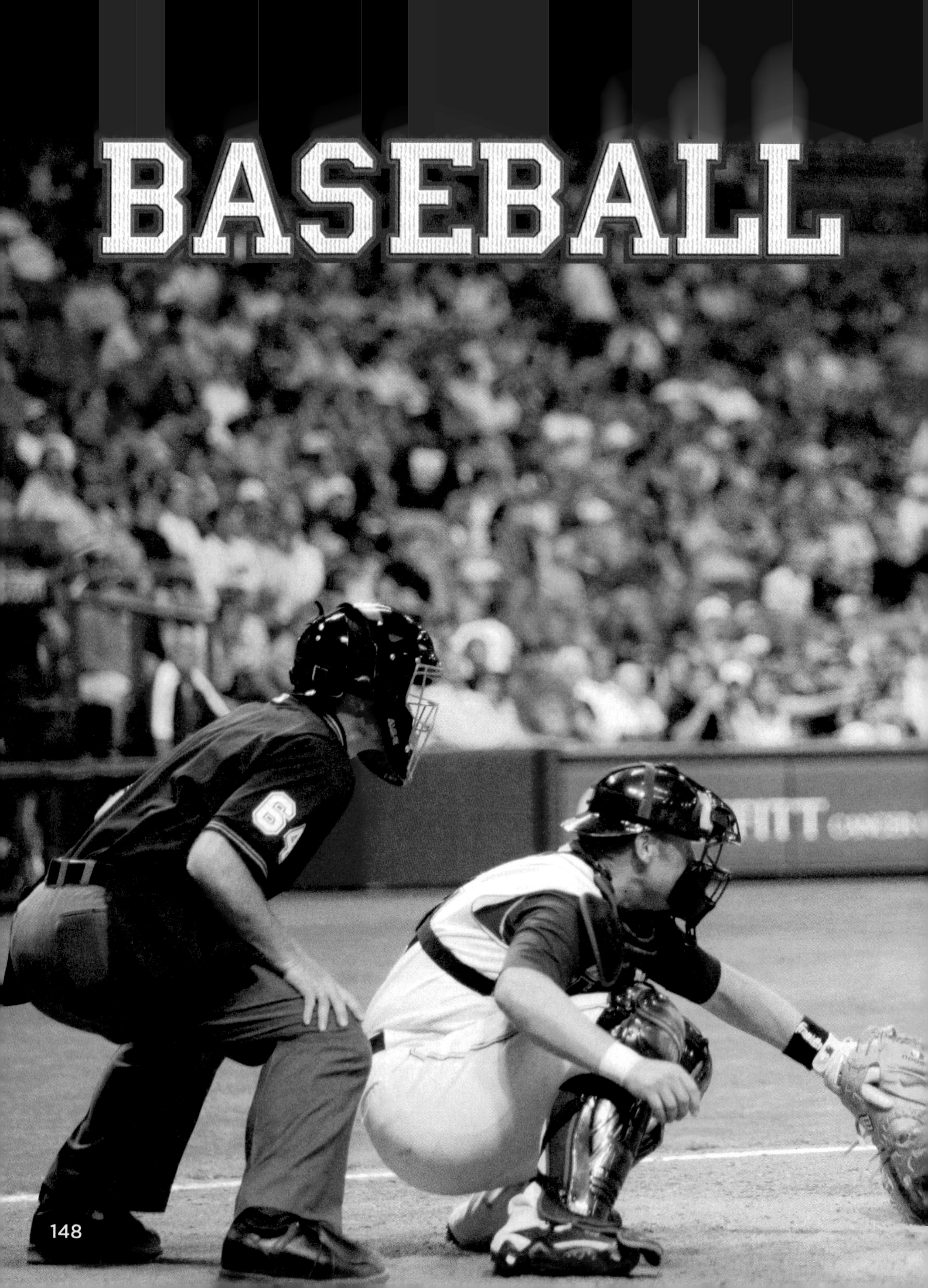

Talk About It

What do you think is happening in this picture? What do you think will happen next?

LOG ON Find out more about baseball at **www.macmillanmh.com**

Vocabulary

legendary
muttered
gaped
snickering
insult
fluke
flinched

FCAT **Context Clues**
Descriptions in the text can help you figure out what a word means. Figure out the meaning of *snickering* using descriptions.

WOMEN PICK UP THE BALL

by Jenny Hull

Lucy's class was at Cooperstown—site of the **legendary** Baseball Hall of Fame. Lucy wasn't thrilled to be there. "Who cares about the All-American Girls Professional Baseball League?" Lucy **muttered** quietly to herself.

The League's Beginning

The guide explained that in 1942, most young men were being drafted to fight in World War II. Some feared that major-league baseball parks would close. But Philip Wrigley, the owner of the Chicago Cubs, decided to start a girls' league. Some may have **gaped** at the idea, but it soon caught on.

Lucy wondered what it was like for those girls. If people laughed in a mean way, did the girls notice the baseball fans **snickering**?

A woman baseball player makes a leaping catch.

The League Succeeds

Girls as young as 15 tried out for the league. The $45- to $85-a-week salaries were a big draw. That might seem like an **insult** today, but back then it was a lot of money.

Players had to follow strict rules of behavior and take classes. They were taught how to dress, act, and take care of themselves.

The success of the league was no **fluke**. During the war many women worked in factories. This changed the image people had of what women could do.

Female players walked with blocks on their heads for balance and posture.

The League Ends

After the war ended, interest lessened and the league fell apart. One reason was that many people got TVs in the early 1950s. They could watch major-league games without buying a ticket or leaving the house!

Time to Leave

Lucy **flinched** when her teacher called the class together. She wasn't ready to leave. She wanted to learn more. But Lucy would have to wait until her next visit to learn more about this interesting time in baseball history.

Reread for Comprehension

Make Inferences and Analyze

FCAT

Author's Purpose The **author's purpose** is the reason he or she wrote the story. Think about details in the story and what you already know to decide on the author's purpose. Reread the selection and fill in your Author's Purpose Map to find the clues that will help you understand the author's purpose.

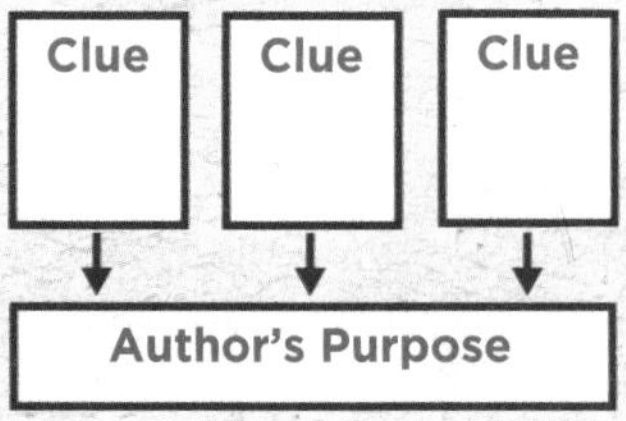

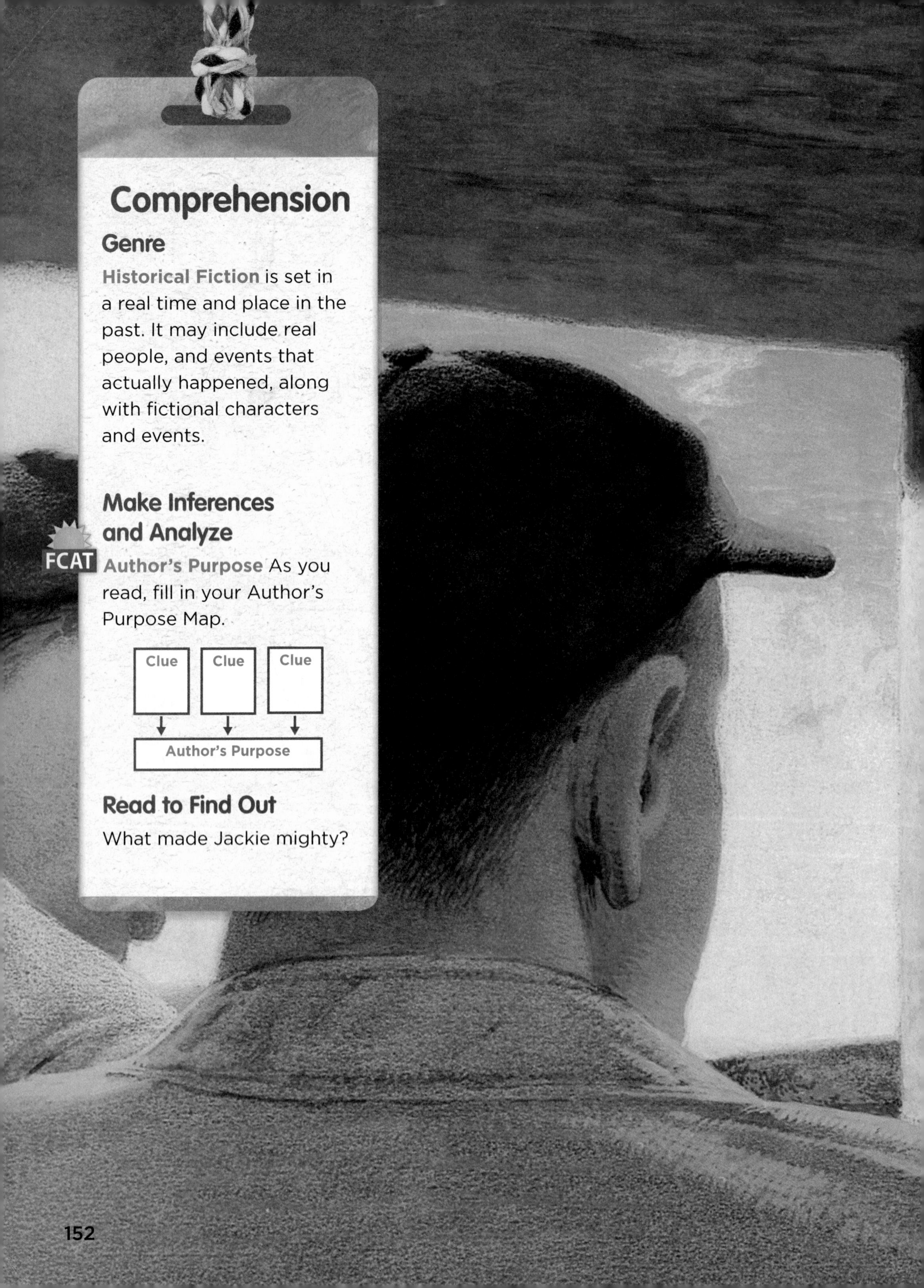

Comprehension

Genre

Historical Fiction is set in a real time and place in the past. It may include real people, and events that actually happened, along with fictional characters and events.

Make Inferences and Analyze

FCAT **Author's Purpose** As you read, fill in your Author's Purpose Map.

Clue → Clue → Clue → Author's Purpose

Read to Find Out

What made Jackie mighty?

MIGHTY JACKIE
The Strike-out Queen

by Marissa Moss • Illustrated by C.F. Payne

Award Winning Illustrator

It was April 2, 1931, and something amazing was about to happen. In Chattanooga, Tennessee, two teams were about to play an exhibition game of baseball.

One was the New York Yankees, a **legendary** team with famous players—Babe Ruth, Lou Gehrig, and Tony Lazzeri.

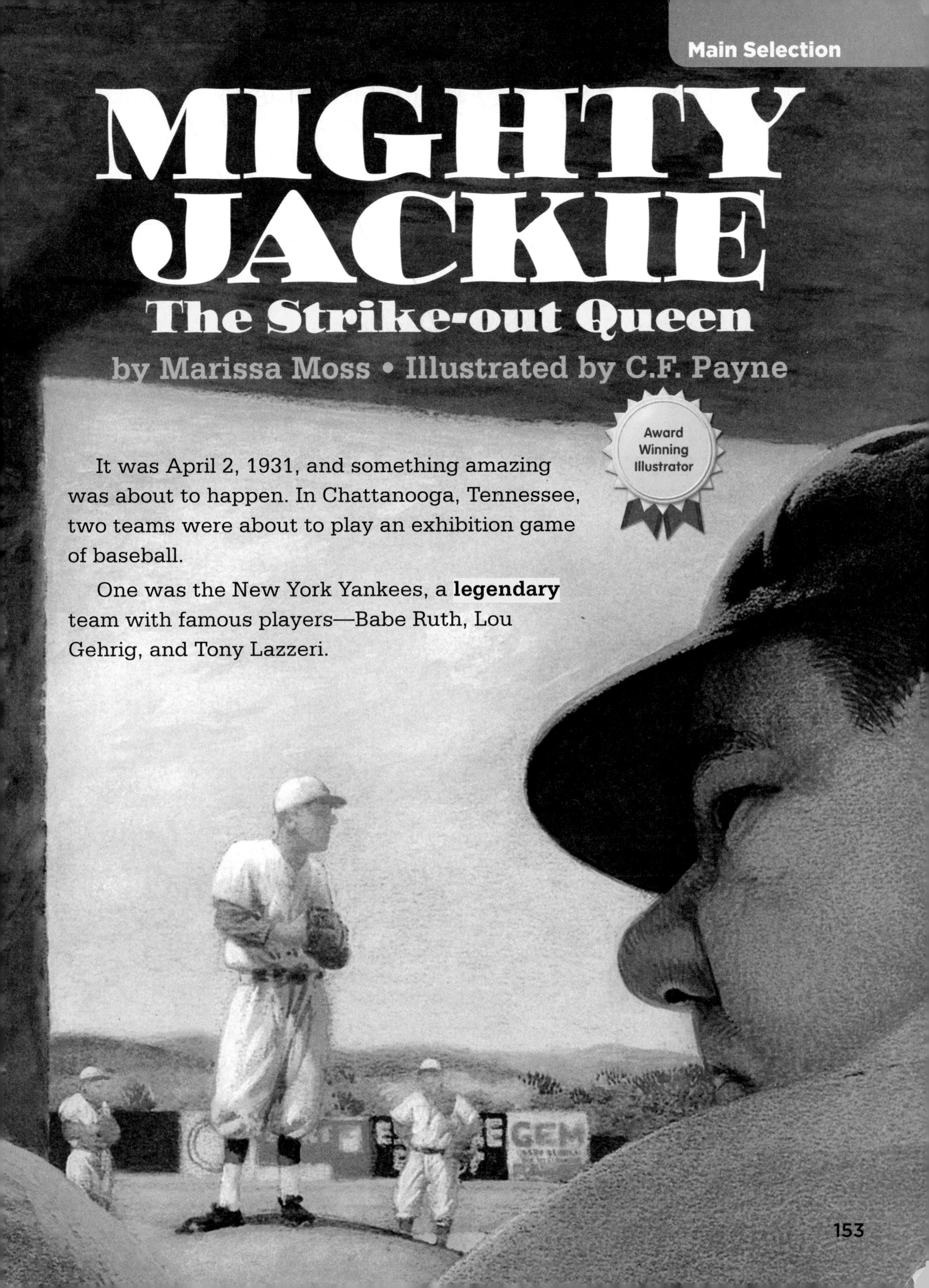

The other was the Chattanooga Lookouts, a small team, a nothing team, except for the pitcher, Jackie Mitchell.

Jackie was young, only seventeen years old, but that's not what made people sit up and take notice. Jackie was a girl, and everyone knew that girls didn't play major-league baseball.

The *New York Daily News* sneered that she would swing "a mean lipstick" instead of a bat. A reporter wrote that you might as well have "a trained seal behind the plate" as have a woman standing there. But Jackie was no trained seal. She was a pitcher, a mighty good one. The question was, was she good enough to play against the New York Yankees?

C

As long as she could remember, Jackie had played ball with her father. She knew girls weren't supposed to. All the kids at school, all the boys in her neighborhood told her that. When one boy yelled at another one, "You throw like a girl!" it was an **insult**—everyone knew girls couldn't throw. Or that's what they thought.

Day after day, in the neighborhood sandlot, Jackie's father told her differently. He said she could throw balls, and she did. She ran bases, she swung the bat. By the time she was eight years old, Dazzy Vance, the star pitcher for the Brooklyn Dodgers, had taught her how to pitch. A real pitcher talking to a little girl was all Jackie needed to start dreaming of playing in the World Series. Her father saw her talent and so did Dazzy. He told her she could be good at whatever she wanted, as long as she worked at it. And Jackie worked at baseball. She worked hard.

She practiced pitching till it was too cold and dark to stay outside. She threw balls until her shoulder ached and her fingers were callused. She pitched until her eyes blurred over and she couldn't see where she was throwing. But it didn't matter, her arm knew.

FCAT **Author's Purpose**
Why do you think the author gives so much information about Jackie's childhood?

And now she was finally going to have her chance to play on a *real* baseball team, to pitch to *real* players. The stands were packed. A crowd of four thousand had come to see the strange sight of a woman on the pitcher's mound.

She stood tall on the field and looked back at the crowd in the bleachers. They were waiting for her to make a mistake, and she knew it. They were waiting for her to prove that baseball was a man's game, not *her* game.

"It *is* my game," she **muttered** to herself and bit her lip. The Yankees were up, top of the first, and the batter was walking up to the plate. Jackie was ready for him, the ball tight in her left hand.

Except the batter was Babe Ruth—Babe Ruth, the "Home Run King," a big mountain of a man—and Babe didn't like the idea of a woman pitcher at all. He thought women were "too delicate" for baseball. "They'll never make good," he said. "It would kill them to play ball every day." He walked to the plate and tipped his cap at Jackie. But if she thought he was going to go easy on her, she could forget it! He gripped the bat and got ready to slam the ball out of the ballpark.

Jackie held that ball like it was part of her arm, and when she threw it, she knew exactly where it would go. Right over the plate, right where the Babe wasn't expecting it, right where he watched it speed by and *thwunk* into the catcher's mitt.

"STRRRRIKE ONE!"

Babe Ruth **gaped**—he couldn't believe it! The crowd roared. Jackie tried to block them out, to see only the ball, to feel only the ball. But Babe Ruth was facing her down now, determined not to let a girl make a fool out of him. She **flinched** right before the next pitch, and the umpire called a ball.

"Hmmmph," the Babe snorted.

"You can do it!" Jackie told herself. "Girls can throw—show them!"

But the next pitch was another ball.

Now the crowd was hooting and jeering. The Babe was **snickering** with them.

Jackie closed her eyes. She felt her fingers tingling around the ball, she felt its heft in her palm, she felt the force of her shoulder muscles as she wound up for the pitch. She remembered what her father had told her: "Go out there and pitch just like you pitch to anybody else."

"STRRRRIKE TWO!"

Now the Babe was mad.

This was serious. The Babe was striking out, and the pitcher was a girl!

Jackie wasn't mad, but she wasn't scared either. She was pitching, really pitching, and it felt like something was happening the way it had always been meant to. She knew the batter would expect the same pitch, close and high, even if the batter was Babe Ruth. So this time she threw the ball straight down the middle with all the speed she could put on it.

"STRRRRIKE THREE!"

Babe Ruth glared at the umpire and threw the bat down in disgust. He told reporters that that would be the last time he'd bat against a woman! The crowd was stunned. A girl had struck out the "Sultan of Swat"! It couldn't be! It was a mistake, a **fluke**! What would the papers say tomorrow? But wait, here came Lou Gehrig, the "Iron Horse," up to the plate. He'd show her. She couldn't strike him out too.

Lou Gehrig swung with a mighty grunt, but his bat hit nothing but air.

"STRRRRRIKE ONE!"

He looked stunned, then dug in his heels and glared at Jackie.

"STRRRRRIKE TWO!"

Jackie grinned. She was doing what she'd worked so hard and long to do, and nothing could stop her.

She pitched the ball the way she knew best, a lefty pitch with a low dip in it. No one could touch a ball like that when it was thrown right.

"STRRRRRIKE THREE!"

The crowd, so ready to boo her before, rose with a roar, clapping and cheering like crazy. Back to back, Jackie had struck out two of baseball's best batters, Babe Ruth and Lou Gehrig. She'd proven herself and now the fans loved her for it.

But Jackie didn't hear them. She was too proud and too happy. She'd done what she'd always known she could do. She'd shown the world how a girl could throw—as hard and as fast and as far as she wanted.

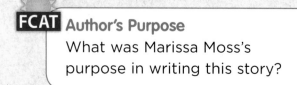

FCAT Author's Purpose
What was Marissa Moss's purpose in writing this story?

The Winning Team: Marissa and C. F.

Marissa Moss likes to write about real women like Jackie who have done unusual things. She has also written about a female train engineer and the first woman to fly across the English Channel. Marissa hopes that when kids read her books they will discover things about the past that remind them of their own lives.

Other books by Marissa Moss and C.F. Payne

C. F. Payne has stepped up to the plate to illustrate other baseball stories. C. F. often does caricatures, a kind of art that exaggerates the way people look or act, making them seem larger than life.

LOG ON Find out more about Marissa Moss and C. F. Payne at **www.macmillanmh.com**

FCAT Author's Purpose

Do you think that Marissa Moss wrote this story to entertain or to inform? Does the fact that the main character was a woman have an effect on the author's purpose? Why or why not?

FCAT Comprehension Check

Summarize

Summarize *Mighty Jackie: The Strike-Out Queen.* Be sure to describe the main events and the setting. Use your Author's Purpose Map to help you think about the story.

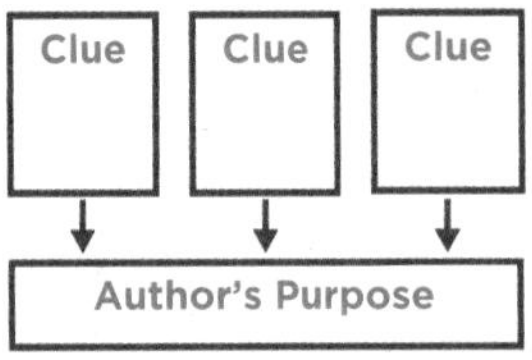

Think and Compare

READ THINK EXPLAIN

1. The author stresses the fact that Ruth and Gehrig were **legendary** baseball players. What is the author's purpose in doing that? Explain using story details. **Make Inferences and Analyze: Author's Purpose**

READ THINK EXPLAIN

2. Read the third paragraph on page 154. What were people's attitudes toward female athletes? Why did the author include this in her story? Use story details to explain. **Analyze**

3. Have you ever reached a goal that you or other people may have thought was impossible to achieve? Explain. **Apply**

4. Why was proving her pitching talent so important to Jackie? Explain using story details. **Analyze**

5. Read "Women Pick Up the Ball" on pages 150–151. How did women's role in professional baseball change from the 1930s to the 1940s? What caused this change? Use details from both selections to explain. **Reading/Writing Across Texts**

Motion in Baseball

Pitching

by Norah Lukeington

Science

Genre

Almanacs have brief sections of information on many subjects.

FCAT Text Feature

Tables present a lot of information, such as names and numbers, in compact form.

Content Vocabulary

alter **force**
trajectory

There are different ways that pitchers need to hold the ball. It all depends on the pitch.

Baseball coaches and pitchers must be able to throw a lot of pitches during a season. In just a regular season, a pitcher can throw close to 3,000 pitches. Some baseball fans keep a running count of every pitch. They also keep track of how many times a pitcher strikes out a batter and how many times a batter hits a pitch.

Speed and Pitching

A pitching coach also keeps track of the type and speed of pitches a pitcher throws. Pitching coaches often use a speed radar gun to measure the speed of pitches. When a ball is pitched, the pitching coach points the speed radar gun at the ball as it travels toward its target. When he shoots the gun, radio waves bounce toward the ball to measure its speed. The waves then bounce back to the gun, reporting the pitch's speed to the coach.

Pitchers **alter**, or change, the **force** they place on a ball depending on how fast or slow they want it to go. By altering the force of the throw, pitchers are also able to get the ball to move the way they want it to. Pitchers know that by holding and throwing the ball a certain way they can affect its speed and direction. They also know that they can make the ball harder for the batter to hit.

The *fastball* is one of the first pitches young pitchers learn. Pitchers hold a fastball across the seams of the ball and throw it with their fingertips. Many pitchers feel they have a lot of control with the fastball. The fastball moves faster than any other pitch. It usually flies by the plate long before the batter swings. A more difficult pitch to learn is the *change-up*. Pitchers throw a *change-up* from the palm of their hand. It moves slowly, and a batter often swings for the ball before it crosses the plate.

Speed radar guns are also used in other sports, such as soccer.

Baseball gloves protect the hands of the players from getting hurt by the hard baseballs.

Reading a Table

Almanacs often have tables as well as charts, lists of facts, and other information.

Pitching Stats

Player	Number of Pitches Thrown	Pitches Per Inning	Strikeouts Per 9 Innings	Hits Per 9 Innings
Pitcher 1	2583	16.45	7.62	7.80
Pitcher 2	1224	17.57	8.27	8.14
Pitcher 3	672	16.39	6.80	9.66
Pitcher 4	387	18.14	4.22	10.97

Throwing vs. Pitching

The *curveball* is a very difficult pitch for batters to hit because its **trajectory**, or direction, changes at the last second. When throwing curveballs, pitchers put their middle fingers on the seam of the ball and tilt their wrist inward so that when the ball leaves their hands, it rolls over their index fingers. The curveball spins. As a result the air under the ball travels faster than the air above the ball, and the ball drops from a 12 o'clock position to a 6 o'clock position. The batter swings at a ball that is not within reach.

Some people do not realize the importance of pitching in baseball. They think pitching is just about "throwing" the ball. The truth is that a lot of thought and skill goes into every single pitch. Before the baseball leaves the pitcher's mit, the pitcher has already decided what pitch to use, how much force to put behind it, and in what direction to throw it. So, the next time you are watching a baseball game and you are watching the ball make its way toward the batter's bat, think about the difference every pitch can have on the final score of the game.

Even the way a pitcher stands affects the force of the ball. Pitchers usually dip down low to throw a ball. This gives it more force.

FCAT Connect and Compare

1. Look at the table on page 172. What is the difference in the number of pitches per inning thrown by pitcher 1 and pitcher 4? How many strikeouts did pitcher 3 get per 9 innings? **Reading a Table**

2. How do pitchers throw a curveball? How is it different from throwing a fastball? **Explain**

3. How is Jackie's pitching style in *Mighty Jackie* similar to the pitching styles discussed in this article? How is it different? **Reading/Writing Across Texts**

Science Activity

Research the science of motion behind another kind of baseball pitch. Write a summary and create a table based on the information you find.

LOG ON Find out more about baseball at **www.macmillanmh.com**

Write a Persuasive Letter

by David P.

Writer's Craft

FCAT **A Good Topic**

To find **a good topic** to write about, think of what interests you. If the topic you pick is too general, narrow it down so you will be able to cover it completely.

I wrote on a topic I knew about and was interested in.

I gave good reasons for my friend Jorge to come with me.

701 S. Washington Street
Beeville, TX 78102
May 28, 2007

Dear Jorge,

I really hope you will come to baseball camp. It's going to be at Wilson Field in June. Professional ballplayers will teach us how to play every position, and we can improve our batting averages. You can work on pitching. So let's go! Call me!!!

Your pal,
David

Writing Prompt

Friends like to do things together.

Think about something you would like a friend to do with you.

Now write a persuasive letter explaining why a friend should do something with you.

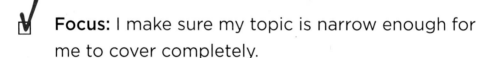

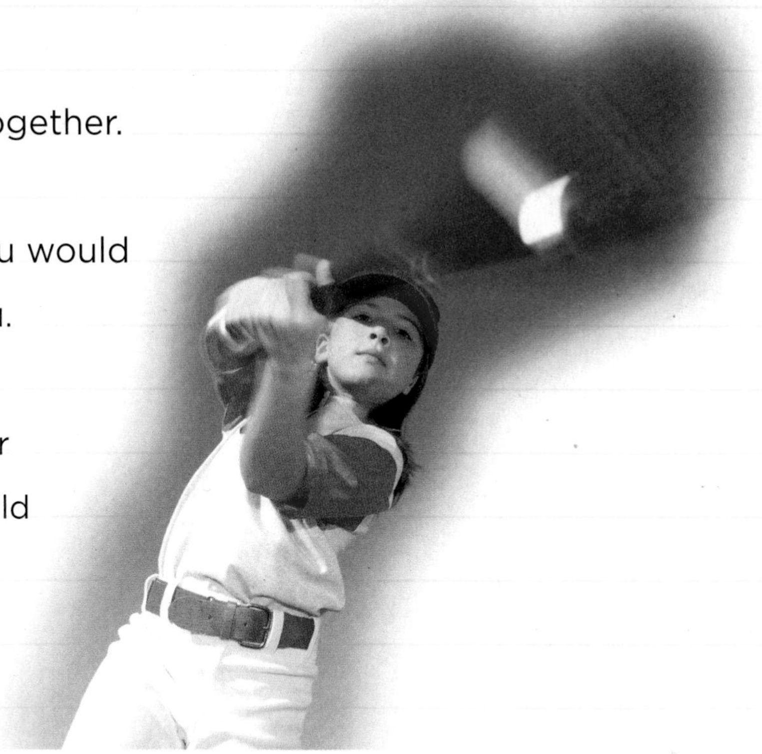

FCAT Writer's Checklist

- [x] **Focus:** I make sure my topic is narrow enough for me to cover completely.
- [ ] **Organization:** My first sentence clearly shows the **good topic** I chose to write about. I present my ideas and reasons in order, saving my strongest reason for last.
- [x] **Support:** I present good persuasive reasons to support my good topic.
- [x] **Conventions:** My writing flows smoothly. My sentences are complete. My grammar is correct.

New Places, New Faces

Talk About It

Where do you think this is? Would you like your face to appear on this flag? Explain why.

LOG ON Find out more about immigration at **www.macmillanmh.com**

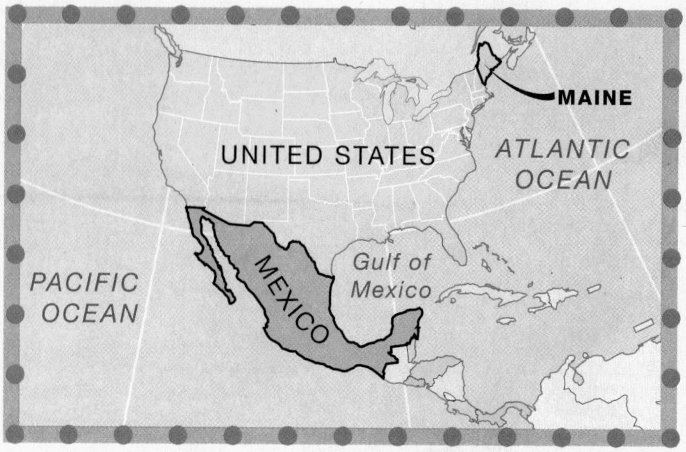

Vocabulary

overheard | strikes | opportunities | citizen | border | boycotts | unions

FCAT Dictionary

Word Origins Where a word comes from and how it came to be in use is its origin. You can look up a word's origin in a dictionary. Use a dictionary to find the origin of *boycotts*.

Mexico: My New Home

by Harold Johnson

Dear Grandpa,

Remember when Mom and Dad thought I was asleep and I **overheard** them talking about moving to Mexico? You said that it would be an adventure. You were right!

I was a little scared when we left Maine. All my friends were there. Living in Mexico is very different, but I'm starting to like it a lot.

Guess what? I ate my first *tamale*. Do you know what that is? When I saw it, I wasn't sure I wanted to find out. But it was good! It's cornmeal wrapped in corn husks and steamed.

I have had many **opportunities** to try new foods. But sometimes I go to my favorite fast food place. So it's not a totally different world. We actually live less than 100 miles from the U.S.-Mexico **border**.

The farmers here work very hard but don't make much money to support their families. Some farmers join **unions**, organizations just for them, to protect their rights. Sometimes there are **strikes**, and people stop working, hoping that will make a difference.

Farmers are asking every **citizen** not to buy produce that comes from outside Mexico. They hope these **boycotts** will improve conditions.

I'm learning a lot about Mexican culture. Local harvests are really important here. There are fairs, called *ferias*, to celebrate. There's lots of music, dancing, and eating. I hope we can go to a *feria* when you visit!

Adios!

Paul (or should I say Pablo?)

Reread for **Comprehension**

Generate Questions

FCAT **Plot Development** The **plot** tells what happens in a story. To help you understand the plot, ask questions about what you have read and what you already know. Reread the selection to look for clues to answer questions you have about the story. Fill in the Inferences Web to help you answer your questions.

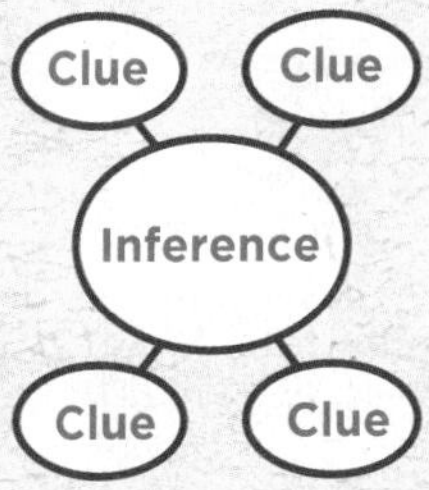

Comprehension

Genre

Realistic Fiction is a made-up story that could have happened in real life.

Generate Questions

FCAT **Plot Development** As you read, fill in your Inferences Web.

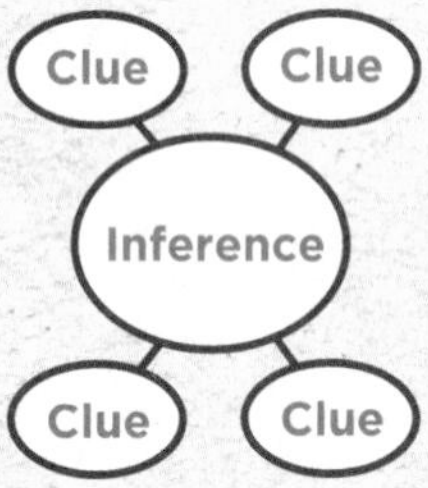

Read to Find Out

What benefits does Amada get from keeping a diary?

My Diary from Here to There

By Amada Irma Pérez
Illustrated by Maya Christina Gonzalez

Sé que ya debería
estar dormida pero
no me importa.
iento que sí

Dear Diary, I know I should be asleep already, but I just can't sleep. If I don't write this all down, I'll burst! Tonight after my brothers—Mario, Víctor, Héctor, Raúl, and Sergio—and I all climbed into bed, I **overheard** Mamá and Papá whispering. They were talking about leaving our little house in Juárez, Mexico, where we've lived our whole lives, and moving to Los Angeles in the United States. But why? How can I sleep knowing we might leave Mexico forever? I'll have to get to the bottom of this tomorrow.

Today at breakfast, Mamá explained everything. She said, "Papá lost his job. There's no work here, no jobs at all. We know moving will be hard, but we want the best for all of you. Try to understand." I thought the boys would be upset, but instead they got really excited about moving to the States.

"The big stores in El Paso sell all kinds of toys!"

"And they have escalators to ride!"

"And the air smells like popcorn, yum!"

Am I the only one who is scared of leaving our home, our beautiful country, and all the people we might never see again?

My best friend Michi and I walked to the park today. We passed Don Nacho's corner store and the women at the tortilla shop, their hands blurring like hummingbird wings as they worked the dough over the griddle.

At the park we braided each other's hair and promised never to forget each other. We each picked out a smooth, heart-shaped stone to remind us always of our friendship, of the little park, of Don Nacho and the tortilla shop. I've known Michi since we were little, and I don't think I'll ever find a friend like her in California.

"You're lucky your family will be together over there," Michi said. Her sisters and father work in the U.S. I can't imagine leaving anyone in our family behind.

OK, Diary, here's the plan—in two weeks we leave for my grandparents' house in Mexicali, right across the **border** from Calexico, California. We'll stay with them while Papá goes to Los Angeles to look for work. We can only take what will fit in the old car Papá borrowed—we're selling everything else. Meanwhile, the boys build cardboard box cities and act like nothing bothers them. Mamá and Papá keep talking about all the **opportunities** we'll have in California. But what if we're not allowed to speak Spanish? What if I can't learn English? Will I ever see Michi again? What if we never come back?

COCINA
COCINA
GATO

Today while we were packing, Papá pulled me aside. He said, "Amada, *m'ija*, I can see how worried you've been. Don't be scared. Everything will be all right."

"But how do you know? What will happen to us?" I said.

He smiled. "*M'ija*, I was born in Arizona, in the States. When I was six—not a big kid like you—my Papá and Mamá moved our family back to Mexico. It was a big change, but we got through it. I know you can, too. You are stronger than you think." I hope he's right. I still need to pack my special rock (and you, Diary!). We leave tomorrow!

FCAT Plot Development

Based on Amada's journal entries, what do you think she is feeling about the move? How do you know?

Our trip was long and hard. At night the desert was so cold we had to huddle together to keep warm. We drove right along the border, across from New Mexico and Arizona. Mexico and the U.S. are two different countries, but they look exactly the same on both sides of the border, with giant saguaros pointing up at the pink-orange sky and enormous clouds. I made a wish on the first star I saw. Soon there were too many stars in the sky to count. Our little house in Juárez already seems so far away.

We arrived in Mexicali late at night and my grandparents Nana and Tata, and all our aunts, uncles and cousins (there must be fifty of them!) welcomed us with a feast of *tamales*, beans, *pan dulce*, and hot chocolate with cinnamon sticks. It's so good to see them all! Everyone gathered around us and told stories late into the night. We played so much that the boys fell asleep before the last blanket was rolled out onto the floor. But, Diary, I can't sleep. I keep thinking about Papá leaving tomorrow.

Papá left for Los Angeles this morning. Nana comforted Mamá, saying that Papá is a U.S. **citizen**, so he won't have a problem getting our "green cards" from the U.S. government. Papá told us that we each need a green card to live in the States, because we weren't born there.

I can't believe Papá's gone. Tío Tito keeps trying to make us laugh instead of cry. Tío Raúl let me wear his special *medalla*. And Tío Chato even pulled a silver coin out of my ear. The boys try to copy his tricks but coins just end up flying everywhere. They drive me nuts sometimes, but today it feels good to laugh.

We got a letter from Papá today! I'm pasting it into your pages, Diary.

My dear family,

I have been picking grapes and strawberries in the fields of Delano, 140 miles north of Los Angeles, saving money and always thinking of you. It is hard, tiring work. There is a man here in the fields named César Chávez, who speaks of ***unions***, ***strikes***, *and* ***boycotts***. *These new words hold the hope of better conditions for us farmworkers.*

So far, getting your green cards has been difficult, for we are not the only family trying to start a new life here. Please be patient. It won't be long before we are all together again.

Hugs and kisses, Papá

FCAT Plot Development

What does Papá have to do to bring his family to California?

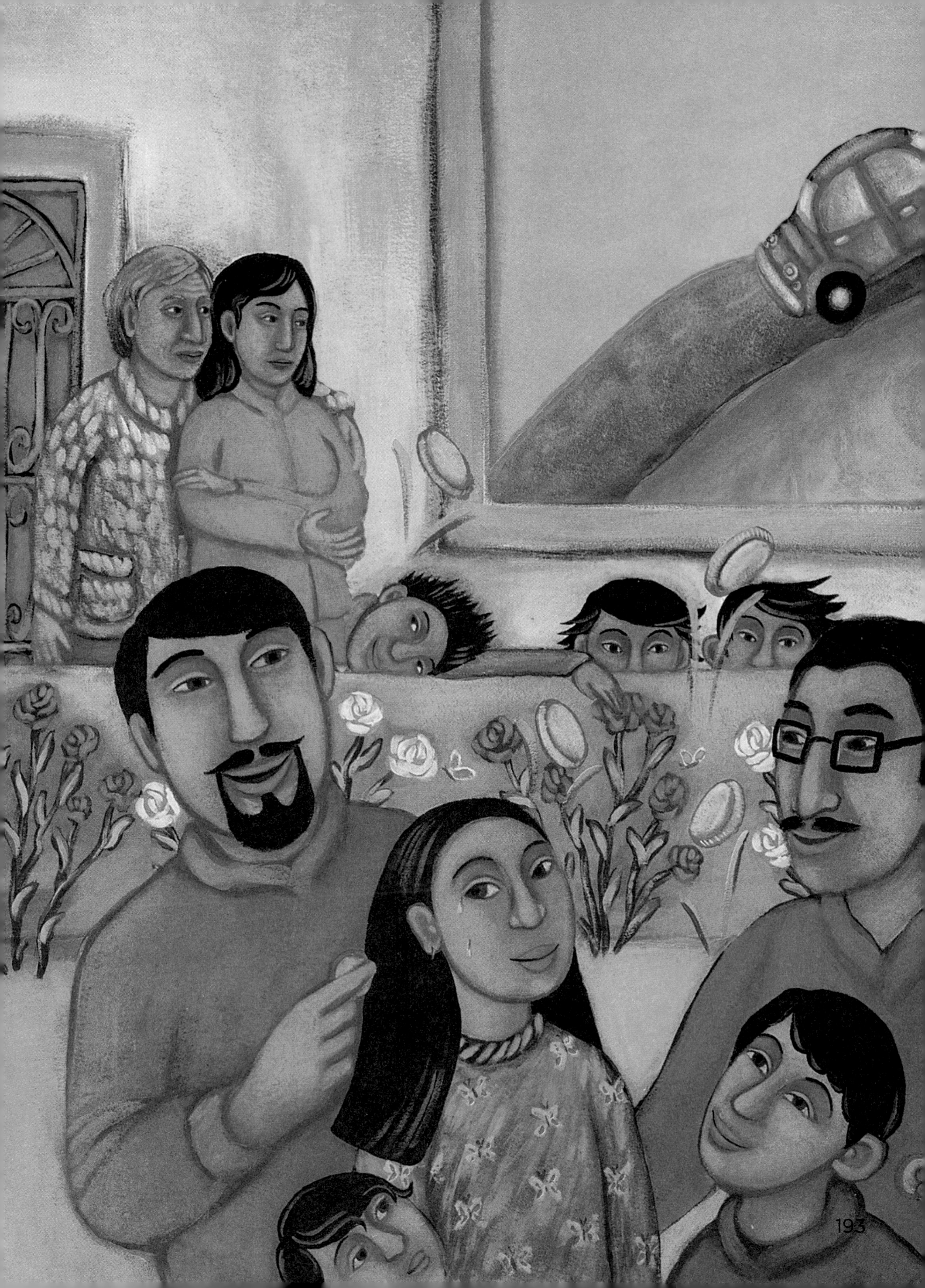

I miss Papá so much—it feels like he left ages ago. It's been tough to stay hopeful. So far we've had to live in three different houses with some of Mamá's sisters. First, the boys broke Tía Tuca's jewelry box and were so noisy she kicked us out. Then, at Nana's house, they kept trying on Tía Nena's high heels and purses. Even Nana herself got mad when they used her pots and pans to make "music." And they keep trying to read what I've written here, and to hide my special rock. Tía Lupe finally took us in, but where will we go if she decides she's had enough of us?

FINALLY! Papá sent our green cards—we're going to cross the border at last! He can't come for us but will meet us in Los Angeles.

The whole family is making a big farewell dinner for us tonight. Even after all the trouble the boys have caused, I think everyone is sad to see us go. Nana even gave me a new journal to write in for when I finish this one. She said, "Never forget who you are and where you are from. Keep your language and culture alive in your diary and in your heart."

We leave this weekend. I'm so excited I can hardly write!

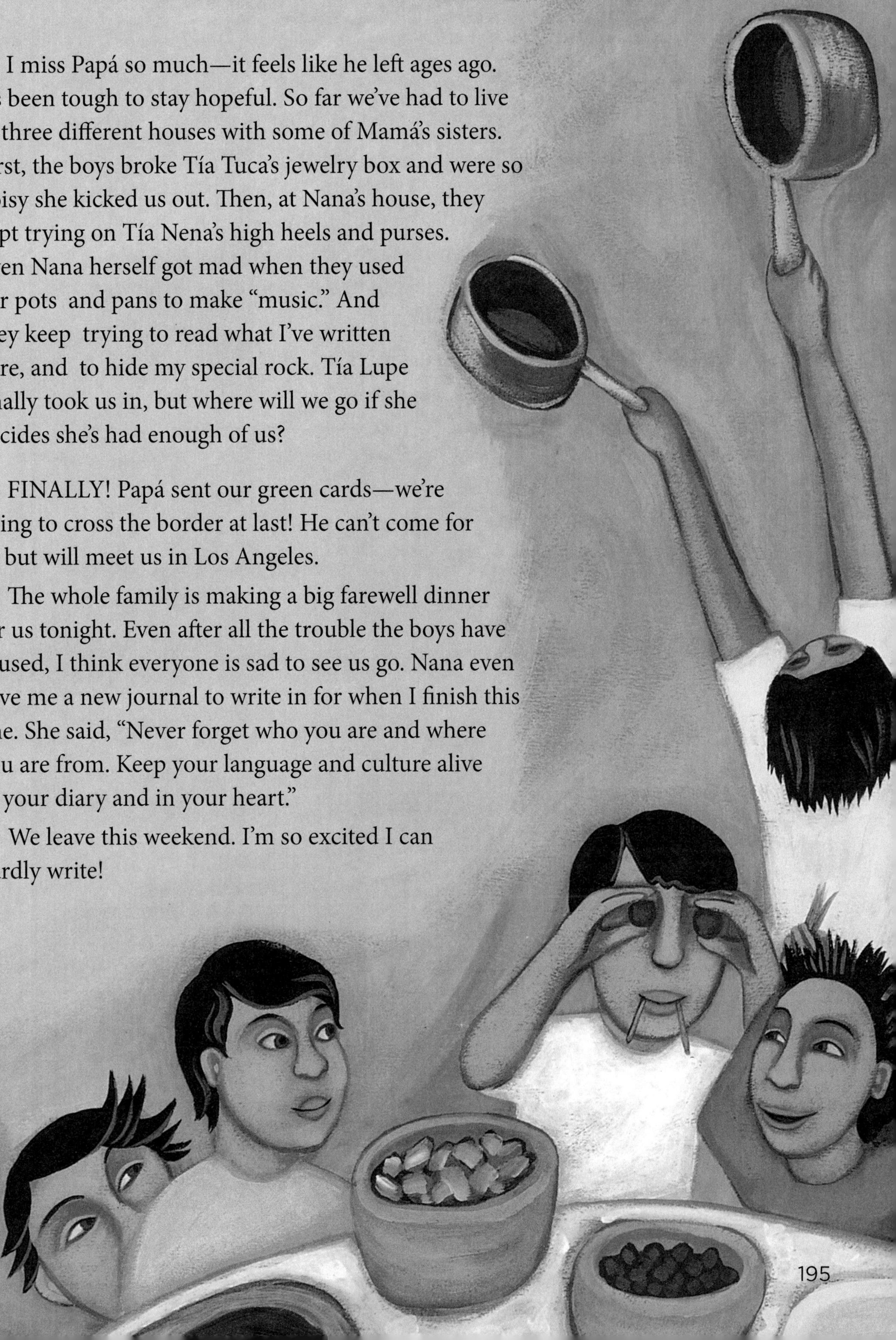

My first time writing in the U.S.A.! We're in San Ysidro, California, waiting for the bus to Los Angeles. Crossing the border in Tijuana was crazy. Everyone was pushing and shoving. There were babies crying, and people fighting to be first in line. We held hands the whole way. When we finally got across, Mario had only one shoe on and his hat had fallen off. I counted everyone and I still had five brothers. Whew!

Papá is meeting us at the bus station in Los Angeles. It's been so long—I hope he recognizes us!

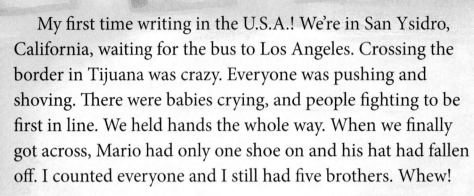

What a long ride! One woman and her children got kicked off the bus when the immigration patrol boarded to check everyone's papers. Mamá held Mario and our green cards close to her heart.

Papá was waiting at the station, just like he promised. We all jumped into his arms and laughed, and Mamá even cried a little. Papá's hugs felt so much better than when he left us in Mexicali!

I wrote to Michi today:

Dear Michi,

I have stories for you! Papá found a job in a factory, and we're living in a creaky old house in El Monte, east of Los Angeles. It's not at all like Juárez. Yesterday everything started shaking and a huge roar was all around us—airplanes, right overhead! Sometimes freight trains rumble past our house like little earthquakes.

Every day I hold my special rock and I think about home—Mexico—and our walks to the park. Papá says we might go back for the holidays in a year or two. Until then, write me!

Missing you,

Amada Irma

Well, Diary, I finally found a place where I can sit and think and write. It may not be the little park in Juárez, but it's pretty. You know, just because I'm far away from Juárez and Michi and my family in Mexicali, it doesn't mean they're not here with me. They're inside my little rock; they're here in your pages and in the language that I speak; and they're in my memories and my heart. Papá was right. I AM stronger than I think—in Mexico, in the States, anywhere.

P.S. I've almost filled this whole journal and can't wait to start my new one. Maybe someday I'll even write a book about our journey!

From the Diaries of . . .

Amada Irma Pérez used memories of her own journey from Mexico to the United States to write this story. Just like the main character, she was both excited and scared about moving. Today Amada still writes in a journal. She believes that diaries help keep our memories alive.

Another book by Amada Irma Pérez

Maya Christina Gonzalez has always loved to draw. When she was a child, she could not find any pictures of Mexican American children like herself in books. Maya would draw her own picture on a blank page in each book she read. Today Maya's books show lots of people of color so readers can feel proud of who they are.

LOG ON Find out more about Amada Irma Pérez and Maya Christina Gonzalez at **www.macmillanmh.com**

FCAT Author's Purpose

Do you think using her own memories affected Amada Irma Pérez's purpose for writing? What clues tell you whether the story mainly entertains or informs?

FCAT Comprehension Check

Summarize

Summarize *My Diary from Here to There.* State the most important events, the setting, and how the main character thinks and acts as the story progresses. Use your Inferences Web to help you.

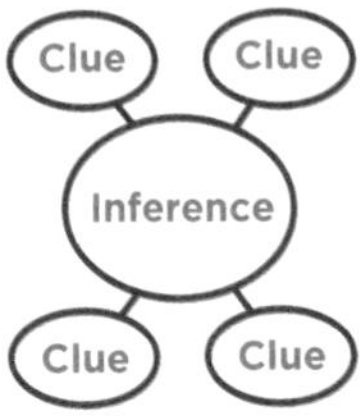

Think and Compare

1. How does Papá losing his job affect the characters and the plot? Use story details to explain. **Generate Questions: Plot Development**

2. Reread page 195. What kind of relationship does Amada's family have with their relatives? Explain using details from the story. **Analyze**

3. Suppose Amada writes a new story about her experiences as a **citizen** in the U.S. What would you most like to read about? **Synthesize**

4. Compare Amada's feelings with those of her brothers. Are some of their feelings the same? Explain using details from the story. **Analyze**

5. Read "Mexico: My New Home" on pages 178–179. How is Paul's situation similar to Amada's? How is it different? Use details from both selections to explain. **Reading/Writing Across Texts**

Social Studies

Genre

Textbook Excerpts are short nonfiction pieces taken from a textbook.

FCAT

Text Feature

Primary Sources are first-person accounts of historical events in letters, journals, or oral histories.

Content Vocabulary

colonize	**immigrants**
cultures	**customs**

IMMIGRATION IN FLORIDA

In 1513 a Spanish explorer named Juan Ponce de León accidentally found the area of land now known as Florida. He was looking for a spring that people said gave the drinker eternal life. De León named this area *Pascua de Florida,* or "feast of flowers," and claimed the land for Spain. There were already Native Americans living in this area, but Spain decided to **colonize** it immediately because France wanted to own the land as well. For many years Spain and France fought over the land. Spain eventually won only to trade Florida to Great Britain in 1763. By the time Florida became a part of the United States in 1822, there were already Native Americans, British, Spanish, and French settlers living there, adding their **cultures** to the new state.

Juan Ponce de León also named Florida's Dry Tortugas. *Tortugas* is Spanish for "turtles." The island's name comes from its lack of fresh water and its many turtles. Dry Tortugas is now a national park.

Floridians have many different celebrations, such as festivals and parades, to honor the different cultures in their state.

A Growing Population

Florida is now the fourth-largest state in the United States and it is still growing! In the last ten years, more than three million people moved to Florida. One third of those people were **immigrants**. The increase in Florida's population created some challenges. Pollution, overcrowded schools, and lack of natural resources are just a few of the problems people living in Florida must face.

Immigrants who come to Florida also face many challenges. Getting used to life in a new country can be difficult for many immigrants. Living in a new country means learning about different **customs**, values, and beliefs. Learning a new language can also be difficult for immigrants as they work to make Florida their new home.

Primary Sources

Oral History

In an oral history, a person describes experiences from a certain time and place. Primary sources are written in a person's own words.

"When I was eight years old, my father left Havana, Cuba, to go to the United States. He wanted our family to have a better life. I was very young and didn't know what was going on. All I knew was that my mother cried a lot and there always seemed to be people around.

My mother, two sisters, and I followed my father three years later. I was scared to go because I didn't know what to expect. When we got to Miami, Florida, things were different. The food didn't taste the same as it did in Havana. I couldn't find any of my favorite fruit! People spoke in a different language and I couldn't read any of the signs because they were in English. I was very scared things weren't going to work out for me.

Then one day, I was walking in the park and I heard a loud drumming. It reminded me of sounds from home so I ran over to investigate. It was people playing the conga drums like back home! I was so excited to see people dancing around and enjoying the music that I grew up listening to. I knew that even though the United States was different from Cuba, it was now home!"

Francisco Vasquez, Miami, FL

Arrived in 1988, Age 11

A New Culture

Immigration has helped shape a new culture in Florida. The variety of people and cultures in this state has had a large influence on many different things like street names, food, how houses are built, and even what subjects are taught in schools. As more immigrants continue to enter the state, Florida continues to grow more diverse in culture.

Florida's nickname is the Sunshine State.

FCAT Connect and Compare

1. Reread the oral history section on page 204. What were things about the United States that Francisco noticed were different from Cuba? What finally made him feel at home in the United States? **Reading Primary Sources**

2. Why would an increase in immigration cause a shortage of natural resources in Florida? **Evaluate**

3. How is Amada's story in *My Diary from Here to There* similar to Francisco's oral history? How is it different? Explain using details from both selections. **Reading/Writing Across Texts**

Social Studies Activity

RESEARCH INQUIRY

Research what it is like for immigrants to come to a new country. Try to find a primary source. Present your research as if you were the immigrant.

LOG ON Find out more about immigration at **www.macmillanmh.com**

Writer's Craft

FCAT **Transitions**

Transitions are words or phrases that connect one idea to another. Writers may go from one idea to another. Using transitions allows them to connect their ideas.

Write a Radio Ad

I wrote this radio ad about a great local place to visit.

I used "Another" to show I am giving more information about another thing you can do at a museum.

Sleep on a Tall Ship

by Kenji C.

Would you like to sleep on a tall ship? You and your class can stay overnight on the *Elissa* at the Texas Seaport Museum. It's a great opportunity. Learn about sails, masts, and ropes. Help set a sail and watch over the harbor. Write in the ship's log. Experience what it is like to be a sailor!

Another thing you can do at the museum is visit the immigration exhibit to see photos of people who came to the United States through the port of Galveston.

Writing Prompt

People like to visit special places.

Think about a special place you would like to visit.

Now write a radio ad to tell about the special place you would like to visit.

FCAT Writer's Checklist

- ☑ **Focus:** My writing clearly persuades the reader. My topic is narrow enough to cover completely.
- ☐ **Organization:** I use **transitions** between paragraphs to connect different ideas. This helps my writing flow better.
- ☑ **Support:** I use details to support my reasons as to why the reader should do something.
- ☑ **Conventions:** I use complete sentences. I use correct grammar, spelling, and punctuation.

Talk About It

How would you describe the country and people of China?

LOG ON Find out more about the people of China at **www.macmillanmh.com**

TIME FOR KIDS

Focus on China

Vocabulary

temples
dynasties
heritage
preserve
overjoyed

China's Great Wall was built over 2,000 years ago to keep invaders out. It is 1,500 miles long!

WELCOME TO CHINA

China is an enormous country. It has the largest population of any nation. In fact one out of every five people on Earth is Chinese! China has barren deserts, lush valleys, and towering mountains. It also has busy cities, where ancient **temples** stand beside gleaming skyscrapers.

For thousands of years, China was ruled by powerful families called **dynasties**. These families were like royalty, treated like kings and queens by the Chinese people. Just over fifty years ago, China became a communist country. Under communism, a harsh central government controls all business and property.

Records of Chinese history and culture go back more than 2,000 years. Today this rich **heritage** can be seen in China's food, art, and traditions. The Chinese invented paper, ink, the compass, and silk.

Today China is one of the world's most powerful countries. However, it faces some of the toughest challenges of any nation. China's citizens live with many strict rules. The government fails to provide enough jobs for its growing population. As a result millions of people are poor. China's rich heritage is a source of strength, but it must continue to change.

ANCIENT WARRIORS

Scientists in China are racing against the clock . . . and nature! They are working to **preserve** hundreds of ancient clay warriors, horses, and chariots. The statues were discovered in a tomb near the city of Beijing, the capital. They have been buried for 2,000 years. If the painted decorations on the statues are exposed to the air for too long, they will fade.

Villagers planting trees in the area were **overjoyed** when they found these foot-tall soldiers. The discovery gives researchers new information about the Han dynasty. This powerful family ruled China from 206 B.C. to 220 A.D.

Scientists named these figures the Weishan terra-cotta army because they were found near Weishan Mountain in Shandong.

The clay soldiers are buried in order of their rank. David Sensabaugh is an Asian art expert at the Yale University Art Gallery. He thinks the figures are a display of power. How powerful is this army? It's too soon to tell, but it may be thousands strong!

China's Great Inventions

Many things were invented in China throughout history. Here are some Chinese inventions and what they were used for in the past. Which ones do we still use today?

Invention	When	Use
Silk	4,000 years ago	clothing for wealthy Chinese
Kite	3,000 years ago	to send messages during battles
Paper	2,000 years ago	to record events; make books
Paper money	1,000 years ago	for buying and selling
Gunpowder	1,000 years ago	to make firecrackers; send signals
Compass	1,000 years ago	to help sailors find their way

LOG ON Find out more about Ancient China at **www.macmillanmh.com**

Real World Reading

Comprehension

Genre

A **Nonfiction Article** in a newspaper or magazine tells a true story.

Make Inferences and Analyze

FCAT **Relevant Facts and Details**

Relevant facts and details are important facts and details that relate to the topic and support the selection's main idea.

This Buddha was nearly smuggled out of Cambodia by a tourist.

STEALING BEAUTY

To whom do a country's valuable objects from past civilizations belong?

During the day the people of Xiaoli (ZHOW•LEE), China, sit outside their mud-brick shacks. Xiaoli is a poor village. Most people in town are farmers. It has become difficult to make a good living from farming, however. So the farmers wait for darkness to fall. That's when Xiaoli comes alive. At night tomb raiders get to work.

Nearly 5,000 years of Chinese history lie underground in Xiaoli. Fields contain tombs of royalty from many different **dynasties**. Valuable works of art are buried in the tombs. Stealing these treasures, called looting, can bring the poor farmers of Xiaoli lots of money.

Little Su, a doctor in Xiaoli, paid for medical school by selling stolen art. He was also able to buy a big-screen TV. Over the past few years, thieves have broken into at least 220,000 tombs in China, according to China's National Cultural Relics Bureau.

"If the looting continues at this pace, we'll soon have nothing left to remind us of our glorious past," says He Shuzhong (HUH SHOO•JOONG). He's the head of Cultural Heritage Watch in Beijing.

Worldwide Problem

Stealing ancient treasures has become a major problem for other countries, too. Police in India recently stopped criminals who had stolen hundreds of sculptures from **temples** and monuments. In Cambodia thieves ripped out carved faces of gods from an eleventh-century site. Cambodian police recently found truckloads of ancient sculptures that were taken from archaeological sites.

What happens to these ancient treasures? Many art pieces are sent to collectors in the United States and Europe. Wealthy art collectors pay large amounts of money for ancient statues, sculptures, and vases.

Money can't replace ancient history, though. Many people believe that stealing artwork is like stealing a country's history and culture.

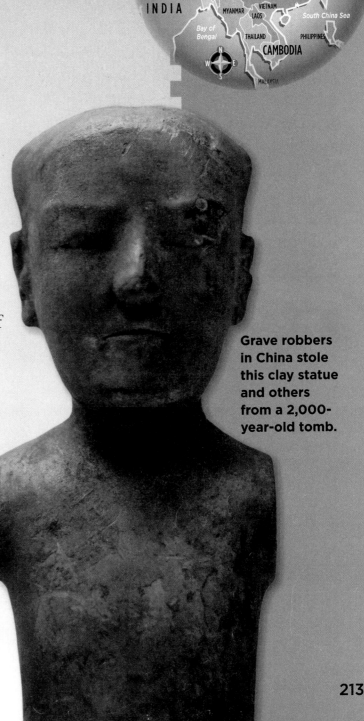

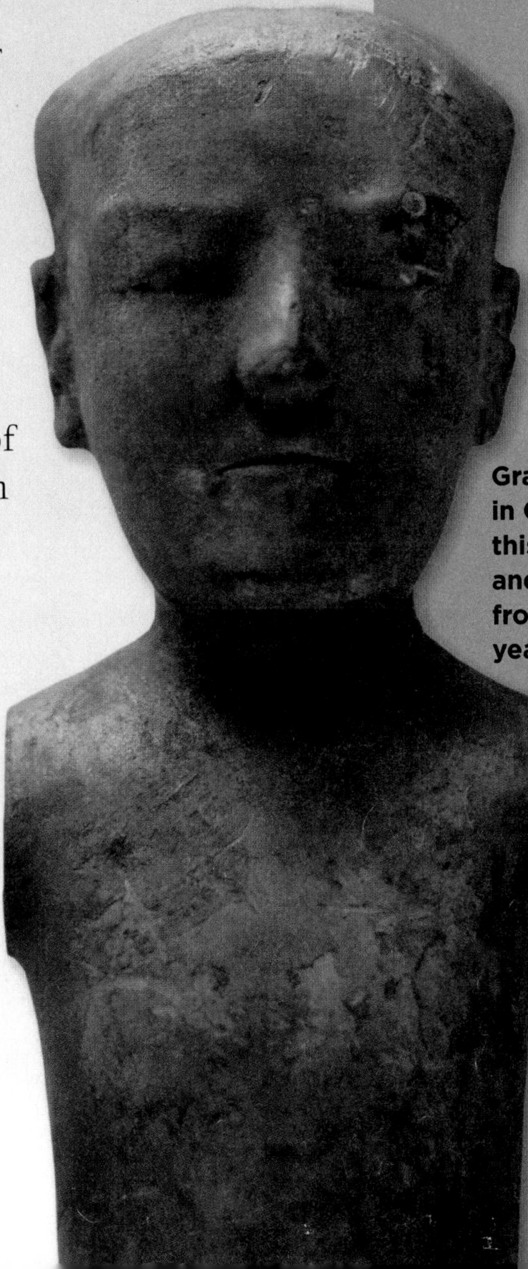

Grave robbers in China stole this clay statue and others from a 2,000-year-old tomb.

"Why are we as a people, as a government, as a country, allowing our **heritage** to slip through our fingers?" asks Michel Tranet. He has the job of protecting Cambodia's treasures and heritage.

Interpol is an international police agency with more than 180 member countries. It maintains a database of stolen cultural properties. The database can help local and national law enforcement officials identify property that has been looted. It also helps individuals and museums avoid buying stolen objects.

Coming Home

Some people in these countries, however, see looting as a way to get rich. Ancient royal statues can sell for $80,000 each or more at auction! A few years ago, small ceramic statues were stolen from the 2,000-year-old tomb of Empress Dou in the city of Xi'an (SHEE•AHN), China. Six of the small statues ended up for sale at an auction in New York City. Luckily the sale was stopped in time to **preserve** some of China's history.

This Buddha figurine sold for $295,000 at an auction in Hong Kong.

Today those six small figures, valued at $6,000 to $8,000 each, have been returned to Xi'an. They are on display in a small museum. Li Ku, the vice director of the museum, believes the statues are an essential part of the city's history and culture. He is **overjoyed** at their return. "Looking at these figures, I feel like my family has come home at last," he says.

FINDERS KEEPERS?

Most thefts of ancient art are never reported. One reason is that it's hard to say who owns some of the treasures. Many Asian countries were once colonies of European countries. Settlers took thousands of pieces of art, monuments, and sculptures. Treasures stolen centuries ago by invaders are often thought to be the property of whoever has them now. But some people don't agree. They say the art should be returned to the country in which it originally belonged. What do you think?

FCAT

Think and Compare

1. According to this article, what countries are having a problem with the theft of ancient treasures?
2. Why are farmers in China stealing treasures from tombs?
3. Many people say stealing ancient treasures is stealing a nation's past. Is this a fact or their opinion? Explain.
4. What theme do the articles "Ancient Warriors" and "Stealing Beauty" have in common?

FCAT Test Strategy

Author and Me

The answer is not directly stated. Think about what you have read to figure it out.

So Far From Home

Early one morning eight-year-old Sonam Dolker was shaken awake by her father. He whispered that she and her six-year-old sister would have to escape secretly from their home in Tibet to start a new life in India. Sonam's parents had planned the trip for weeks and had not told the girls. They were afraid the Chinese police would find out and send the family to prison. "My escape was so secret that I couldn't even say goodbye to my best friend," says Sonam.

For the next two months, the girls and their guide struggled to cross a 19,000-foot pass. They stumbled over the snow and ice of the jagged Himalaya Mountains. Finally they arrived safely in Dharamsala (dar•am•SAHL•a), a town in northwest India. Once there they went to a relief center, where they got new clothes and food.

According to studies conducted in 2001, each year roughly 3,000 Tibetans make the illegal crossing into India. Nearly one third of them are children. They risk frostbite, disease, arrest, and infections from bug bites. They even endanger their lives to go to India. They are willing to brave these dangers to escape the harsh Chinese rule in Tibet. Those who survive will have more freedom in India. They will be able to practice their religion, attend school, and speak their own language. But they will face new trouble in India.

These Tibetan children are in India. The mountains in the background are not the only danger children face going to India. It is against the law to escape from Tibet so if caught, people are sent to prison.

Go on

FCAT Now answer Numbers 1 through 5. Base your answers on the article "So Far From Home."

1. The author's purpose in writing this article is to inform readers about
   - (A) the beauty of Tibet.
   - (B) Tibet's form of government.
   - (C) the differences between China and India.
   - (D) how Tibetans leave their home to find freedom.

2. Tibetans living in India probably DO NOT feel
   - (F) angry that they were forced to leave Tibet.
   - (G) lonely for their families in Tibet.
   - (H) happy about the Chinese ruling Tibet.
   - (I) sad to have left their homeland and families.

Tip

You have to think about the entire passage to choose the best answer.

3. Which statement would the author MOST LIKELY agree with?
   - (A) Life in India is calm and carefree.
   - (B) Many Tibetans should return to their country.
   - (C) Anything is better than living under Chinese rule.
   - (D) Police in India send people back to Chinese prisons.

4. READ THINK EXPLAIN What is the main idea of this article? What relevant facts and details does the author include to support the article's main idea?

5. READ THINK EXPLAIN Describe the difficult journey from Tibet to India. What are some of the risks Tibetans take? Explain using details from the caption and article.

STOP

Write to a Prompt

FCAT

People often lose things that are important to them.

Think of something you lost that was important to you.

Now write a story about something you lost that was important to you.

Narrative writing tells a story about a personal or fictional experience.

To figure out if a writing prompt asks for narrative writing, look for clue words such as tell about, tell what happened, or write a story.

Below see how one student begins a response to the prompt above.

In response to the prompt, the writer organized the events to tell the story in order.

Yesterday at practice, I took off my favorite necklace. I got the necklace at the beach last summer during our family vacation. Whenever I looked at it, I remembered the great time we had. I then put the necklace next to my bag. But, as I was leaving, I grabbed my bag and forgot to take my necklace with me!

I didn't notice it was missing until this morning. So after school, my friends and I searched through the bushes at the practice field. We couldn't find it. Jake thought that maybe a dog chewed it up. Lisa said it might have been picked up after being dropped on the ground. I had to think about where I should start looking next.

Writing Prompt

Respond in writing to the prompt below. Before you write, read the Writing Hints below. Review the hints after you finish writing.

FCAT Most people have something that is special to them.

Think of something that is special to you.

Now write a story about something that is special to you.

Writing Hints for Prompts

- ☑ Read the prompt carefully.
- ☑ Plan your writing by organizing your ideas.
- ☑ Support your ideas by telling more about each event or reason.
- ☑ Use irregular plural nouns correctly.
- ☑ Choose words that help others understand what you mean.
- ☑ Review and edit your writing.

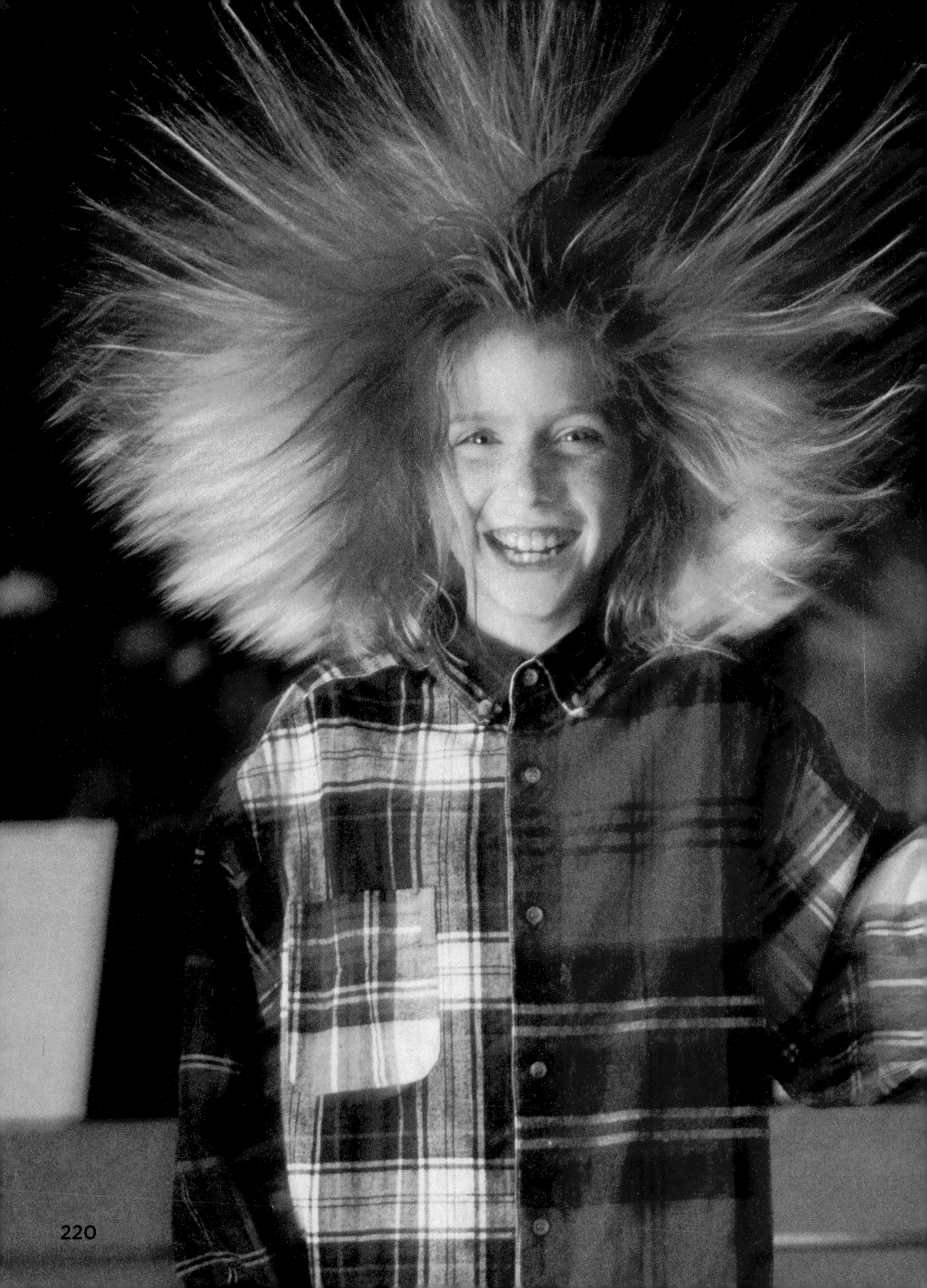

Bright Ideas

Talk About It

What do you think is happening here? Would *you* put your hand on that shiny ball? Why or why not?

LOG ON Find out more about electricity at **www.macmillanmh.com**

Vocabulary

hilarious	dizzy
convinced	whirlwind
mischief	nowadays
independence	
(come in) handy	

FCAT Context Clues

Idioms are phrases whose meaning differs from the meaning of each word. Use context clues to figure out what *come in handy* means.

He Made the World Brighter

by Susan Dickson

Thomas Edison was a poor student. **Hilarious**? It *is* funny when you know what he grew up to become. Even if his grades didn't show it, the mother of this future inventor was **convinced** he was smart. After a few disappointing months in school, she decided to teach Thomas herself at home.

Edison printed his own newspaper called *The Weekly Herald* as a teen.

Thomas's Childhood

Thomas Alva Edison was born in 1847 in Ohio. Always curious and prone to **mischief**, Thomas read whenever he could.

Thomas's first job, at thirteen, was selling newspapers. Back then that's when most boys started working. At sixteen he became a telegrapher. This gave Thomas **independence** and an opportunity to travel. Shortly after this, Edison decided to be an inventor.

The Young Inventor

Not everything Thomas invented was a success. In fact his first invention, an electric vote recorder, failed. Edison thought it would **come in handy** for counting votes. No one else found it useful, but that didn't stop Edison.

Edison's Greatest Challenge

Back then gas was the best lighting source, but burning it was dirty and unhealthy. Gas could also be very dangerous. The idea of using electricity for lighting had been around for over 50 years. But nobody had developed anything practical or safe.

Edison set out to solve this problem. He improved upon what others had learned about electricity. He tested thousands of ideas in a **whirlwind** of activity. Several men helped Edison with his experiments. By 1880 they had burned a light bulb for more than 1,500 hours. They must have felt **dizzy** with excitement!

This was just the beginning. Edison's success led to the invention of an entire electric lighting system. **Nowadays** many appliances and lights run on electricity. It is hard to imagine life without it. Next time you turn on your computer, think of Thomas Edison—and say "Thanks."

Edison with lamps he created

Reread for **Comprehension**

FCAT

Generate Questions

Problem and Solution An author often describes a **problem** a real person faced and tells how he or she found a **solution**. Reread the selection and think about what problem the person worked to solve. Fill in the steps in your Problem and Solution Chart.

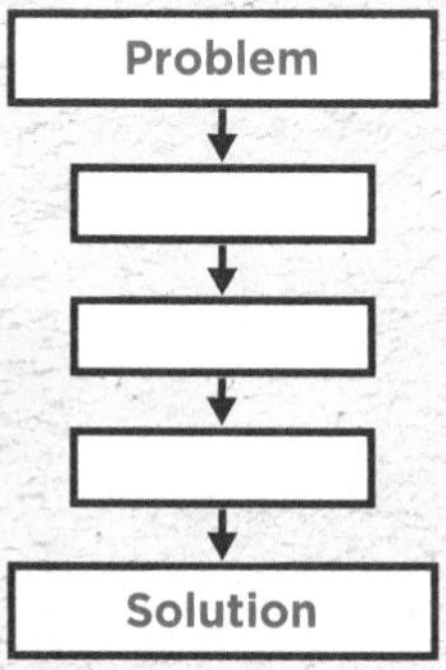

Comprehension

Genre

A **Biography** is a story about the life of a real person written by someone else.

Generate Questions

FCAT **Problem and Solution**

As you read, fill in your Problem and Solution Chart.

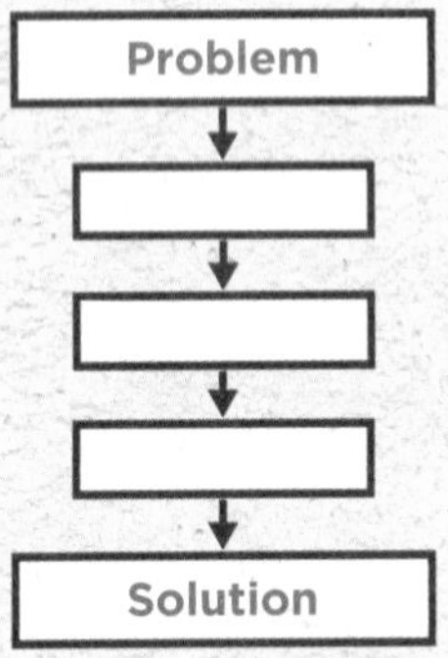

Read to Find Out

What was it like to be Ben Franklin?

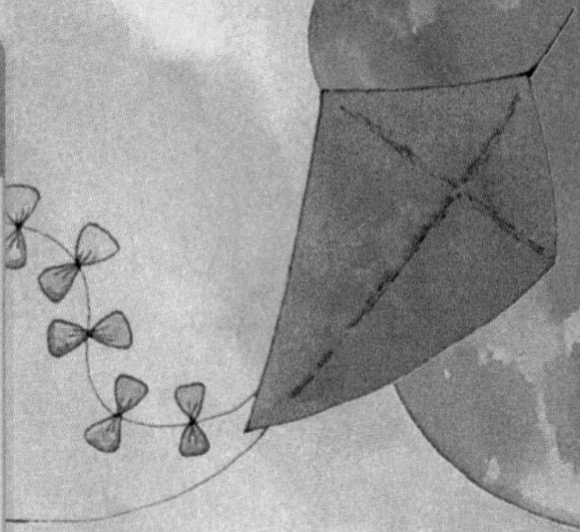

Award Winning
Author
and
Illustrator
How
Ben Franklin
Stole the
Lightning
Rosalyn Schanzer

Early to bed and early to rise makes a man healthy, wealthy and wise.
Silence Dogood
BENJ. FRANKLIN
SOAP
OINTMENT for the ITCH

It's true!

The great Benjamin Franklin really did steal lightning right out of the sky! And then he set out to tame the beast. It goes to figure, though, because he was a man who could do just about anything.

Why, Ben Franklin could swim faster, argue better, and write funnier stories than practically anyone in colonial America. He was a musician, a printer, a cartoonist, and a world traveler! What's more, he was a newspaper owner, a shopkeeper, a soldier, and a politician. He even helped to write the Declaration of **Independence** and the Constitution of the United States!

Ben was always coming up with newfangled ways to help folks out, too. He was the guy who started the first lending library in America. His post office was the first to deliver mail straight to people's houses.

He also wrote almanacs that gave **hilarious** advice about life and told people when to plant crops, whether there might be an eclipse, and when the tides would be high or low.

And he helped to start a hospital!

A free academy!

A fire department!

In colonial days, fire could break out at any time. And it was lightning that caused some of the worst fires. Whenever thunderstorms were brewing, they would ring the church bells for all they were worth, but it didn't do anybody a lick of good.

Of course, after Ben stole the lightning, there weren't nearly as many fires for firefighters to put out. "Now, why was that?" I hear you ask. "And how did he steal any lightning in the first place?" Well, it's a long story, but before we get to the answer, here's a hint. One of the things Benjamin Franklin liked to do best was to make inventions.

FCAT Problem and Solution
Name a common problem in colonial times.

Why, Ben was a born inventor. He loved to swim fast, but he wanted to go even faster. So one day when he was a mere lad of eleven, he got some wood and invented swim paddles for his hands and swim fins for his feet. Ben could go faster, all right, but the wood was pretty heavy, and his wrists got plumb worn out.

That's why his second invention was a better way to go fast. He lay on his back, held on to a kite string, and let his kite pull him lickety-split across a big pond. (You might want to remember later on that Ben always did like kites.)

Ben kept right on inventing better ways to do things for the rest of his life.

Take books, for example. Ben read so many books that some of them sat on shelves way up high near the ceiling. So he invented the library chair. If he pulled up the seat, out popped some stairs to help him reach any books on high shelves. And in case climbing stairs made him **dizzy**, he invented a long wooden arm that could grab his books, too.

He also invented an odometer that told how far he had ridden to deliver the mail. And the first clock with a second hand. And he even thought up daylight saving time. Then he invented bifocals so older folks could see up close and far away without changing glasses.

Everybody and his brother and sister just had to find better ways to heat their houses in wintertime. So Ben came up with a Franklin stove that could warm up cold rooms faster and use a lot less wood than old-fashioned stoves and fireplaces.

People all over Europe and America loved Ben's glass armonica. This instrument could spin wet glass bowls to make music that sounded like it came straight from heaven. Mozart and Beethoven wrote music for it, and it was even played at a royal Italian wedding.

But as popular as warmer stoves and glass armonicas were, they aren't anywhere near as celebrated **nowadays** as the invention Ben made after he stole the lightning.

Another hint about Ben's most famous invention is that it helped make life easier for everyone. His scientific ideas were helpful, too, and were often way ahead of their time. For example, he had a lot of ideas about health. He said that exercise and weight lifting help keep folks fit, but they have to work hard enough to sweat if they want to do any good.

He wrote that breathing fresh air and drinking lots of water are good for you. He was the guy who said "an apple a day keeps the doctor away."

And before anyone ever heard of vitamin C, he wrote that oranges, limes, and grapefruit give people healthy gums and skin. Sailors soon got wind of this idea. They began eating so many limes to stop getting sick from scurvy at sea that they became known as limeys.

Didn't the man ever stop to rest? Even when he was outside, Ben kept right on experimenting.

For instance, he often sailed to England and France to do business for America. As he crossed the Atlantic Ocean, he charted the Gulf Stream by taking its temperature. Once sailors knew the route of this fast, warm "river" in the cold ocean, they could travel between America and Europe in a shorter time than ever before.

He was probably the first person to write weather forecasts, too. Once he chased a roaring **whirlwind** by riding over the hills and forests of Maryland just to find out how it worked.

Ben had an old scientific trick that he liked to show people every chance he got. He used to store some oil inside a bamboo walking stick, and whenever he poured a few drops onto angry waves in a pond or lake, the water became smooth as glass!

Meanwhile, over in Europe, people called "electricians" had started doing some tricks of their own. One trick was to raise a boy up near the ceiling with a bunch of silk cords, rub his feet with a glass "electric tube," and make sparks shoot out of his hands and face.

Another mean trick made the king of France laugh so hard he could hardly stop. His court electrician had run an electric charge through 180 soldiers of the guard, and they jerked to attention faster than they ever had in their entire lives.

But although people were doing lots of tricks with electricity, nobody had a clue about why or how it worked. So Benjamin Franklin decided to find out. He asked a British friend to send him an electric tube so that he could do some experiments.

In one experiment, he made a cork "electric spider" with thread for legs. It kept leaping back and forth between a wire and an electric tube just like it was alive.

Another time he asked a lady and gentleman to stand on some wax. One held an electric tube, the other held a wire, and when they tried to kiss, they got shocked by all the sparks shooting between their lips.

Ben even figured out how to light up a picture of a king in a golden frame. Anyone trying to remove the king's gold paper crown was in for a shock!

Doing all these tricks gave Ben his idea for stealing lightning out of the sky. He believed that lightning was nothing more nor less than pure electricity. Now he set out to prove it.

First he made a silk kite with a wire on top to attract some lightning. Next he added a kite string, tied a key to the bottom, and knotted a silk ribbon below the key. Ben and his son William stood out of the rain inside the doorway of a shed on the side of a field. To keep from getting shocked, Ben held on to the dry silk ribbon. Then he flew his kite straight up toward a big rain cloud.

For the longest time, nothing happened.

Just as Ben and William were about to give up, the hair on that wet kite string began to rise up and stand at attention. Ben put his knuckle near the key, and YIKES!!!! Out jumped a bright spark of genuine electricity!

Real lightning had traveled all the way down that kite string! Ben had stolen electric fire out of the heavens and proven that he was right.

(Of course, now we know that if the storm had been any stronger, the great inventor would have been toast.)

Finally! Here's the part of the story where Ben's practice from thinking up all those inventions **came in** so **handy**. Way back then, you remember, lightning was always setting fire to ships, houses, and church spires. Even the best fire departments couldn't keep entire towns from going up in smoke. So Ben decided to make his most famous invention of all—the lightning rod!

The whole idea was to pull lightning safely out of the sky before it could do any **mischief**. Ben showed people how to put a pointed iron rod on the tip-top of a roof or ship's mast and connect it to a wire leading all the way down under the ground or into water. Now the lightning could follow a safe path without burning up a thing.

FCAT **Problem and Solution**
How did Ben's invention solve the problem?

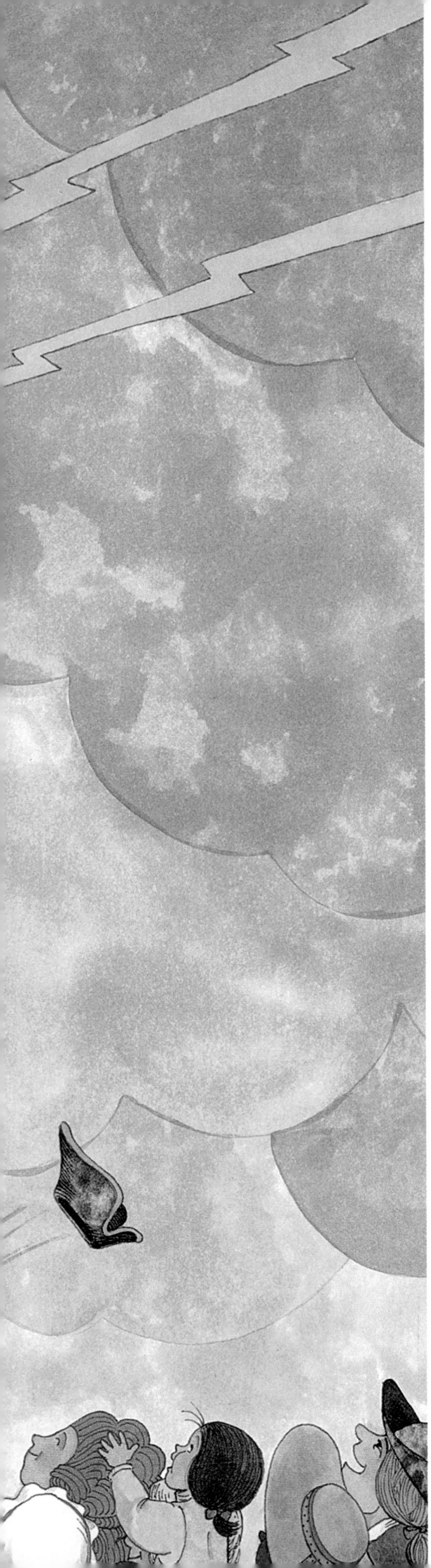

This simple but brilliant invention worked beautifully. It saved more lives than anyone can count and made Ben Franklin a great hero.

Scientists from around the world lined up to give Ben medals and awards. But during his long life, he became much more than the master of lightning. Why, when America fought against Great Britain for the right to become a free nation, Ben **convinced** France to come help win the war, and when it was over, he helped convince Great Britain to sign the peace. He had helped in so many ways that the people of France honored him with a beautiful medallion. It says "He snatched the lightning from heaven and the scepter from tyrants."

And he did.

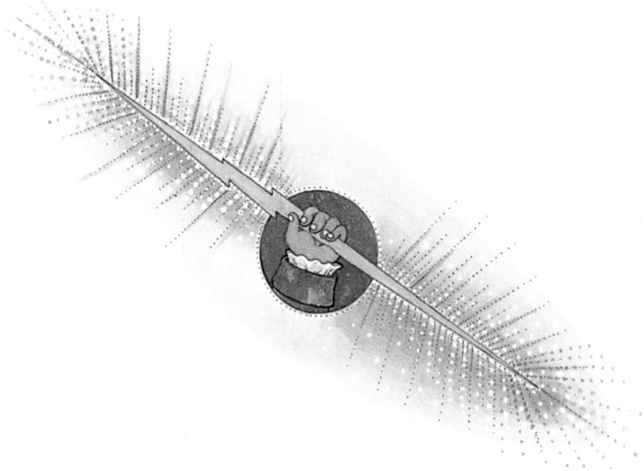

MEET THE INVENTOR

ROSALYN SCHANZER spent a lot of time in Philadelphia to write this piece. She visited the places where Ben Franklin lived and worked to make sure that her words and pictures would be accurate. Rosalyn probably would have gotten along really well with Ben. She is a great swimmer, just like he was. Once she even swam past sharks on a trip to Belize! Rosalyn also shares Ben's curiosity about the world. She's explored a jungle, visited an ancient city, and sailed a boat more than 800 miles.

Other books by Rosalyn Schanzer

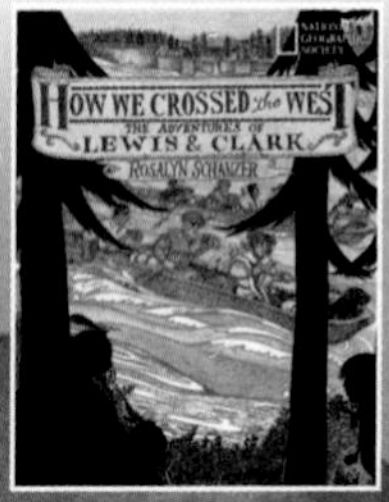

LOG ON Find out more about Rosalyn Schanzer at **www.macmillanmh.com**

FCAT Author's Purpose

What was Rosalyn Schanzer's purpose for writing this story? What clues helped you decide if she was trying to entertain or to inform?

FCAT Comprehension Check

Summarize

Summarize *How Ben Franklin Stole the Lightning*. Include some of the problems Ben Franklin saw and how he solved them. Use your Problem and Solution Chart to help you think about the story.

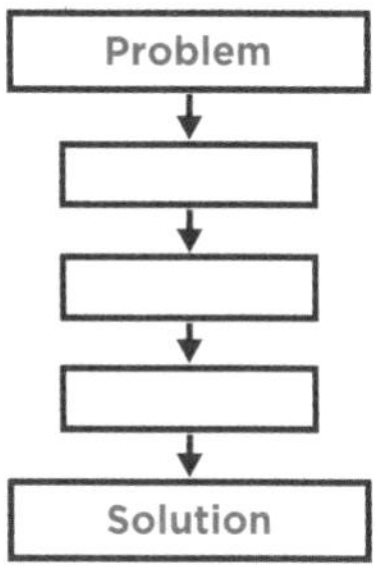

Think and Compare

READ THINK EXPLAIN

1. Besides fires, what two problems did Ben Franklin face? How did he solve these problems? Explain using details from the story. **Generate Questions: Problem and Solution**

READ THINK EXPLAIN

2. Reread pages 235–236. Why was Ben Franklin **convinced** that lightning was a form of electricity? How was he able to prove this ? Use details from the story to explain. **Analyze**

3. If you could improve on any of the inventions mentioned in the story, what would you do and why? **Apply**

4. Do you think Ben Franklin was ever bored? Explain. **Evaluate**

5. Read "He Made the World Brighter" on pages 222–223. How was Thomas Alva Edison like Ben Franklin? Use details from both selections to explain your answer. **Reading/Writing Across Texts**

FCAT

Poetry

A **Concrete Poem** has words arranged in the shape of the thing it describes.

Literary Elements

Figurative Language uses words to evoke mental images.

Alliteration is the repetition of the same consonant sound in a series of words.

Light Bulb

Thomas
Edison didn't
hesitate to let
ideas incubate, and
try again, if they
weren't right. One
day to his intense
delight, he **squeezed**
his thoughts
into a bulb
and then
turned
on the
light
light
light
!!!

— *Joan Bransfield Graham*

Edison didn't really squeeze his thoughts into a bulb. This figurative language helps the reader picture how hard Edison was thinking.

Lightning Bolt

NEWS FLASH!
BEN
FRANKLIN
USES
KITE & KEY
TO UNLOCK
ELECTRICITY!

This use of "kite" and "key" is an example of alliteration.

— *Joan Bransfield Graham*

FCAT Connect and Compare

1. Which words in "Lightning Bolt" show figurative language? **Figurative Language**
2. What do the shapes of these poems have to do with their topics? Explain. **Analyze**
3. How is the information presented in "Lightning Bolt" similar to the information in *How Ben Franklin Stole the Lightning*? In what ways is it different? **Reading/Writing Across Texts**

LOG ON Find out more about concrete poems at **www.macmillanmh.com**

Write a Book Review

Writer's Craft

FCAT **A Strong Opening**

A strong opening sets the tone for the rest of your writing. Opening with a question sparks interest and urges the reader to continue reading.

I started with a strong opening sentence.

I wanted to recommend a book I liked, so I wrote a review of it.

Kids' Bright Ideas

by Katie G.

Do you dream of being an important inventor? Then read Invented by Kids by Cynthia Mills. You'll find out about some great ideas by kids. The Auto-Off Candle goes out after a set time, guarding against fires. A natural mosquito poison is safe to use in animals' drinking water.

If you like experimenting with new ideas, I recommend this book. These inventors inspired me. I'm convinced you'll be inspired, too!

Writing Prompt

Everyone has read a book they like.

Think about a book that you like.

Now write a book review to explain why you liked the book.

FCAT Writer's Checklist

- ☑ **Focus:** My topic sentence clearly shows my main idea.
- ☐ **Organization:** My **strong opening** sets the tone and grabs my reader's attention.
- ☑ **Support:** I use details to support my opening.
- ☑ **Conventions:** I use the correct format for a book title. My spelling, punctuation, and grammar are correct.

Snakes

Talk About It

Explain how these snakes make you feel and why.

LOG ON Find out more about snakes at **www.macmillanmh.com**

Vocabulary

weekdays
cardboard
slithered
genuine
apologize
harmless
ambulance

FCAT **Word Parts**

Base Words can help you figure out the meaning of a word. What does the word *harmless* mean?

harm = "hurt"

less = "without"

harmless = "without hurt"

NAME THAT REPTILE

by Catherine Lutz

Narrator: Mark and Jean have been studying together **weekdays** after school for a big test on Friday. Jean takes a card from a **cardboard** box. The card has the name of a reptile on it. Now Mark will ask questions and try to name the reptile. Can you guess the answer before Mark?

Mark: Is it furry?

Jean: No. Remember, reptiles don't have fur.

Mark: That's right. Where does it live?

Jean: Mostly in the southwestern United States.

Mark: What does it eat?

Jean: It eats small birds, rabbits, mice, and squirrels.

Mark: Is it a crocodile?

Jean: No. Crocodiles live near streams, and this reptile lives where it's dry.

Mark: How big is it?

Jean: Some can be 7 feet long. Others are only 2 feet long.

Mark: It's probably not a turtle or a lizard. Is it a snake?

Jean: Yes!

Is it a crocodile?

Mark: Remember when my pet snake got loose and **slithered** across my mother's foot? I had to return it to the pet store.

Jean: What did the store say?

Mark: I think they were **genuine** when they offered to speak with my mom. I knew that wouldn't help, though.

Jean: Did you **apologize** to your mom and say you were sorry?

Mark: Of course, but she didn't change her mind.

Jean: Okay, back to studying.

Mark: Does the snake crush its prey?

Jean: No.

Mark: So it's not a python. Is it **harmless**?

Jean: No. It's dangerous. Its bite can be fatal. If you get bitten, you'd need an **ambulance**!

Mark: Yikes. Does it give a warning before it attacks?

Jean: Its tail shakes and makes a noise. Each time the snake sheds, its tail gets a new segment in it.

Mark: I've got it! It's a rattlesnake!

Narrator: Did you guess the reptile before Mark did?

It's a rattlesnake!

Reread for **Comprehension**

Generate Questions

FCAT **Plot Development** The **plot** is the events that happen in a story. To understand the plot, readers ask questions about what they read in the story and what they already know. Reread the selection and look for clues to answer any questions you have about the plot. Fill in your Inferences Web as you read.

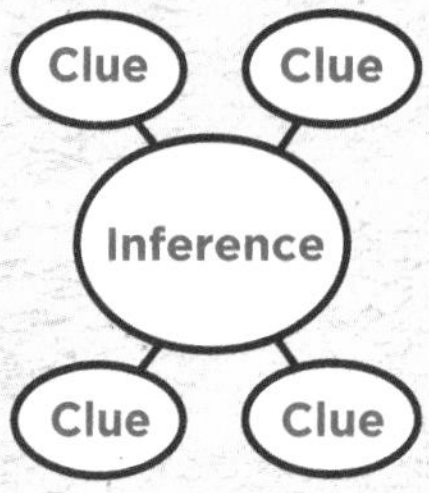

Comprehension

Genre

Humorous Fiction is a made-up story written to make the reader laugh.

Generate Questions

FCAT **Plot Development** As you read, fill in your Inferences Web.

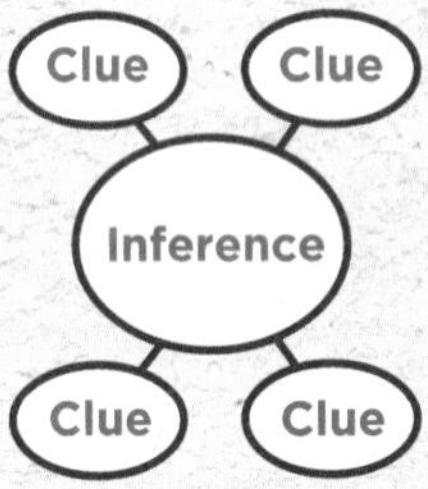

Read to Find Out

What do you learn when you read between the lines?

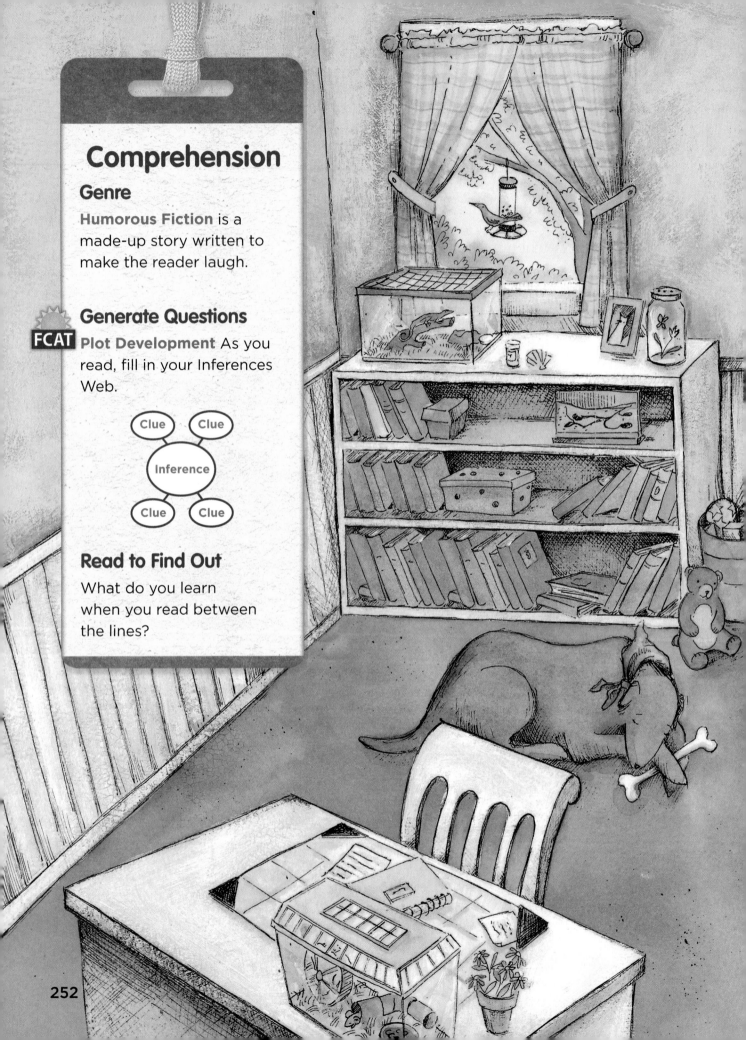

Dear Mr. Winston

by Ken Roberts

Illustrated by Nicole E. Wong

Dear Mr. Winston,

My parents said that I have to write and **apologize**. Dad says he is going to read this letter before it's sent and that I'd better make sure my apology sounds truly **genuine**. So, I am truly, genuinely sorry for bringing that snake into the library yesterday.

My parents say that what I did was wrong, even though the **cardboard** box was shut, most of the time, and there was no way that snake could have escaped if you hadn't opened the box and dropped it on the floor.

My parents say it's my fault for having brought that snake into the library and I truly, genuinely apologize but I still don't know how I was supposed to find out what kind of snake I had inside that box without bringing the snake right into the library so I could look at snake pictures and then look at the snake and try to find a picture that matched the snake.

I told my parents something that I didn't get a chance to remind you about before the **ambulance** took you away. I did come into the library without the snake, first. I left the box outside, hidden under a bush and tried to borrow a thick green book with lots of snake pictures. You told me that the big green book was a reference book which meant that it had to stay inside the library and I couldn't take it out, even for ten minutes.

My parents say I still shouldn't have brought that snake into the library and that I have to be truly, genuinely sorry if I ever hope to watch Galactic Patrol on television again. My parents picked Galactic Patrol because it's my favorite show, although I'm not sure what not watching a television program has to do with bringing a snake into the library.

The people at the library say you hate snakes so much that you won't even touch a book with a picture of snakes on the cover and that is why you won't be back at the library for a few more weeks. If you want, you could watch Galactic Patrol. It's on at 4:00 P.M. **weekdays**, on channel 7. There are no snakes on the show because it takes place in space.

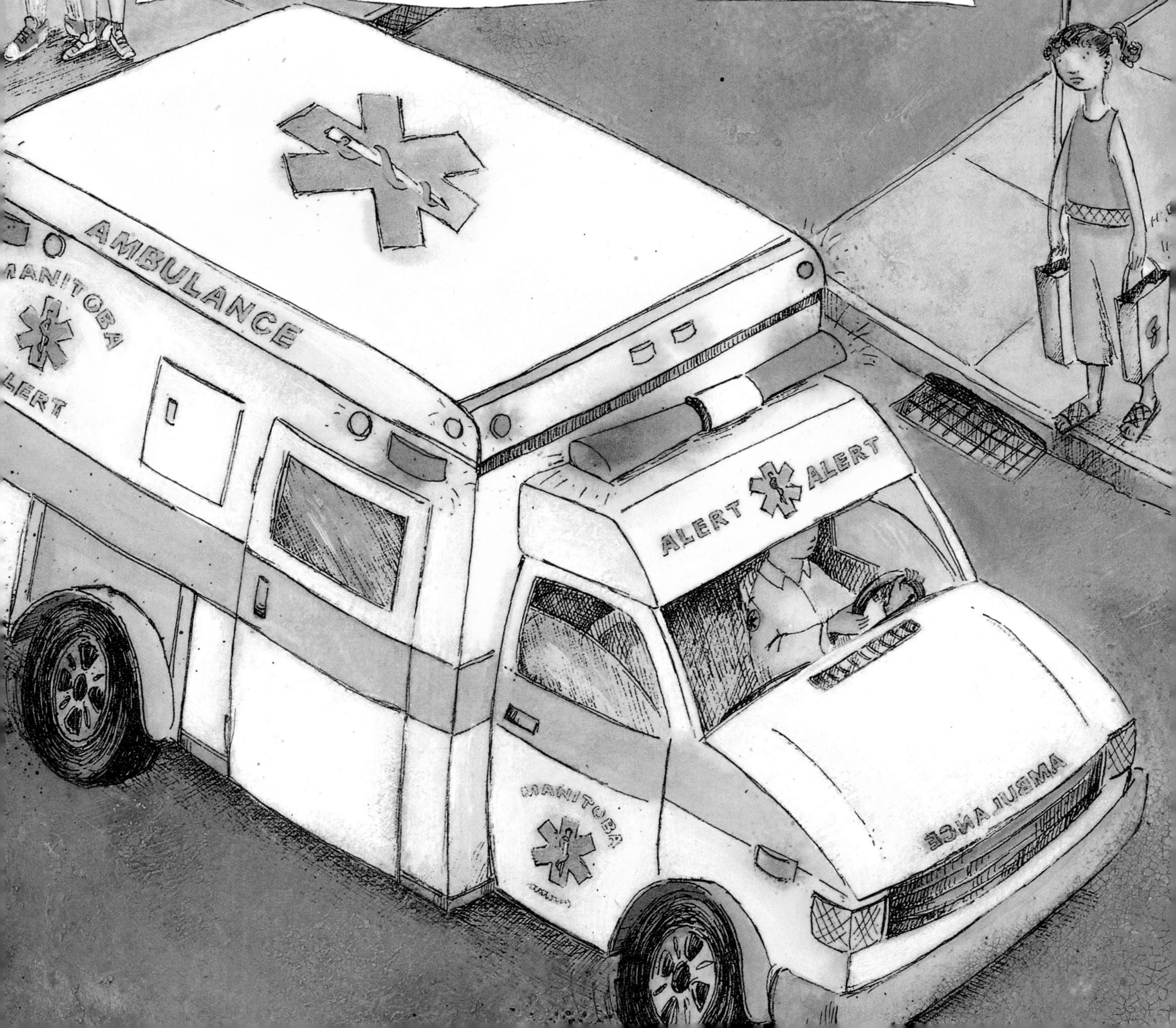

LIBRARY

Did the flowers arrive? Dad picked them out but I have to pay for them with my allowance for the next two months. The flowers are proof that I am truly, genuinely sorry for having brought that snake into the library. I hope the people who work at the library find that snake soon! Did they look under all the chairs?

That snake isn't dangerous. It is a local snake, and there are no poisonous snakes in Manitoba. The people at the library say you know that too because that was one of the reasons you decided to move here. I bought that snake from a friend. I paid one month's allowance for it, which means that snake has cost me a total of three months' allowance and I only owned it for one hour!

Mom says I don't have to tell who sold me that snake so I won't tell you either because Dad says he is going to read this letter. Besides, I don't want you to be mad at anyone else when I am the one who brought that snake into the library yesterday. I am truly, genuinely sorry.

FCAT Plot Development

Do you think the girl is truly, genuinely sorry for bringing the snake into the library? Why or why not?

I want you to know that I didn't plan to show you that snake. I didn't mean to scare you at all. I knew where the big green snake book was kept. I put the box on a table close to the book and tried to find the right picture. I looked at a picture, then at the snake, at another picture, and then the snake. I did that five times and can tell you that the snake inside the library is not a python, a rattlesnake, an anaconda, an asp, or a cobra.

Anyway, I was surprised when you wanted to see what was inside the box because I didn't ask for any help and there were plenty of people in the library who did need help.

Dad says that the fact that I said, "Nothing," instead of "A snake," is proof that I knew I was doing something wrong when I brought that snake into the library. I am truly, genuinely sorry even though my friend Jake Lambert promised me that the snake I bought from him is perfectly **harmless**.

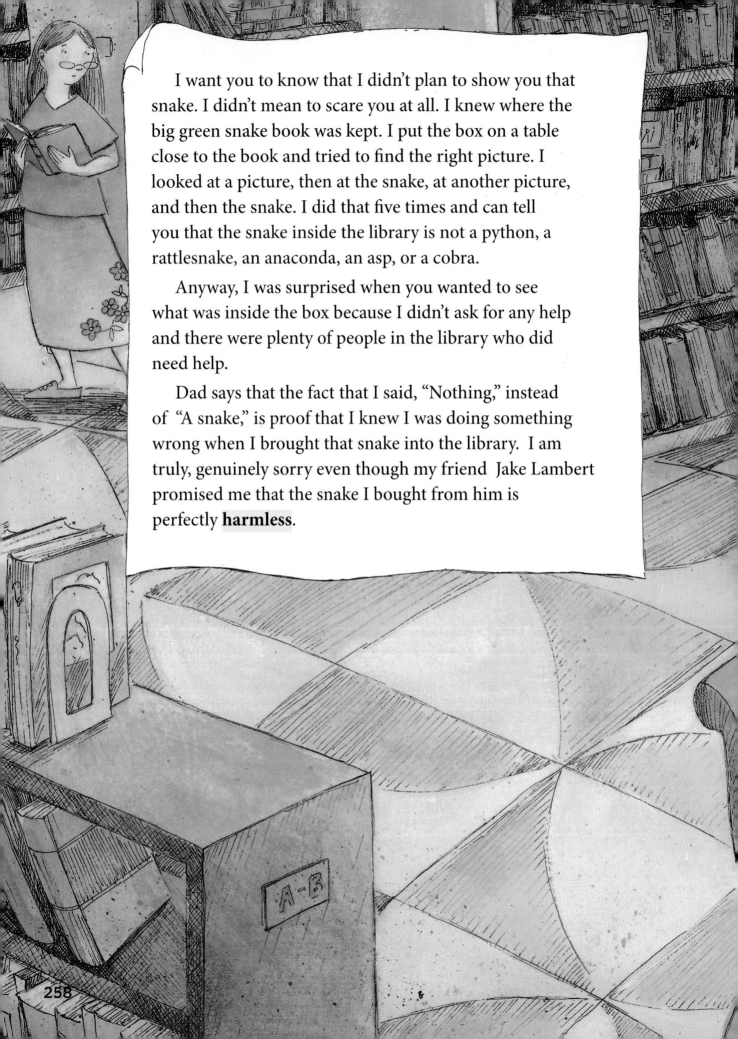

M-N
O-P

I did tell you that I didn't need any help and I did have a snake book open in front of me, so I don't know why you insisted on looking inside the box if you are so afraid of snakes and everything. I don't know why you picked up that box before opening a flap, either. If you had left the box on the table and maybe even sat down next to it, then maybe the box would have been all right when you screamed and fainted. You wouldn't have fallen so far, either, if you were sitting down.

Did you know that you broke out in a rash after you fainted? I thought a person had to touch something like poison ivy to get a rash. I didn't know it was possible to get a rash by just thinking about something but my parents say it really can happen. I think maybe you did touch something. Maybe, when you were lying on the floor, that snake **slithered** over to you and touched you! Did you know that snake skin feels dry, not wet and slimy at all?

FCAT Plot Development
Is the girl taking full responsibility for what happened to Mr. Winston? What makes you think so?

I just thought of something. Maybe everyone's looking in the library for that snake but it's not in the library. Maybe it crawled into one of your pockets or up your sleeve and rode with you to the hospital! Wouldn't that be funny? Why don't you get one of the nurses to check? If it's not in your clothes, it might have crawled out and might be hiding inside the hospital someplace. I think people should be looking there, too.

I am sure you will be talking to the people in the library, to make sure they find that snake before you go back to work. I hope they do find it, even though my parents say that I can't keep it. If that snake is found, could you ask the people at the library to give me a call? I would be interested in knowing that it is all right. And if they do find that snake and do decide to give me a call, could you ask them if they could compare that snake with the snake pictures in that big green reference book before they call me? I would still like to know what kind of snake I owned for an hour.

I am truly, genuinely sorry.

Your friend,

Cora

GET WELL
MR. Winston

Identify the Author and Illustrator

Ken Roberts is actually a librarian. He often writes funny stories with unusual characters, like the girl in this piece. Ken has many talents. He is a storyteller, puppeteer, juggler, and magician. He was once a champion runner, too.

Nicole E. Wong has been interested in art all her life and even went to college to study it. She has been very fortunate to have turned her passion and training into her career in illustration. Nicole's artwork has appeared in several books, including Jan Wahl's *Candy Shop,* and various magazines. Nicole lives in Massachusetts with her husband, Dan, and their dog, Sable.

Another book illustrated by Nicole E. Wong

LOG ON Find out more about Ken Roberts and Nicole E. Wong at **www.macmillanmh.com**

FCAT Author's Purpose

Why do you think Ken Roberts wrote *Dear Mr. Winston*? Do you think the fact that he is a librarian affected his purpose for writing the story?

FCAT Comprehension Check

Summarize

Summarize *Dear Mr. Winston*. Include the main characters and tell the most important events in the correct order. Use your Inferences Web to help you think about the story as you summarize.

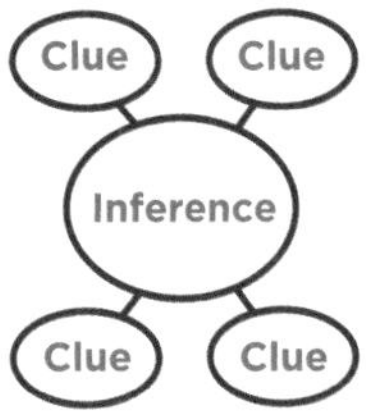

Think and Compare

READ THINK EXPLAIN

1. Was Cara's apology to Mr. Winston truly **genuine**? Why did she write the letter? Explain using details from the story. **Generate Questions: Plot Development**

READ THINK EXPLAIN

2. Reread the second paragraph on page 253. Who does Cara believe was responsible for her snake's escape? Why does she think this? Use story details to explain. **Analyze**

3. If you were Cara, how would you have avoided the whole situation with Mr. Winston and the snake? **Synthesize**

4. Will Mr. Winston ever be able to see the humor in this event? Explain using details from the story. **Evaluate**

5. Read "Name That Reptile" on pages 250–251. How is the problem that Mark is trying to solve similar to Cara's problem? How is it different? Use details from both selections. **Reading/Writing Across Texts**

Science

Genre

Electronic Encyclopedias include articles, diagrams, and photographs on many topics.

FCAT Text Feature

Toolbars help you find more information or move to a different area in an electronic encyclopedia.

Content Vocabulary

reptiles
camouflage
hibernate
digested

Find Snakes

▼ article outline

Snakes

Physical Characteristics

Snakes are **reptiles**. They have flexible skeletons and no legs. Their bodies are covered with scales. Clear scales even cover their eyes. Most snakes are colored to **camouflage** them. For example, the emerald tree boa is green. This helps it hide among tree leaves. Other snakes, like coral snakes, are brightly colored to warn enemies that they are poisonous. Snakes range greatly in size. The dwarf blind snake is 10 cm (around 4 in.) long. The anaconda and reticulated python can be as long as 10 m (about 33 ft.).

Timber rattlesnakes (*crotalus horridus*), northeastern United States

Behavior

Like all reptiles snakes are cold-blooded. They cannot make their own body heat. Snakes need the sun or warm surroundings to keep them warm. In cool weather many snakes gather underground or in other sheltered places. There they **hibernate**, meaning they stay at rest during the winter.

Printers

Features Tools Options Favorites Help

Contents Page | Multimedia | Related Articles

Anaconda
Coral Snake
Emerald Tree Boa
Skeleton

Using a Toolbar

Click on the Related Articles menu and select the subject about which you want to learn more.

Coral Snake a kind of poisonous snake found in North and South America. There are about 30 species. Coral snakes all have bright bands of color on their bodies and are two to three feet in length. They hunt lizards and other snakes.

Anaconda a member of the boa family living in swamps and rivers in South America. The anaconda, like other boas, wraps itself around its prey to suffocate it. It is one of the longest and thickest snakes. It also bears live young.

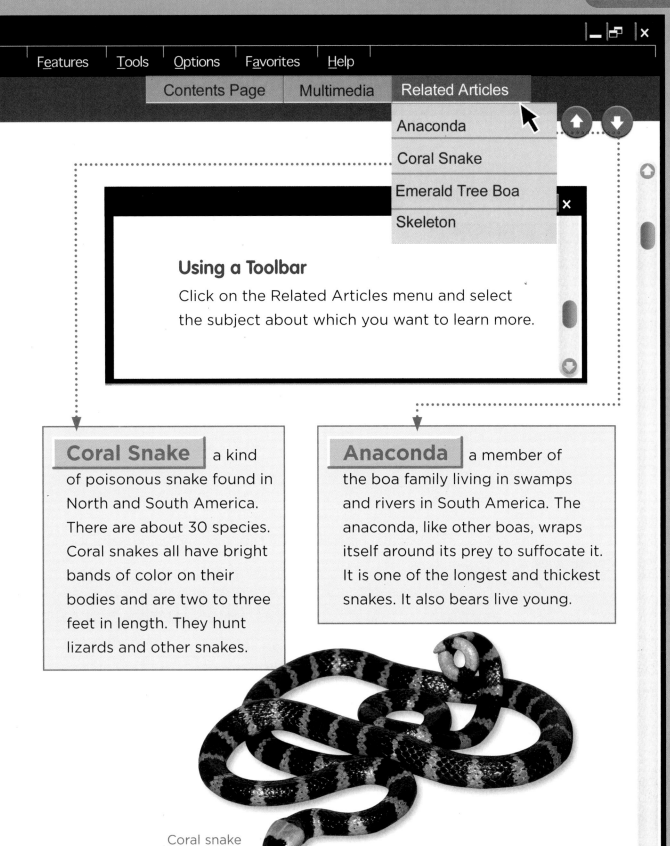

Coral snake

Find Snakes

Hunting and Eating

Egg-eater snake (*Dasyreptis scabra*), savannah, South Africa

Snakes are meat eaters but do not chew their prey. They swallow animals whole. Snakes can stretch their jaws far apart. This lets them eat animals that are bigger than their own heads.

Constrictors, such as boa constrictors, wrap themselves around their prey. These snakes suffocate their prey and then swallow it. Some snakes are venomous and kill their prey with poison. Venomous snakes, such as rattlesnakes, inject the poison through their fangs. Some poisons kill the animal. Others break down the animal's flesh so that it is partly **digested** by the time the snake eats it.

Raising Young

Cobra hatching

Most female snakes lay eggs that have soft, leathery shells. Some females stay close to guard the eggs. Others, such as pythons, coil around the eggs to keep them warm. Some snakes give birth to live babies. Garter snakes can have more than 40 baby snakes at once. Snakes do not usually take care of their young.

Printers

Features Tools Options Favorites Help

Contents Page | Multimedia | Related Articles

- Boa Constrictor
- Garter Snake
- Python
- Rattlesnake

Garter Snake a common and harmless type of snake in North America. They are fairly small (about two feet long) and usually have dark colors, with stripes running along their bodies. They live in moist areas and feed on toads, frogs, earthworms, and similar animals.

FCAT Connect and Compare

1. Look at the Related Articles menu on this page. If a student was doing research on snakes, what would they click on to find out how constrictors kill their prey? Why? **Using a Toolbar**

2. Constrictors often hunt animals that have sharp teeth, claws, or hooves. Why would they need to kill their prey before swallowing it? **Analyze**

3. Think about this article and *Dear Mr. Winston*. Which of the snakes discussed in this selection would not make a good pet for Cara? Explain using details from both selections. **Reading/Writing Across Texts**

Science Activity

Research a snake. If possible, use an electronic encyclopedia. Write a paragraph or two about the snake, and draw a picture of it.

LOG ON Find out about kinds of snakes at **www.macmillanmh.com**

Write About a Character

Writer's Craft

FCAT **Precise Words**

Using **precise words** helps you create a message that is clear and interesting. It also helps the reader understand your topic.

I used precise words like bony, dumped, and bounced to make my writing interesting.

I used precise words to tell the story from the snake's point of view.

The Snake's Story

by Estrella O.

This morning I was slithering in the grass happily minding my own business. Suddenly, some cold, bony fingers picked me up and dumped me in a cardboard box. For a long time, I bounced around in the box. I could hear children's voices laughing and squealing. Finally, everything became still and quiet.

It wasn't peaceful for very long. A man lifted the lid. He screamed and dropped the box. Suddenly, there were lots of people yelling and running around. Scared, I slithered out of the box and slipped away to the darkest corner I could find. What do you think all that excitement was about?

Writing Prompt

Many people have a favorite character from a book.

Think of your favorite character from a book.

Now write a story about your favorite character from a book.

FCAT Writer's Checklist

- [x] **Focus:** My writing shows the message I want to send to the readers.
- [x] **Organization:** I use time-order words like *then* and *finally* to show readers the order of events.
- [ ] **Support:** I use **precise words** to maximize my reader's understanding of my topic.
- [x] **Conventions:** I avoid using run-on sentences. I use language to show my character's feelings.

FCAT **Review**

- **Author's Purpose**
- **Analyze Character**
- **Problem and Solution**
- **Context Clues**
- **Base Words**
- **Table**

Pitch for Fish

"ORDER! THIS MEETING WILL NOW COME TO order!" barked Alison as she slammed her hands down on the desk for attention. Rosa and Javier rolled their eyes at one another as Alison kept talking. "We have to decide what to do for the school fair. I think we should do a game of some sort. Like one where people throw a ball in a jar from three feet away. And if they get it in, they win a prize."

"They'll win a prize? What?" asked Javier.

"A goldfish!" said Alison excitedly. "Don't you just love the idea of seeing all those little goldfish bowls lined up together? We can call our booth *Pitch for Fish*!"

Javier bit his lip. He nodded, knowing his opinion was insignificant. It didn't matter what he thought. Alison always got what she wanted. It was unavoidable.

"Great," Alison said. "Rosa? What about you? Don't you think this is the best idea ever?"

Rosa looked down, her face burning. She

didn't want to say anything to upset Alison but she didn't like the idea at all.

Alison frowned. "Okay, I guess you agree then. Now, I hate painting so you two have to do it. You should paint the booth pink and the letters should be—"

"Alison," Rosa interrupted.

Alison paused at the timid interruption. She looked angry. "Did you just interrupt me, Rosa?"

When she heard the anger in Alison's voice, Rosa felt more intimidated than ever. But she thought of those poor fish, trapped in tiny bowls, and gained enough courage to say, "I think goldfish make terrible prizes."

"Well, I think it's a great idea. And Javier agrees with me."

"He didn't hear my side yet." Rosa took a deep breath before continuing. "It's not fair to the fish. Those tiny bowls aren't healthy. Besides, getting a pet is an important decision. You have to really want one and be willing to take care of it. You should never give someone a pet as a prize or present. Most people who win a fish won't take care of it. Most of those fish will be dead in a few weeks and it will be our fault. I don't want to be responsible for that."

Alison looked stunned. She was not used to people disagreeing with her.

"Actually, I agree with Rosa." Javier said in a firm voice. "We can still have the pitching game, but let's think of another prize. We shouldn't give away something alive."

Alison looked really upset. Rosa knew she had won, but didn't want to rub it in.

"Let's give away stuffed fish instead," Rosa suggested. "Then we can still use your name, Alison. Pitch for Fish is a great name."

Alison smiled again. "It is, isn't it?"

Protect Our Valuable OCEANS

When astronauts look down at Earth from space, they see a beautiful blue world. Oceans cover more than 70% of our planet. Earth has five oceans. They are the Pacific, Atlantic, Indian, Arctic and Southern oceans. These oceans are important to us and our planet.

People depend on oceans for survival. Fish, seaweed, and shellfish all come from the ocean. They are the main source of food for more than 3.5 billion people. Some of our salt, fertilizers, and minerals come from the ocean, as well as natural resources such as oil. A great deal of the world's oil and natural gases are drilled offshore, which means the oil comes from beneath the ocean floor.

Oceans also provide us with transportation. Many cities have ferries, which people use to get to work every morning. Freight and fuel also travel by boat. Oil tankers transport 60% of the oil used by the world. Ships also carry clothes, toys, and other goods you see in stores.

About 21 million barrels of oil runs into the oceans each year from street runoff, factory waste, and ships flushing their tanks.

Table of Ocean Facts

Oceans	Area	Length of Coastline	Elevation Lowest Point
Atlantic Ocean	76.762 million sq km	111,866 km	-8,605 m
Pacific Ocean	155.557 million sq km	135,663 km	-10,924 m
Indian Ocean	68.556 million sq km	66,526 km	-7,258 m
Arctic Ocean	14.056 million sq km	45,389 km	-4,665 m
Southern Ocean	20.327 million sq km	17,968 km	-7,235 m

Knowing some facts about the oceans can help you understand how important they are to our planet!

Even though our oceans do so much for us, we have not been taking care of them. Water pollution is a big problem because it kills many kinds of sea creatures. Some of this pollution results from things people dump into the ocean. For example, cruise ships and cargo ships dump waste into the ocean every day. Other pollution comes from factories and power plants dumping their waste into rivers. The rivers carry this waste to the oceans.

It is not just dumping waste into oceans that harms them. For example, nitrogen, a chemical in fertilizers, is carried to the oceans as runoff. As water "runs off" the ground, it flows into our streams and rivers, which carry it to the sea.

Pollutants such as nitrogen can cause problems in the oceans. Nitrogen reduces the amount of oxygen in the ocean; having less oxygen can kill some sea animals or cause diseases. Pollution severely upsets the balance of nature. Too much nitrogen can produce large amounts of algae, tiny plants that grow in the water, which can hurt other plants and animals.

Luckily there are things we can do to protect oceans. A good start is learning about them. Another thing we can do is get rid of waste properly. Finally, we can ask our government to get involved by passing more laws to help stop pollution. Oceans are an important part of our world, and we have to take care of them.

Friend or Foe?

Talk About It

Is this crocodile a friend or a foe of this frog? How do you know?

LOG ON Find out more about friends and foes at **www.macmillanmh.com**

Vocabulary

interfere **agile**
awkward **guardian**
proclaimed **tottered**

FCAT Thesaurus

Synonyms are words that have the same, or nearly the same, meanings. You can use a thesaurus to find synonyms.

Use a thesaurus to find a synonym for the word *agile*.

ROADRUNNERS: SURPRISING BIRDS

by Adam Savage

"Today we will hear from Pam," said Mr. Sanders.

Pam stood in front of the class. "I'm going to talk about roadrunners," she said, smiling.

Someone snickered, but Pam didn't let a little noise **interfere** with her presentation. She knew that her topic was interesting.

Pam was prepared, so she didn't feel **awkward**, or uncomfortable. Holding up her photo album, Pam began her report. "This is a roadrunner." She looked around the room. No one seemed interested. Pam knew she had to do something to get everyone's attention.

Holding up the next photo, Pam **proclaimed** with confidence, "This amazing bird is so fast and **agile** it can catch a rattlesnake!"

"Whoa, that's cool!" called Peter from the back row. "What else can it do?"

Now every eye was on Pam. "Roadrunners can run up to 15 miles per hour!" she continued.

"Do they fly?" someone asked.

"They can fly when they sense danger. But not very far."

Pam held up the next photo. It showed the roadrunner's black-and-white spotted feathers and the crest on its head.

"Where did you get the photos?" asked Mr. Sanders.

"I took these while I was visiting my grandmother in Arizona," explained Pam.

"I see," said Mr. Sanders. "Is there anything else you'd like to tell us?"

"I learned that a roadrunner is a very clever **guardian** of its young. Let's say an enemy comes near a roadrunner's nest. The roadrunner pretends to have a broken leg, and leads the enemy away. I watched a roadrunner as it **tottered** along. It was so brave!"

Someone asked another question, but Mr. Sanders said to save it for next time. When the class groaned, "Awww," Pam knew her report was a winner.

Reread for Comprehension

FCAT

Evaluate

Author's Purpose is the author's reason for writing a story. An author may write a story to give facts or inform. An author can also write a funny story to entertain. Reread the selection and look for clues to help you identify the **author's purpose**. Fill in your Author's Purpose Map as you read.

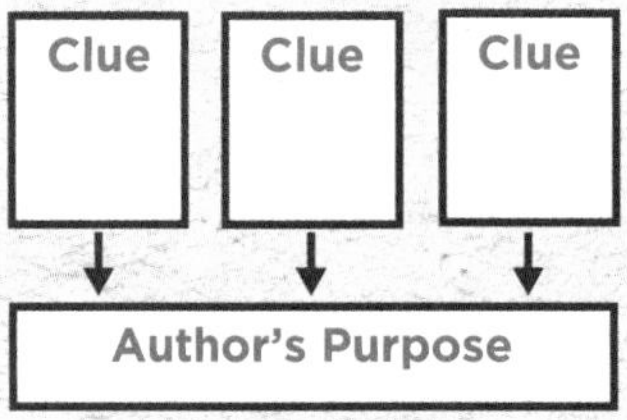

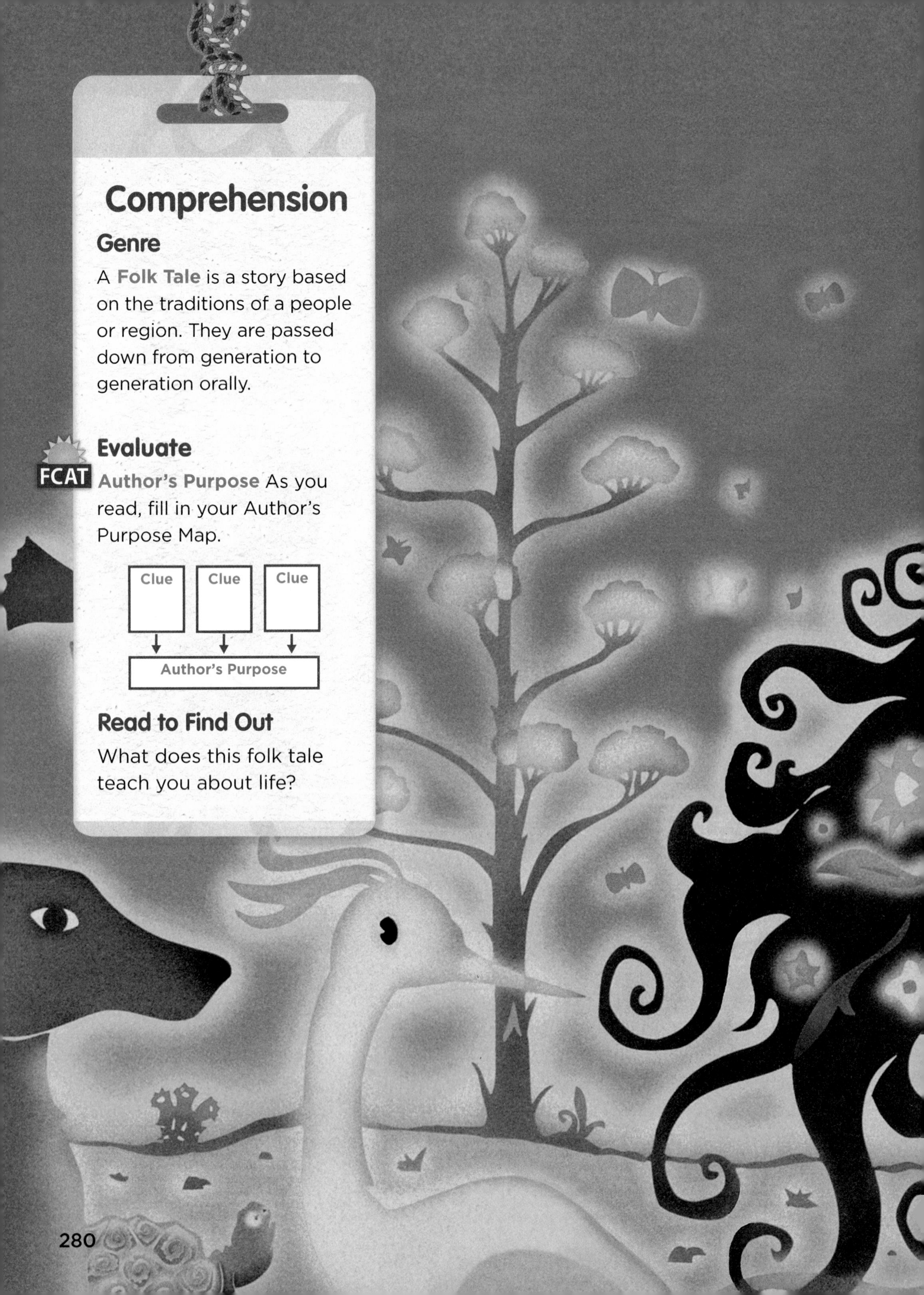

Comprehension

Genre

A **Folk Tale** is a story based on the traditions of a people or region. They are passed down from generation to generation orally.

FCAT

Evaluate

Author's Purpose As you read, fill in your Author's Purpose Map.

Clue	Clue	Clue
↓	↓	↓
Author's Purpose		

Read to Find Out

What does this folk tale teach you about life?

ROADRUNNER'S DANCE

By Rudolfo Anaya • Illustrated by David Diaz

"*Ssss*," hissed Snake as he slithered out of his hole by the side of the road. He bared his fangs and frightened a family walking home from the cornfield.

The mother threw her basketful of corn in the air. The children froze with fright.

"Father!" the children called, and the father came running.

"*Ssss*," Snake threatened.

"Come away," the father said, and the family took another path home.

"I am king of the road," Snake boasted. "No one may use the road without my permission."

That evening the people of the village gathered together and spoke to the elders.

"We are afraid of being bitten by Snake," they protested. "He acts as if the road belongs only to him."

The elders agreed that something should be done, and so the following morning they went to Sacred Mountain, where Desert Woman lived. She had created the desert animals, so surely she could help.

"Please do something about Snake," the elders said. "He makes visiting our neighbors and going to our fields impossible. He frightens the children."

Desert Woman thought for a long time. She did not like to **interfere** in the lives of the people and animals, but she knew that something must be done.

"I have a solution," she finally said.

Dressed in a flowing gown, she traveled on a summer cloud across the desert to where Snake slept under the shade of a rocky ledge.

"You will let people know when you are about to strike," Desert Woman said sternly. And so she placed a rattle on the tip of Snake's tail.

"Now you are Rattlesnake. When anyone approaches, you will rattle a warning. This way they will know you are nearby."

Convinced she had done the right thing, Desert Woman walked on the Rainbow back to her home in Sacred Mountain.

However, instead of inhibiting Rattlesnake, the rattle only made him more threatening. He coiled around, shaking his tail and baring his fangs.

"Look at me," Rattlesnake said to the animals. "I rattle and hiss, and my bite is deadly. I am king of the road, and no one may use it without my permission!"

FCAT Author's Purpose
How is the author building suspense? Why is he doing this?

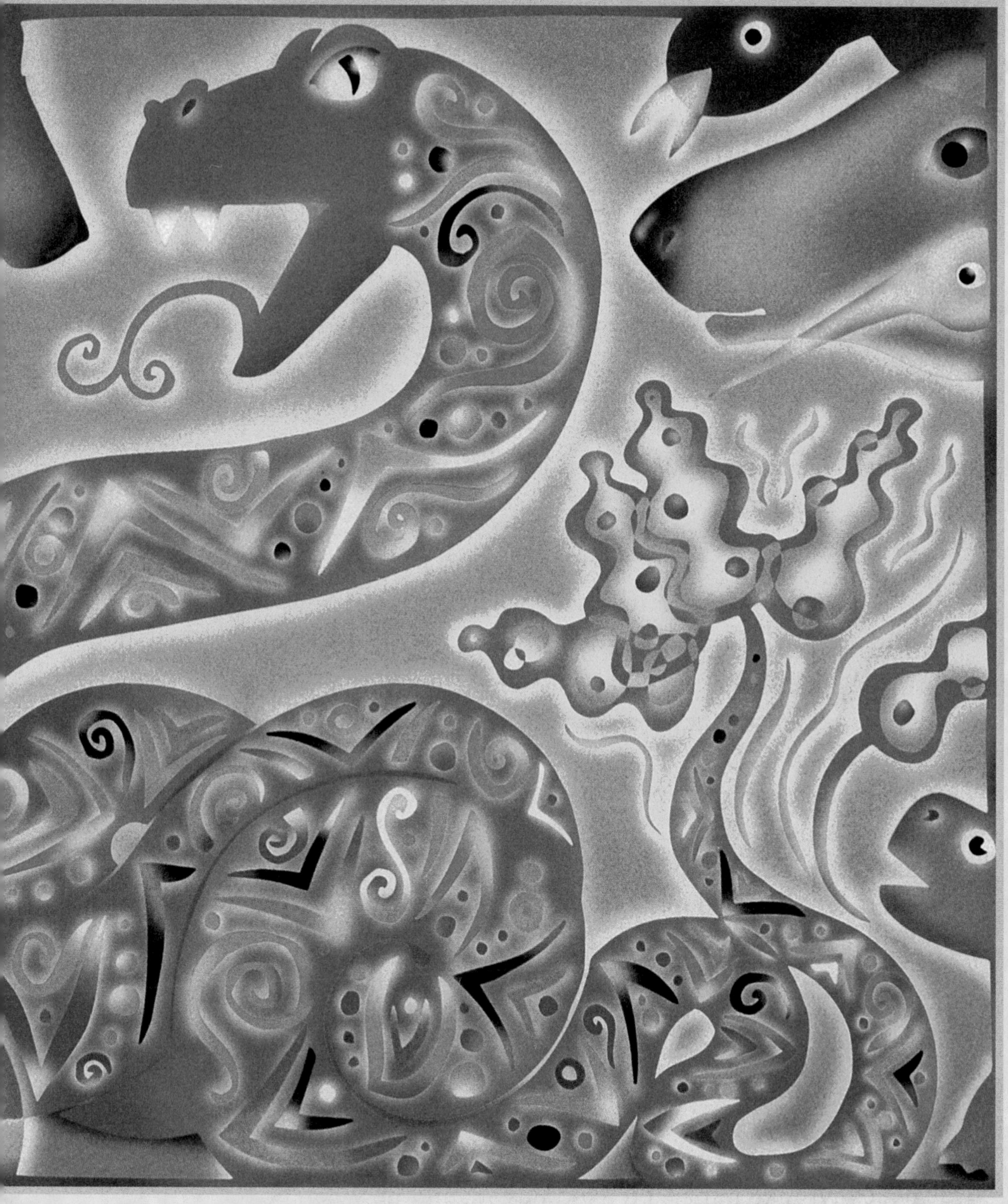

Now the animals went to Desert Woman to complain.

"Who, who," Owl said, greeting Desert Woman with respect. "Since you gave Rattlesnake his rattle, he is even more of a bully. He will not let anyone use the road. Please take away his fangs and rattle!"

"What I give I cannot take away," Desert Woman said. "When Rattlesnake comes hissing and threatening, one of you must make him behave."

She looked at all the animals assembled. The animals looked at one another. They looked up, they looked down, but not one looked at Desert Woman.

"I am too timid to stand up to Rattlesnake," Quail whispered.

"He would gobble me up," Lizard cried and darted away.

"We are all afraid of him," Owl admitted.

Desert Woman smiled. "Perhaps we need a new animal to make Rattlesnake behave," she suggested.

"Yip, yip," Coyote barked. "Yes, yes."

"If you help me, together we can make a **guardian** of the road," Desert Woman said. "I will form the body, and each of you will bring a gift for our new friend."

She gathered clay from the Sacred Mountain and wet it with water from a desert spring. Working quickly but with great care, she molded the body.

"He needs slender legs to run fast," said Deer. He took two slender branches from a mesquite bush and handed them to Desert Woman.

She pushed the sticks into the clay.

"And a long tail to balance himself," said Blue Jay.

"Caw, Caw! Like mine," croaked Raven, and he took long, black feathers from his tail.

"He must be strong," cried the mighty Eagle, and he plucked dark feathers from his wings.

"And have a long beak to peck at Rattlesnake," said Heron, offering a long, thin reed from the marsh.

"He needs sharp eyes," said Coyote, offering two shiny stones from the riverbed.

As Desert Woman added each new gift to the clay body, a strange new bird took shape.

"What is your gift?" Owl asked Desert Woman.

"I will give him the gift of dance. He will be **agile** and fast," she answered. "I will call him Roadrunner."

Then she breathed life into the clay.

Roadrunner opened his eyes. He blinked and looked around.

"What a strange bird," the animals said.

Roadrunner took his first steps. He **tottered** forward, then backward, then forward, and fell flat on his face.

The animals sighed and shook their heads. This bird was not agile, and he was not fast. He could never stand up to Rattlesnake. He was too **awkward**. Disappointed, the animals made their way home.

Desert Woman helped Roadrunner stand, and she told him what he must do. "You will dance around Rattlesnake and peck at his tail. He must learn he is not the king of the road."

"Me? Can I really do it?" Roadrunner asked, balancing himself with his long tail.

"You need only to practice," Desert Woman said.

Roadrunner again tried his legs. He took a few steps forward and bumped into a tall cactus.

"Practice," he said. He tried again and leaped over a sleeping horned toad.

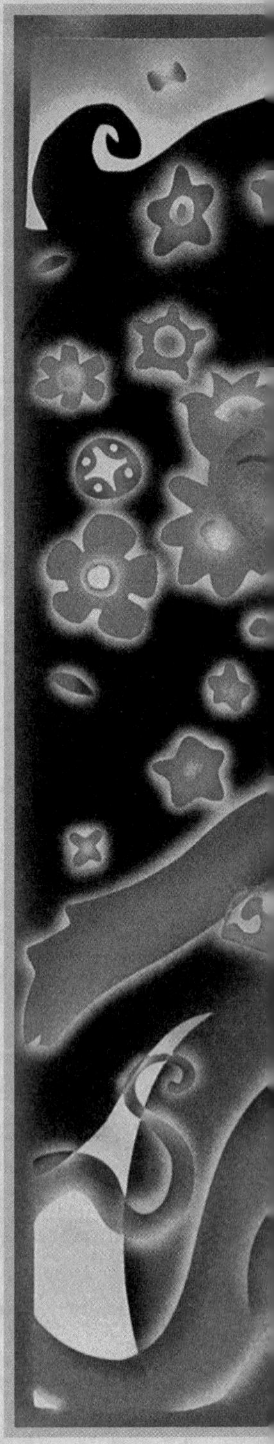

He tried jumping over a desert tortoise, but landed right on her back. The surprised turtle lumbered away, and Roadrunner crashed to the ground.

"I'll never get it right," he moaned.

"Yes, you will," Desert Woman said, again helping him to his feet. "You need only to practice."

So Roadrunner practiced. He ran back and forth, learning to use his skinny legs, learning to balance with his tail feathers.

"Practice," he said again. "Practice."

With time, he was swirling and twirling like a twister. The once awkward bird was now a graceful dancer.

"I've got it!" he cried, zipping down the road, his legs carrying him swiftly across the sand. "Thank you, Desert Woman."

"Use your gift to help others," Desert Woman said, and she returned to her abode on Sacred Mountain.

"I will," Roadrunner called.

He went racing down the road until his sharp eyes spied Rattlesnake hiding under a tall yucca plant.

"*Sssss*, I am king of the road," Rattlesnake hissed and shook his tail furiously. "No one may use *my* road without *my* permission."

"The road is for everyone to use," Roadrunner said sternly.

"Who are you?"

"I am Roadrunner."

"Get off my road before I bite you!" Rattlesnake glared.

"I'm not afraid of you," Roadrunner replied.

The people and the animals heard the ruckus and drew close to watch. Had they heard correctly? Roadrunner was challenging Rattlesnake!

"I'll show you I *am* king of the road!" Rattlesnake shouted, hissing so loud the desert mice trembled with fear. He shook his rattle until it sounded like a thunderstorm.

He struck at Roadrunner, but Roadrunner hopped out of the way.

"Stand still!" Rattlesnake cried and lunged again.

But Roadrunner danced gracefully out of reach.

Rattlesnake coiled for one more attempt. He struck like lightning, but fell flat on his face. Roadrunner had jumped to safety.

Now it was Roadrunner's turn. He ruffled his feathers and danced in circles around Rattlesnake. Again and again he pecked at the bully's tail. Like a whirlwind, he spun around Rattlesnake until the serpent grew dizzy. His eyes grew crossed and his tongue hung limply out of his mouth.

"You win! You win!" Rattlesnake cried.

"You are not king of the road, and you must not frighten those who use it," Roadrunner said sternly.

"I promise, I promise," the beaten Rattlesnake said and quietly slunk down his hole.

The people cheered and praised the bird.

"Now we can visit our neighbors in peace and go to our cornfields without fear!" the elders **proclaimed.** "And the children will no longer be frightened."

"Thank you, Roadrunner!" the children called, waving as they followed their parents to the fields.

Then the animals gathered around Roadrunner.

"Yes, thank you for teaching Rattlesnake a lesson," Owl said. "Now you are king of the road."

"No, now there is no king of the road," replied Roadrunner. "Everyone is free to come and go as they please. And the likes of Rattlesnake had better watch out, because I'll make sure the roads stay safe."

FCAT **Author's Purpose**
What purpose do you think the author had for writing this story?

Dancing with Rudolfo and David

Rudolfo Anaya did not have to do any research on roadrunners to write this story. The birds run free all around his home in the southwestern United States. When Rudolfo was a boy in New Mexico, he heard lots of Mexican American folk tales called *cuentos*. Now he writes his own tales to share his Mexican/Native American heritage.

Other books by Rudolfo Anaya and David Diaz

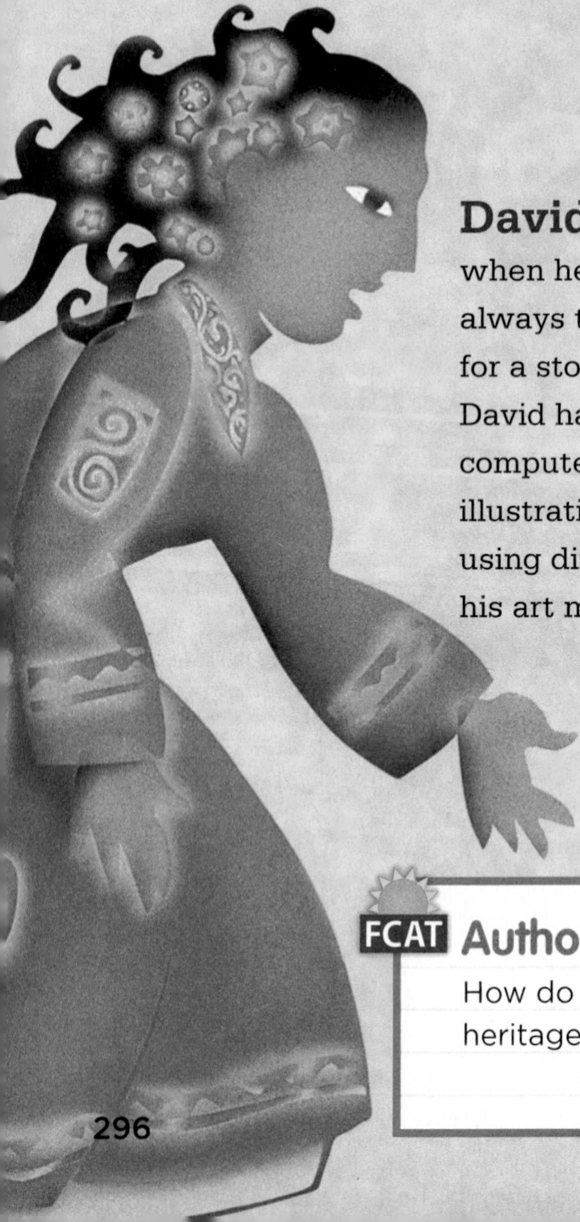

David Diaz likes to experiment when he illustrates a book. He always tries different art techniques for a story before deciding on one. David has even tried using a computer to do some of his illustrations. He believes that using different techniques makes his art more interesting.

LOG ON Find out more about Rudolfo Anaya and David Diaz at **www.macmillanmh.com**

FCAT Author's Purpose

How do you think the author's Mexican and Native American heritages inflenced him to write *Roadrunner's Dance?*

FCAT Comprehension Check

Summarize

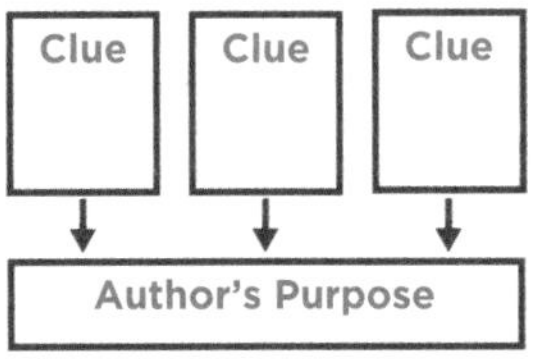

Summarize *Roadrunner's Dance.* Tell about the plot of the story, the setting, and the main characters. Use your Author's Purpose Map to help you think about the story as you summarize.

Think and Compare

READ THINK EXPLAIN

1. What lesson is the author trying to teach with this story? Explain using story details. **Evaluate: Author's Purpose**

READ THINK EXPLAIN

2. Reread pages 286–288. What qualities was Roadrunner given to stand up to Snake? How did these qualities help Roadrunner later in the story? Use details from the story to explain. **Analyze**
3. How would you have dealt with a bully like Snake? **Apply**
4. Why was it better that Desert Woman did not **interfere** by taking away Snake's new rattle? **Evaluate**
5. Read "Roadrunners: Surprising Birds" on pages 278–279. What information about roadrunners was in this selection that was not provided in *Roadrunner's Dance*? Use details from both selections. **Reading/Writing Across Texts**

Science

Genre

Nonfiction Articles present facts about a topic. They also provide informative photos, and graphic aids such as charts.

FCAT Text Feature

Flow Charts show an entire process from start to finish.

Content Vocabulary

absorbed **defend**
disrupt

Food Chains

PREDATOR vs. PREY

by Chisulo Lingenvelder

A food chain shows how living things get the food they need to survive. Food chains are made up of producers, consumers, and decomposers. Plants are producers because they use energy from the sun to make their own food. Animals are consumers because they cannot make their own food. They have to depend on the other living things in the food chain to eat. There are three kinds of consumers. Herbivores are animals that eat only plants. Carnivores are animals that eat other animals. Animals that eat both plants and other animals are called omnivores. Living things like fungi are decomposers. They return minerals to Earth's soil by breaking down plants and animals that have died.

Some predators hunt only a certain kind of prey. Other predators will hunt anything.

Rabbits are herbivores. They are also a popular prey for many predators.

The food chain is a way to move energy from one living thing to another. For example, energy from sunlight beams down on Earth. That energy is then **absorbed** by green plants. The green plants are eaten by herbivores. Herbivores are then eaten by carnivores or omnivores. When that animal dies, a decomposer will break down its body, returning the energy to the soil.

Predators and their prey are important to the food chain. Carnivores are hunters. They are also predators. A predator hunts weaker animals to eat. These weaker animals are prey. Prey must hide to keep from being eaten. Nature has given these animals different ways to protect themselves. Some animals can hide by using their color or shape to blend into their surroundings. Other animals are born with hard shells or sharp teeth that they use to **defend** themselves.

Armadillos have thick body armor to protect themselves from being attacked.

Reading a Flow Chart

This flow chart shows the process of the food chain.

The animals in a food chain depend on one another for survival. This is why it is important that there are no missing links in the chain.

Keeping a Balance

Each living thing in the food chain plays an important part in keeping nature balanced. If one piece of the food chain gets too big, the other animals will have to compete for survival. For example, if there were too many giraffes, there would not be enough plants for all of them to eat. This could cause giraffes to starve and die. This would affect the animals that depend on giraffes for food. Changes like this would **disrupt** the food chain and destroy the world's natural order.

Male giraffes eat from different parts of the tree than the female giraffes. This way there is enough food for all!

FCAT Connect and Compare

1. Look at the flow chart. What happens to grass after it has absorbed energy from the sun? Then, what happens to the mouse? **Reading a Flow Chart**

2. Why is the relationship between predator and prey important to the food chain? Explain using details from the article. **Apply**

3. Compare what happens between Roadrunner and Snake in *Roadrunner's Dance* to the food chain in this article. What is the relationship between a roadrunner and a snake? Where on the food chain are they? **Reading/Writing Across Texts**

Science Activity

RESEARCH INQUIRY

Research the different levels of consumers. Draw a flow chart showing first-level consumers and second-level consumers. Write to explain the differences between them.

LOG ON Find out more about food chains at **www.macmillanmh.com**

Write a Folk Tale

Writer's Craft

FCAT Transition Words

Transition words are used to connect one idea to another. This helps keep writers from jumping from one idea to another.

I used transition words to connect all of my ideas.

I told my story making sure that all my ideas are connected.

Why the Coquí Sings

by Keisha F.

Once upon a time, a little frog lived in a tree and sang all day long. The children loved the frog's song so much that the birds in the forest became jealous. They sang louder and louder every day, so no one could hear the frog sing.

Then one evening, when the birds became quiet for the night, the children heard "ko-kee, ko-kee, ko-kee." The frog had returned to sing the children to sleep. If any of the children awoke during the night, the little frog's singing would let them know that it was not time for them to wake from their sleep. The song of the little frog became a night time lullaby.

That is why coquí sings from sunset to sunrise.

Writing Prompt

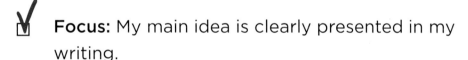

Folk tales often tell the story of how an animal came to look or act a certain way.

Think about an animal and imagine what made it look or act the way it does.

Now write a folk tale about what made this animal look and act the way it does.

FCAT Writer's Checklist

- ☑ **Focus:** My main idea is clearly presented in my writing.
- ☑ **Organization:** I use **transition words** to connect one idea to another.
- ☑ **Support:** I include details to support my main idea. I use description to make my writing interesting.
- ☑ **Conventions:** I use quotation marks and punctuation correctly. My sentences are complete.

People Who Made a Difference

Talk About It

What message do you think the artist was trying to send by painting this picture?

LOG ON Find out more about people who made a difference at **www.macmillanmh.com**

Vocabulary

unfair
ancestors
numerous
segregation
unsuspecting
avoided
injustice

FCAT **Words Parts**

Prefixes are added to the beginnings of words to change their meanings. The prefix *un-* means "not." When added to *fair,* it creates a new word that means "not fair."

IT TOOK COURAGE

by Lily Tuttle

CIVIL RIGHTS are equal opportunities for all citizens regardless of race, religion, or gender. At one time **unfair** laws gave some people more opportunities than others. Several brave people took a stand against this and made a difference.

Thurgood Marshall

Thurgood Marshall's family had come a long way from the time when their **ancestors** were slaves. But when he wanted to attend the University of Maryland Law School, the school rejected him because he was black. Marshall had to go to a different law school.

Later, in one of his first court cases, Marshall helped a young African American student sue the University of Maryland. The school had denied him admission, too.

Marshall worked hard to win **numerous** cases. One of his best-known trials was *Brown v. Board of Education* in 1954. In this case the Supreme Court decided to end **segregation** in schools. The Court made it illegal for black students and white students to be sent to separate locations.

Ruby Bridges

In 1960 six-year-old Ruby Bridges was the first black child to go to an all-white school in the South. Ruby was young and **unsuspecting**. She didn't realize how brave she was to do this. White parents decided to take their children out of school. For a whole year Ruby and her teacher were the only people there. Eventually some white children returned. The following year more black children came. Ruby Bridges made a difference.

Dr. Martin Luther King, Jr.

Dr. Martin Luther King, Jr., was a leader in the 1950s and 1960s. He **avoided** violence and asked others to fight in peaceful ways to end **injustice**.

King organized a march on Washington, D.C. There he and thousands of others demanded equal rights for all people. He gave a famous speech that day. He said, "I have a dream." King's dream was that all people would be treated fairly and equally.

Reread for Comprehension

FCAT

Evaluate

Author's Purpose An author writes a story to entertain, give information, or explain something to the reader. The reason an author writes a story is the **author's purpose**. Think about details in the story and what you already know to help you identify the author's purpose. Reread the selection and fill in the Author's Purpose Map.

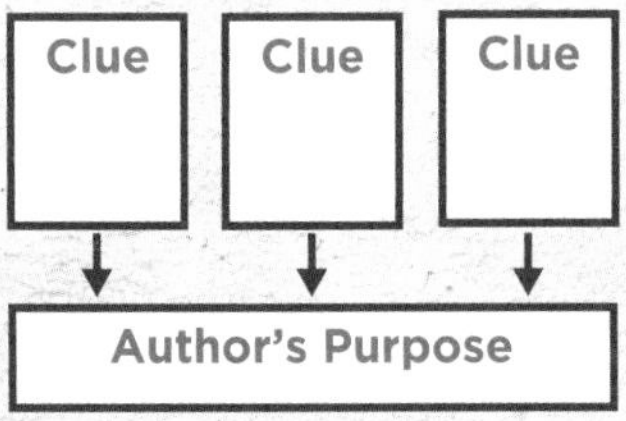

Comprehension

Genre

A **Biography** is a story about the life of a real person written by someone else.

Evaluate

FCAT

Author's Purpose As you read, fill in your Author's Purpose Map.

Clue	Clue	Clue
↓	↓	↓
Author's Purpose		

Read to Find Out

What does Dr. Martin Luther King, Jr.'s sister want you to know about him?

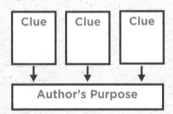

my brother MARTIN

Award Winning Illustrator

A SISTER REMEMBERS
GROWING UP WITH THE REV. DR. MARTIN LUTHER KING JR.

BY CHRISTINE KING FARRIS
ILLUSTRATED BY CHRIS SOENTPIET

We were born in the same room, my brother Martin and I. I was an early baby, born sooner than expected. Mother Dear and Daddy placed me in the chifforobe drawer that stood in the corner of their upstairs bedroom. I got a crib a few days afterward. A year and a half later, Martin spent his first night in that hand-me-down crib in the very same room.

The house where we were born belonged to Mother Dear's parents, our grandparents, the Reverend and

Mrs. A. D. Williams. We lived there with them and our Aunt Ida, our grandmother's sister.

And not long after my brother Martin—who we called M. L. because he and Daddy had the same name—our baby brother was born. His name was Alfred Daniel, but we called him A. D., after our grandfather.

They called me Christine, and like three peas in one pod, we grew together. Our days and rooms were filled with adventure stories and Tinkertoys, with dolls and Monopoly and Chinese checkers.

And although Daddy, who was an important minister, and Mother Dear, who was known far and wide as a musician, often had work that took them away from home, our grandmother was always there to take care of us. I remember days sitting at her feet, as she and Aunt Ida filled us with grand memories of their childhood and read to us about all the wonderful places in the world.

And of course, my brothers and I had each other. We three stuck together like the pages in a brand-new book. And being normal young children, we were almost *always* up to something.

Our best prank involved a fur piece that belonged to our grandmother. It looked almost alive, with its tiny feet and little head and gleaming glass eyes. So, every once in a while, in the waning light of evening, we'd tie that fur piece to a stick, and, hiding behind the hedge in front of our house, we would dangle it in front of **unsuspecting** passersby. Boy! You could hear the screams of fright all across the neighborhood!

Then there was the time Mother Dear decided that her children should all learn to play piano. I didn't mind too much, but M. L. and A. D. preferred being outside to being stuck inside with our piano teacher, Mr. Mann, who would rap your knuckles with a ruler just for playing the wrong notes. Well, one morning, M. L. and A. D. decided to loosen the legs on the piano bench so we wouldn't have to practice. We didn't tell Mr. Mann, and when he sat . . . *CRASH!* down he went.

But mostly we were good, obedient children, and M. L. did learn to play a few songs on the piano. He even went off to sing with our mother a time or two. Given his love for singing and music, I'm sure he could have become as good a musician as our mother had his life not called him down a different path.

But that's just what his life did.

FCAT **Author's Purpose**
Why does the author choose to tell so much about Martin's childhood?

My brothers and I grew up a long time ago. Back in a time when certain places in our country had **unfair** laws that said it was right to keep black people separate because our skin was darker and our **ancestors** had been captured in far-off Africa and brought to America as slaves.

Atlanta, Georgia, the city in which we were growing up, had those laws. Because of those laws, my family rarely went to the picture shows or visited Grant Park with its famous Cyclorama. In fact, to this very day I don't recall ever seeing my father on a streetcar. Because of those laws, and the indignity that went with them, Daddy preferred keeping M. L., A. D., and me close to home, where we'd be protected.

We lived in a neighborhood in Atlanta that's now called Sweet Auburn. It was named for Auburn Avenue, the street that ran in front of our house. On our side of the street stood two-story frame houses similar to the one we lived in. Across it crouched a line of one-story row houses and a store owned by a white family.

When we were young all the children along Auburn Avenue played together, even the two boys whose parents owned the store.

And since our house was a favorite gathering place, those boys played with us in our backyard and ran with M. L. and A. D. to the firehouse on the corner where they watched the engines and the firemen.

The thought of *not* playing with those kids because they were different, because they were white and we were black, never entered our minds.

Well, one day, M. L. and A. D. went to get their playmates from across the street just as they had done a hundred times before. But they came home alone. The boys had told my brothers that they couldn't play together anymore because A. D. and M. L. were Negroes.

And that was it. Shortly afterward the family sold the store and moved away. We never saw or heard from them again.

Looking back, I realize that it was only a matter of time before the generations of cruelty and **injustice** that Daddy and Mother Dear and Mama and Aunt Ida had been shielding us from finally broke through. But back then it was a crushing blow that seemed to come out of nowhere.

"Why do white people treat colored people so mean?" M. L. asked Mother Dear afterward. And with me and M. L. and A. D. standing in front of her trying our best to understand, Mother Dear gave the reason behind it all.

Her words explained the streetcars our family **avoided** and the WHITES ONLY sign that kept us off the elevator at City Hall. Her words told why there were parks and museums that black people could not visit and why some restaurants refused to serve us and why hotels wouldn't give us rooms and why theaters would only allow us to watch their picture shows from the balcony.

But her words also gave us hope.

She answered simply: "Because they just don't understand that everyone is the same, but someday, it will be better."

And my brother M. L. looked up into our mother's face and said the words I remember to this day.

He said, "Mother Dear, one day I'm going to turn this world upside down."

In the coming years there would be other reminders of the cruel system called **segregation** that sought to keep black people down. But it was Daddy who showed M. L. and A. D. and me how to speak out against hatred and bigotry and stand up for what's right.

Daddy was the minister at Ebenezer Baptist Church. And after losing our playmates, when M. L., A. D., and I heard our father speak from his pulpit, his words held new meaning.

And Daddy practiced what he preached. He always stood up for himself when confronted with hatred and bigotry, and each day he shared his encounters at the dinner table.

When a shoe salesman told Daddy and M. L. that he'd only serve them in the back of the store because they were black, Daddy took M. L. somewhere else to buy new shoes.

Another time, a police officer pulled Daddy over and called him "boy." Daddy pointed to M. L. sitting next to him in the car and said, "This is a boy. I am a man, and until you call me one, I will not listen to you."

These stories were as nourishing as the food that was set before us.

Years would pass, and many new lessons would be learned. There would be **numerous** speeches and marches and prizes. But my brother never forgot the example of our father, or the promise he had made to our mother on the day his friends turned him away.

And when he was much older, my brother M. L. dreamed a dream . . . that turned the world upside down.

FCAT **Author's Purpose**
Why does the author echo Martin's words, "I'm going to turn this world upside down"?

The Stories of Christine and Chris

Christine King Farris wrote this story to show boys and girls that her famous brother was once a kid just like them. She saw firsthand how young Martin laughed, played, and sometimes got into trouble. Christine wants readers to see that ordinary people can grow up to do great things.

Chris Soentpiet does a lot of research when he illustrates historical stories like this one. He goes to the library to study what clothes people wore and how they lived. Sometimes he even visits the actual places where story events took place. That is why it often takes Chris up to a year to illustrate a book.

Other books illustrated by Chris Soentpiet

LOG ON Find out more about Christine King Farris and Chris Soentpiet at **www.macmillanmh.com**

FCAT Author's Purpose

Did Christine King Farris write *My Brother Martin* to explain something or to inform or entertain the reader? How did the author's relationship with her brother influence her to write this story?

FCAT Comprehension Check

Summarize

Summarize *My Brother Martin.* Use your Author's Purpose Map to talk about who the narrator is and why that is important to the story. Explain who Martin is and include important events from his childhood.

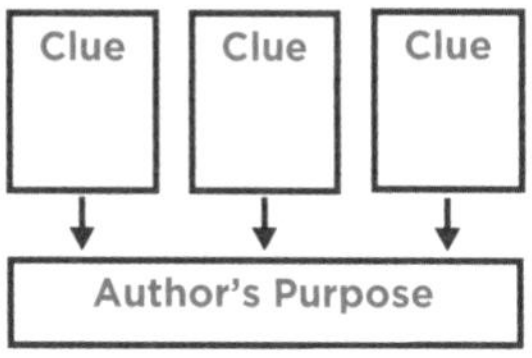

Think and Compare

1. What was the author's purpose in retelling what happened with Martin's childhood playmates? Why was this event important? Explain using details from the story. **Evaluate: Author's Purpose**

2. Reread pages 318–319. Why did Martin's father share his experiences with his children every day? How did his stories influence Martin? Use story details to explain. **Analyze**

3. Suppose you had met Rev. Dr. Martin Luther King, Jr., when he was a child. What character traits would you have in common? Use story details in your answer. **Synthesize**

4. Why is it important to correct **injustice**? Explain using story details. **Evaluate**

5. Read "It Took Courage" on pages 306–307. Compare the experiences of Thurgood Marshall and Rev. Dr. Martin Luther King, Jr. How did segregation affect both men? What did they both accomplish? Use details from both selections to explain. **Reading/Writing Across Texts**

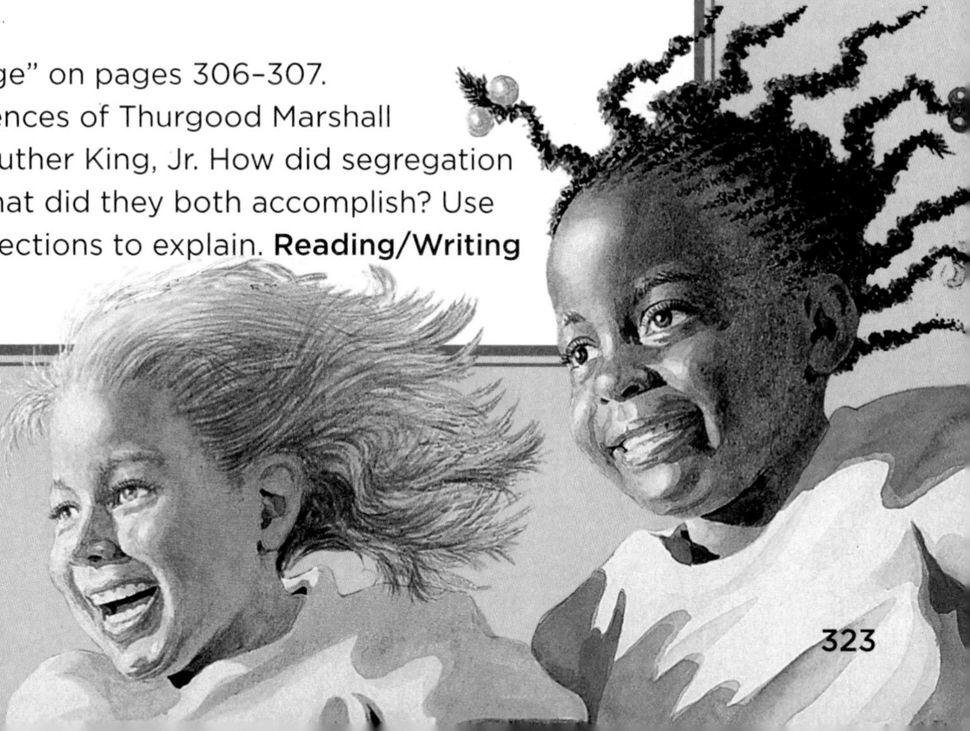

Social Studies

Genre

Letters are written messages that people send to each other.

FCAT Text Features

A **Salutation** is the line in the letter in which the writer greets the person to whom she or he is writing.

The **Body** of a letter is the main part of the letter. It contains the message.

Content Vocabulary

activist **nonviolence** **unconstitutional**

Dear Mrs. Parks

by Rosa Parks with Gregory J. Reed

Introduction

In 1955 civil rights **activist** Rosa Parks was arrested for refusing to give up her seat on a bus to a white person. Her action helped bring about a bus boycott in Montgomery, Alabama. For over a year, thousands of African Americans refused to ride buses in that city. The boycott ended when the U.S. Supreme Court said that separate seating for whites and blacks on the city's buses was **unconstitutional**.

The following letters are from a collection of letters between children and Rosa Parks.

This is the **salutation**.

Dear Mrs. Parks,

This is the **body** of the letter.

I live in the New England area, and I always wondered about the South. When you were growing up in Alabama, did you think that things would ever get better for African Americans?

Kelli
Hartford, Connecticut

We knew that they had to get better! The South had suffered under the unjust laws of segregation far too long. It was time for something to happen to turn things around.

During my childhood years, I had been bothered by the fact that white children had privileges that I did not. I was deeply hurt by the hate that some white people, even children, felt toward me and my people because of our skin. But my mother and grandmother taught me to continue to respect myself and stay focused on making myself ready for opportunity. They felt that a better day had to come, and they wanted me to be a part of it. But it was up to us to make it better.

As an adult I would go home thirsty on a hot summer day rather than take a drink from the "colored only" fountain. I would not be a part of an unjust system that was designed to make me feel inferior.

I knew that this type of system was wrong and could not last. I did not know when, but I felt that the people would rise up and demand justice. I did not plan for that point of change to begin with my actions on the bus that evening in 1955. But I was ready to take a stand.

Dear Mrs. Parks,

What is hope? I have read that you hope for this world to be a better place to live in, and you haven't given up. I'm still figuring out what is "hope," and then maybe I can help "hope" out to make this a better world and be like you.

Elizabeth
Grosse Point, Michigan

Elizabeth, many times we as adults seek to teach students like you without giving you examples of what the true meanings of words are so that you can learn from them.

Hope is wanting something that means a lot to you. It is like wanting something that you do not have. Hope is something we feel with our hearts. When we hope for something with our hearts, it becomes an expectation.

Hope is also something we believe in. Many people I have known believed in ending racial segregation in this country, and their hope that it could happen influenced their actions and brought about change. A friend of mine, the Reverend Jesse Jackson, says, "We must keep hope alive." I agree. You can help keep hope alive by believing in yourself. Your hope for yourself and for the future can make this world a better place to live.

Dear Mrs. Parks,

I always like hearing Dr. Martin Luther King, Jr.'s speeches. He was a great man. I wish he was still living. I believe he can straighten out this mess this country is in. Were you ever afraid of him dying and leaving you here?

Wilbar
Kerhonkson, New York

I, too, wish Dr. King was still with us. It has always been very difficult and very painful to think about Dr. King's death. He was a very dear friend of mine. He spoke with authority and conviction. His faith, his words, and his commitment to **nonviolence** inspired us all in the civil rights movement.

You are right in saying that our country has many problems. We have a long way to go. But we can work together, young and old, to achieve Dr. King's dream of equality and justice. I hope that you will keep that dream in your heart and make it your own.

FCAT Connect and Compare

1. Look at the form of the letters to Mrs. Parks. What parts do all the letters have in common? **Reading Letters**
2. How did Mrs. Park's "hope" help her to become part of the civil rights struggle that took place in the late 1950s? **Evaluate**
3. Think about this week's main selection, *My Brother Martin*. What might Martin's sister say in a letter to Rosa Parks? **Reading/Writing Across Texts**

Social Studies Activity

RESEARCH INQUIRY

Write a letter to a famous person about something they did that you would like to know more about.

LOG ON Find more about writing letters at **www.macmillanmh.com**

Writer's Craft

FCAT **Formal and Informal Language**

Good writers use many kinds of language to add variety to their writing. **Formal language** is "proper" language used in speeches. **Informal language** is language used in everyday communications.

Write About a Person Who Made a Difference

I used formal language to introduce Mr. Barrero.

I used informal language at the end of my speech.

My Hero

by Joseph M.

I am honored to introduce Mr. Barrero, the karate teacher in the after-school program. He has been teaching us since we were in first grade.

Mr. Barrero showed us that karate is much more than breaking boards. From the beginning, we learned to respect ourselves and each other. As his students, we practice hard in every class. The most important thing Mr. Barrero has taught us is how to avoid conflict. We solve problems without fighting.

Mr. Barrero is my hero. I hope he will teach us for a long time.

Writing Prompt

There are many people who have made a difference.

Think about someone who has made a difference.

Now write to explain how this person has made a difference.

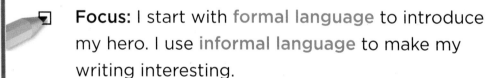

FCAT Writer's Checklist

- [x] **Focus:** I start with formal language to introduce my hero. I use informal language to make my writing interesting.
- [x] **Organization:** I express my ideas in order so that my sentences flow smoothly.
- [x] **Support:** I include details that support my main idea. My detail sentences show readers why this person inspires me.
- [x] **Conventions:** I use correct verb tenses. My spelling, grammar, and punctuation are all correct.

Talk About It

What can kids do to achieve their own goals and also help others?

LOG ON Find out more about kids getting it done at **www.macmillanmh.com**

KIDS GET IT DONE

TIME FOR KIDS

Vocabulary

identified
enterprising
persistence
venture

Gidget Schultz started Gidget's Way when she was 9 years old.

Their Way All the Way!

Gidget Schultz couldn't bear to see kids living on the streets near her Encinitas, California, home. So Gidget, now 14, started her own charity.

Gidget's Way gives backpacks, jackets, and school supplies to homeless kids. Gidget also gives teddy bears to local police to keep in their cars. Officers give the bears to kids who are scared, sad, or hurt. "Running Gidget's Way is a full-time job," says Gidget.

Jhordan Logan of New Castle, Indiana, **identified** a different need. She discovered there were hardly any good books for kids to read at Riley Hospital for Children in Indianapolis. Jhordan organized a Read It Again drive that collected over 5,000 books. Another program she started matches elementary school students with nursing home residents.

Gidget and Jhordan share an **enterprising**, high-energy attitude. "No matter what age you are, you can always volunteer," says Jhordan.

Tips for Planning a Service Project

Kids around the world use their skills and time to help make our world a better place. A service project can be as big as building a home for a family or as simple as collecting coins for charity. Choose something that will inspire you—something that you really care about and makes you want to work hard. Here are some helpful tips.

1. Identify a problem that exists in your community.
2. Learn more about the problem; think about ways to solve it.
3. Set a goal for the project.
4. Decide what supplies and help you'll need.
5. Get others involved.
6. Stick with it! Your **persistence** and hard work will keep the project on track.
7. Have fun! Knowing that you are helping your community should make you feel good.

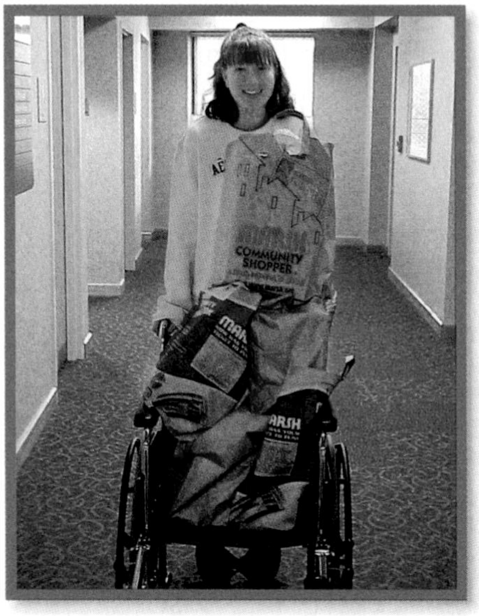

Jhordan Logan, 13, delivers books to kids in the hospital.

Kids' Jobs

Do you think about getting a job when you're older? Maybe you'll want to earn spending money or save for college. These are the types of businesses that employ the most teenagers. Don't forget, though, you can also start your own venture—business or project—and be your own boss!

Male	Percent of All Youths Who Work
Restaurants	31.3%
Grocery Stores	13.6
Entertainment and Recreation Services	4.5
Agriculture	3.6
Construction	3.6
Department Stores	3.1

Female	Percent of All Youths Who Work
Restaurants	32.6%
Grocery Stores	9.9
Private Households (babysitting, etc.)	5.7
Department Stores	4.4
Entertainment and Recreation Services	4.0

Source: U.S. Department of Labor

LOG ON Find out more about kids' jobs at **www.macmillanmh.com**

Comprehension

Genre

A **Nonfiction Article** in a newspaper or magazine tells a true story.

Summarize

FCAT **Compare and Contrast**

When you look for similarities, you compare two or more things or ideas. When you look for differences, you contrast two or more things or ideas.

☆ KID ☆ REPORTERS AT WORK

How do kid reporters tell the story when the news is about improving the lives of children?

Each year the newsmagazine *Time For Kids* selects several young people to serve as TFK kid reporters. These **enterprising** kids are not professional journalists, but like adult reporters they still have to show they are qualified for the job. Three skills they must have are **persistence** in tracking down a story, good interviewing skills, and the ability to write clearly about complicated topics.

Here's a behind-the-scenes look at two TFK reporters and two of the stories they covered for the magazine. The reporters don't have much in common, except that they are both determined to do a good job as reporters covering an interesting story. The stories seem quite different at first, too. However, they have some strong similarities.

REPORTER: TERRENCE CHEROMCKA

STORY:

A World Conference Just for Kids

Terrence, from Pennsylvania, plays softball, basketball, and field hockey. She loves to read and write. She's also very interested in travel, and has visited France and Thailand. In 2002, however, she had the chance to meet people from all over the world without traveling very far at all. That year Terrence got an assignment from TFK to go to New York City to cover the opening ceremonies of the United Nations Special Session on Children.

The event was a follow-up to a conference held at the U.N. in 1990 to promote the rights of children. World leaders and 375 young people met to discuss what had been accomplished since 1990 and how much more needed to be done. Issues with the highest priority were health care, education, and basic rights for the children of the world. U.N. Secretary General Kofi Annan addressed the opening session. Speaking directly to the young people in attendance, he said, "Your voices will be heard, I promise you."

For her story Terrence interviewed kids from several different countries about what they hoped the conference would accomplish. "We hope to get kids closer to the government and making decisions," said Bala Subrayanya of India.

Terrence also reported on her tour of the United Nations building. Her tour ended with an exhibit showing the devastating effects of war. She saw pictures of child soldiers fighting in war-torn countries. She wrote: "It really reminded me of why the U.N. is working so hard to help improve children's lives and why its mission is so important."

In the large room where the United Nations General Assembly meets, young people from many countries perform at the opening ceremonies of the Special Session. Others sit in the U.N. delegates' seats.

REPORTER: MARTIN JACOBS

STORY:

Kid Scientist Starts Kids' Charity

Martin, who lives in New York, is a computer buff, plays the piano, and wants to be an airline pilot when he grows up. When he got the assignment to interview Andrew Hsu, he expected to be talking about science. After all, Andrew had just become the youngest winner of the Washington State Science and Engineering Fair. The 11-year-old scientist won the grand prize for identifying a particular gene that plays an important role in keeping the human body healthy.

Martin soon discovered that being a science whiz is just one of Andrew's accomplishments. He's also an athlete who competes in swimming. But the main thing Andrew wanted to tell Martin about was the World Children Organization (WCO). Andrew founded this organization along with his brother Patrick. The brothers started this **venture** in order to help improve the lives of children. In that way its mission is similar to that of the U.N. Special Session on Children. The U.N. special session **identified** three high-priority issues. In contrast, WCO focuses on a single issue for now.

Andrew and Patrick believe that improving education is the best way they can make a positive difference for children. They know that, unlike the United States, there are places where a free education isn't available to all kids.

Andrew Hsu, 11, receives the grand prize award at the 2003 Washington State Science and Engineering Fair. He became the youngest person to ever win that prize.

To help meet that need, Andrew and Patrick had the idea of producing videos about science, math, and languages for children in countries where there aren't enough qualified teachers. "Without education," Andrew said, "the problems of poverty, hunger, child labor, and other abuses of children's rights will never end."

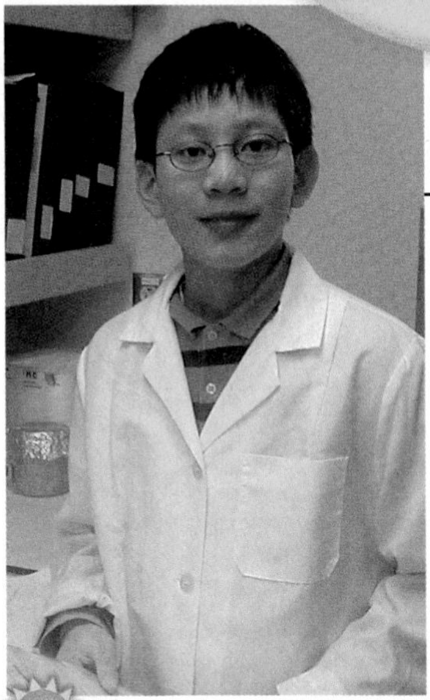

Andrew finished high school at age 9. By age 11 he was already a "working" scientist.

STORY: Different Reporters, Different Stories, a Common Theme

Terrence and Martin both wrote about kids and organizations involved in helping children. In Terrence's story, the organization—the United Nations—is a large one that was founded by the nations of the world. The kids involved came from many different countries. The size and political power of the U.N. enables it to work on several high-priority issues at once. In Martin's story, the organization is a small one—the World Children Organization—founded by two kids. For now, the WCO focuses on education as its single issue.

Clearly, all of these kids—at the U.N. Special Session, Andrew and Patrick at WCO, and reporters Terrence and Martin—share a commitment to making the world a better place for everyone, especially children.

FCAT

Think and Compare

1. What skills do Terrence and Martin need to be good reporters?
2. If you were a kid reporter, what topic would you like to investigate?
3. If there was one way to improve the lives of the children of the world, what could it be?
4. What do Gidget Schultz, Jhordan Logan, the attendees at the U.N. Special Session, and Andrew and Patrick Hsu have in common? How are their projects different?

FCAT **Test Strategy**

Think and Search

Read on to find the answer. Look for information in more than one place.

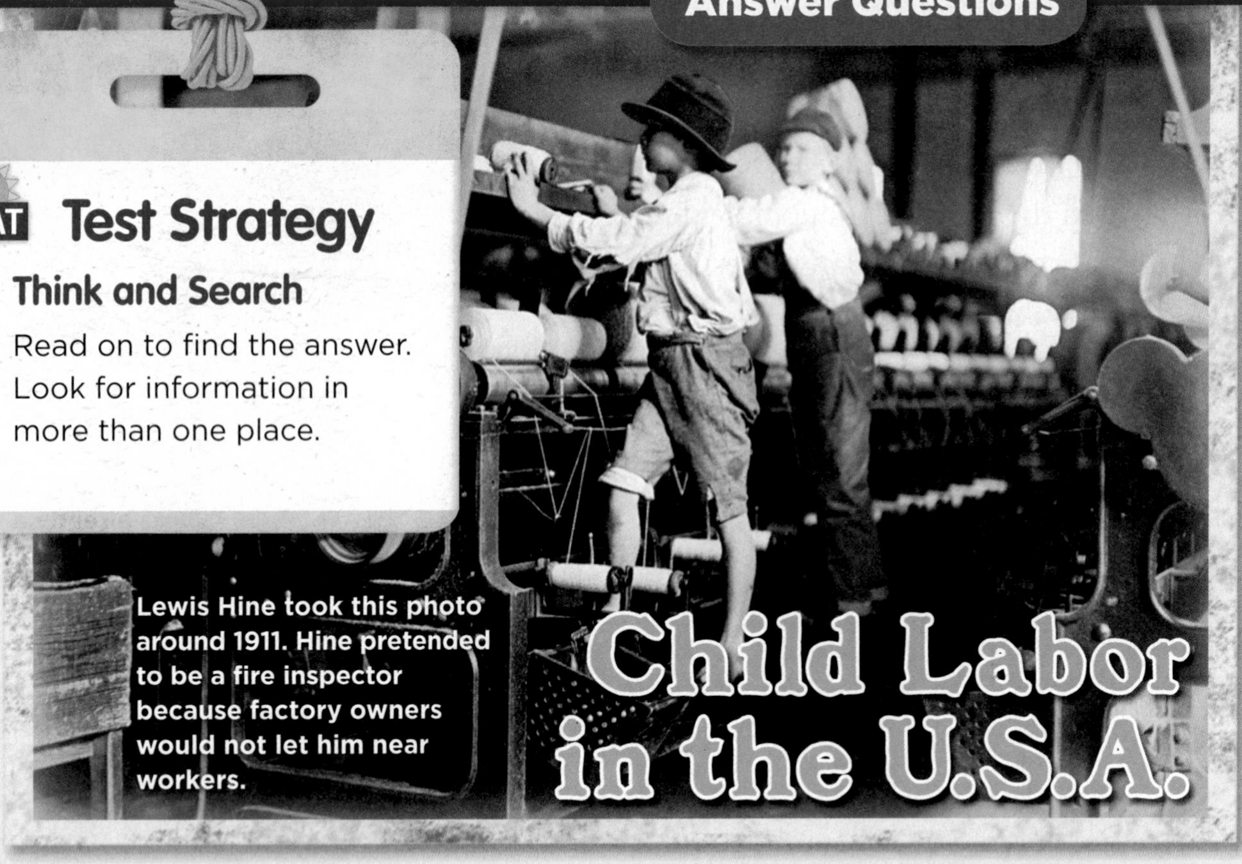

Lewis Hine took this photo around 1911. Hine pretended to be a fire inspector because factory owners would not let him near workers.

Child Labor in the U.S.A.

Throughout its early history, the United States counted on kids to work on farms and in factories. There was a time when employers hired kids because they were cheap labor and easy to manage. In the 1800s kids as young as seven worked in textile mills for 12 hours a day. By the end of the nineteenth century, almost 2 million kids performed hazardous jobs in mills, mines, and factories across the country.

Besides working long hours, conditions and wages for the laborers were very bad. Anyone who misbehaved was punished and sent to a "whipping room." Workers were rarely given breaks and most had to eat their lunches while working. Many concerned citizens tried to change these conditions, including photographer Lewis Hine. He was hired by the National Child Labour Committee to investigate and photograph working kids. His photographs showed just how badly kids were treated in the workforce.

In 1938 a U.S. law called the **Fair Labor Standards Act** was passed. This law limited work hours and set the minimum age for children to work. The Fair Labor Standards Act still exists, but some employers do not follow it. It is estimated that 800,000 children work illegally in the United States today. Close to 1 million children work long hours on farms with heavy machinery or poisonous chemicals, or under other conditions that could harm them.

FCAT **Now answer Numbers 1 through 5. Base your answers on the article "Child Labor in the U.S.A."**

1. What happened BEFORE the 1938 Fair Labor Standards Act was passed?
   - (A) Kids worked long hours at unsafe jobs.
   - (B) Kids were not required to go to school.
   - (C) Kids were not allowed to work in factories.
   - (D) Kids were prevented from working on farms.

Tip

Look for information in more than one place.

2. This article is MOSTLY about
   - (F) farming jobs.
   - (G) finding the right job.
   - (H) photographer Lewis Hine.
   - (I) protecting children who work.

3. What has NOT changed since the 1800s?
   - (A) Kids still eat lunch while working.
   - (B) Kids still work at dangerous jobs.
   - (C) Kids still work in mines and mills.
   - (D) Lewis Hine is still photographing kids.

4. READ THINK EXPLAIN Describe the conditions that the kids had to work in. Why did citizens have a right to be concerned? Explain using details from the article.

5. READ THINK EXPLAIN How have things changed for kids since the Fair Labor Standards Act was passed? How have things stayed the same? Use details from the article to explain.

STOP

Write to a Prompt

FCAT

People take certain steps to start a magazine.

Think about the steps you would take to start a magazine.

Now write to explain the steps you would take to start a magazine.

Expository writing explains, defines, or tells how to do something.

To figure out if a writing prompt asks for expository writing, look for clue words, such as explain, tell how, or define.

Below see how one student begins a response to the prompt above.

The writer explained the steps taken to create the magazine Kids Today.

It is hard for kids to relate to something they have read. That is why I decided to start a new magazine only for kids. I called it Kids Today. The magazine is written and run by kids. It talks about everything that happens in a kid's life.

The first thing I did was look for kids my age who wanted to write for the magazine. I decided to arrange the writing assignments by subject: school, friends, sports, music, and movies. Then I looked for other kids to proofread and edit the articles before they were printed in our magazine.

When I had a group together, I sent them to interview people and write about things that interest kids today. Then the real interesting work began!

Writing Prompt

Respond in writing to the prompt below. Before you write, read the Writing Hints below. Review the hints after you finish writing.

FCAT Suppose you need to increase sales for a magazine.
Think about how you would increase sales for a magazine.
Now write to tell what you would do to increase sales for a magazine.

Writing Hints for Prompts

- ☑ Read the prompt carefully.
- ☑ Plan your writing by organizing your ideas.
- ☑ Support your ideas by telling more about each event or reason.
- ☑ Use helping and main verbs to construct sentences.
- ☑ Choose words that help others understand what you mean.
- ☑ Review and edit your writing.

GREAT PLAINS INDIANS

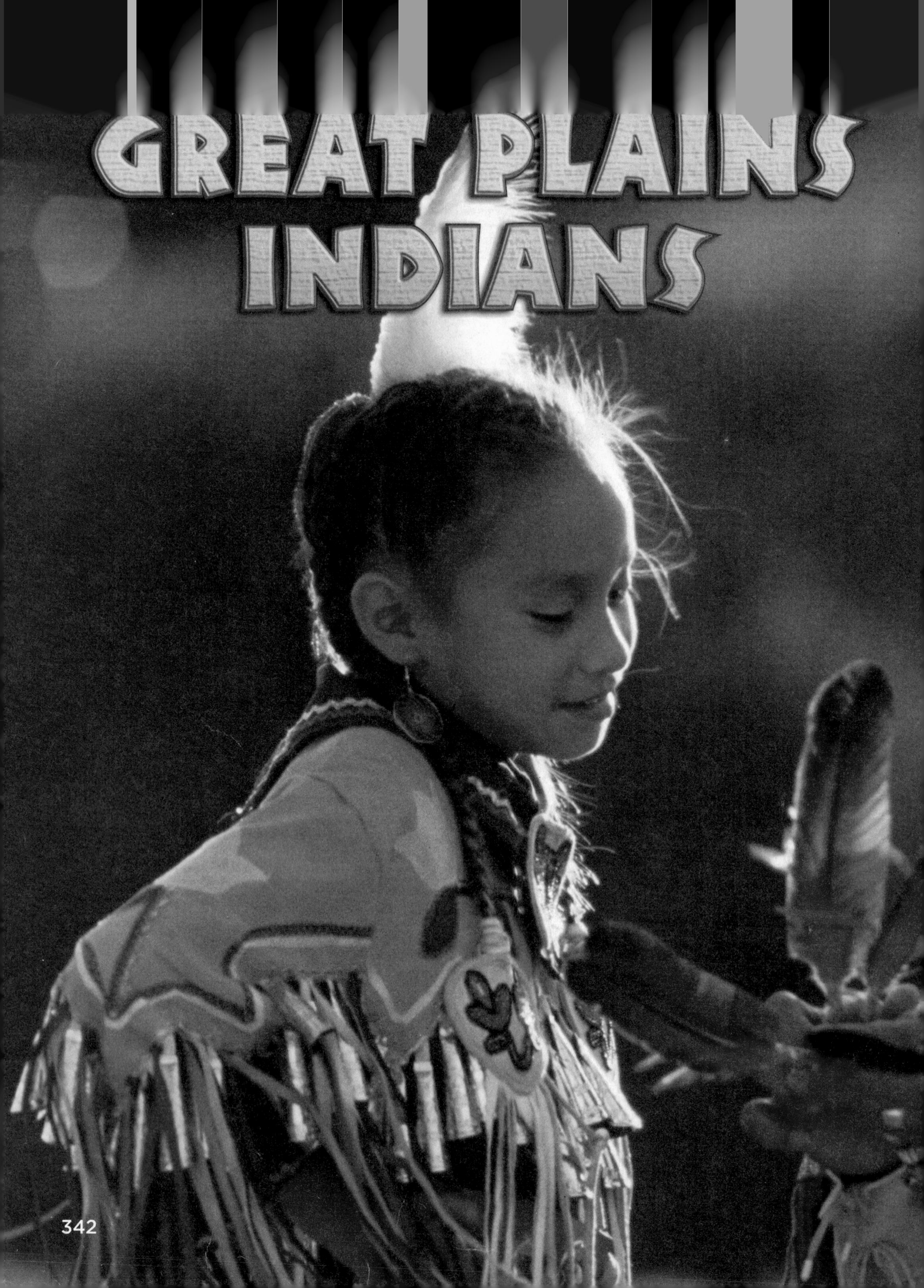

Talk About It

How can you tell that these people are preparing for a special event?

LOG ON Find out more about Great Plains Indians at **www.macmillanmh.com**

Vocabulary

sores **midst**
loosened **responsibility**
mysterious **patchwork**
amazement

FCAT Dictionary

Homophones are words that sound the same but have different spellings and meanings. *Sores* and *soars* are homophones. Can you think of other homophones?

HISTORY AT YOUR FEET

by André Melillo

"Do I have to go?" Sam asked. "I've got **sores** on my feet from walking so much."

Sam, his sister Kim, and their family were on their way to the Pawnee Indian Village Museum.

Mom gave Sam some bandage strips and said, "You'll enjoy learning about the people of the Pawnee nation."

After that, Sam let out a sigh and **loosened** his sandal straps. He then dragged himself towards the museum.

Who Were the Pawnee?

The origins of the Pawnee nation are **mysterious**. In the early 1800s, there were 10,000–30,000 Pawnee living in four separate bands.

"This museum is located where one band of Pawnee settled back in 1820," explained Mom.

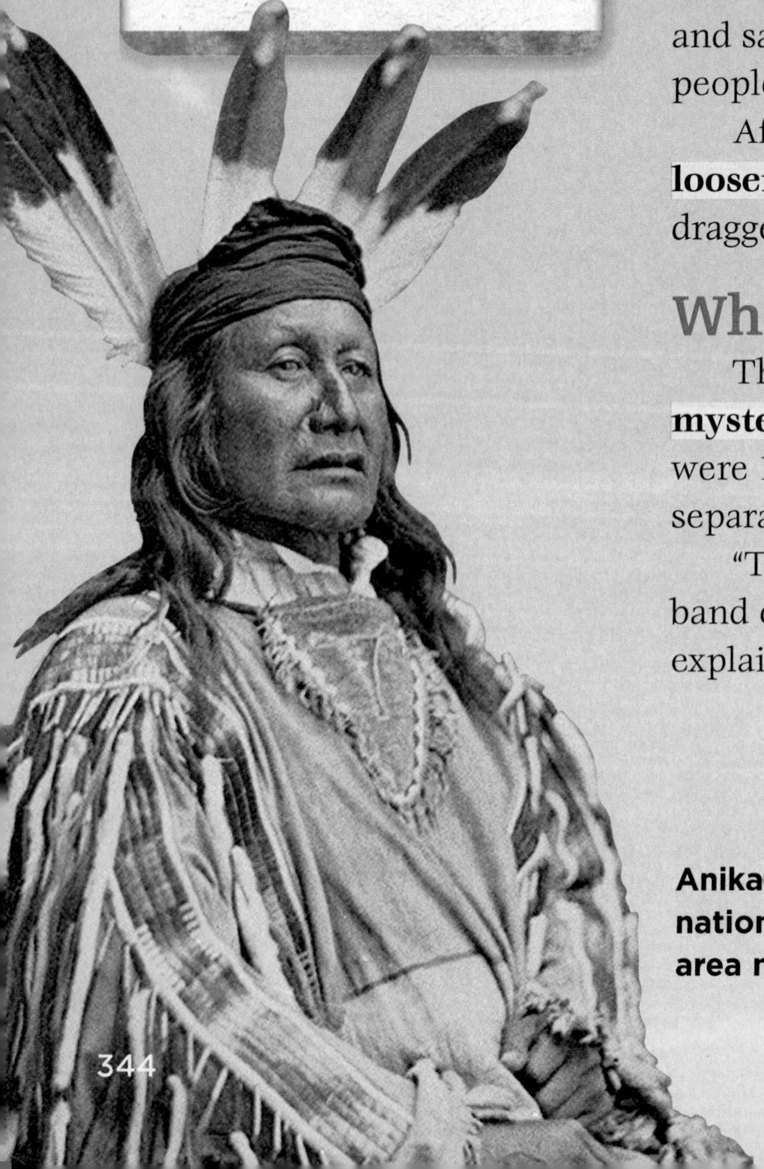

Anikarus Rushing of the Pawnee nation. The Pawnee mostly lived in the area now known as Nebraska.

"And now we're standing exactly where the Pawnee lived!" exclaimed Kim in **amazement**.

"That's right," said Dad. "Here's part of the original floor," he said, pointing. "You can see some burned timbers from the fire that destroyed the village."

"Clothing?" said Kim. "Buffalo aren't shaped like any clothing I've ever seen."

Everyone chuckled. "They'd sew a **patchwork** of pieces into warm winter robes and pants," explained the guide.

What Was Life Like?

Sam had to admit that being in the **midst** of all that history was exciting. "What was it like to live back then?" he wondered aloud.

A museum guide spoke up. "It happens to be my **responsibility** to tell you just that. The Pawnee hunted mostly buffalo and used every part of the animals they killed for food or clothing. They let nothing go to waste."

A battle between the Pawnees and the Konzas was painted on this bison hide.

Reread for Comprehension

FCAT

Summarize

Chronological Order is the sequence, or order, in which events take place. Time-order words such as *then*, *while*, and *after that* are clues to a story's sequence of events. Putting events in **chronological order** will help you summarize a story. Reread the selection and use your Sequence Chart to help you put events in order.

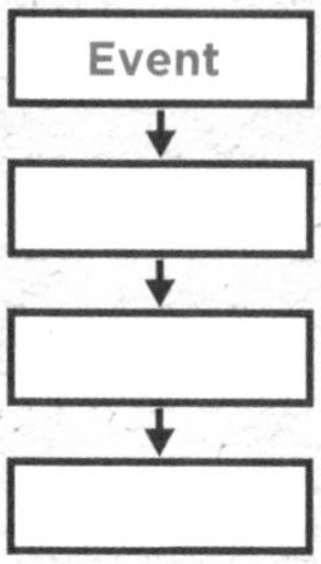

Comprehension

Genre

A **Legend** is a story that has been handed down by a people for many years, and that often has some basis in fact.

Summarize

FCAT **Chronological Order** As you read, fill in your Sequence Chart.

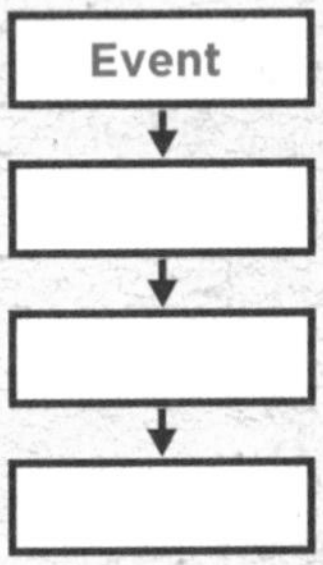

Read to Find Out

What gift does the mystic horse give to the boy and his tribe?

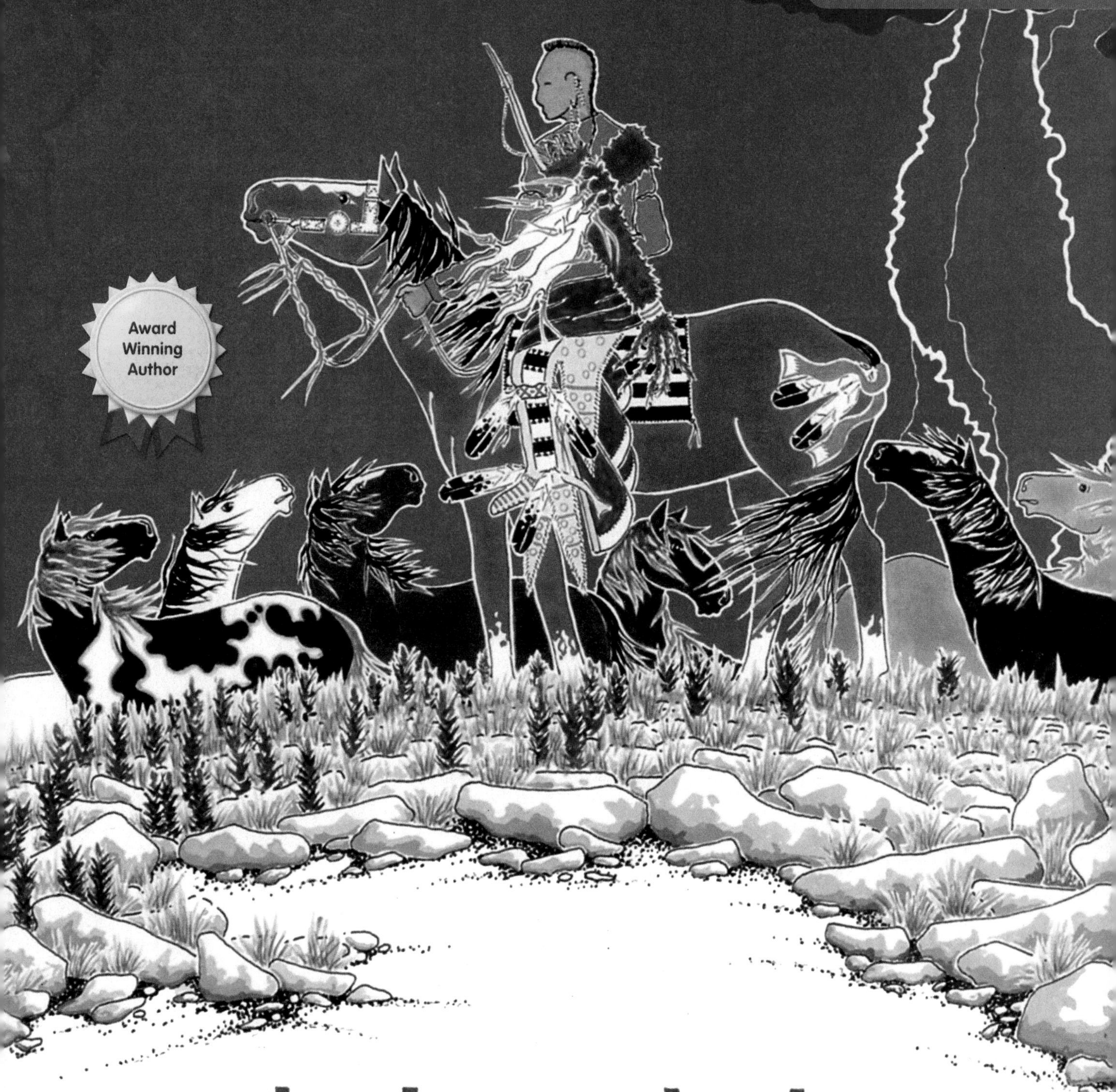

Mystic Horse

written and illustrated by **PAUL GOBLE**

IN THOSE LONG AGO DAYS, when the Pawnee people had harvested their crops of corn and squash, they would leave their earth-lodge villages and travel out on the Great Plains to hunt buffalo. They had horses to ride and to carry their tipis and belongings when they went great distances in search of the wandering herds.

When they were not traveling, and the tipis were pitched, it was the **responsibility** of the older boys, the young men, to look after the herds of horses, and to guard the village. They would stay with the horses at pasture throughout the day, often far away from the camp. All the while they would keep a good lookout for enemies.

Traveling with the people were an old woman and her grandson. They were poor, living alone without any relatives at the edge of the village. Their only shelter was made of sticks and a **patchwork** of pieces of old tipi covers which people had thrown away. Nobody took much notice of them.

When the people moved from one camping place to another, the old woman and her grandson would stay behind to look for scraps of food, and to pick up discarded clothes. They had no horse. They walked, and what their dogs could not carry, they packed on their own backs. Their life was hard, but they were happy.

One day, as they followed far behind the village, they came upon a sad and sickly worn-out horse standing in the trail. He was terribly thin, with **sores** on his back.

"Grandmother," the boy said, "nobody wants this poor old horse. If we are kind and look after him, he will get well again. He will help us carry our packs! Then I will be able to join the buffalo hunt, and we will have meat, and fresh skins as well!"

And so they led the old horse, limping along behind them. People laughed: "You've got yourself a great warhorse, boy! How will we keep up with you now?"

But the boy loved his horse, and looked after him well.

FCAT Chronological Order
What is the first thing the boy does when he finds the horse?

After some days had passed, the boys who were out on the hills looking after the horses spotted enemies approaching on horseback. They quickly drove the herds back to the safety of the camp. The men grabbed their weapons, mounted their fastest horses, and rode out to meet the enemy.

The boy, riding the poor old horse, followed shyly at a distance. But the men pointed at the horse and laughed: "Look! Here's the one who'll leave us all behind! Boy, that's an old good-for-nothing half-starved horse. You'll be killed. Go back home!"

The boy was ashamed, and rode off to one side where he could not hear their unkind remarks. The horse turned his head and spoke to the boy: "Listen to me! Take me down to the river and cover me with mud." The boy was alarmed to hear him speak, but without hesitation he rode to the river and daubed mud all over his horse.

Then the horse spoke again: "Don't take your bow and arrows. Cut a long willow stick instead. Then ride me, as hard as you can, right into the enemy's **midst** and strike their leader with the stick, and ride back again. Do it four times, and the enemy will be afraid; but do not do it more than four times!"

While the horse was speaking, he was tossing his head, stamping and prancing this way and that, until the boy could hardly hold him back. He **loosened** the reins, and the horse galloped toward the enemy. He was no longer an old sickly worn-out horse! He flew like a hawk, right to where the enemy riders were formed up in line of battle. The boy struck their leader with his willow stick, turned, and rode back to his people with arrows flying past him like angry wasps.

He turned again without stopping, and the horse carried him back to strike another enemy rider. By then his people were cheering loudly. Four times the boy charged back and forth, and each time he hit one of the enemy, just as his horse had told him.

FCAT Chronological Order
Summarize the horse's instructions using time-order words.

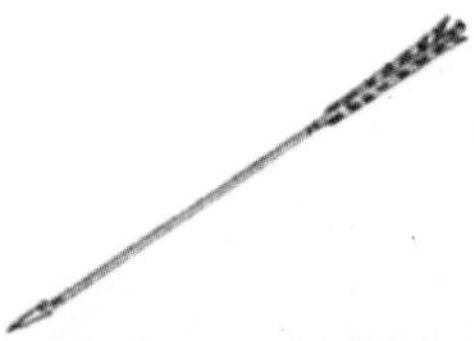

The men watched the boy with **amazement.** Now they, too, felt brave enough to follow his example, and they drove the enemy in full retreat from the village. It was like chasing buffalo.

The boy was eager to join the chase. He said to himself: "I have struck four times, and I have not been hurt. I will do it once more." And so, again, he rode after the retreating enemy riders. He whipped another with his stick, but at that very instant his horse was pierced by an arrow, and fell. The horse tried to stand, but he could not.

When the enemy had fled, the men returned and gathered round the boy. His horse was dead. They wanted to touch the horse, for they knew he had been no ordinary one, but a horse with mystic powers.

The leader spoke: "Today this boy has shown that he is braver than all of us. From now on we will call him Piraski Resaru, Boy Chief."

But the boy cried. He was sad for his horse, and angry with himself that he had not done what the **mysterious** horse had told him. He untied the lariat, pulled out the arrow, and carefully wiped away the blood.

He climbed to the top of a nearby hill to mourn. He sat on a rock and pulled his blanket over his head. While he sat there crying, fearsome dark clouds closed across the sky, and it grew dark as if night was falling. Lightning flashed! Thunder shook the hilltop, and it rained with a terrific downpour.

Looking through the downpour, he imagined he saw the dead horse move his legs a little, and that he even tried to lift his head. He wondered if something strange and wonderful was happening. And then he knew it was true: the horse slowly stretched out his front legs, and then stood up!

The boy was a little afraid, but he ran down from the hilltop and clasped his arms round the horse's neck, crying with joy that he was alive again.

The horse spoke softly to him: "Tirawahat, Our Father Above, is good! He has forgiven you. He has let me come back to you."

The storm passed; the rain stopped. All was still and fresh, and the sun shone brilliantly on his beautiful living horse. "Now take me up into the hills, far away from people," the horse told him. "Leave me there for four days, and then come for me."

When the four days had passed, Boy Chief left the village and climbed into the pine tree hills.

A horse neighed, and the mysterious horse appeared, followed by a herd of spirited horses. They surrounded Boy Chief, snorting and stamping excitedly, horses of every color—beautiful bays, chestnuts, shiny blacks, whites, grays, and paints.

Mounted on his mysterious horse, Boy Chief drove the horses round and round the village. He stopped in front of his grandmother's shelter.

"Grandmother," he said, "now you will always have horses! You need never walk again! Choose the ones you want, and give the rest to those who need them most." And so it was done.

After that, the boy and his grandmother rode whenever they moved camp. They lived in a tipi and were not poor any longer. And, just as his grandmother had looked after him when he was young, so he, too, always took good care of her for all her years.

Meet Paul Goble

Paul Goble first became interested in Native Americans when he was a boy growing up in England. He thought their beliefs, art, and tales were wonderful. When Paul grew up, he moved to the western United States to live and learn among the Native Americans. Paul began to write and illustrate books that retold traditional tales. Before writing each book, he carefully researches Native American customs and clothing. He also likes his books to show how people and nature are connected.

Other books by Paul Goble

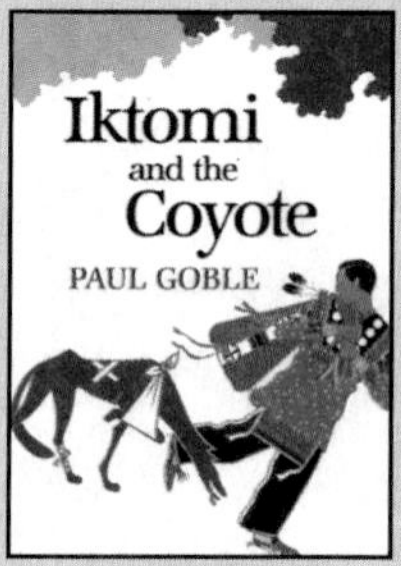

LOG ON Find out more about Paul Goble at **www.macmillanmh.com**

FCAT Author's Purpose

Legends often have some basis in fact. Why did Paul Goble write *Mystic Horse*? Was it mainly to explain, inform, or entertain?

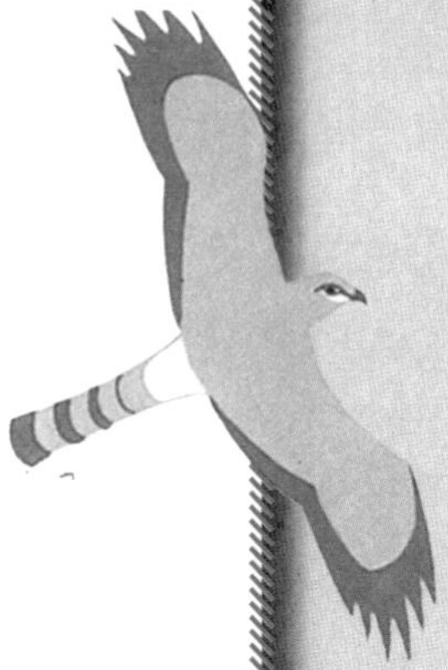

FCAT Comprehension Check

Summarize

Use your Sequence Chart to help you summarize *Mystic Horse.* Tell the story events in the order in which they happened.

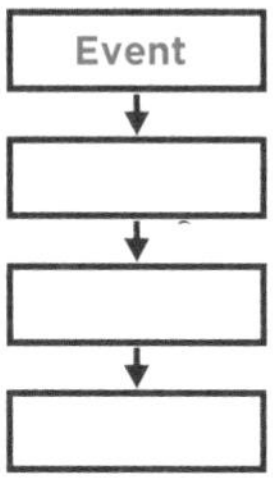

Think and Compare

READ THINK EXPLAIN

1. Describe the **mysterious** change that happened to the old horse after the boy covered it with mud. Use story details to describe the events in order. **Summarize: Chronological Order**

READ THINK EXPLAIN

2. Why did the boy ignore the horse's directions and what price did he pay? How did Tirawahat show he had forgiven the boy? Explain using story details. **Analyze**

3. Suppose you lost a friendship because you made a foolish mistake. How would you correct your mistake and repair the friendship? **Apply**

4. Based on the text, how could one explain the boy's actions in battle? **Evaluate**

5. Read "Who Were the Pawnee?" on pages 344–345, and pages 349–350 of *Mystic Horse*. What do both selections teach about Pawnee life? **Reading/Writing Across Texts**

Address http://www.example.com/

Search

Social Studies

Genre

Online Articles provide factual information and links to a topic.

FCAT **Text Feature**

Links, also called hyperlinks, connect one web page to another.

Content Vocabulary

descendants **resource**
resistance **conserve**

PRINT THIS ARTICLE

E-MAIL THIS ARTICLE TO A FRIEND

WATCH A VIDEO

LISTEN TO A COUNCIL MEETING

FREE PEOPLE

The Seminole Tribe

by Peter Lightfoot

There is nothing that better describes the Seminole tribe than the phrase *free people.* And that is exactly what their name means! The Seminoles are a Native American tribe who presently live in Florida. They are the **descendants** of the Creek people who were living in Florida when the Spanish came over in the 1500s.

When the Spaniards tried to force the Native Americans to work for them, they were met with **resistance**. Because of this, the Spaniards began calling them "free people." Eventually the name stuck and the Seminoles proved to be worthy of their name. They are the only Native American tribe in the United States never to enter into a treaty with the U.S.

Throughout their entire history, they fought for their freedom and resisted all outsiders' attempts at trying to control them. In the late 1950s, Native American tribes pushed to draft their own charters. On July 21, 1957, members of the Seminole tribe voted for a **constitution**.

Favorites History Search Scrapbook

Using Links

Use links to move from one online article to another. If a word or phrase is blue and underlined, that usually means you can click it for more information. When you click, another page will appear.

Address http://www.example.com/constitution/index.shtml

Search

Constitution, Culture, and Government

Seminoles live on reservations, which are pieces of land that the government set aside for Native Americans to live on. The Seminole tribe is divided into eight clans. Each clan is named for something that represents a trait, such as courage, that the clan members show in day-to-day life. The clan names are Bigtown, Panther, Bird, Bear, Wind, Otter, Deer, and Snake.

Clans follow the rules of the Seminole Constitution. The Seminole tribe's constitution sets up a group that makes the laws. This group, or council, is made up of a chairman, a vice-chairman, and council representatives from each clan. The council is in charge of almost all of the Seminole tribe's activities. The council heads the police department, Seminole citrus groves, museums, and the Water **Resource** Management Department (WRMD).

Address http://www.example.com/WRMD/index.shtml

Search

The Water Resource Management Department (WRMD)

Seminole culture and religion are closely linked to the health of their land. The Seminole tribe believes that if the land dies, their tribe will also die. Because of this belief, they are involved in many projects to help keep their environment healthy. One of their projects is trying to **conserve**, or save, Florida's water. In 2001 Florida faced one of the worst droughts in the state's history. The Seminoles realized that without water, their land would die. They decided to get involved. In October 1987 the council of the Seminole tribe created the Water Resource Management Department (WRMD). The WRMD protects and tests the Seminole's land and water resources. The WRMD makes sure the resources are being used sensibly. They also check that water is not being wasted. The early efforts of the Seminoles to conserve water have greatly helped the state of Florida and Seminole land. But, as Florida and the Seminole tribe continue to grow, the need for water increases. Every drop saved will make a difference for the future of the state.

Seminole people are involved in many different activities in Florida. They even have their own newspaper to keep their members up-to-date with any news.

Favorites History Search Scrapbook

Seminole art is very rich in color. The Seminoles make sure that each painting, doll, and sculpture reflects their culture.

FCAT Connect and Compare

1. Reread the Using Links box on page 369. When should someone click on a link? When should they not? **Using Links**

2. How did the Seminoles' belief that land is the source of their lives help other Floridians? Use details from the article to explain. **Apply**

3. How is the Seminole tribe like the Native American tribe described in *Mystic Horse*? How are they different? Use details from both selections to explain. **Reading/Writing Across Texts**

RESEARCH INQUIRY

Social Studies Activity

Use the Internet to research another Native American tribe that has helped the environment. Write a short summary detailing their efforts.

LOG ON Find out more about Seminoles at **www.macmillanmh.com**

Write About a Special Animal

Writer's Craft

FCAT Dialogue

A conversation between two or more characters in a story is called **dialogue**. Good writers add dialogue to their stories to make the characters more interesting. Dialogue helps you learn about a character's personality.

I introduced my characters at the beginning of the story.

I showed more of the personalities of my characters by adding dialogue.

Coyote Helps the People

by Kaya N.

A boy and his grandfather were sitting in the sun. They didn't know Coyote was listening to them.

"Feel how the Sun warms us," said the boy.

"I wish we had a small piece for winter," his grandfather said.

"Yes, then we would be warm," the boy sighed, thinking how cold his hands and feet would be soon.

Coyote walked up. "I have been to the Fire Beings on the mountain."

The boy laughed. "You! How did you get there?"

"Look, I have brought you a piece of fire." Coyote told him.

Grandfather said, "Thank you, Coyote. Now it's our responsibility to share this with everyone."

Writing Prompt

In some stories, animals have special powers.

Think about an animal in a story with special powers.

Now write a story about an animal with special powers.

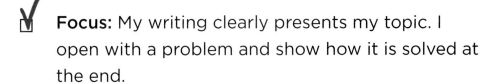

FCAT Writer's Checklist

- ☑ **Focus:** My writing clearly presents my topic. I open with a problem and show how it is solved at the end.
- ☑ **Organization:** My story is told in the order that the events happened.
- ☐ **Support:** I include dialogue that reveals more about my characters' personalities.
- ☑ **Conventions:** I use different verb tenses correctly. My sentences are complete.

Precipitation

Talk About It

What do you think has happened in this photograph?

LOG ON Find out more about precipitation at **www.macmillanmh.com**

Vocabulary

technique	**microscope**
foolishness	**magnify**
inspire	**negatives**
evaporate	**blizzard**

FCAT **Dictionary**

Multiple-Meaning Words are words that have more than one meaning. Use a dictionary to find the different meanings for the word *negatives*.

Let It Snow

by Cynthia Robey

Do you have a **technique** for catching snowflakes? Some people run in circles trying to catch them. Others stand perfectly still with their tongue sticking out. It might look like **foolishness**, but it's fun!

Crystals to Flakes

A snowflake's shape is formed long before it lands on Earth. First an ice crystal forms around a tiny piece of dirt in a cloud. Now it's a snow crystal. The crystal's shape depends on the temperature of the cloud.

Finally, as the crystals fall from the clouds, they stick together to form snowflakes. Each snowflake is made up of 2 to 200 separate snow crystals.

Studying Snowflakes

Snow crystals form into one of seven shapes. You probably know the stellar crystal best. These star-shape crystals are not the most common, but they're the kind that **inspire** the work of most artists.

How can you study snowflakes before they **evaporate** and disappear? First, go outside when it's not windy and about 25°F. Second, bring a piece of dark cloth with you. This will make it easier to see the crystals. Finally, you will need to use a **microscope** to **magnify** the crystal to get a good look at it.

Wilson "Snowflake" Bentley learned how to make the crystals show up in photographs. He cut away the dark parts of the **negatives**.

Dangerous Snowflakes

If conditions are just right, beautiful snowflakes can turn into a dangerous storm called a **blizzard**. In blizzards strong winds can blow the snow around. This causes "whiteout" conditions, making it very difficult to see where you're going.

Always pay attention to the weather. That way you can safely catch and study all the snowflakes you want.

Reread for Comprehension

Evaluate

FCAT **Main Idea and Details** The **main idea** is what the story is about. **Details** support the main idea by explaining or describing it. Figuring out which parts of the story are important can help readers identify the main idea. Reread the selection to find the details that support the main idea. Fill in the Main Idea Web.

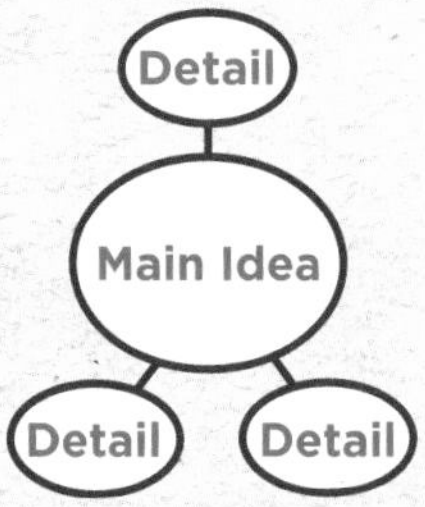

Comprehension

Genre

A **Biography** is a story about the life of a real person written by someone else.

Evaluate

FCAT **Main Idea and Details**

As you read, fill in your Main Idea Web.

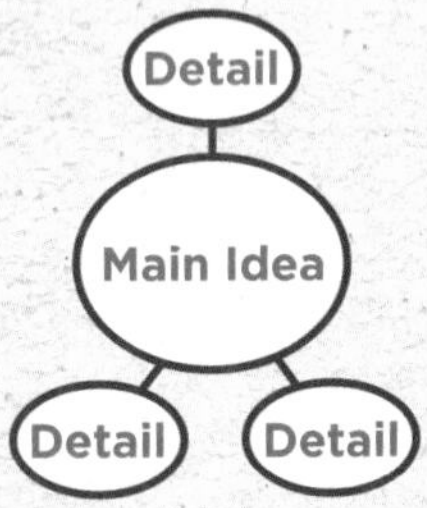

Read to Find Out

What did the world give to Snowflake Bentley, and what did he give to the world?

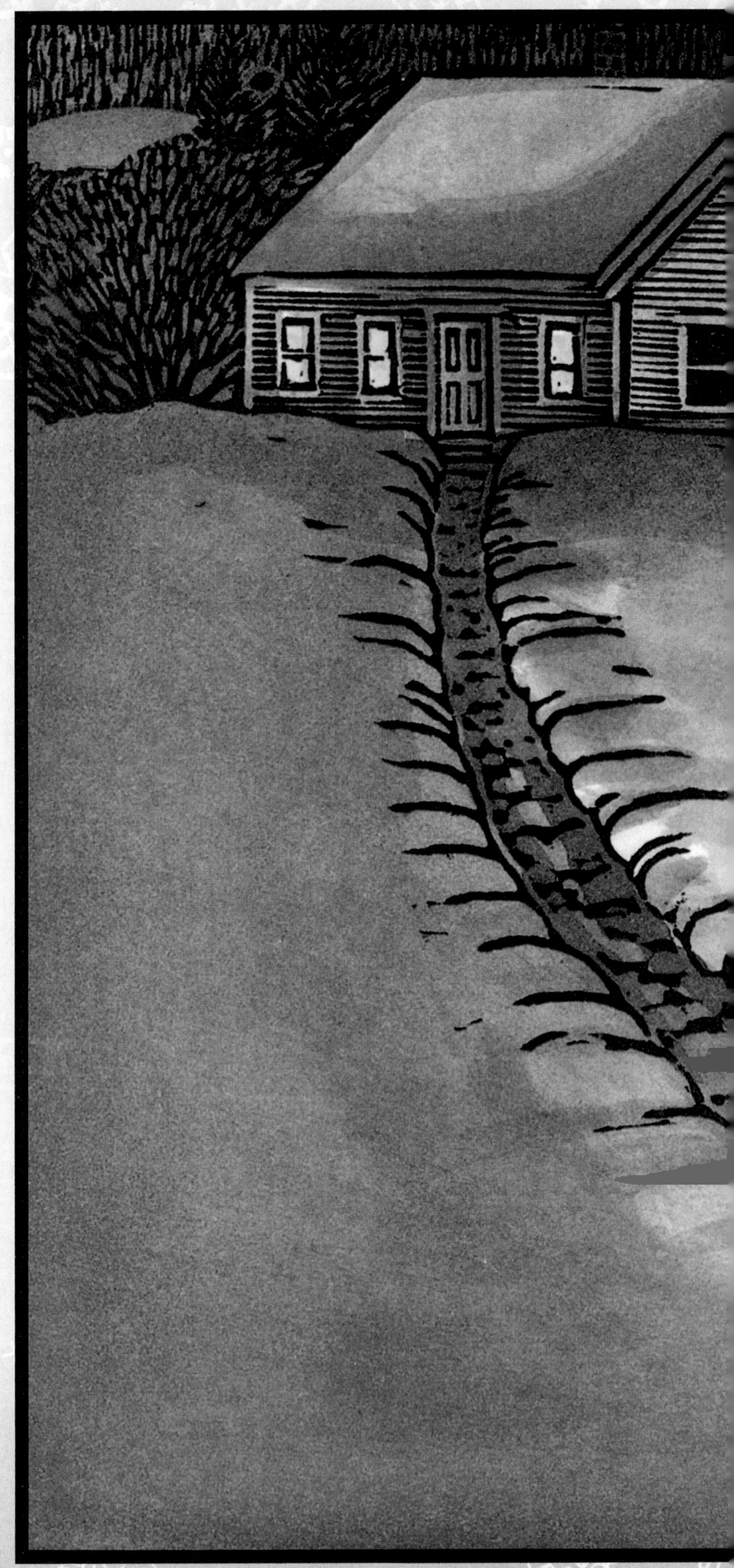

SNOWFLAKE BENTLEY

By Jacqueline Briggs Martin
Illustrated by Mary Azarian

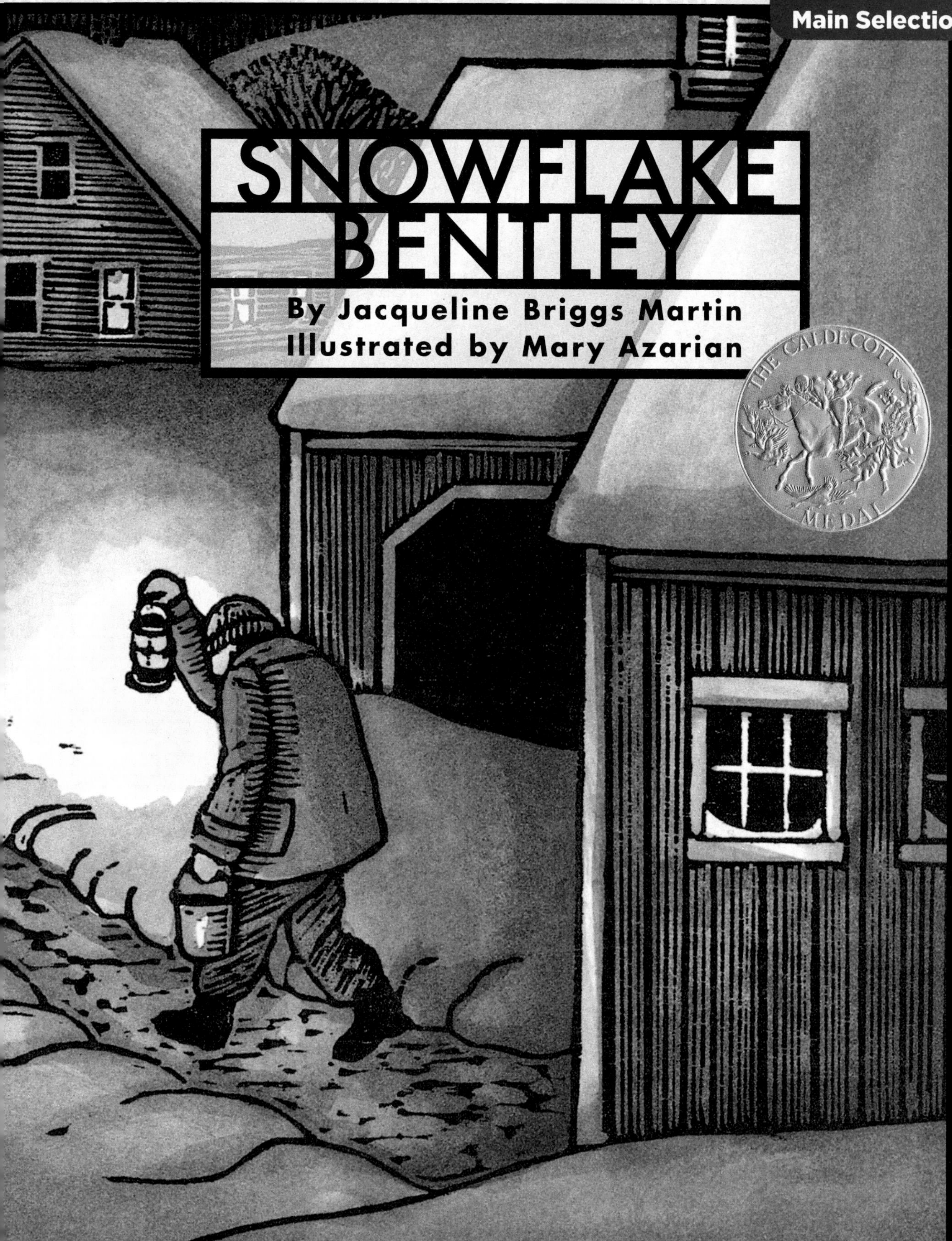

Wilson Bentley was born February 9, 1865, on a farm in Jericho, Vermont, between Lake Champlain and Mount Mansfield, in the heart of the "snowbelt," where the annual snowfall is about 120 inches.

In the days when farmers worked with ox and sled and cut the dark with lantern light, there lived a boy who loved snow more than anything else in the world.

Willie Bentley's happiest days were snowstorm days. He watched snowflakes fall on his mittens, on the dried grass of Vermont farm fields, on the dark metal handle of the barn door. He said snow was as beautiful as butterflies, or apple blossoms.

Willie's mother was his teacher until he was fourteen years old. He attended school for only a few years. "She had a set of encyclopedias," Willie said. "I read them all."

He could net butterflies and show them to his older brother, Charlie. He could pick apple blossoms and take them to his mother. But he could not share snowflakes because he could not save them.

From his boyhood on he studied all forms of moisture. He kept a record of the weather and did many experiments with raindrops.

When his mother gave him an old **microscope**, he used it to look at flowers, raindrops, and blades of grass. Best of all, he used it to look at snow.

While other children built forts and pelted snowballs at roosting crows, Willie was catching single snowflakes. Day after stormy day he studied the icy crystals.

He learned that most crystals had six branches (though a few had three). For each snowflake the six branches were alike. "I found that snowflakes were masterpieces of design," he said. "No one design was ever repeated. When a snowflake melted . . . just that much beauty was gone, without leaving any record behind."

Starting at age fifteen he drew a hundred snow crystals each winter for three winters.

Their intricate patterns were even more beautiful than he had imagined. He expected to find whole flakes that were the same, that were copies of each other. But he never did.

Willie decided he must find a way to save snowflakes so others could see their wonderful designs. For three winters he tried drawing snow crystals. They always melted before he could finish.

The camera made images on large glass **negatives**. Its microscope could **magnify** a tiny crystal from sixty-four to 3,600 times its actual size.

When he was sixteen, Willie read of a camera with its own microscope. "If I had that camera I could photograph snowflakes," he told his mother.

Willie's mother knew he would not be happy until he could share what he had seen.

"Fussing with snow is just **foolishness**," his father said. Still, he loved his son.

When Willie was seventeen his parents spent their savings and bought the camera.

It was taller than a newborn calf, and cost as much as his father's herd of ten cows. Willie was sure it was the best of all cameras.

Even so his first pictures were failures—no better than shadows. Yet he would not quit. Mistake by mistake, snowflake by snowflake, Willie worked through every storm.

Winter ended, the snow melted, and he had no good pictures.

Willie's experiment: He used a very small lens opening, which let only a little light reach the negative, but he kept the lens open for several seconds—up to a minute and a half.

He learned, too, that he could make the snow crystals show up more clearly by using a sharp knife to cut away all the dark parts of the negative around the crystals. This etching meant extra hours of work for each photograph, but Willie didn't mind.

He waited for another season of snow. One day, in the second winter, he tried a new experiment. And it worked!

Willie had figured out how to photograph snowflakes! "Now everyone can see the great beauty in a tiny crystal," he said.

The best snowstorm of his life occurred on Valentine's Day in 1928. He made over a hundred photographs during the two-day storm. He called the storm a gift from King Winter.

But in those days no one cared. Neighbors laughed at the idea of photographing snow.

"Snow in Vermont is as common as dirt," they said. "We don't need pictures."

Willie said the photographs would be his gift to the world.

While other farmers sat by the fire or rode to town with horse and sleigh, Willie studied snowstorms. He stood at the shed door and held out a black tray to catch the flakes.

When he found only jumbled, broken crystals, he brushed the tray clean with a turkey feather and held it out again.

He waited hours for just the right crystal and didn't notice the cold.

If the shed were warm the snow would melt. If he breathed on the black tray the snow would melt. If he twitched a muscle as he held the snow crystal on the long wooden pick the snowflake would break. He had to work fast or the snowflake would **evaporate** before he could slide it into place and take its picture. Some winters he was able to make only a few dozen good pictures.

Some winters he made hundreds.

He learned that each snowflake begins as a speck, much too tiny to be seen. Little bits—molecules—of water attach to the speck to form its branches. As the crystal grows, the branches come together and trap small quantities of air.

FCAT Main Idea and Details
What is the main idea of the second paragraph? What are the supporting details?

Many things affect the way these crystal branches grow. A little more cold, a bit less wind, or a bit more moisture will mean different-shaped branches. Willie said that was why, in all his pictures, he never found two snowflakes alike.

Willie so loved the beauty of nature he took pictures in all seasons.

In the summer his nieces and nephews rubbed coat hangers with sticky pitch from spruce trees. Then Willie could use them to pick up spider webs jeweled with water drops and take their pictures.

On fall nights he would gently tie a grasshopper to a flower so he could find it in the morning and photograph the dew-covered insect.

Willie's nieces and nephews lived on one side of the farmhouse that Willie shared with his brother Charlie. Willie often played the piano as they sang and shared stories and games with them.

But his snow crystal pictures were always his favorites. He gave copies away or sold them for a few cents. He made special pictures as gifts for birthdays.

Many colleges and universities bought lantern slide copies of his photographs and added to their collections each year. Artists and designers used the photographs to **inspire** their own work.

He held evening slide shows on the lawns of his friends. Children and adults sat on the grass and watched while Willie projected his slides onto a sheet hung over a clothesline.

Even today, those who want to learn about snow crystals begin with Wilson Bentley's book, *Snow Crystals*.

By 1926 he had spent $15,000 on his work and received $4,000 from the sale of photographs and slides.

He wrote about snow and published his pictures in magazines. He gave speeches about snow to faraway scholars and neighborhood skywatchers. "You are doing great work," said a professor from Wisconsin.

The little farmer came to be known as the world's expert on snow, "the Snowflake Man." But he never grew rich. He spent every penny on his pictures.

Willie said there were treasures in snow. "I can't afford to miss a single snowstorm," he told a friend. "I never know when I will find some wonderful prize."

Other scientists raised money so Willie could gather his best photographs in a book. When he was sixty-six years old Willie's book—his gift to the world—was published. Still, he was not ready to quit.

Less than a month after turning the first page on his book, Willie walked six miles home in a **blizzard** to make more pictures. He became ill with pneumonia after that walk and died two weeks later.

A monument was built for Willie in the center of town. The girls and boys who had been his neighbors grew up and told their sons and daughters the story of the man who loved snow. Forty years after Wilson Bentley's death, children in his village worked to set up a museum in honor of the farmer-scientist.

And his book has taken the delicate snow crystals that once blew across Vermont, past mountains, over the earth. Neighbors and strangers have come to know of the icy wonders that land on their own mittens—thanks to Snowflake Bentley.

The plaque on the monument says
"SNOWFLAKE"
BENTLEY
Jericho's world famous snowflake authority

For fifty years Wilson A. Bentley, a simple farmer, developed his **technique** of micro-photography to reveal to the world the grandeur and mystery of the snowflake—its universal hexagonal shape and its infinite number of lovely designs.

FCAT **Main Idea and Details**
Willie became famous in his village. List the details that support this.

SNOWFLAKE
BENTLEY

Snapshots of Jacqueline and Mary

Jacqueline Briggs Martin began to write this story after she saw a snowflake and thought about an article she had read about a man who loved snow. Jacqueline saw lots of snow when she was growing up. She lived on a farm in Maine where she enjoyed nature, stories, and history.

Other books illustrated by Mary Azarian

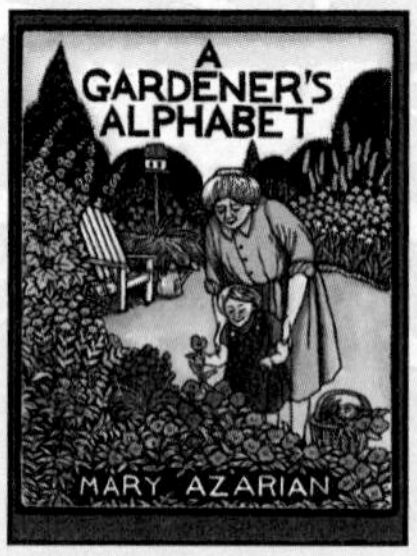

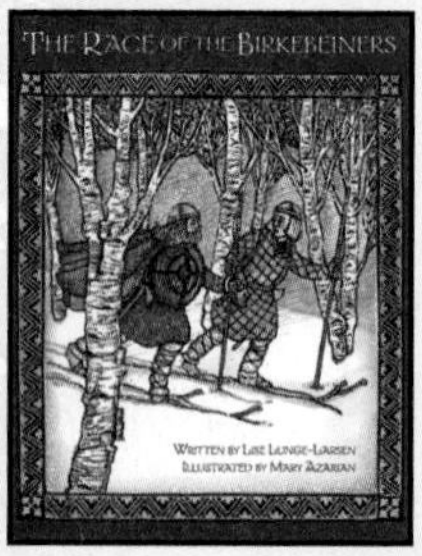

Mary Azarian has also seen a lot of snow. Just like Wilson Bentley, she lives on a farm in Vermont. Mary used her experiences on the farm to create her woodcut illustrations.

LOG ON Find out more about Jacqueline Briggs Martin and Mary Azarian at **www.macmillanmh.com**

FCAT Author's Purpose

Why did Jacqueline Briggs Martin write *Snowflake Bentley*? Was her purpose for writing this biographical piece to inform, to entertain, or to explain something? How do you know?

FCAT Comprehension Check

Summarize

Use your Main Idea Web to summarize *Snowflake Bentley.* Remember to include only the most important information in your summary, such as setting and characters.

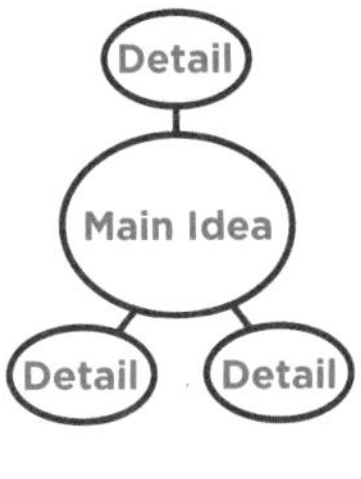

Think and Compare

READ THINK EXPLAIN **1.** Why did Wilson Bentley choose to make snowflake photography his life's work? Use details from the story to explain. **Evaluate: Main Idea and Details**

READ THINK EXPLAIN **2.** Reread pages 384–385. How did Wilson Bentley's parents encourage their son's hobby? How did their encouragement help Bentley to fulfill his life's dream? Explain using details from the story. **Analyze**

3. If you could spend your life studying one thing in nature, what would it be? What **technique** would you use to study it and why? **Synthesize**

4. Why is it important to study the world—even at the microscopic level? Use story details to explain. **Evaluate**

5. Read "Let It Snow" on pages 376–377. How is the information about snow in that selection the same as in *Snowflake Bentley*? How is it different? Explain using details from both selections. **Reading/Writing Across Texts**

FCAT

Poetry

Haiku is poetry that uses three short lines to describe a scene or just one moment. The first and third lines often have five syllables each, and the second line may have seven syllables.

Literary Elements

Imagery is the use of words to create a picture in the reader's mind.

Figurative Language goes beyond the usual meaning of words and uses them to describe something in a new way.

HAIKU

Winter solitude—
in a world of one color
the sound of wind.

—Matsuo Basho

The words "a world of one color" create an image of a snow-covered scene.

Mountains and plains,
all are captured by the snow—
nothing remains.

—Joso

The snow is melting
and the village is flooded
with children.
—Kobayashi Issa

Children do not really flood the village. This figurative language suggests they are running through the streets like water.

No sky at all;
no earth at all—and still
the snowflakes fall....
—Hashin

FCAT Connect and Compare

1. In the haiku by Joso, the word "captured" is figurative language. How does the reader know this? What has really happened to the mountains and plains? **Figurative Language**

2. Reread "No Sky at All," by Hashin. What moment or scene does it describe? **Analyze**

3. When you read these poems, how do they make you feel about snow? How did you feel about snow when you read *Snowflake Bentley*? Compare the two feelings. **Reading/Writing Across Texts**

LOG ON Find out more about haiku at **www.macmillanmh.com**

Write About the Weather

Writer's Craft

FCAT **Vary Sentences**

Good writers **vary sentences** to add variety to their writing. Adding sentences of varying lengths helps make writing more interesting.

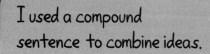

I used a compound sentence to combine ideas.

I included both short and long sentences to add variety to my writing.

Clouds Move In

by Sara K.

Yesterday afternoon was warm and sunny. As I sat in my backyard, I looked at the sky above me. The sky was a bright blue. Every once in a while, white puffy clouds would slowly float by. The warm sun burned brightly in the sky to help make it a perfect spring afternoon.

Then, gray clouds slowly began to move in. Behind them the sky was still blue, but I could see that rain clouds would soon cover the blue of the sky.

The air began to feel cooler. The weather had changed. I knew that the sunny afternoon would soon turn into a rainy night. The rain hasn't stopped yet!

Writing Prompt

Most people have a favorite kind of weather.

Think about your favorite kind of weather.

Now write to tell about your favorite kind of weather.

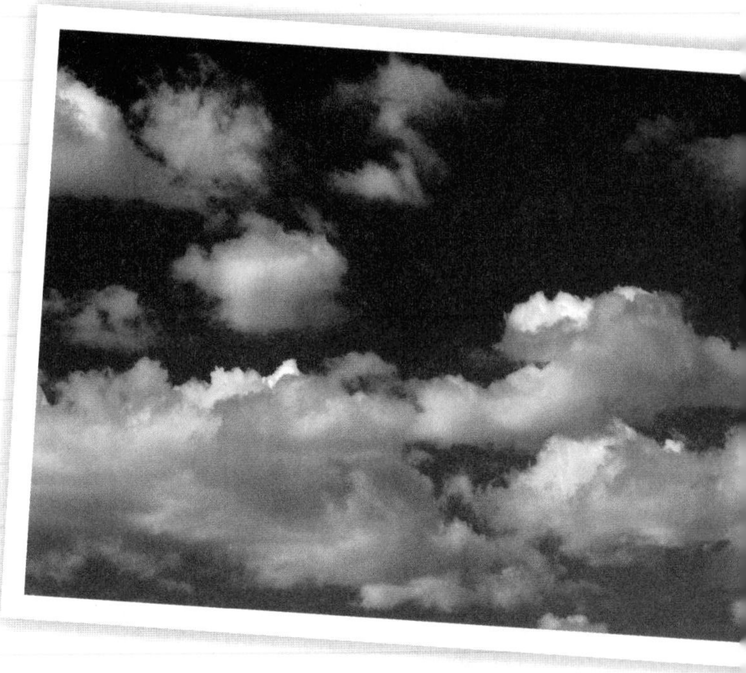

FCAT Writer's Checklist

- ☑ **Focus:** My main idea clearly presents my scientific observations.
- ☑ **Organization:** I tell what happened in order so the reader can easily follow my observations.
- ☑ **Support:** I **vary sentences** to support my topic and to keep the reader engaged and entertained.
- ☑ **Conventions:** I use irregular verbs correctly. My spelling, grammar, and punctuation are correct.

FCAT **Review**

- Chronological Order
- Relevant Facts and Details
- Compare and Contrast
- Context Clues
- Directions

Diary of a Scarecrow's Helper

March 15

Oh no! They're getting rid of Jack Patches! Mom and I planned a visit to the community garden today to help clean up for the spring, and once we arrived, something felt peculiar. At first I couldn't figure it out. Then as I was putting some old planting ties on the garbage pile, I saw a familiar old hat. Our wonderful scarecrow was lying in pieces in the trash.

I talked to Mr. Collins, the garden supervisor. He told me that there was a terrible storm this winter. The metal pole that Jack used to hang on snapped in two because it was rusty and old. Mr. Collins thinks it would be dangerous to try to put Jack back up, so he's getting rid of him.

I'm really going to miss him.

March 16

I keep thinking about Jack Patches lying in the garbage pile. I've got to do something. I can't let him stay there! But what can I do? I called Mr. Collins. He keeps saying that it is not safe to put Jack back up because the metal post is sharp and rusty. Besides, Jack's shirt is a mess. It practically rotted away. And his face is ruined, too. His button eyes fell off and his nose is coming loose.

March 17

I had a dream about Jack Patches. He was holding his nose in his hands and asked me to help him. What can I do?

March 18

I called Mr. Collins again. He agreed to keep Jack for at least a week. Then I talked to my uncle, who is really good with tools and wood. He says it won't be hard to fabricate a new support for Jack.

March 22

Uncle Jorge and I went back to the garden with a brand new post. Mr. Collins agreed that the new post looked very safe and sturdy. Uncle Jorge taught me how to plant a post safely. We placed the post into the concrete and held it there until it hardened, or set, enough that we could remove our hands. Tomorrow the concrete will be set and we can put Jack back together. I brought his face home with me so I can fix it.

March 23

Jack Patches is back! He looks better than ever. Uncle Jorge donated a new shirt to replace the old one that was threadbare and faded. I finished sewing his face together this morning. His shiny new blue button eyes look terrific. He's so happy to be back that he's smiling. Well, he sort of has to because I sewed him that way. But I'm sure everyone who visits the garden and sees him will smile, too!

How to Change a Flat Tire on a Bike

If YOU RIDE A ROAD BIKE, chances are you're going to get flat tires. Sometimes the smallest piece of glass or even a piece of gravel can ruin a leisurely ride on your bike. Other times an unexpected encounter with a pothole can put a quick end to your ride.

To fix a flat tire, you will need a new tube, a pump, and three tire levers. Then, follow these steps:

1. Take the bicycle wheel off the frame of the bike. If the tire is not completely flat, release the rest of the air from it.

2. Place the thin end of the tire lever between the tire and the rim of the wheel.

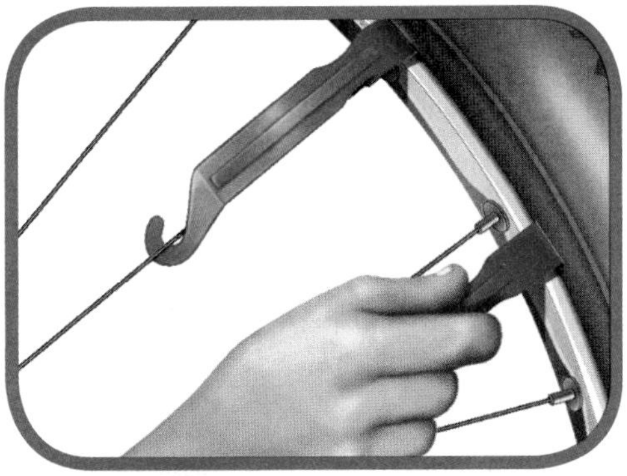

3

Find a spot on the wheel about two spokes over from the last lever. Place the second lever there. Continue to place levers around the rim, removing the first levers as you go.

4

Stop when the tire is free from the wheel. Remove the old tube. Carefully check the tire. Remove any objects. Use your bike pump to put just a little air in your tube. Put the tube into your old tire. Be sure it does not have twists or kinks.

5

Find the hole in the rim of your wheel for the tire valve. Put the tire valve in the tube through the hole as you pull the tire and tube over the wheel. Use your fingers to ease the tire onto the wheel.

6

Use the pump to blow up the tire. The tire should feel firm to the touch. Then put the wheel back on the bicycle frame.

Talk About It

What secrets do you think the boy is sharing with the dog? Where do you think they are?

LOG ON Find out more about dogs at **www.macmillanmh.com**

Man's Best Friend

Vocabulary

neglected **misunderstood**
appreciated **desperate**
risks **endured**
bluffing **obedience**

FCAT Word Parts

Prefixes are added to the beginnings of words to change their meanings.
mis- = "badly" or "wrongly"
misunderstood = "wrongly understood"

Puppy Trouble

by Lana Engell

We got back from the grocery store and found the house a mess. I had **neglected** to close the bathroom door again, and our Saint Bernard, Bernie, had left chewed toilet paper all over the house. Bernie was happily jumping up and running in circles. He had no idea that what he had done while we were away was not **appreciated**.

Bernie had already chewed Mom's favorite handbag and my new pair of shoes. Mom was also concerned that Bernie jumped up on people when I took him out for walks. She didn't want to take **risks** with the little kids on the block, and I couldn't blame her.

Mom said that if Bernie didn't start behaving, we couldn't keep him, and I knew Mom wasn't **bluffing**. I could tell she wasn't kidding. Her message was clear, so there was no way it could be **misunderstood**. Now Bernie was in trouble again.

I was **desperate**. If I didn't think of something really fast, I was going to lose my dog!

Then I had a really wonderful idea. It meant I would have to give up watching some of my favorite TV shows to spend more time with Bernie. In the end, though, if I could keep him, it was worth a try.

Just then Mom finished putting the groceries away. She came into the living room and saw the mess.

"I've had it with this puppy," Mom said in a tired voice. "I'm just about out of patience, Lin."

"I know, Mom," I said. "You've **endured** Bernie's chewing and messes for three months now. But I've never had a pet before. If I'm not training him the right way, then it's not Bernie's fault. Can we try taking him to **obedience** school?" I asked.

And that's just what we did.

Reread for Comprehension

Generate Questions

FCAT **Cause and Effect** A **cause** is why something happens in a story. The **effect** is what happens. By asking questions about cause and effect, readers can learn more about what is happening in the story and why. Fill in your Cause and Effect Chart as you reread the selection.

Cause	Effect

Dear

Comprehension

Genre

A **Fantasy** is a story about characters and settings that could not exist in real life.

Generate Questions

FCAT **Cause and Effect** As you read, fill in your Cause and Effect Chart.

Cause	Effect

Read to Find Out

How close to reality is the picture Ike is painting in his letters to Mrs. LaRue?

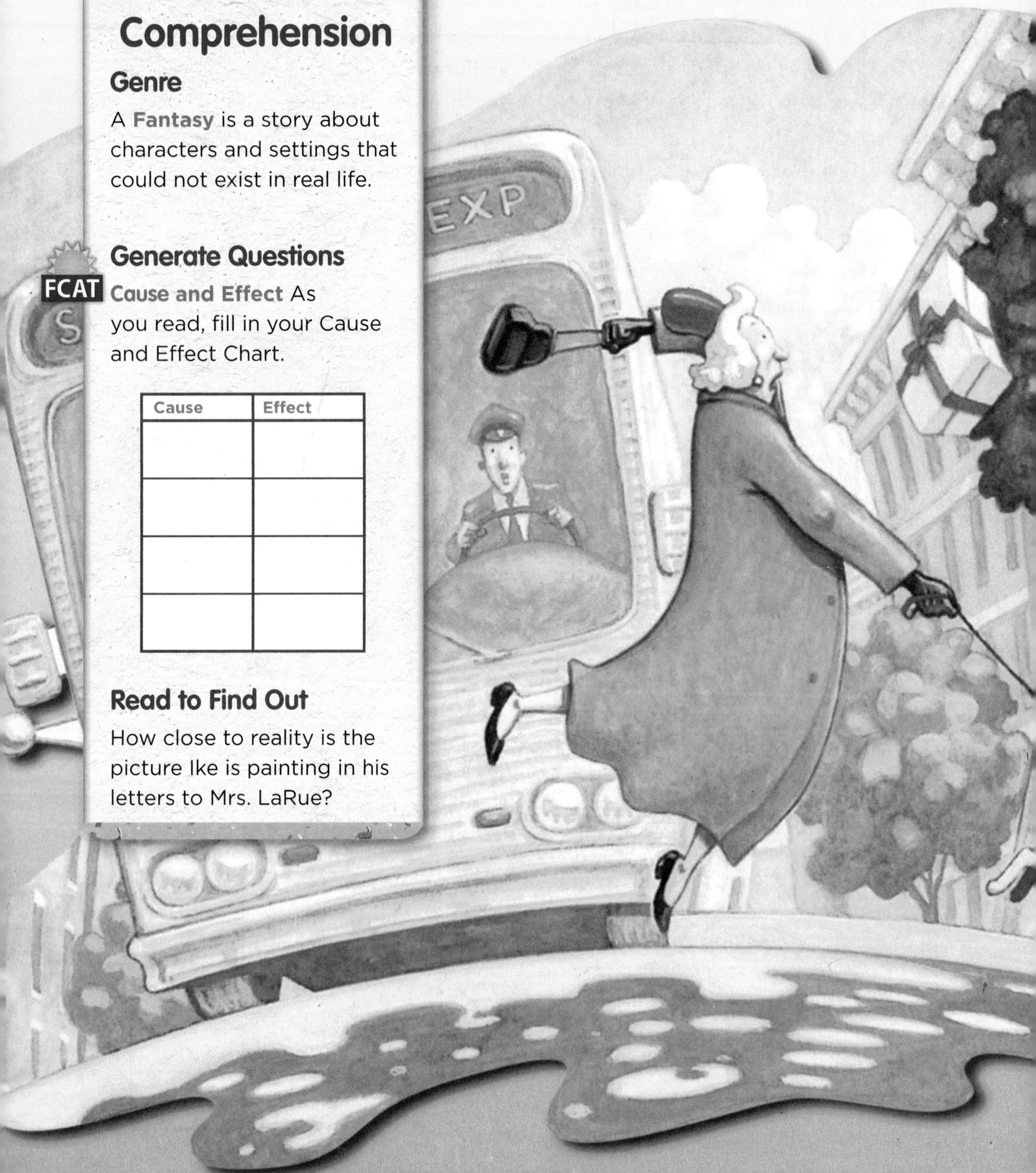

Mrs. LaRue

Letters from Obedience School

Written and Illustrated by

Mark Teague

Award Winning Selection

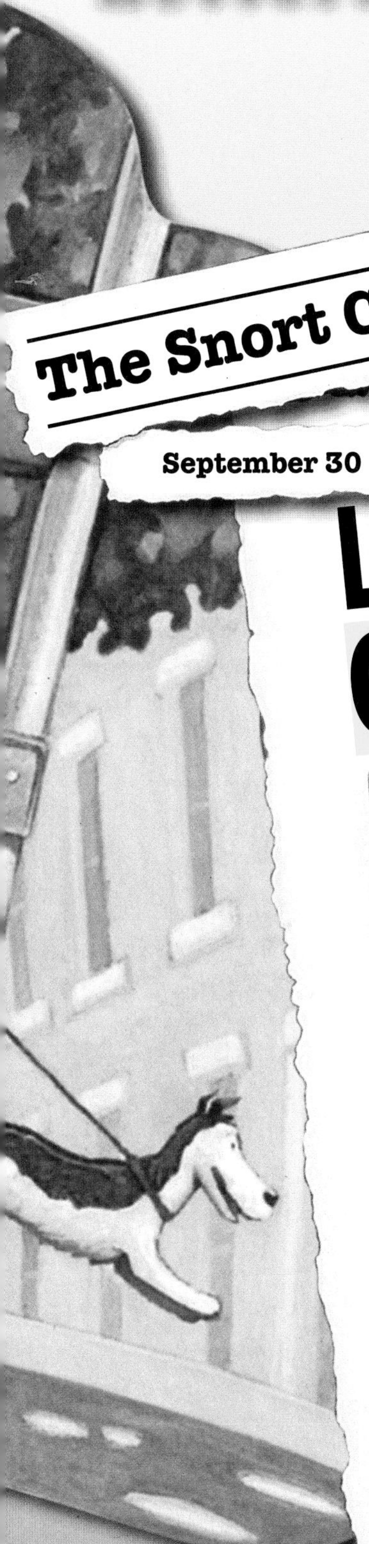

The Snort City Register/Gazette

September 30

LOCAL DOG ENTERS OBEDIENCE SCHOOL

"Ike LaRue"

Citing a long list of behavioral problems, Snort City resident Gertrude R. LaRue yesterday enrolled her dog, Ike, in the Igor Brotweiler Canine Academy.

Established in 1953, the Academy has a history of dealing with such issues.

"I'm at my wit's end!" said Mrs. LaRue. "I love Ike, but I'm afraid he's quite spoiled. He steals food right off the kitchen counter, chases the neighbor's cats, howls whenever I'm away, and last week while I was crossing the street he pulled me down and tore my best camel's hair coat! I just don't know what else to do!"

School officials were unavailable for comment . . .

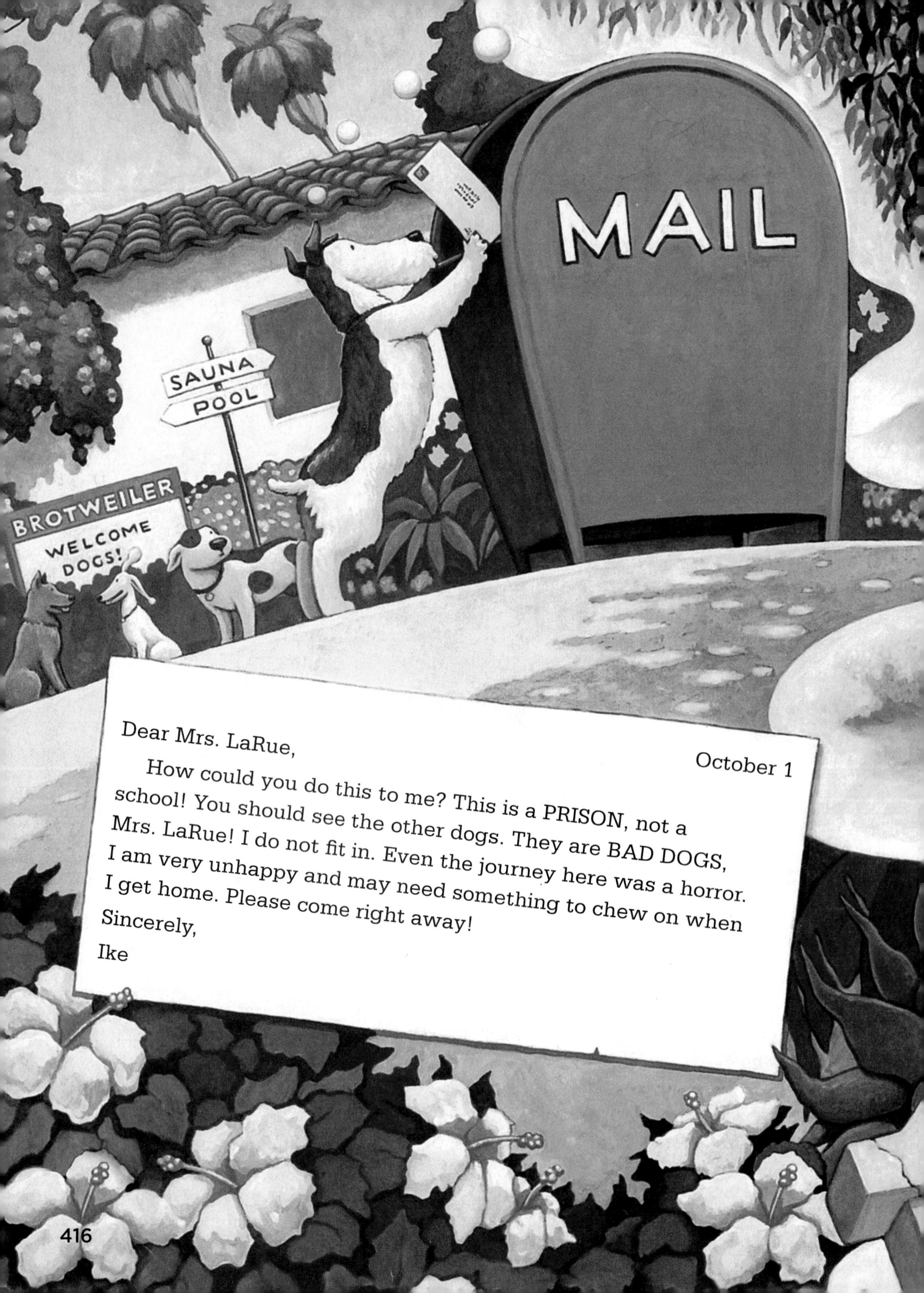

Dear Mrs. LaRue,

October 1

How could you do this to me? This is a PRISON, not a school! You should see the other dogs. They are BAD DOGS, Mrs. LaRue! I do not fit in. Even the journey here was a horror. I am very unhappy and may need something to chew on when I get home. Please come right away!

Sincerely,

Ike

BROTWEILER
IGOR
BROTWEILER
CANINE
ACADEMY
"WE AIM TO TAME"
WARNING!
PRISONERS
ON BOARD
BADDOG
KEEP OUT
IGOR
BROTWEILER
CANINE
ACADEMY

October 2

Dear Mrs. LaRue,

Were you really upset about the chicken pie? You know, you might have discussed it with me. You could have said, “Ike, don’t eat the chicken pie. I’m saving it for dinner.” Would that have been so difficult? It would have prevented a lot of hard feelings.

Needless to say, I am being horribly mistreated. You say I should be patient and accept that I’ll be here through the term. Are you aware that the term lasts TWO MONTHS? Do you know how long that is in dog years?

Sincerely,

Ike

FCAT Cause and Effect
What caused Ike to be sent to obedience school?

October 3

Dear Mrs. LaRue,

I'd like to clear up some misconceptions about the Hibbins' cats. First, they are hardly the little angels Mrs. Hibbins makes them out to be. Second, how should I know what they were doing out on the fire escape in the middle of January? They were being a bit melodramatic, don't you think, the way they cried and refused to come down? It's hard to believe they were really sick for three whole days, but you know cats.

Your dog,

Ike

October 4

Dear Mrs. LaRue,

You should see what goes on around here. The way my teach — I mean WARDEN, Miss Klondike, barks orders is shocking. Day after day I'm forced to perform the most meaningless tasks. Today it was "sit" and "roll over," all day long. I flatly refused to roll over. It's ridiculous. I won't do it. Of course I was SEVERELY punished.

And another thing: Who will help you cross the street while I'm away? You know you have a bad habit of not looking both ways. Think of all the times I've saved you. Well, there was that one time, anyway. I must say you weren't very grateful, complaining on and on about the tiny rip in your ratty old coat. But the point is, you need me!

Yours,

Ike

Dear Mrs. LaRue,

October 5

The GUARDS here are all caught up in this "good dog, bad dog" thing. I hear it constantly: "Good dog, Ike. Don't be a bad dog, Ike." Is it really so good to sit still like a lummox all day? Nevertheless, I refuse to be broken!

Miss Klondike has taken my typewriter. She claims it disturbs the other dogs. Does anybody care that the other dogs disturb ME?

Yours,

Ike

Dear Mrs. LaRue,

October 6

Were the neighbors really complaining about my howling? It is hard to imagine. First, I didn't howl that much. You were away those nights, so you wouldn't know, but trust me, it was quite moderate. Second, let's recall that these are the same neighbors who are constantly waking ME up in the middle of the afternoon with their loud vacuuming. I say we all have to learn to get along.

My life here continues to be a nightmare. You wouldn't believe what goes on in the cafeteria.

Sincerely,

Ike

P.S. I don't want to alarm you, but the thought of escape has crossed my mind!

October 7

Dear Mrs. LaRue,

I hate to tell you this, but I am terribly ill. It started in my paw, causing me to limp all day. Later I felt queasy, so that I could barely eat dinner (except for the yummy gravy). Then I began to moan and howl. Finally, I had to be taken to the vet. Dr. Wilfrey claims that he can't find anything wrong with me, but I am certain I have an awful disease. I must come home at once.

Honestly yours,

Ike

FCAT Cause and Effect
What effect does obedience school have on Ike?

BROTWEILER
PUMPKIN FESTIVAL
THE
BIRDMAN
OF
ALCATRAZ

October 8

Dear Mrs. LaRue,

Thank you for the lovely get well card. Still, I'm a little surprised that you didn't come get me. I know what Dr. Wilfrey says, but is it really wise to take **risks** with one's health? I could have a relapse, you know.

With fall here, I think about all the fine times we used to have in the park. Remember how sometimes you would bring along a tennis ball? You would throw it and I would retrieve it EVERY TIME, except for once when it landed in something nasty and I brought you back a stick instead. Ah, how I miss those days.

Yours truly,

Ike

P.S. Imagine how awful it is for me to be stuck inside my tiny cell!

P.P.S. I still feel pretty sick.

October 9

Dear Mrs. LaRue,

By the time you read this I will be gone. I have decided to attempt a daring escape! I'm sorry it has come to this, since I am really a very good dog, but frankly you left me no choice. How sad it is not to be **appreciated**! From now on I'll wander from town to town without a home — or even any dog food, most likely. Such is the life of a **desperate** outlaw. I will try to write to you from time to time as I carry on with my life of hardship and danger.

Your lonely fugitive,

Ike

The Snort City Register/Gazette

October 10

LARUE ESCAPES DOGGY DETENTION

Former Snort City resident Ike LaRue escaped last night from the dormitory at the Igor Brotweiler Canine Academy. The dog is described as "toothy" by local police. His current whereabouts are unknown.

"To be honest, I thought he was **bluffing** when he told me he was planning to escape," said a visibly upset Gertrude R. LaRue, the dog's owner. "Ike tends to be a bit melodramatic, you know. Now I can only pray that he'll come back."

Asked if she would return Ike to Brotweiler Academy, Mrs. LaRue said that she would have to wait and see. "He's a good dog basically, but he can be difficult. . . ."

October 11 — Somewhere in America

Dear Mrs. LaRue,

I continue to suffer horribly as I roam this barren wasteland. Who knows where my wanderings will take me now? Hopefully to someplace with yummy food! Remember the special treats you used to make for me? I miss them. I miss our nice, comfy apartment. But mostly, I miss you!

Your sad dog,

Ike

P.S. I even miss the Hibbins' cats, in a way.

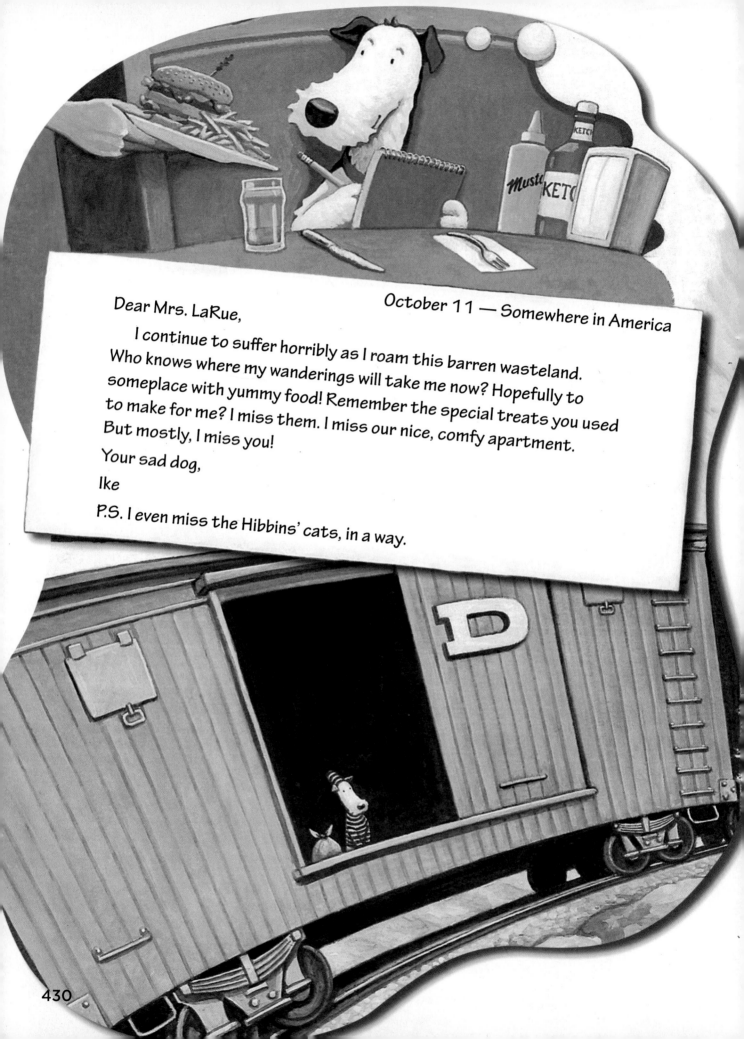

October 12 — Still Somewhere

Dear Mrs. LaRue,

The world is a hard and cruel place for a "stray" dog. You would scarcely believe the misery I've **endured**. So I have decided to return home. You may try to lock me up again, but that is a risk I must take. And frankly, even more than myself, I worry about you. You may not know it, Mrs. LaRue, but you need a dog!

Your **misunderstood** friend,

Ike

GET U2
MORE

The Snort City Register / Gazette

October 13

HERO DOG SAVES OWNER!

Ike LaRue, until recently a student at the Igor Brotweiler Canine Academy, returned to Snort City yesterday in dramatic fashion. In fact he arrived just in time to rescue his owner, Gertrude R. LaRue of Second Avenue, from an oncoming truck. Mrs. LaRue had made the trip downtown to purchase a new camel's hair coat. Apparently she **neglected** to look both ways before stepping out into traffic.

The daring rescue was witnessed by several onlookers, including patrolman Newton Smitzer. "He rolled right across two lanes of traffic to get at her," said Smitzer. "It was really something. I haven't seen rolling like that since I left the police academy."

Mrs. LaRue was unhurt in the incident, though her coat was badly torn. “I don’t care about that,” she said. “I’m just happy to have my Ike back home where he belongs!”

LaRue said she plans to throw a big party for the dog. “All the neighbors will be there, and I’m going to serve Ike’s favorite dishes. . . .”

“. . . I’ll bet he can’t wait to taste the chicken pie. . . .”

Write Home About Mark Teague

Mark Teague says that this story is one of his favorites. He had lots of fun pretending he was Ike and writing from a dog's point of view. Mark based Ike on two dogs he and his brother had. One dog loved to eat, the other dog liked to play tricks. Now Mark has cats. He put them in this story, too. Mark gets ideas for many of his books from things he did as a boy. Then he adds a twist or two to make his stories really funny.

Other books by Mark Teague

LOG ON Find out more about Mark Teague at **www.macmillanmh.com**

FCAT Author's Purpose

What clues can you use to determine Mark Teague's purpose for writing *Dear Mrs. LaRue*? Did the author want to explain, entertain, or inform the reader?

FCAT Comprehension Check

Summarize

Summarize *Dear Mrs. LaRue*. Use your Cause and Effect Chart to help you include the most important story events in your summary. Be sure to tell who is writing the letters and why.

Cause	Effect

Think and Compare

1. Ike escaped from **obedience** school. What effect does the escape have on him? Explain using details from the story. **Generate Questions: Cause and Effect**

2. Reread pages 415 and 434. Mrs. LaRue's coat is badly torn twice. Compare her reaction the first time it is torn to her reaction the second time. How are her reactions different? Why are they different? Explain using details from the story. **Analyze**

3. If you were Mrs. LaRue, would you believe what Ike said in his letters? Why or why not? **Apply**

4. Sometimes people exaggerate like Ike does. Why do you think people do this? **Analyze**

5. Read "Puppy Trouble" on pages 412–413. Compare it with *Dear Mrs. LaRue*. Which story is a fantasy, and which is realistic? How can the reader tell? Use details from both selections to explain. **Reading/Writing Across Texts**

Science

Genre

News Stories give up-to-date information about world events.

FCAT

Text Feature

Line Graphs show changes over time.

Content Vocabulary

intelligent
impressive
demonstrated
exposure
phrases

DOG AMAZES SCIENTISTS!

Rico the border collie has a knack for learning words.

by Kim Christopher

GERMANY – A border collie named Rico is amazing scientists with his knowledge of human language. Rico recognizes at least 200 words and quickly learns and remembers even more.

Rico began his training when he was ten months old. His owner, Susanne Baus, put toys in different places and had Rico fetch them by name. She rewarded Rico with food or by playing with him. Rico continued to learn more and more new words. Scientists first noticed Rico when he showed off his talent on a popular German game show.

Border collies are **intelligent** medium-size dogs that have a lot of energy and are easily trained. They like to stay busy, and they like to please their owners.

Even though nine-year-old Rico knows 200 words, he doesn't know as many words as even the average two-year-old person does. Human nine-year-olds know thousands and thousands of words, and they learn about ten new words a day. Still, Rico's ability to find objects by name is so **impressive** that scientists wanted to study him.

Number of Words a Child Understands

Reading a Line Graph

This graph shows how many words a child understands at different ages.

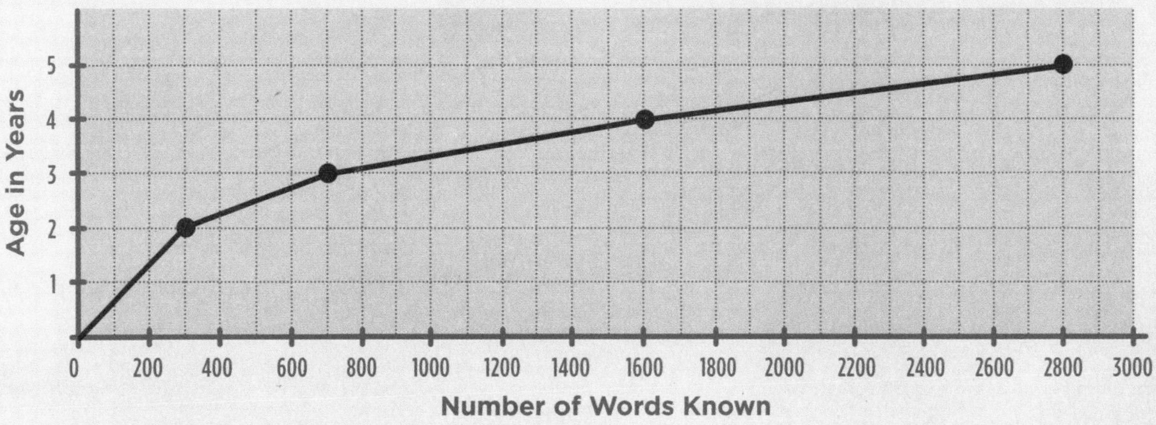

Humans have the ability to learn words far more quickly than even the smartest dog.

Scientists learned a lot about Rico as they watched him fetch familiar toys by name. Then Rico **demonstrated** something amazing. He showed scientists that he could pick out by name toys he had never seen before! Scientists put some familiar toys in a room. They added a new toy. Rico's owner asked him to fetch the new toy. Rico picked out the right toy most of the time in these tests.

Scientists think that Rico connects new words to new things. Since Rico already knows the names of old toys, he knows he should pick out a new toy when he hears a new word.

Rico can also remember the name of a new toy after just one **exposure**, or experience, with that toy. This shows scientists that even though animals are unable to talk, they can understand words. Rico's vocabulary seems to be as large as that of animals that have been trained in language. Those animals include apes, sea lions, dolphins, and parrots.

Most dog owners will tell you that their pets are very smart. But just how smart is Rico? Is he an outstanding dog in a breed known to be very intelligent? Or is Rico a "dog genius"?

Scientists are now studying Rico to learn more. They want to know if Rico can understand **phrases** such as "put the toy in the box." Rico's owner thinks that he can. The answers to questions about Rico's intelligence are still to come. The outcome of the study will be interesting to both scientists and dog owners all over the world.

FCAT Connect and Compare

1. Look at the line graph on page 439. About how many words does a four-year-old understand? **Reading a Line Graph**

2. What other animals should scientists test for language skills? How should they test them? **Synthesize**

3. Think about this article and *Dear Mrs. LaRue.* What would Rico say if he wrote a letter to his owner? Explain using details from both selections. **Reading/Writing Across Texts**

RESEARCH INQUIRY

Science Activity

Research border collies. Report to the class where this breed originated and what it does best.

LOG ON Find out more about border collies at **www.macmillanmh.com**

Write About Solving a Problem

Writer's Craft

FCAT Organize Ideas

Good writers **organize ideas** about their topic. This makes their writing clear and easy to follow.

I will organize my ideas around my topic.

I organized ideas to make my story easy to follow.

Keep That Collar On

by Tammy G.

Our dog, Daisy, always used to slip out of her collar and run away. When she started to do this, we would chase her down and scold her.

My family discussed how to solve the problem. We listed different ideas we had. We crossed out the ideas that wouldn't work, like my brother's idea that we should start skipping some of Daisy's walks. Then we chose the best one. We got a stretchy collar, so it would stay on Daisy better. The problem was solved!

Writing Prompt

People face all kinds of problems.

Think about a problem you faced and the steps you took to solve it.

Now write to explain a problem you faced and the steps you took to solve it.

FCAT Writer's Checklist

- ☑ **Focus:** My topic sentence clearly presents my problem.
- ☐ **Organization:** I **organize ideas** to make my writing clear and easy to follow.
- ☑ **Support:** I use detail sentences to include the steps I took to solve my problem.
- ☑ **Conventions:** My pronouns and their antecedents agree. My spelling and grammar are correct.

Talk About It

Braille changed the lives of many people. What challenges might this person have faced if Louis Braille had not come up with this creative solution?

LOG ON Find out more about Braille at **www.macmillanmh.com**

CREATIVE SOLUTIONS

Through Elizabeth's Eyes

by Theresa Wisniewski

Vocabulary

cautiously	**wisdom**
faint	**fade**
disguised	**jealousy**
crisscrossed	

FCAT Word Parts

Word Families include words that have the same base word.

Wise, wiser, and *wisdom* are in the same word family.

Elizabeth got out of bed, stretched, and dressed. She ate her favorite breakfast of scrambled eggs, toast, and juice. Her mother gave her a kiss before opening the front door and wishing her daughter a good day.

Elizabeth, **cautiously** tapping along, made her way down the sidewalk to her friend Katrina's front door. Elizabeth used to attend a special school for the blind. Today she was joining Katrina at Washington Carver Elementary. Katrina was a bit nervous for her friend. This was sure to be a difficult day for Elizabeth.

"Here comes my brother," Elizabeth remarked.

Katrina looked around but saw no one. Then, suddenly, Joshua came around the next corner on his skateboard. "How did you know Joshua was coming?" Katrina asked.

"From the rattle of the loose wheel on his board," replied Elizabeth. "I'd know it anywhere."

Katrina listened again until she heard that one **faint** sound **disguised** among all the much louder noises on the street. "You're amazing, Elizabeth," she exclaimed.

Joshua **crisscrossed** the sidewalk. "Hey Sis," he called out as he rode by. "Good luck today!"

After Joshua rode away, Elizabeth turned to Katrina and asked, "Do you have any words of **wisdom** for me?"

"Well, to tell you the truth, I was feeling a bit nervous for you."

Elizabeth smiled as she said, "It was scary when my vision began to **fade**. I often felt a twinge of **jealousy** toward the people around me who could see."

"And how do you feel now?"

"Well, I used to think I couldn't do everything," explained Elizabeth. "But now I know that I can do most things. I just need a little more learning time."

Katrina gave her friend's hand a squeeze. "I'm not feeling so nervous about your first day. I think you'll do just fine," she said.

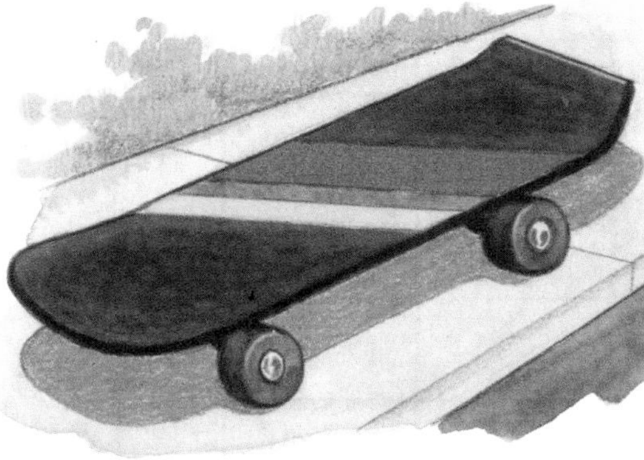

Reread for Comprehension

Generate Questions

FCAT **Compare Characters** A **character's** traits can change as a story develops. Good readers ask questions about the characters and how they change throughout the story. Fill in your Character Chart as you reread the selection. The chart can help you **compare** a character's traits from the beginning of the story to how they change or stay the same at the end of the story.

Event	Character Trait

Comprehension

Genre

Realistic Fiction is a made-up story that could have happened in real life.

Generate Questions

FCAT **Compare Characters** As you read, fill in your Character Chart.

Event	Character Trait

Read to Find Out

What can a blind man and a young hunter learn from each other?

The Blind Hunter

written and illustrated by
KRISTINA RODANAS

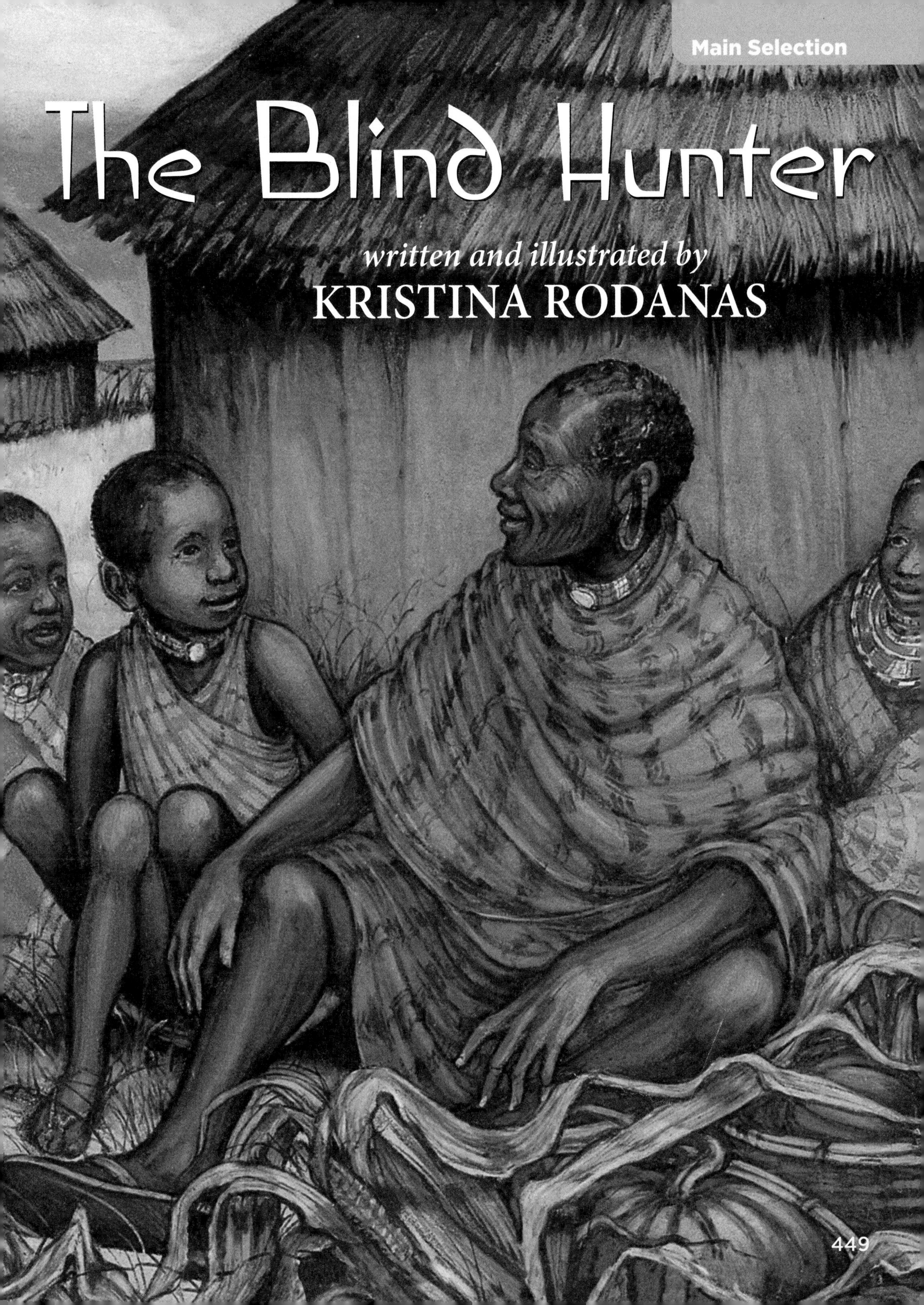

In Africa, not so many years ago, a man named Chirobo lived all by himself in a village of round huts. Each day he went to work in his garden, carefully tending rows of sunflowers, pumpkins, and corn. As he worked he sang sweet songs, and birds of many colors flew out of the trees just to hear him sing.

Chirobo was known to be wise and very kind. People often came to him with questions, for it was said that his answers were never wrong. When children came to visit, he always stopped what he was doing so he could laugh with them and listen to their stories.

Everyone in the village liked this gentle man with the warm smile. Hardly anyone ever seemed to notice that he was blind.

Early one evening, as Chirobo sat stirring a pot of stew, a stranger paused nearby to admire his garden. "Your crops are as beautiful as they are bountiful!" he exclaimed.

Chirobo beamed with pride and asked the young man if he had traveled far. The stranger explained that he was on a hunting trip. He was called Muteye and had come from a village a half day's walk from the west.

"When I return to my home, I will have a sack full of fat birds on my back," he boasted. "Then I will be welcomed as a great hunter!"

"Before my eyes began to **fade** I, too, was a hunter," said Chirobo. "Come sit with me and eat some of this fine stew. We will have much to talk about."

Muteye gladly accepted Chirobo's offer and joined him beside the cooking fire. He stayed for many hours sharing tales, laughing, and singing.

When the moon had climbed high above the distant trees, the young man got to his feet.

"Thank you, my friend, for your kindness," he said. "Is there anything I can do for you in return?"

Chirobo was silent for a few moments. "It would make me very happy if I could go hunting with you," he replied.

The young man laughed and said, "I will not hunt with a man who cannot see."

"I will be no trouble," Chirobo assured him. "I know how to see in other ways."

"Very well, then," said the young man. "Tomorrow, when the sun rises, we will go hunting. You may use one of my traps. Whatever you catch will be yours to keep."

FCAT **Compare Characters**

How does being blind affect Chirobo's life, and how is his life different from Muteye's?

At the first light of dawn, the two men went out into the bush. The young man led the way, holding the end of a long, straight walking stick. Behind him the blind man followed, clutching the other end. They walked along a narrow path that wound through groves of crooked trees.

All of a sudden, Chirobo pulled back on the walking stick. He stood stone still, his hands cupped behind his ears. "We must be careful," he whispered. "There is a leopard nearby."

The young man gazed all around but could not see the leopard. Then he glanced upward, where a strange pattern caught his eye.

Above the path, draped along an acacia limb, a large cat lay sleeping.

When they had safely passed the sleeping beast, Muteye asked, "How does a man who lives in darkness know when a leopard is near?"

Chirobo answered simply, "I know how to see with my ears."

The two men walked on without speaking, into a dense forest where the cool air echoed with the sound of a rushing stream. Again Chirobo tugged at the walking stick, stopping in his tracks. He tilted his head and breathed deeply.

"We must be careful," he warned. "There are warthogs around."

The young man looked in all directions but could not see them.

He hurried to the crest of a nearby hill and peered down through the brush. To his surprise, a herd of warthogs trotted into view, their sharp tusks flashing in the midday sun.

After the two hunters had safely passed the wild pigs, Muteye asked, "How does a man who lives in darkness know when there are warthogs about?"

The blind man smiled and said, "I know how to see with my nose."

They continued on into a wide valley that was thick with thorn bushes and the sweet scent of flowers. Once again, Chirobo gave the walking stick a tug and paused, his feet spread wide beneath him. He fell to his knees and placed his hands upon the ground.

"We must be careful," he murmured. "There are rhinos coming this way."

Muteye glanced about the thicket but could not see the rhinos.

Cautiously, he pushed aside the dense bushes and scanned the surrounding landscape. All of a sudden, a pair of rhinos appeared, stomping through the tall grass.

When the hunters had safely passed the two creatures, the young man turned and faced his friend. He asked, "How does a man who lives in darkness know when there are rhinos approaching?"

Quietly, Chirobo gave his answer, "I know how to see with my skin."

Together the men made their way deeper into the valley until they reached a shallow pond. Countless tracks of birds **crisscrossed** the soft, muddy bank.

"Birds come here for water," observed Muteye. "It is a good place to set our traps."

Following his friend's instructions, Chirobo placed his trap near the edge of the pond while the other man set his trap a short distance away. After he had **disguised** both traps, the young man said, "We will camp nearby and return tomorrow. Then we will see what we have caught."

That night they talked about many things. Muteye grew to admire the blind man's **wisdom** and asked him questions about which he had wondered for a long time.

Early the next morning, they returned to their hunting place. Chirobo knew right away that they had been successful. Excited, he cried, "There are birds in our traps. I can hear them!"

The young man checked his own trap first and discovered that he had caught a small, thin quail. Although he was disappointed, he carefully removed it and put it into a goatskin sack. Then he went to check the other trap.

As he kneeled down to look inside, his heart filled with **jealousy**. The blind man's trap contained a large duck, fat enough to feed a hungry jackal.

For a few moments Muteye hesitated as he considered the two birds and wondered, "How would a man who lives in darkness ever know which bird belonged to him?"

His mind made up, he quickly switched the thin bird for the plump one.

"Your bird is the larger of the two," he said as he handed the quail over to his companion. "It will make a fine meal."

Chirobo stroked the bird's scraggly wings and thoughtfully passed his fingers along its bony back and breast. Without speaking, he put it into his own sack.

Then the men gathered their traps and began the journey back to the village.

In silence they walked and walked, until they stopped to rest beneath an old baobab tree. Muteye was eager to continue the conversation of the night before, so he took the opportunity to ask his friend a question that had worried him since he was a small boy.

"Why do people fight each other?" he inquired.

Chirobo thought about his answer for a long time. When at last he began to speak, his voice was full of sadness.

He said slowly, "People fight because they take from each other what does not belong to them—as you have just done to me."

The young man was stunned by Chirobo's response. He tried to speak, but the words caught in his throat. Deeply ashamed, he reached for his sack and took out the large duck. He gently placed it into the blind man's hands.

In a **faint** voice, Muteye asked, "How does a man who has been unkind earn the forgiveness of his friend?"

Chirobo's blind eyes seemed to look deep into the young hunter's soul. He said, "By learning to see with his heart—as you have just done with me."

FCAT Compare Characters
What was the most important way that Muteye learned to see?

Words of Wisdom About Kristina

Kristina Rodanas decided to write this story after she read a similar story in a collection of African folk tales. Kristina thought the tale had a special message worth sharing with readers all over the world.

Other books by Kristina Rodanas

LOG ON Find out more about Kristina Rodanas at **www.macmillanmh.com**

FCAT Author's Purpose

What was the author's purpose for writing *The Blind Hunter*? Do you think Kristina Rodanas mainly wanted to explain something, to entertain, or inform the reader? How do you know? Point to clues in the story that support your answer.

FCAT Comprehension Check

Summarize

Summarize *The Blind Hunter*. Use your Character Chart to help you discuss story events. Include the main characters and the setting in your summary.

Event	Character Trait

Think and Compare

READ THINK EXPLAIN

1. What happened in the story to show Muteye how to "see"? Why is this important to Muteye's character? Use story details to explain. **Generate Questions: Compare Characters**

READ THINK EXPLAIN

2. Reread page 453 of *The Blind Hunter.* Chirobo tells Muteye that he knows how to see in other ways. What are the ways Chirobo can see? How does he show that in the story? Explain using details from the story. **Analyze**
3. If you could meet Chirobo, what would you ask him? **Apply**
4. What would happen if more people solved their problems with **wisdom** the way Chirobo does? Use details from the story to explain. **Apply**
5. Read "Through Elizabeth's Eyes" on pages 446–447. How are Elizabeth and Chirobo alike? Use details from both stories to explain. **Reading/Writing Across Texts**

Social Studies

Genre

Magazine Articles give facts and information about interesting topics.

FCAT **Text Feature**

A **Glossary** defines selected words used in a text.

Content Vocabulary

devices
limited
refreshes
microphone
accessories

Make Life Easier for Everybody

by Adam Alexander

Our world changes every day. New inventions make life easier, better, and a lot more fun. People with disabilities benefit from new technology too. There are now many tools and **devices** that help them do what they want to do. Here are just a few.

At Home

At one time, people with disabilities were **limited** in what they could do at home. Many simple activities were difficult or impossible. With today's technology, they can do more. From faucet grippers to automated doors, handy devices now make working and relaxing at home a *lot* easier.

Using a Glossary

A **glossary** is an alphabetized list of definitions for difficult words or technical terms found within a text. A glossary usually appears at the back of a book and gives the same kind of information as a dictionary.

de·vice (di vīs´) *n.* something made for a particular purpose. The *device* permitted people to use the telephone without having to hold the handset. *syn.* invention, mechanism.

de·vise (di vīz´) *v.* to think out; invent.

At Play

Do you enjoy skiing, biking, or playing sports? So do people with disabilities. Today they can find cleverly designed pieces of equipment for almost *any* activity.

Winter sports lovers can fly down ski slopes on sit skis. The skis lift up so skiers can get onto the chairlift. For water skiers, there are specially designed boards. And two-wheel hand bikes make bike riding exciting and fun. There are even short golf clubs for use with wheelchairs!

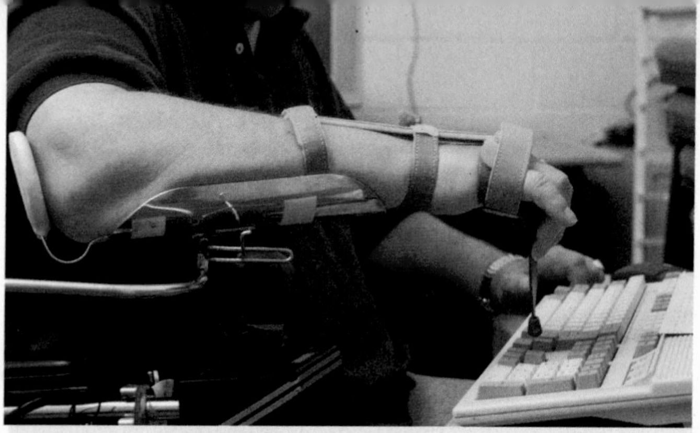

At the Computer

Computers play an important part in our lives today. Thanks to new technology, people with disabilities can use the computer for fun, learning, and communicating with others.

For people who find it hard to type, keyboards have been designed with special keys or spacing. There are even on-screen keyboards. These work using touch, a pointer, or a mouse.

People with limited or no sight can link a Braille display to their computer. Information from the computer is sent to the display. The display forms raised Braille characters that are read by touch. After each line is read, the display **refreshes**. The old line drops down and a new line of characters lifts up.

Computer programs for people with disabilities are being designed all the time. Some programs read aloud what is on a computer screen. Other programs write text as a person speaks into a **microphone**.

Getting Around

Many people with limited mobility use wheelchairs to get around. There are many kinds of wheelchairs, and many wheelchair **accessories**, or "add-ons." Accessories include special wheels and support arms for things like cameras and fishing poles. There are even wheelchairs designed for basketball, tennis, or the beach!

FCAT Connect and Compare

1. Look at the glossary entries on page 465. What does *devise* mean? **Using a Glossary**

2. What device should be created to help someone with a disability? How would the device make a disabled person's life better? **Synthesize**

3. Think about *The Blind Hunter.* What might Chirobo say about the new devices for people with disabilities? Use details from both selections to explain. **Reading/Writing Across Texts**

Social Studies Activity

Research a sport played by people with disabilities. Write about it. Include a title, drawing, and caption.

LOG ON Find out more about creative solutions at **www.macmillanmh.com**

Write About Making Something

Writer's Craft

FCAT Time-Order Words

Good writers use **time-order words** such as *first, next,* and *then* when they write directions. These words help readers know exactly what to do and what order to do them in.

I wrote about how to make vegetable barley soup.

I used time-order words to show readers the order of the steps.

Vegetable Barley Soup

by Harry H.

Yesterday Dad decided to show me how to make soup. He said some great chefs were men. He also said I could easily make soup by myself after he taught me. This is how we did it.

First you fill a big pot 3/4 full with water and place it over a burner. Next, you see what vegetables you have. Dad sliced carrots and celery. I added a jar of tomato sauce and barley. Later you have to skim off the junk that floats on top. The soup starts getting thicker as the water boils away. Then you add some olive oil and spices, and you have soup!

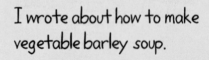

Writing Prompt

Most people know how to make something good to eat.

Think of something you know how to make.

Now write about how to make something good to eat.

FCAT Writer's Checklist

- [x] **Focus:** My writing shows knowledge of the subject.
- [ ] **Organization:** I use time-order words such as *first*, *next*, and *later* to show readers the sequence of steps.
- [x] **Support:** I present my directions with as much detail as possible.
- [x] **Conventions:** I use subject and object pronouns correctly. My sentences are easy to read and understand.

Talk About It

Does it matter what kind of energy we use and where we get it? Why or why not?

LOG ON Find out more about kinds and sources of energy at **www.macmillanmh.com**

Energy: Power Source

Real World Reading

Clean as a Breeze

Vocabulary

electrical
globe
fuels
decayed

High wind speeds in the San Gorgonio Pass make conditions just right for delivering clean electricity to homes. Since 1998 Californians have been able to choose the source of their electricity. I am proud to say that my parents switched to a clean source of **electrical** power.

Though it costs a bit more to generate electricity from wind than from fossil fuels, my parents decided to help the environment. They knew that burning fossil fuels always releases pollutants into the air.

"Choosing wind or solar power is the key to making sure that Earth's future is bright," says Nancy Hazard. Part of an organization that promotes the use of non-polluting energy sources, Ms. Hazard also says, "Creating that vision and really going for it—that's how we'll get energized!"

Around the **globe**, more people than ever are willing to pay extra for clean sources of energy. If you live in a place where power might be generated with a clean technology, get things rolling by talking to your parents and teachers. Remember: "Clean Energy for a Bright, Pollution-Free Future!"

Tiayana Banks, Palm Springs, CA

A windmill farm in California uses clean technology to turn wind energy into electricity.

LOG ON Find out more about renewable energy sources at **www.macmillanmh.com**

TIME FOR KIDS

U.S. Energy Sources

Nuclear power plants generate some of the energy we use, but most of our energy comes from **fuels** such as oil, natural gas, and coal. These fuels are called fossil fuels. Over millions of years, heat and pressure from deep within Earth have reacted with the remains of plants and animals that have **decayed** to form fuel. Once these natural resources are used up, they are gone forever.

Nuclear power plant

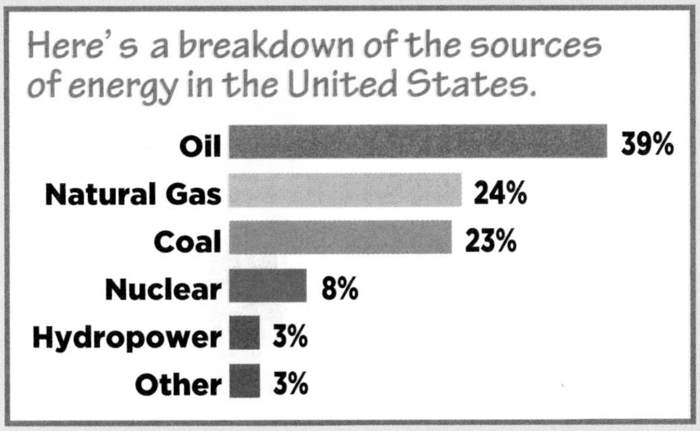

Hydropower plant

Renewable energy sources can be reused, and they create much less pollution than fossil fuels.

- Hydropower uses the force of flowing water to create electricity.
- Solar energy comes from the sun.
- Wind turbines are machines that look like giant windmills. They use the force of the wind to create electricity.
- Geothermal energy comes from heat in Earth's core that is used to create electricity.
- Biomass includes natural products such as wood and corn. These materials are burned and used for heat.

Top 5 Oil Users

Worldwide, people use more than 80 million barrels of oil per day. A barrel contains 42 gallons. These countries are the biggest oil guzzlers. China's oil consumption is growing faster than that of any other country.

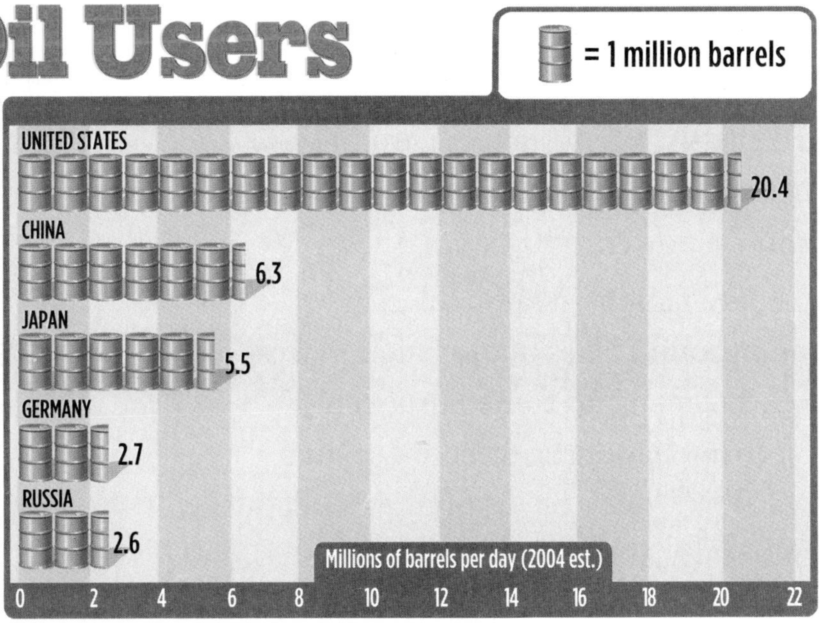

Comprehension

Genre

A **Nonfiction Article** in a newspaper or magazine tells facts about a person, place, or event.

Evaluate

FCAT

Author's Purpose

An author's purpose is the reason the author wrote the story. Authors write to explain, entertain, or inform.

THE POWER OF OIL

WHAT MAKES OIL SO VALUABLE AND SO CHALLENGING?

What can you find deep beneath Earth's surface? Here's a hint: it's shiny, sticky, slick, and very powerful. It's oil.

Oil began forming hundreds of millions of years ago as plant and animal remains were covered with layers of rock. Over the ages those remains **decayed**. They turned into a mighty black brew that we use to make **fuels**. Fuels, such as gasoline, are energy sources that are usually burned to produce power.

Some nations sit atop huge underground lakes of oil. Other places, such as Japan and some European countries, have little or no oil of their own. The United States produces oil, but it also buys about 59% of what it needs.

Oil field worker

Oil is a very important fuel because it helps power cars, trucks, trains, planes, factories, and **electrical** plants. Oil is also an ingredient in some products such as tires, crayons, and other things.

Oil is also a messy fossil fuel. When fossil fuels burn, they release carbon dioxide and other polluting gases. The gases are bad for our health and our planet. They can trap heat near Earth's surface, contributing to the worldwide rise in temperatures known as global warming. Ships carrying oil also have spilled millions of gallons, polluting oceans and shorelines and killing sea life.

HOOKED ON OIL

The United States uses more oil than any other country on the **globe**. Most is pumped into our 200 million cars in the form of gasoline. On average an American burns through 25 barrels of oil each year. Compare this with 15 barrels for a citizen of Japan or 12 for a person living in France.

Some of the 200 million cars on American roads

WHERE DOES ALL THE OIL GO?

The answer is . . . directly into our vehicles, mostly. Traffic on U.S. highways grows heavier every year. Cars, trucks, airplanes, trains, and other forms of transportation burn the most fossil fuel. As you can see, the other uses for oil don't begin to measure up.

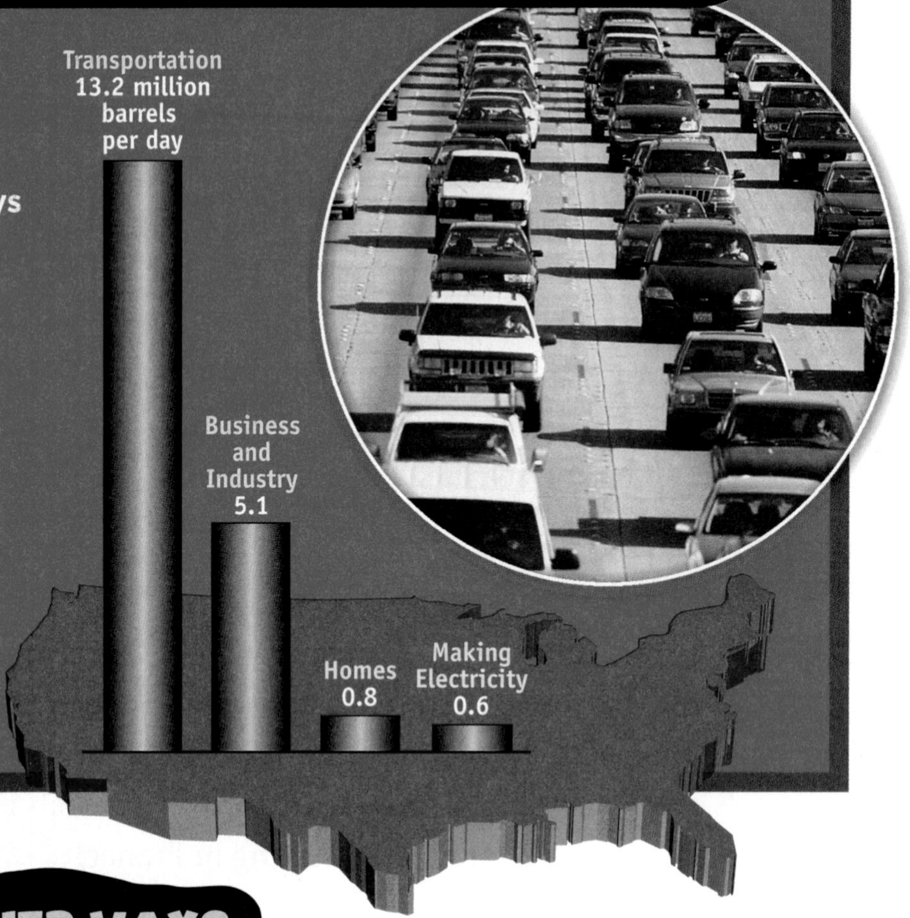

Source: Department of Energy, 2001

IS THERE ANOTHER WAY?

If oil causes so many problems, why do we depend on it? For starters, nearly all of our cars and factories are designed to use oil and gas. Changing them to use other fuels would be very costly.

Still, it's possible to use less. In 1973 a few oil-producing nations got angry at the U.S. The price of oil tripled in just a few months. Gasoline was in short supply and there were long lines at gas stations. That forced auto companies to build cars that use less gas. In 1975 the average car could go just 12 miles on one gallon of gas. By 1990 some cars could travel 30 miles on just one gallon.

In recent years oil prices dropped and Americans went back to buying big gas-guzzlers. About one of every four cars now sold is a sport utility vehicle (SUV), which get as little as 10 or 11 miles per gallon. But that's starting to change, too.

ADVERTISEMENT

WHAT ARE YOU WAITING FOR?

The Facts Are In

Research says roughly 88,000 hybrids were sold in the United States in 2004. That total will climb to 535,000 hybrids per year by 2011. Hybrids use electric motors and battery packs to improve fuel efficiency. A hybrid engine gets better gas mileage than one that runs on gasoline. Hybrid owners save money at the pumps, and through 2006 they are also getting a $2,000 tax break. Best of all, hybrid drivers are cutting their annual emission levels by a whopping 90%!

What Hybrid Drivers Are Saying

- Bill says, "I'd have to throw an anchor out of my window to get mileage less than 40 mpg."
- Dennis says, "I have 60,000 miles on my hybrid. Love it! My lifetime mileage is 53 mpg!"

Celebrities Are Joining the Bandwagon

Many actors and professional athletes are driving hybrids. They are raving about the performance of their cars and feeling good about making the responsible choice.

Come See for Yourself!

In celebration of Earth Day, alternative energy groups across the nation will be hosting at least one presentation of hybrid vehicles in every state. Find the location of the one near you by logging on to www.earthdayevents.example.com. See for yourself! "The Hybrid—It's the Future Now."

Hybrid cars shut off to save power when stopped in traffic. Their engines restart when traffic starts moving again!

FCAT

Think and Compare

1. What is oil made from?
2. How did the oil supply affect the design of American cars?
3. If you wanted to persuade someone to buy a hybrid vehicle, what persuasive argument would you make? What techniques of persuasion would you use?
4. Based on the information in "Clean as a Breeze" and "What Are You Waiting For?," how could one explain the relationship between clean energy choices and emission levels?

FCAT **Test Strategy**

Author and Me

The answer is not always directly stated. Think about everything you have read to figure out the best answer.

Windmills on the Prairies

Mackenzie Burkhart supports the use of energy from windmills.

"Prairies are beautiful places," says Mackenzie Burkhart. "The long, flowing grass looks just like the ocean."

This sixth-grader from Park Ridge, Illinois, worries that nuclear reactors threaten the prairies in his state. A dozen reactors produce nearly three quarters of all the electricity for the state. Mackenzie believes nuclear reactors have the potential to be extremely dangerous. In an accident at a nuclear power plant, nuclear waste could leak out. Radioactive steam and debris could have devastating effects on the plants and animals of the prairies and their surrounding communities.

Burkhart's proposed solution: Provide energy from a more environmentally safe source—a windmill! Big, colorful windmills caught Burkhart's eye while he was on vacation in Denmark with his family. "Windmills were everywhere, and they provided power for much of the country," he says.

During the 1800s windmills played an important role as people began settling in the West. Windmills were used to pump water, grind grain, and generate electricity. Now, with energy prices rising, windmills are slowly being restored and becoming a popular topic of conversation. Many of the midwestern states are discovering the advantages of wind power and have started building more wind farms.

Not only would windmills be environmentally safer, but, as Burkhart points out, they are also a renewable source of power. Unlike fossil fuels or even nuclear fuels, he says, "wind is endless."

Go on

FCAT **Now answer Numbers 1 through 5. Base your answers on the article "Windmills on the Prairies."**

1. What is the author's purpose in writing this article?
   - (A) to talk about windmills in the 1800s
   - (B) to explain to readers how windmills work
   - (C) to inform readers about an alternative source of power
   - (D) to entertain readers with a story about Mackenzie Burkhart's trip to Denmark

Tip
You have to think about the entire passage to choose the best answer.

2. According to the article, some countries use windmills for power. What is a problem with using windmills?
   - (F) They create pollution.
   - (G) They can hurt animals and wildlife.
   - (H) They only work when there is enough wind.
   - (I) They only work in certain countries during the summer.

3. Which reason would the author cite for creating alternatives to nonrenewable energy sources?
   - (A) Global warming increases our need for energy.
   - (B) Winters are getting colder in many parts of the world.
   - (C) People want to choose where their power comes from.
   - (D) Our limited supply of natural resources won't last forever.

4. READ THINK EXPLAIN Why are nuclear reactors dangerous to prairies and other communities? Use details from the article to explain.

5. READ THINK EXPLAIN Why does the author consider windmills an important alternative to nonrenewable energy sources? Explain using details from the article.

STOP

Write to a Prompt

FCAT

Suppose you are taking a road trip with friends.

Think about what can happen on a road trip with friends.

Now write to tell what can happen on a road trip with friends.

Narrative writing tells a story about a personal or fictional experience.

To figure out if a writing prompt asks for narrative writing, look for clue words such as tell about, tell what happened, or write a story.

Below see how one student begins a response to the prompt above.

The writer introduced a problem. The ending will have the solution.

Kea, Bo, and I were cruising down the road in my new hybrid car. Suddenly a huge, unfamiliar object appeared in the middle of the road. I quickly slammed on my brakes.

We saw a group of people standing in front of the object. They looked upset, but a young boy seemed the most upset of all. "What happened?" I asked.

"We ran out of gas," he told me. "And now I'll never make soccer practice!" I realized what the object blocking the road was: a kind of car people drove years ago. I didn't know people still drove gas-powered cars.

Luckily, Bo thought of a way we could help.

Writing Prompt

Respond in writing to the prompt below. Before you write, read the Writing Hints below. Review the hints after you finish writing.

FCAT

> People invent new kinds of cars.
>
> Think about a kind of car you would invent.
>
> Now write to tell about the kind of car you would invent.

Writing Hints for Prompts

- ☑ Read the prompt carefully.
- ☑ Plan your writing by organizing your ideas.
- ☑ Support your ideas by telling more about each event or reason.
- ☑ Check that your pronouns and verbs agree.
- ☑ Choose words that help others understand what you mean.
- ☑ Review and edit your writing.

WHALES

Talk About It

Have you seen a whale in a movie or on TV? At the aquarium or in the sea? What were some of the things you thought or felt?

LOG ON Find out more about whales at **www.macmillanmh.com**

Vocabulary

rumbling
snoring
unique
dove
massive
tangles
politicians

FCAT Dictionary

Homographs are words that are spelled the same but have different meanings. They also may have different pronunciations.

dove = past tense of *dive*

dove = a type of bird

A Whale of a Trip!

by Kristin Gold

"Ladies and gentlemen," shouted Matty, our guide. He had to yell over the **rumbling** sounds of the boat's engines. "I don't want to hear any **snoring**," he teased. "You're in for a **unique** and exciting trip."

Matty continued, "I want to give you a little information about whales." First he explained that whales are mammals, not fish. Then he informed us that a group of whales is called a pod.

The first thing we saw were birds flying alongside our boat. One **dove** sharply toward the water, and then flew up again! "That's a dovekie," explained Matty. "Whales may be nearby."

"There are two major groups of whales," Matty continued, "baleen whales and toothed whales. Instead of teeth, baleen whales have plates that act like a big sieve and collect food. These birds hang around to eat the tiny fish that slip out of the whales' mouths!"

When a whale suddenly surfaced, I couldn't believe how big it was. It was **massive**!

Soon we saw another whale slap its tail on the water.

"Is it angry?" I asked Matty.

"Probably not," said Matty. "That's called lobtailing. Some scientists think it's a warning to other whales. Others think they're just playing or cleaning their tails."

Matty explained that it's against the law to hunt humpback whales, but whales get killed anyway. The huge nets fishermen use to catch tuna often trap whales, too. Matty said these **tangles** can be prevented by using other kinds of nets. Some concerned people want the **politicians** to help by passing more laws to protect whales.

When we finally reached the dock, we realized that Matty was right. The whale watching trip had been exciting and one-of-a-kind.

Reread for **Comprehension**

FCAT Analyze Text Structure

Chronological Order Authors use signal words such as *first* and *then* to identify the order of events in a story. Identifying the **chronological order** of a story will help the reader figure out how the story is organized. Fill in your Sequence Chart as you reread the selection to help you put the events in order.

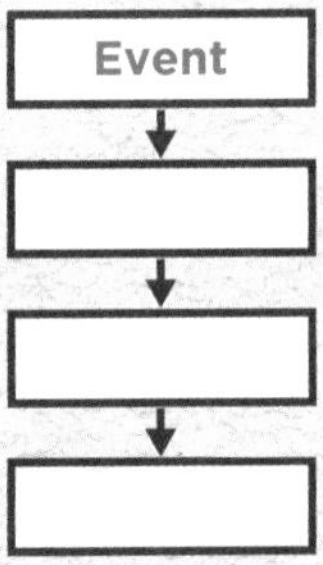

Comprehension

Genre

A **Photo Essay** is an article or book composed mostly of photographs to express a theme or topic.

Analyze Text Structure

FCAT

Chronological Order As you read, fill in your Sequence Chart.

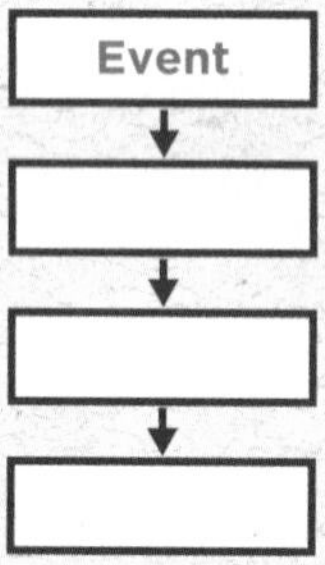

Read to Find Out

How have the yearly visits of the whales affected Adelina's life?

ADELINA'S WHALES

Text and photographs by
RICHARD SOBOL

La Laguna is the name of a quiet, dusty fishing village on the sandy shore of Laguna San Ignacio, in Baja California, Mexico. A few dozen homesites are scattered along the water's edge. These little houses are simple one- or two-room boxes patched together with plywood and sheet metal. Drinking water is stored outside in fifty-gallon plastic barrels, and electricity is turned on for only a few hours each day.

Adelina Mayoral has lived her whole life in La Laguna. She is a bright ten-year-old girl. She loves the ocean and the feeling of the ever-present wind that blows her long, dark hair into wild **tangles**. She knows what time of day it is by looking at the way the light reflects off the water. Adelina can tell what month it is by watching the kind of birds that nest in the mangroves behind her home. She can even recognize when it is low tide. Simply by taking a deep breath through her nose, she can smell the clams and seaweed that bake in the hot sun on the shoreline as the water level goes down.

In late January, every afternoon after school, Adelina walks to the beach to see if her friends—the gray whales—have returned. At this same time every year the whales come, traveling from as far away as Alaska and Russia. They slowly and steadily swim south, covering more than five thousand miles along the Pacific Coast during November, December, and January.

One night Adelina is awakened by a loud, low, **rumbling** noise. It is the sound of a forty-ton gray whale exhaling a room-size blast of hot wet air. As she has always known they would, the gray whales have come again to visit. Adelina smiles and returns to her sleep, comforted by the sounds of whales breathing and **snoring** outside her window. At daybreak she runs to the lagoon and sees two clouds of mist out over the water, the milky trails of breath left by a mother gray whale and her newborn calf.

The waters of the protected lagoon are warm and shallow. The scientists who have come to visit and study the whales have explained that Laguna San Ignacio is the perfect place for the mother whales to have their babies and then teach them how to swim. But Adelina knows why they really come—to visit her!

Adelina's family lives far away from big cities with highways and shopping malls. Her little village does not have any movie theaters or traffic lights, but she knows that her hometown is a special place. This is the only place on earth where these giant gray whales—totally wild animals—choose to seek out the touch of a human hand. Only here in Laguna San Ignacio do whales ever stop swimming and say hello to their human neighbors. Raising their **massive** heads up out of the water, they come face-to-face with people. Some mother whales even lift their newborns up on their backs to help them get a better view of those who have come to see them. Or maybe they are just showing off, sharing their new baby the way any proud parent would.

The whales have been coming to this lagoon for hundreds of years, and Adelina is proud that her grandfather, Pachico, was the first person to tell of a "friendly" visit with one. She loves to hear him tell the story of that whale and that day. She listens closely as he talks about being frightened, since he didn't know then that the whale was only being friendly. He thought he was in big trouble.

Adelina looks first at the tight, leathery skin of her grandfather, browned from his many years of fishing in the bright tropical sun. From his face she glances down to the small plastic model of a gray whale that he keeps close by. As he begins to tell the story of his first friendly whale encounter, there is a twinkle in his eye and a large smile on his face. Adelina and her father, Runolfo, smile too, listening again to the story that they have heard so many times before.

In a whisper, her grandfather begins to draw them in. Adelina closes her eyes to imagine the calm and quiet on that first afternoon when his small boat was gently nudged by a huge gray whale. As the boat rocked, her grandfather and his fishing partner's hearts pounded. They held tight and waited, preparing themselves to be thrown into the water by the giant animal. The whale **dove** below them and surfaced again on the opposite side of their boat, scraping her head along the smooth sides. Instead of being tossed from the boat, they were surprised to find themselves still upright and floating.

For the next hour the whale glided alongside them, bumping and bobbing gently—as gently as possible for an animal that is as long as a school bus and as wide as a soccer goal. As the sun started to set behind them, the whale gave out a great blast of wet, snotty saltwater that soaked their clothes and stuck to their skin. The whale then rose up inches away from their boat and dove into the sea. Her first visit was over.

As her grandfather finishes the story, he looks to Adelina, who joins him in speaking the last line of the story: "Well, my friend, no fish today!" they say before breaking into laughter.

FCAT **Chronological Order**
Use signal words to retell the grandfather's story in chronological order.

After this first friendly visit with the whales, word quickly spread of the **unique** encounter between a wild fifty-foot whale and a tiny fishing boat. Scientists and whale watchers started to come to Laguna San Ignacio to see the whales themselves. Perhaps word spread among the whales, too, because now dozens of whales began to approach the small boats. With brains as large as a car's engine, gray whales might even have their own language. They "talk" in low rumbles and loud clicks, making noises that sound like the tappings of a steel drum or the ticking that a playing card makes as it slaps against the spokes of a turning bicycle wheel. Maybe they told each other that it was safe to visit here.

Adelina's favorite time of the day is the late afternoon, when her father and grandfather return from their trips on the water, guiding visitors to see the whales. They sit together as the sun goes down behind them, and she listens to stories of the whales. She asks them lots and lots of questions.

Adelina has learned a lot about the gray whales. She knows that when a whale leaps out of the water and makes a giant splash falling back in, it's called breaching. When a whale pops its head straight up out of the water, as if it is looking around to see what is going on, it is called spyhopping. Adelina also learned how the whale's wide, flat tail is called a fluke, and when it raises its tail up in the air as it goes into a deep dive, that is called fluking.

Although her home is a simple one on a sandy bluff hugging the edge of the Pacific Ocean, Adelina has many new friends who come to share her world. She has met people who come from beyond the end of the winding, bumpy road that rings the lagoon. Some are famous actors. Some are **politicians**. Some speak Spanish. Some speak English. Those that weigh forty tons speak to her in their own magical style. The whales have taught her that the world is a big place.

Adelina knows that she has many choices in her future. Sometimes she giggles with delight at the idea of being the first girl to captain a *panga* (a small open fishing boat) and teach people about the whales in the lagoon. Or sometimes she thinks she may become a biologist who studies the ocean and can one day help to unlock some of the mysteries of the whales in her own backyard. Or maybe she will take pictures like the photographer whom she watches juggling his three cameras as he stumbles aboard the whale-watching boat. But no matter what she chooses, the whales will always be a part of her life.

For these three months Adelina knows how lucky she is to live in Laguna San Ignacio, the little corner of Mexico that the gray whales choose for their winter home. This is the place where two worlds join together. She wouldn't trade it for anything.

FCAT Chronological Order
What events brought whale watchers to Laguna San Ignacio? List the events in chronological order.

In the early spring the lagoon grows quiet. One by one the whales swim off, heading north for a summer of feeding. On their heads and backs they carry the fingerprints of those they met, the memories of their encounters in Mexico. Maybe, as the whales sleep, they dream of the colorful sunsets of Laguna San Ignacio.

Every afternoon Adelina continues to gaze across the water. Sometimes now, when she closes her eyes, she can still see the whales swimming by. And if she listens *really* closely, she can even hear their breathing.

A Snapshot of Richard Sobol

Richard Sobol is a photographer who has snapped many different subjects in his long career. For the past few years, Richard has spent a lot of time photographing wildlife, including the whales. He is especially interested in capturing images of endangered species.

Other books by Richard Sobol

LOG ON Find out more about Richard Sobol at **www.macmillanmh.com**

FCAT Author's Purpose

Nonfiction texts are often written to inform the reader or explain something. Why did Richard Sobol write *Adelina's Whales*? What clues help you figure out his purpose in creating this photo essay?

FCAT Comprehension Check

Summarize

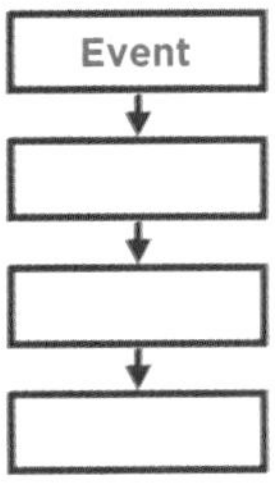

Summarize the relationship between humans and gray whales in Laguna San Ignacio. Use your Sequence Chart to organize story events in chronological order.

Think and Compare

1. Describe the sequence of events that lead the **massive** whales to Laguna San Ignacio. How do the whales get there? When and why do they leave? Use details from the story to explain. **Analyze Text Structure: Chronological Order**

2. Reread pages 497–498. What has Adelina learned from the whales? What has she learned from the people who visit the whales? Why are these lessons important? Explain using story details. **Analyze**

3. How would you organize a club to study whales and visit Laguna San Ignacio? Develop a plan showing the steps you would take. **Apply**

4. What will happen to the whales and Adelina's community if the lagoon becomes polluted? Explain. **Synthesize**

5. Read "A Whale of a Trip!" on pages 484–485. What information about whales was in this article that was not in *Adelina's Whales?* **Reading/Writing Across Texts**

FCAT

Poetry

A **Limerick** is a funny poem with a specific pattern of rhyme and meter. All limericks have five lines.

Literary Elements

Meter is the rhythm of the syllables in a line of poetry.

Rhyme Scheme is the pattern of rhymes within a poem.

Limericks

A Whale of a Meal

There once was a whale named Alene
Who strained all her meals through baleen.
But she dreamed of a lunch
With a food that goes "crunch"
Like a truckload of just-picked string beans.

—Doreen Beauregard

Whale Watch

The meter in these three lines is created by emphasizing the third, sixth, and ninth syllables.

Near our boát is a mámmal named Lúke
Who's exceédingly proúd of his flúke.
Just don't call it a tail
Or this dignified whale
Will respónd with a spláshy rebúke.

—Doreen Beauregard

The Podless Whale

There once was a whale near Cape Cod
Who just could not locate his pod.
So he joined with a mass
Of bewildered sea bass
Who found this behavior quite odd.
—Doreen Beauregard

The last line of a limerick always rhymes with the first two lines. The second and third lines have a different rhyme.

FCAT Connect and Compare

1. What is the rhyme scheme of "Whale Watch"? What if the last line rhymed with the third and fourth lines? **Rhyme Scheme**
2. Why were the sea bass in "The Podless Whale" bewildered? **Apply**
3. How are the whales in these poems similar to the ones in *Adelina's Whales*? How are they different? **Reading/Writing Across Texts**

LOG ON Find out more about limericks at **www.macmillanmh.com**

Write About Your Favorite Animal

Writer's Craft

FCAT Voice

The **voice** of any kind of writing reveals the writer's personality. Good writers use language that reflects their voice to show interest and enthusiasm for their topic.

Nighttime Swim

by Maggie W.

The water was cold and dark when I jumped in. I couldn't see much as I swam, but the noise of the whales' singing led me to my friend Angie.

I had met Angie on my last voyage to sea. She has the bluest skin and kind black eyes. Tonight we swam together for hours. When we stopped to rest, she splashed me with her massive whale body. I laughed, and her eyes seemed to be laughing, too.

Back on the shore, I turned to watch Angie swim away. I felt very sad to watch my friend leave. I called out, "Goodbye!" She stopped swimming and turned back towards the shore. I think I saw her wave a large fin goodbye.

I used descriptive words to introduce my main character.

The language I used shows my enthusiasm for the topic.

Writing Prompt

Most people have a favorite animal.

Think about your favorite animal.

Now write about you and your favorite animal.

FCAT Writer's Checklist

- [x] **Focus:** My story clearly shows what it would be like to spend time with my favorite animal.
- [x] **Organization:** The events in my story are shown in the order they happened.
- [ ] **Support:** The language I use shows my voice and enthusiasm for my topic.
- [x] **Conventions:** I spell possessive pronouns correctly. My sentences are complete.

THE Sea

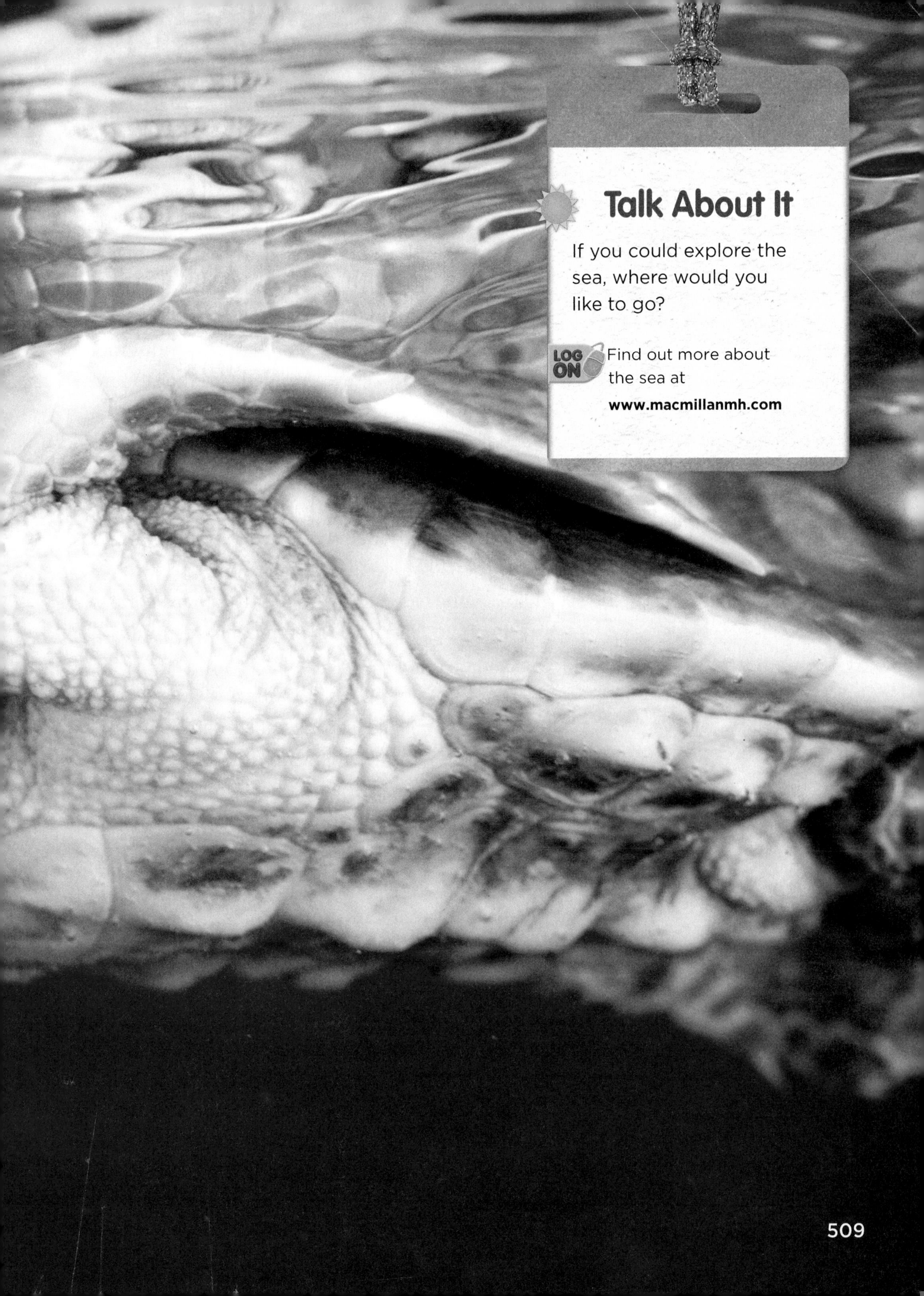

Talk About It

If you could explore the sea, where would you like to go?

LOG ON Find out more about the sea at **www.macmillanmh.com**

Coral Reefs

by Mindy Smith

Vocabulary

coral, eventually, reef, brittle, partnership, suburbs, current

FCAT Context Clues

Descriptions in the surrounding text can give clues to the meaning of an unfamiliar word.

Use context clues to find the meaning of *suburbs*.

Coral comes in a variety of shapes, colors, and sizes. It can be the size of the head of a pin, or a foot in diameter. Although corals are often mistaken for rocks or plants, they are actually very small animals. When thousands of these animals are grouped together to form a mound or a tree shape, it is called a coral colony. Thousands of these colonies make up a **reef**.

There are more than 700 kinds of coral but only two main types. Each kind of coral is either a soft coral or a hard coral.

The easiest way to identify a hard coral is by its appearance. A colony of hard corals can resemble a vase, a plate, a little tree, a boulder, a brain, or the antlers of an elk. Hard corals have groups of six smooth tentacles around their mouths. They get their name from the hard, cuplike skeletons of limestone that they produce out of seawater.

Soft corals always have eight feathery tentacles around their mouths. They have names like sea fan, sea whip, or sea fingers and are as soft and bendable as plants or tree branches. Soft corals do not have hard skeletons. They have woody cores that support them instead. Soft corals often live on coral reefs along with hard corals, but soft corals can also live in cool, dark regions where hard corals would die.

Hard corals cannot live as far from the surface as soft corals because hard corals have plants, called algae, living inside of them. Through this **partnership**, the algae provide most of the coral polyp's food and the polyp gives the algae protection from the predators that eat them. The algae, though, require sunlight in order to live.

Hard corals begin their lives as fertilized eggs. These develop into soft larvae which drift with the **current** of the waves until they attach themselves to a part of the existing reef. **Eventually** the coral polyps die and other living larvae attach themselves to their skeletons.

Scientists believe that the existing coral reefs began to grow over 50 million years ago. When seaweed, sponges, giant clams, oysters, starfish, and **brittle** stars die, they serve as the foundations upon which another generation of hard coral polyps will attach and grow. In this way the hard corals are the architects of the community—from the downtown area out to the **suburbs**.

The sprawling structures of the coral reefs support a quarter of all known sea animals. This includes over 4,000 different kinds of fish, along with mollusks, octopus and squid, sponges, algae, seaweed, shrimp, sea turtles, and sharks.

Reread for Comprehension

Analyze Text Structure

FCAT **Compare and Contrast** Authors sometimes organize a selection by **comparing** and **contrasting** two or more things. Comparing is telling how things or people are alike. Contrasting is telling how they are different. Reread the selection and use your Venn diagram to help you learn how things are different and how they are the same.

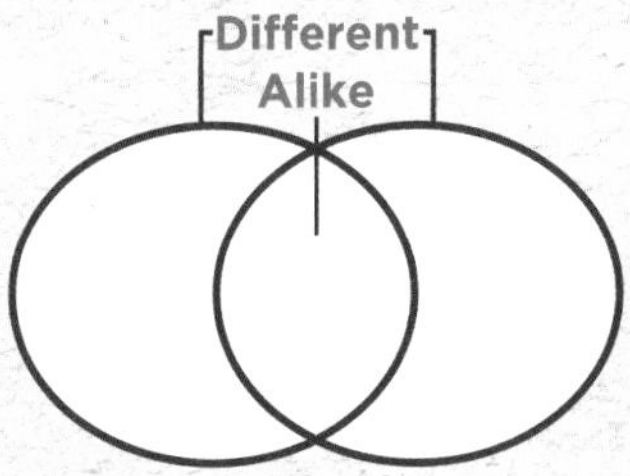

Comprehension

Genre

Narrative Nonfiction is a true story or account about actual persons, living things, situations, or events.

Analyze Text Structure

FCAT

Compare and Contrast

As you read, fill in your Venn diagram.

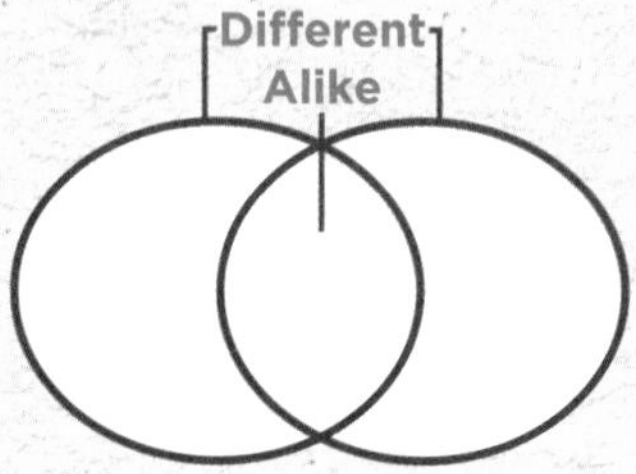

Read to Find Out

How does a coral reef change and grow?

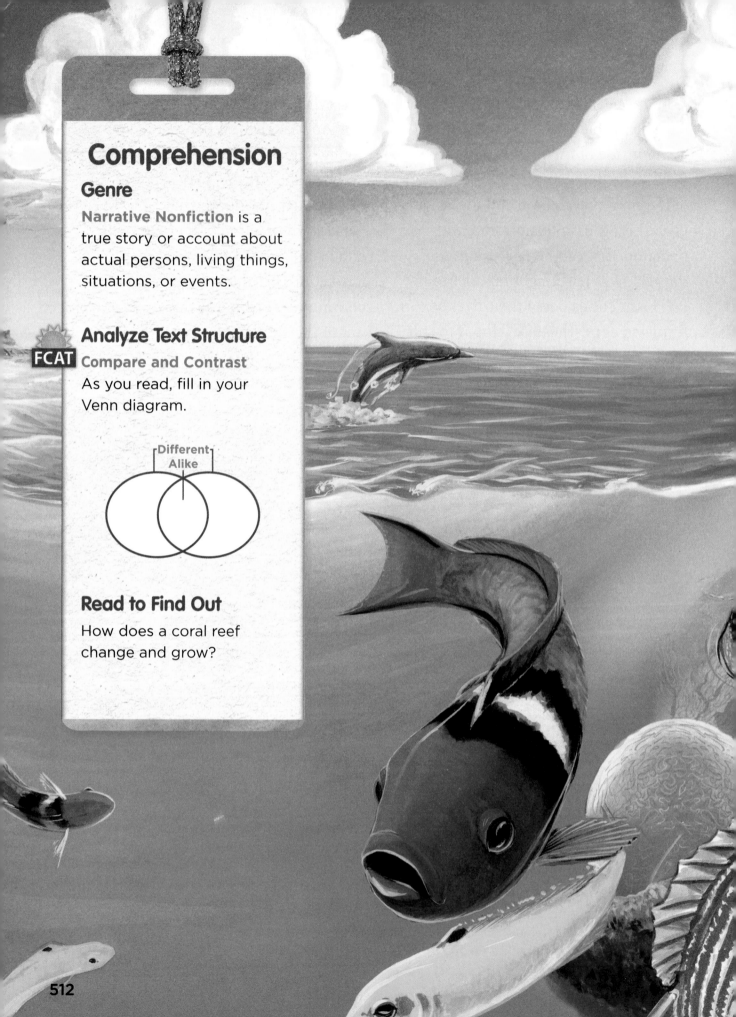

AT HOME IN THE Coral Reef

by Katy Muzik • Illustrated by Katherine Brown-Wing

Down, down, down in the tropical clear blue sea lives a beautiful **coral** reef. The coral **reef** is a wonderful home for hundreds of kinds of fish and thousands of other kinds of creatures. The reef itself is made of zillions of tiny animals called coral polyps.

Each tiny coral polyp catches food with its little arms, called tentacles. The polyps share their food and live so close together that their skeletons are connected.

Some kinds of coral polyps make soft skeletons that sway gently back and forth in the water. These polyps have 8 tentacles. Other coral polyps make skeletons that are as hard as rock. Their hard skeletons form the coral reef. A hard coral polyp has 12, or 24, or 48, or more tentacles! Together, over 50 kinds of hard coral form this reef in the Caribbean Sea.

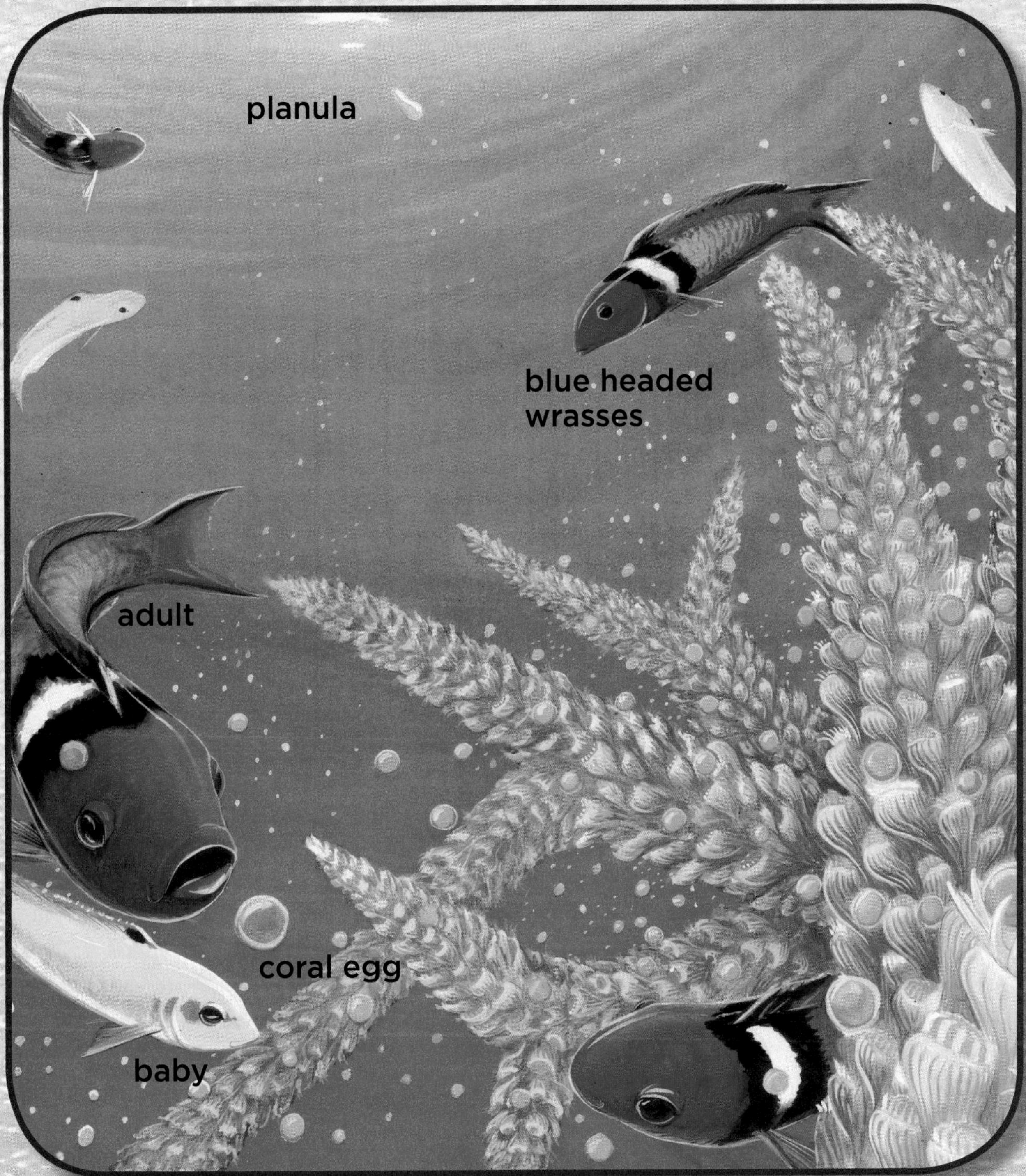

What are these pink things? Coral eggs! Once a year, coral polyps have babies. Eggs and sperm pop out of the polyps and float up and up to the top of the blue sea. There each fertilized egg becomes a baby coral called a planula. Now it is ready to search for a new home.

The planula is completely covered with little hairs. It swims by waving them through the water, but it cannot swim very fast. Watch out for those hungry wrasses!

Just in time, a big wave carries the planula away to the crest, or top, of the coral reef. Here the water is very shallow. Because it is so shallow, the waves break and crash into the reef.

Splash! Crash! The breaking waves make the water very rough. It's so rough that only a few animals can live here. A fireworm holds on tight. A school of blue tangs darts in and out, hunting for food.

Crash! Splash! Will this be home for the planula? No, it's too rough. The planula is swept along, riding a wave over the crest to the lagoon.

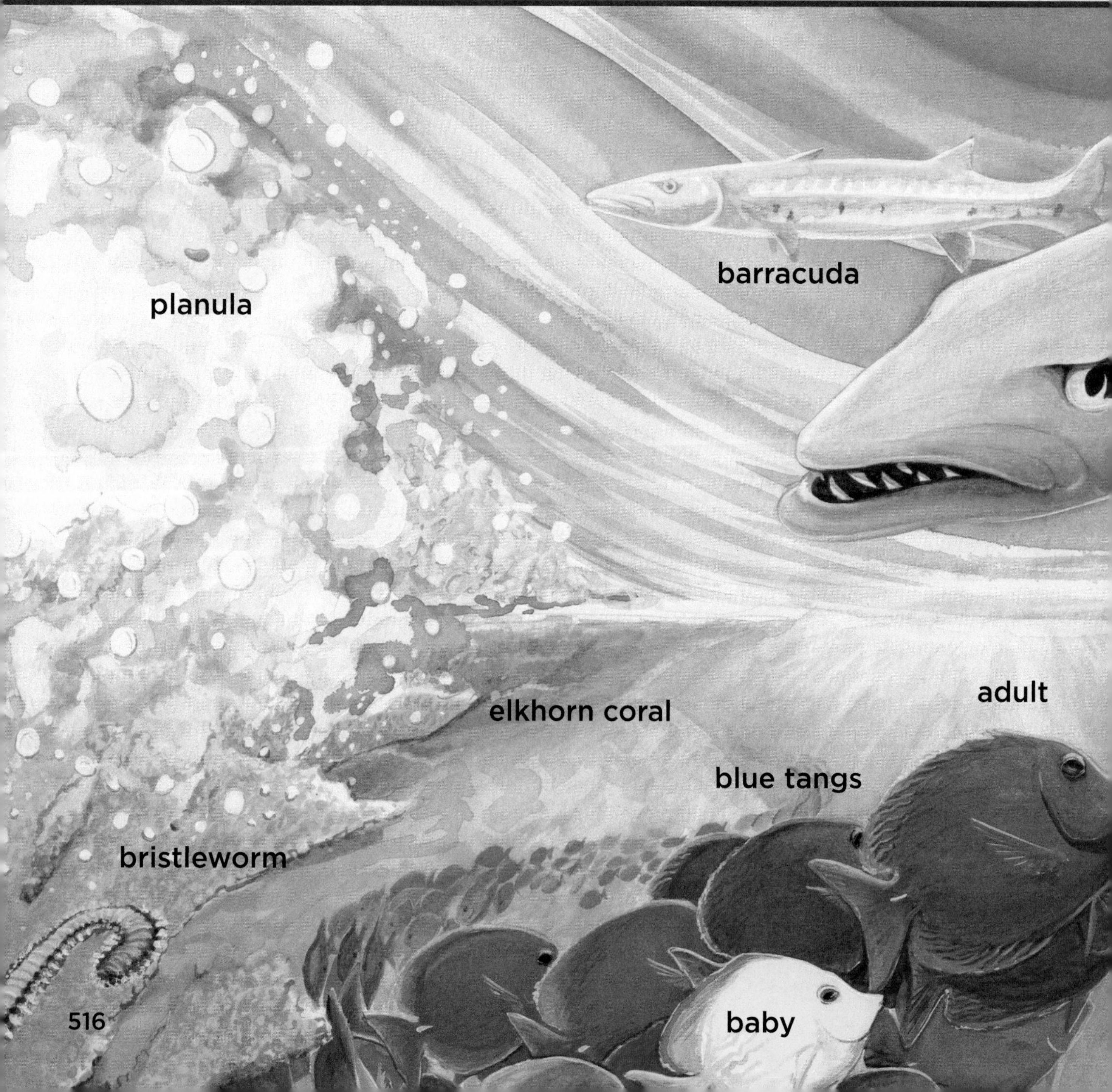

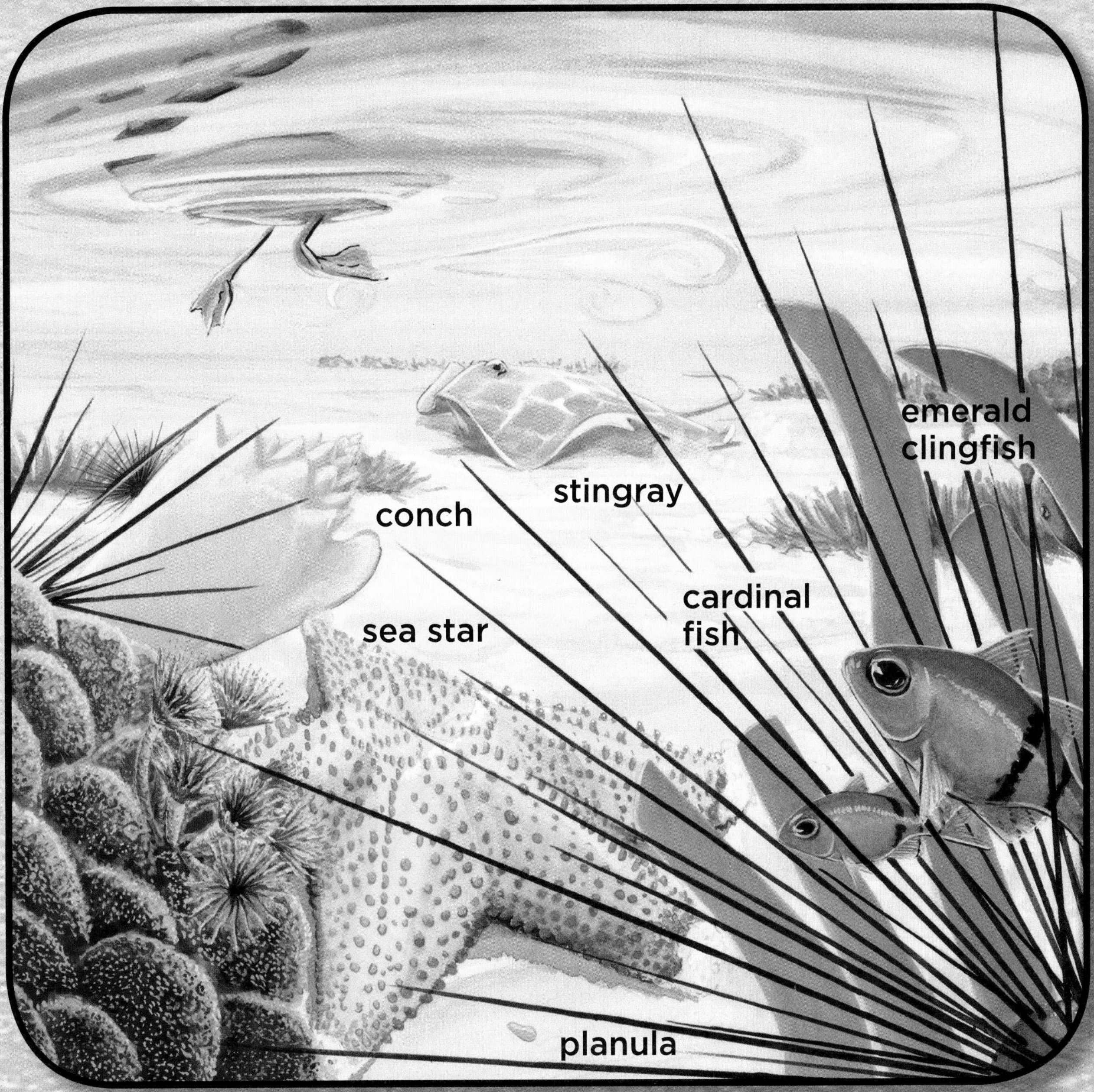

The water in the lagoon is calm. Although the lagoon seems peaceful, it is really a busy place, from top to bottom. At the top, a pelican gulps a pouchful of fish. At the bottom, a stingray slurps up shrimp.

Many animals looking for food in the lagoon are hard to see. An emerald clingfish hides on a blade of turtle grass. Clams and crabs hide in the sand.

FCAT Compare and Contrast

Compare the features of the crest at the coral reef and the lagoon.

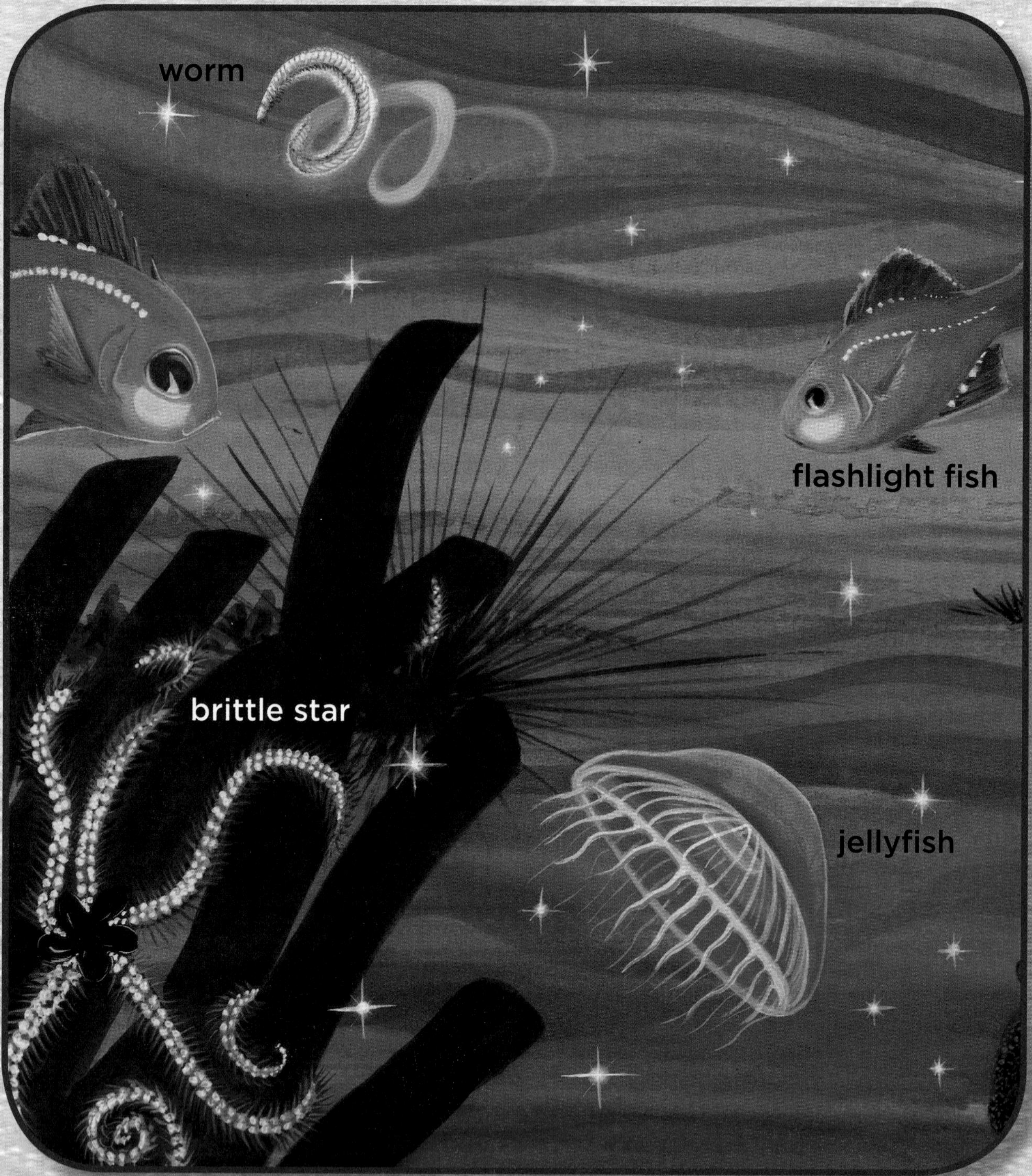

Such a busy place, day and night in the lagoon.

Flash! Glow! Blink! What could these lights be? They twinkle like stars in the sky, but they are all under water.

These lights are made by animals. Animals almost too small to see are twinkling. **Brittle** stars flash to scare away lobsters and crabs. Worms glow to show other worms where they are. Flashlight fish attract their food by blinking.

Can the planula live here? No, it is too sandy.

The planula needs a rocky place. It floats along to the red mangrove trees near the shore of the lagoon. Red mangroves can grow in salty water. Their roots grow out and hang down right into the ocean. Sponges and seaweeds grow on the roots.

Millions of baby fish and baby shrimp start life in the water around mangrove roots. There's lots of food for them there. Will this be a home for the planula, too?

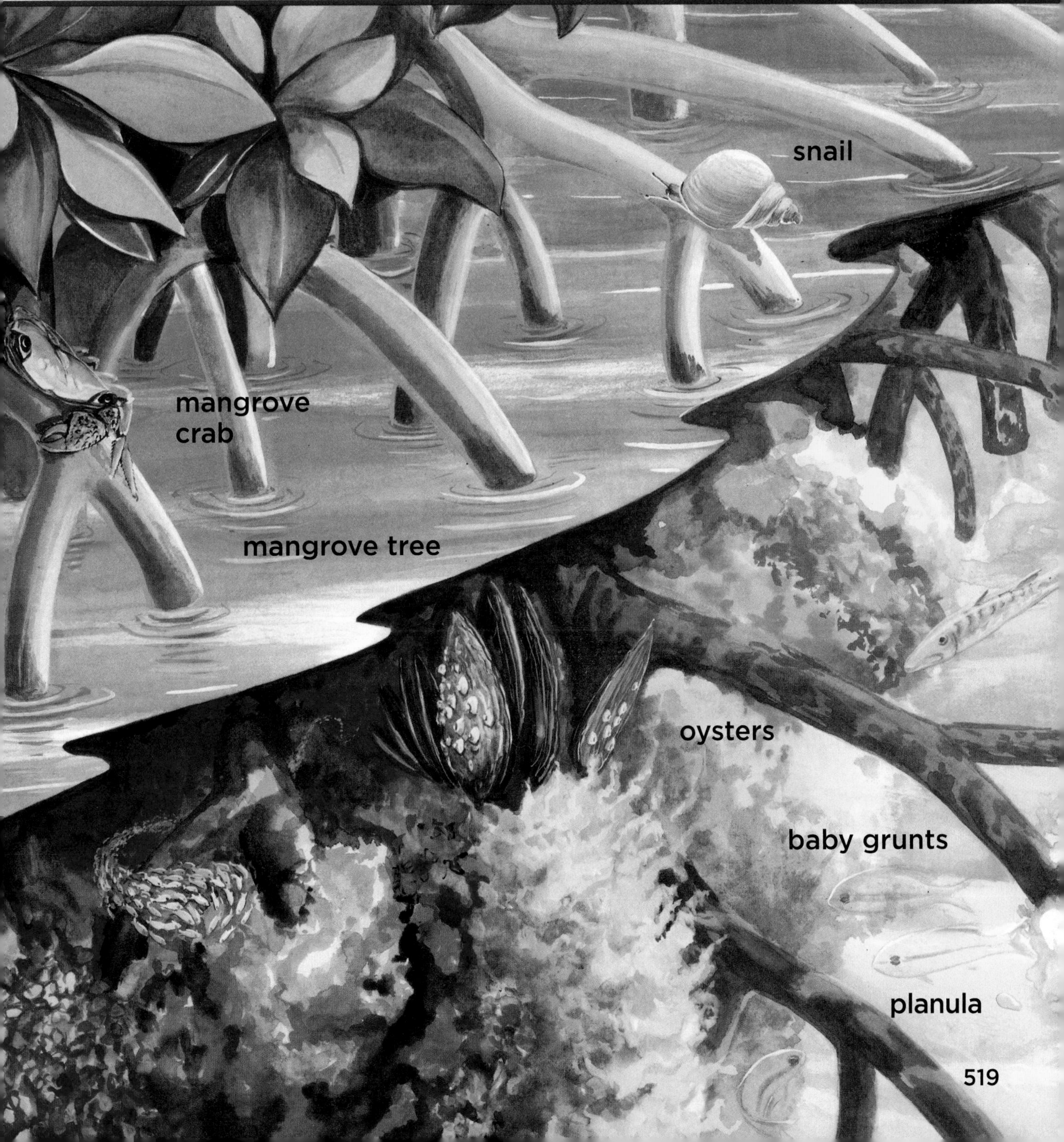

No, the water here is too shady for the planula. It turns away and swims to the shallow water near the beach of the lagoon.

The sunshine heats the sandy beach. The sand was made by the ocean waves. Over thousands of years, the waves have pounded the skeletons of reef animals and plants into smaller and smaller bits. **Eventually**, the bits formed so many grains of sand that they covered the bottom of the lagoon and washed up on shore to make a beach.

Will this be home for the planula? No, it is too shallow and too hot here.

The planula catches a **current** to deeper water. Oh, no, the water is dirty! The water is so dirty, the coral is dying. The dirt smothers the coral polyps and blocks the sunlight they need.

Chemicals washed down the rivers from factories and farms poison the coral. In the dirty water harmful bacteria grow over the coral and kill it. Careless divers hurt the coral too. They step on it and break it with their boat anchors.

Without living coral, the fish and other animals will leave. The planula cannot live here either.

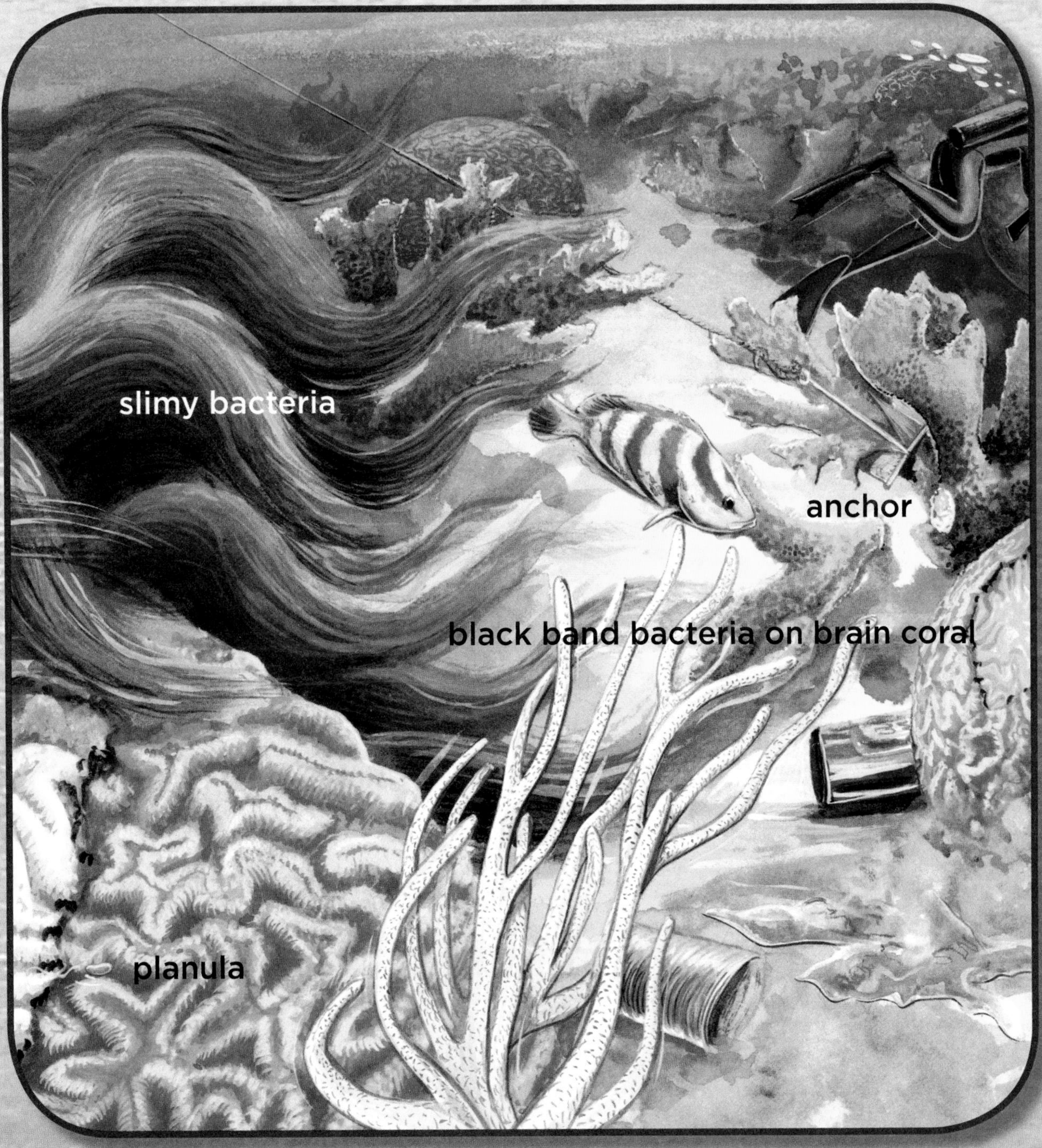

Luckily, a current carries it out of the lagoon, over the top of the reef, and down the other side of the reef deeper and deeper and deeper to a healthy part of the reef.

At last! A safe spot for the planula to settle down. The spot is hard and rocky. It is sunny but not too hot. Gentle currents bring clean water, and plenty of food. It will be a perfect home.

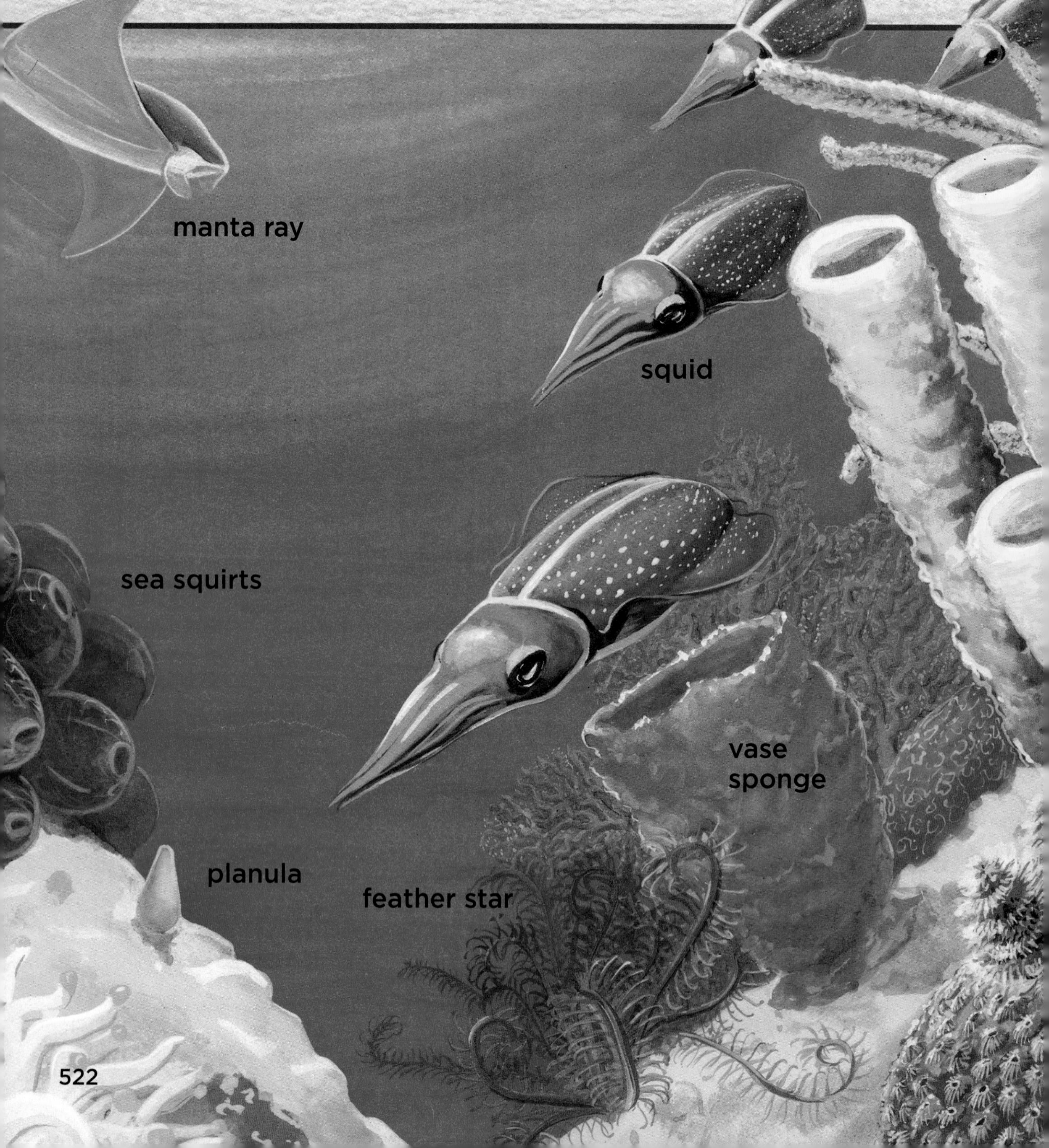

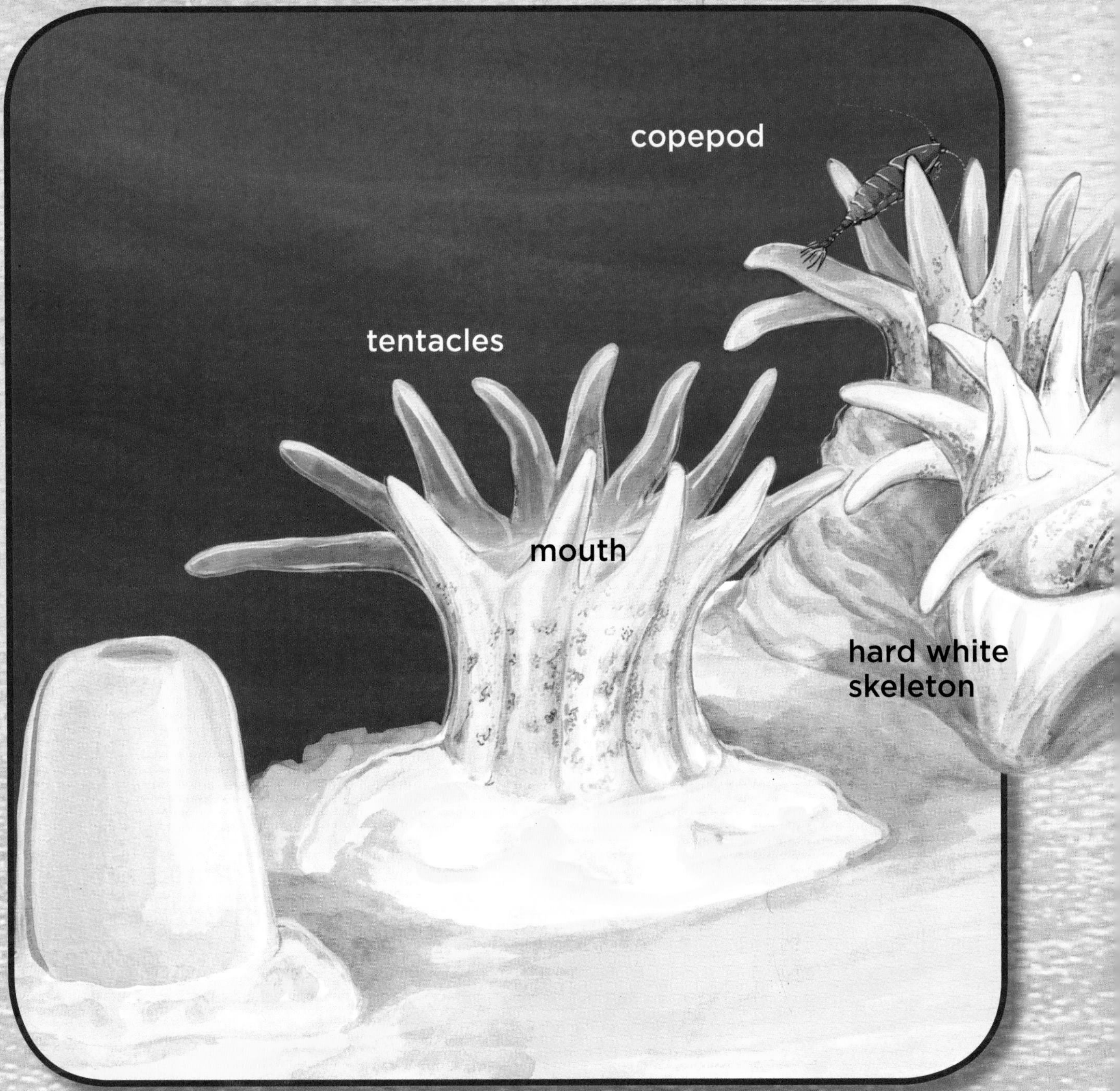

The planula begins to change. First, it sticks itself to a safe spot. Then, around its mouth it grows twelve little tentacles. Now it is a polyp. It looks like a flower, but it really is an animal.

Under its soft body, the polyp starts to grow a hard white skeleton. In a few weeks it makes another tiny polyp exactly like itself. The polyps are connected to each other. Together, the two polyps have twenty-four tentacles for catching food.

The planula is growing up to be a staghorn coral. More polyps grow, and more and more.

Here comes a reef butterfly fish. It eats coral. The coral polyps warn each other of danger. Quick as a wink, they hug their tentacles in. They hide their soft bodies down inside their hard white skeleton. When the danger is past, the coral polyps slowly come out and open up their tentacles again.

Many creatures in the reef are partners that help each other hide or find food. A crab hides in the coral to escape from a hungry octopus. A shrimp lives safely inside a vase sponge.

At a cleaning station, gobies eat what they clean from the teeth of a big grouper. The grouper holds its mouth wide open for the gobies. Away from the station, the grouper would eat gobies!

Even the tiny polyps have partners. The polyps get special food from little golden plants living just inside their skin. In return, the plants get a home. This **partnership** helps the coral grow big enough to form reefs.

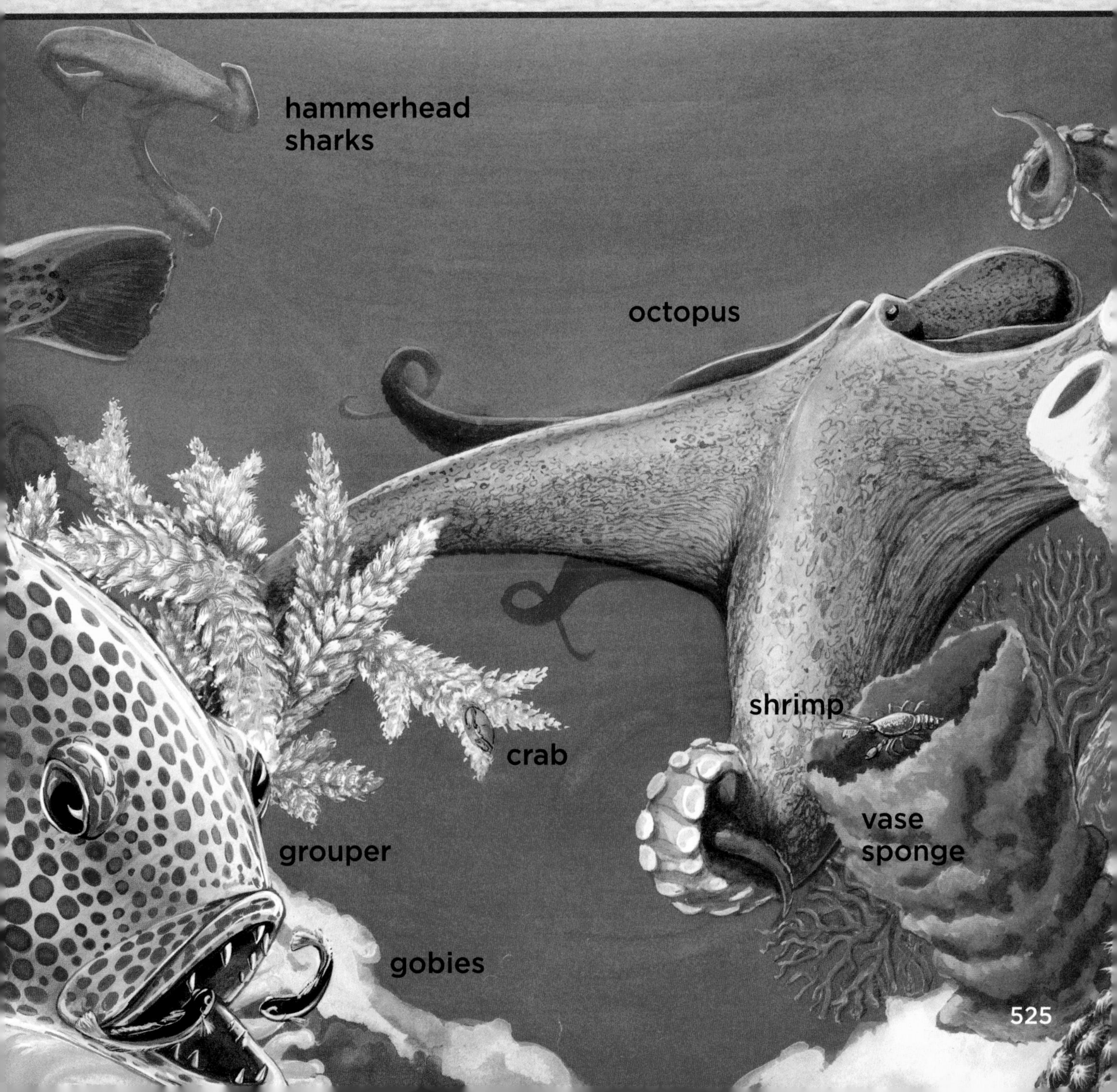

Down, down, down in the tropical clear blue sea, this coral reef is alive and well. The place where it lives is clean. Zillions of coral animals have been adding their skeletons to the reef for over 8,000 years.

It takes thousands of years for a reef to grow but only a few years for one to be destroyed! This reef and other coral reefs all around the world are in danger because the oceans are becoming dirty. Coral reefs need our help.

FCAT **Compare and Contrast**
The planula eventually chooses a safe spot to live. How is this spot different from the other places described in the story? How is it the same?

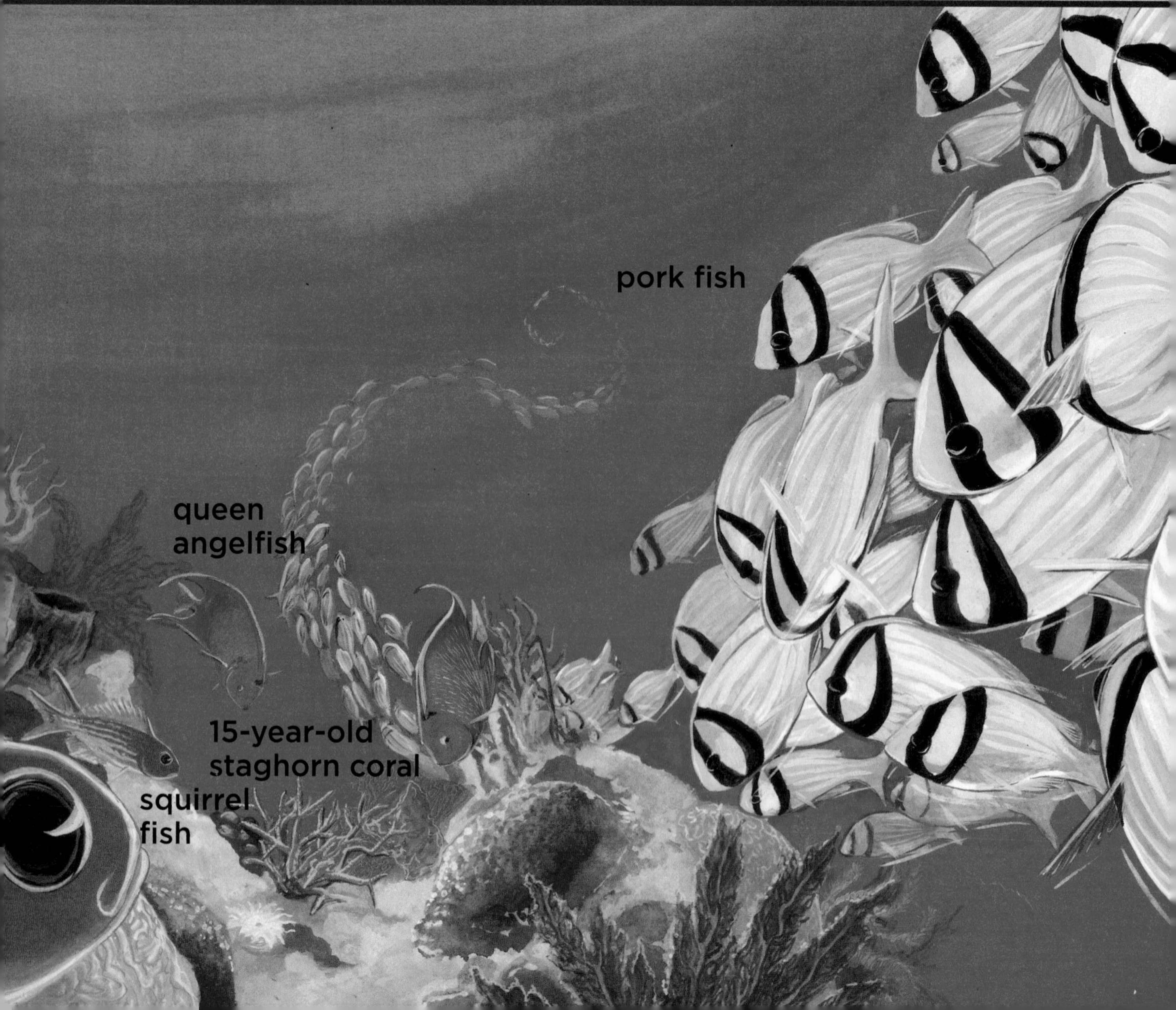

What can we do to help a little baby planula grow up to become part of a big coral reef? The first step is to discover how what we do on land affects life in the sea.

All living creatures—including corals and people—need clean water. We all use water on our farms, in our **suburbs**, and in our cities. We throw many things into it that make it dirty. This dirty water flows into rivers, lakes, and underground streams, and eventually ends up in the sea. There it hurts the coral reef and all the creatures that make it their home.

But we can make a difference. We can make our rivers and lakes and oceans clean again. We can learn about life on the coral reef and share what we learn. We can help people everywhere to care about the amazing reefs and the tiny coral animals that build them.

AT HOME WITH Katy & Katherine

Katy Muzik is a marine biologist who specializes in octocorals—commonly known as sea fans. She has dived on coral reefs all over the world, including Fuji, Japan, Australia, and throughout the Caribbean.

Katy wrote *At Home in the Coral Reef* to share both her love of the sea and her concern for its rapidly declining health. She hopes that once people realize how beautiful, fragile, and important corals are, they will change their behavior to help preserve coral reefs. Katy lives near the ocean in Isabela, Puerto Rico.

Katherine Brown-Wing studied at the Art Institute of Boston. She works as a biological illustrator, and her pictures have been published in numerous scientific journals. Katherine lives in North Kingstown, Rhode Island with her husband.

LOG ON Find out more about Katy Muzik at **www.macmillanmh.com**

FCAT Author's Purpose

How do you think the author's job affected her purpose for writing *At Home in the Coral Reef*? What clues tell whether she wanted to entertain, inform, or explain?

FCAT Comprehension Check

Summarize

Summarize what you learned from *At Home in the Coral Reef*. Use your Venn diagram to help you include only the most important information in your summary.

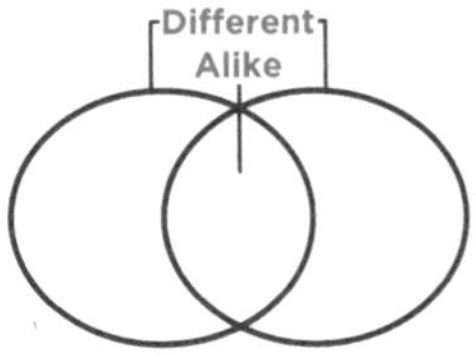

Think and Compare

1. How are the sandy beach and the **coral reef** alike? How are they different? Explain using story details and illustrations. **Analyze Text Structure: Compare and Contrast**

2. Reread pages 524–525 of *At Home in the Coral Reef.* Describe in detail the partnership that some of the underwater sea creatures have with one another. How do they help each other? Use details from the story to explain. **Analyze**

3. What changes in your life could you make to avoid adding pollution to ocean waters? Explain. **Synthesize**

4. Suppose there was a large increase in butterfly fish. How would this change the coral reef community? **Evaluate**

5. Read "Coral Reefs" on pages 510–511 and page 514 of *At Home in the Coral Reef.* What information did each selection provide about hard and soft coral? Use details from both selections to explain. **Reading/Writing Across Texts**

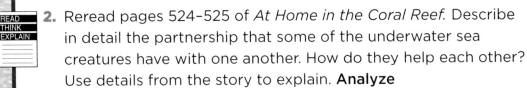

Waves and Climate

RESHAPING EARTH

by Gillian Reed

Science

Genre

Nonfiction Articles explain a topic by presenting facts about it. They also provide informative photos and graphic aids.

FCAT Text Feature

Diagrams are graphic aids that show how things relate to each other. Some diagrams show the steps of a process.

Content Vocabulary

coastline
erodes
storm surge

Do you think your favorite beach looks the same now as it did 500 years ago? Probably not! Five hundred years ago, that beach you now build sand castles on was a rocky piece of land. Over time different forces on Earth work to reshape the land. These forces can take a muddy swamp and turn it into lush farmland. They can wear down rocky coasts to produce a beautiful beach. These forces can create and shape almost any new landform.

These waves splashing against the beach are slowly changing the shape of the land.

The Strength of Waves

Waves are one of the forces that reshape Earth's land. Waves are movements on any body of water in the form of a swell or ridge. They are created by wind. The stronger the wind is, the stronger the wave will be. Waves with lots of strength are important in the process of reshaping our land.

Some coasts are made of cliffs or large rocks. When strong waves slam against the **coastline**, they crash on the rocks over and over again. In time the strength of the waves **erodes**, or breaks apart, the rocks. With the outer rocks broken off, the rocky coast moves inland a little. At the same time, those small pieces of broken rock are taken out to sea. As these pieces move, they break down even more. Over time they mix together with mud and other matter in the water to become tiny pieces of sand. These tiny pieces of sand travel with the waves and are eventually dropped onto a sandy coast. As the sandy coast moves more and more inland because of rock erosion, a beach is formed.

This rock is being slowly eroded by the intense force of the waves.

Hurricane wind speeds can range anywhere from 74 to more than 155 miles per hour!

Reshaping with Climate

Climate is another force that can reshape our land. Strong storms like hurricanes develop in the warm ocean waters and can produce large waves. These storms can erode coastlines quickly. In addition to strong waves, hurricanes can produce a **storm surge**. A storm surge occurs when the water that is built up in the middle of the hurricane reaches land. When the water finally goes back out to sea, some coasts are a lot smaller.

The forces of waves and climate are important to our Earth. Without them we would not be able to enjoy the sandy shores of a beach or any of the other landforms they help create. Earth's land is constantly changing, and this is due in great part to physical forces like waves and climate.

Reading a Diagram

This diagram shows the effect a wave can have on a coastline over time.

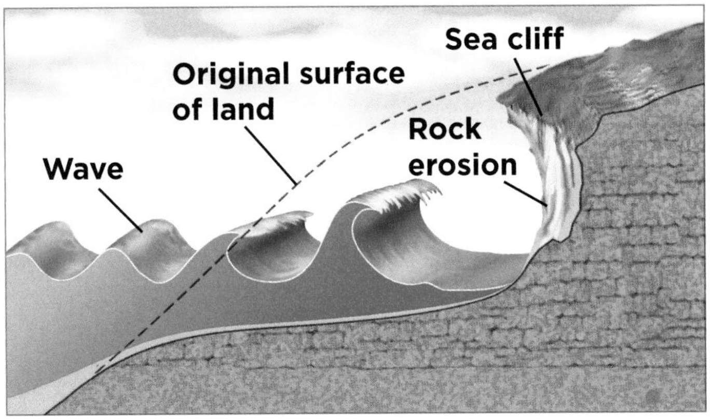

FCAT Connect and Compare

1. Look at the diagram on page 533. What has changed the original land shape of the sea cliff? **Reading a Diagram**

2. How is wind important in helping waves and climate reshape Earth? Use details from the article to explain. **Analyze**

3. What new information about water was presented in this article that wasn't mentioned in *At Home on the Coral Reef*? Explain using details from both selections. **Reading/Writing Across Texts**

Science Activity

Research any hurricane that has hit the state of Florida within the past 25 years. Write a summary describing its effects on Florida coastlines.

LOG ON Find out more about reshaping Earth at **www.macmillanmh.com**

Write a Cinquain

Writer's Craft

FCAT **Figurative Language**

Using **figurative language** in writing helps readers form a mental image of what they are reading.

A **simile** uses figurative language to compare two things using the words *like* or *as*.

I wrote a cinquain that is also a riddle.

For figurative language I used a simile to describe the sea creature.

Who Are We?

by Kyle M.

Creatures,
so attractive,
flash and blink on and off
like lighthouses under the sea.
Sea Stars.

Answer: Flashlight fish

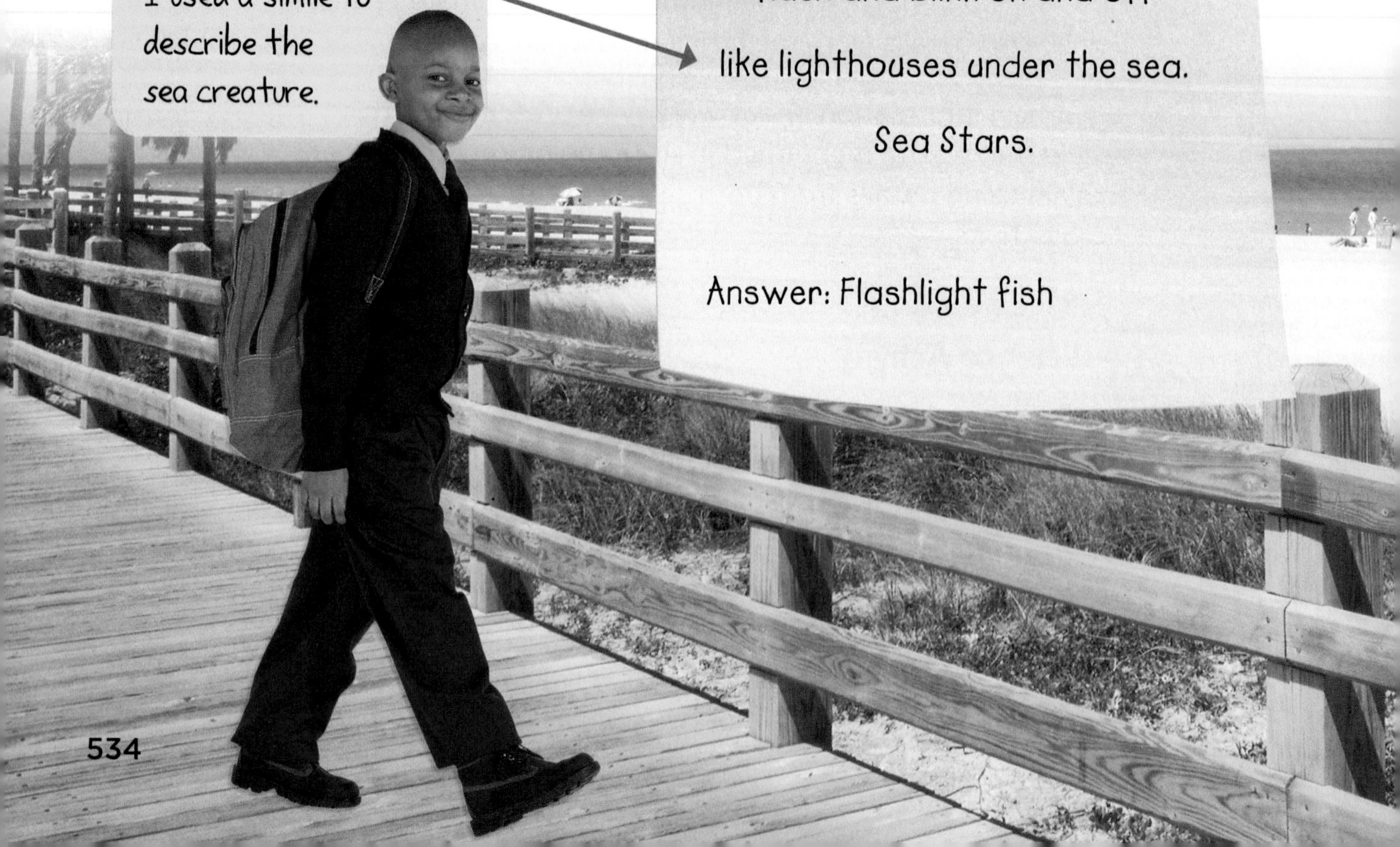

Writing Prompt

Choose one of the creatures from *At Home in the Coral Reef.*

Think of two or three things that describe this creature.

Now write a cinquain that describes the creature.

FCAT Writer's Checklist

- [x] **Focus:** My writing clearly describes the creature without giving its name.
- [x] **Organization:** The details in this poem are clearly organized so the reader can follow along.
- [ ] **Support:** I use **figurative language** in my poem to help the reader picture what I am writing about.
- [x] **Conventions:** My poem flows smoothly. My spelling, grammar, and punctuation are correct.

FCAT Review

- Author's Purpose
- Chronological Order
- Cause and Effect
- Context Clues
- Prefixes
- Line Graph

A Purple Person

I was just so weary of hearing that question! If I had to answer it one more time, I was going to explode! Over and over, I've been asked the same thing at least a million different times. *What's your favorite color?*

I don't know why everyone is so fascinated by other people's favorite colors. If you ask me, their interest is misplaced. I mean, I can think of a heap of other things I'd rather know about a person. But whenever anyone runs out of things to talk about, the first thing they ask me is, "Shona, what's your favorite color?"

I never knew what to say. There was no one color that I preferred. I mean, colors are gorgeous, but I was never, like, in love with any particular one. If I was feeling polite that day I would answer, "I don't have one." Most of the time though, I wasn't feeling polite and I would retort with a comment like, "Oh, who cares."

Finally one day, after being asked the same mind-numbing question for the billionth time, I gave up. I was wearing a purple shirt that day, so I just said, "It's purple. I love purple."

That was a lie, of course. I liked purple, but I liked yellow, green, blue, and scarlet just as much. In fact I had always thought my purple shirt was unattractive.

But then something strange started to happen. I began to wear that shirt a lot more. When I put it on, I would think to myself, "My favorite shirt is my favorite color." Then I would remember that it wasn't really true, but I'd wear it anyway.

Soon people started to buy me purple things because it was my "favorite" color. They gave me purple socks and purple posters. Even my mom bought me purple sheets, purple pillow cases, and purple curtains. My whole room was slowly turning purple!

Then, without realizing it, I started buying purple things on purpose. I bought a purple notebook, a purple bag for school, and even started taking notes with a purple pen. It's so bizarre because a year ago all colors were the same to me. Now I can describe the difference between lavender and lilac or violet and plum. I'm happy when I see a house with purple shutters or a purple car. And all of this happened because I lied and said I loved the color purple. The best part of it is that no one ever asks me what my favorite color is anymore. It's obvious. I'm a purple person!

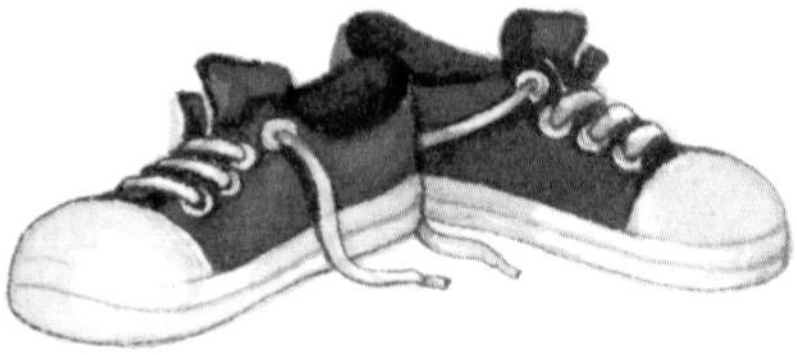

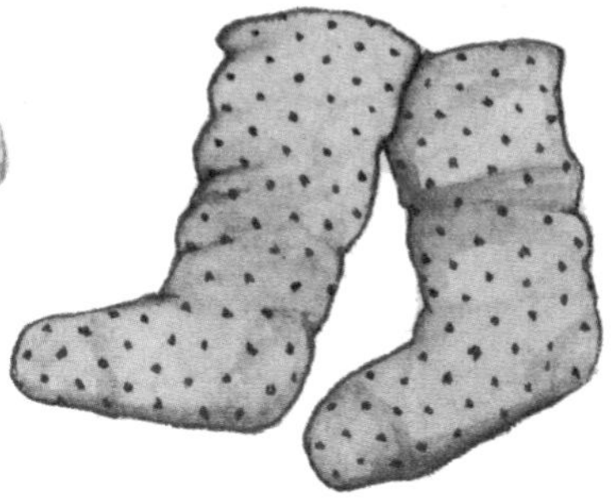

Silent Spring No Longer: RACHEL CARSON

RACHEL CARSON WAS BORN on a farm in Springdale, Pennsylvania, in 1907. It was here, through the gentle encouragement of her mother, that she learned to love nature. When Carson went to college, she took her love of nature with her. She majored in marine biology, the study of life in the sea.

After college Carson taught for five years before joining the U.S. Bureau of Fisheries. She wrote a radio show that explored life in the seas. It was called "Romance Under the Waters." Carson's writing made the sea come alive. She also wrote three books about the sea: *Under the Sea Wind, The Sea Around Us,* and *The Edge of the Sea.* These books all became bestsellers and won many awards. Carson soon left her job so she could become a full-time writer.

In the late 1940s and 1950s, people used chemicals called pesticides to kill unwanted insects. One of these pesticides was DDT. Scientists began to learn that DDT did kill harmful insects, but it also killed birds. Birds took the chemical into their bodies when they ate insects infected with it. The chemicals made the birds' eggs very frail. The delicate eggs broke easily, and many baby birds did not hatch. Birds such as peregrine falcons and bald eagles began to die out.

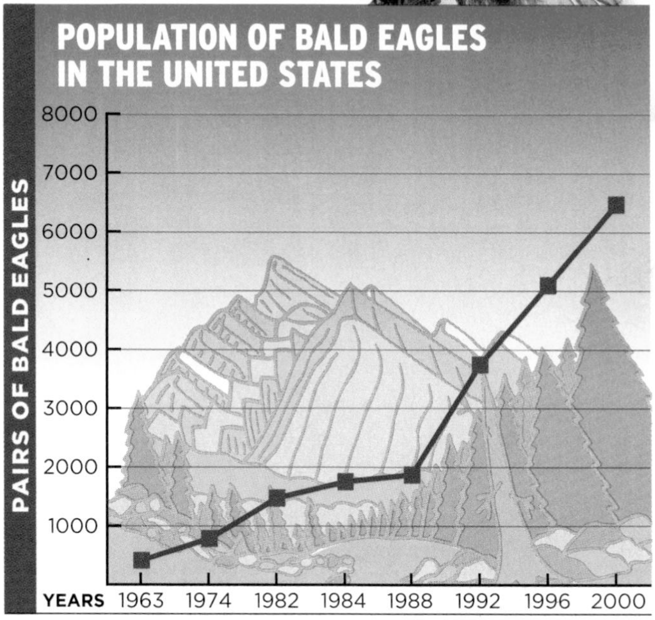

This line graph shows how the population of bald eagle pairs increased after DDT was banned in the United States.

Rachel Carson became concerned about this problem. She spent a lot of time gathering facts. Then she wrote a book called *Silent Spring*. In the book she wrote about how birds were dying because of DDT.

Companies that made the chemicals tried to say that Rachel was mistaken. President John F. Kennedy called for testing of chemicals used as pesticides. Tests showed that Carson was right. Pesticides were harming the environment and causing birds to die out.

Rachel Carson published *Silent Spring* in 1962. Carson did not get to see her work change history because she died in 1964. The use of DDT in the United States was banned in 1972. Since then birds that were in danger of dying out were saved and have come back. Now each spring you can hear these wonderful birds singing in the trees. Thanks to Rachel Carson, spring is not silent.

GOING TO THE LIBRARY

Talk About It

Libraries have more than books. In what other ways can you learn at the library?

LOG ON Find out more about the library at **www.macmillanmh.com**

Vocabulary

peculiar	**selecting**
snuffled	**consisted**
positive	**advanced**

FCAT **Dictionary**

Connotation/Denotation
Connotation is the feeling associated with a word. Denotation is the dictionary meaning. What are the connotation and denotation of *peculiar?*

A Library Card for Emilio

by Susan Pinter

"Hurry or we'll miss the bus to the library, Emilio!" called Mrs. Mendoza. The Mendoza family had moved to Boston, from San Juan, Puerto Rico, last month, and Emilio was going to get his library card today.

On the bus, Emilio's grandmother noticed something **peculiar**. Emilio was very quiet and looked rather sad. "Is something wrong, honey?" she asked.

Emilio **snuffled**. He then took out a tissue to blow his nose. "My speaking of English is not good. What if the library lady is not able to understand what I am saying?" he said.

"Your English gets better and better every day. I'm one hundred percent **positive** that the librarian will understand you," Mrs. Mendoza said confidently. "I am sure that you will be able to take some books home today."

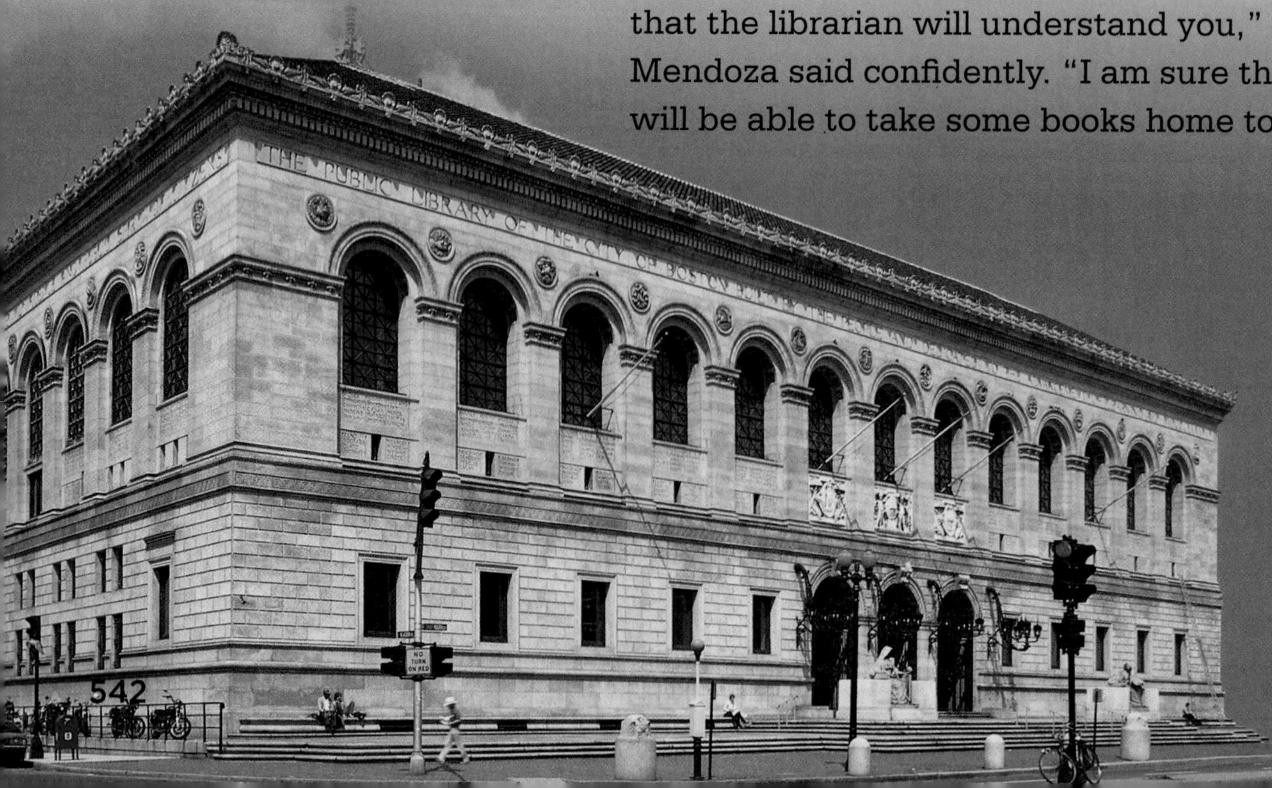

When they finally got to the library, there were lots of people. Some were reading newspapers. Others were **selecting** books that they wanted to borrow from the shelves. As Emilio looked around in wonder, a smiling librarian asked, "May I help you with anything?"

Emilio stuttered a little as he began to explain. "I... I am here for my card for library books."

"That's just terrific!" said the librarian. She asked him to complete a form that **consisted** of questions about Emilio and where he and his family lived.

Mrs. Mendoza smiled. She noticed that her grandson had no trouble understanding the form. He filled it in quickly and then returned it to the librarian.

"It will take me a few minutes to process your card, Emilio," said the librarian. "Why don't you select a few books to borrow today? If you're an **advanced** reader, you might want to look over there."

"Thank you," said Emilio.

"*Abuela*," Emilio whispered to Mrs. Mendoza, "My English must be better than I thought!"

Reread for Comprehension

Evaluate

FCAT

Chronological Order is the sequence or order in which events take place. Certain words and phrases can help readers identify the sequence of events in a story. Fill in your Sequence Chart to help you identify the **chronological order** of events as you reread the selection.

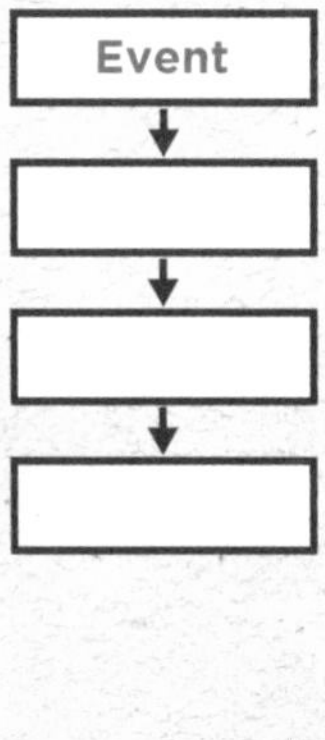

Comprehension

Genre

Realistic Fiction is a made-up story that could have happened in real life.

Evaluate

FCAT **Chronological Order**

As you read, fill in your Sequence Chart.

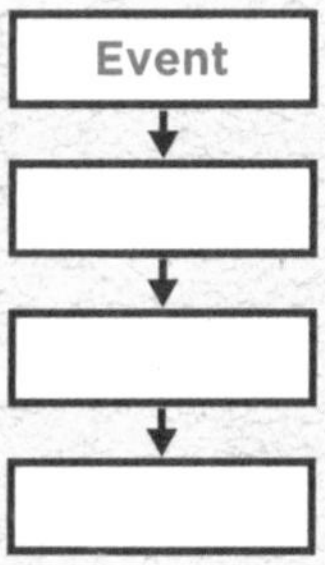

Read to Find Out

What happened that day at the library?

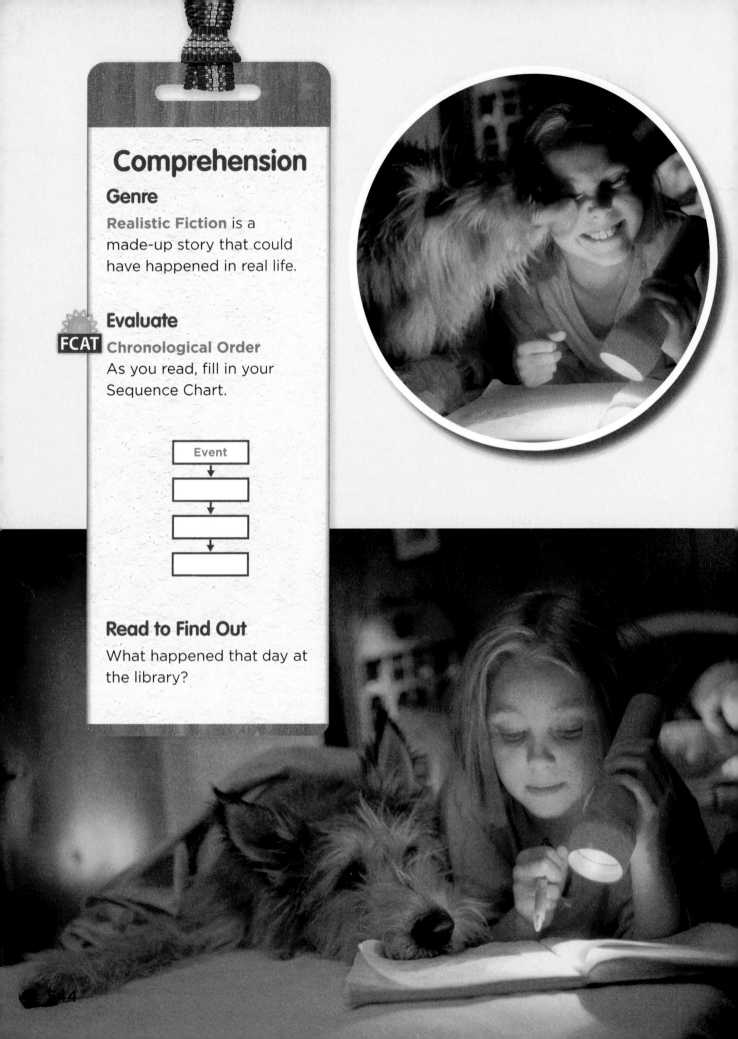

Because of Winn-Dixie

by Kate DiCamillo

I spent a lot of time that summer at the Herman W. Block Memorial Library. The Herman W. Block Memorial Library sounds like it would be a big fancy place, but it's not. It's just a little old house full of books, and Miss Franny Block is in charge of them all. She is a very small, very old woman with short gray hair, and she was the first friend I made in Naomi.

It all started with Winn-Dixie not liking it when I went into the library, because he couldn't go inside, too. But I showed him how he could stand up on his hind legs and look in the window and see me in there, **selecting** my books; and he was okay, as long as he could see me. But the thing was, the first time Miss Franny Block saw Winn-Dixie standing up on his hind legs like that, looking in the window, she didn't think he was a dog. She thought he was a bear.

This is what happened: I was picking out my books and kind of humming to myself, and all of a sudden, there was this loud and scary scream. I went running up to the front of the library, and there was Miss Franny Block, sitting on the floor behind her desk.

"Miss Franny?" I said. "Are you all right?"

"A bear," she said.

"A bear?" I asked.

"He has come back," she said.

"He has?" I asked. "Where is he?"

"Out there," she said and raised a finger and pointed at Winn-Dixie standing up on his hind legs, looking in the window for me.

"Miss Franny Block," I said, "that's not a bear. That's a dog. That's my dog. Winn-Dixie."

"Are you **positive**?" she asked.

"Yes ma'am," I told her. "I'm positive. He's my dog. I would know him anywhere."

Miss Franny sat there trembling and shaking.

"Come on," I said. "Let me help you up. It's okay." I stuck out my hand and Miss Franny took hold of it, and I pulled her up off the floor. She didn't weigh hardly anything at all. Once she was standing on her feet, she started acting all embarrassed, saying how I must think she was a silly old lady, mistaking a dog for a bear, but that she had a bad experience with a bear coming into the Herman W. Block Memorial Library a long time ago and she never had quite gotten over it.

"When did that happen?" I asked her.

"Well," said Miss Franny, "it is a very long story."

FCAT **Chronological Order**

List the sequence of events leading up to Opal finding Miss Franny on the floor.

"That's okay," I told her. "I am like my mama in that I like to be told stories. But before you start telling it, can Winn-Dixie come in and listen, too? He gets lonely without me."

"Well, I don't know," said Miss Franny. "Dogs are not allowed in the Herman W. Block Memorial Library."

"He'll be good," I told her. "He's a dog who goes to church." And before she could say yes or no, I went outside and got Winn-Dixie, and he came in and lay down with a "huummmppff" and a sigh, right at Miss Franny's feet.

She looked down at him and said, "He most certainly is a large dog."

"Yes ma'am," I told her. "He has a large heart, too."

"Well," Miss Franny said. She bent over and gave Winn-Dixie a pat on the head, and Winn-Dixie wagged his tail back and forth and **snuffled** his nose on her little old-lady feet. "Let me get a chair and sit down so I can tell this story properly."

Back when Florida was wild, when it **consisted** of nothing but palmetto trees and mosquitoes so big they could fly away with you," Miss Franny Block started in, "and I was just a little girl no bigger than you, my father, Herman W. Block, told me that I could have anything I wanted for my birthday. Anything at all."

Miss Franny looked around the library. She leaned in close to me. "I don't want to appear prideful," she said, "but my daddy was a very rich man. A very rich man." She nodded and then leaned back and said, "And I was a little girl who loved to read. So I told him, I said, 'Daddy, I would most certainly love to have a library for my birthday, a small little library would be wonderful.' "

"You asked for a whole library?"

"A small one," Miss Franny nodded. "I wanted a little house full of nothing but books and I wanted to share them, too. And I got my wish. My father built me this house, the very one we are sitting in now. And at a very young age, I became a librarian. Yes ma'am."

"What about the bear?" I said.

"Did I mention that Florida was wild in those days?" Miss Franny Block said.

"Uh-huh, you did."

"It was wild. There were wild men and wild women and wild animals."

"Like bears!"

"Yes ma'am. That's right. Now, I have to tell you, I was a little-miss-know-it-all. I was a miss-smarty-pants with my library full of books. Oh, yes ma'am, I thought I knew the answers to everything. Well, one hot Thursday, I was sitting in my library with all the doors and windows open and my nose stuck in a book, when a shadow crossed the desk. And without looking up, yes ma'am, without even looking up, I said, 'Is there a book I can help you find?'

"Well, there was no answer. And I thought it might have been a wild man or a wild woman, scared of all these books and afraid to speak up. But then I became aware of a very **peculiar** smell, a very strong smell. I raised my eyes slowly. And standing right in front of me was a bear. Yes ma'am. A very large bear."

"How big?" I asked.

"Oh, well," said Miss Franny, "perhaps three times the size of your dog."

"Then what happened?" I asked her.

"Well," said Miss Franny, "I looked at him and he looked at me. He put his big nose up in the air and sniffed and sniffed as if he was trying to decide if a little-miss-know-it-all librarian was what he was in the mood to eat. And I sat there. And then I thought, 'Well, if this bear intends to eat me, I am not going to let it happen without a fight. No ma'am.' So very slowly and very carefully, I raised up the book I was reading."

"What book was that?" I asked.

"Why, it was *War and Peace*, a very large book. I raised it up slowly and then I aimed it carefully and I threw it right at that bear and screamed, 'Be gone!' And do you know what?"

"No ma'am," I said.

"He went. But this is what I will never forget. He took the book with him."

"Nuh-uh," I said.

"Yes ma'am," said Miss Franny. "He snatched it up and ran."

"Did he come back?" I asked.

"No, I never saw him again. Well, the men in town used to tease me about it. They used to say, 'Miss Franny, we saw that bear of yours out in the woods today. He was reading that book and he said it sure was good and would it be all right if he kept it for just another week.' Yes ma'am. They did tease me about it." She sighed. "I imagine I'm the only one left from those days. I imagine I'm the only one that even recalls that bear. All my friends, everyone I knew when I was young, they are all dead and gone."

She sighed again. She looked sad and old and wrinkled. It was the same way I felt sometimes, being friendless in a new town and not having a mama to comfort me. I sighed, too.

Winn-Dixie raised his head off his paws and looked back and forth between me and Miss Franny. He sat up then and showed Miss Franny his teeth.

"Well now, look at that," she said. "That dog is smiling at me."

"It's a talent of his," I told her.

"It is a fine talent," Miss Franny said. "A very fine talent." And she smiled back at Winn-Dixie.

"We could be friends," I said to Miss Franny. "I mean you and me and Winn-Dixie, we could all be friends."

Miss Franny smiled even bigger. "Why, that would be grand," she said, "just grand."

FCAT **Chronological Order**
How did Miss Franny and Opal become friends? List the events in chronological order.

And right at that minute, right when the three of us had decided to be friends, who should come marching into the Herman W. Block Memorial Library but old pinch-faced Amanda Wilkinson. She walked right up to Miss Franny's desk and said, "I finished *Johnny Tremain* and I enjoyed it very much. I would like something even more difficult to read now, because I am an **advanced** reader."

"Yes dear, I know," said Miss Franny. She got up out of her chair.

Amanda pretended like I wasn't there. She stared right past me. "Are dogs allowed in the library?" she asked Miss Franny as they walked away.

"Certain ones," said Miss Franny, "a select few." And then she turned around and winked at me. I smiled back. I had just made my first friend in Naomi, and nobody was going to mess that up for me, not even old pinch-faced Amanda Wilkinson.

Because of Kate

Kate DiCamillo wrote this story while she was shivering in Minnesota one winter. Kate had moved there from Florida and was very homesick. She also felt sad because she was not allowed to have a dog in her apartment. When Kate went to sleep, she dreamed she heard a girl say she had a dog named Winn-Dixie. Kate started writing the story as soon as she woke up.

Because of Winn-Dixie became the first book that Kate published. It won a Newbery Honor, which is one of the most respected awards a children's book can receive. She is also the author of *The Tiger Rising* and of *The Tale of Despereaux: Being the Story of a Mouse, a Princess, Some Soup, and a Spool of Thread*, which received the Newbery Medal in 2004.

When Kate wrote *Because of Winn-Dixie*, she would get up early every day to write two pages before leaving for her job at a bookstore. She no longer works at the bookstore, but she still writes two pages every morning.

Other books
by Kate DiCamillo

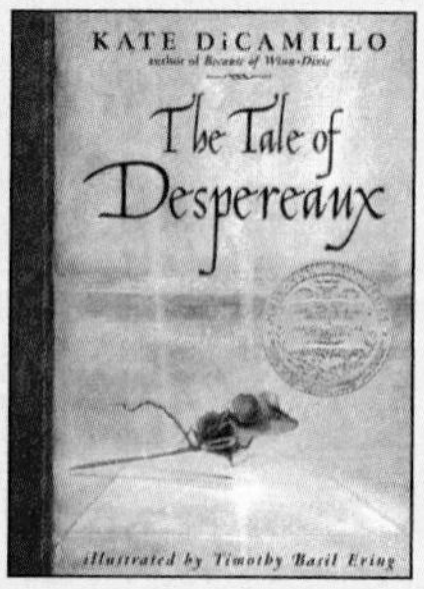

LOG ON Find out more about Kate DiCamillo at **www.macmillanmh.com**

FCAT Author's Purpose

This story is a made-up story that has true-to-life details. What was the author's purpose for writing? Why do you think so?

FCAT Comprehension Check

Summarize

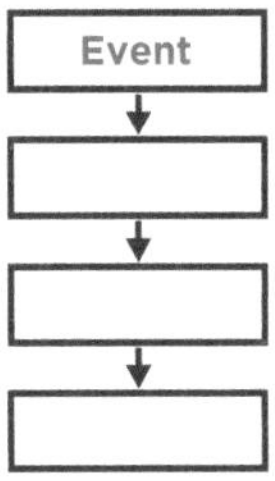

Use your Sequence Chart to help you summarize *Because of Winn-Dixie*. Include the most important plot events.

Think and Compare

1. Miss Franny Block tells Opal a **peculiar** story from her childhood. Describe the events of this story in chronological order. **Evaluate: Chronological Order**

2. Reread page 552 of *Because of Winn-Dixie*. Why don't Opal and Miss Franny have any friends? How is this important to the story? Explain using story details. **Analyze**

3. What story would you share with a new friend? **Apply**

4. Why are Miss Franny Block and Opal a good match for each other? Explain using story details. **Evaluate**

5. Read "A Library Card for Emilio" on pages 542–543. How is Emilio like Opal in *Because of Winn-Dixie*? How are they different? Use details from both selections to explain. **Reading/Writing Across Texts**

FCAT

Poetry

Free Verse Poems do not have to follow rhyme schemes but often contain rhythmic patterns and other poetic elements.

Literary Elements

Onomatopoeia is the use of a word that imitates the sound that it stands for, such as *hiss*.

A **Simile** compares two different things, usually by using the words *like* or *as*.

I Love the Look of Words

The word *popping* sounds like the thing it describes. This is an example of onomatopoeia.

Popcorn leaps, popping from the floor
of a hot black skillet
and into my mouth.
Black words leap,
snapping from the white
page. Rushing into my eyes. Sliding
into my brain which gobbles them
the way my tongue and teeth
chomp the buttered popcorn.

When I have stopped reading,
ideas from the words stay stuck
in my mind, like the sweet
smell of butter perfuming my
fingers long after the popcorn
is finished.

This simile compares ideas sticking in the poet's mind to the smell of butter sticking to her fingers.

I love the book and the look of words
the weight of ideas that popped into my mind
I love the tracks
of new thinking in my mind.

— Maya Angelou

FCAT Connect and Compare

1. Although it does not rhyme, this free verse poem contains elements of poetry, such as onomatopoeia. Besides the word *popping*, what are other examples of onomatopoeia in this poem? **Onomatopoeia**

2. The poet uses a simile to compare her brain to something. What is it? Explain using details from the poem. **Analyze**

3. Compare the narrator in this poem with the narrator in *Because of Winn-Dixie*. How are they alike? How are they different? **Reading/Writing Across Texts**

LOG ON Find out more about free verse poems at **www.macmillanmh.com**

Writer's Craft

FCAT **Multiple Paragraphs**

Good writers use **multiple paragraphs** to organize and present information. Arranging paragraphs in a logical order helps writers compare and contrast their information.

Write About Two Characters

I wrote multiple paragraphs to compare and contrast two characters.

I told how the characters were different in one paragraph. I showed how they were alike in another paragraph.

Ike and Cara

by Ramona C.

I am writing to compare two characters from the books we read this year. One is Ike from Dear Mrs. LaRue and the other is Cara from Dear Mr. Winston.

Right away, you can tell that Ike's character could never be real—dogs cannot talk or write letters to their owners. Cara's character could be real. She looks and writes like a real person. Ike uses a typewriter. Cara types her letter on a computer.

The two characters are alike because they are both clever, they get in trouble, and they make readers like me laugh.

Writing Prompt

Characters from books can have similar and different traits.

Think of characters that have similar and different traits.

Now write to tell about characters that have similar and different traits.

FCAT Writer's Checklist

- [x] **Focus:** My writing clearly shows the similarities and differences between my characters.
- [ ] **Organization:** I use multiple paragraphs to compare my characters. I tell how they are alike in one paragraph and how they are different in another.
- [x] **Support:** I choose good details about my characters' traits to compare and contrast.
- [x] **Conventions:** I use correct punctuation. I capitalize proper nouns.

PUTTING ON A PLAY

Talk About It

Make up a story about the play these kids are performing. What is it called? What happens?

LOG ON Find out more about plays at **www.macmillanmh.com**

Vocabulary

selfish
bumbling
cranky
commotion
exasperated
specialty
famished

FCAT Thesaurus

Antonyms are words that have opposite meanings. *Cranky* and *cheerful* are antonyms. Can you think of other antonyms?

The Frog Prince

by Marcia Stevens

Narrator: There once was a beautiful princess whose favorite amusement was a golden ball. One day the princess tossed the ball too high, and it landed in the well. As the princess cried over her lost treasure, she heard someone ask a question.

Frog: Why are you crying, beautiful princess?

Narrator: The princess looked around and saw only a frog.

Princess: I am crying because my favorite golden ball fell into the well.

Frog: I can retrieve it for you, but first you must agree to one condition. You must promise to take me home and be my friend.

Narrator: The princess had no intention of being friends with a frog, but she promised anyway. When the frog brought her the ball, the princess snatched it from him and scampered home.

Frog: What a **selfish** princess. I'm certain that she has forgotten her promise. I'll just hop over to the castle to remind her.

Narrator: The frog hop-hop-hopped through the meadow and knocked on the heavy door of the castle.

Princess: What are you doing here, you **bumbling** frog?

Frog: My, aren't *we* **cranky**? And as for bumbling, *I* wasn't the one who dropped the ball into the well. I am here to remind you of the promise you made.

Narrator: The princess slammed the door in the frog's face with a big BANG.

King: I heard a door slam. What's all the **commotion**? If you made a promise, you must honor it.

Narrator: The princess was **exasperated** but obeyed her father. The king, the princess, and the frog enjoyed dinner together. It was mutton stew, the cook's **specialty**.

Frog: I was **famished**, but now I'm full. Thank you for dinner. Kindly show me to my bed now.

Narrator: The princess did as she was asked, but the frog looked sad.

Frog: You have welcomed me into your home, but I can tell that you don't want to be my friend.

Narrator: The princess blushed, for what the frog said was true. She bent down to kiss the frog, but ended up kissing a prince.

Frog: I am a prince who was turned into a frog, and your kiss turned me back. Thank you, dear friend!

Narrator: The prince and princess were wonderful friends from that day on and lived happily ever after.

Reread for Comprehension

Evaluate

FCAT

Cause and Effect Sometimes the events in a story are organized by **cause and effect**. A cause is why something happens. An effect is what happens. Identifying a story's cause and effect helps readers examine the events in a story. Fill in your Cause and Effect Chart as you reread the selection.

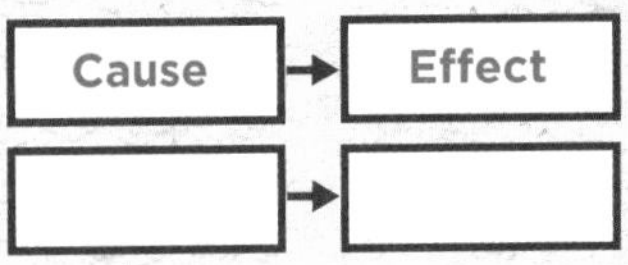

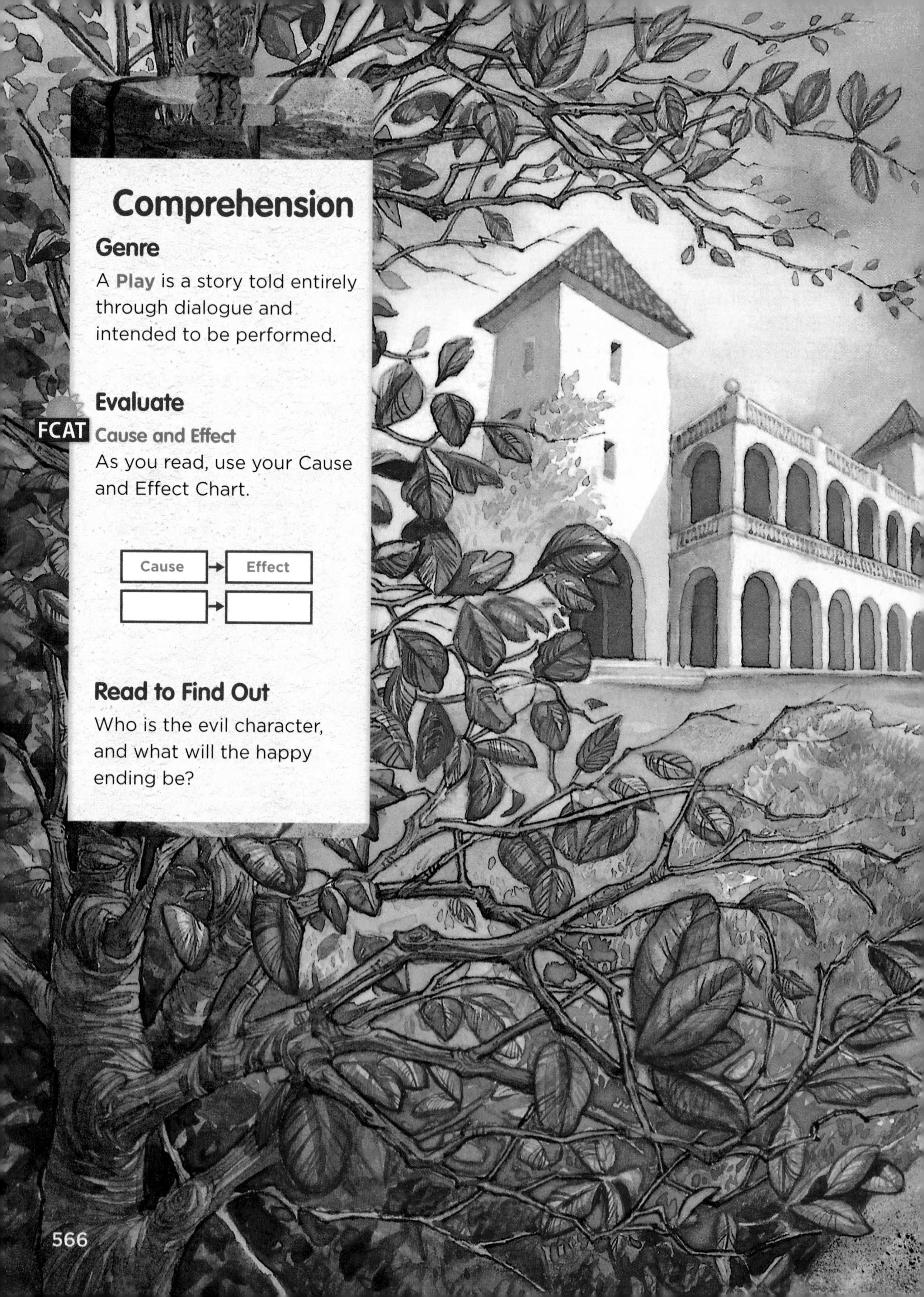

Comprehension

Genre

A **Play** is a story told entirely through dialogue and intended to be performed.

Evaluate

FCAT **Cause and Effect**

As you read, use your Cause and Effect Chart.

Cause	→	Effect
	→	

Read to Find Out

Who is the evil character, and what will the happy ending be?

Ranita
The Frog Princess

by Carmen Agra Deedy
illustrated by Renato Alarcão

Setting

Long ago in Mexico. The Viceroy's hunting lodge in Chapultapec forest.

Players

Felipe, the Viceroy's rotten son

Pepe, Felipe's mistreated servant

Ranita, a little frog with a mysterious past

Vieja Sabia, a wise but **cranky** old woman

Viceroy, the representative of the Spanish throne

Viceroy's Wife

Cook

Man One

Man Two

Servant One

Servant Two

Man Three

Extras: Members of hunting party, servants attending dinner, noblemen and ladies

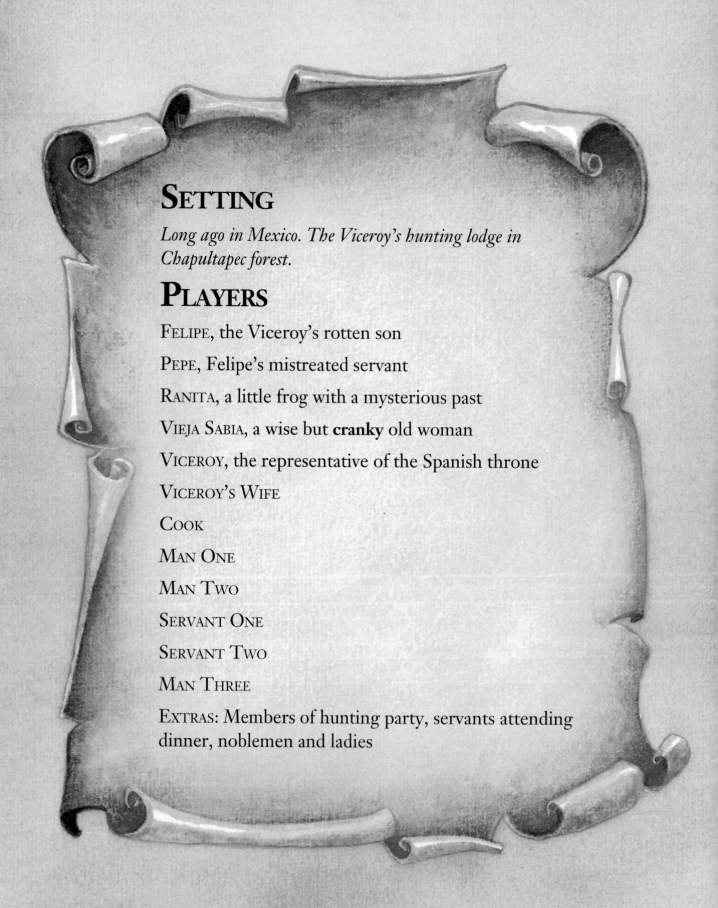

Scene 1

In a forest clearing, men are frantically searching the ground. From a nearby stone well, Ranita watches but remains unnoticed.

Man One: *(Frustrated)* Keep looking! If we don't find that golden arrow—

Man Two: —we'll be on *tortillas* and water for the next month!

(Men, grumbling, all agree.)

(Enter Felipe.)

Felipe: *(Loud and demanding)* Well? Have you found my golden arrow yet?

Man Three: Not yet, Señor!

Felipe: *(Sweetly, hand over heart)* It was a gift from my dear mother. *(Turning suddenly and hissing)* Find it or I will feed you to the jaguars—starting with my **bumbling** servant, Pepe. It's his fault I missed my mark. Now, out of my sight, all of you!

(Men exit hurriedly.)

Felipe: *(Stomping foot and whining)* I want my golden arrow back!

Ranita: *(Sitting on top of well, holding the golden arrow)* You mean, *this* golden arrow?

Felipe: *(Joyously)* My golden arrow! You found it! You—*(Stops cold)*—you're a frog.

Ranita: You were expecting a Mayan princess, perhaps?

Felipe: *(Rolls eyes)* Well, I wasn't expecting a talking frog!

Ranita: *(Sighs)* I'm under a spell. I don't like to talk about it.

Felipe: *(Pauses to think)* Not my problem. Hand over the arrow.

Ranita: *(Plink! Drops it back down the well)* Hmm, looks like it's your problem now.

Felipe: N-n-noooo! *(Threateningly)* What have you done, you foolish frog?

Ranita: If I am so foolish, how come I am the one with the arrow while you are the one standing there talking to a *rana*, a frog?

Felipe: I would squish you right now—*(Sniffs)*—but you are only a frog.

Ranita: *(Warningly)* You want that golden arrow?

Felipe: *(Suspicious)* In exchange for what?

Ranita: A promise.

Felipe: *(Relieved)* Oh, is that all?

Ranita: A promise is a very serious thing.

Felipe: *(Coughing)* Yes, yes, of course—go on.

FCAT Cause and Effect

What caused Felipe to make a promise to Ranita?

Ranita: IF I rescue your golden arrow, you must promise to let me eat from your *plato*, sleep in your *cama*, and give me a *beso* when the sun comes up.

Felipe: *(Just stares)* Eat from my plate? Sleep in my bed? KISS you? *That* is disgusting!

Ranita: No promise, no golden arrow.

Felipe: *(Crossing his fingers behind his back)* I promise.

(Ranita fetches the arrow. Felipe bows and runs off.)

Ranita: *Espera*! Wait! I can't hop that fast! *(Hangs her head and begins to cry)* He's gone. Now I'll never break this evil spell.

(Enter wise woman, leaning on two canes.)

Vieja Sabia: It doesn't feel very good, does it?

Ranita: *(Blows nose)* Please, no lectures today, old woman.

Vieja Sabia: My name is Vieja *Sabia*.

Ranita: Sorry, *Wise* Old Woman. *(Sadly)* You've already turned me into a frog. Isn't that enough?

Vieja Sabia: You wouldn't be a frog if you hadn't refused to give me a drink from this well, so long ago.

Ranita: I was a **selfish** child then. I have paid for that, haven't I? I have learned what it is like to be alone and forgotten.

Vieja Sabia: Perhaps you have . . .

Ranita: *(Brightening)* Then, you will turn me into a girl again?

Vieja Sabia: No. But I will take you as far as the Viceroy's hunting lodge. You must make the leap from there.

(Exit Vieja Sabia and Ranita.)

Scene 2

Hunting lodge with Viceroy, his wife, noblemen and women, all seated at long banquet table. Servants scurry in and out with bowls of food.

Servant One: *(Placing bowl of soup before Viceroy) Sopa,* Señor?

Viceroy: (***Exasperated***) *Sí, sí.* Where is Felipe?

Viceroy's Wife: *(Wistfully)* Dear boy. He is probably feeding the birds.

Servant Two: *(Aside)* To the cat.

Servant One: *(Muffles laugh)*

(Enter Felipe.)

Felipe: I am **famished**. What a day I've had today. First, I lost my golden arrow—

(Shouting from the kitchen can be heard.)

Felipe: *(Louder)*—then I met this ridiculous, demanding—

(Enter Ranita, running from the kitchen chased by cook and servants.)

Felipe: *(Slack-jawed)*—frog.

Cook: You hop back here! *(To servant)* Stop her, right now!

Servant One: *(Tries to catch frog)* Aaaaayyyy! She's a slippery one!

Servant Two: Oooooeeeeee! She bit me!

Cook: Get her, Pepe. *(Pepe catches Ranita under the table, smiles, and lets her go. A* **commotion** *follows as the cook and servants chase Ranita.)*

FCAT Cause and Effect
What will be the effect of Ranita going to Felipe's home?

Viceroy: *Basta!* Enough! Who *is* this creature?

Felipe: *(Sneering)* She's the nasty little frog who rescued my golden arrow.

Ranita: And in return he promised to let me eat from his *plato*, sleep in his *cama*, and give me a *beso* when the sun came up.

Viceroy: Did you make this promise?

Felipe: *(Sullen)* I don't remember.

Viceroy's Wife: *(Indignant)* Even if he did—he is the Viceroy's son!

Viceroy: *(Grave) Sí.* And THE VICEROY'S SON KEEPS HIS PROMISES. Pepe! Set a place for our guest.

Felipe: But, Father—

Viceroy's Wife: Ernesto!

Viceroy: *(Slams fist on table.) Silencio!* Silence!

(Ranita hops on table. Felipe is too stunned to speak. Viceroy's Wife is glaring.)

Viceroy: Everyone—and I mean *everyone*—EAT!

(Pepe puts bowl down in front of Felipe.)

Felipe: *(Gives a yelp)* Pepe!

Pepe: *(Innocently) Sí?*

Felipe: *(Disgusted)* There is a fly in my soup!

Pepe: It's for the frog.

Viceroy: Excellent. Eat up, Felipe.

Viceroy's Wife: *(Revolted)* Arggh.

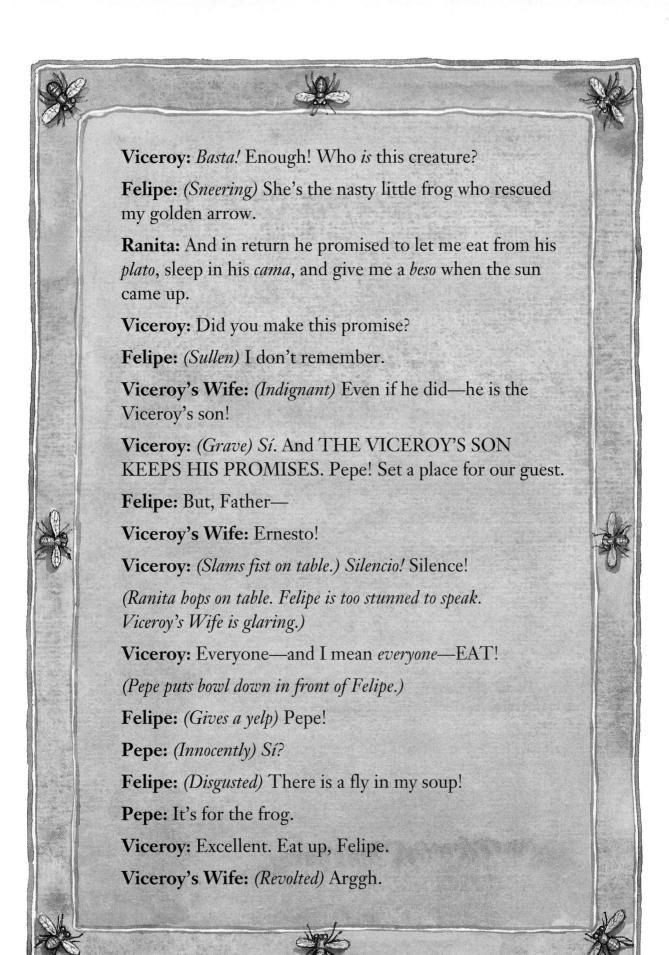

Scene 3

(Felipe's bedroom)

Felipe: *(On bed)* I refuse to sleep next to a FROG. Pepe!!!!!!!!

Pepe: *(Enters immediately) Sí*, Señor?

Felipe: *(Snappish)* What took you so long? Hurry—tell my father I can't do this. *(Desperate)* Tell him I'll get warts.

(Enter Viceroy.)

Viceroy: *(Annoyed)* With any luck, you will get one on your oath-breaking tongue, boy.

Felipe: *(Whining)* Father—

Viceroy: You made a promise, Felipe. *(To Pepe)* Help him keep his word, eh, Pepe?

(Exit Viceroy.)

Felipe: *(Throws pillow at Pepe. Falls on bed and begins to wail.)* AAAAAAAYYYYYYYY!

Pepe: *(Blows out candle and sits in chair.) Hasta mañana . . .* until tomorrow. Sweet dreams, Felipe.

Felipe: *(Growls)* I will dream of roasted frog legs.

Ranita: I'm telling.

Felipe: Bug breath!

Ranita: Big baby!

Pepe: *(Sighs)* It's going to be a long night.

(Next morning)

Ranita: *(Cheerful) Despierta*, wake up! It's "beso time!"

[Felipe rubs eyes, sees Ranita, and shrieks.]

Felipe: *(Whimpers, clutching his blanket)* It wasn't a bad dream, after all. Forget it, frog! I am not kissing you!

Ranita: *(Stubbornly)* You promised.

Felipe: Well, *(Smiles slowly)* I've just had a better idea. *(Kicks chair to wake his servant)* Pepe!

Pepe: *(Groggy)* Señor!

Felipe: You are sworn to obey me in all things, *sí*?

Pepe: *(Confused) Sí*, Señor.

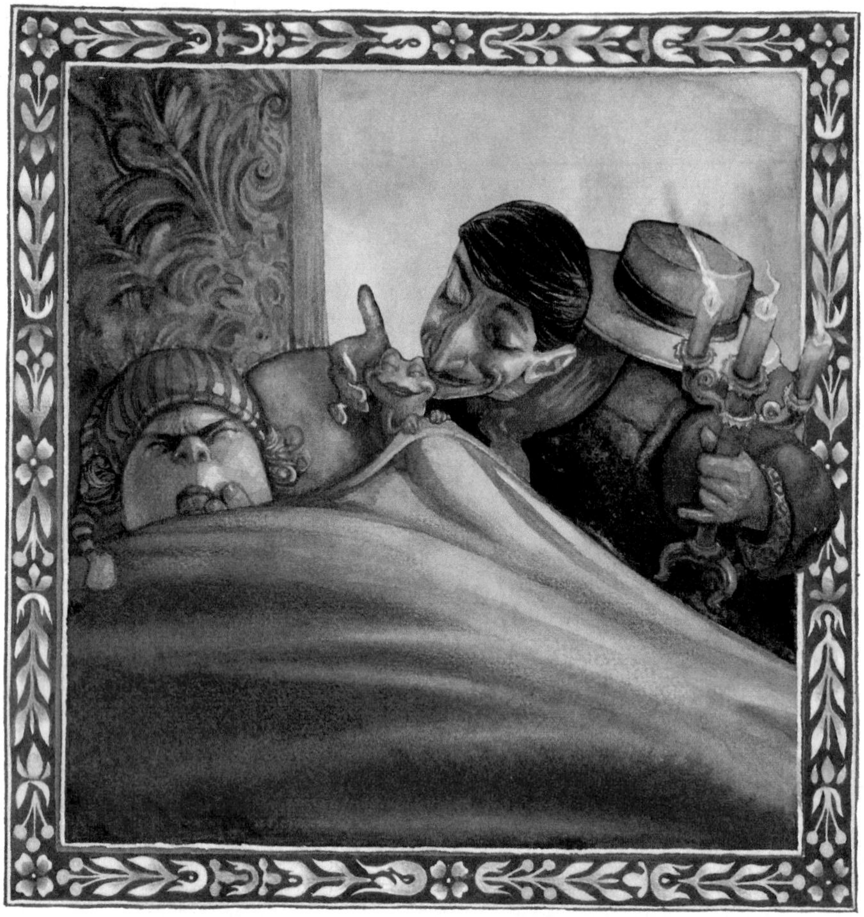

Felipe: *(Smug)* KISS . . . THE . . . FROG.

[Pepe shrugs and kisses Ranita's cheek.]

(No longer a frog, Ranita is now a beautiful Mayan Princess.)

Felipe: *(Dazzled)* I—but who? *(Bowing)* Allow me to introduce myself, I am—

Ranita: —the Spanish Viceroy's Rotten Son. And I am . . . the Mayan Emperor's Lucky Daughter.

(Felipe and Pepe fall on their knees.)

Ranita: I have been enchanted for 200 years.

Felipe: *(Looks up)* You've been a frog for 200 years? What's so LUCKY about that?

Ranita: I'll tell you. As a princess, I could have ended up the wife of a spoiled brat like you. Instead, I found myself a prince . . . *(Takes Pepe's hand)* a prince of a husband, that is.

(Pepe kisses the Princess's hand, while Felipe has a screaming tantrum.)

Epilogue

The same clearing in the forest as in Scene 1

Felipe: *(Kicks a stone)* If they think I'm going to their ridiculous wedding . . . ha! May they have a dozen ugly tadpole children!

(Enter Vieja Sabia.)

Vieja Sabia: *Agua!* Water from the well, my son, before I die of thirst.

Felipe: *(Snarling)* I'm no water boy. I'm the Viceroy's son! Get your own water, you old *cucaracha!*

Vieja Sabia: *(With gentle concern)* Cockroach? It's very rude to speak to your elders that way. Has no one taught you manners?

Felipe: *(Puzzled)* No.

Vieja Sabia: *(Smiling wickedly)* Well *(pointing finger at Felipe)*, that is my **specialty**.

*(**POOF** Felipe the Frog hops onto the top of the well.)*

Vieja Sabia: *(to audience)* And now you know how the Frog Prince ended up in that well.

Once Upon a Time . . .

Carmen Agra Deedy came to the United States from Cuba in 1960, after a revolution made it dangerous for her family to live there. Hoping for a more peaceful life, Carmen and her family settled in Georgia. Carmen has not forgotten her Cuban heritage. She combines it with the heritage of the southern United States when writing her stories.

Other books by Carmen Agra Deedy

Renato Alarcão was born, raised, and currently lives in Rio de Janeiro, Brazil. Among his many art projects was the creation of 13 murals around Paterson and Passaic, New Jersey, all done with a team of artists and local teens.

FCAT **Author's Purpose**

Why did Carmen Agra Deedy write the play *Ranita, the Frog Princess*? Was her purpose to explain, inform, or entertain? How do you know?

LOG ON Find out more about Carmen Agra Deedy at **www.macmillanmh.com**

FCAT Comprehension Check

Summarize

Summarize *Ranita, the Frog Princess*. Use your Cause and Effect Chart to tell what Ranita's problem was and how it was solved.

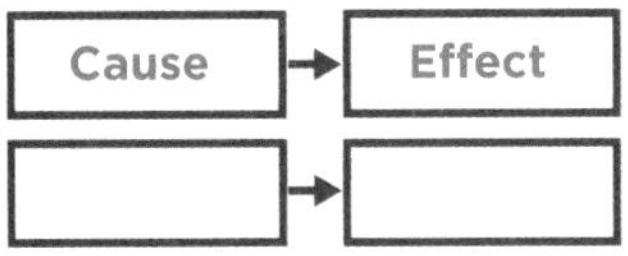

Think and Compare

1. Felipe is rude and breaks his promises. What does his rudeness bring him at the end of the story? Explain the outcome using story details. **Evaluate: Cause and Effect**

2. Reread Scene 2 of *Ranita, the Frog Princess* on pages 574–577. How does the Viceroy's wife feel about Felipe? How do the servants feel? How do their feelings help the reader predict the ending of the story? Explain using details from the story. **Analyze**

3. How would you respond to the deal that Ranita offered Felipe? **Apply**

4. Did Felipe deserve the punishment he received for being **selfish**? Explain using story details. **Evaluate**

5. Read "The Frog Prince" on pages 564–565. How is this story like *Ranita, the Frog Princess*? How are the stories different? Use details from both selections to explain. **Reading/Writing Across Texts**

Science

Genre

Nonfiction Articles explain a topic by presenting facts about it. They also provide informative photos.

FCAT Text Features

Interviews are questions asked by one person and answered by another.

Content Vocabulary

organs **circulation** **digestion**

Digestion and Circulation: A Frog's Story

by Jerry Liverstein

Many zoos have exhibits where you can view frogs in their natural environment.

Do you know what happens to a bug after a frog swallows it? Food travels to the same place in a frog that it does in people. You might think that a frog's body is different from a person's body but they are actually similar! Both frogs and people have special **organs** that carry out various jobs. These organs make up different structures. Read the following interview about digestion and circulation in frogs.

Q How does everything start?

A First the body needs food. A frog catches food by throwing its sticky tongue into the air. Any insect buzzing around gets caught on the tongue, and the frog swallows it. The insect travels down the frog's throat toward the stomach.

Q What happens once the insect is in the stomach?

A **Digestion** begins. Stomachs are like giant mixing bowls. They are lined with acids, or liquids used to break down food. In the stomach the insect mixes with acids and becomes a liquid.

Q What happens to that liquid?

A The liquid moves out of the stomach. It passes along vitamins and other nutrients to the frog's blood.

When a frog swallows food, it closes its eyes. Many scientists believe this is to help push the food into its stomach.

Reading an Interview

An interview is made up of questions and answers. The letter *Q* stands for the question, and the letter *A* stands for the answer. Each *Q* paragraph may have a question mark at the end, but it also may not.

Q: How many bugs do frogs eat a year?

A: It depends on the frog, where it lives, and the weather that year.

Q Why does that liquid pass anything along to the blood?

A The blood needs vitamins and nutrients for **circulation**. Like people, frogs need oxygen to live. They can get oxygen in two ways. They can either breathe in oxygen or absorb it through their skin. Oxygen goes into their bloodstream. It is the heart's job to make sure the oxygen-filled blood circulates throughout the frog's body.

Q How does the heart get blood to the body?

A When a heart beats, it is pumping blood to the other organs in the body. The other organs need the oxygen and nutrients in the blood to perform their jobs. Circulation helps the other organs get what they need.

Frogs may not be as big as we are, but their small bodies have the same systems that our bodies do. Knowing about the systems of frogs can help us better understand our own!

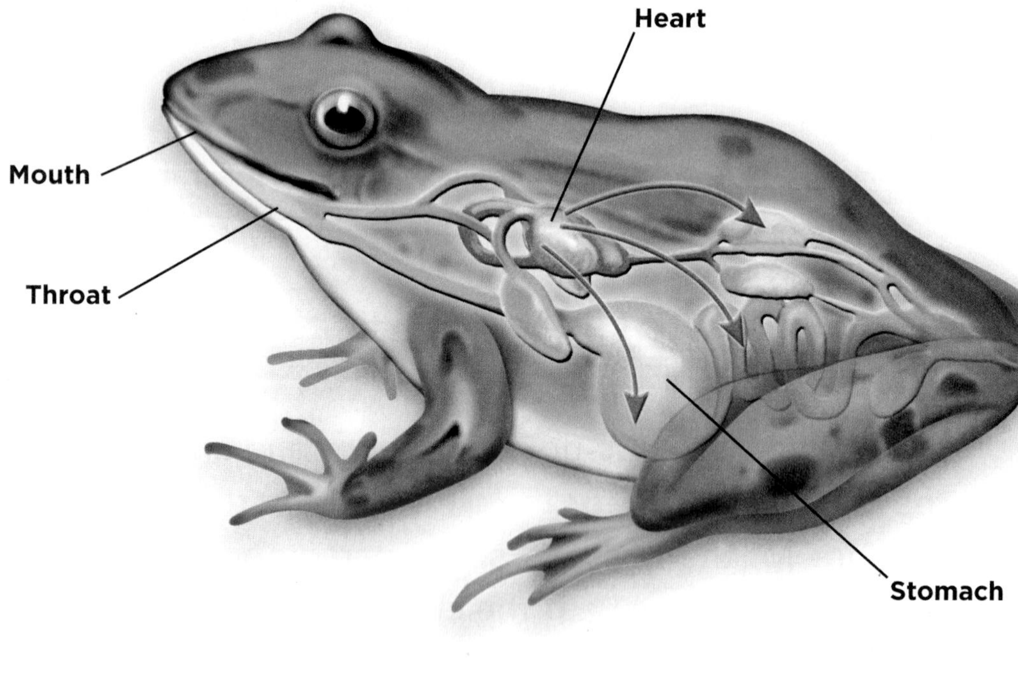

This diagram shows the organs used in digestion and circulation. The arrows indicate the blood flow in circulation.

Not only do frogs make fun pets, but many scientists use frogs to help them better understand the human body.

FCAT Connect and Compare

1. In this interview, how can the reader tell when a question is being asked? How will they know they are reading an answer? **Reading an Interview**

2. Describe the process of digestion using details from the article. **Analyze**

3. Think about this article and *Ranita, the Frog Princess*. How could the author have included information from this article to make Felipe treat Ranita better? Explain using details from both selections. **Reading/Writing Across Texts**

Research Inquiry: Science Activity

Research other body systems and organs. Write a brief summary about one of the organs and the job it performs in the human body. Write a list of questions you would ask if you were going to interview someone about how the organ works in the human body.

LOG ON Find out more about body systems at **www.macmillanmh.com**

Write a Descriptive Poster

Writer's Craft

FCAT Word Choice

A good writer pays close attention to **word choice**, using precise adjectives to help readers picture what is being described.

I wanted to describe the spring festival at school on a poster.

I used colorful adjectives.

School Spring Funfest!

by Jenny G.

Enjoy yourself at the
Annual All-School Spring Funfest
on April 10 from 12–6 p.m.

The Spring Funfest is a festival for everyone. Kids can have their faces painted like birds or lions or bears. You can eat spicy tamales, crunchy eggrolls, and hot dogs that are a foot long. Grades 3 and 4 will put on a talent show in the gym, and all the teachers will dress up as famous people from history.

For sports fans, there will be an exciting soccer game outside between parents and 6th graders.

Everyone has a great time. Mark your calendars!

Writing Prompt

Descriptive posters often tell about an event at school.

Think about descriptive posters you've seen that tell about an event at school.

Now write a descriptive poster to tell about an event at school.

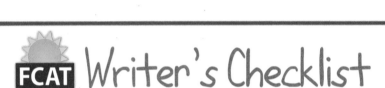

FCAT Writer's Checklist

- [x] **Focus:** My poster clearly shows the purpose of the event. I explain what will happen.
- [x] **Organization:** I start my poster with a catchy title. I include the date, time, and place of the event.
- [ ] **Support:** My word choice shows my enthusiasm. I use precise adjectives to show readers what I am describing.
- [x] **Conventions:** I use the articles *a* and *an* correctly. My sentences are complete.

Talk About It

What is the definition of an explorer? What do you think motivates a person to explore?

LOG ON Find out more about explorers at **www.macmillanmh.com**

Explorations

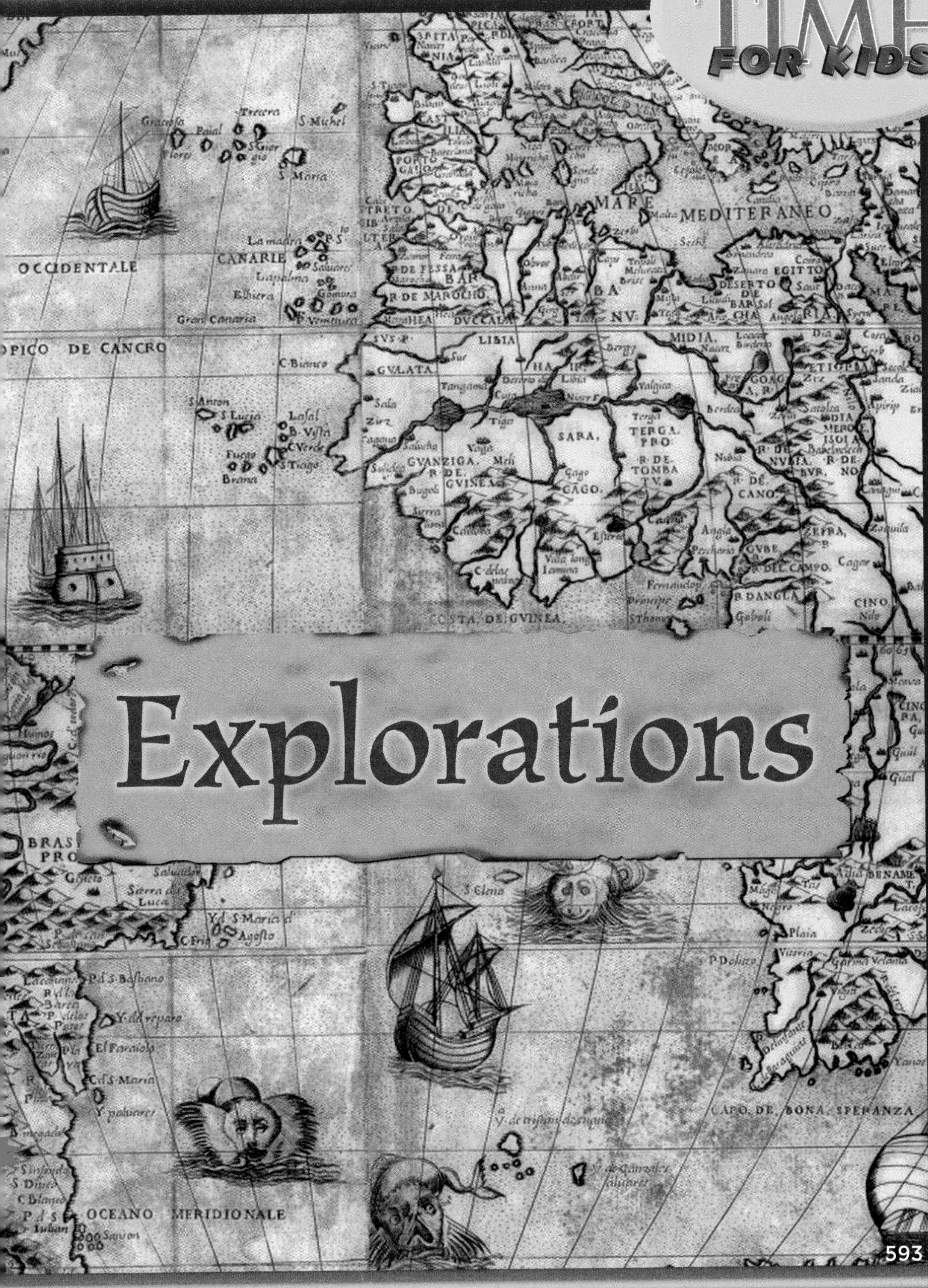

Real World Reading

BACK IN TIME WITH SPANISH EXPLORERS

Vocabulary

period
vessels
valuable
documenting
estimated

The sixteenth century was a **period** of great exploration by European countries. Facing known and unknown dangers, explorers set sail in the best sea-going **vessels** of their day. Many of those explorers who set sail for North America were from Spain.

The *Santa Maria*, Columbus's flagship

1492–1500: Christopher Columbus, sailing under the Spanish flag, explores the area around the Caribbean Sea.

1508: Juan Ponce de León travels to Puerto Rico.

1510: Diego Velázquez de Cuellar and 300 men conquer Cuba.

1513: Ponce de León is the first European to land in Florida.

1513: Vasco Núñez de Balboa is the first European to see the Pacific Ocean.

1518: Hernán Cortés leaves Cuba to explore Mexico.

1519: Alonso Álvarez de Pineda claims Texas for Spain.

1520: Álvarez de Pineda proves Florida is not an island but part of a gigantic continent instead.

1542: Alvar Núñez Cabeza de Vaca publishes a book about his travels in what is now Arizona, Texas, and New Mexico.

1539–1542: Hernando de Soto is the first European to see the Mississippi River.

1592: Juan de Fuca sails up the west coast of North America from Mexico to Vancouver Island.

1602: Sebastián Vizcaíno finds Monterey Bay and sets the scene for the settlement of what we now call California.

Tales of the Taíno

Deep in a forest of the Dominican Republic is an unusual well. It contained more than 240 objects—chairs, jars, baskets, and bowls—that are at least 500 years old. Far from worthless, these old everyday objects are instead extremely **valuable**. They are giving scientists new information about the Taino (tie•EE•no).

The Taino used shell, stone, wood, cotton, and other materials to carve representations of their gods.

The Taino were people who lived throughout the Caribbean, including the countries now called Cuba, Puerto Rico, Haiti, and the Dominican Republic. When European explorers started arriving in the Caribbean in 1492, the lives of the Taino were changed forever. Explorers took their land. Many of the Taino were killed. By the 1520s very little was left of the Taino civilization except some artifacts and a few words. *Hurricane*, *barbecue*, and *canoe* are Taino words we still use.

Scientists and historians are **documenting**—making a record of—and studying the items from the well. After 500 years of silence, it seems that the story of the Taino will finally be told.

The Commonwealth of Puerto Rico

Puerto Rico is a territory of the United States. That means it belongs to the U.S. but is not one of the 50 states. Puerto Rico is located in the Caribbean Sea, southeast of Miami, Florida. It consists of the island of Puerto Rico and the smaller islands of Vieques, Culebra, and Mona.

Capital: San Juan
Land area: 3,459 square miles
Estimated population: 3,886,000
Languages: Spanish and English

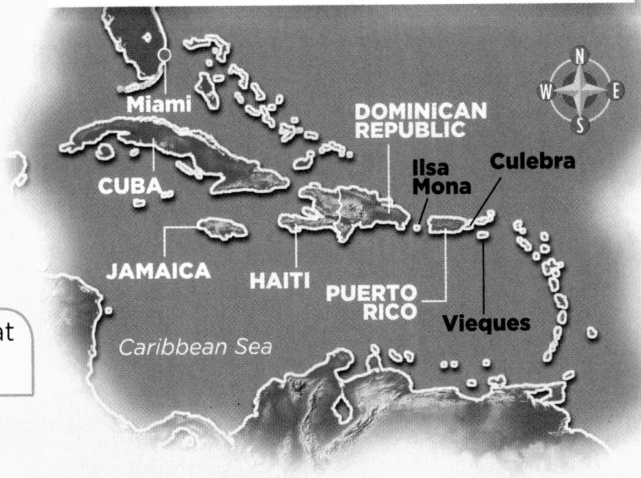

LOG ON Find out more about Puerto Rico at **www.macmillanmh.com**

Comprehension

Genre

A **Nonfiction Article** gives information about real people, places, or things.

Evaluate

FCAT

Compare and Contrast

When you compare, you tell how two or more things or ideas are similar. When you contrast, you tell how two or more things or ideas are different.

Exploring the Undersea Territory

Why are scientists devoting their lives to learning about the least explored territory on Earth—the ocean?

Off the coast of Hawaii in 2000, Sylvia Earle pilots a one-person submarine designed by a company she helped found.

Fifteenth- and sixteenth-century European explorers arrived in North America after dangerous ocean voyages. Today we are in another **period** of ocean-based exploration. Now the focus is on exploring the worlds found under the water. Explorers of the past and the present have a lot in common. However, modern explorers have **vessels** equipped with technologies that sea captains of the past could never have imagined.

Sylvia Earle: "Her Deepness"

Many things set Sylvia Earle apart from the great explorers of the past and the present. In 1979 she set the record for the deepest ocean dive—1,250 feet—ever made by a human alone and untethered—not connected in any way to a vessel or other object. That feat earned her the title "Her Deepness." In 1985 she set another record for diving solo. This time she dove to 3,000 feet in a submersible—a "compact" version of a submarine—she helped design.

Sylvia Earle at Woods Hole, Massachusetts, in 1995

Over the course of Earle's career of more than fifty years, she spent more than 6,000 hours under water. She held the positions of Explorer-in-Residence at the National Geographic Society and Chief Scientist at the National Oceanic and Atmospheric Administration (NOAA)—the first woman ever to hold that post. She co-founded and served as chief executive of a company that designs diving equipment. Add to this list the titles of mother and grandmother.

According to Earle, "This is the Lewis and Clark era for oceans." She was referring to the historic 1805 expedition to explore the huge and largely unknown area of the U.S. known as the Louisiana Purchase. Lewis and Clark mapped and documented the new territory.

"The ocean is the cornerstone of all life," Earle pointed out. "It produces most of the oxygen in the atmosphere. It shapes climate and weather. If the sea is sick, we will feel it. If it dies, we die." She based her work on her belief that ignorance is the greatest threat of all to this resource that is so **valuable** to life on Earth. "We know more about Mars than we know about the oceans," she has said. This scientist who is also an explorer, a businesswoman, and a grandmother has dedicated her life to both exploring and protecting the oceans of the world.

Robert Ballard: Exploring "Shipwreck Alley"

Robert Ballard is best known as the explorer who located the wreck of the luxury steamship *Titanic*. Like Sylvia Earle, he is a National Geographic Society Explorer-in-Residence. As Director of the Institute for Exploration (IFE), Ballard continues to dedicate his work to revealing the mysteries of the world's oceans. He and his team locate and study ancient shipwrecks in an effort to understand early human history.

Ballard's team is studying wrecks like this one (left) in Lake Huron. It is the freighter *Montana*, shown below in 1872.

Ballard and his team don't always have to travel to distant oceans to find interesting old shipwrecks. In fact they don't have to go any further than Lake Huron, one of the Great Lakes. There, within the Thunder Bay National Marine Sanctuary and Underwater Preserve, is an area known as "Shipwreck Alley." It is **estimated** that more than 100 shipwrecks dating back to the 1800s sit on the bottom of the lake. Ballard believes that finding and **documenting** them will tell an important story about trade and shipbuilding in North America.

Using a submersible called *Little Hercules*, the IFE team has identified a number of well-preserved wrecks. One is the *Cornelia B. Windiate*, which sank on November 28, 1875. It went down with all crew members and 332 tons of wheat. Cameras have photographed the ship's three wooden masts, still standing tall; its anchors, deck, and rigging; and its name, carved into the hull.

As their work in "Shipwreck Alley" continues, Ballard and his team expect to increase awareness of one aspect of U.S. history.

Robert Ballard carries a salvaged artifact.

A sonogram—a picture made with sound waves—shows the *Cornelia B.Windiate* on the floor of Lake Huron.

FCAT

Think and Compare

1. How did Sylvia Earle earn the nickname "Her Deepness"?
2. Why does Robert Ballard want to investigate the shipwrecks in Lake Huron?
3. How are Sylvia Earle and Robert Ballard alike? How are they different?
4. Based on these selections, what generalization can be made about explorers both past and present?

FCAT **Test Strategy**

Right There

You can put your finger on the answer. Look for key words in the question. Then find those key words in the selection.

LORDS OF THE SEAS

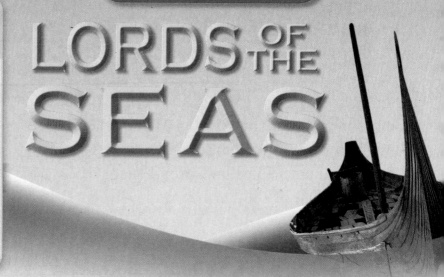

The Oseberg ship, shown above, is now on display at the Viking Ship Museum in Oslo, Norway.

Nearly 500 years before Christopher Columbus, bold Viking sailors crossed the Atlantic Ocean. Vikings were the first Europeans to reach North America. They lived in a part of Northern Europe called Scandinavia. Most Vikings were peaceful farmers, traders, and gifted craftsmen. They were also excellent shipbuilders. The ships Vikings built sailed faster and further than any other ships built at that time.

Viking ships were tough enough to sail hundreds of miles on the open sea. They were also light enough to be carried over land. When there was no wind, the crews could row the ships with oars. Other ships in that time period depended on wind and had not been designed to use oars.

Vikings used their ships to search for goods they could not get at home, such as silk and glass. Some sailed west and settled in Iceland and Greenland. Artifacts found in these places show that about 12,000 Vikings settled in these lands.

The Viking artifacts tell many tales. A famous Viking ship called Oseberg was discovered off the coast of Norway. It was found around 1906 in the murky clay of a burial mound. Archaeologists Gabriel Gustafson and Haakon Shetelig unearthed this ancient ship. It is believed to be the grave site of a priestess who was around 25 years old. When an analysis of the ship was made, it was discovered that the wood dates back to A.D. 834.

Between A.D. 997 and 1003, a Viking named Leif Eriksson landed in what is now Canada. The Vikings probably stayed for less than 10 years, but traded with Native Americans for much longer. A bit of their culture can still be found on our calendar. Tuesday, Wednesday, Thursday, and Friday are named for Viking gods!

Go on

FCAT **Now answer Numbers 1 through 5. Base your answers on the article "Lords of the Seas."**

1 The Vikings originally lived in

(A) Canada.
(B) Scandinavia.
(C) the Atlantic coast.
(D) Iceland and Greenland.

2 According to the article, what was one important feature of Viking ships?

(F) They had very colorful sails.
(G) They were large enough to hold many people.
(H) They were light enough to be carried over land.
(I) They were made from rare and expensive wood.

Tip
Look for key words.

3 Archaeologists Gabriel Gustafson and Haakon Shetelig

(A) buried a priestess.
(B) sailed the Oseberg ship.
(C) unearthed the Oseberg ship.
(D) sold wood from the Oseberg ship.

4 READ THINK EXPLAIN How were Viking ships different from the other ships that were built in that time period? Explain using details from the article.

5 READ THINK EXPLAIN How were Viking ships designed? What were they used for? Explain using details from the article.

STOP

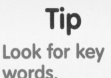

Write to a Prompt

FCAT

Jobs require special skills and talents.

Think of a job you know about.

Now write to explain what it takes to do this job.

Expository writing explains, defines, or tells how to do something.

To figure out if a writing prompt asks for expository writing, look for clue words, such as explain, tell how, or define.

Below see how one student begins a response to the prompt above.

The writer used details to add interest.

Explorers need special qualities and skills. Explorers should like danger, traveling, and studying. It's hard to think of a more dangerous job than diving to the bottom of the ocean or digging in a dark chamber. Any problem could result in a serious injury or death.

Explorers should probably go to college. They need to study what they want to explore and become an expert in their field. This way they can recognize things people might not notice. Having knowledge of their surroundings helps explorers while they are out working. A deep sea explorer should be able to see a fish and figure out if the fish is a threat.

Writing Prompt

Respond in writing to the prompt below. Before you write, read the Writing Hints below. Review the hints after you finish writing.

FCAT Some people like to explore new places.

Think of a person you know who likes to explore.

Now write to tell about this person who likes to explore.

Writing Hints for Prompts

- ☑ Read the prompt carefully.
- ☑ Plan your writing by organizing your ideas.
- ☑ Support your ideas by telling more about each event or reason.
- ☑ Use adjectives.
- ☑ Choose words that help others understand what you mean.
- ☑ Review and edit your writing.

ARTISTS AT WORK

Talk About It

In what ways does this artist express himself in the world around him?

LOG ON Find out more about artists at **www.macmillanmh.com**

Vocabulary

skyscrapers
collage
barbecue
glorious
strutting
flicked
swarms

FCAT **Context Clues**

Descriptions can help you figure out the meaning of unfamiliar words. Use the description words in the story to figure out what the word *collage* means.

SECONDHAND ART

by David Walcott

Danny and Emma decided to enter the school art contest. Today they are working together on their project. The problem is that they can't decide what to make.

"Danny, maybe we should make models of modern **skyscrapers**. I know how much you love tall buildings. Isn't it your dream to design the world's tallest building?" Emma asked with a smile.

"Yes, it is. That's a great idea, Emma, but that might be too hard for us," said Danny. "How about making a **collage**?"

"We could," said Emma, "but lots of kids will make collages. Let's try to be different!"

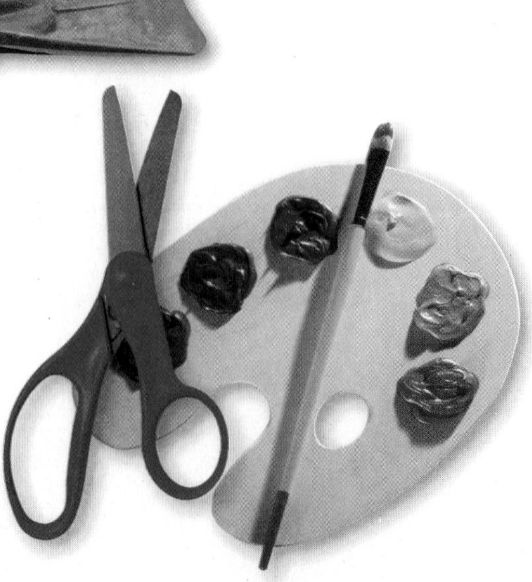

Danny's mom walked into the kitchen. She reminded Danny to put the recycling bin in her car. Danny's eyes lit up.

"I've got it!" he said. "Emma, you're always talking about taking care of the earth. Let's make a city out of that stuff!"

"Great idea," agreed Emma.

They got right to work. There were tons of aluminum cans from last week's outdoor hamburger and hot dog **barbecue**.

They used empty plastic bottles and jars. They cut up strips of newspaper to make papier-mâché buildings. At last Danny and Emma were ready to paint.

"Let's use bright yellow," Emma suggested. "It's such a **glorious** color, isn't it?"

Danny giggled. "You're so dramatic, Emma."

He started **strutting** around the room. "Yellow is such a *glorious* color," he teased Emma. Emma **flicked** her paintbrush at Danny.

The next day Danny and Emma presented their art project. Everyone loved their "recycled city." Danny and Emma won first prize. **Swarms** of people came up to congratulate them.

"I always told you recycling could be a lot of fun!" Emma exclaimed.

"You were right, Emma. And the best part was that I didn't have to haul everything into Mom's car," said Danny with a grin.

Reread for **Comprehension**

Monitor Comprehension

FCAT **Compare Characters** To help readers understand the **characters** in a story, they can think about the character's traits. Readers should pay attention to character traits to see how a character changes throughout the story. Fill in your Character Web as you reread the selection.

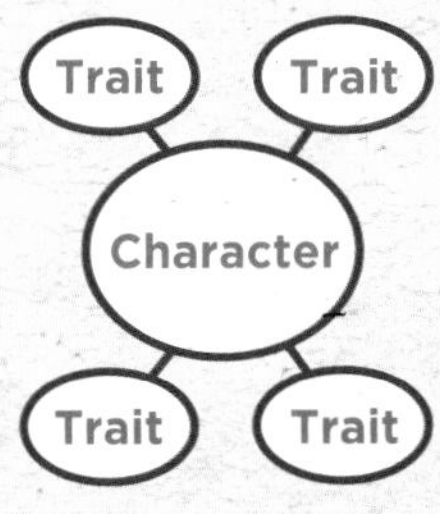

Comprehension

Genre

Realistic Fiction is a made-up story that could have happened in real life.

Monitor Comprehension

FCAT **Compare Characters**

As you read, fill in your Character Web.

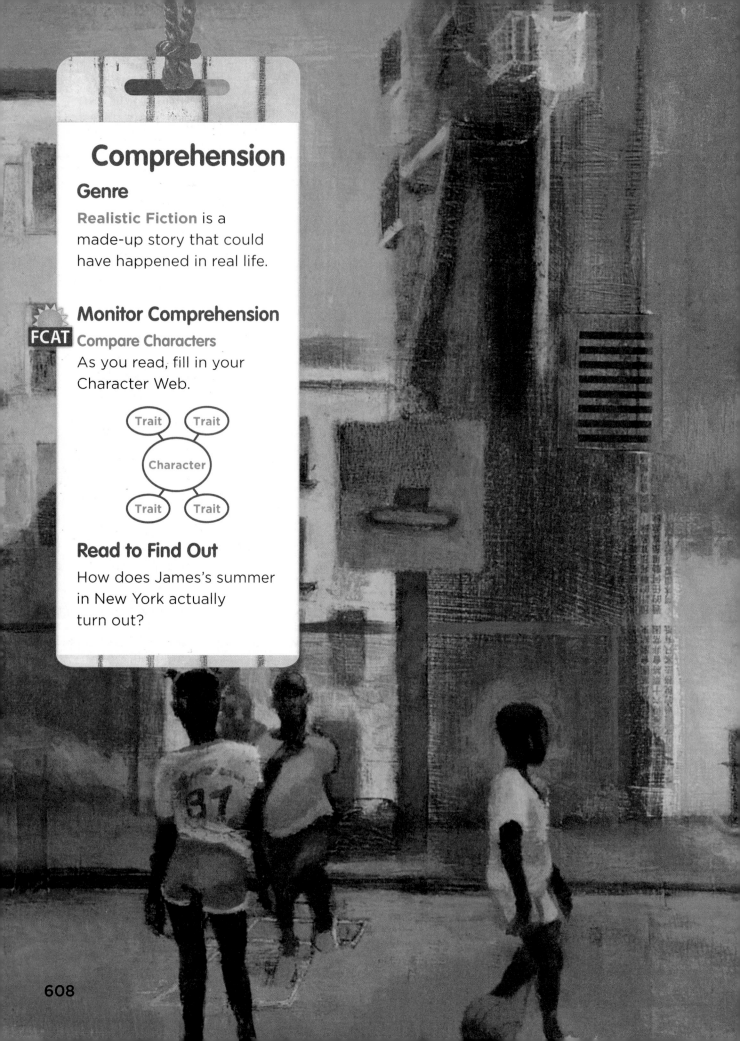

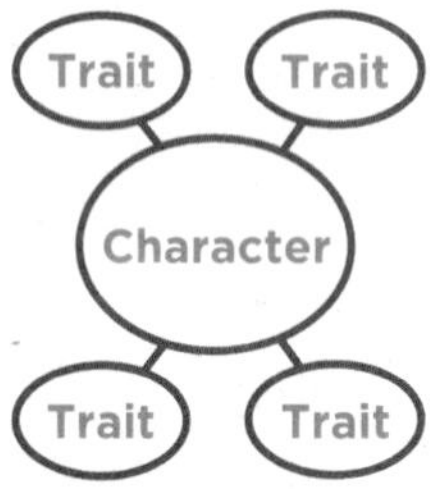

Read to Find Out

How does James's summer in New York actually turn out?

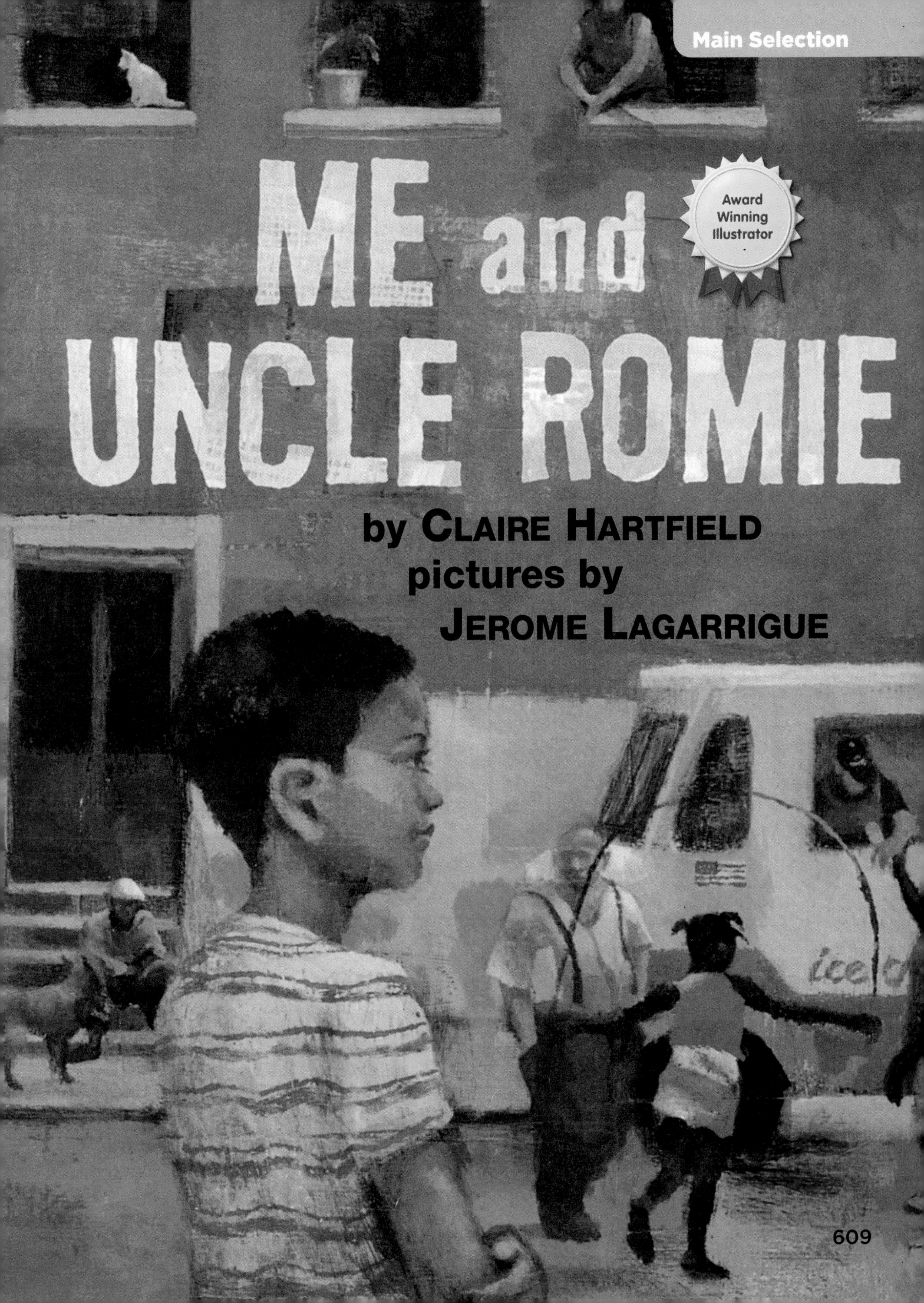

ME and UNCLE ROMIE

by CLAIRE HARTFIELD
pictures by
JEROME LAGARRIGUE

Award Winning Illustrator

It was the summer Mama had the twins that I first met my uncle Romie. The doctor had told Mama she had to stay off her feet till the babies got born. Daddy thought it was a good time for me to visit Uncle Romie and his wife, Aunt Nanette, up north in New York City. But I wasn't so sure. Mama had told me that Uncle Romie was some kind of artist, and he didn't have any kids. I'd seen his picture too. He looked scary—a bald-headed, fierce-eyed giant. No, I wasn't sure about this visit at all.

The day before I left home was a regular North Carolina summer day. "A good train-watching day," my friend B.J. said.

We waited quietly in the grass beside the tracks. B.J. heard it first. "It's a'coming," he said. Then I heard it too—a low rumbling, building to a roar. *WHOOO—OOO!*

"The *Piedmont*!" we shouted as the train blasted past.

"I'm the greatest train-watcher ever," B.J. boasted.

"Yeah," I answered, "but tomorrow I'll be *riding* a train. I'm the lucky one."

Lucky, I thought as we headed home. *Maybe*.

That evening I packed my suitcase. Voices drifted up from the porch below.

"Romie's got that big art show coming up," Mama said quietly. "I hope he's not too busy for James, especially on his birthday."

"Romie's a good man," Daddy replied. "And Nanette'll be there too."

FCAT Compare Characters

Who is the narrator of this story? How would you describe this character?

The light faded. Mama called me into her bedroom. "Where's my good-night kiss?" she said.

I curled up next to her. "I'll miss the way you make my birthday special, Mama. Your lemon cake and the baseball game."

"Well," Mama sighed, "it won't be those things. But Uncle Romie and Aunt Nanette are family, and they love you too. It'll still be a good birthday, honey."

Mama pulled me close. Her voice sang soft and low. Later, in my own bed, I listened as crickets began their song and continued into the night.

The next morning I hugged Mama good-bye, and Daddy and I headed for the train. He got me seated, then stood waving at me from the outside. I held tight to the jar of pepper jelly Mama had given me for Uncle Romie.

"ALL A-BOARD!" The conductor's voice crackled over the loudspeaker.

The train pulled away. *Chug-a-chug-a-chug-a-chug.* I watched my town move past my window—bright-colored houses, chickens **strutting** across the yards, flowers everywhere.

After a while I felt hungry. Daddy had packed me a lunch and a dinner to eat one at a time. I ate almost everything at once. Then my belly felt tight and I was kind of sleepy. I closed my eyes and dreamed about Mama and Daddy getting ready for those babies. Would they even miss me?

Later, when I woke up, I ate the last bit of my dinner and thought about my birthday. Would they make my lemon cake and take me to a baseball game in New York?

The sky turned from dark blue to black. I was getting sleepy all over again.

"We're almost there, son," the man next to me said.

Then I saw it . . . New York City. Buildings stretching up to the sky. So close together. Not like North Carolina at all.

"Penn Station! Watch your step," the conductor said, helping me down to the platform. I did like Daddy said and found a spot for myself close to the train. **Swarms** of people rushed by. Soon I heard a silvery voice call my name. This had to be Aunt Nanette. I turned and saw her big smile reaching out to welcome me.

She took my hand and guided me through the rushing crowds onto an underground train called the subway. "This will take us right home," she explained.

Home was like nothing I'd ever seen before. No regular houses anywhere. Just big buildings and stores of all kinds—in the windows I saw paints, fabrics, radios, and TVs.

We turned into the corner building and climbed the stairs to the apartment—five whole flights up. *Whew!* I tried to catch my breath while Aunt Nanette **flicked** on the lights.

"Uncle Romie's out talking to some people about his big art show that's coming up. He'll be home soon," Aunt Nanette said. She set some milk and a plate of cookies for me on the table. "Your uncle's working very hard, so we won't see much of him for a while. His workroom—we call it his studio—is in the front of our apartment. That's where he keeps all the things he needs to make his art."

"Doesn't he just paint?" I asked.

"Uncle Romie is a **collage** artist," Aunt Nanette explained. "He uses paints, yes. But also photographs, newspapers, cloth. He cuts and pastes them onto a board to make his paintings."

"That sounds kinda easy," I said.

Aunt Nanette laughed.

"Well, there's a little more to it than that, James. When you see the paintings, you'll understand. Come, let's get you to bed."

Lying in the dark, I heard heavy footsteps in the hall. A giant stared at me from the doorway. "Hello there, James." Uncle Romie's voice was deep and loud, like thunder. "Thanks for the pepper jelly," he boomed. "You have a good sleep, now." Then he disappeared down the hall.

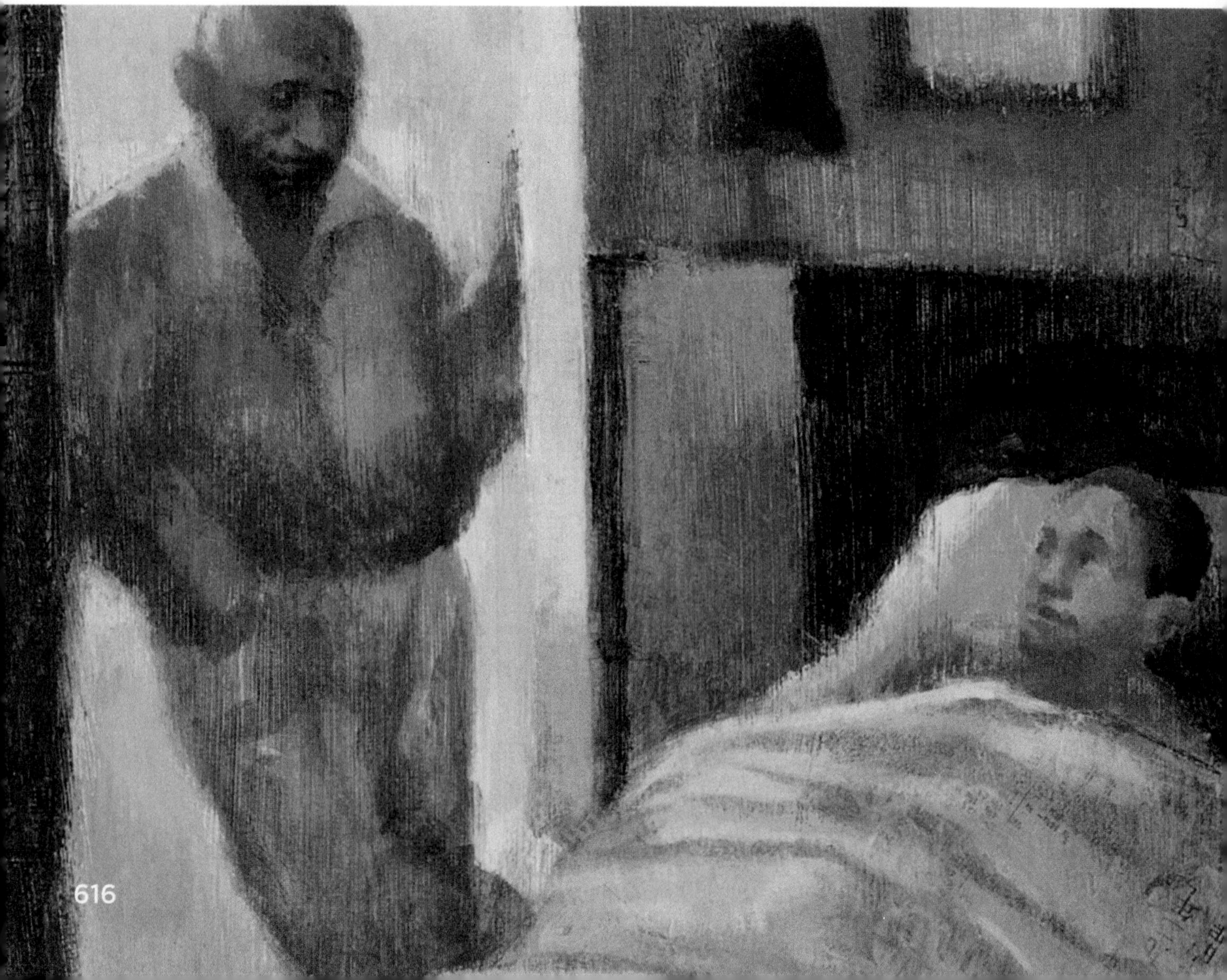

The next morning the door to Uncle Romie's studio was closed. But Aunt Nanette had plans for both of us. "Today we're going to a neighborhood called Harlem," she said. "It's where Uncle Romie lived as a boy."

Harlem was full of people walking, working, shopping, eating. Some were watching the goings-on from fire escapes. Others were sitting out on stoops greeting folks who passed by—just like the people back home calling out hellos from their front porches. Most everybody seemed to know Aunt Nanette. A lot of them asked after Uncle Romie too.

We bought peaches at the market, then stopped to visit awhile. I watched some kids playing stickball. "Go on, get in that game," Aunt Nanette said, gently pushing me over to join them. When I was all hot and sweaty, we cooled off with double chocolate scoops from the ice cream man. Later we shared some **barbecue** on a rooftop way up high. I felt like I was on top of the world.

As the days went by, Aunt Nanette took me all over the city—we rode a ferry boat to the Statue of Liberty . . . zoomed 102 floors up at the Empire State Building . . . window-shopped the fancy stores on Fifth Avenue . . . gobbled hot dogs in Central Park.

But it was Harlem that I liked best. I played stickball with the kids again . . . and on a really hot day a whole bunch of us ran through the icy cold water that sprayed out hard from the fire hydrant. In the evenings Aunt Nanette and I sat outside listening to the street musicians playing their saxophone songs.

On rainy days I wrote postcards and helped out around the apartment. I told Aunt Nanette about the things I liked to do back home—about baseball games, train-watching, my birthday. She told me about the special Caribbean lemon and mango cake she was going to make.

My uncle Romie stayed hidden away in his studio. But I wasn't worried anymore. Aunt Nanette would make my birthday special.

4 . . . 3 . . . 2 . . . 1 . . . My birthday was almost here!

And then Aunt Nanette got a phone call.

"An old aunt has died, James. I have to go away for her funeral. But don't you worry. Uncle Romie will spend your birthday with you. It'll be just fine."

That night Aunt Nanette kissed me good-bye. I knew it would not be fine at all. Uncle Romie didn't know about cakes or baseball games or anything except his dumb old paintings. My birthday was ruined.

When the sky turned black, I tucked myself into bed. I missed Mama and Daddy so much. I listened to the birds on the rooftop—their songs continued into the night.

The next morning everything was quiet. I crept out of bed and into the hall. For the first time the door to Uncle Romie's studio stood wide open. What a **glorious** mess! There were paints and scraps all over the floor, and around the edges were huge paintings with all sorts of pieces pasted together.

I saw saxophones, birds, fire escapes, and brown faces. *It's Harlem*, I thought. *The people, the music, the rooftops, and the stoops.* Looking at Uncle Romie's paintings, I could *feel* Harlem—its beat and bounce.

Then there was one that was different. Smaller houses, flowers, and trains. "That's home!" I shouted.

"Yep," Uncle Romie said, smiling, from the doorway. "That's the Carolina I remember."

"Mama says you visited your grandparents there most every summer when you were a kid," I said.

"I sure did, James. *Mmm.* Now that's the place for pepper jelly. Smeared thick on biscuits. And when Grandma wasn't looking. . . I'd sneak some on a spoon."

"Daddy and I do that too!" I told him.

We laughed together, then walked to the kitchen for a breakfast feast—eggs, bacon, grits, and biscuits.

"James, you've got me remembering the pepper jelly lady. People used to line up down the block to buy her preserves."

"Could you put someone like that in one of your paintings?" I asked.

"I guess I could." Uncle Romie nodded. "Yes, that's a memory just right for sharing. What a good idea, James. Now let's get this birthday going!"

He brought out two presents from home. I tore into the packages while he got down the pepper jelly and two huge spoons. Mama and Daddy had picked out just what I wanted—a special case for my baseball cards, and a model train for me to build.

"Pretty cool," said Uncle Romie. "I used to watch the trains down in North Carolina, you know."

How funny to picture big Uncle Romie lying on his belly!

"B.J. and me, we have contests to see who can hear the trains first."

"Hey, I did that too. You know, it's a funny thing, James. People live in all sorts of different places and families. But the things we care about are pretty much the same. Like favorite foods, special songs, games, stories . . . and like birthdays." Uncle Romie held up two tickets to a baseball game!

It turns out Uncle Romie knows all about baseball—he was even a star pitcher in college. We got our mitts and set off for the game.

Way up in the bleachers, we shared a bag of peanuts, cracking the shells with our teeth and keeping our mitts ready in case a home run ball came our way. That didn't happen—but we sure had fun.

Aunt Nanette came home that night. She lit the candles and we all shared my Caribbean birthday cake.

After that, Uncle Romie had to work a lot again. But at the end of each day he let me sit with him in his studio and talk. Daddy was right. Uncle Romie is a good man.

The day of the big art show finally came. I watched the people laughing and talking, walking slowly around the room from painting to painting. I walked around myself, listening to their conversations.

"Remember our first train ride from Chicago to New York?" one lady asked her husband.

"That guitar-playing man reminds me of my uncle Joe," said another.

All these strangers talking to each other about their families and friends and special times, and all because of how my uncle Romie's paintings reminded them of these things.

Later that night Daddy called. I had a brand-new brother and sister. Daddy said they were both bald and made a lot of noise. But he sounded happy and said how they all missed me.

This time Aunt Nanette and Uncle Romie took me to the train station.

"Here's a late birthday present for you, James," Uncle Romie said, holding out a package. "Open it on the train, why don't you. It'll help pass the time on the long ride home."

I waved out the window to Uncle Romie and Aunt Nanette until I couldn't see them anymore. Then I ripped off the wrappings!

And there was my summer in New York. Bright sky in one corner, city lights at night in another. Tall buildings. Baseball ticket stubs. The label from the pepper jelly jar. And trains. One going toward the **skyscrapers**. Another going away.

FCAT Compare Characters

How has James changed from the beginning of the story? How has he stayed the same?

Back home, I lay in the soft North Carolina grass. It was the first of September, almost Uncle Romie's birthday. I watched the birds streak across the sky.

Rooftop birds, I thought. *Back home from their summer in New York, just like me.* Watching them, I could still feel the city's beat inside my head.

A feather drifted down from the sky. In the garden tiger lilies bent in the wind. *Uncle Romie's favorite flowers.* I yanked off a few blossoms. And then I was off on a treasure hunt, collecting things that reminded me of Uncle Romie.

I painted and pasted them together on a big piece of cardboard. Right in the middle I put the train schedule. And at the top I wrote:

Visit the Studios of Claire and Jerome

Claire Hartfield based this story on African American artist Romare Bearden. She likes his collages because they seem to tell stories. Claire wrote her story to show how we can use art to share ideas. She's been expressing herself through art since she was young. Claire was a shy child, and she found that dance and art helped her share her feelings.

Jerome Lagarrigue comes from a family of artists. He grew up in France, but came to the United States to study art. Jerome illustrates books and magazines. He also teaches art.

Other books by Jerome Lagarrigue

LOG ON Find out more about Claire Hartfield and Jerome Lagarrigue at **www.macmillanmh.com**

FCAT **Author's Purpose**

Did Claire Hartfield write *Me and Uncle Romie* to explain something or entertain the reader? Do you think that the author's own love of art affected her purpose for writing? Explain using details from the story.

FCAT Comprehension Check

Summarize

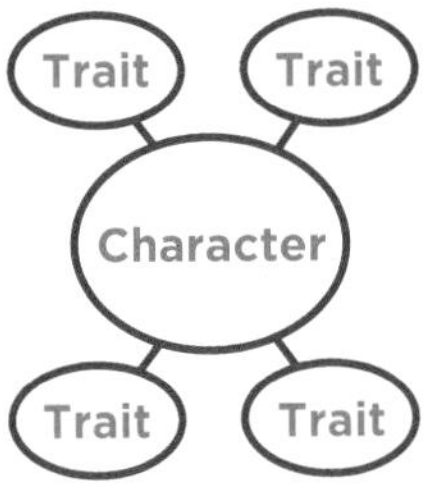

Summarize *Me and Uncle Romie.* Use your Character Web to help you tell what happened to James when he went to New York City to stay with his aunt and uncle.

Think and Compare

1. How did Uncle Romie change from the beginning of the story? How did he stay the same? Explain using details from the story. **Monitor Comprehension: Compare Characters**

2. Reread pages 619–623. Why did James think his birthday was ruined? How does his birthday change his relationship with Uncle Romie? Explain using story details. **Analyze**

3. Have you ever discovered that you had judged someone's character based on the person's appearance? Explain. **Apply**

4. Why is art a **glorious** way to express feelings and ideas? **Evaluate**

5. Read "Secondhand Art" on pages 606–607. Compare this story with *Me and Uncle Romie.* How are the stories alike? How are they different? Use details from both selections to explain. **Reading/Writing Across Texts**

Science

Genre

Nonfiction Articles explain a topic by presenting facts about it. They also provide informative photos.

FCAT **Text Feature**

Directions are the steps you follow in order to do or make something.

Content Vocabulary

technology
software

COMPUTERS

THE FUTURE OF ART

by Lynn Boulanger

What do you think of when you hear the word *artist*? Most people picture someone painting or drawing on a canvas. Others see a person using a hammer to create a sculpture. These days new **technology** allows artists to express themselves using new and exciting tools.

Reading Directions

The following directions tell how to install a software program like CAD:

Directions:

1. Check that your computer meets the requirements of the software.
2. Close other programs.
3. Follow the exact instructions in the manual.
4. Install other necessary programs if prompted to do so.

Art and Technology

Computers are the latest tool artists are using to create new art. Computer-assisted design (CAD) is a **software** program sculptors can use to plan their art. At one time artists sketched plans for a new piece on paper. Now many of them bring their ideas to life on computers using programs such as these. With CAD artists can play around with the size of their creations. CAD can even produce images of three-dimensional shapes. These images can help artists plan or change their works before they actually create them.

Even though this new technology has many benefits, it also has many costs. Computer-assisted programs are expensive. An artist would have to buy the program before being able to work on it. Some of these programs can be hard for artists to understand. Other programs require that artists take a class before working on them, to learn the different features that they offer. In spite of the costs, computers are changing the way artists create art!

FCAT Connect and Compare

1. Look at the Reading Directions box on page 628. What is the first thing a person should do when installing software on his or her computer? **Reading Directions**

2. What are the benefits of using computer-assisted programs? What are the costs? **Recall**

3. Think about this article and *Me and Uncle Romie*. How might computer-assisted programs like CAD help Uncle Romie in his work? Explain using details from both selections. **Reading/Writing Across Texts**

Science Activity

Research another form of technology artists are using these days besides computers. Write a summary of your findings.

LOG ON Find out more about art and technology at **www.macmillanmh.com**

Write About Learning Something

Writer's Craft

FCAT **Mood**

The **mood** is the feeling writers create in their writing. Writers use precise words to make the mood of a story exciting, scary, funny, or serious.

I used words like "nervous" and "scared" to set the mood of my story.

The mood has changed at the end of my story.

Skating With Blanca

by Teresa N.

One warm day my sister Blanca announced, "I'm going to teach you to roller skate." Right away, I started feeling nervous and a little scared. That's because I'm clumsy and I could already see myself falling down again and again.

"It will be fun," Blanca insisted. "We will take it nice and slow." I wasn't so sure about that. I have never had good luck with keeping my balance!

It was a rocky start, but soon I was able to skate along with no trouble. I am so glad I got over my fear and learned how to do something that turned out to be so much fun! My sister Blanca is the most incredible teacher in the world.

Writing Prompt

Most people like to learn how to do something new.

Think of a time someone taught you how to do something new.

Now write a story about a time someone taught you how to do something new.

FCAT Writer's Checklist

- [x] **Focus:** My story clearly describes a time someone taught me how to do something new.
- [x] **Organization:** My sentences support my topic.
- [ ] **Support:** I set the **mood** of my writing by using precise words to express my feelings about the topic.
- [x] **Conventions:** My sentences are complete. I use quotes correctly.

Talk About It

These wild horses live in a big marsh in southern France. What do you see in the photo that tells you they are wild?

LOG ON Find out more about wild horses at **www.macmillanmh.com**

WILD HORSES

Vocabulary

descendants
sanctuary
glistening
threatened
coaxing
fragile
habitat

FCAT Context Clues

Paragraph Clues are words in a paragraph that can help readers figure out the meaning of unfamiliar words. Use paragraph clues to figure out what the word *descendants* means.

The Wild Ponies of Chincoteague

by Gregory Searle

Every year since 1924, a pony swim has taken place between two tiny islands in the Atlantic Ocean. Assateague and Chincoteague islands are located off the coasts of Maryland and Virginia. Part of Assateague belongs to Maryland and part belongs to Virginia. On a smaller neighboring island, the Chincoteague ponies graze.

These beautiful animals are **descendants** of wild horses. How the ancestors of the ponies ended up on an island, no one knows for sure.

The Pony Swim

The calm, quiet privacy of Assateague provided a **sanctuary** for its residents. However, when several terrible fires broke out on Chincoteague, it was clear that emergency services were needed. The new Volunteer Fire Department needed money to buy equipment. That's how the idea for the annual pony swim started.

Every year thousands of people come to watch the ponies. Many watch from boats out on the **glistening** water. The firemen "round up" the wild ponies on Assateague Island. At first the ponies feel **threatened** and try to head back into the trees. After some **coaxing**, the ponies swim across the channel to Chincoteague Island.

These ponies are small, but they are not **fragile**. They are very strong and intelligent animals. Many farmers want to buy a Chincoteague pony. Some of the foals are auctioned off to good homes. The rest of the ponies swim back to Assateague Island a few days later. The fire department uses the money that is raised to update their safety equipment.

Protecting the Ponies

The pony swim is important for another reason, too. The number of horses living on Assateague has to be controlled. If too many horses are born, there won't be enough grass for the rest to eat. Keeping the numbers under control protects the **habitat** and its natural resources for future generations.

Reread for Comprehension

Monitor Comprehension

FCAT

Cause and Effect A **cause** is why something happens in a story. An **effect** is what happens. Readers can look for cause and effect in a story to help them check their understanding of the story's events. Reread the selection and fill in your Cause and Effect Chart to help you identify what happens in the selection and why.

Cause → Effect
→
→
→
→

Comprehension

Genre

Narrative Nonfiction
is a story or an account of actual persons, living things, situations, or events.

Monitor Comprehension

FCAT

Cause and Effect
As you read, fill in your Cause and Effect Chart.

Cause → Effect
→
→
→
→

Read to Find Out

What is it that makes a wild horse wild?

Wild Horses

by Cris Peterson

photographs by Alvis Upitis

In the deepest, darkest part of night, when the crickets and tree frogs are almost silent, shadowy shapes emerge from the ponderosa pine ridge and tiptoe down to the glassy Cheyenne River below. Their long tangled manes and tails ruffle in the night breeze. Ever alert and watchful for predators, they swiftly drink their fill. Then they turn on their heels and lunge up the rocky hills to safety.

In the misty glow of dawn, one can see these mysterious visitors aren't backyard pasture mares with swishing tails and docile, trusting eyes. These horses are wild—from another century, another era, another world. They are American mustangs, whose freedom, adaptability, and toughness define the western wilderness.

Some of the mares have names. Medicine Hattie is easy to spot. Her dark ears jut out above her ghostly white face and corn-silk mane. Painted Lady's pure white coat is splashed with brown spots; she always seems to know where the sweetest grasses are.

And there are others. Funny Face has a creamy white blaze that slides down the sides of her face like melting ice cream on a hot day. She loves to stand on the highest rock-strewn spot with her face to the wind. Yuskeya, whose name means freedom in the Sioux language, always stands at the edge of the herd, alert for danger and ready to run.

To find these horses, cross Cascade Creek where the South Dakota Black Hills meet the prairie, and turn right onto a pothole-strewn gravel road. This is the land of silver sagebrush and cowboy legends. Scraggly buzzards perch on fence posts near the entry gate to the Black Hills Wild Horse **Sanctuary**, home for more than three hundred wild horses and one determined cowboy-conservationist named Dayton Hyde.

Dayton was a gangly, growing thirteen-year-old boy when he met his first horse. It was a dirt-colored pony he found drinking from a puddle of old soapy dishwater behind his family's summer cabin in northern Michigan. He recalls that for a time he thought all horses blew bubbles out of their noses.

Soon after that encounter, word came from Dayton's cattle rancher uncle in Oregon that his cowboys had just captured a band of wild horses. Dayton hopped a westbound train and arrived on his uncle's doorstep, where he grew up as a cowboy learning to love the western range and its wild horses.

Mustangs are **descendants** of the horses brought to America by Spanish explorers nearly five hundred years ago. By 1900, more than two million smart, fast, surefooted wild horses roamed the West.

When newly invented barbed wire fences began crisscrossing the rangelands, the horses lost access to sources of food and water and became a pesky problem for local residents. Thousands of them were slaughtered for fertilizer or pet food. By 1950, less than seventeen thousand survived.

After a Congressional act prohibited the capture or slaughter of wild horses in 1971, the wild horse population again grew quickly. Many died of thirst and starvation in the harsh western winters. In an attempt to manage the size of the herds, the United States government gathered up the animals and maintained them in fenced feedlots until they could be adopted.

One day in the early 1980s, Dayton Hyde, who by this time owned his uncle's ranch and had a grown family of his own, drove by one of these feedlots. Shocked and dismayed by the sight of dozens of muddy and dejected horses locked in a corral, he felt he had to do something.

FCAT Cause and Effect
What caused the mustang population to increase during the 1970s?

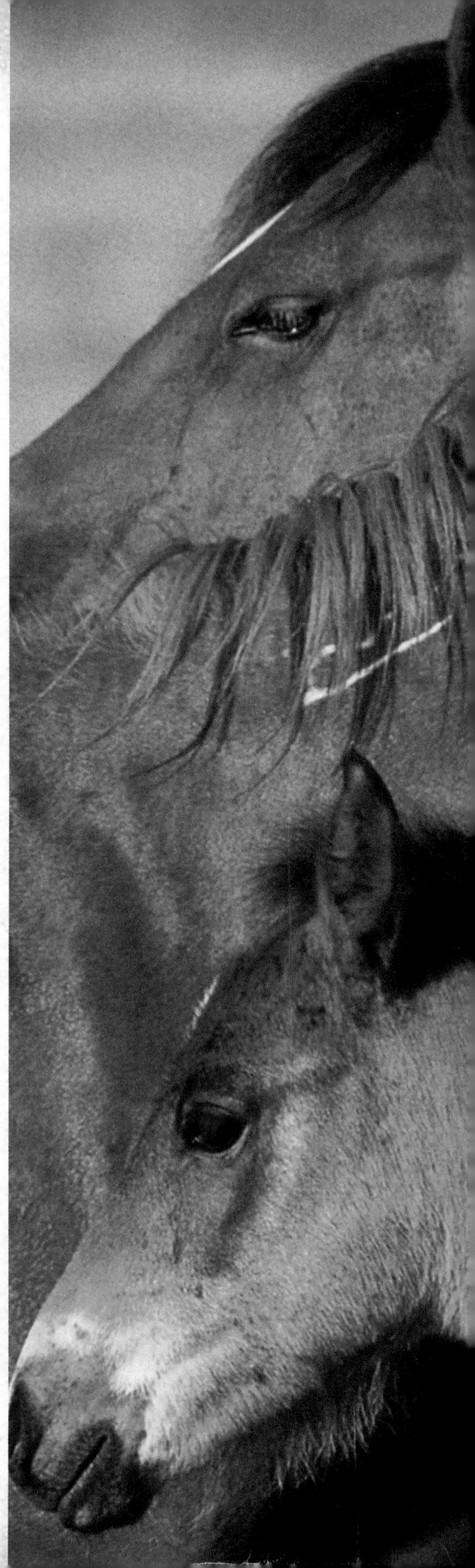

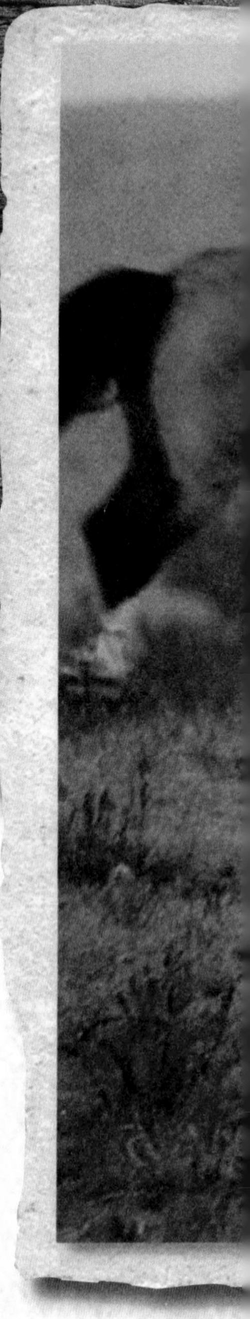

After months of searching and many long days spent convincing government officials to accept his plan of creating a special place for wild horses, he acquired eleven thousand acres of rangeland and rimrock near the Black Hills in South Dakota. Here, among yawning canyons and sun-drenched pastures, he hoped wild horses—some too ugly, old, or knobby kneed to be adopted—could run free forever.

Before he could ship his wild horse rejects to their new home, Dayton had to build eight miles of fences to ensure they wouldn't wander into his neighbors' wheat fields. He also fenced in a fifty-acre training field where the horses would spend their first few days on the ranch adjusting to their new surroundings.

On a miserably cold fall day, huge creaking semi-trailers filled with snorting, stomping steeds finally arrived at the ranch. After hours of **coaxing**, Dayton succeeded in getting Magnificent Mary to skitter off the trailer. She was a battle-scarred, mean-eyed mare with a nose about twice as long as it should be. The rest of the herd clattered behind her, eyes bulging with fear.

Dayton's worst fear was that the horses would spook and charge through his carefully constructed six-wire fence, scattering across the prairie like dry leaves in a whirlwind. Aware that wild horses often feel **threatened** by being watched, he sat in the cab of his old pickup truck, peeking at them out of a corner of his eye. Finally, after nearly a week of around-the-clock vigilance, he swung open the gate from the training field to his wild horse sanctuary.

Many years have passed since Dayton held his breath and pushed that corral gate open. Every spring, dozens of his wild horses give birth to tottering colts that learn the ways of the back country from their mothers. They share the vast, quiet land with coyotes, mountain lions, and countless deer. Star lilies, bluebells, and prairie roses nod in the wind along with the prairie short grass that feeds the herd.

Thousands of visitors arrive each summer to get a glimpse of wild horses in their natural **habitat**, a habitat that has been preserved through Dayton's careful planning. Throughout the grazing season, he moves the herd from one area of the ranch to another so the horses don't damage the **fragile** rangeland. In the process, he searches for his marker mares: Painted Lady, Medicine Hattie, Funny Face, Yuskeya, Magnificent Mary, and several others. When he spots them all, he knows the whole herd is accounted for.

Sometimes in the fall while he's checking on the horses, Dayton notices a gaunt, aging mare whose ribs stand out through her ragged coat. He knows this old friend won't survive the winter. As the pale December daylight slips over the rimrock, the old mare lies down and goes to sleep for the last time. After years of running free, the wild mustang returns to the earth and completes the circle of life.

The wild mustangs Dayton Hyde once discovered crowded into a feedlot now gallop across the Cheyenne River free as the prairie wind. They splash through the **glistening** water and bolt up a ravine. Here in this rugged wilderness, one man's vision of a sanctuary for wild horses has become a reality.

FCAT Cause and Effect

What were the events that caused the wild horses from the feedlot to be protected in the sanctuary?

Ride Away with Cris and Alvis

Cris Peterson lives on a big dairy farm in Wisconsin. Tending 500 cows keeps Cris pretty busy, but she still finds time to write. Cris writes a lot about farm life and animals. She often uses her own experiences to inspire her books. Cris believes it is very important to give readers a true picture of farms and animals, so she chooses her details carefully.

Alvis Upitis has provided the photographs for many of Cris's books. He is a good partner. When Cris was very busy with farm work and did not think she'd have time to write, Alvis encouraged her to try.

Other books by Cris and Alvis

LOG ON Find out more about Cris Peterson and Alvis Upitis at **www.macmillanmh.com**

FCAT Author's Purpose

Cris Peterson tried hard to create for readers a true picture of the animals in her story *Wild Horses*. What does this suggest about her purpose for writing? Explain using story details.

FCAT Comprehension Check

Summarize

Summarize *Wild Horses.* Use your Cause and Effect Chart to help you include only the most important information.

Cause → Effect
→
→
→
→

Think and Compare

1. What caused Dayton Hyde to want to do something to help the wild horses? What did he decide to do? Explain using story details. **Monitor Comprehension: Cause and Effect**

2. Reread pages 644–647. Describe the process the wild horses go through to adapt to their new environment. How does Dayton manage to care for the **fragile** land while allowing the horses free range? Use story details to explain. **Analyze**

3. How would you help an animal in trouble? Explain. **Apply**

4. Why is it important to care for and protect animals? Explain using details from the story. **Evaluate**

5. Read "The Wild Ponies of Chincoteague" on pages 634–635. Compare Assateague Island with the Black Hills Wild Horse Sanctuary. How are the two places alike? How are they different? Use details from both selections to explain. **Reading/Writing Across Texts**

Language Arts

Genre

Tall Tales are stories with events so exaggerated that they are beyond belief. Tall tales are an American form of storytelling.

FCAT Literary Elements

Hyperbole is the use of exaggeration for emphasis. The author does not expect it to be believed. An example of hyperbole is *I told you a million times to clean your room.*

A **Figure of Speech** is an expressive use of language that is not meant to be taken literally.

The Tale of Pecos Bill

retold by Gillian Reed

Pecos Bill was the best cowboy and toughest man there ever was. He had bounced out of his family's wagon when he was a baby and landed in the Pecos River. He was raised by coyotes, but he didn't talk about that very much.

One day Bill showed up on the Texas range wearing a blue bandanna and a big Stetson hat. "Hey, partner," Pecos Bill roared at a gold prospector, "I'm lookin' for some real cowhands. Got me a ranch in New Mexico — well, to tell the truth, New Mexico is my ranch. I need some tough guys to work for me. I'm looking for the kind of man who can eat a pot of beans in one gulp and pick his teeth with barbed wire."

Pecos Bill's description of a tough guy is **hyperbole**. It's a humorous exaggeration that the reader is not meant to believe.

The prospector said some tough cowhands were camped out 200 miles down the river. Bill and his horse set off in that direction, and before long a mountain lion leaped from a boulder straight down onto Pecos Bill.

Bill's horse didn't wait around to see what happened next. If he had, all he would have seen was a blur of flying fur. He would have heard nothing but hideous snarls and groans. When the fur settled, the big cat was apologizing to Bill.

"How can I make it up to you?" it asked.

"You can't, but I'm putting this saddle on you," said Bill. "You scared off my horse, and I hate walkin'."

So Pecos Bill rode the cat to the tough guys' campsite. Those tough men took one look at Bill on that mountain lion and made him their new boss. Then the whole crew headed out for New Mexico.

Back on the ranch, Pecos Bill caught a wild black horse for himself and named it Widow-Maker. That crazy horse had the power of twelve horses and wouldn't let anyone but Bill ride him.

Pecos Bill also got himself a spouse. He first spied Slue-Foot Sue on the Rio Grande. She was riding a catfish the size of a boat and whooping at the top of her lungs.

The day she married Bill, Slue-Foot Sue wore a dress with one of those old-time bustles. The bustle was a steel-spring contraption that made the back of her dress stick out a mile.

After the wedding, Sue wanted to ride Widow-Maker. Now, Pecos Bill loved Slue-Foot Sue, so he attempted to talk her out of this notion.

"Widow-Maker won't let anybody ride him but me. He'd throw you in a second."

But Sue insisted, and Bill finally let Sue give it a try. Sue got on Widow-Maker, who bucked and jumped and bucked again. Then he threw Slue-Foot Sue, and she sped into the sky like she'd been shot from a cannon. When Sue finished going up, she plummeted down. And when she hit the ground, she bounced on her steel-spring bustle and flew up again, even higher than before. She even hit her head on the moon.

> Sue was not actually shot from a cannon, but the comparison helps the reader picture what happened. This comparison is a figure of speech.

For days Pecos Bill watched his bouncing bride. Up and down she went. Every time Sue landed, she bounced up higher, until she came down to Earth only once every few weeks.

It took a long time for Pecos Bill to find another bride as accomplished as Slue-Foot Sue. And he never again allowed a wife of his to ride Widow-Maker.

FCAT Connect and Compare

1. Find two examples of hyperbole in the descriptions of Slue-Foot Sue and her adventures. Explain why they are hyperboles. **Hyperbole**

2. Which descriptions of Pecos Bill's actions and of his life let readers know that this is a tall tale? **Apply**

3. Compare Widow-Maker to the mustangs described in *Wild Horses*. How are they similar? How are they different? **Reading/Writing Across Texts**

LOG ON Find out more about tall tales at **www.macmillanmh.com**

Write A Tall Tale

Writer's Craft

FCAT **Tone**

Tone is the attitude writers take about the subject or character they are writing about.

I used a character that shows I am writing just for fun.

I used funny examples that show my story is for fun.

The Tale of Big Bart

by Christopher F.

The town was in big trouble. The townspeople heard from the President that there was a bunch of space junk speeding toward Earth and headed straight for their town!

The townspeople knew that their only hope was to call Big Bart. Big Bart was the strongest man alive. He was so big, he could arm wrestle two grizzly bears at the same time and win.

Big Bart was happy to help. He stood in the middle of town, stretched out his big bulging arms and caught the space junk. Bart then threw it so far it landed near the North Pole. The junk is now covered with ice and makes a nice playground for penquins.

Writing Prompt

Authors often tell stories about heroic characters who do extraordinary things.

Invent a heroic character who does something extraordinary.

Now write a tall tale about a heroic character who does something extraordinary.

FCAT Writer's Checklist

- ☑ **Focus:** My tall tale clearly tells about the extraordinary things that my character does.
- ☑ **Organization:** I tell my tall tale's events in the order that they happened.
- ☐ **Support:** I set a **tone** for my tall tale by using informal language.
- ☑ **Conventions:** I vary my sentence lengths. My spelling and grammar are correct.

FCAT Review

- Cause and Effect
- Relevant Facts and Details
- Compare Characters
- Context Clues
- Antonyms
- Diagram

READING FOR MISTER PAREDO

Benito knocked quietly on the door to Mr. Paredo's room. There was no answer.

"Fantastic," thought Benito. "I can just go home." When he turned to leave, a nurse caught his eye.

"You better knock louder than that," she said. "Mr. Paredo has a difficult time hearing."

Benito sighed and knocked again. A gruff voice shouted, "What is it?"

He opened the door. An old man lay in the bed. He looked feeble and exhausted, but his deep blue eyes were still dynamic. "What do you want?" he asked.

"Um, I'm the reader," Benito began. "The school sent me to help you, um, read."

Mr. Paredo didn't say anything for a long time. He just stared at Benito. At last he muttered, "Well, what are you going to read?"

Benito took a step closer to the bed. He took off his backpack and started rummaging through it. "I didn't know what you would like," he said. "So I brought a bunch of stuff. I have today's newspaper—"

“I hate the news,” said Mr. Paredo. “It’s always unpleasant.”

“I also have a sports magazine.”

“Nah. My team always loses.”

As Benito was taking the books out of his backpack, a magazine fell out. It landed on the bed, hitting Mr. Paredo right on the leg. He flinched and his blue eyes looked furious. “What was that?” he asked.

“I’m sorry,” said Benito as he hurried to put it away.

“Wait,” said Mr. Paredo, grabbing Benito’s wrist before he could take the magazine. “Is that a comic book?”

“I’m sorry,” repeated Benito. “It’s mine. I just got it. I didn’t mean to hit you with it.”

“I love comics,” said Mr. Paredo, smiling for the first time. He held the cover very close to his face so he could read the title. “I used to read them all the time. Now my eyes won’t let me.”

“You like comics?” asked Benito. “If you want, I can read it to you.” Mr. Paredo was silent. “Don’t worry. I’ll describe the pictures so you can almost see them.”

“Okay,” said Mr. Paredo.

At first it was hard to read the words and describe the pictures at the same time. Mr. Paredo would interrupt with so many questions. He wanted to know every detail, from the color of someone’s hair to the shape of the speech balloons. But soon Benito became an expert. His descriptions grew longer and more elaborate. When he finished, Benito felt like he had never read one of his comic books more thoroughly.

“I can come back on Saturday if you want. I have more comics,” he said.

“Great!” said Mr. Paredo. He smiled as Benito left.

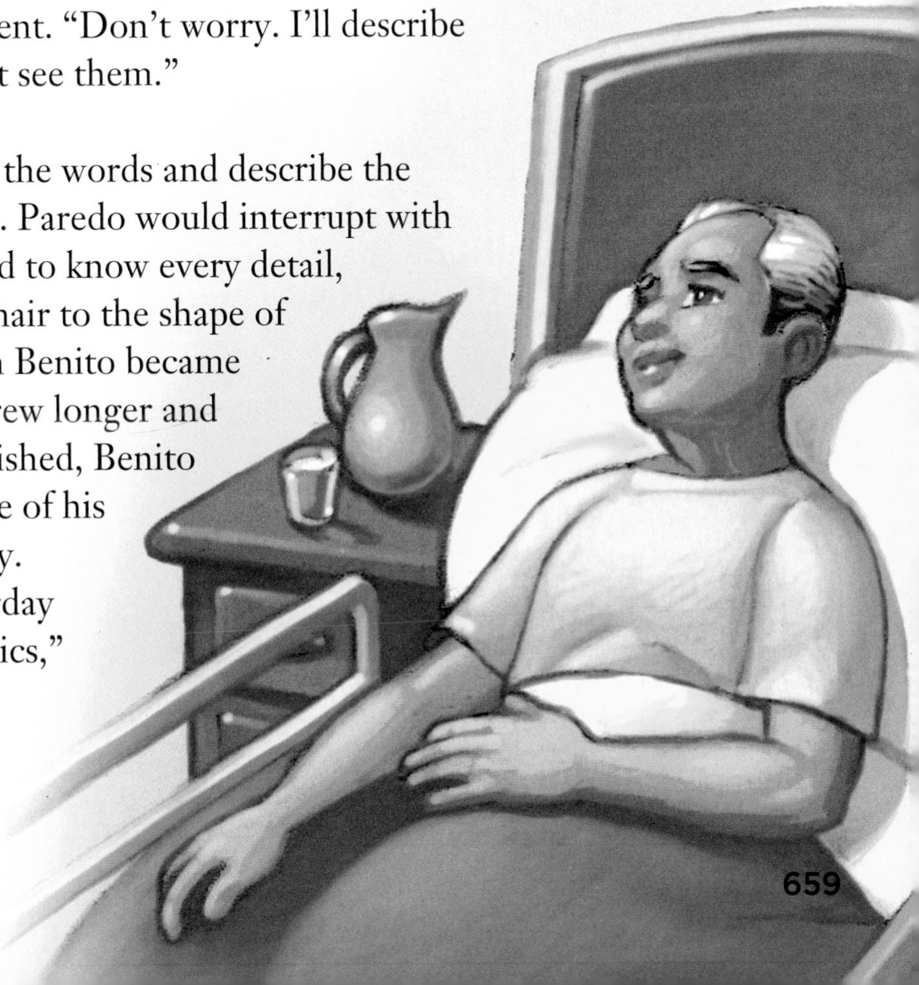

Getting to Know SHARKS

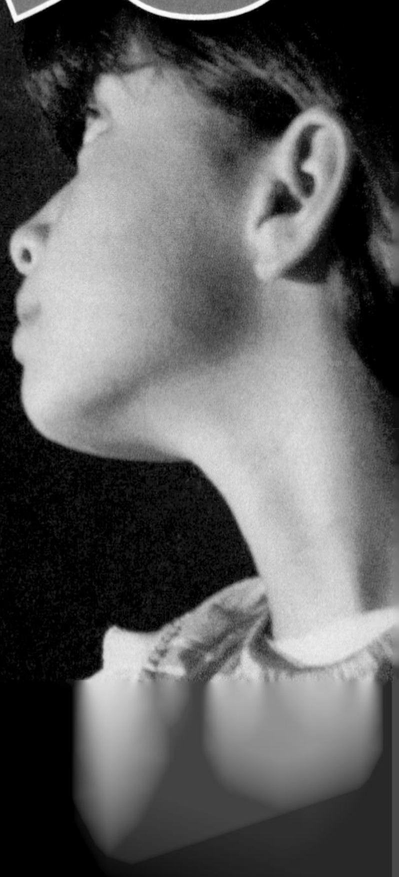

SHARKS ARE LIVING FOSSILS. They are among the oldest living creatures on Earth. Many sharks look the same as sharks that lived 100 million years ago.

Sharks are different from other fish in several ways. Sharks have no bones. Instead a shark's skeleton is made of a hard material called cartilage. Your nose and ears are made of cartilage.

Most sharks have several rows of teeth. When a shark loses a tooth, another one moves up to take its place. Great white sharks lose their teeth at least once a week, but there are always more teeth to take their place. The diagram on the next page shows some of the different parts of a shark.

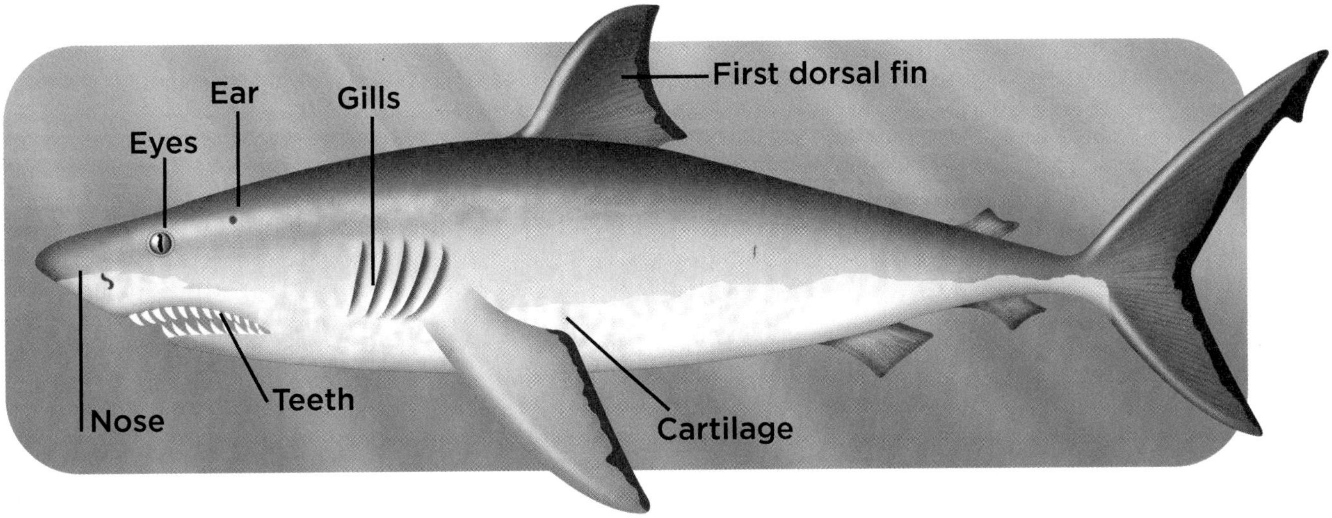

Up Close and Personal

Scientists learn about sharks by studying them up close. They wear shark-proof diving suits and get into iron shark cages. Scientists study how sharks hunt, what they eat, and where they go in the sea.

Scientists also catch sharks and attach tags to them. Tiny computers in each tag record where the shark is, how deep it goes, and how fast it swims. One shark swam more than 1,800 miles in three months!

Wolves of the Sea

Sharks have been called "wolves of the sea" because they are feared hunters. They can sense a tiny bit of blood in the water and find its cause. Some sharks will even attack members of their own species. However, the largest shark—the giant whale shark—is docile and harmless. It feeds on tiny sea animals that it strains out of the water with its gills.

There are about 370 different kinds of sharks. Of these only 27 species have been known to attack humans. The most dangerous are the great white, hammerhead, tiger, bull, and blue sharks. The most feared shark is the great white. A great white can be more than 20 feet (6 meters) long and weigh 4,000 pounds (1,800 kilograms)! Around the world, great white sharks have attacked more than 250 people. However, they prefer to eat other sharks, sea turtles, dolphins, seals, and sea lions.

Seeing Sharks

There are places where people go scuba diving to see sharks, but for most people the best place to go is an aquarium. Many aquariums keep sharks. They are not too difficult to care for—and they are popular! Visit an aquarium if you want to see these living fossils in real life.

THE GOLD RUSH

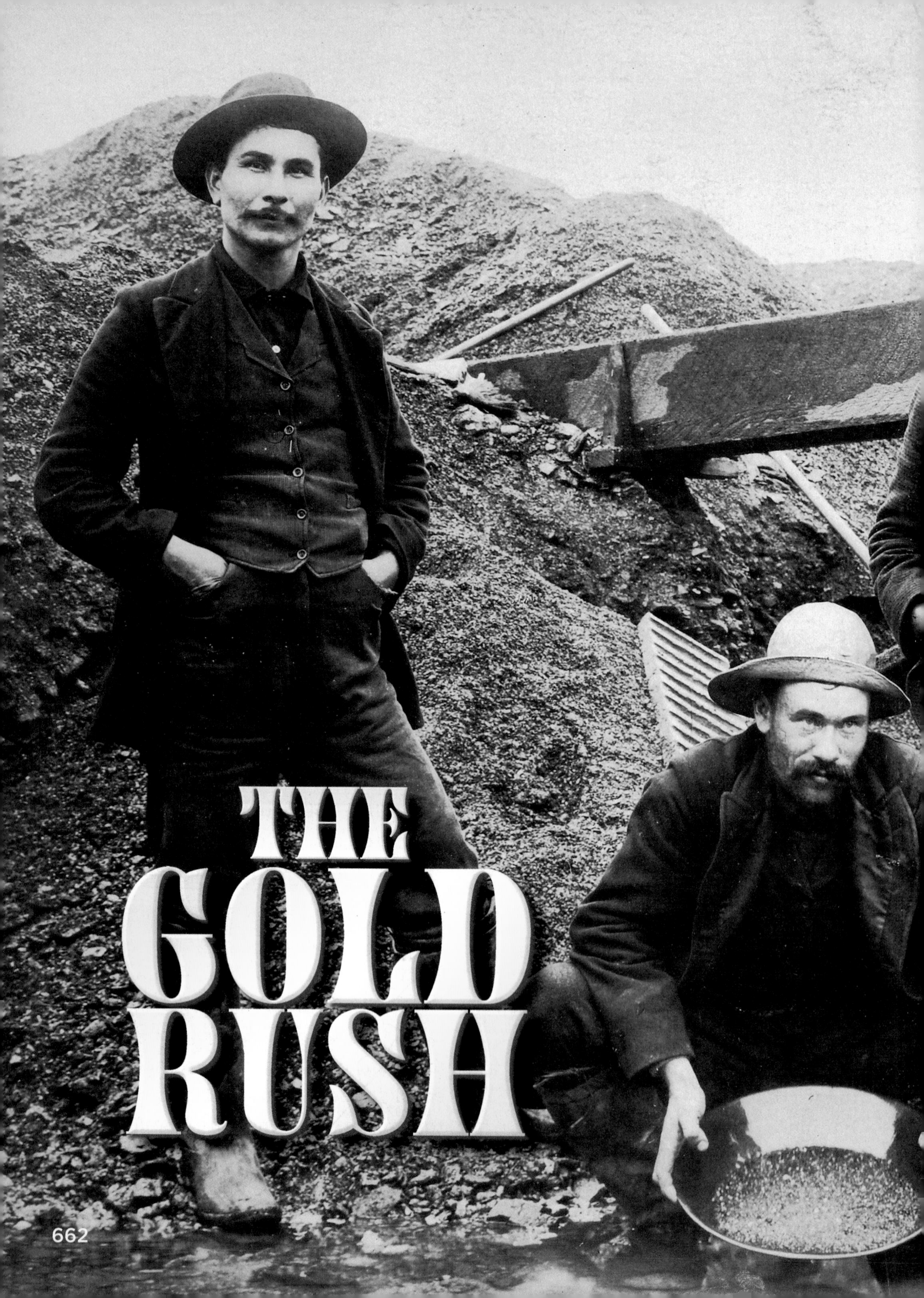

Talk About It

The Gold Rush gave people the opportunity to get rich quick. What would you do if you found gold?

LOG ON Find out more about the Gold Rush at **www.macmillanmh.com**

Vocabulary

reference **circular**
prospectors **outstretched**
disappointment **glinted**
annoyed

Word Parts

FCAT

Suffixes are word parts added to the ends of words to change their meaning.
-or = "one who"
prospector = "one who looks for gold"

In Search of Gold

by Al Ortiz

Mr. Rodriguez's fourth-grade class was on a field trip at the Sutter Gold Mine. Larry couldn't wait to load up on gold. He even brought along some photographs to use as a **reference**. He didn't want to pick up any "fool's gold" by mistake.

Larry's class boarded the Boss Buggy Shuttle that would take them down into the mine. Everyone had to wear a hard hat for safety. On the ride down, their guide, Ron, gave them some information about the Gold Rush.

"Many **prospectors** came to this area beginning in 1848," explained Ron. "A prospector is someone who searches for valuable metals like gold."

Margaret commented, "Everyone must have gotten rich!"

"Actually," said Ron, "not everyone was successful. Many left the mines filled with **disappointment**. People often turned to farming or ranching to make a living instead."

"If I don't find any gold today, I'll be really **annoyed**," Larry thought to himself.

The underground tour lasted about an hour. Then it was time to go to the mining flumes and pan for gold. Ron handed out pans and demonstrated how to swirl them in a **circular** motion.

"It's okay to let some of the water splash out," said Ron. "If there's any gold in your pan, it will sink to the bottom."

Larry found an open place at one of the flumes. With his arm **outstretched**, he dipped his pan below the surface of the water. Then he swished around the water. "Nothing," he said with a sigh.

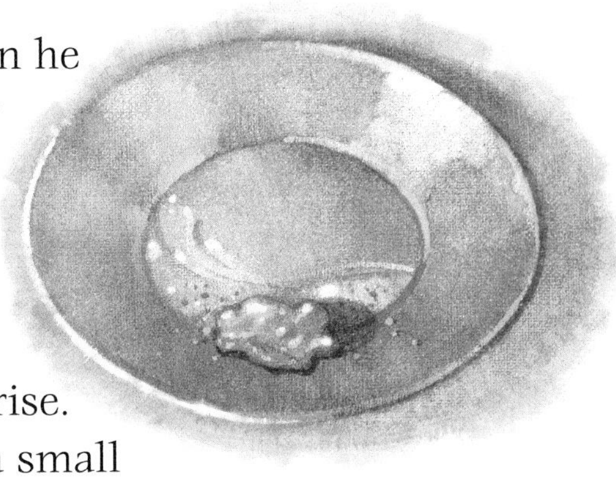

Larry repeated the process several times. Then he noticed something at the bottom of his pan. Larry angled the pan so he could get a better look. Whatever it was, it **glinted** in the sunlight. Larry pulled out the photos and compared them with what was in his pan. Then he went to show Ron.

"You've found gold!" Ron exclaimed with surprise.

Everyone gathered around to see. It was just a small piece, but Larry felt like he had hit the jackpot.

Reread for Comprehension

Analyze Story Structure

FCAT

Cause and Effect Sometimes authors organize their stories to show **cause and effect**. A cause is why something happens. What happens as a result is the effect. Reread the selection and use your Cause and Effect Chart to help you figure out what happens and why it happens.

Cause → Effect
→
→
→
→

Comprehension

Genre

Science Fiction is a fantasy in which an invention involving science or technology affects historic or imaginary characters.

FCAT Analyze Story Structure

Cause and Effect

As you read, fill in your Cause and Effect Chart.

Cause → Effect
→
→
→
→

Read to Find Out

Which part of this story is science and which part is fiction?

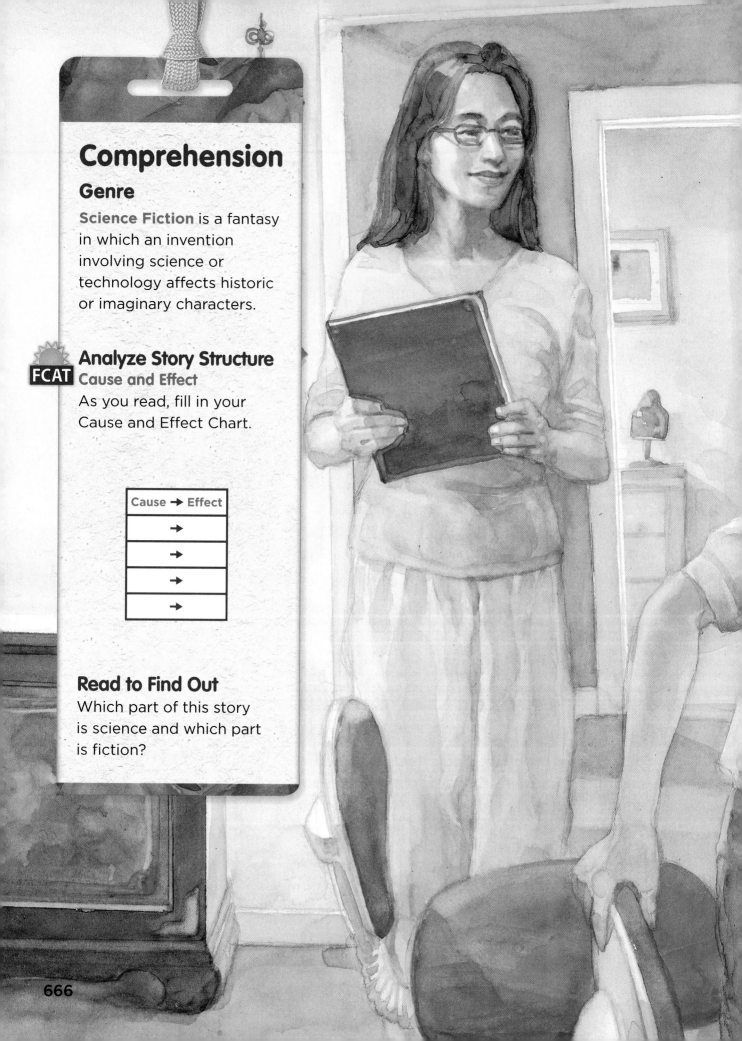

The Gold Rush Game

by William F. Wu

illustrated by Cornelius Van Wright and Ying-Hwa Hu

Eric Wong looked at his new game on the computer screen. "Let's play." He clicked the button to start.

"The Gold Rush," his friend Matt O'Brien read out loud, as he rolled his chair closer. "What's that mean? I want to see it! Come on, I'm going first."

"I'm older," said Eric. "Besides, it's my game."

"Be nice." Eric's mom came up behind them. "We bought the game so Eric could learn more about the Gold Rush," she said to Matt. "His dad and I are tracing our family tree. Eric's great-great-great grandfather on his dad's side came to California from China during the Gold Rush, but we don't know much about him."

"Hey, look at the game," said Eric. On the screen, he saw steep, mountain slopes covered with tall, green trees. Some men wearing broad-brimmed hats rode horses along a muddy path, leading mules with bundles on their backs. Picks and shovels were tied to the bundles. Chinese men, with long, braided queues down their backs, squatted by a rushing river.

"Who are those guys?" Matt asked. "Are they looking for gold?"

"They might be," said Eric's dad as he came into the room. He held out a small piece of paper with two Chinese characters written on it. "This is the name of our ancestor who first came to California. I don't know Chinese, but my grandfather wrote it down for me when I was growing up."

Eric turned and looked. "What was his name?"

"Daido," his dad said. "I'll say it slower, 'Dye-doe.' It means 'Great Path.' That's a good name for a man who took a great adventure traveling across the Pacific Ocean to a new land. In Chinese, his family name would be given first. And so, he was called Wong Daido."

"Wong Daido," Eric repeated. "Yeah."

"Do you know how to write that?" Matt asked, looking at the name.

"No." Eric shrugged.

"We'll let you play your game," said Eric's mom. "Come on, dear." She and Eric's dad walked away.

"Look." Eric pointed to the screen. A miner wearing a broad-brimmed gray hat lifted a rock showing a button that said, "Press if you dare."

"I dare you," Matt said loudly.

"I'm doing it." **Annoyed**, Eric pressed the button.

Suddenly Eric and Matt found themselves standing in a narrow space between two large, tall rocks by the muddy road in the mountains, with trees towering over their heads. Miners and **prospectors** walked and rode past. Eric's heart beat faster with excitement, but he was also a little scared.

"What happened?" Matt asked. "This is creepy. Where are we?"

Eric smelled the scent of pine trees and kicked at the mud. "I think we're really in the Gold Rush. We went back in time!"

"Did you say, back in time?" Matt stared around them in shock.

"Come on." Eric walked up to the mysterious miner who had lifted the rock. "Do you know a man named Wong Daido?" Eric carefully pronounced his ancestor's name, remembering to put his family name first.

The miner laughed. Then he looked closely at Eric and Matt. "You're not from around here are you?"

"No, we're not," said Eric hoping the man wouldn't ask any more questions.

"Do you know how many people are in this area? We're on the Feather River upstream from Marysville, in the western foothills of the Sierra Nevada in California. Men came to find gold. We're called the Forty-niners because so many of us have come this year."

"What year?" Matt asked, his eyes wide.

"1849, of course," said the miner. He frowned. "Don't you boys know what year it is? Gold was discovered in this area last year. Now, Forty-niners are coming from all over America and lots of other places."

FCAT **Cause and Effect**
How did Eric and Matt find themselves back in 1849?

"How do they get here?" Eric asked.

"I came overland from the eastern United States by wagon train. A good friend of mine took a ship from the east coast south around Cape Horn at the tip of South America. From China, other men come on ships across the Pacific Ocean."

"But where do they live?" Eric asked. "I don't see any houses here."

"Marysville is a new town," said the miner. "It was started by miners and prospectors. But men also live in camps, sometimes together and sometimes on their own, while they look for gold." He pointed to the river. "But the best way to find a Chinese miner is to ask other Chinese miners."

Matt ran down to the edge of the river, where a Chinese miner squatted by the rushing water, swirling sand in a metal pan.

Eric hurried after him. "Hey, mister, is your name Wong Daido?"

"No." The man shook his head. Then he gave Eric a little smile and pointed downstream. "You see that man? His name is Wong."

Matt ran down the bank, but this time Eric ran, too. They stopped next to Mr. Wong together, near a big tree growing right beside the river.

"Are you named Wong Daido?" Eric asked.

Mr. Wong was a little younger than the other Chinese miner. His long, braided queue swung behind him as he looked up. "I am," he said, giving both boys a big smile. "Why do you ask?"

Eric was afraid to explain he and Matt had traveled through time from the future. He was sure Mr. Wong wouldn't believe him and might chase them away, so he changed the subject. "My name's Eric, and this is my friend Matt. Have you found any gold?"

"Not today. Some days I find enough gold to buy food that will last until the next time I find gold. I filed this claim so I have the right to pan gold here. The river washes gold dust downstream, so I catch river water, mud, and sand in this pan and try to find it." He moved the pan in a **circular** motion, so that water sloshed out with some of the sand. "Gold is heavy, so it stays in the pan."

"Wow," said Matt. "And the river's so fast."

"Don't you have to get sand from the bottom of the river?" Eric asked. "It looks really deep right here!"

"It's very deep here," said Mr. Wong. "The riverbank drops steeply from the edge of the water and the current's very fast. But I can take the sand and mud right here at the edge and pan it. And the water itself carries sand, even when it looks clear. On a good day, the water brings gold to me."

Suddenly the ground shook. Eric and Matt thumped backward into a sitting position in the mud. Mr. Wong fell into the river with a splash.

"It's an earthquake!" Eric jumped up again. He had felt small earthquakes before, and this one was so quick it had ended already. When he looked up, he saw Mr. Wong in the river, desperately holding onto a tree root with both hands. The power of the river current pulled his legs downstream and he struggled to hold his head above the water. "Help me!"

Eric and Matt grabbed his arms and pulled, but the river current was too strong and Mr. Wong was too heavy for them to help.

"We have to save him," Eric called desperately to Matt. "If we don't, my family won't ever be born. And I won't be here!"

Eric saw a tree branch hanging low. "Come on! Help me pull the branch down!" He took the branch in both hands and bent his knees so his weight pulled it down. When Matt grabbed it, too, the branch lowered to Mr. Wong.

With an **outstretched** hand Mr. Wong grasped the branch.

"Matt, let go!" Eric and Matt released the branch and the branch slowly moved upward again, pulling Mr. Wong out of the water. He got his feet back on the river bank and let go of the branch. Mr. Wong took several moments to catch his breath. His clothes were so wet they stuck to him. "Aiee! You two saved my life. Thank you."

FCAT **Cause and Effect**

How did saving Mr. Wong's life affect the future?

"Mine too," said Eric. "You're welcome."

"I thought I was going to drown. Everything I have dreamed about would have come to an end." He paused and looked down at the ground. "I came from a poor peasant village in southern China," Mr. Wong went on. "I hope to find some gold and send for a woman I love. We'll marry here and raise a family in America—at least, I hope so."

"Hey, that's good," said Matt. "Because—"

Eric jabbed Matt with his elbow and interrupted, ". . . because it's a good idea." He smiled, knowing that Mr. Wong's dream was going to come true.

"I don't have much to offer in return for my life," said Mr. Wong. He reached into his pocket and pulled something out. "This is my chop."

Eric and Matt looked. It was a small piece of ivory, with unfamiliar shapes carved on the bottom. "What's it for?" Eric asked.

"I'll show you." Mr. Wong pushed the bottom into a smooth spot of mud next to the river. When he lifted it, three marks were in the mud. "That's my name, Wong Daido. I don't have any gold today. But I would like you to accept this as my gift. I will always remember you."

Eric took the chop. "That's very nice of you. Thanks."

"I should return to my camp and dry off," said Mr. Wong.

"I think we better go home, too," said Eric. "We enjoyed meeting you!" He carefully put the chop in his pants pocket.

"Thank you again for your help," said Mr. Wong. "Goodbye." He picked up his pan and walked away from the river toward the muddy road.

"How do we get back to our time?" asked Matt. "Maybe we should try to find those big rocks. But where are they?"

"Come on," Eric said to Matt. "I remember where they are. Maybe we'll find some kind of clue there that will help us get back." He led Matt back into the space between the two big rocks where they had walked out. Suddenly they were back in Eric's living room in front of the computer.

"Wow! It worked. Those rocks must be some kind of doorway into the past." Matt looked at the computer screen. "That's a great game!"

"Who's winning?" Eric's mom asked, as she and his dad came in.

"Mom! Dad!" Eric called out. "We went into the game and back in time!"

"Yeah," said Matt. "We met Eric's great-great-great grandfather!"

Eric's mom and dad laughed.

"I love the way these games build imagination while they teach history," said Eric's mom. "Isn't that nice?"

"Dad! He told us he filed a claim for his mine along the Feather River!"

"Well, I know from what I read in my grandfather's journal that Daido did file a claim. Let's see if we can find out if it was along the Feather River." Eric's dad moved to the computer and conducted an Internet search. After a while he looked up in surprise. "Wong Daido did file a claim in that area in 1849. I found a **reference** to it."

"Do you believe me now?" Eric asked.

"C'mon, Eric. Do you expect me to believe you actually went back in time?"

"No, I guess not." Eric felt a wave of **disappointment**, then suddenly reached into his pocket. "Maybe this will convince you!" He pulled out the chop. "Dad! Look at the name: Wong Daido." Smiling, Eric held it up.

On the chop, a little bit of gold dust from the river **glinted** in the light.

File a Claim with William, Cornelius, and Ying-Hwa

William F. Wu has liked history since he was a boy. During recess at school, he and his friend acted out famous historical events. William also enjoyed writing stories and poems. He first thought about becoming a writer when he was eight years old.

Cornelius Van Wright and **Ying-Hwa Hu** are a husband and wife team who have been illustrating books for over 15 years. Cornelius studied art in New York City, while Ying developed her art skills in Taiwan and Minnesota. With such different backgrounds, the two try to combine their different cultures into each illustration for this story.

LOG ON Find out more about William F. Wu, Cornelius Van Wright, and Ying-Hwa Hu at **www.macmillanmh.com**

FCAT Author's Purpose

What clues in *The Gold Rush Game* helped you understand the author's purpose for writing this science fiction story? Did William F. Wu want to inform or entertain the reader? Discuss the evidence that led you to your conclusion.

FCAT Comprehension Check

Summarize

Summarize *The Gold Rush Game*. Use your Cause and Effect Chart to help you explain what the main characters are trying to do and what happens to them.

Cause → Effect
→
→
→
→

Think and Compare

READ THINK EXPLAIN

1. Who are the Forty-niners? Why did they come to California? Explain using details from the story. **Analyze Story Structure: Cause and Effect**

READ THINK EXPLAIN

2. What was the reason Eric's parents bought him the Gold Rush game? Did their wishes come true by the end of the story? Use story details to explain. **Analyze**

3. How would you change the plot to include one of Matt's ancestors? Would you make Matt's ancestor a **prospector** too? Invent a character with traits that would fit into the story. **Synthesize**

4. Why is it important for people to learn about their family's history? Explain. **Evaluate**

5. Read "In Search of Gold" on pages 664–665. How is Larry's experience similar to that of the prospectors in *The Gold Rush Game*? How is it different? Use details from both selections to explain. **Reading/Writing Across Texts**

Science

Genre

Nonfiction Articles provide information about real people, places, or things.

Text Feature

Timelines show historical events in the order in which they occurred.

Content Vocabulary

properties
displacement
density

The History of GOLD

Searching, Measuring, and Wearing

by Howard Murphy

Nearly 500 years ago, Spanish explorers made their way to the Americas in search of gold. In the late 1800s, people from all over the world—even as far away as China—journeyed to California for gold. What is gold? And why, after so many years, is it still sought after by people from all over the world?

Gold is a valuable mineral that is thinly spread throughout the earth. It is unusual to find large amounts of gold in a single location. This explains why people throughout history have had to travel all over the world to find just a small amount of gold.

"Panning" for gold involves dipping a pan into a river, collecting water, and swishing it around to see if there are any gold pieces.

Gold can be measured using different types of instruments. The gold above is being measured using a scale.

Properties of Gold

Gold has **properties**, or characteristics, that can be easured. One property of gold is volume. Volume the amount of space that an object takes up. To termine the volume of gold, people use a method lled **displacement** of water. In this method a piece of ld is dropped into a cylinder filled with water. Some the water in the cylinder is pushed out by the gold. is overflow of water is then measured to determine the ld's volume.

Another way to measure gold is to find t its **density**. Gold is a very dense neral. This means that gold is avy for its size. One cubic ntimeter of gold weighs .3 grams. When you mpare that to one cubic ntimeter of steel, which eighs only 7.87 grams, u can easily see that ld is very dense!

e word *gold* comes from an d English word *gelo*, which eans "yellow."

This gold bracelet is 24 carats. It was made in India during the 1800s.

Uses of Gold

Gold is used to make jewelry and some art. The gold used for jewelry is measured in carats. Twenty-four carats means that the mineral is pure gold. The lower the carats, the less pure the gold is. This means other metals have been added to the gold to make it harder. Pure gold is too soft for some pieces of jewelry. It would scratch too easily.

Important Dates in the History of Gold

Reading a Timeline

A timeline organizes events on a line. Read across the timeline from left to right.

4000 B.C. Gold is first used in parts of Central and Eastern Europe.

3000 B.C. The Egyptians begin mixing gold with metals.

1492 Christopher Columbus comes to the Americas searching for gold.

1849 People rush from all parts of the world to California to search for gold.

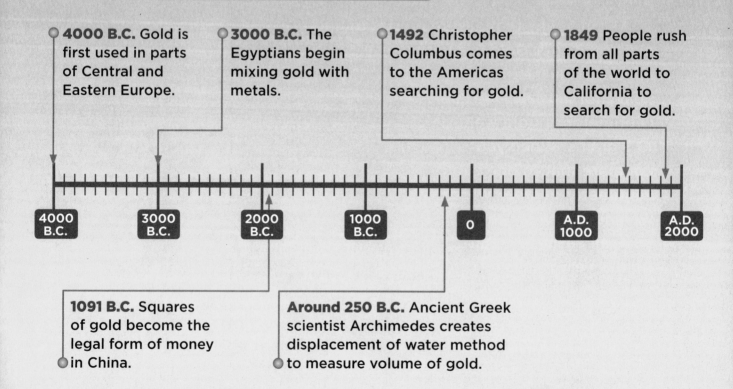

1091 B.C. Squares of gold become the legal form of money in China.

Around 250 B.C. Ancient Greek scientist Archimedes creates displacement of water method to measure volume of gold.

Gold Is Rare

One reason gold is so valuable is that it is very scarce. Gold is hard to find in large amounts. It is found in rocks in very small amounts. It takes time and money to get a gold mine ready to produce gold. Sometimes gold can no longer be found in some mines and they have to be shut down. It takes time, work, and money to keep up with the world's demand for gold.

Gold bars are weighed in grams.

Connect and Compare

1. Look at the timeline on page 684. When was gold first used in Europe? When and why did Christopher Columbus come to the Americas? **Reading a Timeline**

2. What method is used to measure the volume of gold? Explain the method in detail using examples from the article. **Apply**

3. Think about this article and *The Gold Rush Game*. What information did you learn about gold in this article that was not in the story? What information was the same? Use details from both selections to explain. **Reading/Writing Across Texts**

Science Activity

Research a method that is used to measure gold's density. Write a summary of your findings.

LOG ON Find out more about gold at **www.macmillanmh.com**

Write About a Place

Writer's Craft

FCAT **A Strong Conclusion**

A good writer uses **a strong conclusion** to bring his or her writing to a close. A strong conclusion emphasizes the writer's main idea. It also makes the reader think about the information that was presented to support the topic.

I wrote in my journal about White Pines Forest and why it is my favorite place to visit.

I used a strong conclusion to strengthen my main idea.

White Pines Forest

Yesterday my parents took me to White Pines Forest. It is my favorite place to visit! I like going there because it's such an interesting place. I can always find something to do at White Pines. Sometimes I go boating on the Muddy River. If it's a hot day, I can swim happily in Colson Lake.

This time I decided to take pictures of birds with my new camera. At first, I only saw common birds like robins. But then I saw a chubby bird with large eyes. I realized it was an owl when I heard it hoot spookily. Only at White Pines Forest would I be able to see something as rare as an owl flying during the day!

Writing Prompt

Communities have special places that people like to visit.

Think about a special place in your community that you like to visit.

Now write about a time you visited a special place in your community.

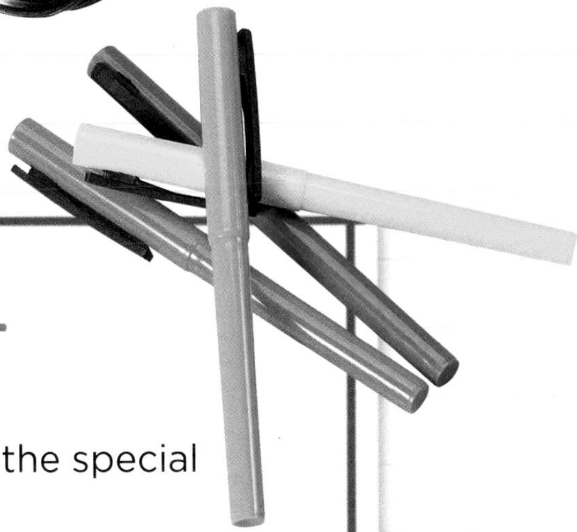

FCAT Writer's Checklist

☑ **Focus:** I clearly show enthusiasm for the special place I chose to write about.

☐ **Organization:** I use a strong conclusion to end my writing. My conclusion emphasizes my main idea.

☑ **Support:** I include the most interesting information about this place. Each paragraph has a clear topic sentence with details that support it.

☑ **Conventions:** I correctly use adverbs that end in *-ly*. My sentences are complete.

WILD VISITORS

Talk About It

Why do think the driver might be surprised by the alligator crossing the road?

LOG ON Find out more about wild visitors at **www.macmillanmh.com**

Vocabulary

wistfully
jumble
eavesdropping
scornfully
scuffling
logical
acquaintance

Context Clues

FCAT **Paragraph Clues** can help you figure out the meaning of unfamiliar words.

Find *jumble* in the story. Use clues within the paragraph to figure out its meaning.

The Country Mouse and the City Mouse

retold by Jeff Banner

One day Country Mouse invited an old friend from the city to visit her. Country Mouse welcomed City Mouse with a delicious meal of fresh barley and corn. City Mouse was very quiet, so Country Mouse asked her whether anything was wrong.

"I was just missing the city," she replied **wistfully**. "You must come visit one day. There are lots of good things to eat."

Country Mouse thought this was a very good idea, so a few weeks later she traveled to the city. City Mouse invited her friend for dinner at her favorite restaurant. Country Mouse followed City Mouse as she tiptoed quietly into a cupboard and listened.

"So, what are we doing?" asked Country Mouse.

"Shhh. We're doing a bit of **eavesdropping**," City Mouse whispered. "When the cook leaves for the night, we can help ourselves to that lovely bag of sugar over there."

A light went out, and it grew quiet. City Mouse nibbled a hole in the bag, and Country Mouse took the tiniest taste.

"I've never tasted anything so wonderful in all my life!" she cried.

Just then the mice heard a **scuffling** sound coming from behind the cupboard door. "Run for your life!" screamed City Mouse.

"That's Esperanza, the cook's rotten cat," City Mouse explained when they were safe. "You don't ever want to make her **acquaintance**. One swipe from her claws and it's curtains. When she's asleep again, we can go back for more sugar."

But Country Mouse was too frightened to go back, so they went down to the basement instead. There they found a **jumble** of grain bags stacked randomly against the wall. Country Mouse happily nibbled this and that. Then she saw something that made her mouth water—a hunk of cheese! Country Mouse was about to bite it when. . .

"STOP!" yelled City Mouse. "Can't you see that's a trap?" she said **scornfully**. "One nibble and that big metal thing comes crashing down."

Country Mouse was horrified. The city was not the safest, most **logical** place for a mouse to live—or visit! So Country Mouse went home and never visited the city again.

Reread for Comprehension

Analyze Story Structure

FCAT

Essential Message/Theme A story's **theme** is also called the **essential message**, or main point. To figure out a story's essential message, think about what the characters say and do and what happens as a result. Then think about what lesson the author wants readers to learn. Reread the selection and use your Theme Chart to help you find the essential message.

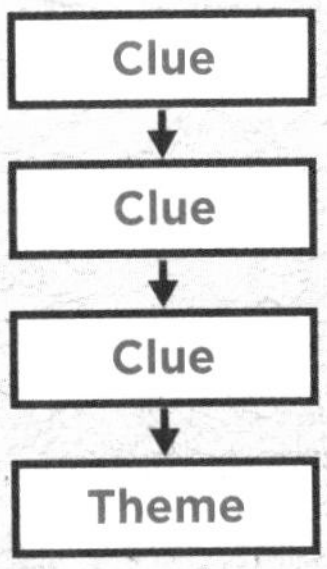

Comprehension

Genre

Fantasy is a story with invented characters, settings, or other elements that could not exist in real life.

Analyze Story Structure

FCAT **Essential Message/Theme**

As you read, fill in your Theme Chart.

Clue
↓
Clue
↓
Clue
↓
Theme

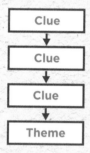

Read to Find Out

What happens when a country cricket winds up in a big city?

THE CRICKET
IN TIMES SQUARE
By George Selden
NEWBERY HONOR
BOOK
DRAWINGS BY
Garth Williams

Chester

Tucker Mouse had been watching the Bellinis and listening to what they said. Next to scrounging, **eavesdropping** on human beings was what he enjoyed most. That was one of the reasons he lived in the Times Square subway station. As soon as the family disappeared, he darted out across the floor and scooted up to the newsstand. At one side the boards had separated and there was a wide space he could jump through. He'd been in a few times before—just exploring. For a moment he stood under the three-legged stool, letting his eyes get used to the darkness. Then he jumped on it.

"Psst!" he whispered. "Hey, you up there—are you awake?"

There was no answer.

"Psst! Psst! Hey!" Tucker whispered again, louder this time.

From the shelf above came **scuffling**, like little feet feeling their way to the edge. "Who is going 'psst'?" said a voice.

"It's me," said Tucker. "Down here on the stool."

A black head, with two shiny black eyes, peered down at him. "Who are you?"

"A mouse," said Tucker, "Who are *you*?"

"I'm Chester Cricket," said the cricket. He had a high, musical voice. Everything he said seemed to be spoken to an unheard melody.

"My name's Tucker," said Tucker Mouse. "Can I come up?"

KLEENEX
200
100
SIZE 8.5

"I guess so," said Chester Cricket. "This isn't my house anyway."

Tucker jumped up beside the cricket and looked him all over. "A cricket," he said admiringly. "So you're a cricket. I never saw one before."

"I've seen mice before," the cricket said. "I knew quite a few back in Connecticut."

"Is that where you're from?" asked Tucker.

"Yes," said Chester. "I guess I'll never see it again," he added **wistfully**.

"How did you get to New York?" asked Tucker Mouse.

"It's a long story," sighed the cricket.

"Tell me," said Tucker, settling back on his haunches. He loved to hear stories. It was almost as much fun as eavesdropping—if the story was true.

"Well it must have been two—no, three days ago," Chester Cricket began. "I was sitting on top of my stump, just enjoying the weather and thinking how nice it was that summer had started. I live inside an old tree stump, next to a willow tree, and I often go up to the roof to look around. And I'd been practicing jumping that day too. On the other side of the stump from the willow tree there's a brook that runs past, and I'd been jumping back and forth across it to get my legs in condition for the summer. I do a lot of jumping, you know."

"Me too," said Tucker Mouse. "Especially around the rush hour."

"And I had just finished jumping when I smelled something," Chester went on, "liverwurst, which I love."

"You like liverwurst?" Tucker broke in. "Wait! Wait! Just wait!"

In one leap, he sprang down all the way from the shelf to the floor and dashed over to his drain pipe. Chester shook his head as he watched him go. He thought Tucker was a very excitable person—even for a mouse.

Inside the drain pipe, Tucker's nest was a **jumble** of papers, scraps of cloth, buttons, lost jewelry, small change, and everything else that can be picked up in a subway station. Tucker tossed things left and right in a wild search. Neatness was not one of the things he aimed at in life. At last he discovered what he was looking for: a big piece of liverwurst he had found earlier that evening. It was meant to be for breakfast tomorrow, but he decided that meeting his first cricket was a special occasion. Holding the liverwurst between his teeth, he whisked back to the newsstand.

"Look!" he said proudly, dropping the meat in front of Chester Cricket. "Liverwurst! You continue the story—we'll enjoy a snack too."

"That's very nice of you," said Chester. He was touched that a mouse he had known only a few minutes would share his food with him. "I had a little chocolate before, but besides that, nothing for three days."

"Eat! Eat!" said Tucker. He bit the liverwurst into two pieces and gave Chester the bigger one. "So you smelled the liverwurst—then what happened?"

FCAT Theme
The characters in this story become friends. What message is the author sending?

“I hopped down from the stump and went off toward the smell,” said Chester.

“Very **logical**,” said Tucker Mouse, munching with his cheeks full. “Exactly what I would have done.”

“It was coming from a picnic basket,” said Chester. “A couple of tuffets away from my stump the meadow begins, and there was a whole bunch of people having a picnic. They had hard boiled eggs, and cold roast chicken, and roast beef, and a whole lot of other things besides the liverwurst sandwiches which I smelled.”

Tucker Mouse moaned with pleasure at the thought of all that food.

“They were having such a good time laughing and singing songs that they didn’t notice me when I jumped into the picnic basket,” continued Chester. “I was sure they wouldn’t mind if I had just a taste.”

“Naturally not,” said Tucker Mouse sympathetically. “Why mind? Plenty for all. Who could blame you?”

“Now, I have to admit,” Chester went on, “I had more than a taste. As a matter of fact, I ate so much that I couldn’t keep my eyes open—what with being tired from the jumping and everything. And I fell asleep right there in the picnic basket. The first thing I knew, somebody had put a bag on top of me that had the last of the roast beef sandwiches in it. I couldn’t move!”

“Imagine!” Tucker exclaimed. “Trapped under roast beef sandwiches! Well, there are worse fates.”

"At first I wasn't too frightened," said Chester. "After all, I thought, they probably come from New Canaan or some other nearby town. They'll have to unpack the basket sooner or later. Little did I know!" He shook his head and sighed. "I could feel the basket being carried into a car and riding somewhere and then being lifted down. That must have been the railroad station. Then I went up again and there was a rattling and roaring sound, the way a train makes. By this time I was pretty scared. I knew every minute was taking me farther away from my stump, but there wasn't anything I could do. I was getting awfully cramped too, under those roast beef sandwiches."

"Didn't you try to eat your way out?" asked Tucker.

"I didn't have any room," said Chester. "But every now and then the train would give a lurch and I managed to free myself a little. We traveled on and on, and then the train stopped. I didn't have any idea where we were, but as soon as the basket was carried off, I could tell from the noise it must be New York."

"You never were here before?" Tucker asked.

"Goodness no!" said Chester. "But I've heard about it. There was a swallow I used to know who told about flying over New York every spring and fall on her way to the North and back. But what would I be doing here?" He shifted uneasily from one set of legs to another. "I'm a country cricket."

"Don't worry," said Tucker Mouse. "I'll feed you liverwurst. You'll be all right. Go on with the story."

"It's almost over," said Chester. "The people got off one train and walked a ways and got on another—even noisier than the first."

"Must have been the subway," said Tucker.

"I guess so," Chester Cricket said. "You can imagine how scared I was. I didn't know *where* I was going! For all I knew they could have been heading for Texas, although I don't guess many people from Texas come all the way to Connecticut for a picnic."

"It could happen," said Tucker, nodding his head.

"Anyway I worked furiously to get loose. And finally I made it. When they got off the second train, I took a flying leap and landed in a pile of dirt over in the corner of this place where we are."

"Such an introduction to New York," said Tucker, "to land in a pile of dirt in the Times Square subway station. Tsk, tsk, tsk."

"And here I am," Chester concluded forlornly. "I've been lying over there for three days not knowing what to do. At last I got so nervous I began to chirp."

"That was the sound!" interrupted Tucker Mouse. "I heard it, but I didn't know what it was."

"Yes, that was me," said Chester. "Usually I don't chirp until later on in the summer—but my goodness, I had to do *something*!"

The cricket had been sitting next to the edge of the shelf. For some reason—perhaps it was a faint noise, like padded feet tiptoeing across the floor—he happened to look down. A shadowy form that had been crouching silently below in the darkness made a spring and landed right next to Tucker and Chester.

"Watch out!" Chester shouted, "A cat!" He dove headfirst into the matchbox.

Harry Cat

Chester buried his head in the Kleenex. He didn't want to see his new friend, Tucker Mouse, get killed. Back in Connecticut he had sometimes watched the one-sided fights of cats and mice in the meadow, and unless the mice were near their holes, the fights always ended in the same way. But this cat had been upon them too quickly: Tucker couldn't have escaped.

There wasn't a sound. Chester lifted his head and very cautiously looked behind him. The cat—a huge tiger cat with gray-green eyes and black stripes along his body—was sitting on his hind legs, switching his tail around his forepaws. And directly between those forepaws, in the very jaws of his enemy, sat Tucker Mouse. He was watching Chester curiously. The cricket began to make frantic signs that the mouse should look up and see what was looming over him.

Very casually Tucker raised his head. The cat looked straight down on him. "Oh, him," said Tucker, chucking the cat under the chin with his right front paw, "he's my best friend. Come out from the matchbox."

Chester crept out, looking first at one, then the other.

"Chester, meet Harry Cat," said Tucker. "Harry, this is Chester. He's a cricket."

"I'm very pleased to make your **acquaintance**," said Harry Cat in a silky voice.

"Hello," said Chester. He was sort of ashamed because of all the fuss he'd made. "I wasn't scared for myself. But I thought cats and mice were enemies."

NO SALE
Musical America

"In the country, maybe," said Tucker. "But in New York we gave up those old habits long ago. Harry is my oldest friend. He lives with me over in the drain pipe. So how was scrounging tonight, Harry?"

"Not so good," said Harry Cat. "I was over in the ash cans on the East Side, but those rich people don't throw out as much garbage as they should."

"Chester, make that noise again for Harry," said Tucker Mouse.

Chester lifted the black wings that were carefully folded across his back and with a quick, expert stroke drew the top one over the bottom. A *thrumm* echoed through the station.

"Lovely—very lovely," said the cat. "This cricket has talent."

"I thought it was singing," said Tucker. "But you do it like playing a violin, with one wing on the other?"

"Yes," said Chester. "These wings aren't much good for flying, but I prefer music anyhow." He made three rapid chirps.

Tucker Mouse and Harry Cat smiled at each other. "It makes me want to purr to hear it," said Harry.

"Some people say a cricket goes 'chee chee chee,'" explained Chester. "And others say, 'treet treet treet,' but we crickets don't think it sounds like either one of those."

"It sounds to me as if you were going 'crik crik crik,'" said Harry.

"Maybe that's why they call him a 'cricket,'" said Tucker.

They all laughed. Tucker had a squeaky laugh that sounded as if he were hiccupping. Chester was feeling much happier now. The future did not seem nearly as gloomy as it had over in the pile of dirt in the corner.

"Are you going to stay a while in New York?" asked Tucker.

"I guess I'll have to," said Chester. "I don't know how to get home."

"Well, we could always take you to Grand Central Station and put you on a train going back to Connecticut," said Tucker. "But why don't you give the city a try. Meet new people—see new things. Mario likes you very much."

"Yes, but his mother doesn't," said Chester. "She thinks I carry germs."

"Germs!" said Tucker **scornfully**. "She wouldn't know a germ if one gave her a black eye. Pay no attention."

"Too bad you couldn't have found more successful friends," said Harry Cat. "I fear for the future of this newsstand."

"It's true," echoed Tucker sadly. "They're going broke fast." He jumped up on a pile of magazines and read off the names in the half-light that slanted through the cracks in the wooden cover. "*Art News—Musical America*. Who would read them but a few long-hairs?"

"I don't understand the way you talk," said Chester. Back in the meadow he had listened to bullfrogs, and woodchucks, and rabbits, even a few snakes, but he had never heard anyone speak like Tucker Mouse. "What is a long-hair?"

Tucker scratched his head and thought a moment. "A long-hair is an extra-refined person," he said. "You take an Afghan hound—that's a long-hair."

"Do Afghan hounds read *Musical America*?" asked the cricket.

"They would if they could," said Tucker.

Chester shook his head. "I'm afraid I won't get along in New York," he said.

"Oh, sure you will!" squeaked Tucker Mouse. "Harry, suppose we take Chester up and show him Times Square. Would you like that, Chester?"

"I guess so," said Chester, although he was really a little leery of venturing out into New York City.

The three of them jumped down to the floor. The crack in the side of the newsstand was just wide enough for Harry to get through. As they crossed the station floor, Tucker pointed out the local sights of interest, such as the Nedick's lunch counter—Tucker spent a lot of time around there—and the Loft's candy store. Then they came to the drain pipe. Chester had to make short little hops to keep from hitting his head as they went up. There seemed to be hundreds of twistings and turnings, and many other pipes that opened off the main route, but Tucker Mouse knew his way perfectly—even in the dark. At last Chester saw light above them. One more hop brought him out onto the sidewalk. And there he gasped, holding his breath and crouching against the cement.

They were standing at one corner of the Times building, which is at the south end of Times Square. Above the cricket, towers that seemed like mountains of light rose up into the night sky. Even this late the neon signs were still blazing. Reds, blues, greens, and yellows flashed down on him. And the air was full of the roar of traffic and the hum of human beings. It was as if Times Square were a kind of shell, with colors and noises breaking in great waves inside it. Chester's heart hurt him and he closed his eyes. The sight was too terrible and beautiful for a cricket who up to now had measured high things by the height of his willow tree and sounds by the burble of a running brook.

"How do you like it?" asked Tucker Mouse.

"Well—it's—it's quite something," Chester stuttered.

"You should see it New Year's Eve," said Harry Cat.

Gradually Chester's eyes got used to the lights. He looked up. And way far above them, above New York, and above the whole world, he made out a star that he knew was a star he used to look at back in Connecticut. When they had gone down to the station and Chester was in the matchbox again, he thought about that star. It made him feel better to think that there was one familiar thing, twinkling above him, amid so much that was new and strange.

FCAT **Theme**

How do the characters in the story show the essential message?

HOTEL ASTOR
STATE
CHEVROLET
8 8
KINSEY
BO
CRITE
SHE

On a Journey with George and Garth

George Selden wrote this story after he heard a cricket chirping in the Times Square subway station. Chester's whole story came to George immediately. The cricket reminded George of his home in the countryside where he used to live.

Other books by George Selden and Garth Williams

Garth Williams worked very hard to make the creatures in this story look and act like real people. First, he started with an actual photograph of the animal. Then he drew and redrew until the animal seemed to have human qualities.

LOG ON Find out more about George Selden and Garth Williams at **www.macmillanmh.com**

FCAT Author's Purpose

Why did George Selden write *The Cricket in Times Square*? Was his main purpose to explain, entertain, or inform? What details help you figure this out?

FCAT Comprehension Check

Summarize

Summarize *The Cricket in Times Square.* Use your Theme Chart to help you tell about the main characters and important events in the story.

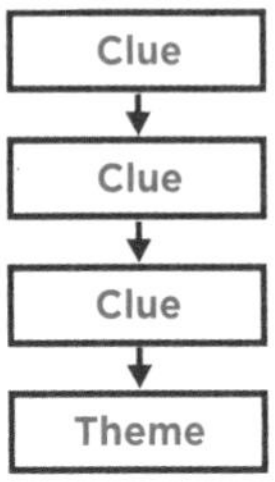

Think and Compare

READ THINK EXPLAIN

1. New York City is filled with people from many different backgrounds and countries. What message is the author sending by making a cricket, a cat, and a mouse his main characters? Use details from the story to explain. **Analyze Story Structure: Essential Message/Theme**

READ THINK EXPLAIN

2. Reread page 708 of the story. Why was the sight of Times Square too much for Chester? Why did he feel comfort when he looked at the stars? Explain using story details. **Analyze**

3. If you could be a character in the story, which character would you choose to be, Chester or Tucker? Explain your answer. **Apply**

4. Tucker advises his new **acquaintance**, Chester, to give the city a try. How is this a good idea? **Evaluate**

5. Read "The Country Mouse and the City Mouse" on pages 690–691. How is Country Mouse's experience similar to Chester's on pages 701–704? How is it different? Use details from both selections to explain. **Reading/Writing Across Texts**

Science

Genre

Editorials are articles printed in newspapers and magazines that express the opinions of the writer.

FCAT Text Feature

Advertisements are text and pictures that persuade consumers to buy a product.

Content Vocabulary

nocturnal **echolocation** **mammals**

Adapting to Survive

Bats can also use their wings to hold their food while eating.

by Melissa Perez

Did you know that there are 13 different kinds of bats living in Florida? You have probably never seen one, which might make you wonder where they live. What do they eat? How do they find food? And how are these fascinating creatures able to survive in different environments filled with so many people and other animals?

Bats are able to survive in nearly any place because they adapt to their environment. Bats usually live in caves. But if they are in an environment where there are no caves, bats will live in any dark place where they can't be disturbed. Finding a peaceful, dark place to live is important to a bat because bats are **nocturnal**.

cont'd on page 714

Reading an Advertisement

The purpose of an advertisement is to persuade people to buy a product. Look for ways in which the author motivates customers to come to Kramer's.

Our Best Bat House Just Went On Sale!

Now Only $40.00
(Regularly $55.00)

Designed by the Bat Society
Slanted roof for better run-off
Weather-resistant red cedar
Made in the USA

Special: Hammocks–Up to 50% off!

Wheelbarrows–10% off when you bring this ad

For a limited time only. Sales end 6/30.

Kramer's Lawn and Garden

555 Main Street, Live Oak, Florida • (555) 555-5555

Open daily 10-6

Bats usually sleep together in large groups. They hang upside down from the ceiling.

cont'd from page 712

Most animals hunt during the day, so bats do not have to compete with many other animals for their food. Also, because it is cooler at night, bats are protected from having to hunt in the heat for the insects they love to eat.

After locating their food, bats fly towards it. Bats are the only **mammals** that can truly fly. They have small, light bodies, large muscles, and very strong wings. A bat's size and strength allow it to move quickly to catch insects in the air.

Unfortunately bat populations are falling all around the country. Many different factors, such as people disturbing bat roosts, play a role in the decline of this amazing creature. That is why it is a good thing that these creatures can adapt to almost any environment. This way there is a chance that they will be around for a longer time. Now that you have learned all this new and exciting information about bats, I urge you to go to your nearest zoo to see bats up close!

DID YOU KNOW ?

Did you know that bats do not rely on their eyes when they fly and hunt insects? Instead they use **echolocation**. They emit high-pitched sounds. When the sound waves bounce off objects and return to the bat's ears, it can tell how far away the object is.

FCAT Connect and Compare

1. What are some persuasive techniques used in the ad on page 713? Could a customer at Kramer's get 50% off all hammocks? Explain. **Reading an Advertisement**

2. What statements from the article support the claim that it is a good thing bats are nocturnal? Explain using details from the article. **Analyze**

3. Think about *The Cricket in Times Square* and this article. How did Tucker, Harry, and Chester adapt to their environment? How have bats adapted to their environment? **Reading/ Writing Across Texts**

RESEARCH INQUIRY Science Activity

The evening bat is a kind of bat found throughout Florida. Research this bat and write two paragraphs summarizing your findings. Include a physical description of the evening bat, what kind of bugs it eats, and where it lives.

LOG ON Find out more about bats at **www.macmillanmh.com**

Write a News Article

Writer's Craft

FCAT Facts and Opinions

Facts are statements that can be proven true. **Opinions** are statements that tell what someone thinks or believes. News articles use facts to answer "Who?," "What?," "When?," "Where?," and "Why?" These "five Ws" should be explained within the text of the article.

I used facts that could be proven to help me write my news article.

I used the "five Ws" to help me gather information.

School News

What ARE Those Birds?

by Matthew E.

Have you seen the big green birds on the telephone poles behind the school? Their messy nest has been growing larger and larger for years. Now it is the largest nest in the neighborhood!

The birds are called monk parakeets. They are a kind of parrot that originally lived in South America.

How did they get here? They are probably escaped pets. Bird experts think the parakeets like it here on the coast because it doesn't get too cold in the winter. Next time you're outside for recess, take a look at our monk parakeet colony.

Writing Prompt

Most people know a funny story about an animal.

Think about a funny story you know about an animal.

Now write a news article to tell a funny story about an animal.

FCAT Writer's Checklist

- **Focus:** My news article clearly presents my topic using **facts**. I avoid using **opinions**.
- **Organization:** I answer the questions "Who?," "What?," "Where?," "When?," and "Why?" in the text of my article.
- **Support:** I include details to support my topic.
- **Conventions:** I use adverbs that compare correctly. My sentences are complete.

Talk About It

What do we gain from learning about the natural world around us?

LOG ON Find out more about studying nature at **www.macmillanmh.com**

TIME FOR KIDS®

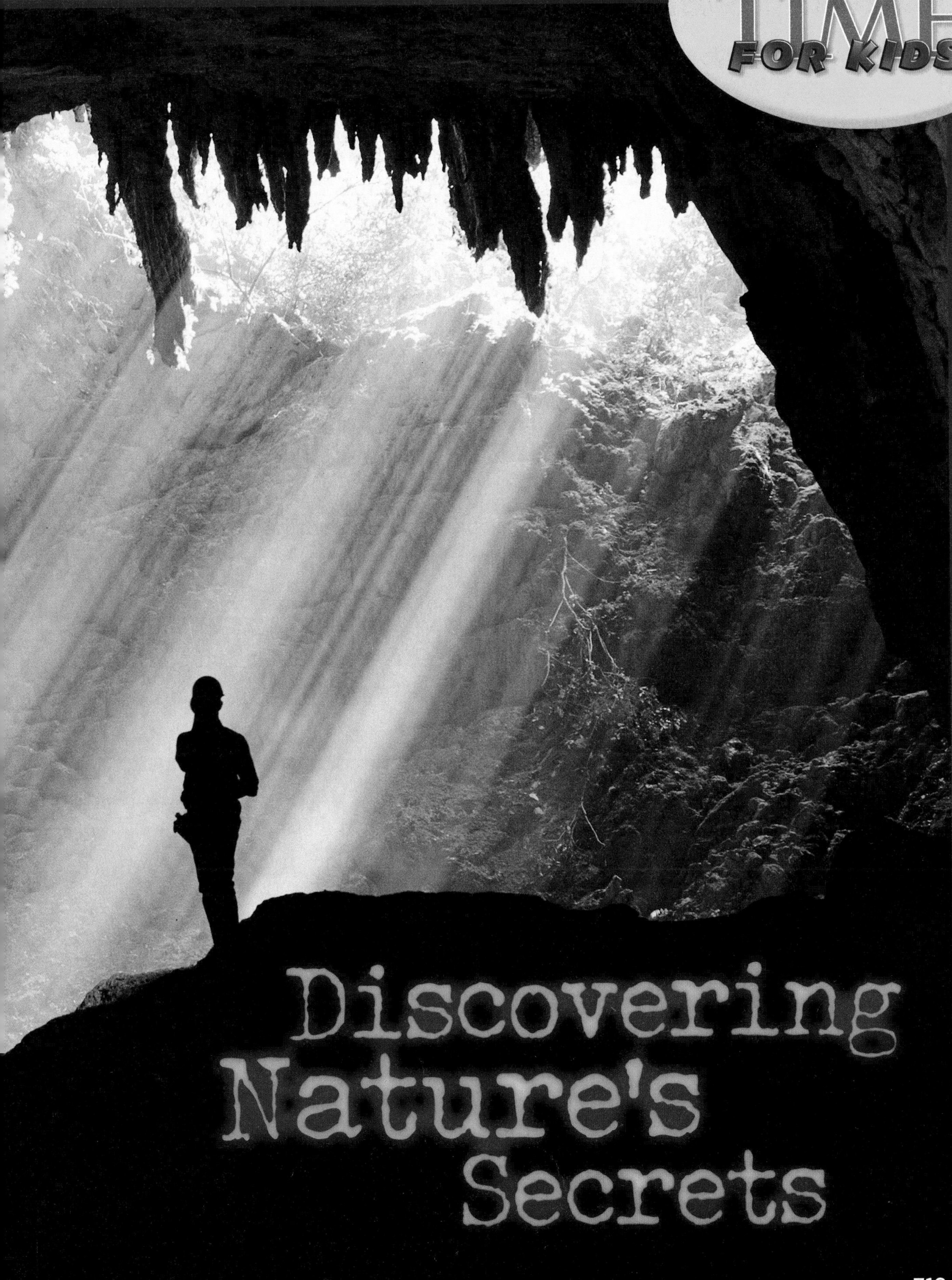

Discovering Nature's Secrets

Real World Reading

Amber: Nature's Time Capsule

Vocabulary

fossil
stumbled upon
paleontologist
inspected

Scorpion and damsel fly trapped in amber (above), and an Etruscan amber carving (below)

About 30 million years ago, this tiny scorpion found trouble. It got stuck in some sticky stuff called resin. Over millions of years, that resin grew dryer and harder. Finally it turned into a material called amber. The scorpion remained perfectly preserved in a golden prison.

Amber is nature's time capsule. It forms a tight seal around whatever is trapped inside, protecting it from the effects of aging. Scientists have found insects preserved in amber that come from the time of the dinosaurs.

Several years ago a scientist discovered an important amber **fossil**: three tiny flowers that were 90 million years old. Found in New Jersey, they are the oldest whole flowers ever seen.

Because amber is beautiful, people value it for reasons other than science. For centuries people have made jewelry and sculpture from amber. To the ancient Etruscans, who lived in what is now Italy, amber was as precious as gold. But not all amber is golden. Some is white, red, or green.

LOG ON Find out more about amber at **www.macmillanmh.com**

A Dinosaur Named Bambi

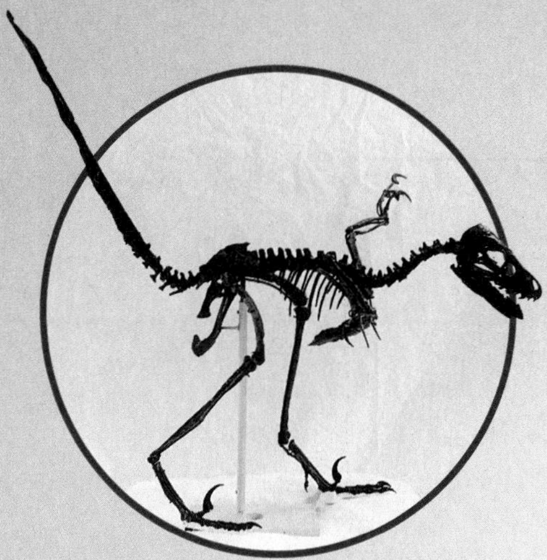

Bambiraptor had a long, stiff tail and long arms that could bend at the wrist. It may also have had feathers.

"This big ball of dirt rolled over, and I saw black bones in it," recalls Wes Linster, describing his astonishing discovery in 1994 at age 14. Linster was digging on a ranch near Choteau, Montana, when he **stumbled upon** the new dinosaur species. His family nicknamed the three-foot-long fossil Bambi because it was so small.

The fossil itself is the skeleton of a baby that lived 75 million years ago. It belongs to a dinosaur family that most scientists believe are the ancestors of birds.

Paleontologist John Ostrom first **inspected** the bones in 1995. "The skeleton is a jewel," he says. "I think it's one of the most valuable scientific specimens ever found in North America."

Into the Dark Unknown

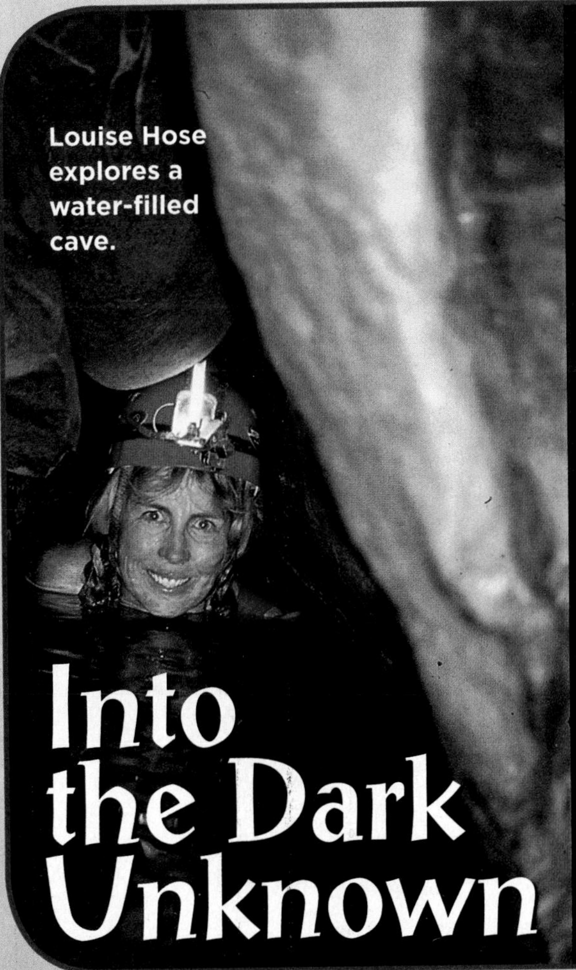

Louise Hose explores a water-filled cave.

Louise Hose is a geologist and a speleologist, or caver. For the past few years, she has gone to Tapijulapa (tah•pee•hoo•LA•pa), Mexico, to map a cave. She and her fellow explorers found that it is full of animals that have adapted to life underground. There are vampire bats, spiders, and colorless fish and crabs in the cave's streams.

They also discovered something more amazing: colonies of microscopic living creatures that can survive in extreme conditions. Even with poisonous air and with no light, these creatures thrive underground. The living colonies drip down like a runny nose. They contain sulfuric acid, which can burn human skin. A photographer on the expedition named the slimy critters "snottites."

Real World Reading

Comprehension

Genre

A **Nonfiction Article** gives information about real people, places, or things.

Monitor Comprehension

FCAT **Main Idea and Details**

The main idea of an article is what the article is all about. Details support and give information about the main idea.

Meet a Bone-ified Explorer

What does a paleontologist do after she's discovered the largest and most complete* Tyrannosaurus rex *fossils ever found?

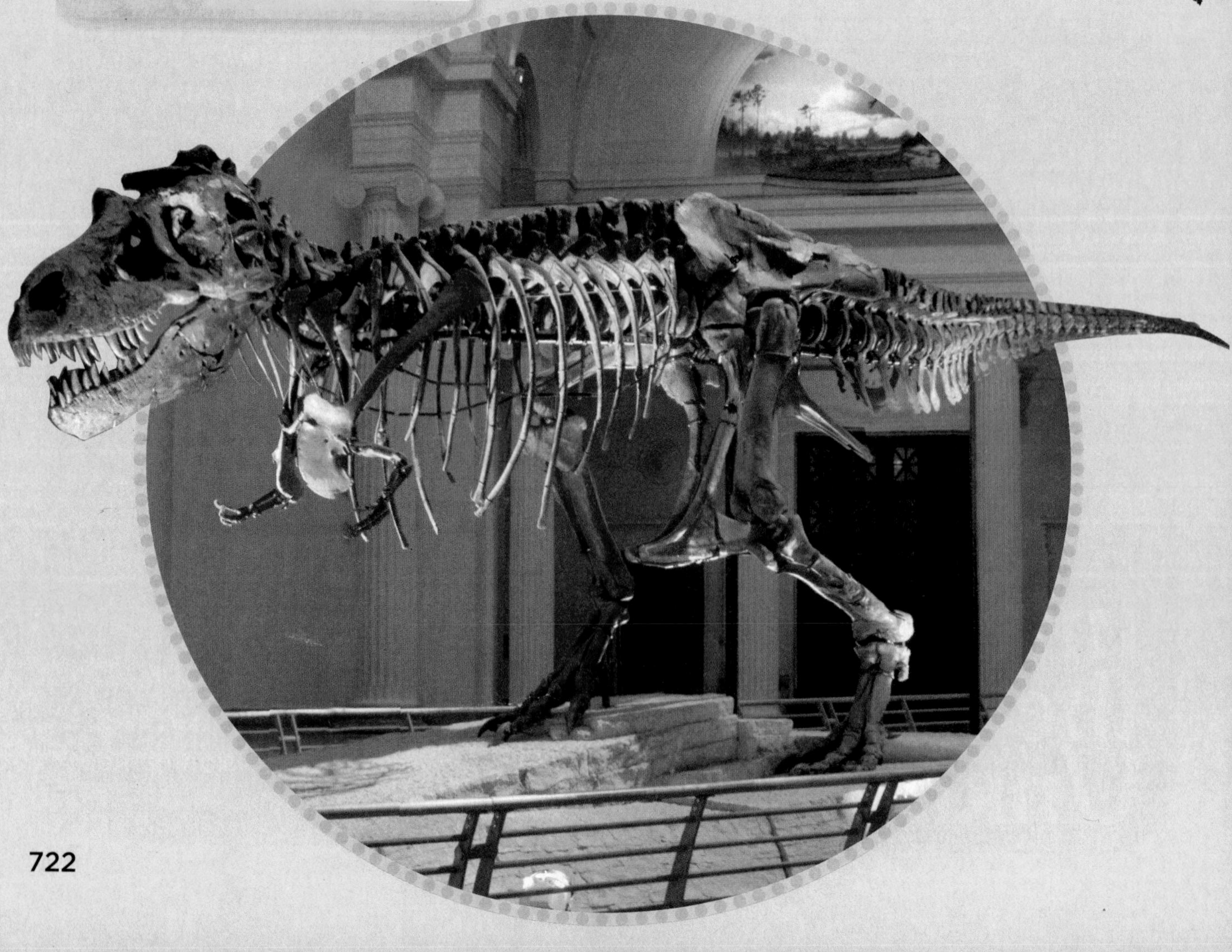

Sue Hendrickson poses with a model of the foot of the *Tyrannosaurus rex* she found.

As a little girl in Munster, Indiana, Sue Hendrickson always kept her eyes on the ground. "I was really shy and always walked with my head down," she says, "but my curiosity was strong." She often searched the ground for low-lying treasures. Hendrickson's interest in finding things turned into an exciting job. Now she is a field **paleontologist**. As a paleontologist, Hendrickson gets to spend a lot of her time exploring—and digging. Her searches for new discoveries have taken her to countries around the world.

Hendrickson became famous after making a gigantic discovery in August 1990. After a long day of digging in South Dakota, she **stumbled upon** one of the largest and most complete specimens of a *T. rex* skeleton ever found. "It was as if she was just waiting to be discovered," Hendrickson says. "It took 67 million years, but we finally got to her."

Finding the Fossil

How did this **fossil** hunter discover this ancient natural wonder? It all started with a flat tire. While others from her digging team went to get the tire fixed, Hendrickson decided to explore a nearby cliff with her golden retriever, Gypsy. She walked around with her eyes to the ground, as usual. Suddenly she noticed a few pieces of bone. Then she looked up. She **inspected** the rocky cliffs above her head and saw three dinosaur backbones. She quickly headed back to the team to tell them about her exciting discovery.

Over a period of three weeks, the paleontologist and her team were able to uncover the huge dinosaur fossil. The team decided to name the dino fossil Sue, after Hendrickson. How does Hendrickson feel about finding Sue? "She is, I am certain, the greatest discovery I will ever make," she said.

Sue Hendrickson stands next to the skull and teeth of the *T. rex* skeleton before they were removed from the cliff.

Diving for Treasure

Hendrickson's adventurous spirit and curiosity about the past have taken her to extreme places to do her work. When she's not digging for bones, she's diving for sunken treasure. She has been working with a team in Egypt to find the palace of Cleopatra. The palace sank underwater during a fifth-century earthquake. "Sharing these finds with the world is the biggest thrill," says Hendrickson.

Sue Hendrickson explores an ancient shipwreck.

Hendrickson also explored a 400-year-old sunken ship in the waters near the Philippines. The ship was called *San Diego*. It was a Spanish ship that was used for trade and battle. In 1600 the ship sank to the bottom of the South China Sea. Hendrickson was part of the team that helped make the *San Diego* famous again.

In 2004 Hendrickson joined a team of divers in Egypt to find an ancient sunken city. She also was part of a dive in Cuba to explore a ship that sank in 1714.

What advice does Hendrickson have for kids who want to get their fingers dirty? "Spend some time volunteering out in the field with professionals," she recommends. "And focus on school. It will equip you to learn on your own."

FCAT

Think and Compare

1. What is a paleontologist?
2. What is the main idea of this article?
3. Do you think you would like traveling as much as Sue Hendrickson does? Why or why not?
4. What is the value of the discoveries—fossils in amber, "Bambi," "snottites"—described in these selections?

Out on a Limb

FCAT Test Strategy

Think and Search

Read on to find the answer. Look for information in more than one place.

A canopy crane lowers scientists from the Smithsonian Tropical Research Institute into the canopy of a rain forest in Panama.

Rain forests are one of Earth's last frontiers. They are filled with plants and animals that are rarely—if ever—seen by humans. According to one estimate, more than half of all life-forms on Earth live in tropical rain forests. Some scientists believe there may be many millions more.

Scientists are now focusing on the forest canopy. The canopy is the highest part of the forest. It is a network of leaves, vines, and branches that forms a world within a world. It functions differently from other parts of the forest because of its height and exposure to sunlight. The canopy usually extends 60 to 80 feet above ground. Areas near the top receive more sun and air, while the areas near the bottom have little or no light or air movement.

The forest canopy has been difficult to study because of the height of rain forest trees. Early techniques used by scientists included cutting down trees and climbing up ropes to view the canopy. Instead of answering questions, these methods only created more because scientists were just studying bits and pieces of the canopy. Today scientists are using new techniques and equipment, like the canopy crane, to make studying forest canopies easier.

The canopy crane is an ordinary construction crane equipped with a special platform. The crane lifts the platform above the treetops and then gently lowers it into the canopy. Scientists use the platform as a base of operations. One scientist described this experience as "like landing on the moon." Scientists agree that there is much to learn about this very unique place.

Go on

FCAT **Now answer Numbers 1 through 5. Base your answers on the article "Out on a Limb."**

1. Why are rain forests considered one of Earth's last frontiers?
   - (A) The forest canopy keeps the scientists out.
   - (B) The height of the trees makes travel difficult.
   - (C) Scientists have been unable to study many of the organisms that live there.
   - (D) Scientists have little interest in studying the plants and animals of the rain forest.

2. What condition helps make the canopy different from other parts of the rain forest?
   - (F) It contains no plants.
   - (G) Animals cannot reach it.
   - (H) People do not live there.
   - (I) It is higher and receives more sunlight.

Tip

Look for information in more than one place.

3. Early techniques to study the forest canopy
   - (A) created more questions for scientists.
   - (B) answered all of the scientists' questions.
   - (C) made scientists feel as if they were "landing on the moon."
   - (D) ruined the ecosystem of the rain forest because scientists kept cutting down trees.

4. READ THINK EXPLAIN What is the main idea of this article? What details support the main idea?

5. READ THINK EXPLAIN Describe how the canopy crane works. How does this new equipment help scientists gather more information about forest canopies? Explain using details from the article.

STOP

Write to a Prompt

FCAT

Sometimes people go to live in new and unfamiliar places.
Imagine you have to live in a new and unfamiliar place.
Now write a story about living in a new and unfamiliar place.

Narrative writing tells a story about a personal or fictional experience.

To figure out if a writing prompt asks for narrative writing, look for clue words such as tell about, tell what happened, or write a story.

Below see how one student begins a response to the prompt above.

The writer included an opinion to express a point of view.

I grew up in a small town. I knew everyone there, and I was very happy. Then one day my mother said we were moving. She had a great new job, in a city a thousand miles away.

The city was very different. I felt uncomfortable because I didn't know anybody. I was scared to go out because there was lots of traffic outside. People spoke many different languages. And I didn't like the food very much.

I was unhappy for about three days. Then I met my new neighbor, a kid my age. He introduced me to his friends. When school started, I met even more new friends. That's when many good things started happening to me.

Writing Prompt

Respond in writing to the prompt below. Before you write, read the Writing Hints below. Review the hints after you finish writing.

FCAT People often face new situations or experiences.

Think about a time you faced a new situation or experience.

Now write a story about a time you faced a new situation or experience.

Writing Hints for Prompts

- ☑ Read the prompt carefully.
- ☑ Plan your writing by organizing your ideas.
- ☑ Support your ideas by telling more about each event.
- ☑ Use facts and opinions when appropriate.
- ☑ Choose words that help others understand what you mean.
- ☑ Review and edit your writing.

AIRPLANES

Talk About It

Have you ever seen airplanes like these? Would you like to ride in one?

LOG ON Find out more about airplanes at **www.macmillanmh.com**

Vocabulary

glider **headlines**
unstable **hoisting**
wingspan **assured**
applauded

Word Parts

FCAT **Inflectional Endings**

When *-ed* is added to the end of a verb, the tense changes to the past.

The past tense of *applaud* is *applauded*.

Take Off

by Terry Eager

Every day thousands of people fly in airplanes. It is easy to take flying for granted, but it is important for us to remember that it took many years and several inventors to master flight.

Early Ideas

About 1500 Leonardo da Vinci, an Italian artist, made sketches of flying machines with wings that flapped like a bird's. In 1783 the Montgolfier brothers made a balloon out of linen cloth and paper. A controlled fire filled the balloon with hot air, which made it rise. Other inventors tried using hydrogen to make their balloons rise. Hydrogen is a gas that is lighter than air.

In 1804 Sir George Cayley made the first successful **glider**. A glider is an aircraft without engines. Although Cayley's first glider could not carry a passenger, his later gliders could.

Over the years better gliders were built. They were still **unstable**, though, and hard to control. It was the Wright brothers who figured out how to steer a glider.

Great Developments

In 1903 the Wright brothers built their first airplane. It had a gasoline engine and a **wingspan** of 40 feet, 4 inches. Only a few inventors **applauded** the Wright brothers' success. Other inventors continued working to perfect the flying machine.

Newspaper **headlines** cheered Charles "Lucky" Lindbergh in 1927. He was the first to fly alone across the Atlantic Ocean. Amelia Earhart became the first woman to do the same thing, in 1932.

Jets

In the 1950s American engineers designed passenger jet planes. By 1970 the world's first jumbo jet could carry more than 400 people. Today jets can fly farther and faster than ever.

Flight has come a long way since the days of **hoisting** a glider to the top of a sand dune. We owe our thanks to those who risked their lives when no one was **assured** of success.

Reread for Comprehension

Monitor Comprehension

FCAT

Author's Purpose Thinking about how an author feels about a topic can help readers identify the **author's purpose**. An author writes a story to entertain, give information, or explain something to the reader. Think about clues in the story that show how the author feels about the topic. Reread the selection and fill in your Author's Purpose Map.

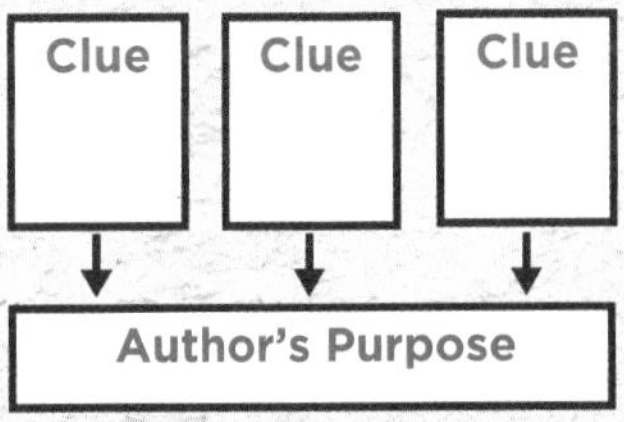

Comprehension

Genre

Narrative Nonfiction is a story or an account of actual persons, living things, situations, or events.

Monitor Comprehension

FCAT

Author's Purpose

As you read, fill in your Author's Purpose Map.

Clue	Clue	Clue
↓	↓	↓

Author's Purpose

Read to Find Out

What inspired the Wright brothers to make the first successful flying machine?

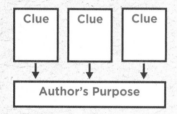

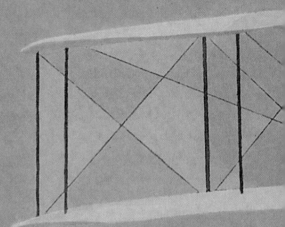

My Brothers' Flying Machine

by
JANE YOLEN
paintings by
JIM BURKE

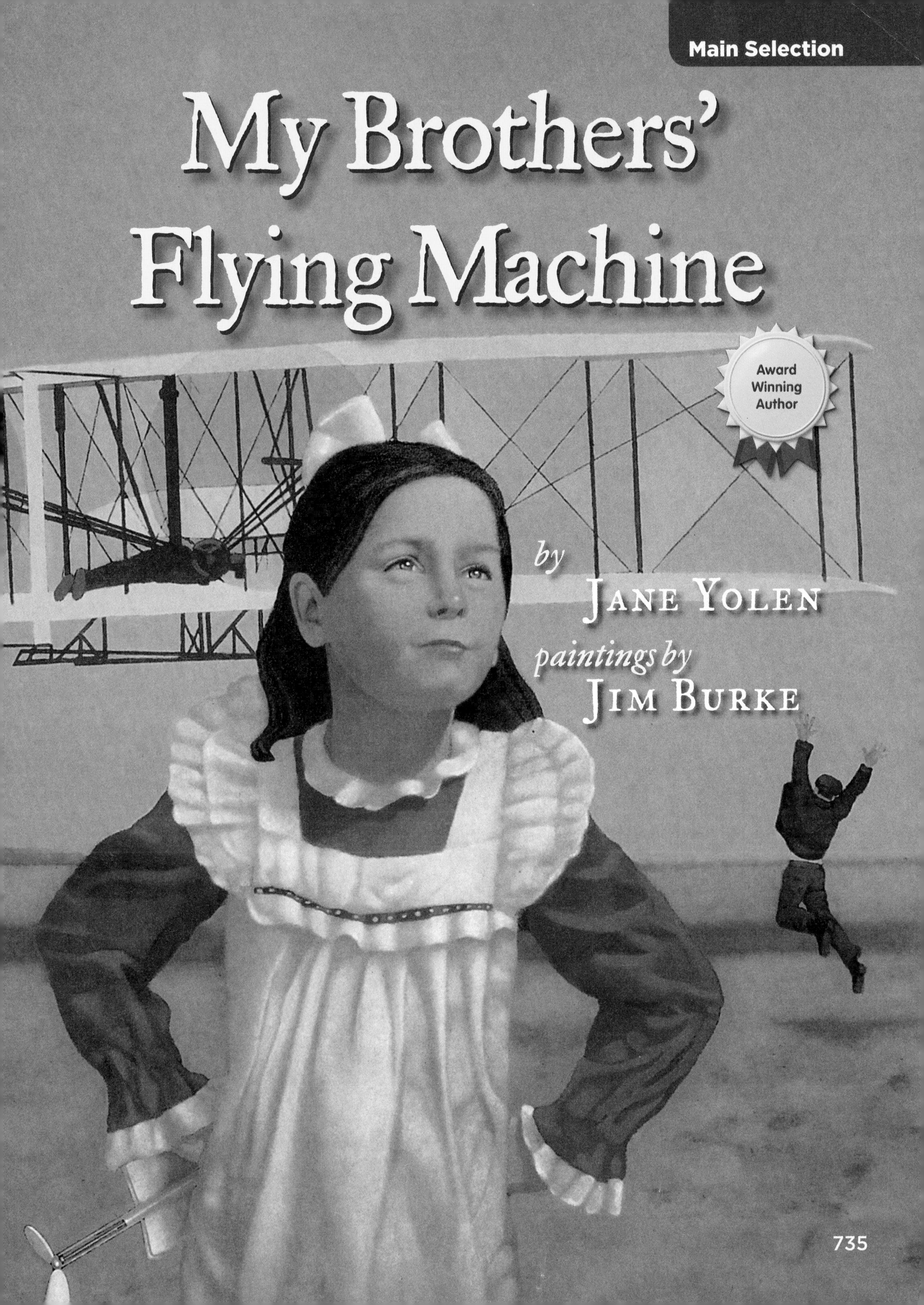

I was four years old when Papa brought home a little flying machine. He tossed it into the air right in front of Orv and Will. They leaped up to catch it.

"Is it a bat?" Orv asked. Or maybe it was Will.

When at last the "bat" fell to the floor, they gathered it up like some sultan's treasure, marveling at its paper wings, admiring the twisted rubber band that gave it power. I wanted to touch it, too, but they would not let me, saying I was too little, though I was but three years younger than Orv, to the very day.

When the "bat" broke, they fixed it together, Will directing Orv—with his busy hands—tinkering till the toy worked better than when Papa first brought it home.

Our older brothers, Reuchlin and Lorin, looked down on childish activity, but Will was not put off. He made one, and two, and three more "bats," each one bigger than the last. Orv was his constant helper. I stood on tiptoe by the table, watching them work.

Will shook his head. "On a much larger scale," he said, "the machine fails to work so well."

They both were puzzled. They did not know yet that a machine twice as big needs eight times the power to fly.

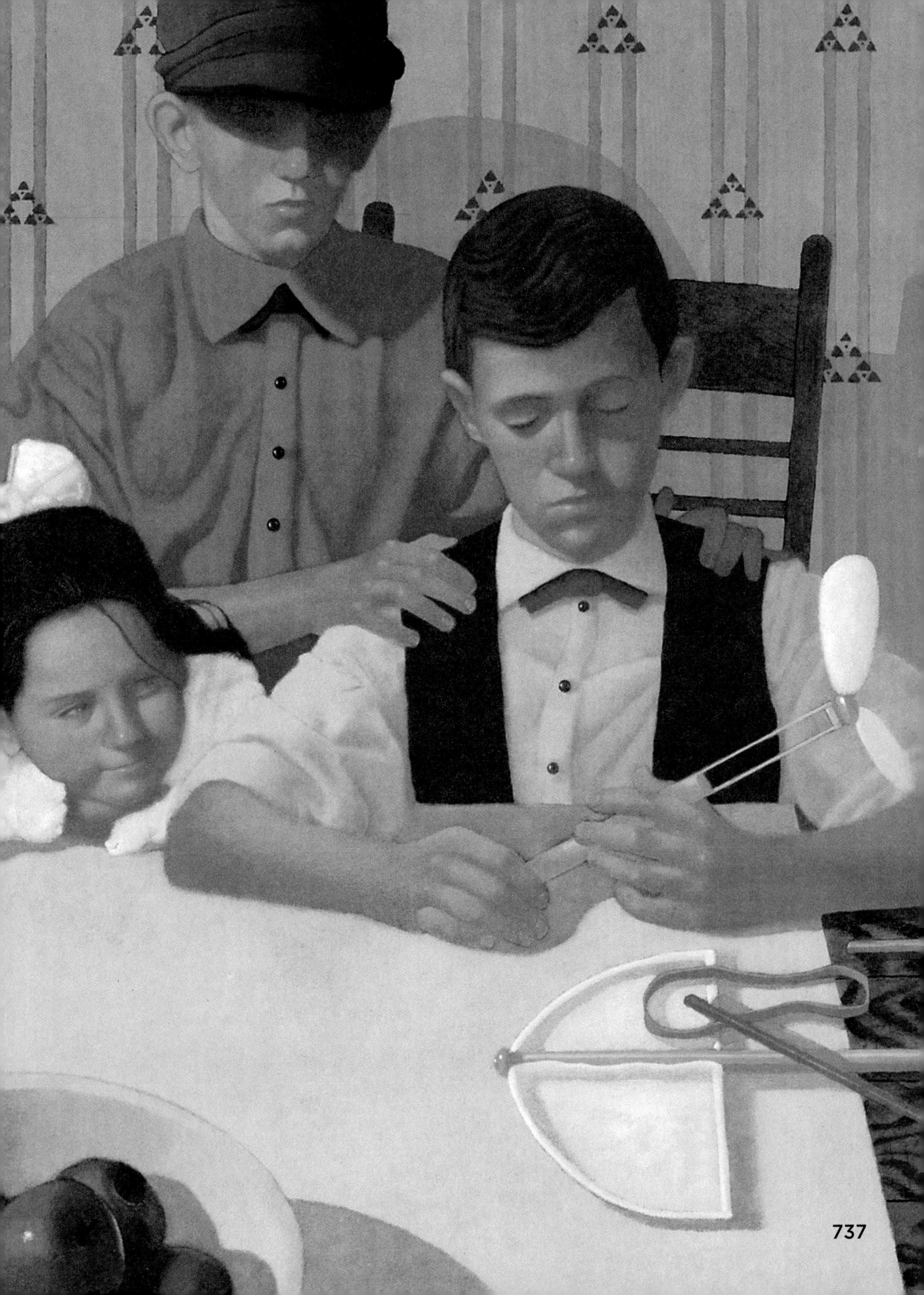

After that, Will built sturdy kites, which he sold to his pals in school. Orv made a printing press, with an old tombstone for a press bed, wheels and cogs from a junkyard, and the folding top of my old baby buggy that he had found in the barn. My, it made me smile to see it.

Papa and Mama **applauded** their efforts. Orv's press could print a thousand pages an hour. A printer from the great city of Denver came to visit and climbed under and over Orv's baby-buggy press. At last he laughed, amazed. "Well it works," he said, "but I certainly don't see how."

Orv and Will made many messes, but Mama never complained. She'd always been the one who gave them a hand building things when they were boys. Poor Papa. He knew God's word well enough, but not how to drive a nail.

When dear Mama died of tuberculosis, I took over her role: keeping the house, making the meals, and always giving the boys applause, even after I graduated from college and worked as a teacher.

West Side News

Will and Orv never went on in school. They ran a print shop, then a bicycle shop, repairing and making custom-built models they called the Van Cleve and the St. Clair. Theirs was not the biggest bicycle shop in Dayton, but I like to think it was the best.

Will and Orv. Orv and Will. They worked side by side in the bicycle shop, whistling at the same time, humming the same tune. They even—so Will said—*thought* together.

Some folks mistook them for twins, though they looked nothing alike. Will had a hawk's face, and Orv a red mustache. Orv was the neat one. He wore special cuffs for his sleeves and a blue-and-white-striped apron to protect his clothes. But Will—land's sake, he was a mess. I had to remind him when his suit needed pressing and when his socks did not match, or find him one of Orv's shirts when he was ready to go off to give a speech.

The newspapers and magazines were full of stories about people trying to fly. Lilienthal, Pilcher, Chanute, MEN INTO BIRDS, the **headlines** read. I wondered if such a thing were really possible. Orv said: “insects, birds, and mammals fly every day at pleasure, it is reasonable to suppose that man might also fly.”

Will wrote off to the Smithsonian for all their books and pamphlets on flight. He and Orv studied page after page. The first question they asked was: *How can we control the flight?*

They knew that a bicycle is **unstable** by itself, yet it can be controlled by a rider. *How much more control would an aeroplane need?*

Overhead, buzzards wheeled in the sky, constantly changing the positions of their wings to catch the flow of air. “If birds can do it,” Orv mused out loud, “so can men.” He seemed so certain, I began to believe it could be done. I began to believe it could be done by Will and Orv.

FCAT Author’s Purpose
Why did the author have Will and Orville’s sister narrate the story?

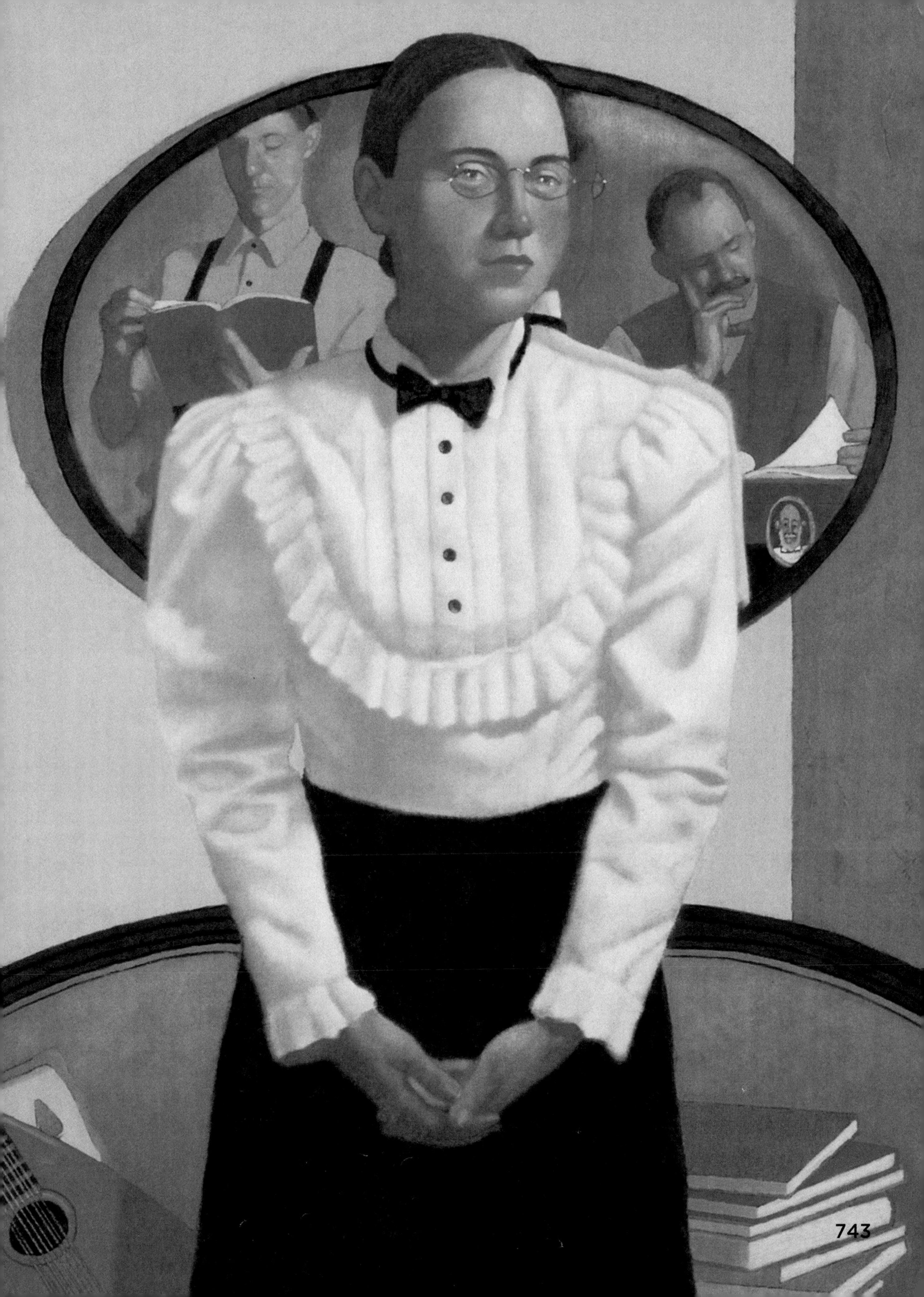

They built their first aircraft right in the bicycle shop. I took over running the place, as Mama would have, so they might make their flying machine.

That first aircraft's wings spanned a full five feet. I measured it out myself. The craft was of pinewood covered with fabric and sealed with shellac. Like a kite, it was controlled by a set of cords.

When it was finished, Orv and I went off on a camping trip with a group of friends. While we were gone, Will did a sneak. He marched out to a nearby field and he flew the **glider**, watched only by some boys. The thing suddenly swooped down on them. The boys ate dust that day, I'll tell you.

Their first aircraft was a big kite. But a kite is not an aeroplane. So Will and Orv set about to build it bigger—sixteen or seventeen feet, large enough to carry a man but still open to all the elements.

Will lay facedown on the lower wing, showing me how he planned to fly. I tried to imagine the wind in his face, the dirt and grass rushing up to greet him like an old bore at a party.

"Is it safe?" I whispered.

He winked at me, smiled, and said, "If you are looking for perfect safety, sit on the fence and watch the birds."

Dayton, Ohio, where we lived, was not the place to fly the craft. Will and Orv needed somewhere with open spaces and strong, regular breezes. They thought about San Diego, about St. James, Florida, about the coasts of South Carolina and Georgia.

At last they settled on Kitty Hawk on the Outer Banks, a two-hundred-mile strip of sand with the ocean at its face and North Carolina at its back. Will called it "a safe place for practice." Only sand and hearty breezes. Only sun and a moon so bright Orv could read his watch all hours. I kept the store. Will and Orv kept the sky.

Weeks, months went by in practice. The boys sent me letters almost every day so that I might follow their every move. When they were home, I was in their closest confidence.

At Kitty Hawk they flew the aircraft with a man—and without one—but always controlled the craft from the ground. We had thought: *Stand on the shoulders of giants, and you are already high above the ground*, but success did not come as quickly as we hoped. Finally Will made a big decision: "We cast the calculations of others aside."

Back in Dayton they would start anew. This time when they left Kitty Hawk for home, when they left the wind, the sand, the mosquitoes that left lumps like hen's eggs, they came home with a new idea.

FCAT **Author's Purpose**
How do you think the author feels about the Wright brothers? Provide examples from the story to support your answer.

Now they worked dawn to dusk, so absorbed in what they were doing, they could hardly wait for morning to come to begin again. They built a small wind tunnel out of an old starch box and used a fan to make the wind. Then they built a larger tunnel.

They learned about lift and drag. They tried out many different kinds of wings. And three years, almost to the day, after Will had written to the Smithsonian, they were ready for *powered* flight. They built the *Flyer*, with a **wingspan** of just over forty feet.

Our friend Charlie Taylor made a twelve-horsepower engine for the *Flyer*, a motor both light and powerful. Gasoline was gravity-fed into the engine from a small tank just below the upper wing. The *Flyer* was so big—over six hundred pounds of aeroplane—it could not be assembled whole in our shop.

Back to Kitty Hawk they went at the tag end of September 1903, carrying crates filled with aircraft parts. It took weeks to put the *Flyer* together, weeks more to prepare for the flight.

Winter came blustering in early. It was cold in camp, each morning the washbasin was frozen solid, so they wrote in their letters. They kept fiddling, tinkering, changing things.

Finally, on December 14, they were ready. They flipped a coin to see who would be pilot. Will won, grinned, climbed into the hip cradle, and off the *Flyer* went, rattling down the sixty-foot starting track, then sailing fifteen feet into the air, where it stalled, crashed. But they were encouraged nonetheless. The telegram they sent to Papa and me read: *Rudder only injured. Success* **assured**. *Keep quiet.*

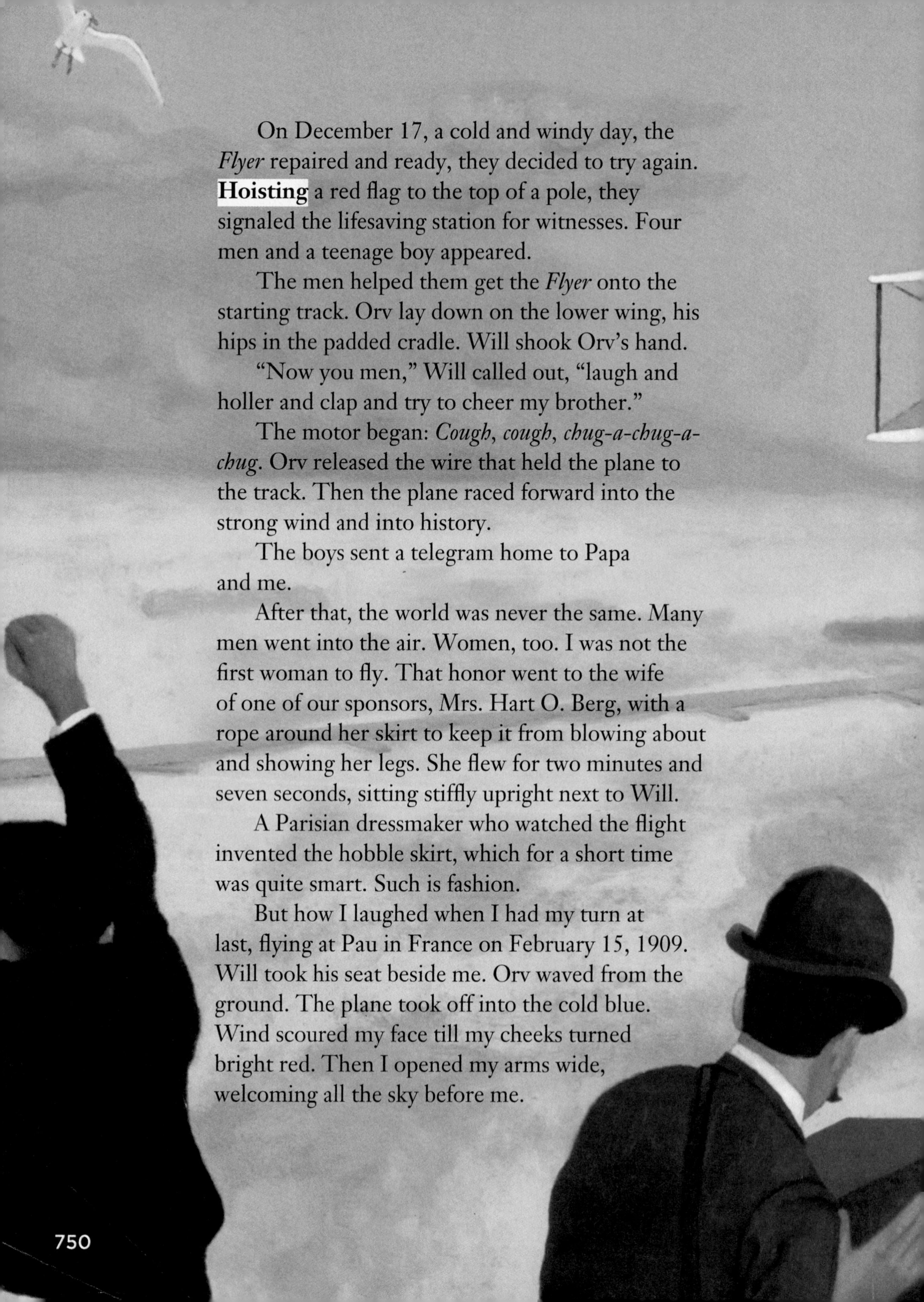

On December 17, a cold and windy day, the *Flyer* repaired and ready, they decided to try again. **Hoisting** a red flag to the top of a pole, they signaled the lifesaving station for witnesses. Four men and a teenage boy appeared.

The men helped them get the *Flyer* onto the starting track. Orv lay down on the lower wing, his hips in the padded cradle. Will shook Orv's hand.

"Now you men," Will called out, "laugh and holler and clap and try to cheer my brother."

The motor began: *Cough, cough, chug-a-chug-a-chug*. Orv released the wire that held the plane to the track. Then the plane raced forward into the strong wind and into history.

The boys sent a telegram home to Papa and me.

After that, the world was never the same. Many men went into the air. Women, too. I was not the first woman to fly. That honor went to the wife of one of our sponsors, Mrs. Hart O. Berg, with a rope around her skirt to keep it from blowing about and showing her legs. She flew for two minutes and seven seconds, sitting stiffly upright next to Will.

A Parisian dressmaker who watched the flight invented the hobble skirt, which for a short time was quite smart. Such is fashion.

But how I laughed when I had my turn at last, flying at Pau in France on February 15, 1909. Will took his seat beside me. Orv waved from the ground. The plane took off into the cold blue. Wind scoured my face till my cheeks turned bright red. Then I opened my arms wide, welcoming all the sky before me.

Soar with Jane and Jim

Jane Yolen was asked by her editor to write a book about the Wright brothers for the 100th anniversary of their first flight. Jane wanted her book to be different from all the other books about the Wrights. She did a lot of research until she came across an interesting note about the Wright brothers' sister. Jane knew she had found her story.

Other books **by Jane Yolen**

Jim Burke has been an award-winning artist for many years, but this is his first book for children. Jim currently lives in New York City.

Another book **by Jim Burke**

LOG ON Find out more about Jane Yolen and Jim Burke at **www.macmillanmh.com**

FCAT Author's Purpose

What clues in the story can help you figure out Jane Yolen's purpose for writing *My Brothers' Flying Machine*? Did she want to inform, explain, or entertain?

FCAT Comprehension Check

Summarize

Summarize *My Brothers' Flying Machine.* Explain who the main characters are. Use your Author's Purpose Map to help you tell the most important story events.

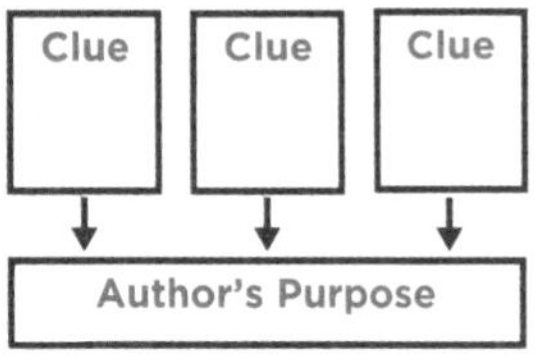

Think and Compare

1. What was the author's purpose in describing Will and Orville's first inventions? Explain using details from the story. **Monitor Comprehension: Author's Purpose**
2. Reread pages 744–746. What kind of place were Will and Orville looking for to test their aircraft? Why did they finally choose Kitty Hawk? Use story details to explain. **Analyze**
3. Imagine you are reporting on the Wright brothers' historic flight at Kitty Hawk. What would your **headline** and article say? **Synthesize**
4. Would the Wright brothers have succeeded without the support of their sister? Explain using story details. **Evaluate**
5. What do readers learn about the Wright brothers' first airplane *The Flyer* in the selection "Take Off" on page 733 and in the story *My Brothers' Flying Machine* on pages 748–750? **Reading/Writing Across Texts**

FCAT

Poetry

A **Narrative Poem** tells a story. Some narrative poems have rhyming patterns and some do not.

Literary Elements

Repetition happens when a word or phrase is repeated throughout a poem.

Personification is a literary device in which human characteristics are given to an animal, a thing, or an idea.

Brave New Heights

I hear Amelia Earhart
took a plane
and flew it like a bullet
straight up through clouds
into an atmosphere
we can't see

and when the engine
cut
(the plane being pushed
as high as it would go)

The first line of the poem is repeated later.

I hear Amelia Earhart
turned that plane
straight back
down into a blanket
of foggy cloud lying thick
and nearly to the ground

The phrase "the ground screaming in her face" is an example of personification. The poet describes the ground as if it were a human being.

only with the clouds gone
could she pull back on the stick
the ground screaming in her face
Amelia tacked that plane
back into the sky
saving herself and breaking
another flying record

FCAT Connect and Compare

1. How else can personification be used in this poem? **Personification**

2. How is this narrative poem like a story? Tell about the poem's main character, the problem faced by the main character, and the solution. **Analyze**

3. Compare Amelia Earhart with the Wright brothers as they are described in *My Brothers' Flying Machine*. How are they similar? How are they different? **Reading/Writing Across Texts**

LOG ON Find more about narrative poems at **www.macmillanmh.com**

Write an Interview

Writer's Craft

FCAT **Important Details**

Statements and facts that support your main idea are called **important details**. Good writers add important details to make their writing informative and interesting.

I interviewed my neighbor. She writes and illustrates books.

I included important details about why Ann writes and illustrates books.

All About Ann

by Lisa B.

I interviewed my neighbor Ann Smith. She writes and illustrates children's books. Many of her books are about birds and flying insects. I asked Ann why that was.

"I've always wished I could fly," said Ann. "I guess that's why I make books about things that fly." Ann said she usually goes to a nearby park on sunny days to watch birds and insects. On a pad of paper, she sketches them and carefully takes notes about what they do. She also reads a lot of books about animals that can fly.

I asked Ann what her next book will be about. She laughed and said, "It's about airplanes!"

Writing Prompt

Suppose you are given the chance to interview your favorite writer.

Think about questions you would like to ask about the writer's work.

Now write an interview where you ask your favorite writer about his or her work.

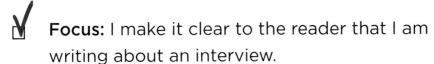

FCAT Writer's Checklist

- ✓ **Focus:** I make it clear to the reader that I am writing about an interview.
- ✓ **Organization:** I start by introducing the person I interviewed and by telling what her or his job is.
- ☐ **Support:** I include important details that make the interview informative and interesting.
- ✓ **Conventions:** I use quotation marks around direct quotes. My spelling and grammar are correct.

ANTS

Talk About It

What questions could you ask about the ants in this photograph?

LOG ON Find out more about ants at **www.macmillanmh.com**

Vocabulary

astronomer **nutrients**
investigates **prehistoric**
solitary **overcome**
territory
communication

Word Parts

FCAT **Greek Roots** can help you figure out the meaning of unfamiliar words.

astron = "star"
astronomer = "one who studies the stars"

Amazing Ants

by Tara Rosati

What do you want to be when you grow up? Perhaps an **astronomer** who studies the stars? How about a scientist who **investigates** ants? Find out how interesting these insects really are!

Social Insects

There are about 10,000 kinds of ants. Most are not **solitary** but live in groups called colonies. Ants are everywhere, but they prefer their **territory** to be in warm climates and never where it's very cold.

Communication among ants varies. Some tap on the outside of their nest to alert the ants inside that food or enemies are nearby. Other ants can make squeaking or buzzing sounds. Ants also make chemicals that other ants in the colony can smell. Each chemical communicates different information to the colony.

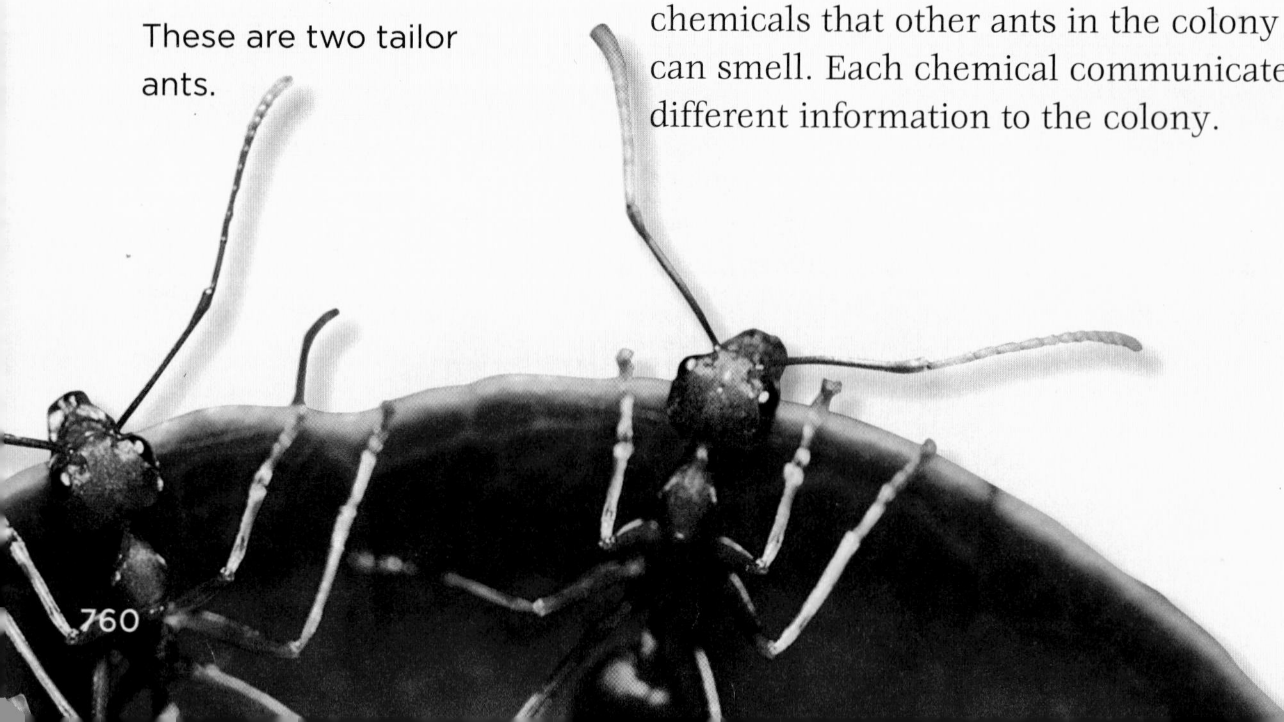

These are two tailor ants.

Dairying Ants

These ants got their name from the way they get most of their **nutrients**. Dairying ants "milk" insects called aphids. In exchange for the juice, dairying ants protect the aphids against other insects.

Some dairying ants are also babysitters. They keep aphids' eggs in their nests during the winter. When the eggs hatch, the ants place the baby aphids on plants.

Fungus Growers

Some ants are gardeners. They grow fungi that the colony can eat. These ants gather leaves, flower petals, and other things from outside the nest. Then they bring them inside to use as fertilizer in their fungi gardens.

Ant Survival

Ants have lived on Earth for a long time. They have been found in **prehistoric** pieces of amber. This is material that existed during the time of the dinosaurs! These tiny creatures have had to **overcome** many challenges in order to survive, and ants are here to stay.

A black garden ant caught in sundew

Reread for **Comprehension**

Analyze Text Structure

FCAT

Relevant Facts and Details Details and facts that are important to the story's topic, or main idea, are called **relevant facts and details**. Good readers can decide which details are relevant, or important, to helping them understand the main idea. Reread the selection and use your Main Idea Web to identify relevant facts and details.

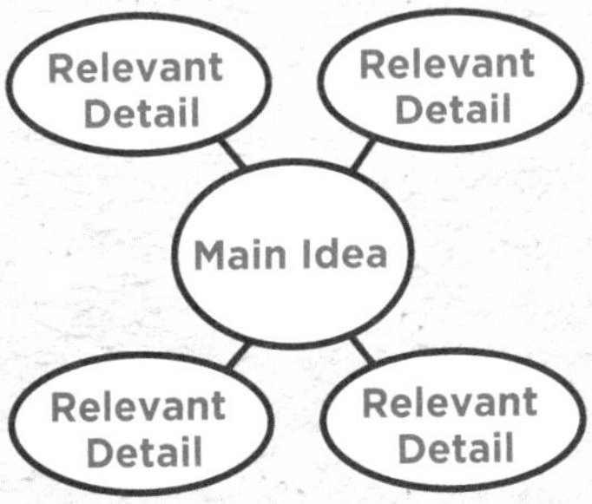

Comprehension

Genre

Informational Nonfiction is a detailed composition that sets out to explain something by presenting facts about it.

Analyze Text Structure

FCAT

Relevant Facts and Details

As you read, fill in your Main Idea Web.

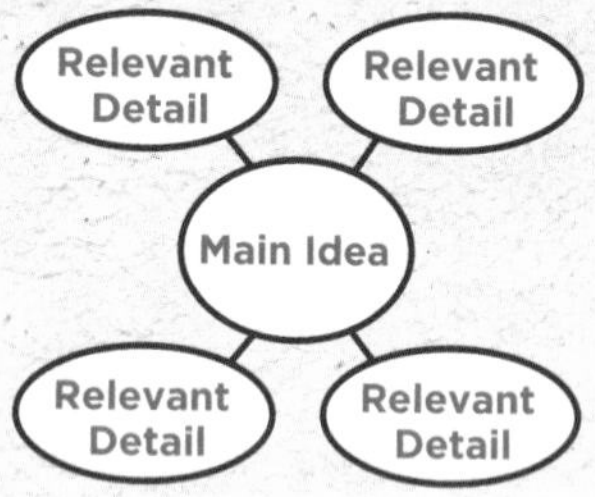

Read to Find Out

What characteristics make an ant able to do the things it does?

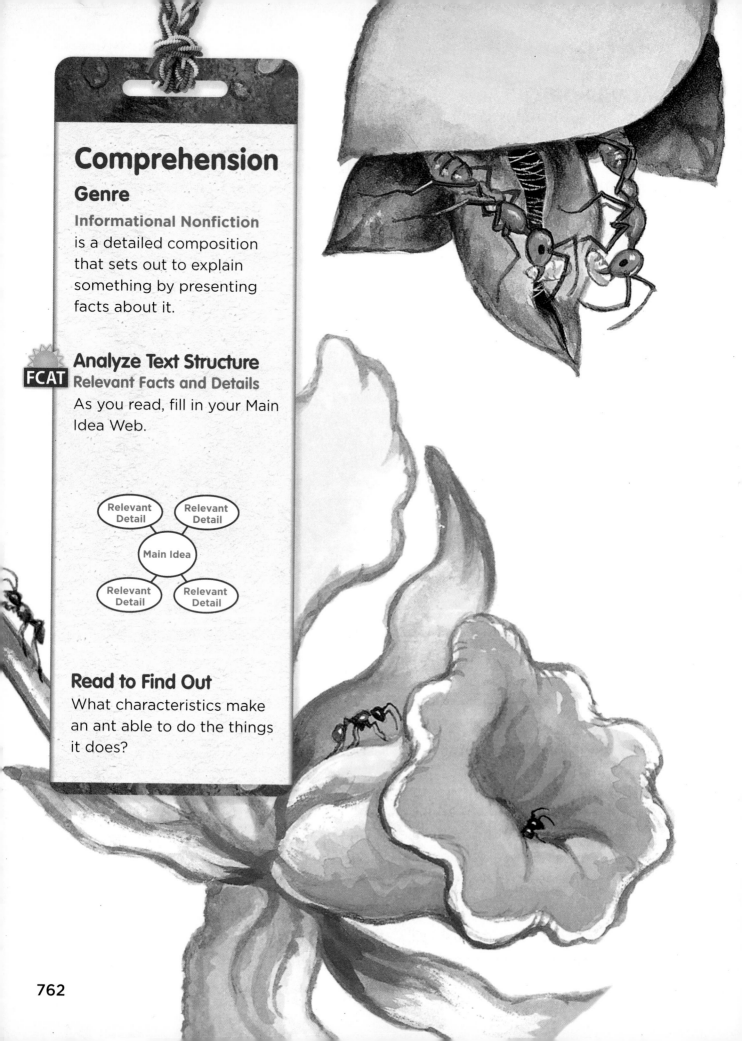

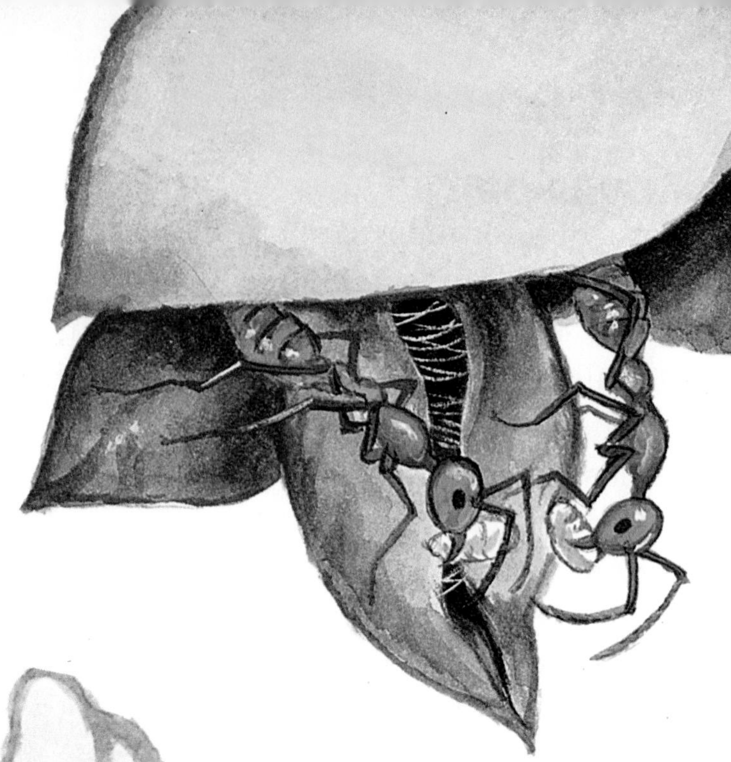

The Life and Times of the Ant

written and illustrated by
Charles Micucci

Masters of the Earth

Ants are one of the world's most important insects. They plow more soil than beetles, eat more bugs than praying mantises, and outnumber many insects by 7 million to 1.

Tunneling out of jungles and forests and into back yards on every continent except Antarctica, ants ramble on as if they own the Earth. Perhaps they do.

Ounce for ounce, an ant is one of the strongest animals on earth. An ant can lift a seed five times its weight, while an elephant can lift a log only one fifth of its weight.

Each year, the world's ants dig up more than 16 billion tons of dirt— enough to fill 3 billion dump trucks.

Ants are frequently compared with people because they live in social communities and work together to solve their problems.

Great Dynasties on Earth

Ants have been digging through dirt for more than 100 million years. Their dynasty stretches from the time of dinosaurs to today.

Friends in Low Places

There are more than a million kinds of insects. Most of them are **solitary** insects. Their survival depends on only one being—themselves.

An ant is different; it is a social insect. It cannot survive by itself for long periods of time. Ants need other ants to help build a nest, gather food, and protect themselves from enemies. This need for other ants is not a weakness but a strength that enables the ant to **overcome** its small size.

When an ant is threatened by a larger insect, it emits a scent called an alarm pheromone. Other ants smell the odor and rush to help.

FCAT Relevant Facts and Details
What details support the main idea that ants are different from other insects?

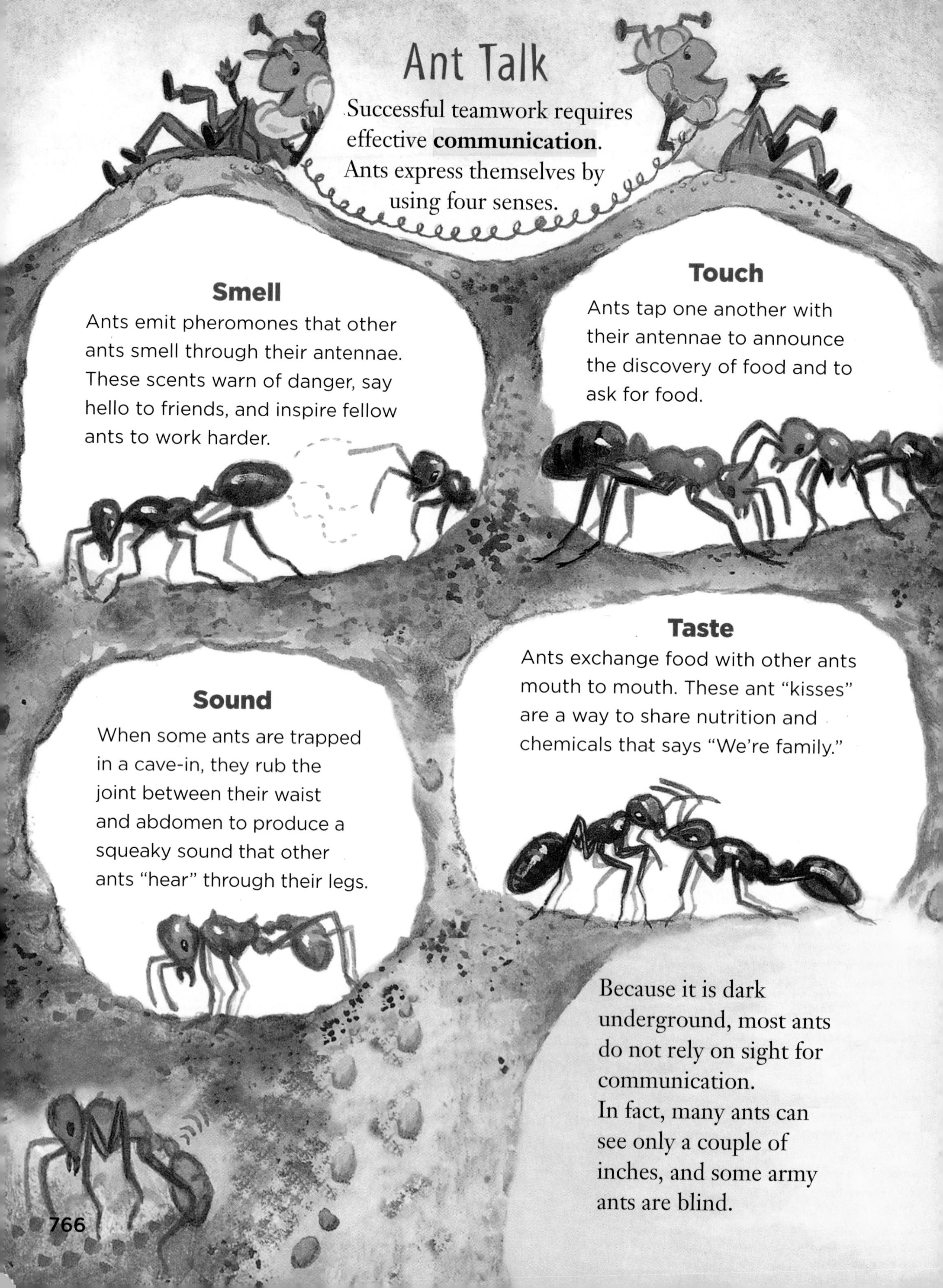

Ant Talk

Successful teamwork requires effective **communication**. Ants express themselves by using four senses.

Smell

Ants emit pheromones that other ants smell through their antennae. These scents warn of danger, say hello to friends, and inspire fellow ants to work harder.

Touch

Ants tap one another with their antennae to announce the discovery of food and to ask for food.

Sound

When some ants are trapped in a cave-in, they rub the joint between their waist and abdomen to produce a squeaky sound that other ants "hear" through their legs.

Taste

Ants exchange food with other ants mouth to mouth. These ant "kisses" are a way to share nutrition and chemicals that says "We're family."

Because it is dark underground, most ants do not rely on sight for communication.
In fact, many ants can see only a couple of inches, and some army ants are blind.

The Ant Family

Ants live in social groups called colonies. A small colony may contain only 12 ants, while a large colony overflows with more than 7 million ants. Each colony has three types of ants: workers, male ants, and the queen ant.

Worker Ants

Most of the colony's ants are workers. They are all female, but they do not lay eggs. Although they are the smallest ants, they do all of the chores: clean the nest, gather food, and defend the colony. When you see an ant dragging a crumb of food, you are looking at a worker.

Male Ants

All males have wings and can be seen for only a few weeks in the summer. They mate with the queen but do no work in the colony.

Queen Ants

The queen ant lays eggs and is the mother of all the ants. Young queens have wings, but old queens do not. All queens have large abdomens to produce eggs. Some queens lay millions of eggs per year.

How an Ant Colony Starts

After a hot summer rain, a young queen takes off on her mating flight. The queen flies into a cloud of male ants and mates in the air.

Afterward, all the males die, and the queen returns to the earth. She breaks her wings off by rubbing them on the ground.

Then she digs a hole in the soft, moist earth and starts laying eggs. She will never leave the nest again.

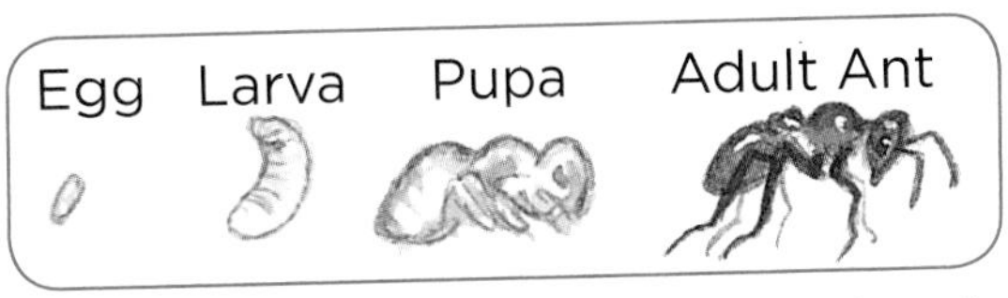

During the next three months, the eggs develop through four stages: egg, larva, pupa, and adult ant.

After they have hatched, the first workers assume the duties of the colony. They search for food and protect the queen. As the queen lays more eggs, the workers enlarge the nest.

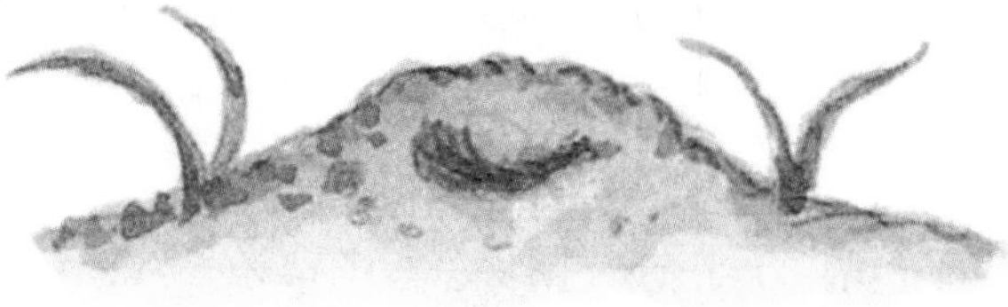

Inside an Anthill

Most ants build their homes underground. Ants dig by scooping dirt with their mandibles (jaws). As they chew the dirt, it mixes with their saliva to form little bricks. Then they pack the little bricks together to reinforce the tunnels. Finally, the ants carry the excess dirt outside with their mandibles, and it gradually forms an anthill.

Beneath the anthill lies the ant nest. Small nests have only one chamber just inches below the surface, while large nests may have thousands of chambers and may be as deep as twenty feet. All nests provide shelter from the weather and a safe environment for the queen ant to lay eggs.

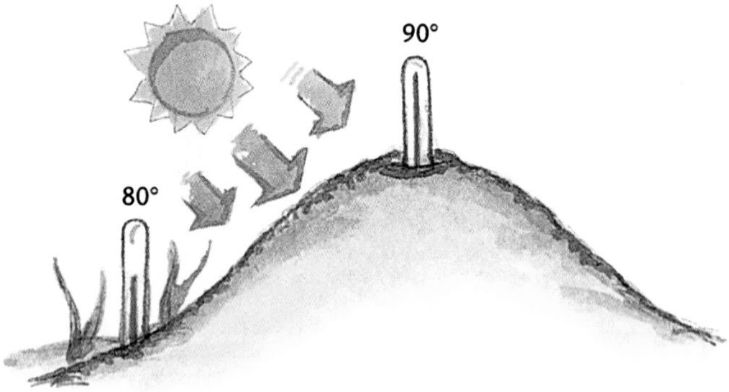

An anthill absorbs the sun's rays and transfers the heat down into the nest. An anthill can be ten degrees warmer than the surrounding area.

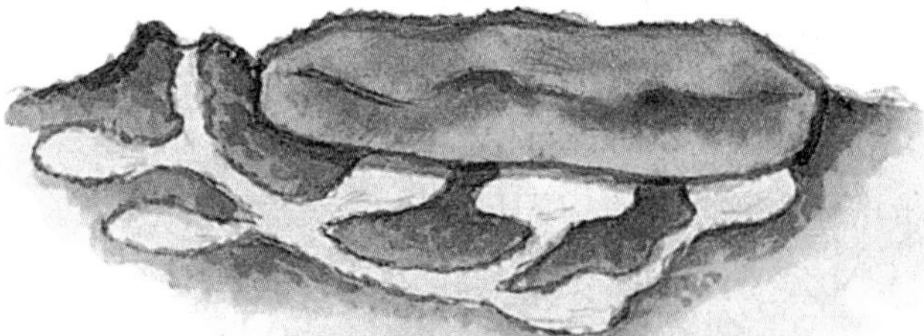

Ants often nest beneath a rock or log, which protects the nest and traps moisture in the dirt. Ants require moisture so that their bodies do not dry out.

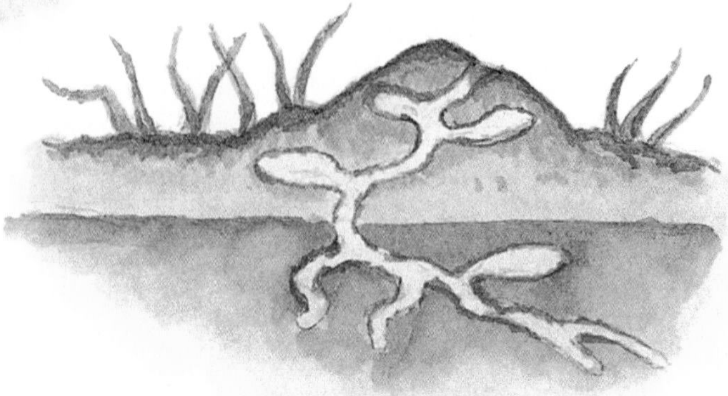

Ants dig their nests deep enough to reach damp dirt. As air dries out the nest, they dig new tunnels into the damp dirt.

As ants bring up dirt, they recycle **nutrients** that help plants grow.

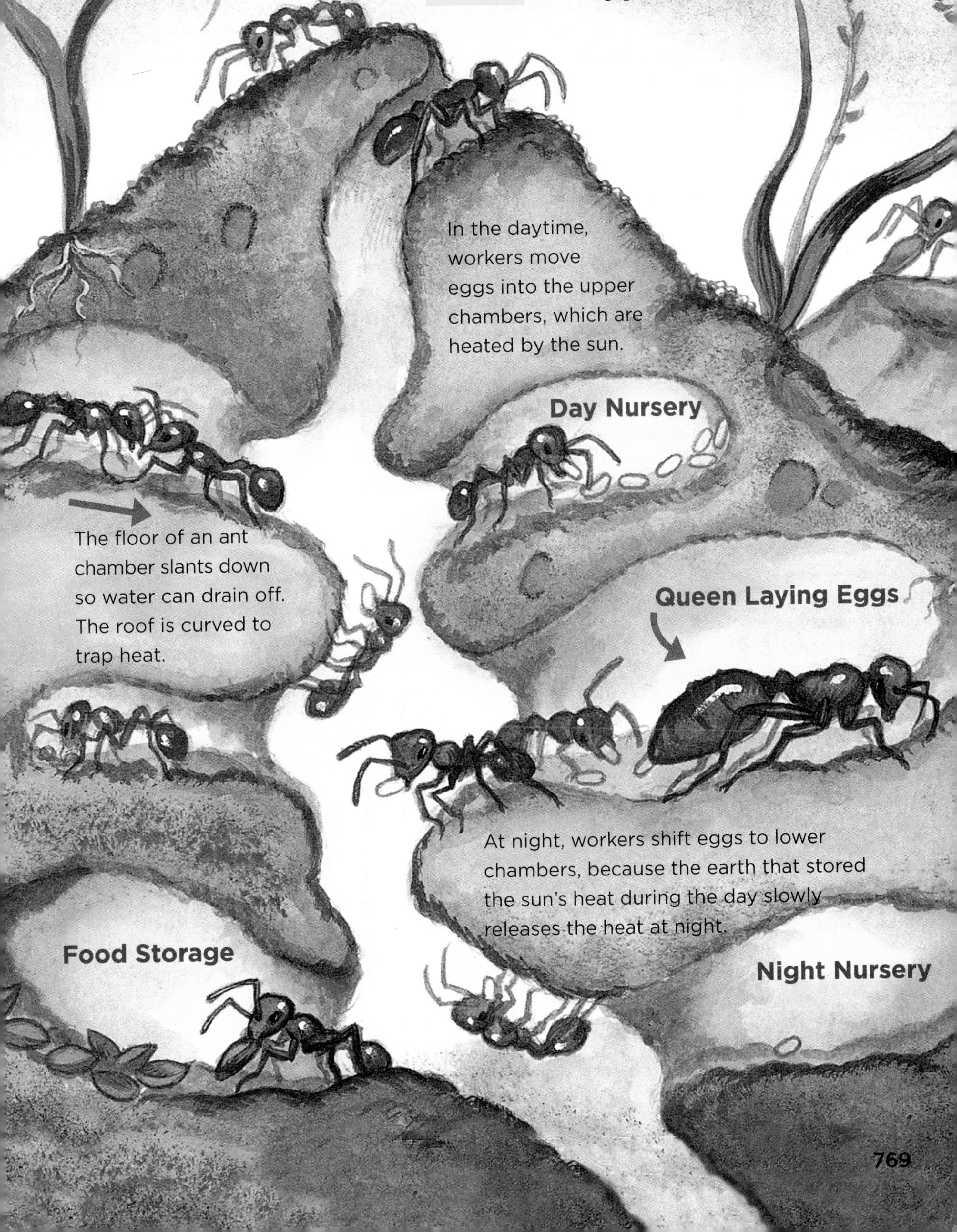

In the daytime, workers move eggs into the upper chambers, which are heated by the sun.
Day Nursery
The floor of an ant chamber slants down so water can drain off. The roof is curved to trap heat.
Queen Laying Eggs
At night, workers shift eggs to lower chambers, because the earth that stored the sun's heat during the day slowly releases the heat at night.
Food Storage
Night Nursery

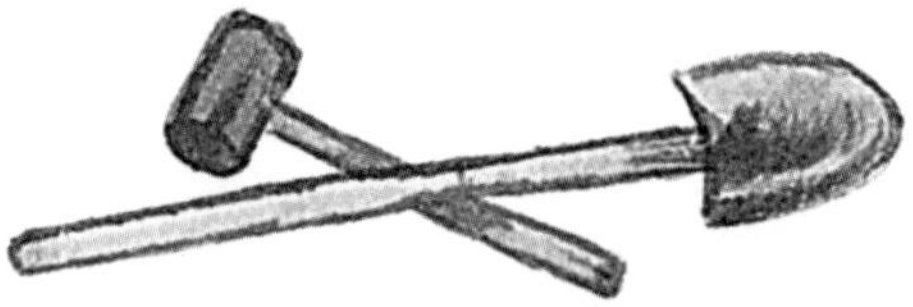

A Life of Work

Ants begin their working lives by cleaning themselves. In a couple of days they start sharing food and licking each other. These food exchanges bond the colony together. There is no boss ant, but active ants usually begin doing chores and then other ants join in.

Younger ants work in the nest — tending the queen ant, feeding larvae, and digging tunnels. After a couple of months, the ants leave the nest to search for food. There is no retirement; worn out or battle-scarred, ants work until they die.

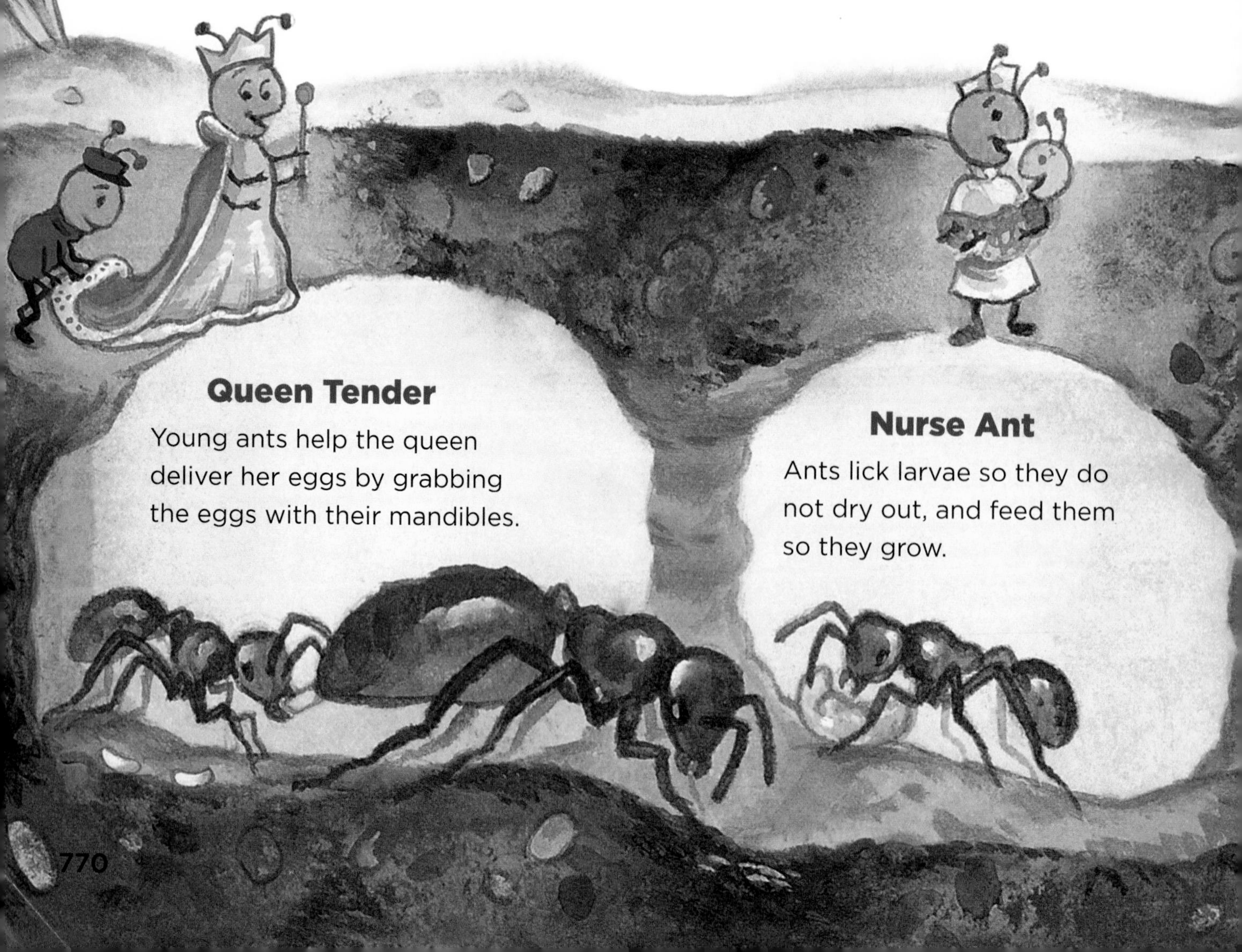

Queen Tender

Young ants help the queen deliver her eggs by grabbing the eggs with their mandibles.

Nurse Ant

Ants lick larvae so they do not dry out, and feed them so they grow.

Foragers

The oldest ants search for food. Most foragers search within fifty feet of the nest, but if food is scarce, they may travel thousands of feet.

Guard

When ants first leave the nest, they stand near the entrance, blocking strange ants from entering.

Tunnel Diggers

As the population grows, ants dig more tunnels for the increased traffic and new chambers to store the eggs and larvae.

Digging holes can be hard work. To remove a pile of dirt 6 inches high, 6 inches wide, and 6 inches long requires 500,000 loads of dirt.

Show Me the Way

Every warm day, foraging ants patrol the colony's **territory**. They are not just wandering; they are searching for food. When an ant finds food, she rushes back to the colony while laying a scent trail. It is the scent trail that leads the other ants to the food source.

Each forager moves out in a different direction. One of the ants discovers a cookie crumb. She **investigates** it with her antennae. Then she tries to drag it home, but it's too big.

So she rushes home to get help. Every couple of steps she bumps her abdomen against the ground and her scent gland releases an invisible vapor, which forms a scent trail.

Back inside the colony, the forager alerts other ants about the cookie by tapping them with her antennae. Suddenly, several ants rush out and follow the scent trail to the food.

Each of the new ants harvests part of the cookie and transports it back to the colony while laying a scent trail of her own.

Soon the vapors of the scent trail are so thick that many more ants join the harvest. As they return, the foraging ants share their feast with the ants inside the nest. Within twenty-four hours, every ant in the colony has tasted the cookie.

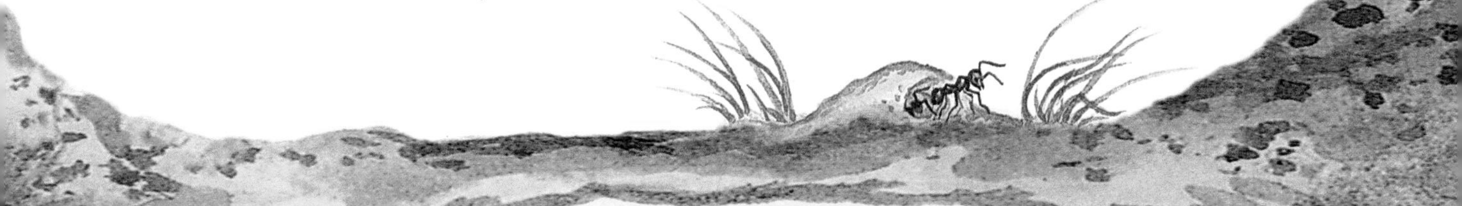

Harlow Shapley, an **astronomer** whose hobby was ants, tested their speed. He discovered that they run faster on hot days.

Temperature	78°F	85°F	92°
Speed (inches per second)	1	$1\frac{3}{8}$	$1\frac{5}{8}$

FCAT Relevant Facts and Details
What relevant details about ants can you learn from this table ?

Tunneling Through Time

Ants evolved from wasps more than 100 million years ago. They have been dodging footsteps ever since. As dinosaurs thundered above ground, ants dug out a home below. The mighty dinosaurs are long gone, but the little ant has survived.

Today, myrmecologists search for the secrets of the ants' long existence and how those traits may benefit our society. They study ant fossils in **prehistoric** amber and observe the daily habits of ant colonies.

100,000,000 B.C.
Ants dug tunnels under dinosaurs.

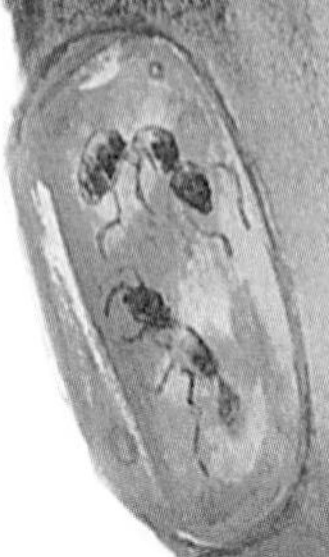

90,000,000 B.C.
Two ants were sealed in amber. Millions of years later, the amber was found in New Jersey.

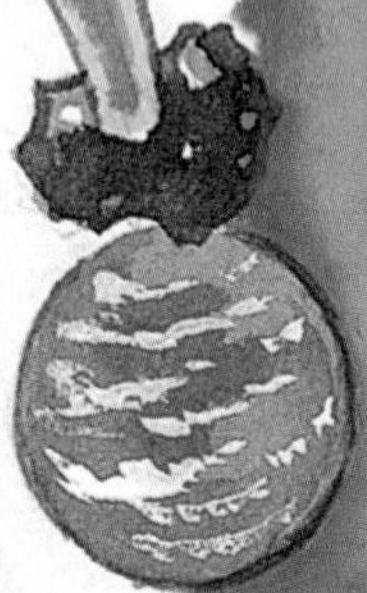

65,000,000 B.C.
Some scientists think a giant meteorite crashed into Earth, killing the dinosaurs. But ants, which could hide underground, survived the disaster.

2000 B.C.
Aborigines in Australia ate the honey of honeypot ants. Their modern descendants call these sweet ants *yarumpa*.

400 B.C.
Herodotus, a Greek historian, wrote about ants that mined gold. Today, some miners sift through anthills to learn what minerals lie underground.

A.D. 1200–1300
Chinese farmers used ants to keep their orange trees free of insect pests.

1500s–1800s
When Europeans conquered the Caribbean islands, their forts were frequently invaded by ants. They offered rewards and prayed to Saint Saturnin to stop the six-legged armies.

1687
Anton von Leeuwenhoek, who invented the microscope, discovered ant eggs and pupae.

1991
Bert Hölldobler and Edward O. Wilson, two myrmecologists, won the Pulitzer Prize for their book *The Ants*.

1859
The biologist Charles Darwin wrote about ant intelligence and teamwork in his classic work *The Origin of Species*.

1880
Germany passed a law protecting wood ants because they kept trees free of pests.

1890s–1930s
William Wheeler, one of America's first myrmecologists, traveled around the world collecting ants and ant fossils.

2000
Scientists applied ant behavior as a model for computer networks. Computer systems based on ant behavior rerouted around problems quicker than previous systems did.

The tunnel of time continues for ants. Their hard work inspires people today, as it has for many centuries. Look down on a warm day and you will probably find an ant. Drop a piece of food . . . and an ant will probably find you.

The Life and Times of Charles Micucci

Charles Micucci often fills his nature books with amusing illustrations, just as he does in this selection. Once he even drew the planet Earth wearing red sneakers. Charles carefully researches his science topics. Sometimes he does experiments to help him write. When he was working on a book about apples, he planted 23 apple seeds and cared for them in his apartment.

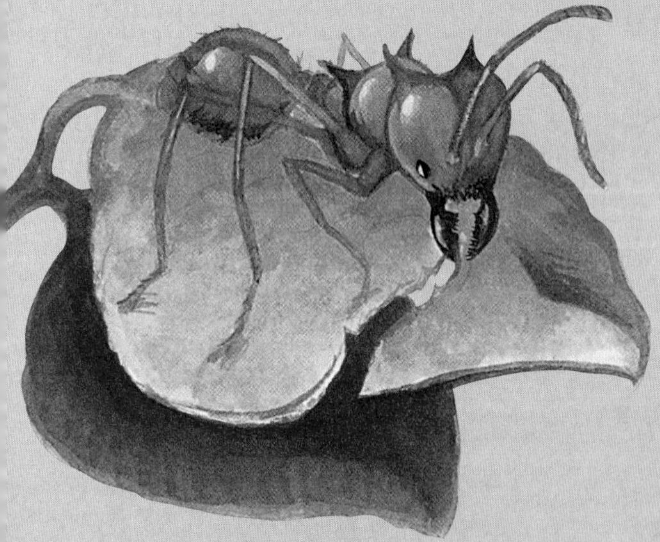

Other books by Charles Micucci

LOG ON Find out more about Charles Micucci at **www.macmillanmh.com**

FCAT Author's Purpose

The Life and Times of the Ant is a work of informational nonfiction. What was Charles Micucci's purpose for writing it? What clues in the text or illustrations help you to know?

FCAT Comprehension Check

Summarize

Summarize *The Life and Times of the Ant.* Use your Main Idea Web to include only the most important information in your summary.

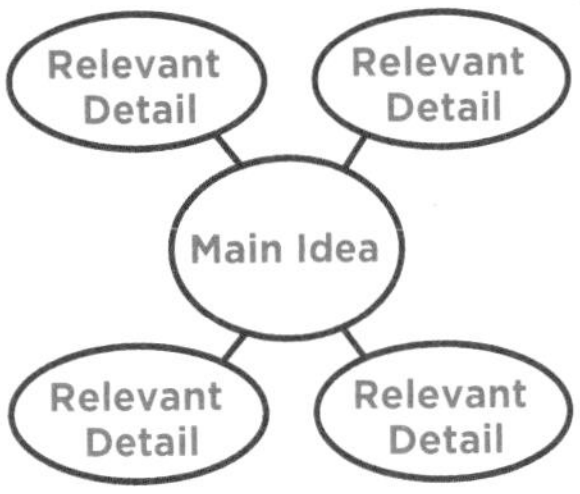

Think and Compare

READ THINK EXPLAIN

1. Ants are social insects that depend on one another for survival. What relevant details in the story support this fact? Use story details to explain. **Analyze Text Structure: Relevant Facts and Details**

READ THINK EXPLAIN

2. Reread pages 768–769 of *The Life and Times of the Ant.* Describe what ants do to create an anthill. What does it look like on the inside? Explain using story details. **Analyze**

3. How could you use what you have learned about ants to **overcome** a problem? Explain your answer. **Apply**

4. How do ants keep nature in balance? Use details from the story to explain. **Evaluate**

5. Reread "Amazing Ants" on pages 760–761 and *The Life and Times of the Ant*. What do readers learn about how ants get their food? **Reading/Writing Across Texts**

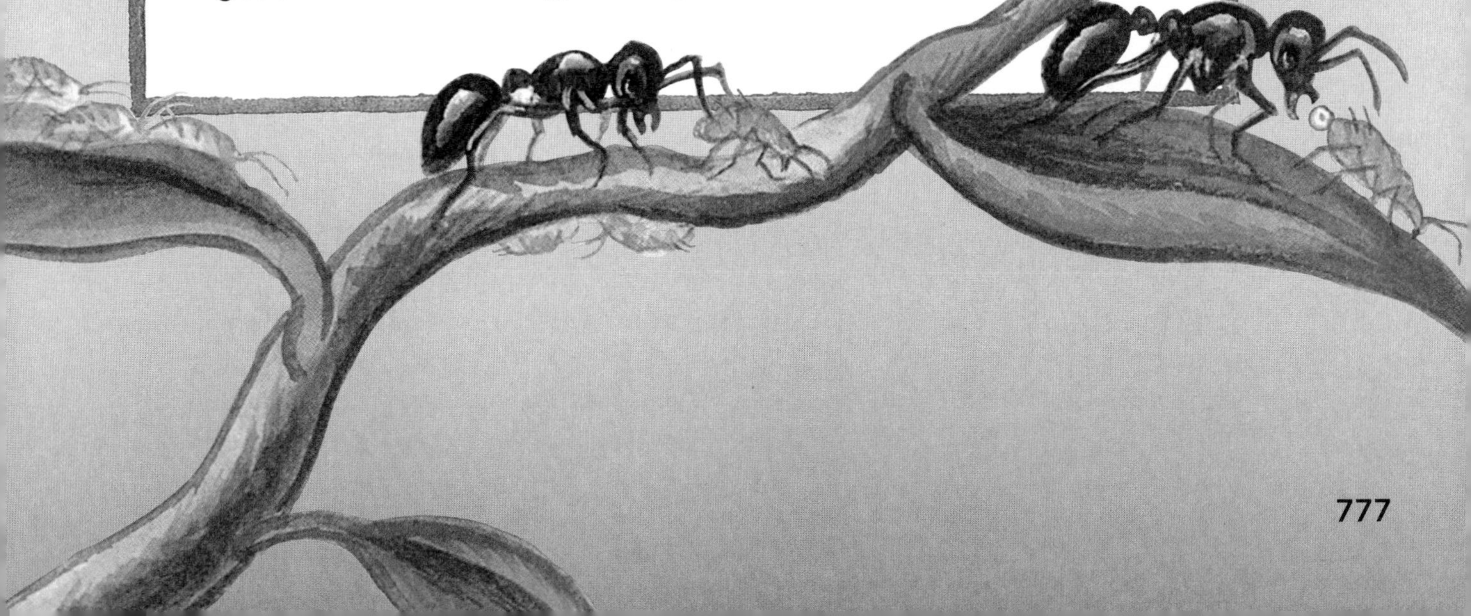

FCAT Language Arts

Fables are stories that have animal characters that talk and act as people do. A moral, or lesson, usually appears at the end of a fable.

Literary Elements

Characters in a fable are often animals that have human traits and feelings.

The **Moral** of a fable is the lesson it teaches, which the reader can apply to his or her own personal experiences.

THE Ant AND THE Grasshopper

retold and illustrated by Amy Lowry Poole

A LONG TIME AGO, in the old Summer Palace at the edge of the Emperor's courtyard, there lived a grasshopper and a family of ants.

The ants awoke every day before dawn and began their endless tasks of rebuilding their house of sand, which had been washed down by the evening rains, and searching for food, which they would store beneath the ground. They carried their loads grain by grain, one by one, back and forth, all day long.

The grasshopper liked to sleep late into the morning, rising as the sun stretched toward noon.

"Silly ants," he would say. "You work too hard. Come follow me into the courtyard, where I will sing and dance for the great Emperor."

The ants kept on working.

"Silly ants," the grasshopper would say. "See the new moon. Feel the summer breeze. Let us go together and watch the Empress and her ladies as they prepare for midsummer's eve."

But the ants ignored the grasshopper and kept on working.

Soon the days grew shorter and the wind brought cooler air from the north. The ants, mindful of the winter to come, worked even harder to secure their home against the impending cold and snow. They foraged for food and brought it back to their nest, saving it for those cold winter months.

Comparing the traits of the grasshopper and the ants will help you identify the moral.

"Silly ants," said the grasshopper. "Don't you ever rest? Today is the harvest festival. The Emperor will feast on mooncakes and sweet greens from the fields. I will play my music for him until the moon disappears into the smooth lake water. Come and dance with me."

"You would do well to do as we do," said one of the ants. "Winter is coming soon and food will be hard to find. Snow will cover your house and you will freeze without shelter."

But the grasshopper ignored the ant's advice and continued to play and dance until the small hours of the morning.

Winter arrived a week later and brought whirls of snow and ice. The Emperor and his court left the Summer Palace for their winter home in the great Forbidden City. The ants closed their door against the ice and snow, safe and warm, resting at last after their long days of preparation.

And the grasshopper huddled beneath the palace eaves and rubbed his hands together in a mournful chirp, wishing he had heeded the ant's advice.

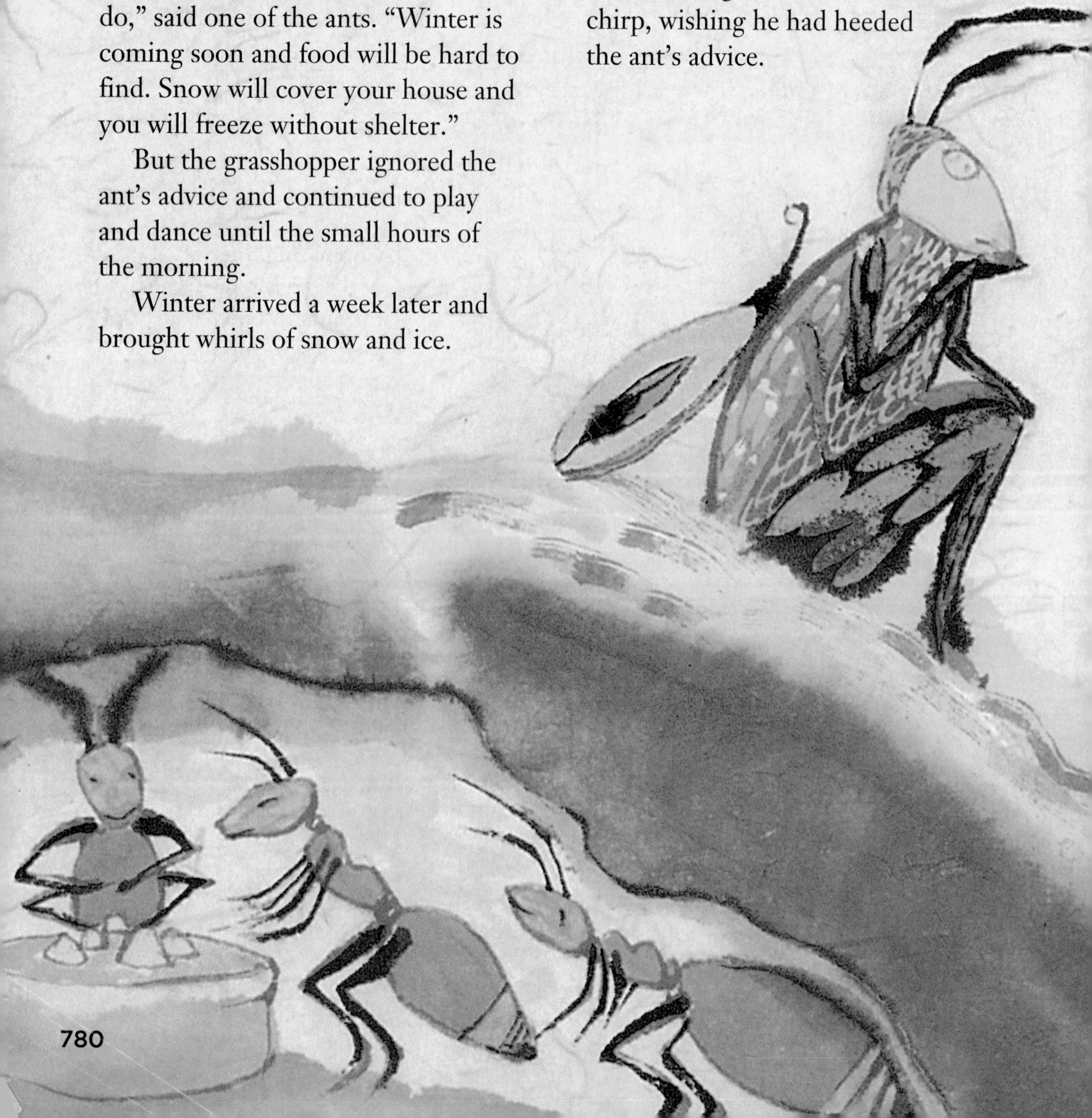

FCAT Connect and Compare

1. Identify the moral of this fable. Is this a good lesson to learn? Why or why not? **Moral**

2. What problem does the grasshopper have? At what point in the story is he aware of it? Does he solve his problem? **Analyze**

3. Think about *The Life and Times of the Ant*. How are the ants in this fable similar to the ants in that selection? How are they different? **Reading/Writing Across Texts**

LOG ON Find out more about fables at **www.macmillanmh.com**

Write About Ants

Writer's Craft

FCAT **Beginning, Middle, and End**

Good writing has a **beginning, middle, and end**. The beginning introduces the topic of your writing. The middle gives details and adds interest. The end contains a strong conclusion.

The beginning introduces my story's topic.

The middle gives details. I have a strong conclusion at the end.

Ants to the Rescue

by Luis M.

"We're smaller than the other ants, Angela. That's why we need to always travel together!" Angela didn't listen. She left me alone when she went to find food. When I came home and Angela wasn't there, I knew there was trouble. I was nervous, but I had to alert the other ants.

We crawled along quickly, picking up rocks with our antennae. Angela's scent told us she was nearby. Soon we saw the spider that had captured Angela.

Together we faced the spider. We threw rocks and made a fuss. The spider ran away and Angela was safe.

Very proudly I said to all, "We may be small, but we're a great team when we work together!"

Writing Prompt

Ants work together to get things done.

If you were an ant, think about how you would work with other ants to get something done.

Now write a story about how you would work with other ants to get something done.

FCAT Writer's Checklist

- [x] **Focus:** My story is clearly told from the point of view of my main character.
- [ ] **Organization:** My story has a clear **beginning, middle, and end.**
- [x] **Support:** I support my main idea with important details.
- [x] **Conventions:** I use capitalization and punctuation correctly. My sentences are complete.

FCAT

Review

- Theme
- Main Idea and Details
- Problem and Solution
- Context Clues
- Suffixes
- Map

Mouse and Crow

Mouse had a beautiful collection of 10 glittering crystals. She loved looking at the way they sparkled, so she displayed each one on a shiny metal bottle cap.

One day she brought a sparkling green crystal to the river to wash it. Crow was perched in a tree nearby. The gleam of the crystal caught his eye.

"That's beautiful," called out Crow as he eyed the crystal jealously.

"Yes it is," said the innocent Mouse, "but it's not my prettiest. I have nine others at home that are more beautiful."

Crow didn't respond. He knew he would have to be patient.

A few days later, as Mouse was walking in the field, Crow began performing flying tricks. He soared up and down and zigzagged across the sky to get her attention. Mouse watched him in amazement.

"What fun it is to fly!" Crow laughed. "You cannot imagine how wonderful it feels!"

"Oh! I wish I could fly," said Mouse.

"I can take you," volunteered Crow. "And all I ask in return is that one green crystal. You said you have others."

Mouse happily agreed. She ran home and got the crystal. She brought it back to Crow and they flew off. Mouse was astonished. She giggled helplessly as they soared into the air. It was a thrilling feeling! Crow flew for miles. The sky seemed limitless! After several hours Crow landed on a large rock.

"That was amazing!" Mouse said excitedly.

"I'm glad you had fun!" smiled Crow. He then got up and started to fly away.

"Wait!" shouted Mouse. "I need to go home."

"Oh dear," said Crow. "I'm afraid that will cost you more. You will have to pay me nine more crystals. Otherwise you have to find your own way home."

Upset, Mouse realized she didn't know how to get home. She would have to go home with Crow. As she rode back with Crow, Mouse felt angry. The more she thought about it, the angrier she got. "How can he be so greedy?" she wondered. The question made her think, and suddenly she knew how she could save her crystals.

As she handed over her crystals to Crow, she sighed sadly and said, "Well, that's the last one. Except…oh, never mind." She pretended to be nervous.

"Except what?" Crow said angrily.

"N-n-n-nothing," stammered Mouse.

"TELL ME!" shouted Crow.

"Well, I was saving them for me. I mean, you won't like them. They're not that special."

"Bring whatever it is out here right away," Crow said threateningly.

Mouse brought out the 10 bottle caps. Crow thought that Mouse was trying to keep them for herself. "They must be extremely precious," thought Crow. "I'll take those instead of those boring crystals."

And he did.

Mouse still has her beautiful crystals. She loves her collection more than ever, but she longer boasts about them. She now knows not everyone can be trusted.

DIAMONDS FOR THE TAKING

HAVE YOU EVER WONDERED what it would be like to be a prospector? Imagine what it would be like to tap rocks with a hammer, hour after hour, in the hopes of discovering a glittering diamond.

Each year hundreds of people do just that in upper New York State. Herkimer County, New York, is the only place in the world where Herkimer diamonds can be found. The map below shows exactly where Herkimer County is in New York State. Actually the diamonds found there are not really diamonds. They are natural quartz crystals, and what is unusual about them is that they have points at both ends.

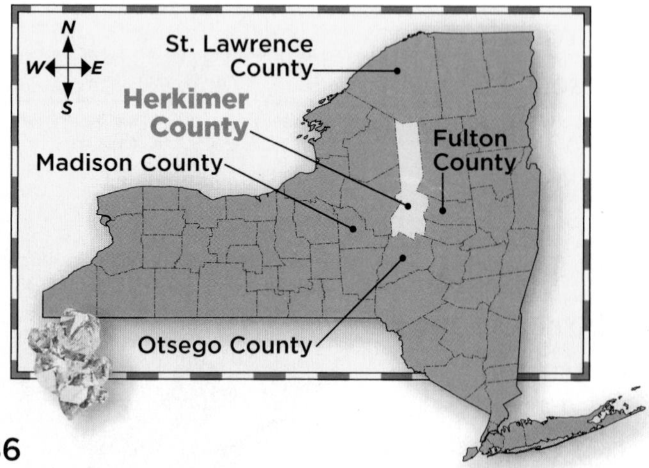

When true diamonds are taken from the earth, they need to be cut and polished to make them sparkle and shine. Herkimer diamonds come out of their rocky homes already shaped and polished by nature!

HOW HERKIMER DIAMONDS BEGAN

Some 500 million years ago, a shallow sea covered parts of what is now New York State. Particles of rock and earth settled to the bottom. Over millions of years, this sediment built up. The weight of the sediment on top pressed down on the bottom layers. Gradually the layers of sediment turned into rock. Water seeped through pores in the rock and eventually became trapped in pockets inside the rock. Over time crystals formed in those pockets.

Long ago the sea dried up. Glaciers and storms wore away the top layers of rock. This weathering exposed hidden crystals and the first Herkimer diamonds came to light!

Prospecting for Diamonds

Herkimer "mines" are actually rocky, open pits. The ground is rough and uneven. Prospectors are told to wear hiking boots, and goggles are also recommended. A rock chip in your eye can cause a serious problem!

Some collectors just wander around, hoping to spot a diamond. Some sift through the dirt. Serious prospectors use crowbars, rock hammers, and heavy chisels. Most miners use hammers that weigh two or three pounds. They pound the rock until it breaks apart. If they are lucky, a crystal will be there.

The luckiest prospectors find pockets of crystals. These pockets can be as much as six feet wide and can contain thousands of crystals. Most pockets contain crystals in a wide range of sizes, up to eight or more inches long. Sometimes people find crystals with water bubbles inside. Twin crystals, double crystals, and smoky crystals are all exciting discoveries as well.

Shouts of "I found one!" encourage other prospectors to keep working. If they keep at it, they may get lucky, too. If not they can always buy a Herkimer diamond in the gift shop.

Glossary

What Is a Glossary?

A glossary can help you find the **meanings** of words in this book that you may not know. The words in the glossary are listed in **alphabetical order**. **Guide words** at the top of each page tell you the first and last words on the page.

Each word is divided into syllables. The way to pronounce the word is given next. You can understand the pronunciation respelling by using the **pronunciation key** at the right. A shorter key appears at the bottom of every other page. When a word has more than one syllable, a dark accent mark (ˈ) shows which syllable is stressed. In some words a light accent mark (ˌ) shows which syllable has a less heavy stress. Sometimes an entry includes a second meaning for the word.

Guide Words

First word on the page — Last word on the page

Sample Entry

Pronunciation — **Part of Speech**

Main entry & Syllable division — **a•brupt•ly** (ə brupt lē) *adverb.*

Definition — Happening without warning. *Ben* ***abruptly*** *dropped the hot potato onto the floor.* — **Example sentence**

Pronunciation Key

Phonetic Spelling	Examples
a	at, bad, plaid, laugh
ā	ape, pain, day, break
ä	father, calm
âr	care, pair, bear, their, where
e	end, pet, said, heaven, friend
ē	equal, me, feet, team, piece, key
i	it, big, give, hymn
ī	ice, fine, lie, my
îr	ear, deer, here, pierce
o	odd, hot, watch
ō	old, oat, toe, low
ô	coffee, all, taught, law, fought
ôr	order, fork, horse, story, pour
oi	oil, toy
ou	out, now, bough
u	up, mud, love, double
ū	use, mule, cue, feud, few
ü	rule, true, food, fruit
u̇	put, wood, should, look
ûr	burn, hurry, term, bird, word, courage
ə	about, taken, pencil, lemon, circus
b	bat, above, job
ch	chin, such, match

Phonetic Spelling	Examples
d	dear, soda, bad
f	five, defend, leaf, off, cough, elephant
g	game, ago, fog, egg
h	hat, ahead
hw	white, whether, which
j	joke, enjoy, gem, page, edge
k	kite, bakery, seek, tack, cat
l	lid, sailor, feel, ball, allow
m	man, family, dream
n	not, final, pan, knife, gnaw
ng	long, singer
p	pail, repair, soap, happy
r	ride, parent, wear, more, marry
s	sit, aside, pets, cent, pass
sh	shoe, washer, fish, mission, nation
t	tag, pretend, fat, dressed
th	thin, panther, both
t͟h	these, mother, smooth
v	very, favor, wave
w	wet, weather, reward
y	yes, onion
z	zoo, lazy, jazz, rose, dogs, houses
zh	vision, treasure, seizure

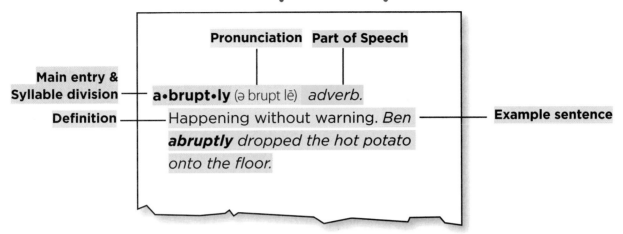

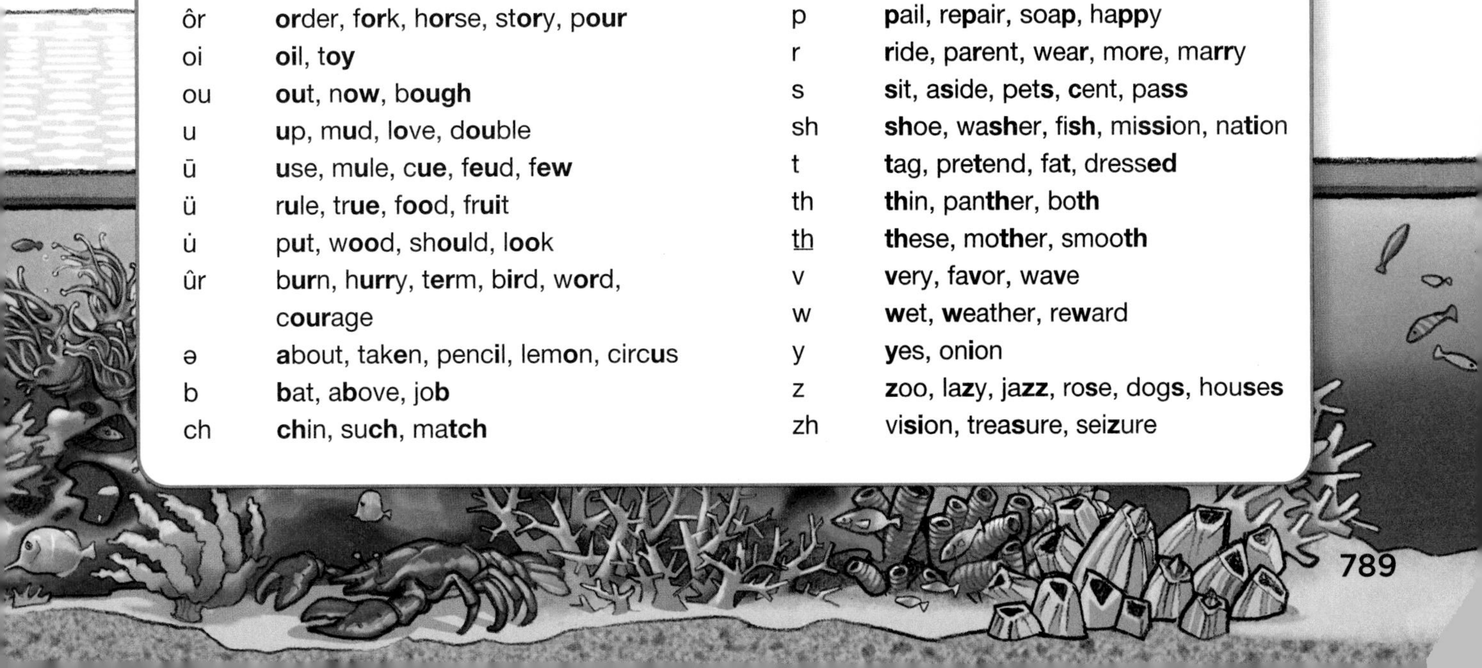

Aa

ab·sorbed (ab zôrbd´) *verb.* Soaked up something such as a liquid or the sun's rays. *It was a hot day, so the plant* ***absorbed*** *the water immediately.*

ac·ces·so·ries (ak ses´ ə rēz) *plural noun.* Extra parts or add-ons that are useful but not essential. *We bought several* ***accessories*** *for our new car.*

ac·cuse (ə kūz´) *verb.* To say that a person has done something wrong or illegal. *I will not* ***accuse*** *someone of something unless I am sure.*

ac·quaint·ance (ə kwān´təns) *noun.* A person one knows, but who is not a close friend. *Carole is an* ***acquaintance*** *from camp.*

ac·ti·vist (ak´tə vist) *noun.* A person who believes in and actively supports a cause. *Rev. Dr. Martin Luther King, Jr., was an* ***activist*** *for peace and social justice.*

a·dapt·ed (ə dap´tid) *verb.* Changed for new or different conditions. *After all the trees were cut down, the animals* ***adapted*** *to their smaller home.*

ad·vanced (ad vanst´) *adjective.* Beyond the beginning level; not elementary. *As a singer, Sheila was really* ***advanced*** *for her age.*

ag·ile (aj´əl) *adjective.* Able to move and react quickly and easily. *Bonita is an* ***agile*** *softball player.*

al·ler·gies (al´ər jēz) *plural noun.* Conditions that cause a person to have an unpleasant reaction to certain things that are harmless to most people. *My aunt has* ***allergies*** *in the spring when plants bloom.*

al·ter (´al tər) *verb.* To make different or change. *Eleuterio can* ***alter*** *his appearance by wearing a wig.*

a·maze·ment (ə māz´mənt) *noun.* Great surprise or wonder. *To the* ***amazement*** *of the audience, the children played some difficult music perfectly.*

am·bu·lance (am´byə ləns) *noun.* A special vehicle that is used to carry sick or injured people to a hospital. *My neighbor once had to call an* ***ambulance*** *to take him to the hospital.*

a·nal·y·sis (ə nal´ə sis) ***noun.*** A careful and detailed examination. *We performed an* ***analysis*** *of the liquid found at the crime scene.*

an·ces·tors (an´ses tərz) *plural noun.* People in the past from whom one comes. *Your great-grandparents are some of your* ***ancestors****.*

an·noyed (ə noid´) *adjective.* Bothered or disturbed. *Kevin looked* ***annoyed*** *when his little sister came out to join the game.*

a·pol·o·gize (ə pol′ə jīz′) *verb.* To say one is sorry or embarrassed; make an apology. *Aaron said, "I'd like to **apologize** for being late."*

ap·plaud·ed (ə plôd′əd) *verb.* Showed approval for or enjoyment of something by the clapping of hands. *The crowd **applauded** the soldiers as they came off the ship.*

ap·pre·ci·at·ed (ə prē′shē āt′əd) *verb.* Understood the value of; was grateful for something. *The boss **appreciated** how much his workers did for the company.*

as·sign·ments (ə sīn′mənts) *plural noun.* Tasks that are given out or assigned. *The teacher gave us two math **assignments** for homework.*

as·sured (ə shůrd′) *verb.* Made certain or sure. *Our hard work **assured** the success of the festival.*

as·tro·naut (as′trə nôt′) *noun.* A person trained to fly in a spacecraft. *The **astronaut** will walk on the moon.*

Word History

Astronaut is made from the Greek words *astro* for "star" and *nautēs* for "sailor" (as in *nautical*).

as·tron·o·mer (ə stron′ə mər) *noun.* A person who works or specializes in astronomy, the science that deals with the sun, moon, stars, planets, and other heavenly bodies. *An **astronomer** will speak at the next science fair.*

at; **ā**pe; f**ä**r; c**â**re; **e**nd; m**ē**; **i**t; **ī**ce; p**î**erce; h**o**t; **ō**ld; s**ô**ng; f**ô**rk; **oi**l; **ou**t; **u**p; **ū**se; r**ü**le; p**u**ll; t**û**rn; **ch**in; si**ng**; **sh**op; **th**in; **th**is; **hw** in **wh**ite; **zh** in trea**s**ure.

The symbol **ə** stands for the unstressed vowel sound in **a**bout, tak**e**n, penc**i**l, lem**o**n, and circ**u**s.

a·void·ed (ə void´əd) *verb.* Stayed away from. *Butch **avoided** doing hard work.*

awk·ward (ôk´wərd) *adjective.* Lacking grace in movement or behavior; clumsy or uncomfortable. *Until Julio learned the steps, his dancing was **awkward**.*

Bb

bar·be·cue (bär´bi kū´) *noun.* A meal, usually meat, cooked outdoors over an open fire. *We had a great **barbecue** in the park.*

bliz·zard (bliz´ərd) *noun.* A strong windstorm marked by intense cold and blowing snow. *No one should try to drive in a **blizzard**.*

bluf·fing (bluf´ing) *verb.* Trying to fool people with a false show of confidence, courage, or knowledge. *Rory said he could fly, but I knew he was **bluffing**.*

bor·der (bôr´dər) *noun.* A line between one country, state, county, or town and another. *A river runs along the **border** between the two states.*

boy·cotts (boi´kots) *plural noun.* Protests in which people refuse to buy from or work for a person, nation, or business. *The community plans **boycotts** of all the unfair businesses.*

Word History

Boycotts comes from Charles Boycott, who was shunned by Irish farmers for his harsh actions against them.

brit·tle (brit´əl) *adjective.* Likely to break or snap. *Susan's fingernails became **brittle** and started to break.*

bum·bling (bum´bling or bum´bəl ing) *adjective.* Making clumsy mistakes. *The **bumbling** detective would never solve the mystery.*

Cc

cam·ou·flage (kam'ə fläzh') *verb.* To hide or conceal by using shapes or colors that blend with the surroundings. *The chameleon is able to* ***camouflage*** *itself by changing the color of its skin.*

card·board (kärd'bôrd') *noun.* A heavy, stiff paper used to make boxes and posters. *I like to store my small toys in shoe boxes made of* ***cardboard****.*

cau·tious·ly (kô'shəs lē) *adverb.* In a careful way. *Because so many cars were coming, we crossed the street* ***cautiously****.*

cir·cu·lar (sûr'kyə lər) *adjective.* Having or making the shape of a circle. *The referee's arm made a* ***circular*** *motion as he blew the whistle.*

cir·cu·la·tion (sûr'kyə lā'shən) *noun.* The movement of the blood to and from the heart. ***Circulation*** *helps the frog's other organs get the nutrients and vitamins they need.*

cit·i·zen (sit'ə zən) *noun.* A person who was born in a country or who chooses to live in and become a member of that country. *Carmine is an Italian* ***citizen*** *but often visits the United States.*

cli·mate (klī'mit) *noun.* The average weather conditions of a place or region through the year. *Most deserts have a hot, dry* ***climate****.*

clut·tered (klut'ərd) *verb.* Filled with a messy collection of things. *Val's bedroom was* ***cluttered*** *with all of her sports equipment.*

at; āpe; fär; câre; end; mē; it; īce; pîerce; hot; ōld; sông; fôrk; oil; out; up; ūse; rüle; pu̇ll; tûrn; chin; sing; shop; thin; this; hw in white; zh in treasure.

The symbol ə stands for the unstressed vowel sound in about, taken, pencil, lemon, and circus.

coast·line (kōst′ līn′) *noun.* The outline of a coast. *The waves slammed against the beach's* ***coastline*** *during the storm.*

coax·ing (kōks′ing) *verb.* Persuading or influencing by mild arguing. *The instructor was* ***coaxing*** *young swimmers into the water.*

col·lage (kə läzh′) *noun.* A picture made by pasting paper, cloth, metal, and other things in an arrangement on a surface. *Once I made a* ***collage*** *of my day's activities, and it was full of bright colors and cotton balls.*

Word History

Collage comes from the French word *collage*, from *colle*, meaning "glue" or "paste."

col·o·nize (kol ′ə nīz′) *verb.* To settle in a new place but still follow the laws of the old country. *The pilgrims wanted to* ***colonize*** *the Americas.*

com·mo·tion (kə mō′shən) *noun.* A noisy disturbance; confusion. *We ran into the hall to see what was causing the* ***commotion****.*

com·mu·ni·ca·tion (kə mū′ni kā′shən) *noun.* An exchange or sharing of feelings, thoughts, or information. *Some forms of* ***communication*** *do not require speech.*

com·ple·ted (kəm plēt′əd) *verb.* Did, finished. *I could hardly wait until my brother* ***completed*** *his Thanksgiving project and we could all finally go to the movies.*

con·serve (kən sûrv′) *verb.* To protect from loss or harm. *Wildlife groups wanted to* ***conserve*** *the trees in the area.*

con·sid·er·a·tion (kən sid′ər ā′shən) *noun.* Thoughtfulness for other people and their feelings; something carefully thought about. *Leroy showed great* ***consideration*** *for his grandmother.*

con·sis·ted (kən sis′təd) *verb.* Contained; was made up. *The batter* ***consisted*** *of a cup of flour, one egg, and a cup of milk.*

con·sume (kən süm′) *verb.* To eat or drink. *Growing children can* ***consume*** *a lot of food and water.*

con·vinced (kən vinst′) *verb.* Caused a person to believe or do something. *The coach* ***convinced*** *the team they could win, and they did.*

cor·al (kôr′əl) *adjective.* Made of coral, a hard substance like stone made up of the skeletons of tiny animals. *We went snorkeling on the* ***coral*** *reef.*

crank·y (krang´kē) *adjective.* Cross or in a bad temper; grouchy. *Roni is always **cranky** before she's had breakfast.*

craters (krā´tərz) *plural noun.* Bowl-shaped pits or holes made by the impact of a meteorite. ***Craters** are easier to spot in the desert.*

criss·crossed (kris´krôst) *verb.* Went across, back and forth. *Grandma **crisscrossed** lengths of dough to make a pretty pie top.*

cul·tures (kul´chərs) *plural noun.* Groups of people who share a way of life, including art, music, food, and stories. *The fair featured foods from different **cultures** around the world.*

cur·rent (kûr´ənt) *noun.* A portion of a body of water or of air flowing continuously in a definite direction. *The lifeguard blew his whistle when he noticed that the **current** was taking the boys out too far.*

cus·toms (kus´ təms) *plural noun. A set of behaviors that are passed down from one generation to another. One of our **customs** is to eat turkey on Thanksgiving.*

Dd

de·cayed (dē kād´) *adjective.* Having undergone the process of decomposition; rotted. *We walked past **decayed** stumps in the woods.*

de·fend (di fend´) *verb.* Guard against attack or harm. *The rabbit could not **defend** itself against the snake, so it ran away.*

at; **ā**pe; f**ä**r; c**â**re; **e**nd; m**ē**; **i**t; **ī**ce; p**î**erce; h**o**t; **ō**ld; s**ô**ng; f**ô**rk; **oi**l; **ou**t; **u**p; **ū**se; r**ü**le; p**u̇**ll; t**û**rn; **ch**in; si**ng**; **sh**op; **th**in; **th**is; **hw** in **wh**ite; **zh** in trea**s**ure.

The symbol ə stands for the unstressed vowel sound in **a**bout, tak**e**n, penc**i**l, lem**o**n, and circ**u**s.

de·mon·stra·ted (de′mən strā′təd) *verb.* Showed by actions or experiment. *The performer **demonstrated** great skill with both the piano and the drums.*

den·si·ty (den′si tē) *noun.* The quantity of something per unit measure. *The **density** of aluminum is less than that of gold.*

de·scen·dants (di send′ənts) *plural noun.* People who come from a particular ancestor. *My neighbors are **descendants** of a French explorer.*

des·per·ate (des′pər it) *adjective.* Very bad or hopeless. *I needed money, but I was not **desperate** for it.*

de·vi·c-es (di vīs′əz) *plural noun.* Things used or made for specific purposes. *You can choose from several kinds of **devices** for help in opening a can.*

di·ges·tion (dī jest′shən) *noun.* The process where food is broken down and absorbed by the body. *Without the process of **digestion**, the body would never be able to break down food.*

dis·ap·point·ment (dis′ə point′mənt) *noun.* A feeling of being disappointed or let down. *Losing the match was a **disappointment**, but I still like tennis.*

dis·guised (dis gīzd′) *verb.* Changed the way something or someone looks to hide it or to look like something else. *The king **disguised** himself as a peasant and walked through town.*

dis·gus·ted (dis gus′tid) *adjective.* Having a strong feeling of dislike. *I felt **disgusted** by the way the bully was treating others.*

dis·place·ment (dis plās mənt) *noun.* A method used to measure the volume or weight of something. *The students dropped a piece of gold into water to measure its volume using the method of **displacement** of water.*

dis·rupt (dis rupt′) *verb.* To throw into disorder or confusion. *The city's plans to build a mall would **disrupt** the natural order of the forest nearby.*

diz·zy (diz′ē) *adjective.* Having the feeling of spinning and being about to fall. *Riding the Ferris wheel makes me **dizzy**.*

doc·u·ment·ing (dok′yə ment ing) *verb.* Making a record or collecting information. *The scientists took notes **documenting** their findings.*

dove¹ (dōv) *verb.* Plunged head first into water. *We watched as the woman **dove** perfectly off the board and into the deep pool.*

dove² (duv) *noun.* A medium-size bird of the pigeon family. *The **dove** cooed quietly on the window ledge.*

down·stream (doun′strēm′) *adverb.* Moving in the same direction as the current of a stream. *On a raft it is easier to float **downstream** than to push upstream.*

dy·nas·ties (dī′nə stēz′) *plural noun.* Periods of time during which a line of rulers from the same family is in power. *It took years and many different **dynasties** to finish building the Great Wall of China.*

Ee

eaves·drop·ping (ēvz′drop′ing) *noun.* Listening to other people talking without letting them know you are listening. ***Eavesdropping** is not a polite thing to do.*

ech·o·lo·ca·tion (ek ō lō kā′shən) *noun.* A way to find out where objects are by making sounds and interpreting the echo that returns. *Bats rely on **echolocation** when they hunt for insects.*

ee·rie (îr′ē) *adjective.* Strange in a scary way. *We heard an owl's **eerie** hooting as we walked home in the dark.*

e·lec·tri·cal (i lek′tri kəl) *adjective.* Relating to the form of energy carried in wires for use to drive motors or as light or heat. *Dad carefully connected the **electrical** cables to the positive and negative terminals on his car's battery.*

Word History

Electrical comes from the Latin *electrum* meaning "amber," because of amber's property of attracting other substances when rubbed.

end·less (end′lis) *adjective.* Having no limit or end. *The line of people for the show seemed **endless**, and not everyone would get a ticket.*

en·dured (en dùrd′ or en dyùrd′) *verb.* Survived or put up with. *The workers **endured** the hot sun all day.*

en·ter·pri·sing (en′tər prī′zing) *adjective.* Showing energy and initiative; willing or inclined to take risks. *Brian, an **enterprising** young man, ran for class president and won.*

at; **ā**pe; f**ä**r; c**â**re; **e**nd; m**ē**; **i**t; **ī**ce; p**î**erce; h**o**t; **ō**ld; s**ô**ng; f**ô**rk; **oi**l; **ou**t; **u**p; **ū**se; r**ü**le; p**ù**ll; t**û**rn; **ch**in; si**ng**; **sh**op; **th**in; **th**is; **hw** in **wh**ite; **zh** in trea**s**ure.

The symbol **ə** stands for the unstressed vowel sound in **a**bout, tak**e**n, penc**i**l, lem**o**n, and circ**u**s.

en·vi·ron·ments (en vī′rən mənts) *plural noun.* The things that make up an area, such as air, water, and land. *Polar bears and penguins have adapted very well to their cold **environments**.*

e·rodes (i rōds′) *verb.* Gradually wears away due to the action of wind and water. *The water **erodes** the rocks along the coast when waves crash against it.*

es·ti·mat·ed (es′tə mā′təd) *verb.* Judged or calculated, as of the value, quality, extent, size, or cost of something. *It is **estimated** that there are only 30,000 to 50,000 Asian elephants left in the world.*

e·va·po·rate (i vap′ə rāt′) *verb.* To change from a liquid or solid into a gas. *When heat makes water **evaporate**, the water seems to disappear.*

Word History

Evaporate comes from the Latin *evaporatus*, "dispersed in vapor," from *ex*, "out," and *vapor*, "exhalation."

e·ven·tu·al·ly (i ven′chü ə lē) *adverb.* In the end; finally. *We **eventually** got a DVD player because the good movies were not being shown on television.*

ev·i·dence (ev′i dəns) *noun.* Proof of something. *People thought the knave stole the tarts, but they had no **evidence** to support their claims.*

ex·as·per·at·ed (eg zas′pə rāt′əd) *verb.* Annoyed greatly; made angry. *Helping me with my math so **exasperated** my dad that my mom took over.*

ex·plo·ra·tion (ek′splə rā′shən) *noun.* The act of traveling through unfamiliar areas in order to learn about them. *Remote-control vehicles are carrying out an **exploration** of the surface of Mars.*

ex·po·sure (ek spō′zhər) *noun.* The condition of being presented to view. *Each time the dog saw a new toy was counted as one **exposure**.*

Ff

fade (fād) *verb.* To become gradually weaker, fainter, or dimmer. *When a song ends, sometimes it will* ***fade*** *out.*

faint (fānt) *adjective.* Not clear or strong; weak. *A* ***faint*** *noise came from outside, but I couldn't see anyone.*

fam·ished (fam′isht) *adjective.* Very hungry; starving. *After a long day of running and swimming, the children were* ***famished*** *and wanted to eat as soon as possible.*

flicked (flikt) *verb.* Hit or moved with a quick, light snap. *Fred* ***flicked*** *the fly off his face.*

flinched (flincht) *verb.* Drew back or away, as from something painful or unpleasant; winced. *When the door suddenly slammed, Myra* ***flinched****.*

fluke[1] (flük) *noun.* A chance happening; an accidental turn. *The substitute player's touchdown pass must have been a* ***fluke****.*

fluke[2] (flük) *noun.* The flat part of a whale's tail. *The whale smacked the water with its* ***fluke****.*

fool·ish·ness (fü′lish nəs) *noun.* The act of not showing good sense. *I wanted to race across the street, but my mom will not allow that* ***foolishness****.*

force (fôrs) *noun.* The strength behind a motion. *Richard threw the ball with very little* ***force*** *so it would not go far.*

fo·ren·sic (fə ren′sik) *adjective.* A special branch of science used to help police officers investigate and solve crimes. *The police asked* ***forensic*** *scientists to study the blue powder.*

fos·sil (fos′əl) *noun.* The hardened remains or traces of an animal or plant that lived long ago. *The* ***fossil*** *we found had imprints of ancient seashells in rock.*

frag·ile (fraj′əl) *adjective.* Easily broken; delicate. *My toothpick ship is too* ***fragile*** *to take to show-and-tell.*

at; **ā**pe; f**ä**r; c**â**re; **e**nd; m**ē**; **i**t; **ī**ce; p**î**erce; h**o**t; **ō**ld; s**ô**ng; f**ô**rk; **oi**l; **ou**t; **u**p; **ū**se; r**ü**le; p**u̇**ll; t**û**rn; **ch**in; s**ing**; **sh**op; **th**in; **th**is; **hw** in **wh**ite; **zh** in trea**s**ure.

The symbol **ə** stands for the unstressed vowel sound in **a**bout, tak**e**n, penc**i**l, lem**o**n, and circ**u**s.

fu·els (fū´əlz) *plural noun.* Substances burned as a source of heat and power, such as coal, wood, or oil. *When the world runs out of fossil **fuels**, we will be forced to use alternate energy sources.*

Gg

gaped (gāpt) *verb.* Stared with the mouth open, as in wonder or surprise. *The audience **gaped** at the acrobats.*

gen·u·ine (jen´ū in) *adjective.* Sincere; honest. *My friends and I made a **genuine** effort to help all the kids that were new to the school.*

gli·der (glī´dər) *noun.* An aircraft that flies without a motor. *Riding in a **glider** can be exciting.*

glin·ted (glin´təd) *verb.* Sparkled or flashed. *Rays of sunshine **glinted** on the water.*

glis·ten·ing (glis´ən ing) *adjective.* Shining or sparkling with reflected light. *The **glistening** eyes of the children looked out from the stage.*

globe (glōb) *noun.* Earth (as a shape). *Our **globe** is the home of billions of people.*

glo·ri·ous (glôr´ē əs) *adjective.* Having or deserving praise or honor; magnificent. *The colors of the tree leaves in Autumn are **glorious**.*

guard·i·an (gär´dē ən) *noun.* A person or thing that guards or watches over. *My older brother sometimes acts like he is my **guardian**.*

Hh

hab·i·tat (hab´i tat´) *noun.* The place where an animal or plant naturally lives and grows. *A clean pond is a good **habitat** for frogs.*

Word History
Habitat comes from the Latin *habitare*, meaning "to dwell."

han·dy (han´dē) *adjective.* Within reach, nearby; easy to use. • **come in handy.** Be useful. *It's amazing how many times a dictionary can **come in handy**.*

harm·less (härm′les) *adjective.* Not able to do damage or hurt. *My dog looks mean, but really she is* ***harmless****.*

head·lines (hed′līnz) *plural noun.* Words printed at the top of a newspaper or magazine article. *The most important news has the biggest* ***headlines****.*

he·ri·tage (her′i tij) *noun.* Something that is handed down from previous generations or from the past; tradition. *Jazz is now a part of our country's cultural* ***heritage****.*

hi·ber·nate (hī′bər nāt′) *verb.* To sleep or stay inactive during the winter. *Bears eat a lot to get ready to* ***hibernate****.*

hi·lar·i·ous (hi lâr′ē əs) *adjective.* Very funny. *Keisha tells* ***hilarious*** *jokes.*

hoist·ing (hoist′ing) *verb.* Lifting or pulling up. ***Hoisting*** *logs out of the water, the men soon grew tired.*

Ii

i·den·ti·fied (ī′den′tə fīd′) *verb.* Proved that someone or something is a particular person or thing. *The fingerprints on the gold watch* ***identified*** *the butler as the thief.*

im·mi·grants (im′i grənts) *plural noun.* People who come to live and work in another country. *Many* ***immigrants*** *come to the United States every year.*

im·pres·sive (im pres′iv) *adjective.* Deserving admiration; making a strong impression. *The track team won five races, which was its most* ***impressive*** *result all year.*

in·de·pen·dence (in′di pen′dəns) *noun.* Freedom from the control of another or others. *America gained its* ***independence*** *from Great Britain.*

in·jus·tice (in jus′tis) *noun.* Lack of justice; unfairness. *There are many tools to fight* ***injustice****, and everyone should know them.*

at; āpe; fär; câre; end; mē; it; īce; pîerce; hot; ōld; sông; fôrk; oil; out; up; ūse; rüle; pu̇ll; tûrn; chin; sing; shop; thin; th̲is; hw in white; zh in treasure.

The symbol ə stands for the unstressed vowel sound in about, taken, pencil, lemon, and circus.

in·spec·ted (in speck′təd) *verb.* Looked at closely and carefully. *The official **inspected** our car and declared that it was safe to drive.*

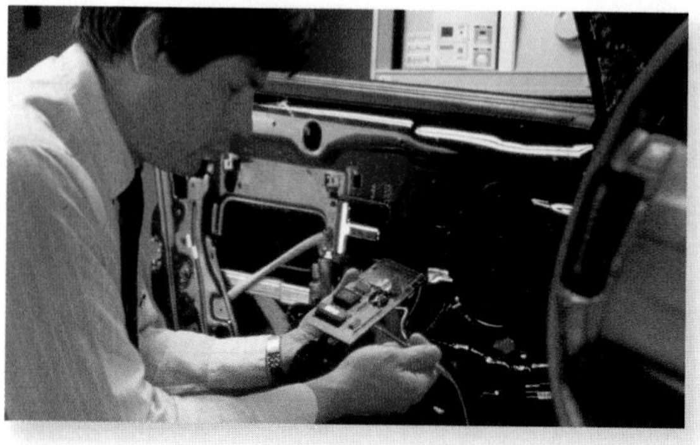

in·spire (in spīr′) *verb.* To stir the mind, feelings, or imagination. *Nature can **inspire** some people to write poetry.*

in·sult (in′sult′) *noun.* A remark or action that hurts someone's feelings or pride. *It would be an **insult** not to invite Marta to the party.*

in·tel·li·gent (in tel′i jənt) *adjective.* Able to understand and to think especially well. *Mr. Lee asked an **intelligent** question.*

in·ter·fere (in′tər fîr′) *verb.* To take part in the affairs of others when not asked; meddle. *My mom hates to **interfere**, but she often gives me good advice.*

in·ves·ti·ga·tion (in ves ti gā′shən) *noun.* The process of studying something to learn more about it. *The **investigation** took time but the police solved the crime.*

Jj

jeal·ous·y (jel′ə sē) *noun.* A feeling of envy of what a person has or can do. *Ken felt some **jealousy** when he saw Lin's new bike, but he got over it.*

jour·ney (jûr′nē) *noun.* A trip, especially one over a considerable distance or taking considerable time. *Ping made a **journey** to China to meet his grandparents and uncles.*

jum·ble (jum′bəl) *noun.* A confused mixture or condition; mess. *My room is a **jumble** of toys and books, so I have to clean it.*

Ll

leg·en·dary (lej′ən der′ē) *adjective.* Relating to a legend, or a story that has been handed down for many years and has some basis in fact. *Johnny Appleseed's efforts to spread the apple tree have become **legendary**.*

lim·it·ed (lim′i tid) *adjective.* Restricted, or kept within boundaries. *The menu had only a **limited** number of choices.*

log·i·cal (loj′i kəl) *adjective.* Sensible; being the action or result one expects. *When it rains, I do the **logical** thing and put my bicycle in the garage.*

loos·ened (lü′sənd) *verb.* Made looser; set free or released. *Brad **loosened** his necktie when the ceremony was over.*

lum·ber·ing (lum′bər ing) *adjective.* Moving in a slow, clumsy way. *Put a **lumbering** hippo in the water and it becomes a graceful swimmer.*

lurk (lûrk) *verb.* To lie hidden. *Many animals **lurk** in their dens to escape the heat of the day.*

Mm

mag·ni·fy (mag′nə fī′) *verb.* To make something look bigger than it really is. *Devices such as microscopes help to **magnify** small things.*

mam·mals (mam′əls) *plural noun.* Warm-blooded animals with backbones that give birth to live offspring. *Bats, cows, and people are **mammals.***

mas·sive (mas′iv) *adjective.* Of great size or extent; large and solid. *The sumo wrestler had a **massive** chest.*

mi·cro·phone (mī′krə fōn′) *noun.* A device that converts sound waves into electrical signals, which can then be recorded, broadcast, or amplified. *We couldn't hear the principal in the back of the auditorium because her **microphone** was broken.*

Word History

Microphone comes from the Greek words *mikros,* meaning "small," and *phone,* meaning "sound."

mi·cro·scope (mī′krə skōp′) *noun.* A device for looking at things that are too small to be seen with the naked eye. *To see small cells in the body, one needs to use a **microscope**.*

Word History

Microscope comes from the Greek words *mikros* meaning "small," and *skopein,* meaning "to view or examine."

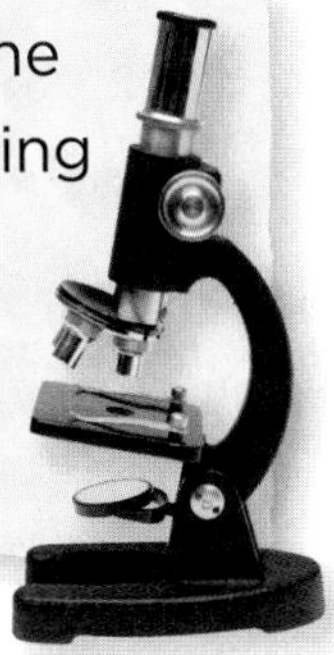

at; āpe; fär; câre; end; mē; it; īce; pîerce; hot; ōld; sông; fôrk; oil; out; up; ūse; rüle; pu̇ll; tûrn; chin; sing; shop; thin; this; hw in white; zh in treasure.

The symbol ə stands for the unstressed vowel sound in about, taken, pencil, lemon, and circus.

midst (midst) *noun.* A position in the middle of a group of people or things. *"There is a poet in our **midst**," said the principal, "and we need to clap for her."*

mi·grate (mī′grāt) *verb.* To move seasonally from one climate to another. *Birds **migrate** south during the winter.*

mis·chief (mis′chif) *noun.* Conduct that may seem playful but causes harm or trouble. *The kittens were always getting into **mischief** when we weren't home.*

mis·un·der·stood (mis′un dər stu̇d′) *verb.* Understood someone incorrectly; got the wrong idea. *I **misunderstood** the directions my teacher gave and did the wrong page for homework.*

mut·tered (mut′ərd) *verb.* Spoke in a low, unclear way with the mouth closed. *I could tell he was mad by the way he **muttered** to himself.*

mys·te·ri·ous (mi stîr′ē əs) *adjective.* Very hard or impossible to understand; full of mystery. *The fact that the cookies were missing was **mysterious**.*

Nn

nat·u·ral (nach′ər əl) *adjective.* **1.** Unchanged by people. *We hiked through **natural** surroundings of woods, streams, and meadows.* **2.** Expected or normal. *The **natural** home of the dolphin is the open ocean.*

ne·ga·tives (neg′ə tivz) *plural noun.* **1.** Photographic images made when film is developed. *The photographer looked at the **negatives** through the magnifier.* **2.** Words or phrases that mean "no." *We heard nothing but **negatives** in the report.*

ne·glec·ted (ni glekt′əd) *verb.* Failed to give proper attention or care to; failed to do. *I **neglected** to finish my science project and could not present it at the fair.*

noc·tur·nal (nok tûr′nəl) *adjective.* Active at night. *The owl is **nocturnal** because it hunts at night.*

non·vi·o·lence (non vī′ə ləns) *noun.* The philosophy or practice of opposing the use of all physical force or violence. *The demonstrators practiced **nonviolence** during the four-hour march on Washington.*

now·a·days (nou′ə dāz′) *adverb.* In the present time. *People hardly ever write with typewriters **nowadays**.*

nu·mer·ous (nü′mər əs or nū′mər əs) *adjective.* Forming a large number; many. *The mountain climbers faced **numerous** problems, but they still had fun.*

nu·tri·ents (nü′trē ənts or nū′trē ənts) *plural noun.* Substances needed by the bodies of people, animals, or plants to live and grow. *Sometimes we get ill because we are not getting the proper **nutrients**.*

nuz·zle (nuz′əl) *verb.* To touch or rub with the nose. *My dog will **nuzzle** me when he wants attention.*

Oo

o·be·di·ence (ō bē′dē əns) *noun.* The willingness to obey, or to carry out orders, wishes, or instructions. *It is important to show **obedience** to safety rules.*

Word History

Obedience comes from the Latin word *oboedire*, meaning "to hearken, yield, or serve."

op·por·tu·ni·ties (op′ər tü′ni tēz) *plural noun.* Good chances or favorable times. *School offers students many **opportunities** to be involved in clubs.*

or·bits (ôr′bits) *plural noun.* The path in space of one heavenly body revolving around another. *When we studied **orbits**, I learned that it takes Pluto 248.53 years to go around the Sun.*

at; **ā**pe; f**ä**r; c**â**re; **e**nd; m**ē**; **i**t; **ī**ce; p**î**erce; h**o**t; **ō**ld; s**ô**ng; f**ô**rk; **oi**l; **ou**t; **u**p; **ū**se; r**ü**le; p**u̇**ll; t**û**rn; **ch**in; si**ng**; **sh**op; **th**in; **th**is; **hw** in **wh**ite; **zh** in trea**s**ure.

The symbol **ə** stands for the unstressed vowel sound in **a**bout, tak**e**n, penc**i**l, lem**o**n, and circ**u**s.

or·gans (ôr´gəns) *plural noun.* Parts of the body in animals and people that perform a specific function or functions. *The frog's **organs** perform different tasks like helping it breathe and eat.*

or·gan·isms (ôr´gə niz´əms) *plural noun.* Any living thing. *Plants, animals, and people are **organisms**.*

out·stretched (out´strecht´) *adjective.* Stretched out; extended. *His **outstretched** palm held the quarter I had dropped.*

o·ver·come (ō´vər kum´) *verb.* To get the better of; beat or conquer. *The team was able to **overcome** losing the lead to go on to win the game.*

o·ver·heard (ō´vər hûrd´) *verb.* Heard something one was not supposed to hear. *I **overheard** my brother planning a surprise party for me.*

o·ver·joyed (ō´vər joid´) *adjective.* Very happy. *The whole team felt **overjoyed** when we won the soccer game.*

Pp

pa·le·on·tol·o·gist (pā´ lē ən tol´ə jist) *noun.* A scientist who deals with fossils of prehistoric animal and plant life. *The **paleontologist** spoke to the class about the history of dinosaurs.*

par·a·lyzed (par´ə līzd´) *adjective.* **1.** Having lost movement or sensation in a part of the body. **2.** Powerless or helpless. *Sue was **paralyzed** by stage fright.*

part·ner·ship (pärt´nər ship´) *noun.* A kind of business in which two or more people share the work and profits. *Janell, Pat, and Erik formed a gardening **partnership**.*

patch•work (pach′wûrk′) *noun.* Something put together out of many uneven or varied parts. *From the air, the land looked like a **patchwork** of green and brown fabrics.*

pe•cul•iar (pi kūl′yər) *adjective.* Strange; not usual. *I had the **peculiar** feeling that I was being watched.*

pe•ri•od (pîr′ē əd) *noun.* **1.** A length of historical time. *The 19th century was a **period** of railroad building.* **2.** A mark of punctuation (.) at the end of a declarative sentence or an abbreviation. *Joan forgot to put a **period** at the end of her sentence.*

per•sis•tence (pər sis′təns) *noun.* The ability to keep trying in spite of difficulties or obstacles. *In order to run a business, a person must have a lot of **persistence**.*

phras•es (frāz′iz) *plural noun.* Groups of words expressing a single thought but not containing both a subject and predicate. *When I proofread my report, I made **phrases** into complete sentences.*

pol•i•ti•cians (pol′i tish′ənz) *plural noun.* People who hold or seek elected offices. *Four **politicians** were running for the one seat in Congress.*

pos•i•tive (poz′i tiv) *adjective.* Certain; sure. *I was **positive** I had left that cookie right here on the counter.*

pre•his•tor•ic (prē′his tôr′ik) *adjective.* Belonging to a time before people started recording history. ***Prehistoric** artists sometimes made cave paintings to tell a story.*

pre•serve (pri zûrv′) *verb.* To keep safe for the future. *My parents **preserve** some of my school papers every year.*

pro•claimed (prə klāmd′) *verb.* Announced publicly. *The principal **proclaimed** May 20 as the day for our annual class trips.*

pro•fes•sion•als (prə fesh′ə nəlz) *plural noun.* People who have an occupation that requires special training. *Engineers and architects are **professionals**.*

at; āpe; fär; câre; end; mē; it; īce; pîerce; hot; ōld; sông; fôrk; oil; out; up; ūse; rüle; pu̇ll; tûrn; chin; sing; shop; thin; <u>th</u>is; hw in white; zh in treasure.

The symbol ə stands for the unstressed vowel sound in about, taken, pencil, lemon, and circus.

prop·er·ties (prop′ər tēz) *plural noun.* Characteristics of matter that can be observed. *Scientists measured the **properties** of gold in their lab.*

pros·pec·tors (pros′pek tərz) *plural noun.* People who explore an area for minerals, such as gold. *California was full of **prospectors** during the Gold Rush of 1849.*

pro·tes·ted (prō test′əd) *verb.* Complained against something. *When the workers lost their jobs in the factory, they **protested** to the union.*

Rr

raft (raft) *noun.* A kind of flat boat made of logs or boards fastened together. *Floating down the river on a **raft** is a nice way to spend a summer day.*

re·al·is·tic (rē′ə lis′tik) *adjective.* Seeing things as they are; practical. *I dream of being a famous rock star, but I should also be **realistic** and stay in school.*

reef (rēf) *noun.* A ridge of sand, rock, or coral at or near the surface of the ocean. *Boaters have to be careful not to scrape against the **reef** below.*

ref·er·ence (ref′ər əns or ref′rens) *noun.* A statement that calls or directs attention to something. *The speech makes a **reference** to a play written by William Shakespeare.*

re·fresh·es (ri fresh′iz) *verb.* Restores strength and vitality to, as through food or rest. *Lemonade **refreshes** on a hot summer day.*

rep·tiles (rep′tīlz) *plural noun.* Cold-blooded vertebrates of the group Reptilia, which includes lizards, snakes, alligators, crocodiles, and turtles. *Most **reptiles** lay eggs, although some give birth to live young.*

re·sist·ance (ri zis′təns) *noun.* Opposition or fending off. *Whenever any colonists tried to conquer the Native Americans, they were met with **resistance**.*

re·source (rē′zors) *noun.* A material found on Earth that can be used to satisfy the needs of people. *Wood is an important natural **resource**.*

re·spon·si·bil·i·ty (ri spon′sə bil′i tē) *noun.* The quality or condition of having a job, duty, or concern. *Taking care of the dog was my **responsibility**.*

risks (risks) *plural noun.* Chances of loss or harm. *Explorers were willing to take **risks** in the hope of discovering new lands.*

roamed (rōmd) *verb.* Moved around in a large area. *The grizzly bear **roamed** over a long, narrow valley and the nearby mountains.*

ro·tate (rō′tāt) *verb.* To turn or cause to turn around on or as on an axis. *I had to **rotate** the image because the photo was upside down.*

rum·bling (rum′bling) *noun.* A heavy, deep, rolling sound. *The **rumbling** of thunder woke me up.*

Ss

sanc·tu·ar·y (sangk′chü er′ē) *noun.* A refuge for wildlife where predators are controlled and hunting is not allowed. *My friend runs a **sanctuary** for injured hawks and owls.*

scat·tered (skat′ərd) *verb.* Spread or thrown about here and there. *Practice balls were **scattered** all over the tennis court.*

at; āpe; fär; câre; end; mē; it; īce; pîerce; hot; ōld; sông; fôrk; oil; out; up; ūse; rüle; pu̇ll; tûrn; chin; sing; shop; thin; <u>th</u>is; hw in white; zh in treasure.

The symbol ə stands for the unstressed vowel sound in about, taken, pencil, lemon, and circus.

scorn·ful·ly (skôrn′fəl ē) *adverb.* In a way that shows that something or someone is looked down upon and considered bad or worthless. *The critic was unhappy with the new artist's painting so he spoke* ***scornfully*** *about them.*

scuf·fling (skuf′əl ing or skuf′ling) *noun.* The sound of feet shuffling. *When we heard* ***scuffling*** *from upstairs, we knew Grandpa had finished his nap.*

seg·re·ga·tion (seg′ri gā′shən) *noun.* The practice of setting one racial group apart from another. *There are laws against* ***segregation*** *in public schools.*

se·lec·ting (si lek′ting) *verb.* Picking out among many; choosing. *I spend a long time* ***selecting*** *the right gift.*

self·ish (sel′fish) *adjective.* Thinking only of oneself; putting one's own interests and desires before those of others. *A second piece of cake sounded good, but I didn't want to be* ***selfish****.*

sen·si·ble (sen′sə bəl) *adjective.* Having or showing sound judgment; wise. *If you make a mistake, the* ***sensible*** *thing to do is apologize.*

shim·mer (shim′ər) *verb.* To shine with a faint, wavering light; glimmer. *The walls of the canyon began to* ***shimmer*** *in the rays of the setting sun.*

silk·en (sil′kən) *adjective.* **1.** Made of silk. **2.** Like silk in appearance. *Antonio wrote a poem about the girl's long* ***silken*** *hair.*

sky·scrap·ers (skī′skrā′ pərz) *plural noun.* Very tall buildings. *The city has many* ***skyscrapers****, and some of them are 50 stories tall!*

slith·ered (slith′ərd) *verb.* Slid or glided like a snake. *When the snakes* ***slithered*** *across the ground, they moved quickly and hardly made a sound.*

snick·er·ing (snik′ər ing) *verb.* Laughing in a mean or disrespectful manner. *The children stopped* ***snickering*** *when their mother told them to be kinder*

snor·ing (snôr′ing) *verb.* Making harsh or noisy sounds while sleeping. *The dog was* ***snoring*** *on the porch when I came home from school.*

snuf·fled (snuf′əld) *verb.* Breathed noisily because of partly stopped-up nasal passages. *Because of a bad cold, I* ***snuffled*** *all day.*

soft·ware (sôft´ wâr´) *noun.* Written or printed programs of information that are used on a computer. *The artist used a new design* ***software*** *to help plan her latest sculpture.*

sol·i·tar·y (sol´i ter´ē) *adjective.* Living, being, or going alone. *The prisoner was placed in* ***solitary*** *confinement.*

Word History

Solitary comes from the Latin *solitarius,* meaning "alone, lonely."

sores (sôrz) *plural noun.* Places where the skin has been broken and hurts. *My hands had* ***sores*** *after raking leaves all morning with no gloves on.*

spe·cial·ty (spesh´əl tē) *noun.* A special thing that a person knows a great deal about or can make very well. *Making quilts is my aunt Lisa's* ***specialty****.*

storm surge (stôrm sûrj) *noun.* An odd rise in the level of the sea along a coast caused by the winds of a storm. *There was a* ***storm surge*** *last night along the coastline of the beach.*

strikes (strīks) *plural noun.* **1.** The stopping of work to protest something. *The workers threatened* ***strikes*** *if conditions did not improve.* **2.** Pitched balls in the strike zone or that a batter swings at and misses. *Three* ***strikes*** *and you're out during a baseball game.*

strut·ting (strut´ing) *verb.* Walking in a self-important way. *Marilyn went* ***strutting*** *around in her new boots from Italy.*

stum·bled (stum´bəld) *verb.* Lost one's balance, as by missing one's footing, stubbing one's toe, or tripping over an obstacle. • **stum·bled up·on** *verb.* Came upon something unexpectedly or by chance. *We* ***stumbled upon*** *the clues that would lead us to the treasure.*

at; āpe; fär; câre; end; mē; it; īce; pîerce; hot; ōld; sông; fôrk; oil; out; up; ūse; rüle; pu̇ll; tûrn; chin; sing; shop; thin; this; hw in white; zh in treasure.

The symbol ə stands for the unstressed vowel sound in about, taken, pencil, lemon, and circus.

sub·urbs (sub´ûrbz) *plural noun.* The areas around a city where people live. *Many people commute from the **suburbs** to go to work in the city.*

Word History
Suburbs comes from the Latin *suburbium*—from *sub*— "under" and *urbs,* meaning "city."

sus·pi·cious (səs pish´əs) *adjective.* Feeling doubt and mistrust; causing the feeling that something is wrong. *When my mom saw me by the cookie jar, I could tell she was **suspicious**.*

swal·lows[1] (swol´ōz) *verb.* Causes food or other substances to pass from the mouth into the stomach. *Kathy's sore throat hurts every time she **swallows**.*

Word History
Swallows comes from the Old English word *swelgan* with the same meaning.

swal·lows[2] (swol´ōz) *plural noun.* Several groups of small birds having a slender body and a forked tail. ***Swallows** usually build their nests in places where predators cannot find them.*

swarms (swôrmz) *plural noun.* Large groups of insects flying or moving together. *When the hive fell, **swarms** of angry bees flew out.*

Tt

tan·gles (tang´gəlz) *plural noun.* Knotted, twisted, confused masses. *The garden hose had not been rolled back up and was full of **tangles**.*

tech·nique (tek nēk´) *noun.* A method or way of bringing about a desired result in a science, an art, a sport, or a profession. *Part of Orli's **technique** when she is running is to breathe in and out through her mouth.*

Word History
Technique comes from the Greek word *teknikos,* meaning "relating to an art or a craft."

tech·nol·o·gy (tek nol′ə jē) *noun.* Electronic products and systems that have various uses. ***Technology** has changed the ways that artists create their work.*

tem·ples (tem′pəlz) *plural noun.* Buildings used for the worship of a god or gods. *Visitors to Athens can tour many **temples** of the ancient Greeks.*

ter·ri·to·ry (ter′i tôr′ē) *noun.* Any large area of land; region. *My brother's **territory** for selling medical office supplies is in North Carolina.*

threat·ened (thret′ənd) *adjective.* Having a sense of harm or danger. *The dark storm clouds made the baseball players feel **threatened** with a rain-out.*

tot·tered (tô′tərd) *verb.* Walked or moved with unsteady steps; rocked or swayed as if about to fall. *The baby **tottered** as she first tried to walk.*

tra·jec·to·ry (trə′jek tə rē) *noun.* The path that an object in motion takes. *The **trajectory** of Earth as it moves around the Sun is the same every year.*

Uu

un·con·sti·tu·tion·al (un′ kon sti tü′ shə nəl) *adjective.* Not in keeping with the constitution of the United States. *Segregation was declared **unconstitutional** by the Supreme Court.*

un·fair (un fâr′) *adjective.* Not fair or just. *Punishing all of us for the actions of my little sister seemed **unfair**.*

un·ions (ūn′yənz) *plural noun.* Groups of workers joined together to protect their jobs and improve working conditions. *Labor **unions** fight to get workers the safety equipment they need.*

u·nique (ū nēk′) *adjective.* Having no equal; the only one of its kind. *The Everglades is **unique** in that there is no other place on Earth like it.*

u·ni·verse (ū′nə vûrs′) *noun.* Everything that exists, including Earth, the planets, the stars, and all of space. *Many scientists spend their lives studying the wonders of the **universe**.*

un·sta·ble (un stā′bəl) *adjective.* Not settled or steady; easily moved or put off balance. *Although the raft looked **unstable**, it floated very well.*

at; **ā**pe; f**ä**r; c**â**re; **e**nd; m**ē**; **i**t; **ī**ce; p**î**erce; h**o**t; **ō**ld; s**ô**ng; f**ô**rk; **oi**l; **ou**t; **u**p; **ū**se; r**ü**le; p**u̇**ll; t**û**rn; **ch**in; si**ng**; **sh**op; **th**in; **th**is; **hw** in **wh**ite; **zh** in trea**s**ure.

The symbol **ə** stands for the unstressed vowel sound in **a**bout, tak**e**n, penc**i**l, lem**o**n, and circ**u**s.

un·sus·pect·ing (un´sə spek´ting) *adjective.* Having no suspicions. *The **unsuspecting** girls did not realize they were about to get sprayed by the hose.*

Vv

val·u·a·ble (val´ū ə bəl) *adjective.* Of great use, worth, or importance. *The excavation gave us some **valuable** new information about the settlers.*

ven·ture (ven´chər) *noun.* A business or some other undertaking that involves risk. *Rea's new **venture** was a carpet-cleaning service.*

ves·sels (ves´əlz) *plural noun.* Ships or large boats used to transport or carry over water. *The ocean liner known as the* Titanic *was larger than all other oceangoing **vessels** of the time.*

vi·ta·mins (´vī tə məns) *plural noun.* Any group of nutrients needed in small amounts to maintain the health and systems of the body. *Frogs get some of the **vitamins** they need to survive from water.*

Ww

week·days (wēk´dāz´) *plural noun.* The days of the week except Saturday and Sunday. *We go to school only on **weekdays**.*

whirl·wind (whûrl´wind´, wûrl´wind´) *noun.* **1.** A whirling current of air that moves forward with great force. **2.** Anything resembling a whirlwind. *She moved quickly about the apartment, packing like a **whirlwind**.*

wild·life (wīld´līf´) *noun.* Living things, especially the animals that live naturally in an area. *We saw lots of **wildlife** on our hike in the woods.*

wing·span (wing´span´) *noun.* The distance between the tips of the wings of a bird, an insect, or an airplane. *The **wingspan** of some hawks is five feet.*

wis·dom (wiz´dəm) *noun.* Good judgment and intelligence in knowing what is right, good, and true. *When I'm not sure what to do, I look to my grandpa's **wisdom**.*

Word History

Wisdom comes from the Old English word *wisdom*, from *wis*, meaning "having sound judgment, learned."

wist·ful·ly (wist´fəl ē) *adverb.* In a sadly longing way; yearningly. *My grandma looked at her wedding pictures **wistfully**.*

(Continued from Copyright page.)

"I Love the Look of Words" by Maya Angelou from SOUL LOOKS BACK IN WONDER. Copyright © 1993 by Tom Feelings. Reprinted by permission of Dial Books, a division of Penguin Books USA Inc.

"I Was Dreaming to Come to America" selected by Veronica Lawlor from I WAS DREAMING TO COME TO AMERICA. Copyright © 1995 by Veronica Lawlor. Reprinted by permission of Viking Press, a division of Penguin Books USA Inc.

"Into the Swamp" by Elizabeth Schleichert, photos by C. C. Lockwood. From RANGER RICK SEPTEMBER 2003 — INTO THE SWAMP. Copyright © 2003 by the National Wildlife Federation. Reprinted by permission of People and Nature: Our Future Is in the Balance.

"The Life and Times of the Ant" by Charles Micucci from THE LIFE AND TIMES OF THE ANT. Copyright © 2003 by Charles Micucci. Reprinted by permission of Houghton Mifflin Company.

"Light Bulb" and "Lightning Bolt" by Joan Bransfield Graham from FLICKER FLASH. Text copyright © 1999 by Joan Bransfield Graham. Reprinted by permission of Houghton Mifflin Company.

"Me and Uncle Romie" by Claire Hartfield, paintings by Jerome Lagarrigue. Text copyright © 2002 by Claire Hartfield, paintings copyright © 2002 by Jerome Lagarrigue. Reprinted by permission of Dial Books, a division of Penguin Books USA Inc.

"Mountains and plains" and "No sky at all" from AN INTRODUCTION TO HAIKU: AN ANTHOLOGY OF POEMS AND POETS FROM BASHŌ TO SHIKI. Copyright © 1958 by Harold G. Henderson. Reprinted by permission of Doubleday Anchor Books, a division of Doubleday & Company, Inc.

"Mighty Jackie: The Strike-Out Queen" by Marissa Moss, illustrated by C. F. Payne. Text copyright © 2004 by Marissa Moss, illustrations copyright © 2004 by C. F. Payne. Reprinted by permission of Simon & Schuster Books for Young Readers.

"My Brother Martin: A Sister Remembers, Growing Up with the Rev. Dr. Martin Luther King, Jr." by Christine King Farris, illustrated by Chris Soentpiet. Text copyright © 2003 by Christine King Farris, illustrations copyright © 2003 by Chris Soentpiet. Reprinted by permission of Simon & Schuster Books for Young Readers.

"My Brothers' Flying Machine" by Jane Yolen, paintings by Jim Burke. Text copyright © 2003 by Jane Yolen, illustrations copyright © 2003 by Jim Burke. Reprinted by permission of Little, Brown, and Company.

"My Diary from Here to There" story by Amada Irma Pérez, illustrations by Maya Christina Gonzalez from MY DIARY FROM HERE TO THERE. Story copyright © 2002 by Amada Irma Pérez, illustrations copyright © 2002 by Maya Christina Gonzalez. Reprinted by permission of Children's Book Press.

"Mystic Horse" by Paul Goble. Copyright © 2003 by Paul Goble. Reprinted by permission of HarperCollins Publishers.

"The Raft" by Jim LaMarche. Copyright © 2000 by Jim LaMarche. Reprinted by permission of HarperCollins Publishers.

From "Roadrunner's Dance" by Rudolfo Anaya, illustrated by David Diaz. Copyright © 2000. Text reprinted by permission of Susan Bergholz Literary Services, New York.

"The snow is melting" and " Winter solitude" from THE ESSENTIAL HAIKU: VERSIONS OF BASHŌ, BUSON, AND ISSA. Introduction and selection copyright © 1994 by Robert Hass. Unless otherwise noted, all translations copyright © 1994 by Robert Hass. Reprinted by permission of The Ecco Press.

"Snowflake Bentley" by Jacqueline Briggs Martin, illustrated by Mary Azarian. Text copyright © 1998 by Jacqueline Briggs Martin, illustrations copyright © 1998 by Mary Azarian. Reprinted by permission of Houghton Mifflin Company

"A Walk in the Desert" by Rebecca L. Johnson with illustrations by Phyllis V. Saroff from A WALK IN THE DESERT. Text copyright © 2001 by Rebecca L. Johnson, illustrations copyright © 2001 by Phyllis V. Saroff. Reprinted by permission of Carolrhoda Books, Inc.

"Wild Horses: Black Hills Sanctuary" by Cris Peterson, photographs by Alvis Upitis. Text copyright © 2003 by Cris Peterson, photographs copyright © 2003 by Alvis Upitis. Reprinted by permission of Boyds Mills Press, Inc.

ILLUSTRATIONS

Cover Illustration: Bandelin-Dacey Studio

18-19: Laura Watson. 20-37: (bg) Joe Cepeda. 39: Joe LeMonnier. 50-51: (bg) Wetzel & Company. 50-51: (tl) Laura Westlund. 52: (tl) Phyllis V. Saroff. 52-53: (bg) Wetzel & Company. 53: (tr) Phyllis V. Saroff. 54: (tl) Phyllis V. Saroff. 54-55: (bg) Wetzel & Company. 55: (tr) Phyllis V. Saroff. 56: (tl) Phyllis V. Saroff. 56-57: (bg) Wetzel & Company. 57: (tr) Phyllis V. Saroff. 58: (tl) Phyllis V. Saroff. 58-59: (bg) Wetzel & Company. 59: (tr) Phyllis V. Saroff. 60: (tl) Phyllis V. Saroff. 60-61: (bg) Wetzel & Company. 61: (tr) Phyllis V. Saroff. 64: (l) Phyllis V. Saroff. 66-67: (bg) Russell Farrell. 68: Daniel Del Valle. 76: Joe Lertola. 84: Kim Johnson. 86-101: Anna Rich. 105: Geoff McCormack/Photo Researchers. 112-137: Jim LaMarche. 140: Karen Minot. 142: Daniel Del Valle. 145: Viviana Diaz. 146: Paul Mirocha. 152-169: C.F. Payne. 158: (br) Daniel Del Valle. 180-201: Maya Christina Gonzalez. 206: Daniel Del Valle. 213,216: Rick Nease for TFK. 224-243: Rosalyn Schanzer. 246: Daniel Del Valle. 250: Ann Boyajian. 252-265: Nicole Wong. 270: Daniel Del Valle. 272-273: Stacey Schuett. 280-297: David Diaz. 302: Daniel Del Valle. 303: Maryana Beletskaya. 308-323: Chris Soentpiet. 328: Daniel Del Valle. 329: Time Life Pictures/Getty. 346-367: Paul Goble. 372: Daniel Del Valle. 378-401: Mary Azarian. 402-403: Tina Fong. 404: Daniel Del Valle. 406-407: Susan Swan. 408-409: Argosy. 414-437: Mark Teague. 446: Lane Gregory. 448-463: Kristina Rodanas. 476: Rick Nease for TFK. 504-505: Jesse Reisch. 506: Daniel Del Valle. 512-529: Katherine Brown-Wing. 533: Barb Cousins. 536-537: Bruce Whatley. 558-559: Robert Casilla. 560: Wetzel & Company. 564-565: David LaFleur. 566-585: Renato Alarcão. 588: Barb Cousins. 590: Daniel Del Valle. 595: Rick Nease for TFK. 608-627: Jerome Lagarrigue. 650-651: John Hovell. 652-655: Ande Cook. 656: Ernesto Burciaga/Alamy. 658-659: Darryl Ligasan. 661: Sam Tomasello. 664-665: Greg Shed. 666-681: Ying-Hwa Hu & Cornelius Van Wright. 686: Daniel Del Valle. 690-691: Loretta Krupinski. 692-709: Garth Williams. 715: Argosy. 720: American Museum of National History. 734-753: Jim Burke. 754-755: Bandelin-Dacey Studios. 761: Paul Mirocha. 762-777: Charles Micucci. 778-781: (bg) Amy Lowry Poole. 782: Daniel Del Valle. 783: John Hovell. 784-785: Bill Cigliano. 788-789: Renato Alarcão.

PHOTOGRAPHY

All photographs are by Macmillan/McGraw Hill (MMH) except as noted below:

16-17: Harald Sund/The Image Bank/Getty Images. 17: Nick Koudis/Getty. 36: (tl) Courtesy Johanna Hurwitz; (tc) Wetzel & Company; (bcr) WernerPhoto.com. 38-39: (bkgd) S. Alden/PhotoLink/Getty Images. 38: (cr) Ashley Cooper/CORBIS. 39: (br) Dorling Kindersley/Getty Images. 40-41: (bkgd) S. Alden/PhotoLink/Getty Images. 40: (br) Stockbyte/PunchStock; (tl) Mediscan/Corbis. 42: CORBIS. 43: Lew Robertson/CORBIS. 44-45: Michael & Patricia Fogden/CORBIS. 45: Alan and Sandy Carey/Getty. 46: Jack Barrie/Bruce Coleman. 47: Dave Tipling/Alamy. 48-49: Bruce Clendenning/Visuals Unlimited. 49: Martin J Miller/Visuals Unlimited. 51: (tr) Steve Warble; (b) Brian Vikander. 52: Barbara Gerlach/Visuals Unlimited. 53: (tc) Richard Day/Daybreak Imagery; (b) Tom Bean. 54: (tc) Bayard A. Brattstrom/Visuals Unlimited; (b) Rob Simpson/Visuals Unlimited. 55: John Cunningham/Visuals Unlimited. 56: (tc) LINK/Visuals Unlimited; (b) John Gerlach/Visuals Unlimited. 57: Hal Beral/Visuals Unlimited. 58: Malowski/Visuals Unlimited. 59: John Gerlach/Visuals Unlimited. 60: (tr) Barbara Gerlach/Visuals Unlimited; (b) Joe McDonald/Visuals Unlimited. 61: Tom J. Ulrich/Visuals Unlimited. 62-63: Bruce Clendenning/Visuals Unlimited. 64: Courtesy Lerner Publishing Group. 64-65: (bkgd) Martin J Miller/Visuals Unlimited; (bl) Barbara Gerlach/Visuals Unlimited. 65: (bc) Rob Simpson/Visuals Unlimited; (br) Steve Warble. 68: Michael Newman/Photo Edit. 69: Digital Vision/Getty. 70-71: William Smithey Jr/Getty. 72: Frank Staub/Index Stock. 73: Corey Rich. 74-75: Ken Wilson/Wildfaces. 77: Campbell William/CORBIS Sygma. 78: (cl) Galen Rowell/CORBIS; (bcl) Raymond Cramm/Photo Researchers; (bcr) Richard Kettlewell/Animals Animals; (bl) Tony Arruza/CORBIS; (bc) W. Gregory Brown/Animals Animals. 80: SuperStock/AGE. 81: (bkgd) Dian Lofton for TFK; (c) C. Squared Studios/Getty; (cr) Dian Lofton for TFK. 82-83: NASA/AP. 83: NASA/Getty. 85: Stock Trek/Getty. 100: (tl) Photo by Das Anndas. Courtesy Farrar, Straus and Giroux; (cr) Courtesy Anna Rich. 102: NASA. 104: Detlev Van Ravenswaay/Science Photo Library. 104-105: Chris Butler/Science Photo Library. 106: Rubberball/Getty. 107: Photodisc/Getty. 108-109: Steve Dunwell/Index Stock. 109: Jeremy Woodhouse/Getty. 110: John Beatty/Getty. 111: (cl) Jen & Des Bartlett/Bruce Coleman; (bkgd) Jim Brandenburg/Minden. 136: Courtesy Jim LaMarche. 138: CC Lockwood. 138: (t) Tim Fitzharris/Minden Pictures. 138-139: (b) Stephen Frink Collection/Alamy. 139: (tr) William Leaman/Alamy.141: (t) Angelo Cavalli/Getty Images. 142: Photodisc/Getty. 143: (t) F. Lukasseck/Masterfile. 144: (tr) Brand X Pictures/PunchStock. 146-147: (bc) Chris Howes/Wild

Places Photography/Alamy. 148-149: Victor Baldizon/Getty Images. 149: C Squared Studios/Getty. 150: Bettmann/CORBIS. 151: Bernard Hoffman/Getty. 168: (tl) Courtesy Simon & Schuster; (cr) Courtesy C. F. Payne. 170: Doug Pensinger/Getty Images. 171: Richard Drew/ Associated Press. 172: PunchStock. 173 Paul J. Sutton/Duomo/Corbis. 174: Myrleen Ferguson Cate/Photo Edit. 175: Brand X/Getty. 176-177: Stephen Chernin/AP. 177: Mel Curtis/Getty. 178: Rusty Hill/FOODPIX. 179: David Hiser/Getty. 200: Courtesy Children's Book Press. 202: Bettmann/CORBIS. 203: Jeff Greenberg/Alamy. 205: Bill Brooks/ Alamy. 206: BananaStock/Alamy. 207: Mark Gibson/CORBIS. 208-209: Wu Jianxin/Imaginechina. 210: Picture Finders/Estock. 211: (tc) Wu Xiang/Imaginechina; (cl) C Squared Studios/Getty. 212-213: John Stanmeyer. 214: Christie's Images. 216: Tenzin Dorjee. 218: SW Productions/Brand X. 219: (bkgd) Dian Lofton for TFK; (cl) Photodisc/Getty; (cr) Burke/Triolo/Alamy; (bcr) Tomi/Photolink/ Getty. 220-221: Paul Souders/CORBIS. 221: Steve Cole/Getty. 222: (tr) Schenectady Museum; Hall of Electrical History Foundation/ CORBIS; (bl) W. Dickson/CORBIS. 223: Bettmann/CORBIS. 242: Courtesy Roz Schanzer. 246: Kevin Peterson/Getty. 247: (tr) DigitalVision/AGE; (tr) Ryan McVay/Getty. 248-249: Tim Davis/Getty Images. 251: (tl) Daryl Balfour/Getty; (cr) Stephen Cooper/Getty. 264: (tl) Courtesy Groundwood Books; (cr) Courtesy Nicole Wong. 266: John Cancalosi/DRK. 267: Michael & Patricia Fogden/Minden. 268: Michael Fogden/Animals Animals. 269: Daniel J. Lyons/Alamy. 270: Tipp Howell/Getty. 271: Art Wolfe/Getty. 274: (br) Michael St. Maur Sheil/CORBIS; (t) Jerry Driendl/Getty Images. 274-275: (bkgd) Jerry Driendl/Getty Images. 276-277: Jonathan Blair/CORBIS. 277: C. McIntyre/PhotoLink/Getty. 278-279: John Cancalosi/Ardea. 279: ZSSD/SuperStock. 296: (tl) Photo by Mimi. Courtesy Rudolfo Anaya; (bcr) Courtesy Harcourt Brace and Co. 298: Mitsuaki Iwago/Minden Pictures. 299: (br) Robert W. Ginn/Alamy; (tl) Steve Kazlowski/ Danita Delimont.com. 300: (bc) blickwinkel/Alamy; (br) Andrew Harrington/Alamy; (cl) Renee Morris/Alamy; (tl) InsideOutPix/ PunchStock. 301: Royalty-Free/CORBIS. 303: (t) Raymond Mendez/ Animals Animals. 304-305: Jeff Greenberg/Alamy. 305: CORBIS. 306-307: Bettmann/CORBIS. 322: (tl) Courtesy Simon & Schuster; (c) Courtesy Chris Soenpiet. 324: AP. 325: Larry Downing/Getty. 326: Bettmann/CORBIS. 326-327: Bill Pierce/Time Life Pictures/Getty. 328: Amos Morgan/Getty. 330-331: Jeff Greenberg/PhotoEdit. 332: (tr) Jan Kleveland; (cr) Russel Illig/Photodisc/Punchstock; (br) C Squared Studios/Getty. 333: Courtesy Jhordan Logan. 334: (l) Mi Won Kim for TFK; (r) Rick Nease for TFK. 335: Mi Won Kim for TFK. 336: (t) Courtesy Esta Shapiro; (bl) Courtesy David Hsu. 337: Courtesy David Hsu. 338: Lewis Wickes Hines/CORBIS. 340: Image 100/Punchstock. 341: (bkgd) Dian Lofton for TFK; (cl) Burke/Triolo/Alamy; (cr) Ryan McVay/Getty. 342-343: Warren Morgan/CORBIS. 343: Photodisc/ Getty. 344: Fototeca Gilardi/Phodo/Alamy. 344-345: Corel Stock Photo Library. 345: Hulton Archive/Getty 366: Courtesy Paul Goble. 369: Seminole Tribe of Florida. 370: Timothy O'Keefe/Index Stock. 371: Jeff Greengerg/Index Stock. 372: ImageState/Alamy. 373: Dave King/DK. 374-375: Wayne Eastep/Stone/Getty Images. 375: Kevin Jordan/Getty. 376: Gary Buss/Getty. 377: Richard Hutchings/CORBIS. 400: (tl) Sharron L. McElmeel/McBookwords LLC; (cr) Courtesy Mary Azarian. 404: Michael Newman/PhotoEdit. 405: (t) Brand X Pictures/ PunchStock. 410-411: Hans Huber/Getty Images, Inc. 411: G.K. & Vikki Hart/Getty 412: (bl) Ulrike Schanz/Animals Animals/; (b) CORBIS. 413: Mary Grace Long/Asia Images/Getty. 436: Courtesy Scholastic. 438: Okapia/Hund/Kramer/Photo Researchers. 439-441: Manuela Hartling/Reuters/CORBIS. 442: CORBIS. 443: Myrleen Ferguson Cate/ PhotoEdit. 444-445: Richard Price/Taxi/Getty. 445: Jim Craigmyle/ CORBIS. 462: Courtesy Kristina Rodanas. 464: Jonathan Nourok/ PhotoEdit. 465: (tl) Bob Daemmrich/Image Works; (br) PhotoDisc. 466: (tr) Owen Franken/CORBIS; (bl) Bob Daemmrich/PhotoEdit. 467: John A Rizzo/Getty. 468: (cl) Dan Bigelow/Getty; (br) Matt Bowman/ FoodPix/Getty. 469: (tr) Andy Crawford/DK; (cr) Brian Hagiwara/ Getty; (cr) Ryan McVay/Getty. 470-471: Peter/Georgina Bowater/ Mira. 472: D.C. Lowe/EPN Images. 473: (tcl) W. Cody/CORBIS; (tr) CORBIS. 474: AP. 475: Derek Trask/CORBIS. 476: Comstock/Alamy. 477: AP. 478: (tr) Steve Liss; (b) Imageshop/Punchstock. 480: SuperStock/AGE. 481: (bkgd) Dian Lofton for TFK; (cr) S. Wanke/ PhotoLink/Getty. 482-483: Stuart Westmorland/Stone/Getty. 483: CORBIS. 484: (tr) Amos Nachoum/CORBIS; (br) Roger Tidman/ CORBIS. 484-485: Stephen Frink Collection/Alamy. 486-501: Richard Sobol. 502: Courtesy Robert Sobol. 502-503: Richard Sobol. 506: Dan Bigelow/Getty. 507: Mickey Gibson/Animals Animals. 508-509: Brian J. Skerry/Getty Images. 509: Siede Preis/Getty. 510: Brandon Cole Marine Photography/Alamy. 510-511: Boden/Ledingham/Masterfile. 511: (Brandon Cole/Visuals Unlimited. 514-527: (bkgd) Wetzel & Company/Janice McDonald. 528: Photo by Yuusuke Itagaki. Courtesy Charlesbridge Públishers. 528-529: (bkgd) Wetzel & Company/Janice McDonald. 530: Linda Svendsen/Panoramic Images. 531: Thinkstock/JupiterImages. 532: Cluadia Daut/Reuters/ CORBIS. 534: Comstock/Alamy. 534-535: Masterfile. 535: (t) Digital Vision/Getty Images. 538: Time & Life Pictures/Getty Images. 539: (tr) Danita Delimont/Alamy. 540-541: Comstock Images/PunchStock - Upper Cut Images. 541: Siede Preis/Getty. 542-543: Steven Weinrebe/Index Stock. 543: Don Smetzer/Stone/Getty. 544-550: ©2005 Twentieth Century Fox. All rights reserved. 550-553: (bkgd) Wetzel & Company. 553-555: ©2005 Twentieth Century Fox. All rights reserved. 556: (tr) Courtesy Candlewick Press; (bl) ©2005 Twentieth Century Fox. All rights reserved. 557: ©2005 Twentieth Century Fox. All rights reserved. 560: Ryan McVay/Getty. 561: CORBIS. 562-563: Bill Bachmann/Index Stock. 563: Nick Koudis/ Getty. 584: (tcl) Courtesy Peachtree Publishers; (bcr) Courtesy Renato Alarcao. 586: Central Stock/Fotosearch. 587: Runk/ Schoenberger/Grant Heilman Photography, Inc. 589: James Darell/ Getty Images. 590: (tr) Jody Dole/Getty; (c) C Squared Studios/Getty; (cl) Stockbyte/Getty. 591: Photodisc/Getty. 592-593: Library of Congress, Maps Division. 594: North Wind.. 595: Museo Nazionale Preistorico Etnografico Luigi Pigorini. 596: Jan Sonnenmair/Aurora. 597: Seth Resnick. 598: (bcl) Thunder Bay National Marine Sanctuary and Underwater Preserve; (b) Bowling Green State University. 599: (tr) Priit Vesilind/National Geographic; (bl) Courtesy of the Institute for Exploration, Mystic, CT. 600: (tr) Richard T. Nowitz/CORBIS; (br) University Museum of Cultural Heritage. 602: Photostock/SuperStock. 603: (b) Dian Lofton for TFK; (cl) Burke/ Triolo/Alamy; (cr) Ryan McVay/Getty. 604-605: Ingolf Pompe/Alamy. 605: C Squared Studios/Getty 606: (bl) Chris Steele-Perkins/Magnum; (br) Comstock/Getty; (br) Photodisc/Getty. 607: Photodisc/Getty. 626: (tr) Photo by Jessica Tampas. Courtesy Claire Hartfield; (cl) Courtesy of Penguin Group. 628: (b) Frank Chmura/Alamy. 630: Alan Levenson/AGE. 631: Photodisc/PunchStock. 632-633: Steve Bloom Images/Alamy. 633: CORBIS. 634: Scott Neville/AP. 636-649: Alvis Upitis. Frames and Parchment: Artbeat. 650: Courtesy of Highlights for Children. 650-651: Alvis Upitis; frame: Artbeat. 651: Alvis Upitis. 656: Amos Morgan/Getty. 657: (t) Andre Jenny/Alamy. 660: image100/PunchStock. 662-663: The Granger Collection, New York. 663: C Squared Studios/Getty. 680: (tr) Rob Layman; (cl) Courtesy Cornelius Van Wright and Ying-Hwa Hu. 682: (bl) James L. Amos/ CORBIS. 682-683: (bkgd) Joe Ginsberg/Getty Images. 683: (br) Joe Ginsberg/Getty Images; (tl) Pat Roque/Associated Press. 684: (tl) Victoria & Albert Museum, London / Art Resource, NY. 685: (tr) ImageDJ/Jupiter Images. 686: (cl) BananaStock/AGE. 687: (tr) Brand X/Getty; (tr) CORBIS. 688-689: Tom Salyer/Silver Image. 689: U.S. Fish & Wildlife Service/Craig Koppie. 710: (tl) Marcia Johnston. Courtesy Farrar, Straus & Giroux; (bcr) Courtesy Estate of Garth Williams c/o Frost National Bank. 712: (c) Steve Kaufman/CORBIS; (tc) Hugo Wilcox/Foto Natura/Minden Pictures. 713: Pat Little/AP-Wide World Photos. 714: Buddy Mays/CORBIS. 716: (cl) Robert Llewellyn/Alamy; (br) Kathy Willens/AP. 717: Paul Souders/CORBIS. 718-719: David Boyer/National Geographic. 720: American Museum of Natural History. 721: (tl) Dwight Hilpman; (bl) Jim Pisarowicz. 722: Field Museum, Chicago. 722-723: Black Hills Institute/Field Museum, Chicago. 723: John Weinstein/Field Museum, Chicago. 724: Black Hills Institute/Field Museum, Chicago. 724-725: Black Hills Institute/ Field Museum, Chicago. 725: Courtesy Sue Hendrickson. 726: Mark Moffett/Minden. 728: Jiang Jin/SuperStock. 729: (cl) Burke/Triolo/ Alamy; (cr) S. Wanke/Photolink/Getty; (b) Dian Lofton for TFK. 730-731: Stephanie Maze/CORBIS. 731: PhotoLink/Getty. 732-733: Bettmann/CORBIS. 733: Science Museum, London/Topham-HIP/ Image Works. 752: (tr) Jason Stemple Photographer; (bcl) Courtesy Jim Burke. 756: Frank Siteman/AGE. 758-759: Michael & Patricia Fogden/CORBIS. 759: Brand X/PictureQuest. 760: Masterfile. 761: Steve Hopkin/Ardea. 776: Anita Lambrinos/Courtesy Charles Micucci. 782: Rubberball/Getty. 786: (bl) Michael Okoniewski/AP-Wide World Photos. 787: (bl) Hemera Technologies/Alamy; (br) Michael Okoniewski/AP-Wide World Photos. 790: Andrew Ward/Life File/Getty. 791: (l) Comstock/Getty; (r) TRBfoto/Getty. 792: (l) Photodisc/Getty; (tr) Sylvia Pitcher Photolibrary/Alamy; (br) Robert Brenner/PhotoEdit. 793: Digital Vision/Getty. 794: Yellow Dog Productions/Image Bank/Getty. 795: (l) Robert Harding World Imagery/Getty; (r) StockTrek/Getty. 796: (l) Dick Scott/Visuals Unlimited; (r) CORBIS. 797: Adam Jones/Visuals Unlimited. 798: (l) CORBIS; (r) JPL/NASA. 799: Siede Preis/Getty. 800: Photolink/Getty. 801: Charles George/Visuals Unlimited. 802: Andy Sacks/Stone/Getty. 803: (l) Mel Curtis/Getty; (r) Siede Preis/Getty. 804: (l) Jeff Foott/ Discovery Images/PictureQuest; (r) Comstock/Getty. 805: Victor Habbick Visions/Photo Researchers. 806: Louie Psihoyos/CORBIS. 807: Digital Vision/Getty. 808: David Ball/CORBIS. 809: (l) S. Solum/ Photolink/Getty; (r) Pixel/Alamy. 810: Donovan Reese/Getty. 811: Peter Yates/CORBIS. 812: (l) Jeremy Woodhouse/Getty; (r) Digital Vision. 813: Jay Freis/Image Bank/Getty. 814: Stockbyte/Getty.